GW00676619

THE LETTERS
OF
LIAM O'FLAHERTY

Born in 1896 on Inishmore, the largest of the Aran Islands, Liam O'Flaherty grew up in a world of awesome beauty, filled with echoes of the ancient pagan past. From his father, a Fenian, O'Flaherty inherited a rebellious streak; from his mother, a noted *seanchaí* (storyteller), came the deep spiritualism and love of nature that has enraptured readers through the decades.

In France in 1917 O'Flaherty was severely shell-shocked. After a short recuperation, he spent several restless years travelling the globe. In 1922 he supported the Republican cause against the Free State government. Influenced by the Industrial Workers of the World's programme of social revolution, O'Flaherty organised the seizure and occupation of the Rotunda Theatre at the top of Dublin's O'Connell Street in 1922. He hoisted the red flag of revolution, calling himself the 'Chairman of the Council of the Unemployed', but fled three days later to avoid bloodshed. Later that year he moved to London, where his writing skills came to the attention of critic Edward Garnett, who recommended to Jonathan Cape the publication of O'Flaherty's first novel. For the next two decades, O'Flaherty's creative output was astonishing. Writing in English and Irish, he produced novels, memoirs and short stories by the dozen. Remarkable for their literary entertainment and value, O'Flaherty's books are also crucial from an anthropological point of view, charting the ways and beliefs of a peasant world before it was eclipsed by modernity.

Some of O'Flaherty's work was banned in Ireland – he was a rebel in his writing, as in his life. Liam O'Flaherty died in Dublin in 1984, aged 88 years, having enriched forever Irish literature and culture.

Other works by LIAM O'FLAHERTY
From WOLFHOUND PRESS

FICTION
Famine
Short Stories: The Pedlar's Revenge
The Wilderness
Skerrett
Insurrection
The Assassin
Mr. Gilhooley
The Ecstasy of Angus

AUTOBIOGRAPHY
Shame the Devil

FOR CHILDREN
The Test of Courage
All Things Come of Age

Also by A.A. KELLY

Liam O'Flaherty: The Storyteller

Joseph Campbell, Poet and Nationalist 1879-1944
A Critical Biography
(with Norah Saunders)

Mary Lavin: Quiet Rebel

Edited by A.A. KELLY
From WOLFHOUND PRESS

Wandering Women:
Two Centuries of Travel out of Ireland
Pillars of the House: Verse by Irish Women
From 1690 to the Present
The Ecstasy of Angus by Liam O'Flaherty
The Wilderness by Liam O'Flaherty
The Pedlar's Revenge and Other Stories by Liam O'Flaherty
(selected and introduced)
The Wave and Other Stories by Liam O'Flaherty
(selected and introduced)

THE LETTERS
OF
LIAM O'FLAHERTY

Selected and Edited by

A.A. Kelly

WOLFHOUND PRESS

First published 1996 by
WOLFHOUND PRESS
68 Mountjoy Square
Dublin 1

Wolfhound Press receives financial assistance from the Arts Council/
An Chomhairle Ealaíon, Dublin.
British Library Cataloguing in Publication Data
A catalogue record for this book is available from the British Library.

ISBN 0 86327 380 7

Typesetting: Wolfhound Press
Cover design: Joe Gervin
Printed in the UK by Cambridge University Press

CONTENTS

ABBREVIATIONS AND CONVENTIONS

BOM	Boston University (Mugar Memorial Library), Massachusetts
HLH	Houghton Library, Harvard University, Cambridge, Massachussets
HRHRC	Harry Ransom Humanities Research Center, University of Texas at Austin
IS	The *Irish Statesman*
IUL	Indiana University (Lilly Library), Bloomington, Indiana
JR	Joyce Rathbone
KT	Catherine Harding (Kitty) Tailer
McMU	McMaster University (Mills Memorial Library), Hamilton, Ontario
NLD	National Library, Dublin
NLW	National Library of Wales, Aberystwyth
NWUL	Northwestern University Library, Evanston, Illinois
NYUF	New York University (Fales Library), New York
SIUL	Southern Illinois University (Morris Library), Carbondale, Illinois
SLUL	University of London (Sterling Library)
TCD	Trinity College Library, Dublin
VG	Victor Gollancz, Ltd
[ ]	supplied by editor, missing words, letters, names, dates
{ }	indecipherable or obliterated word(s)
ALS	handwritten script
TLS	typed script (except for signature)
n.d.	no date
p.m.	postmark
....	omission of phrase, sentence or passage

INTRODUCTION

IN EDITING THESE LETTERS as few alterations as possible have been made to the original text, though some of the letters to Kitty Tailer have been abbreviated where marked, to avoid offence to living persons, and to cut out repetitive and unimportant domestic detail. The dating of some letters is approximate. Spelling and punctuation, paragraphing, missing pronouns, apostrophes and auxiliary verbs have been supplied where necessary. No translation has been made of short remarks in French and Spanish.

The script varies in size, pressure and decipherability. As much explanatory material as possible is given in the editorial footnotes.

The letters have been numbered consecutively throughout for easy reference. A list of correspondents, to whom the letters were written, precedes the general index. Also a selected list of critical writings on O'Flaherty has been included.

There are no letters extant written in Irish, Liam O'Flaherty's first language.

O'Flaherty was annoyed when his letters to Edward Garnett were sold by David Garnett to the Harry Ransom Humanities Center, University of Texas at Austin, so that in later life he became an extremely cautious letter writer, preferring telegrams, or the telephone. His correspondence with his daughter Pegeen was, at his request, destroyed. He also told Kitty Tailer not to keep his letters to her, but she disobeyed, except for some of the earlier ones, hoping that these letters might later be published. When, upon the death of Mrs Tailer, these letters became available for publication, there were so many that a selection amongst them had to be made.

In his letters to Edward Garnett during his early years as a writer O'Flaherty was not always sincere. He is, for example, flattering about David Garnett whom in truth he did not admire. The Garnett letters reveal O'Flaherty's early struggles and defeats, his temperamental difficulties, caused in part by having been shellshocked, something which he at first feared might affect his brain, and his emergence as an independent writer, who no longer needed fostering, in the early thirties.

There is, of course, more behind the letters which the reader can only guess at, some of which can be gleaned from comparing them with O'Flaherty's autobiographical writing, and his prose pieces (not yet published). It is clear, however, that O'Flaherty was torn between his pride at having fought with the Irish Guards, his horror at trench warfare, and his dislike of British imperialism. An Irish republican, he mocked some aspects of Irish society, especially the influence of the Roman Catholic church. Some of his feelings about man and nature, most fully explored in his short stories, have been vindicated by the worldwide ecological awareness movement, initiated only in O'Flaherty's old age. Allowance always has to be made in his writing for deliberate garbling, or exaggeration, and facts cannot always be taken at their face value. O'Flaherty's philosophy is often incoherent because it sometimes reflects a particular state of mind. He always preferred intuitive response to analytical theory.

In 1926 O'Flaherty wrote notes about himself in E.J. O'Brien (ed.), *Best Short Stories of 1926* as follows:

Life history, so far, of the man known as Liam O'Flaherty. Born Aran Islands, Co. Galway, Ireland, 28th August, 1896, educated Rockwell College, Blackrock College and University College, Dublin. Joined the British Army 1915, served in France therewith. Discharged with shell-shock May 1918. Set out to conquer the world August 1918, from the Aran Islands. Worked in London as foreman in a brewery, a porter in a hotel and as a clerk in an office. Walked out of the office and went to sea as a trimmer on a tramp steamer. Left the steamer at Rio de Janeiro. Did not like the place. Came back in the same capacity on another steamer to Liverpool. Joined another at Cardiff and went east to Italy, Turkey, Greece, etc., then to Montreal, where he left the ship. Wandered over Canada working in the capacity of lumberjack, railway worker, tinned milk maker, miner in coppermines, dock labourer, hobo carpenter. Crossed the American frontier without a passport in November 1919. Joined his brother in Boston. Followed various invocations in various States of the Union, to wit, maker of pastry, telegraph messenger, oyster fisher, houseporter, dishwasher, waiter in a construction camp boarding-house, dynamite worker, shipyard worker, plumber's assistant, printer's assistant, rubber tyre maker, and labourer in a biscuit factory. Joined another ship in New York, August 1920, to return to Ireland. Carried to South America instead. Joined another ship at Santos, Brazil, and travelled to Belgium, Holland and Germany thereon. Came from Hamburg to Cardiff. Came to Ireland from Cardiff in November 1920. Stayed a few weeks in that country and passed to London once more, where he stayed until January 1921, in which month he returned to the Aran Islands without having conquered any part of the world. Meditated for many months on the aforesaid islands on the indefinability of the paregoric, the uncertainty of life, and the constant tribulation to be met in this world. Roused himself to a desire for a further attempt at world conquest in August 1921. Set out for London once more, but returned to Ireland in December of the same year and became active in various manners, to wit, in the organisation of the unemployed and the seizure of the Rotunda, over which he hoisted the Red Flag, and fed the poor, in participation in the Four Courts Rebellion, and later a further departure from the scene of these activities by going once more to London, where, in September 1922, he commenced to write ...

This brings the reader to the period where the letters start.

Edward Garnett read O'Flaherty's short story 'The Sniper' in the *New Leader* (12 January, 1923), and first made contact with him then. O'Flaherty paid tribute to Garnett in his autobiographical note in *Ten Contemporaries, second series*, edited by John Gawsworth, (London, 1933): 'To his kindness, his help, his marvellous critical faculty and his loving friendship, I owe whatever success I have had subsequently in creating my work.' More background detail about O'Flaherty's family and early education can be found in Patrick Sheeran's critique of O'Flaherty's novels.

In 1929 O'Flaherty wrote an introduction to Heinrich Hauser's *Bitter Water* (translated Patrick Kirwan) (New York: Horace Liveright, 1929; London: Wishart & Co., 1930), hailed as the book of the year by Thomas Mann and others. Here he wrote: 'I am always polite to strangers and always suspicious of them. It is a relic of the various wars and revolutions in which I have taken part. Every stranger is a potential enemy, whose capacity for evil is not measured. And politeness is the best weapon with an enemy.' This attitude, except when he lost his temper, increased with age.

It was Edward Garnett who gave O'Flaherty confidence in his artistic destiny, so that at a period when it was still possible to live simply on a writer's modest earnings, he refused offers to write regularly as a journalist. His work as a script-writer in Hollywood was never continued. Regularity and fixed hours or subject matter were anathema to him, and he found teamwork difficult. His erratic nature needed freedom in time and space. These letters give some idea of his frequent movements and writing habits.

Leaving Jonathan Cape affected O'Flaherty's relationship with Edward Garnett, and there would have been more letters here, either missing or unavailable. O'Flaherty was as lucky in his agent, A.D. Peters, as he had been in his literary godfather. For here again he received much support and advice, though at times he must have proved a very tiresome client.

Inspiration for his work often seems to have come from people he knew or met who are sometimes thinly disguised, sometimes transformed, in his fiction. It was his fascination both with natural beauty and with the endless variety of humanity which led him to travel. In the autobiographic note of *Ten Contemporaries* (cf.) he attributes the 'awakening of my conscious mind' to the immense range of men he met in the army, including German prisoners.

O'Flaherty's caustic wit, exercised more often in conversation than in print, sometimes gave offence. Here is a little known piece from his 'Mustard and Cress' column which appeared four times in the *Sunday Referee* (London: December 1933\January 1934):

> A nanny goat named Dolabella has written an account of her experiences with an empty tin of sardines. The result is a little masterpiece which is next month's choice of the Little Book Society founded by James Agate in

opposition to the Big (or Priestley) Book Society. I believe that General Rathcroghan's first public appearance in London will be at a cocktail party given in honour of Dolabella.

This goat's name reminds me of that magnificent sprinter Myrobella, whom Francis Stuart and myself put up for membership of the Irish Academy of Letters last Summer. W.B. Yeats, AE and Lennox Robinson had never heard of the filly, and Senator Oliver St. John Gogarty objected to her on the grounds that she could not stay over the distance of the Nobel prize. The result was that she was blackballed. Stuart and myself were severely reprimanded for contempt of glorified humbug.

What? You think that Sir John Squire or Virginia Woolf is of greater importance to life than Mick the Miller or the Loch Ness monster?

O'Flaherty's personal letters to his longtime companion Catherine Harding Tailer (Kitty), an American divorcée he first met in Santa Barbara in the mid thirties, give intimate glimpses into his character. Their devoted relationship endured to O'Flaherty's death and there is no doubt that Kitty was an immense encouragement and support to him both morally and materially. She also took over the management of his literary affairs, which he had always found irksome and therefore neglected.

O'Flaherty's letters to Kitty reveal his distress at his waning creative powers as old age progressed, though he continued trying to write until his mind failed. His unfinished novel *The Gamblers* is summarised in an appendix to this volume. The novel was to be dedicated to Kitty.

A.A. Kelly

1. HRHRC TLS

41 Fitzroy Street, London W1   n.d. [? April, 1923]

Dear Mr. Garnett,

I received your letter re Tomlinson's indisposition.[1] Very sorry. I have now started *The Black Soul* and am going at it hot and heavy. It's good – that is I like it myself and that is the only thing that is worth while, since a man could pimp in a brothel for a living, and writing if not pleasurable is nowise better than touting on a racecourse. I didn't touch the Yellow Beard since. I am walking around the plot but didn't walk into it yet. I guess a comedy is a big bit of cheese to chew. I wrote an animal story on the lines you told me and sent it to the *Manchester Guardian*. It had an interesting title anyway – A Cow's Suicide – that alone might make the editor look at it.

Yours
Liam O'Flaherty

[1]Henry M. Tomlinson, literary editor of the *Nation*.

---

2. HRHRC ALS

Quaker Farm, North Crawley

Newport Pagnell, Bucks[1]   Friday evening n.d. [? April, 1923]

Dear Mr. Garnett,

Just had your letter mailed on to me. Good news about Tomlinson. Please accept my thanks for your services. The list of my obligations is piling up to a degree that very soon I shall have to commit the indecency of writing an ode to you, {nicaeus?} etc.

Thanks very much.

I am recuperating here on this farm, thirty-five shillings a week, very good. I am working at an alarming rate. I have been here two days and have done two sketches (fifteen hundred each) and have started a third. Have done 'The Fight' and 'Three Lambs'. The last is a bit too raw, describing a sheep giving birth to three lambs. I am eager to see whether they are sketches or not. I am going to do 'Selling a Pig' tomorrow. In the country one can rattle off an eighteen hundred word sketch in two hours without any effort. I am going to do 'Summer' here too. Well!

Damn it Tchekov is the greatest genius ever born. I don't give a damn about your Lawrence, Tchekov is the goods. England should be grateful to your wife for introducing him, and it is a tribute to her art that the translation most undoubtedly seems to lose nothing.[2] I refer particularly to 'Lights'. Remember it? After that I am eager to get at Lawrence. Perhaps he is the apostle of a new era in English literature. Look here, I am willing to lay a wager with you that my present book will knock spots out of him. I say this in confidence because I don't mean it. I am keeping stuff out of *The Black Soul* for it. Still I am not going to let the latter go hungry because it's really your book.

Yours sincerely
Liam O'Flaherty

[1] The MSS of 'The Rockfish', undated, is marked with the Newport Pagnell address (held by HRHRC).

[2] Constance Garnett translated many Russian writers into English.

---

3. HRHRC ALS

Quaker Farm, North Pagnell   Tuesday n.d. [? April, 1923]

Dear Mr. Garnett,

I was awfully pleased to get your letter this morning and the four Tchekovs, thanks so much. I am sending you two sketches and a story 'The Fight', 'Three Lambs' and 'Josephine'. I am awfully sorry they are in pencil and I doubt whether you can read them but you will catch their drift anyway. When you have deciphered them you can drop them down to Connaught St. so that I can type them when I get back. I am doubtful about the 'Lambs' and 'Josephine', but I like 'The Fight'. I had started 'Summer' yesterday but I rather think I am going to leave it till I get back. I am too comfortable here to do justice to *The Black Soul*, so I will do some more sketches and stories. Between yourself and Tchekov I find the sketch as easy as plugging a man at twenty-five yards with a Colt .45 automatic. But even yet I can't differentiate between good and bad. It's a good job I don't or I'd get too conceited.

McCarthy[1] sent me a note to enquire about my health. He is putting my reviews through and said he cut the O'Neill one a little. I sent him the shebeen business. I think we have 'secured' McCarthy all right, although I doubt whether he likes real raw art. Damn it I am looking forward to having a real big talk to you when you get back from {?}. I can just picture you sitting leaning over a table, looking at three or four people and nobody knows whether you are laughing or not. I have been a lucky bastard these last few months. It's just as if somebody thrust a shaft into some unused cellar in my brain and unloosed a store of thought. And after all in this best of all worlds thought is the best thing possible.

I sat for two hours in a field yesterday watching young heifers. It's peculiar the way they lie down. Invariably they {?} the air and blow out their breath. I think it's to clear their nostrils. Or perhaps this bunch suffered from nasal catarrh. I never noticed this before.

Oh I say, do send the bicycle to Connaught St., that will be great. I can always run out then and I wouldn't call Venus my mistress. I'll be a regular General Rathcroghan.[2]

I don't think I could postpone this blasted marriage. Between the two of us – oh well, what's the use talking about it. I gave my word and a word is a word, damn it. It won't affect me much, although I am so quiet and happy here that I can see the difference. A woman is not necessary to my life.[3] I can see that, and I love the country. The wind sighing in the trees is music to me.

Say, sometime when I make a lot of money you must come down to the Aran Islands with me. I say when I make a lot of money because assuredly I would have to buy a quart of whiskey for every man on the island. I was just thinking yesterday of the turf pier at Kilmurvey in summer, lying with hands beneath the head, listening to the boatmen curse and talk about the coarse side of sex in a poetic manner, and then watch some maiden bathe on the sandy beach where the curate stood examining the family history of O'Malley.[4] Well, well! I hope you enjoy {? place name} as much as I am enjoying this.

Liam O'Flaherty

[1] Desmond McCarthy, literary editor of the *New Statesman*.

[2] See Letter No. 9

[3] See Letter No. 5

[4] Characters in *Thy Neighbour's Wife*

---

4. HRHRC TLS
52 Warren Street, London W1   Monday evening n.d.[? May, 1923]

Dear Mr. Garnett,

Just got your letter. Glad that first chapter was right, I was beginning to be afraid of it. I think the chapter I am doing now is better. I have got back more completely into the native Aran Island swing of the *Neighbour's Wife*. I can feel it moving now without effort – the great thing that is necessary for an Irishman, for we have not the gift of concentration that you have. But say, I am writing a story now, inspired by El Ombu. I started out and wrote it in Irish and then translated it into English, using the phraseology that they would use in Aran. I am telling the truth, so it is surprising what similitude there is between the mode of expression and the Spanish one. 'The Black Mare' it's called. I owned the mare myself but I get old Patcheen Saele to tell it, he was the greatest braggart in Aran.

Say, I am beginning to see the light now – about how to write. I can see that the only thing one can write with any merit is the truth – the things one knows. Thanks. I was thinking over that play going down the Edgware Road yesterday. The bloody thing was making great progress and then I lost it going into the lavatory and couldn't resurrect it again. I haven't got those women right. I hope your woman, Mrs. Rice is it, will be in the nature of an inspiration.

Ha, I was right about your son. So he is the man who wrote *Lady into Fox*, I have heard it condemned by a bitch of a woman so it must be good. The same woman told me I was worse than James Joyce and a vulgar fellow. I think the Council of Nicea or was it Trent was right about most of them. Only for the deciding bishop keeping a pretty concubine they would have decided against women having souls. But that is a primitive Irish point of view and not true.

I got a great woman for the second woman in *The Black Soul* I know her better than myself and she's a fine character, a beautiful woman and an ardent Catholic. I am on pins waiting to see herself and the Black Soul getting into spirited handigrips. Is there anything more boring or egoistic than a young writer?

I can't understand Nietzsche. I guess I don't know enough yet for him. Do you [know] what? I was just picturing Christ and Nietzsche having an argument. Christ gesticulating in true Jewish fashion, with the energetic cunning action of a Trotsky and Nietzsche the brilliant profound German. It should be a good debate. I would lay my money on Christ, because I think he knew human nature better and would get the audience with him. But that Nietzche was a marvellous character – must have had Irish blood in him (?).

Sorry to write so much muck, and glad to meet you on Wednesday.

I remain, sincerely yrs
Liam O'Flaherty

P.S. I knew an old chap apropos of writing letters who used to say, 'The matter of writing letters is not the qualification of an Irish gentleman. As long as an Irish gentleman can make himself understood by another gentleman there is no necessity for him to be able to spell or even to write.' Most of them had those qualifications or rather the lack of them.

---

5. HRHRC TLS
258 King's Road, Chelsea, London SW   Saturday n.d [? May, 1923]

Dear Mr. Garnett,

You see I have a typewriter sense. I succeeded in borrowing one for the day from Kirwan.[1] Well, I was jolly glad to get your two letters today and cheque enclosed. Say, we'd better make that debt of twenty five pounds now since the marriage did not come off. I would prefer it that way if you didn't mind. Thanks awfully. I do believe I would be all over the shop if it were not for you. I will be able to have all these things typed by the time you come back, and beginning Autumn of *The Black Soul*. I think 'Summer' is far better than 'Spring'. Tell me, do you think it better to burn 'Spring' and do it all over again? You didn't like it you know. 'Autumn' is strong, that is it has a strong factor in Red John's madness. Say though, a 'Manhood' is going to be bigger than The Black Soul.

I have a wonderful opening. I am half intrigued with the idea of making it into a drama. The beginning has such dramatic possibilities that it would be a pity to waste it on simple prose. You see the party of peasant women on the rocks chanting these hymns with their men out on the raging sea in a storm, the sounds of the sea, the rush of the spray, the hissing of the wind, the eyes of the women, the men fierce {?...} forgetting danger in the raw lust of manhood. But I will tell you about it when I see you. Of course I am not working on it, it is merely simmering in my brain. It's the novel I wanted to write from the beginning. But is it a drama?

I am glad you liked the idea of my falling in love. It's a great sensation and she's a fine girl that.[2] She's the first one that appealed to me that way. I met a lot of women with whom I wanted to sleep for a night, and others with whom I liked to talk, but she is the combination of both. You know what I mean? I have no burning desire to possess her, in fact I believe I would hate to do it in normal mood, but every time I look at her she sends the blood throbbing through me. Such a flexibility of figure. Such a consciousness of beauty perfectly concealed. Perhaps though you will consider her quite common. However we will toast her in a flask of Falnernia when we see her. You will find our first embrace depicted truthfully in the middle of 'Summer' of *The Black Soul*. Yes, she lives down at Quaker Farm. Her brother has some one hundred and fifty acres of land there and her mother keeps this farm house business. Her mother I fancy is just an ordinary what we would call peasant woman. It was from her father that this lady got her beauty, and more than her beauty, her pose. Funny how fathers hand down their character more than women, especially the chacteristics of race or type. The women hand down the characteristics of genius, the waywardness of the mind. Any damn how, I like this girl, and she writes well and sensibly. She thinks all Irishmen crazy, and is under the impression that were it not for the English race the world would be by now a lunatic asylum. So, so!

I have another sketch that I am going to do tomorrow or after called 'The Wren's Nest'. I hope I get it. It will be very difficult to prevent it from being cruel and on the other hand from being sentimental. And finally I may not get it at all. If I get it it will be the best of the bunch.

This place is nice to work in and the people are all right. The lady Miss Russell, I think, asked me for a reference and I gave her you, and she immediately said 'Oh, the father of *Lady into Fox*.'

She knows your son's wife pretty well.

Yours, Liam O'Flaherty

[1] A friend who later typed for O'Flaherty

[2] This woman's name is never mentioned. Evidently she repels O'Flaherty's advances beyond a certain point

6. HRHRC TLS
52 Warren Street, London W1 Saturday morning, n.d. [? early May, 1923].

Dear Mr. Garnett,

I have shifted my digs pursued by those enemies of livers in rooms –
bugs! I got your letter this morning and was delighted to hear that you liked
the cow. It's not the sketch itself but the fact that at last I know what is
wanted to write one that pleases me. Thanks so much for showing me. You
see I was always aiming after this damn cleverness in expression without
bothering about the bones of the corpse upon which I was operating,
probably copying the daily papers, but I imagine the fault is hereditary.
However that damn cow, like all cows, persisted in coming back from the
Manchester Guardian last night.

Now if I had not known you, I would have torn that up considering it to
be a rotten production and only worthy of the basket. But you better not
tell me that I am writing too well or I might get a swelled head, it's swelled
enough already, and we Irish are very prone to enlarging our area above
the neck at the least encouragement or for the lack of it.

Say, I was greatly taken with your son yesterday. He has got a higher
development of the artistic temperament than I have. See what I lose by my
ancestors being all uncivilised.

I think this is a better room for writing, although the noise is greater.

Is mise le meas, Liam O'Flaherty

---

7. HRHRC TLS
52 Warren Street, London W1   Monday morning n.d. [? 14 May, 1923]

Dear Mr. Garnett,

I am going out to the country on Wednesday, at least I expect to go if
things pan out all right. I have had a bad cold since and I guess I had better
beat it and get better. I am staying away for a fortnight and then coming to
live in Connaught St. I think I irritated you last Friday. Excuse me, I am very
hard to put up with when I am nervous. By the way, I have discovered a
good subject for my next book describing the peasant life of Aran. Got the
idea yesterday reading D.H. Lawrence's 'The Fox'. I don't like that fellow
Lawrence's way of writing.

Didn't hear from Tomlinson yet. I saw Cape had a letter in yesterday's
Observer about O'Neill.[1] Clever fellow Cape. He can keep up advertising all
right. And it looked genuine. Went into Westminster Catholic Cathedral
yesterday and asked the attendant had they a statue of the illustrious St.
Michael of Compostella on the premises. He assured me that they hadn't
and inquired into the nationality of the saint. I told him that Voltaire and
he were personal friends and he nearly dropped dead.

Then I lit a candle to Saint Brigid of Ballinamuck and that satisfied the attendant as to my bona fides. I should have asked him whether General Rathcroghan got married there, though it is obvious that he got hitched in the Oratory.

So long
Liam O'Flaherty

[1] This refers to Cape's publication of Eugene O'Neill's plays. 27 May, 1923, p.11. the *Observer*, St. John Ervine wrote a commentary under 'At the Play' on O'Neill's *Anna Christine* (included with *The Hairy Man* and *The First Man* in the Cape volume) then playing at the Strand Theatre.

---

8. HRHRC TLS
52 Warren Street, London W1   Saturday morning n.d. [? end May, 1923]

Dear Mr. Garnett,

I am glad to say that Desmond McCarthy accepted both the sketches. He also gave me a book to review and told me that he might publish selections from *Thy Neighbour's Wife* if they were suitable. He didn't like 'Blood Lust', said it was too pathological for his taste, so I had to sell it to him in American fashion. The other he took right away. This damn book he gave me to review, Nellie Ptaschkina's Diary,[1] has been published by Cape, so if I knock it he won't like it, and if I praise it I will have to get stupidly drunk in order to appease my self-respect. However I will do neither. I'll talk about the weather and the Bulgarian exercise, in the [manner] of reviewing books.

Had a bad night last night.

Sincerely yours
Liam O'Flaherty

[1] This diary, translated by Pauline de Chary, was that of a Russian girl aged seventeen who died in 1920 after a fall in the Alps. No review of this book by O'Flaherty appeared in the *New Statesman*.

---

9. HRHRC TLS
52 Warren Street, London W1   Sunday evening n.d. [? May, 1923]

Dear Mr. Garnett,

Mrs Casey asked me to give you her compliments and would be honoured if you would call at 18 Connaught St. on Thursday after six o'clock and before seven. You would have supper and also have the pleasure of meeting General Michael Rathcroghan,[1] (it's the second turning to the left as you come up Edgware Road from the Marble Arch). The enclosed is the beginning of the masterpiece which is going to make both our reputations for indecency and which will probably land us in the Tower of London until our bones do rot, or otherwise will drop us into a comfortable lunatic asylum.

I feel one hundred per cent better after the visit to Surrey and I am very grateful for your hospitality and especially your introduction to my friend the general.

Seven o'clock Thursday evening, 18 Connaught St.

Yours
General Michael Rathcroghan

[1] See appendix for more about Rathcroghan, O'Flaherty's *alter ego*. Mrs. Casey was a shopkeeper who befriended Irish Republicans.

---

10. HRHRC TLS

52 Warren Street, London W1   Wednesday n.d. [? end May, 1923]

Dear Mr. Garnett,

In this best of all possible worlds your letter was the best thing. Glad to hear that you have begun the preface of {? Tents etc.} That thing I sent to you was merely an indication of how I might be able to be of assistance. But damn it I think that it is most amusing. I told my girl about the idea and she thought it would create a great sensation. And, my dear Sir, as she is typical of a large class of the people who pay contributions to libraries and have standardised intelligences, we might make a few shillings on the profligacy of the General.

Thanks for the cheque. You are really too good to me. I hope that sometime in the near future I may be able to do you an equally bad turn according to the Panglossian system of philosophy. I did that sketch you told me to write about the fellow addressing the mob. I called it 'The Proletariat Unbound'.[1] However, it's not a sketch for sale. I have also written two stories since, three thousand words each, finishing 'The Black Mare', and the other one, 'John Corbett's Treasure', is damn good but I think most unsaleable.

Now I am starting in on *The Black Soul*. Cape sent me an agreement to sign and the manuscript of that novel for revision. I didn't sign the thing yet. I thought I would like to show it to you, because I was never born to be a business man and I'm stupid on these matters.

Hoping to see you on Thursday at seven,

Liam O'Flaherty

[1] There is no trace of this manuscript nor of 'John Corbett's treasure.'

---

11. HRHRC TLS

52 Warren Street, London W1   Saturday morning n.d. [? 29 May, 1923]

Dear Mr. Garnett,

Thanks very much for your appreciation of *Black Soul*. Damn it I am the luckiest curse on earth, for I would rather have your praise than a five million circulation, seventeen whacks of the king's sword and a ducal dinner with knee breeches complete. I didn't get your letter until late last night, because I spent the weekend with an Irish friend, and there I met another Irish friend, the subject for a novel or a drama, I don't know which.

There is matricide in it, and the elopement with a step-sister. This friend I met is the nephew of the matricide, regular Irish romance or tragedy, old Protestant Irish family of the Cromwellian type, weak mouth like a crushed orange. The matricide must have had the same mouth, and this fellow is a successful business man. Well, well! Then I went out yesterday by Windsor Castle and Egham and Staines to get the atmosphere for 'Spring' in the *Black Soul*. I was lucky, saw goats with kids and horses and cows and all sorts, and met a fellow at Egham who told me the history of his life. His life was the making of a bicycle which he rode the day before from Bath to Staines. Then I quarrelled with the girl I was with and came home. She was no relation of the fellow with the mouth like a crushed orange. Her mother just belonged to the same town in Mayo.

Well, well! Another idea has struck me with reference to the *Black Soul*. It is a new idea and I must talk to you about it on Tuesday, and see whether it's too abnormal. By the way I don't think the whole thing would be longer than fifty thousand words or so.

Finished 'Winter' with three more pages, and I guess the remainder of the season would not cover any more ground apiece. You were right in saying that any detailed account of everyday occurrences would spoil the effect. Since then that has become very obvious to me, the petty details in 'Winter' of course were all black and would lend colour to the whole, but too much of them would weary the reader and make him think that it was an ordinary novel.

Anyhow I have lost the vision of 'Winter', so all I wanted to write must have been written. Now my soul is full of 'Spring', so there.

Got a letter from my brother today[1]. He tells me that he is starting a new paper and wants me to edit it. He doesn't want to do it himself as its policy would be different to the one he is doing now, and he tells me that there is nothing in writing novels. I am afraid though that editing a monthly newspaper would be more than I could stomach, so he can go to hell.

I will be delighted to come down on Tuesday. These talks with you buck me up no end. You see every week or so I get an insane desire to go to the North Pole, thinking that I could not possibly write. But I better let up on it and finish.

Crane is fine.[2] I nearly expired laughing at old Bill, the gunman. It's great, but I think he is a bit romantic. The psychology of the men in the open boat I have not come across. But then of course the men were Americans. Irishmen would act altogether differently. The description of the sea is fine in it, especially the mats of seaweed, which I have never seen before.

Sincerely yrs

Liam O'Flaherty

[1]Thomas J. O'Flaherty (1889-1936), O'Flaherty's only brother, had been in Boston since 1912, and was a member of the American Communist Party. He had always encouraged Liam to write. Tom's paper was the *Irish People*. Liam contributed 'The Sniper' to its first number (June 1923); then 'The New Irish Farm Worker' (August 1923), 'A Short Social Survey of Great Britain' (September 1923), 'The Renegade' (November 1923), 'Matchmaking' (April 1924, 'The Salted Goat' (May 1924). In the late 1920s Tom O'Flaherty wrote a *Daily Worker* column 'As we see it'. The editor is indebted to Jim Monaghan, of Dun Laoghaire, for this information.

[2]Stephen Crane's 'The Open Boat'.

---

12. HRHRC TLS

52 Warren Street, London W1   Tuesday morning n.d. [? end May, 1923]

Dear Mr. Garnett,

  Got your letter and cheque last night. Thanks so much. Got your letter re. General Rathcroghan this morning. The poor General is getting it hard, poor fellow. We must see what Cape can do for him. I bet it's that Sheeny we met in the Mont Blanc[1] that ran away with his wife. He looked like it. She couldn't make a cawk-tail for him so he refused to pay her her hire money. Well, well!

  I have done the review and will bring it down. I have done no more sketches, I was getting through with *Thy Neighbour's Wife*.

  I brought it down to Cape yesterday, but I couldn't see him and after a talk with the cashier, another Sheeny, I signed the agreement and left it there. The damn thing irritated me, and I'm glad to be rid of it. I hope I don't have to do much proof correcting on it. Once I have done a thing, I hate to read it again or correct it.

  The Black Soul has advanced twenty one kilometres into 'Spring'. I tried it on Miss Casey with the usual effect but I fear myself that it's weak. I have missed that O'Daly woman somehow or other. I haven't got inside her, although I know her far better than Little Mary. However, to hell with her.

  I'm getting spliced up in three weeks' time. It's much cheaper than living on my own, and I guess if I stay much longer in this kip I would die of the con. or nervous prostration. So I'm going to commit the indecency of living with a woman. That might be worse, for all the women I have ever lived with were a curse. However, long live Rathcroghan and may his shadow never grow less. I will be delighted to come to Mont Blanc on Thursday. By the way, that son of an illegitimate Sheeny, Cape's cashier, said that I had no right to get extracts published in *New Statesman*. He claims Cape has all rights to publicity. How is that?

  Oh yes, I would be tickled to death to get the loan of that bike. I am the devil on a bike. I generally break any bicycle I get hold of. I think it's a horse and ride it everywhere, over hedges and ditches.

Yours sincerely
Liam O'Flaherty

P.S [ALS] The sounds of their horses' hoofs are heard from dawn to dark, the sounds of trotting hoofs, the sounds of galloping hoofs, with sharp whinnies and neighs, and the ringing sounds of steel shoes on smooth stones. Life, life, and the labour of strong hands in Inverara in Spring.

[1] A restaurant in Gerrard Street, Soho.

---

13. HRHRC TLS
[no address]   Thursday morning n.d. [? June, 1923]

Dear Mr. Garnett,

Glad to hear that Tomlinson is coming. If we can capture him for the work of liberating the relative of a Rathcroghan from vile poverty we are well away. I will hawk some stuff along. You gave me a good ending for that story. Thanks very much. I have another sketch that might be of use for *Cassell's Weekly*.[1] I quite agree with the man who said that it was punk. It's worse, it's junk, and that's a step below punk.

I finished the first part of 'Spring', so I will bring it along tomorrow. I guess I am well away with that stuff now. You watch my smoke when I get into 'Summer'. By the way, all indications seem to point to the fact that you are working on Tents and Sheenies.[2] Is there any truth in it? Damn it, the lid will rush off England when they discover that there are two criminals like ourselves threatening them with such a flood of literature in the near future. But like the Aran man who had the illegitimate child, we'll put the blame on Cape. It was he started it.

I will be around at one thirty tomorrow at Mont Blanc. Till then.

Sincerely yours
Liam O'Flaherty

[1] This could be 'Selling Pigs' published *TP's & Cassell's Weekly* 19 January, 1924

[2] E. Garnett was engaged in promoting TE Lawrence's work at the time, *Seven Pillars of Wisdom*. Garnett helped prepare the previous abridgement of this *Revolt in the Desert* (1926).

---

14. HRHRC TLS
258 King's Road, Chelsea   Saturday n.d. [30 June, 1923]

Dear Mr. Garnett,

I got your letter yesterday. This morning I see 'The Cow's Death' in the *New Statesman*. It reads well in print. Well, that's your sketch. You taught me how to write that one. I thank you very much. I have not done anything as good as it since. I don't think 'Three Lambs' comes near it.

I am coming near the end of *The Black Soul*. I didn't want to do 'August' until I got your advice on it, but I got the itch and I had to go ahead with it. I have no idea what it is like. Trust to luck.

Great hounds, you must feel like a warrior of the Milesian type after your stay in Devon. I can just picture the feeling of sprawling full length on top of a cliff watching the sea roll on. It's better than any theatre. One never feels the necessity of doing anything. And then you have so many memories and they all roll up like a film. Even the pleasure of conversation is futile lying on top of a cliff. To my mind I think you should have read Voltaire lying there. Or perhaps you didn't lie there at all. But you must have.

I am feeling elated at the prospect of finishing *The Black Soul*. After that I think I had better attend to the Press for a bit and feed the bread basket. The prospect of starting another novel leaves me cold. It would also leave me very poor I think. But I suppose I have a lot of work to do on *The Black Soul* yet. Wherever in the hell did we get the crazy fellow from? Nobody will believe us when we tell them that he is real. To my mind he has no relation at all to General Rathcroghan. Damn it, wouldn't it be a good idea when we are reconstructing his arrival in Inverara to say that he came there because American Sheenies stole his wife and hid her in a tent?

Apropos of Tents and Sheenies, how much have you done of it since? But I will leave that alone as I think you want to keep it quiet. However, you must let me in on it.

I will be very glad to call up at 8.30 on Tuesday evening.

Thanking you for 'The Cow's Death',

I remain,

Yours sincerely
Liam O'Flaherty

---

15. HRHRC TLS
18 Connaught Street
Hyde Park, London W2   Tuesday morning n.d. [?June 1923]

Dear Mr. Garnett,

Thanks so much for your letter and cheque. I would be dead were it not for you and of course Fr. John O'Reilly would say you were aiding and abetting the devil. Well, I hope to raise the devil with the world yet anyway. The above address would be the best to write to, and Miss Casey would forward the letters.[1] I'm taking my reviews down to McCarthy now and trying to get some books to review while I'm away. I've done him a sketch from the novel too. I'm going to do a lot of work while I'm away, several sketches on Aran that I think will be good.

Damn it, I feel better now at the thought of getting out of London for a few days. You see I am a savage yet and can't breathe well in a city.

I don't think Murry[2] will fall for the 'Mare'. Strikes me from his first number that it's not his style. But I bet Tomlinson will get something into *Cassell's*. He'll be afraid to send them all back, after your telling about Brailsford[3] and the can of petrol plus automatic. He is a good fellow, that Tomlinson. I like them that way. Know what I mean?

I'm going to romp through that *Black Soul* when I come back. Hell, I'm talking about myself all the time, but what the hell else is there to talk about? Women, I suppose, or booze and the damn doctor says I must have no booze, and women don't interest me, so there you are. 'Ah', says he, 'the day I killed Buck,' and he sucked his lips. 'But Buck is still alive,' said the other. 'Oh well, of course,' says he, 'I killed him, for all that was left alive of him.'

Liam O'Flaherty

[1] Mrs and Miss Casey were sympathetic to Irish republicans. Miss Casey discouraged Liam from emigrating to the USA and encouraged him to write.

[2] John Middleton Murry, editor of the new *Adelphi*.

[3] H.N. Brailsford, whose *Socialism for Today* O'Flaherty reviewed in 1926.

---

16. HRHRC ALS
Quaker Farm, North Crawley
Newport Pagnell, Bucks   Friday morning n.d. [? 19 June, 1923]

Dear Mr. Garnett,

Christ, I am in a devil of a mess. I have just written to Miss Casey breaking off my engagement. I couldn't do it. It's awful terrible torture to injure a *friend*. She has been a friend to me, the most sacred thing in life, a friend, a comrade. And to make her unhappy – this is awful. It has been killing me for months. Driving me mad. Wasting my body. Trying to make myself love her because she had been good to me. And now I could do it no longer and it is painful.

Forgive me for telling you this, but I must tell somebody and you are the only friend I have. I suppose I will get over this. To kill a man is nothing — that does not hurt. But to hurt some living thing that is kind is ugly. It's like murdering a dream. O Christ!

Truly I have a black soul. But what of it. It's an awful thing to be sensitive and weak. I wish I were hard and careless, as I try to be. Life would be much easier. To eat and to drink, to sleep and not to care for sorrow. To drink sorrow and fatten on it like milk.

But enough, I expect you have enough troubles of your own without listening to mine. Everybody has. Do write to me though, and tell me to buck up. It's so silent and beautiful here that it's a sin to be sorrowful, and my brain is so clear. Perhaps it is why I have been able to write that letter. It appeared so ugly out here, sitting on a fallen tree, to live with a woman and not to love her. Like living with a prostitute. Dry, sickly smells, the sucked skin of an orange, the entrails of a worm.

I am doing *The Black Soul*. I have five thousand words of Summer done. I think it's good, but then I don't know. Anyhow I am following instructions and giving free rein to feeling and emotion. If there is anything in me it's going into it. So you can see my brave soul and measure its worth when you read. It's the opposite to Winter – Summer, and yet the same. You see the sea before a storm on calm sultry day. It is as if oil were poured on it. Well, that's Summer, Winter with oil poured on it. Lascivious summer.

I have done no more sketches. *The Black Soul* has gripped me, so that I can't think beyond it. *Cassell's Weekly* published 'Matchmaking' . There is nothing much in it. By the way I'd like to see your article on [W.H.] Hudson, I see it's been in last week's issue and I didn't see it.

Oh thanks for the cheque. Thanks dear friend, and I'm glad I'm going to meet the author of Thirteen Stories soon. It's great to meet people who think, real raw men.

Oh hell, I nearly forgot! [D.H.] Lawrence is a master. I read a copy of *Adelphi*, with a short thing by him in it, about trees.[1] Yes, he is the goods. He lives, by Christ he does. Tell me though; I noticed a marked similarity between the style of your speech, your manner of describing things and his method of writing about the trees. You must have had a big influence on him. I think all writers are {?}, and after all thought is half a tradition handed down, transmitted.

L.O'F

P.S. I don't know what the hell arrangements I'm going to make now. However, as long as I am writing 'Summer' I don't worry.

[1] 'Trees and Babies and Papas and Mamas', the *Adelphi* Vol.1, No. 1, June 1923, pp. 20-33.

---

17. HRHRC ALS
77 Charlotte Street, London, W1

Dear Mr. Garnett,

Just landed back. Got your letter this morning and sketches returned. I do believe you didn't get the letter I wrote to you last Thursday. Well, I told you in that letter that my engagement with Miss Casey was finished. I broke it myself. Now I am back in an evil smelling hole in Charlotte Street, that is, I believe, alive with bed bugs, if not vermin. I had to come up to get my kit from Connaught Street. They ordered me to take it away immediately, and now when I came up for it they refused to give it to me. They said they would send it in a few days, so I had to take this room and wait for it. Otherwise I would have gone back to North Crawley. I feel rotten since I came back to town – caught a fresh cold, and every damn thing. While down there I felt fine. Fancy, I finished 'Summer' in a week there, twelve thousand words.

Now for the reason I broke off my engagement. I discovered the reason the day after I broke it off. It was a woman, of course, and I didn't know it then. Now I am in love with her. For the first time in my life, in spite of Tchekov. Now you can laugh at me. You see, she is beautiful, born in the country, can ride a horse, farmer's daughter, fine English type, great grand-father came from France, so naturally I collapsed. It's bloody awful being in love. I wrote 'Summer' under its influence. Wrote the seven thousand words of it in three days, and if I had stayed down there another fortnight I would have finished 'Autumn' and the book. I gave her Tchekov to read – 'Lights'. You remember, 'There were the usual promises without which love seems to be impossible.' We both laughed at that and made the promises. She is twenty-three, was married to an army officer, artillery I think, at nineteen, and divorced last year. Has a daughter two years old. If we still love one another when I make good we will live together. She wouldn't marry any more she says. Well, well! What a crazy animal I am, There is no understanding anything in this world, except beauty.

Thanks so much for your praise of 'Three Lambs' and the others. It made me feel good. Now I can't type them as I haven't got a typewriter. The one I had is at Miss Casey's. It was a hired one so I guess I won't get it again. I guess I am in an awful mess, all of my own making of course. But why in the name of hell, or pride, should I marry a woman out of gratitude? Eh?

The *Daily Herald* published a little sketch of mine on the 11th.[1] I am eagerly awaiting your return, so that we can talk again. At present I am lovesick and can do nothing. It's no use talking to me about Rabelais, I refuse to listen to you, and Voltaire to my mind is a buffoon. General Rath-croghan's past career was the most unmitigated kind of piffle. He was only playing with life. Now he is hit hard on the top of the head. I hope it wears off and yet I hope it doesn't. Christ! I could write under its influence.

Yours
Liam O'Flaherty

P.S. Amn't I an awfully impertinent fellow to worry you with this child-ishness. But you are the only one I can talk to, so forgive me.

---

[1] 'How to behave in Western Ireland'.

---

18. HRHRC ALS

258 King's Road, Chelsea   Friday n.d. [? 22 June, 1923]

Dear Mr. Garnett,

Just a note to let you know my new address. I couldn't stand the stench of Charlotte Street, so I shifted as soon as I got my kit from Miss Casey's.

Am busy changing addresses. Haven't done any work yet. I will type the sketches on Kirwan's typewriter and send them on to you.

Have planned out a fine beginning for *Manhood*, a book about Aran life. Am rather afraid that recent events will cloud the finish of *The Black Soul*, but would like your advice about the ending of it.

Couldn't see McCarthy. He is in France and won't be back until next week.

This is a nice place to work, up on the top of a house. There is a little noise but not much. Noise is sometimes soothing to the writing temperament.

Hope you are enjoying the cliffs. You must tell me about them. I am greedy about cliffs. Wait though, till you see the Hill of Slaughter and The Yellow Gable in Aran. They are what you might call cliffs. We will go round in a curragh.

Yours
Liam O'Flaherty

---

19. HRHRC ALS
258 King's Road, Chelsea   Sunday morning n.d. [? 25 June, 1923]

Dear Mr. Garnett,

I started yesterday to write a story 'Ginger Dick, the fireman', and this morning, when I continued to {deploy?} the conversation it suddenly struck me as a drama. Now I'm full of it. It's my own first trip to sea on the {Romney?}, an awful tub. I went to kill the second engineer. The chief was a peculiar dramatic character, and the {hero?} Robbie McDonald, was the regular goods. He's Ginger Dick. The only thing is that O'Neill[1] has gone before. However, for one's own pleasure it's going to be written. I know these fellows better than O'Neill does. He gives them too much of a literary sense. The Americans are not seamen. Only British seamen are real seamen. See Conrad (not index of Tents and Sheenies). We'll see what can be made of it. Then I can console myself with *Manhood*.

L.O'F

[1] Eugene O'Neill was known for his sea plays at this time, and had won the Pulitzer Prize in 1920 for *Beyond the Horizon*.

---

20. HRHRC ALS
258 King's Road, Chelsea   Tuesday n.d. (? June 26, 1923)

Dear Mr. Garnett,

I got a letter this morning from the editor of *The Best British Short Stories*, to wit Edward J. O'Brien, asking formal permission to publish 'The Sniper'. It's coming out in America. I sent them a reply saying 'yes'. I wonder is it all right? I suppose the only thing we'll get out of it is the honour and glory, that is if it's any honour to be discovered by America. Was it you or Cape told them to take it?

I think I missed the 'Wren's Nest'. I typed 'Summer'. Now I am going to sit down and think out 'Autumn'. I will lead it up to the climax. We will have an argument about the climax. What's your idea about 'Autumn'? 'Autumn' strikes me as a 'wake'. I don't know.

Well, it's only a few days now until you come back and then we shall have a great talk. I am feeling good. I feel like seducing a Pope's daughter, I am that full of life.

Yours sincerely
Liam O'Flaherty

---

21. HRHRC ALS
258 King's Road, Chelsea   n.d. [? 27 June, 1923]

Dear Mr. Garnett,

If you haven't sent 'The Black Mare' to Graham yet hold it up. McCarthy says he'll take it. He will because he hates Murry and I told him Murry turned it down. He wants me to give him a look at the others too. I gave 'Three Lambs' to Mary Agnes Hamilton. She won't take it.

McCarthy is going to duplicate sketches in *N.S.* for me, and will send a note to *Outlook* with one. See you on Friday.

Yours sincerely
Liam O'Flaherty

---

22. HRHRC TLS
258 King's Road, Chelsea   Monday n.d. [? 30 June, 1923]

Dear Mr. Garnett,

I just got your letter. I couldn't post your other letter yesterday, forgot it on Saturday and left it lying on my table. However, I knew you would be vexed at my running about. But I was in such a state of mental torture that I didn't know what I was doing. Now I am better. I am all right here. I'm not going to kick the bucket. I feel good and can work like a horse and eat like a bear. I have done the 'Wren's Nest' and I hope you will like it. I do. I couldn't stay down at Quaker Farm as a permanence on account of my affair with the daughter. It would be embarrassing for her. You know what a country place is like. Besides I guess I would get fed up with it. I put all that stuff into 'Summer'. It's either first class stuff or it's tripe. I don't know which it is, though I fear parts of it are tripe pure and simple. But I wrote it from my heart. Some of it has to be struck out if we want to publish it. It's worse than *Candide*.

I don't know whether I love that woman yet or not. I guess I do. Well, she has given me an inspiration anyway, but they all do. Say nothing till I see you again. You see, I would not like to leave this joint now since I have moved into it, because the lady who owns it is a painter, and it's not fair to inconvenience people in the trade. And damn it, it's an awful trouble moving about. When a man gets a place with a daily bath and no bed bugs he is naturally afraid to leave it. I am working like the devil trying to get my typing up to date and the fool who owns this typewriter is writing a novel and I can only get it at odd moments. I wonder what makes bank clerks write novels. Their wives I suppose. I hate retyping things. There is such a lot that I can do and want to do. The only pleasure is in the moment of creation. There is no pleasure in preparing for the market. I have the 'Wren' ready for the market but none of the other three. I have typed a copy from the pencil script. I will have them ready when you come back and probably 'The First Bream'.

This bloody place, Chelsea, must be a dumping ground for lunatics who can't muster enough human energy to qualify for a legitimate store-room of the insane. Such an artificial respectable place. Fitzroy St. for me only for the bed bugs and the fetid air. My room is a nice one. Plenty of scope to walk about and laugh and strike my chest when an idea hits me. Gee, I will do some work here. My chest is getting better. I guess it was worry more than anything else kept me down. I don't want to die so I am not going to die anyway and that settles it.

Yours
Liam O'Flaherty

---

23. HRHRC TLS
258 King's Road, Chelsea   n.d. [? 9 July, 1923]

Dear Mr. Garnett,

Got your letter this morning. Glad you didn't think that *Manhood* should be a drama. You see, I get foolish ideas now and again and it requires a kick in the back-side to get me back to a correct view of things. I will be able to get it into prose. I have started Autumn, but very slowly. She didn't get going yet, no impetus, no motion.

Damn it, I am beginning to get windy about this place Chelsea. Everybody I told that I was living here said, 'Ha, that's bad, Chelsea is a low lying place, you should have gone to Hampstead somewhere.' You are the fourth that said it. However, damn the place. It will do until we can get somewhere else. My mark is a little cottage in the country somewhere all to myself. About twelve feet by fourteen, with a long lease and a rent of about six shillings a week, that will satisfy my homing instincts. Living in rooms is awful. To hell with them. This room is about the best I have struck.

Thanks very much for sending me that bike. Boy, when I get it I am going to ride out and keep riding. I once did seventy miles in a little over half a day on a bike and then drank a pint of whiskey with Larry De Lacey. Ha! Be Jasus, them were the good ould days. God damn them, they were rotten days if the truth were only told. I got a letter from the young woman this morning. I told her to amuse herself by writing sketches and she sent me two done right off. Damn it, they were the regular tripe for women's journalism. Quite good. So I do really believe that I will be able to make money on that woman. I will write artistic stuff and make the reputation and she will make the money on junk. Very good, then I'll cut my throat. Still better!

This son of a priest, McCarthy, is still in France, so I can't get any books to review. That's bad because I think this is the best season for good books to review. I mean the fifteen shilling ones that you don't read but read the publisher's account on the cover, and then sell for seven and sixpence and a clear conscience. If I could get about ten of them a week I'd be all right. If McCarthy is a sufficiently dishonest Irishman he should give them to me. Damn it, what other use is McCarthy, will ye tell me that! You are supposed to know, as Pat Coleman used to say.

I wish you were back so I could talk to you. I notice some eccentricities coming into my style of writing that I think are artificial and I can't locate them. I think I'm getting too fond of strong words. How is this in the beginning of 'Autumn', 'Goats with their crooked bones sticking out through their skins ran about in their season smelling evilly.' 'Autumn, the withered mistress of nature, ugly as a woman with child.'

I can't get 'Autumn' unless I discuss it with you. Damn it, unless I get this *Black Soul* excellent, I will never get anything right. We should be able to fix up the beginning of the Stranger. I forget now what we did with the poor devil. That should be easy. 'Summer' I think is the best part of it. Now for 'Autumn'. Autumn, damn it, is an awful season, all rain and mist and treachery. How do women feel in Autumn in Inverara? That's the point. I have got rid of Kathleen. Poor girl she was a false alarm. The poor chap couldn't stick her. Little Mary turned out to be the goods. But I rather fancy that she also lost her charm in 'Autumn'. He finishes up by taking her away with him, scratching his head and saying, 'Oh well, damn it, a man has to be born and married and buried. And what's the difference anyway.' To my mind it would be false to do the thoroughly regenerated stunt on him. He is an Irishman. He finished up by saying, to hell with Inverara. Civilisation is the thing after all, and he thirsts for Mooney's in Abbey St. and the fellows spitting into the Liffey.

Yours, Liam O'Flaherty

P.S. [ALS] The 'Wren's Nest' is no good. We can sell it though I think. It's a poor imitation of Mark Twain.

24. HRHRC ALS
marked 'Crawley'   n.d. [? 15 July, 1923]

Dearest Friend [Edward Garnett],

Just got your note. My teeth will close with a snap on your door knocker at 7 o'clock Wednesday. I am sending you some more of Rathcroghan's memoirs. Hold it until I see you. If the sketch is worth typing I want to improve first paragraph. The inventory of pictures in first paragraph is not in the order our friend Montague[1] would desire, although for us two, who are beyond all that kind of second-rate {?} it's all right. There's boasting! Before you know where you are I'll be saying, 'Myself and Edward Garnett'. God forgive me.

I hope you will show me your preface to your book on Hudson[2] I am greatly looking forward to it.

Now I'm hiking off to Mrs Coppard. She is bringing her husband[3] from somewhere. The reason is obvious, 'Fear', said Rathcroghan to me last night, as he was examining a wart on his big toe.

                                                                        Till Wednesday
                                                                        Liam.

[1] C.E. Montague, *Manchester Guardian* critic, whose *A Writer's Notes on His Trade* were collected and published in 1930.

[2] *A Hudson Anthology* published by J.M. Dent, ed. Garrett, 1924

[3] A.E. Coppard, writer of short stories and verses.

---

25. HRHRC ALS to Edward Garnett
4 Council Houses
North Crawley, Newport Pagnell, Bucks   Sunday n.d [? 23 July, 1923]

My Dearest Friend,[1]

You really must allow me to apologise for having been so churlish during my last few meetings with you. It would be unjust for me to excuse my conduct on the plea of ill-health. I think my unspeakable vanity would be a better explanation. However, I trust that you will understand. To an intellectual the case around the instrument is not so important as the instrument itself. And to you I hope that Liam O'Flaherty is of absolutely no importance compared to the artistic soul that sometimes lurks beautiful and gaunt within the ridiculous fellow's body.

So, so! I got out of town just in time to save myself from falling back again into savagery. You will misunderstand this I know, but the fact is that towns demoralise me. It is only when I can feel the vastness of the empty firmament above me and the clean smell of unvarnished nature about me that I can think. I become pure, my conceit vanishes, I soften. There is no necessity to put on armour in the country in the face of nature. One lays bare the breast, the heart, the soul, to drink in God which is beauty. Then only can one sing when the wine of beauty surges against the chords of the brain in myriad waves, jangling them. That is how I felt yesterday lying in the trap that took me out from Newport Pagnell. Like a good Catholic I examined my conscience. Like an O'Flaherty I .... Oh well, let's keep that quiet. Fact is I felt vexed with myself for having been boorish and childish towards you. Please forgive me because you are very good. If you had been an Englishman I wouldn't mind, but you have an Irish soul, I can see it always through your eyes. We go very far back into the past, us two. I expect our ancestors were sometimes boorish to one another too.

I commenced *The Black Soul* this morning. I have done two thousand words and already I have felt fierce over it. I am improving it, I feel it, and now I understand what you meant by the language having to be poetic. I am going to try and raise the tone of the whole thing to the level of the first page, and I have found a new sub theme, i.e., 'So the very soul of Inverara sang in winter, with the sea, the wind and the rain playing a thunderous symphony on its mighty chords. Beauty is the queen of life. She is the eternal joy of Being. She knows no laws. Away with laws, away with sentiment!' This to explain Little Mary's despising of Red John. Let us hope that the *Black Soul* will emerge perfect. But it must. It hurts me as much now as the first day I thought of it. It hurts me like reading Shelley, and I always loved Shelley. It is only the things one loves that hurt, *or that one hurts.*

I am writing it with a pen into a big exercise book with a stiff vellum cover. It will hold the lot, a book in itself.[2] And I tell you what, I will save enough money to get it typed. You see my cigarette money can go to some typist and I will be a gentleman, without a stooped back.

I met my girl yesterday and we spent a good many hours together. She is writing a little sketch which I think is quite good. A clever girl. I had hoped that she was not clever. Tell me, do you believe in intellectual men mating with stupid women, or should they mate with intellectual woman? Supposing this girl becomes intellectual, then I imagine she would become as conceited as myself and it would be, 'pistols for two, coffee for me, gadjooks'.

Well, goodbye and good luck.

Is mise le meas
Liam O'Flaherty

[1] All the following letters beginning *A Chara*, 'My Dearest Friend' are to Edward Garnett.

[2] MSS drafts of *The Black Soul* are held by the Lilly Library, Indiana University.

---

26. HRHRC ALS to Edward Garnett
41 Fitzroy St, London W1   Friday n.d. [end July, 1923]

A Chara,
     You are five times bigger than God. Your letter has been an elixir to me.

I was so much afraid that I had missed the 'Banners of the Dead'. And, here is twenty-six talking, after I left you on Wednesday I became pregnant immediately with the idea of a drama. By nine o'clock it began to grow beyond a one-act comedy and after a sleepless night, it developed into a four-act comedy-tragedy. I have written two thirds of the first act since. Of course I suppose it is an abortion, and, equally of course, I have cried over it and sang over it and laughed over it and think it a masterpiece. But to tell you the truth, now that I look at it, I see Ibsen's *Hedda Gabler* and Euripides' *Alcestis*. But, as the Irishman said after disfiguring his face in a fight, 'Begob, something might come of it'.

I am not going to touch the 'Banners of the Dead' until I see you again. That Marion Phillips woman is all wrong somehow. I heard her talking yesterday in Bertorelli's, but though I tried to pick her up I failed.

I will go down in the morning for those sketches, and I don't know how I can ever thank you, Mr. Garnett, for all you have done for me. I have been thinking at the rate of a thousand miles a minute since I met you.

I am eagerly looking forward to having another talk with you, it's so damn lonely in this street, and the landlady calls me a typewriter man.

I am calling this play 'The Yellow Beard', tearing the scrofulous hide off Figgis's carcase.

Is mise le meas mór
Liam Ó'Flaithbeartaigh

[Neither of these script ideas seemed to have matured]

---

27. HRHRC TLS to Edward Garnett
41 Fitzroy St, London W1   n.d. [? end July, 1923]

A Chara,

By jabers, I think we'll turn that into a comedy. I was reading your letter for about an hour last night and then I commenced to laugh. The laugh lasted well into midnight. Nothing has come so far but I see indications of something. This fellow Fitzgerald is all wrong. I see now that he could not possibly exist. A fellow like Fitzgerald would never give Curtiss his soul. Away with Fitzgerald. His name is Flanagan. Mick Mullen is his name in actual life, a fellow that simply delights in politics, in intrigue, in love affairs and in private life is cynical about the whole thing. Mrs Curtiss is Delia Larkin (who in actual life hires Mullen to boost her brother Jem) and she also delights in intrigue, but her intrigues in this case almost get Curtiss into serious trouble. Curtiss in face of the camera is a hell of a fellow but his wife arranges his bow tie for him and treats him as an infant. His wife is fonder of publicity than he is, a vain but witty woman, a clever woman, who can use everybody. The other woman would be an English woman, her name is Tilly something or other in real life, and she was prominent in the suffragette movement in England and belongs to an upper middleclass Kentish family. I forget her other name or you might know her. She is a bosom friend of Delia Larkin. This fellow Mullen used, in fact, to make love to her and to Delia Larkin too. How in the hell you discovered that I don't know! This fellow Hanley is also hand in glove with Curtiss and finally they arrange to sell the election, the one to the other, each being afraid of getting elected, for fear of assassination by the other fellow's gunmen.

Mary O'Reilly will be the wife of one of the 'chiefs of police' and overhears the beard-cutting adventure and comes to Curtiss to tell it, for money; but Harley also tells Curtiss and the beard-cutting might be organised by Curtiss's wife in conjunction with Mullen and Tilly.

Now this is impossible to understand, but it could develop into a regular interesting mix-up and in point of fact I knew a case like it in Dublin, where everybody is intriguing against the whole of the rest of the population. I have it, by God, if I can get it out. The second act under this plan would have to be changed. The American reporter could be dispatched but I would like him to stay as he also was making love to Delia Larkin.

But one point I would disagree with, Curtiss's wife, as an Irishwoman, would never fight against Curtiss. She would commit any kind of an indecency on Curtiss to get him elected, but she would desire, through her own vanity, to help him, merely as a tool to get herself cheers and bouquets. Whereas Mullen, being a regular unscrupulous fellow would commit an indecency on anybody maliciously out of pure devilment. Mullen, according to my judgment, would be the hero of the piece, setting everybody at the other fellow's throat and always wangling out of it. He would plot the whole thing and have all the women using him, while he was using them.

Anyhow, by the time I meet you on Tuesday, I will have my idea of the plot written out to see what you think of it.

It's great fun anyway.

Is mise le meas mór
Liam O'Flaherty

[The ideas in this letter do not seem to have been developed]

----

28. HRHRC ALS to Edward Garnett
North Crawley,
Newport Pagnell   Wednesday noon n.d. [25 July, 1923]

A Chara Go Buan,

I was delighted with your letter. I am indeed lucky to have you as a friend, because, as you say, you understand me. That is the great test of friendship, understanding. The only other person on earth that understands

me is my sister Delia. Even the worst of us have something good down
below the rust that gathers through the storms and the hard struggling
through the slime and mud of life, and it is only the eye of real friendship
that can shine down through the rust to the pure metal, just like a sun ray
shines down through the heart of a deep well to find the pearl that has been
hidden there by a miser. So your letter consoled me. I had begun to lose
hope in myself, I mean in the existence of that thin layer of pure metal. As
Conrad would say, if that thin layer is reached by the rust a man ceases to
be 'One of us'. But he, he, O Rabelais – why do I speak thus. Let us hide
these things from our tongues and let them speak for themselves through
our actions; just to murmur them on occasion over a handclasp, as our
ancestors would, is sufficient.

I am working on *The Black Soul* like a Jew making money. It pleases me
now. I am just taking the old M.S. as a rough mould and slashing at it with
a huge hammer, giving it shape. It speaks to me. I am making Little Mary
move now. In the old M.S. she didn't satisfy. I am remodelling the Stranger
and O'Daly I am going to recast altogether. He was 'bad form' I think,
before. I think I have caught the style completely now. I read the first
eighteen pages to my girl and I got the desired effect. She leaned on my
shoulder and wept. It will {three words} but no matter, the Stranger is now
'one of the craven O'Connors of Ballymilis, a descendant of him who fled
with a bloodless sword in the heat of battle'. I think he would carry better.
And O'Daly ... well, we will talk about O'Daly when I bring you the first
part of Winter completed. I rather think he is going to be like you.

I got the bicycle yesterday and it's splendid. I thank you so much for
sending it. Now I can run into London on it. I can ride it into Leighton
Buzzard and train from there. Would tomorrow week, i.e. Thursday August
2nd, be a suitable day to see you, or the following day? I will bring the first
part of the M.S. I did a little sketch yesterday about a seagull. It's {rather?}
light and I think weak, but I will send it to you with 'The Failure!' when I
finish the latter.[1]

I am reading Conrad's *Lord Jim*, it's fine but I think I prefer *The Outcast*.[2]
There is more fire in *The Outcast*, more abandonment. But *Lord Jim* is
wonderful too. I didn't start Turgenev yet. I have not much time to read,
only in bed at night. In the morning I lie in a field to do the *Black Soul*, and
in the afternoon I exercise my body and fiddle with sketches.

How is David getting on? Remember me to him, and to Miss Heath.[3] I
think she has a fine soul too. I can remember her smile. If I can remember
a woman's smile she is a fine woman. It's curious. But that deplorable
character Rabelais would crack his fingers at all these simple tests and shout
out, 'Ha! my jolly topers this poor fellow is in a very bad way. Obviously
he is in need of a dose of Pantagruelism.' You are quite right, Mrs Morris is
not that kind of an intellectual woman, but she thinks better than I have met

so far. I gave her my sketches. She liked the 'Cow' best and 'Blood Lust' and the 'Death Grip' (dog fight) next best. 'Josephine' and 'The Wren's Nest' she thought poor stuff. I don't think I will encourage her writing. She would be far better occupied loving.

Well, *au revoir*,

With best regards
Liam O'Flaherty

[1] Held by HRHRC is a 3 page MS of *The Failure* marked 'Chapter I' and bearing the Newport Pagnell address. It is about John Francis Dillon, a medical student son of a Portadown farmer, who has been five years trying to pass his first year medical studies in Dublin, and his father cuts his allowance down to fifty pounds a year. Dillon spends his money on drink. The chapter describes his return to Dublin and his sense of failure. By the end of the chapter he has decided to go home and farm. He is known as a teetotaller at home. His brothers are Joseph (a priest) and Peter (a farmer).

[2] In fact *An Outcast of the Islands* (1896)

[3] David is Edward's son. Nellie Heath, with whom Edward Garnett had a long-standing relationship.

---

29. HRHRC ALS to Edward Garnett
North Crawley,
Newport Pagnell   Monday morning n.d. [30 July, 1923]

My Dearest Friend,

I bet you are certain that I have changed the 'Stranger' for the worse, but 'the divil a change', I am merely solidifying him. I am giving a 'particular' cause instead of a general one. After all, the old copy was awful bosh when one comes to look at it closely. Only the basis of the first part of Winter remains with the best of the phrases. It was very crude. The new copy is better. The first ten thousand words ran with the lilt of a song and then it became a bit on a lower key to my ear. But I will raise the last thousand or so to a height again. O'Daly to my mind is much better now. He is a character now. Before he was merely a *scale*. I have seventeen hundred words done. I think the whole will reach ninety thousand now. I have very little for anything else but *The Black Soul* now. It has a far greater grip on me than when I did it before. Let us hope it is not mirage fruit. However, I found time for {Russian name?}. It is miraculous. Ah yes, Turgenev makes even a conceited {?gouger} like myself murmur with humility 'those heights are unattainable'. The lucidity of the pictures are {?ghastly}, the dogs tearing the horse's carcase, the hare being killed by the hounds, etc. Conrad perhaps reaches the same height in *Typhoon*, but nobody else I am sure.

The *Daily Herald* published an article of mine this morning,[1] and double headlined and spaced it beside Evelyn Sharp – there's an honour for you.

I will shoot them another. That anti-clerical fellow Ryan is better than

that degenerate son of a loose woman, McCarthy. I will never forgive him
for holding back 'Blood Lust'.[2] If I were in town I would go in and take it
away from him and horse whip him into the bargain. The unmitigated
scoundrel.

I will be at your place at 6.30 Thursday pronto. The bicycle is splendid,
I murmur at every mile I finish on it, 'Edward Garnett, damn it, is a
gentleman.' I did thirty on it yesterday, into Bedford, etc., rowed for two
hours up and down in a glider skiff and licked everybody on the river Ouse.
Then I drank a bottle of Bass to my own health, came home and did two
thousand words of *The Black Soul* describing a man in a state of despair. I
think the ill-health plea for writing is false. I feel as fit as a fiddle.

Hoping your dear self is likewise,

I remain,

Yours
Liam O'Flaherty

[1] 'Islanders who never go swimming, the queer bathing customs of western Ireland.'

[2] This story was published in *New Statesman*, 4 August, 1923.

---

30. HRHRC ALS to Edward Garnett
North Crawley,
Newport Pagnell   Saturday n.d. [? August, 1923]

My Dearest Friend,

Thanks ever so much for your delightful letter. Really I can never thank
you sufficiently for all you have done for me. I mean, apart from the other
things, the material things, in keeping my feet treading the artistic road. I
was almost lost. It was only yesterday as I was coming back from London
(I had to go to Hoppé the photo man at Cape's request) that I realised it. I
stopped at a wayside inn for a cup of tea, and just as I was sitting down to
the meal a hurdy gurdy began to play in the street outside. You know what
effect music has on us Irish. Well, it seemed that something fermented in
my bowels and that I had to vomit it or bust. It was painful but excruciat-
ingly wonderful, and it cried out, 'You fool, you are deserting life for the
pig's trough.' I jumped on my bicycle without eating and cycled home
yelling like a madman. And since then I feel the pain down in my heart,
that you say a woman makes you feel. I have begun to write *The Black Soul*
again. It is giving me the same sad joy that it gave me in Warren Street. Now
I have only to beware of the verbal pitfalls. But apart from the writing of it,
or anything I write, I am eternally grateful to you for keeping me true to
my own soul. It's black, curse it, and I don't want it to get yellow, or white
or the colour of a bank account.

I will pay attention to your memorandum re. 'style' and wording and
the Stranger.

I have the idea of 'Chaos' thought out. It will be in a similar vein to *The Black Soul*, i.e. the *sound* will be the same, but the method will be different. It has too many characters in it for a similar method. But I will make them all dance demonaically to the same mad comedy, some of them bravely, some of them cowardly, etc. It's a fine subject and it has not been treated yet. I hope you will help me with that too, because I will run the danger of becoming didactic, patriotic and a host of other things that don't belong to art. I tore up Black Michael, I couldn't do it.

I had the honour of meeting David's wife while I was in London, at Miss Russell's place. How very like David! Splendid woman, that is I mean she is an artist genuinely. I said something about a tree and a light came into her eyes. It's funny, the soul in a person.

I am going to make O'Daly my father with certain changes, and foist myself into my mother's people, that is, of course, the Stranger.[1] And I will make it no longer. I think Winter will only require verbal changes excepting Stranger's youth.

Now, here's to life and let us tear huge strips from its living body and eat them raw to the sound of the wild music of the sea. We were conceived ferociously in a gentle womb. Let not the mob terrify us by their shouts and suck the strength from our loins with their bribes.

Yours
Liam O'Flaherty

[1] O'Flaherty's mother, Margaret Ganly, came from Antrim forebears who came to Aran to build lighthouses. She eloped, aged 16, with Michael O'Flaherty aged 26.

---

31. HRHRC ALS to Edward Garnett
North Crawley,
Newport Pagnell   n.d. [? August, 1923]

My Dearest Friend,

I am enclosing a little sketch. I am afraid it's a transposition of the 'Death Grip', but it might do for the papers. I guess I am coming near the end of my tether in these sketches, repeating myself and using a fixed formula. I am trying one in the personal style about fishermen. I am not meeting with very much success, but if I get in on it I will have a wide field telling stories about all the funny people and customs in Inverara.

I am finding *The Black Soul* rather hard work, but I am plugging away at it. By the way I find my affair with Mrs Morris was not an affair of an hour. I tried to leave her and found I was madly in love with her. So weep for me. Still, I am happy. I am going to live with her, 'Fool,' you say. Very well, I am a fool. I am going to take Mrs Coppard's cottage if I can get it. Then we are going to live on three pounds a week. She is going to leave the child at her house for the winter, and then in spring if we are tired of one another, we part. It's a good time for writing 'Chaos' next winter, eh? Still, I can't see how I could do better. She is beautiful, at least to my eyes. She has no prejudices about anything. She is obedient, very loving, and there is no nonsense about her. So I run as good a chance of not dying of neurasthenia with her as I would without her.

I read Turgenev's 'Clara Millitch'. It's wonderful art – magnificent. I didn't like the story. I don't like any of Turgenev's stories. He adopts the same attitude towards life as I do myself (within my own soul), so I don't like his attitude. He hurts in the heart.

I got something for your index: 'Popular author, see soon: soon, see forgotten: forgotten, see blatherskite: blatherskite, see popular author.'

L.O'F

---

32. HRHRC ALS to Edward Garnett
North Crawley,
Newport Pagnell   n.d. [? August, 1923]

My Dearest Friend,

I got those sketches. Thanks very much. I sent 'Beauty' to McCarthy.[1] I pulled off a trick on Murry – sent him a letter thanking him for having published 'The Ass of St. Joseph', saying it was a splendid story. He sent me a letter saying he would be sure to accept a story of mine shortly and very sorry to have to reject 'Josephine'. I'll fool the fellow. After all an Englishman is pretty easy food for an Irishman. I noted his scoundrel's attack on David – very good.

I finished 'Spring' and will probably have 'Summer' finished in another week. I like the *B.S.* very much now. Red John has improved immensely. However, it will be a great load off my chest to have finished with it.

Hoping you and yours are feeling quite fit?

Yours
Liam O'Flaherty

[1]The MS of 'Beauty', held by HRHRC, bears the following undated note:

My Dearest Friend,

This is a page from Rathcroghan's memoirs. He sanctioned my giving it to the public. 'But,' he said, with the chuckle which we know so well, 'you may tell Edward what happened when I got back. God! I found my fiancée under a tree in another fellow's arms.' 'What did you do then, General?' I asked him. 'Begob,' he said, 'I was going after the beggar to murder him when I fell over a fallen tree and hurt my crotch. I had to lie there groaning for half an hour.'

L.O'F.

---

33. HRHRC ALS to Edward Garnett
North Crawley,
Newport Pagnell   Saturday morning n.d. [? 11 August, 1923]

My Dearest Friend,

I have decided to start *The Black Soul* again and do it carefully, sticking to the old copy, excepting, as far as the construction of the sentences is concerned, the 'solicitor' business and the second last two pages of Autumn. Further I am now doing a short story or rather a longish compressed short sketch (about four thousand words boiled intensely). It's real true life. It happened, every word of it. I know the man, the place, the very words uttered, the psychology. I am weighing every word, gesture, sound and mood. And if it is not right I am going to chuck writing and take to journalism. (That is, of course, when I have finished correcting *The Black Soul*.) The point is that Murry may be right, that I can write fairly well, but that I am not in the first line and could never get there. This sketch will effectively try me. It's not a thing that would get published in this country, for political reasons, but I am doing it merely as a test of myself. And I will take your verdict. It was madness for Tchetof Hanov to try and make the second 'Malek' take the ditch the first 'Malek' took, i.e. of course if they were two different horses, or two horses from the same sire and dam. The second failure at the moment might have been due to bad oats, a stone in the hoof or simply a cold. We shall see. the *Statesman* published 'Blood Lust'.

About a book on the Aran Islands. I have got the characters and the material but no plot and no theme. If a theme strikes me I will tell you. Any theme that I could think of for the moment would be trite. The plot, of course, works out of the theme, or do they call it the first motif? When I finish 'Black Michael Derrane' I will think of it. That is if 'Black Michael Derrane' is worth the mother's milk he drank. Here's good luck to him. I can see now I was all wrong about new copy of *Black Soul*. Reading Conrad did the damage. I am going to read no more of him while I am working. I'm reading Gogol now. [unfinished]

———————————

34. HRHRC ALS to Edward Garnett
North Crawley,   17 August, 1923
Newport Pagnell

My Dearest Friend,

I got your letter this morning. I hope there is nothing serious the matter with your knee. Something told me you were ill. What were you doing? Trying to imitate Tchichikoff when he found that he possessed two hundred Dead Souls?

Thank you for getting 'The Fight' accepted. that's another stronghold carried by assault.[1] I'm a lucky devil to have your friendship. I hope I may be able to do something in return for your kindness yet. But I was never able to do anything for anybody.

I am very glad David's wife liked me. See how you have civilised me in the last six months.

I am doing the second part of 'Winter' of the *B.S.* It's great stuff the second part of 'Winter'. I feel that somebody else had written it and that I want to know the chap. If I could only have written the whole thing like that! I'm not touching it except for the style, and the words. I catch your point about the 'indirect picture'. I will pay attention to it. It's my individuality that, but I didn't see it until you pointed it out. If I could only get rid of my blasted conceit it would be plain sailing, but at times it almost overwhelms me.

Say, you mustn't let Rathcroghan get away with the whole fowl. The govt. contractor, Nick Carmody, tore a piece of the wing and swallowed it. The General struck the table with the end of his knife, 'If you don't cough up that wing, Carmody,' he said, 'I'll rip it out of your dirty guts.'

We have struck Autumn here. There is a tearing wind and the leaves are showing their white backs. It is just as if Autumn were driving the summer before it. Energy is coming back to me. Summer is the worst time for the intellect. The long Winter nights are the best for work. One can lie back and snatch up pictures in profusion from the past. There are no bright suns, or dewy dawns or sounds of women's laughter to distract me.

I expect do great work next winter on 'Chaos'. By the way am I to send you the *B.S.* bit by bit or will I wait until I have it all rewritten? I intend to go over it a third time in winter before it is submitted to Cape. You never know what ideas a man might get about style and words after a rest of a few months. If you would be so kind as to be merciless with the new copy I would be pleased.

I am going to see Mrs Coppard's cottage on Monday. I would like to see you next week to have a talk about 'Spring' of the *B.S.* It's about the Stranger possessing Little Mary. The point is, would she allow him to possess her before she was certain that he loved her, as a strong woman? I have some personal data on the matter from the private autobiography of Gen. Michael Rathcroghan, given under seal to me on his departure to arrest De Valera at Ennis at the request of the F.G. govt.[2] I think we should stick as closely to reality as possible. To my mind if she were an intellectual city woman, imbued with logic and theories she would allow him to do so. Gen. Rath. was positive that he had an affair with Little Mary's prototype and she resisted all his attempts. 'Why is that?' said the General. 'No', she said with tears in her eyes, 'not until I can have you all to myself. Until you are mine forever. If I let you possess me now it would spoil everything. If you are a gentleman you won't tempt me further.' Of course the General, being a boor of a fellow, did tempt her. But the Stranger being a neurasthenic chap, fond of theories and 'fine feeling', tore his hair and ran up to the shebeen and got drunk 'to drown the pangs of conscience'. Then he waited till summer when he really fell in love with her. As soon as she saw the light in his eyes she said, 'Ha, I didn't see that light in Rathcroghan's eyes.'

Yrs
Liam O'Flaherty

P.S. What day next week could I have a talk with you about 'Spring'?

[1] The *Manchester Guardian*.

[2] Fine Gael.

---

35. HRHRC ALS to Edward Garnett
North Crawley,
Newport Pagnell   n.d. [? August, 1923]

My Dearest Friend,

I met McCarthy and spent the day with him. We got on very well, in fact we were both pretty drunk in Irish fashion when we parted. He is taking 'The Black Mare' and wants some more sketches. I think he would publish one every five weeks or so. He is also going to look after a good review for my novel. I think I had better give him 'Beauty' if you have not sent it elsewhere. I think it's the best kind of a sketch for that crowd of readers. 'Blood lust' was as great a failure, he tells me, as 'The Cow's Death' was a success. They are a weak, cowardly bunch of pacifists and don't like anything real. They believe anything as long as there is a touch of sentiment in it. If there is no sentiment in it they say it's not true to life. To hell with them – but one must earn a living.

I am beginning on 'Spring'. It's not as bad as I thought. I guess I will have the whole manuscript finished in a month. I move to Chinnor on October 1st with my girl. Then I will begin to work on 'Chaos'. It's gathering shape in my head very fast. About another month I think I will be able to begin it. It's a far better subject than the *B.S.*, but I don't think it will be as good a book. I am no good at portraying character. Anyway, I'm going to spend a long time at it, because it's my last novel for a long time. It begins with 'The axle snapped', and it ends with 'Dead'. The rest is easy. By the way, I don't think De Lacey is the central figure and he didn't die. It's not natural that he should. And in life he was too wily a character to be the central figure in anything. We'll have to get a buffoon, brave, sincere, reckless, idealistic, for the central figure, with De Lacey in the background. De Lacey is the wind that lashes the sea. It comes and goes. You can't touch it, neither can you see it. But its power is felt everywhere.

I will open my political campaign this winter. McCarthy will introduce me to Yeats the poet. I think Yeats's crowd would be nearly the best for me to join. They are not deeply afflicted with partisanship. Then you can watch a cunning Irishman moving with all the wiles of the fox. I think it's the game that appeals to us most – like the French. The French persuade the world that they are fighters and then win wars by intrigue. The English, the only decent fighting race in the world, always preen themselves on their diplomatic talent, a game at which they are miserable charlatans. The writing of a book would be more interesting to an Englishman than the advertising of it. The latter is more interesting to an Irishman. It demands a greater power over men. If a thousand lies are necessary to write a book five thousand are necessary to advertise it and telling lies is a game at which only very clever men can play with any hope of success.

Liam

---

36. HRHRC ALS to Edward Garnett
North Crawley
Newport Pagnell   30 August, 1923

My Dearest Friend,

I was very much bucked by your letter this morning. I am so glad that 'Winter' has passed inspection. I felt myself that it was right, or almost right this time. I am doing 'Spring' in the same spirit but somehow it's not as strong as 'Winter'. The action is too varied and snatchy. But we never expected great things of 'Spring'. I haven't got sufficient power yet to treat *lust* in a manner that will make it *real* without being rude. This blasted public, I mean the so-called intellectual one, is like a nightmare over my head and that brings me to Montague's[1] very gross appreciation of 'Three Lambs'. I think he very blatantly exposes his own weakness in saying that he didn't like it because of its unreserve. It sounds so pharisaical. Such an argument is always used by the man who is loving to his wife and tells filthy stories on weekends to his kept mistress. As for the inventories, well, everyone finds an excuse for his cowardice, or rather for his jealousy. To hell with the bastard. He might have written 'His First Flight' himself, so I expect he took it for that reason. But we will see ourselves living on dogfish skins, cooked with the grease of a mongrel's vomit before we are sidetracked from what we consider pure art to please a mountebank or a Montague.

The *New Leader* accepted 'The Wren's Nest'. There you are; we are going to beat the blighters. And when we have got them on the run we are going to give them as large a dose of obstetrics as would cleanse bowels ever more substantially corroded with the virus of puritanical hypocrisy than the old maidenish bag of worms which passes as the innards of the British Intellect. To hell with them. To my young mind, respect for any convention, even the convention that is most sacred and the only one that is sacred, the honour of my father's name, is suicidal to truthfulness and art. Therefore, like

General Rathcroghan when he scaled the convent walls with two bottles of good wine in his lordly stomach, I am going to respect neither young nor old, ugly nor beautiful, but deflower everything within reach.

Cape has asked me to write a descriptive account of *Thy Neighbour's Wife* for the wrapper. I will enclose it to you, and you can give it to him. I would be very much obliged if you would look over it and change things if unsuitable as I am liable to make a fool of myself in these things.

If we can keep a hold on these three papers, the *Manchester Guardian, New Statesman* and *New Leader*, we will be able to live fairly well until our boat comes in, whenever that is. I am greatly afraid that *The Black Soul* will meet the fate of James Joyce's *Ulysses*. But I believe Joyce made a lot of money on that. At least so I am told. I am going to work McCarthy from now on carefully. Mum's the word between the two of us. Some day yet we'll give champagne to our hounds instead of sour milk, or if we don't we'll give them a good kick, like Tchetof Hanov used to do.

I got Borrow's *Lavengro* from McCarthy. That fellow Borrow[2] was a wonderful genius, though an uncommon liar. In fact he is one of the best liars I have ever met. He is among the first water men in my opinion, one of the very few Englishmen who can claim that distinction. I don't say by their writing but in their attitude towards their fellow men and more especially their attitude towards themselves. There is a certain innocuous conceit that is inseparably connected with a first rate genius, and a certain sparkle of melancholy wit that comes uncalled for like a flea under a lady's armpit. Ha, ha! Now we return to 'Spring'. Remember me to David,

Sincerely yrs
Liam O'Flaherty

P.S. For fear you might be gone to the country before you get this I am sending 'wrapper' straight to Cape.

[1] C.E. Montague, *Manchester Guardian* reviewer and critic.

[2] George Borrow's *Lavengro* was first published in 1851

---

37. HRHRC ALS to Edward Garnett
North Crawley,
Newport Pagnell   13 September, 1923

My Dearest Friend,

Delighted to get your letter. I was beginning to think that something had happened to you or that I had said something that vexed you. Instead I find that you have been delightfully busy preparing to spread your fame across the American continent. Congrats, and thanks for turning down Mrs Coppard's document. These women are a nuisance, they *will* keep writing.

There now, the numerous points in your letter are so important, and each in itself calls for 'thanks' or 'you are very good', so that if I were to deal with them in detail under their proper heading my script would look like a hymn to the Virgin Mary instead of a friendly chat with a heartless sinner like yourself. Still, it was good of you to get hold of Garwin and your self-sacrifice on my behalf in having lunch with Lynd[1] deserves a V.C. or something like it. When the two capture our hereditary estates in Clare and Galway, then we can bestow decorations on one another.

I am going to Chinnor on October lst and I don't think I will be in town until then. When I change abode I will be able to run in any day. My girl is getting on all right, but she is down with a cold now or rather just getting up. I am still very much in love with her. Where it is going to end I don't know. As Butler says, 'All reason is against love, but all healthy instinct is for it, and in this case instinct is the older and safer guide.'

I have finished 'Spring' long ago and am half way through 'Summer'. I would have finished 'Winter' by now, but I couldn't touch *The Black Soul* for the last eight days. It revolted me completely. I will try again today. I enclose two sketches I have done. 'The Salted Goat' gave me a great deal of satisfaction. I think it's the best thing I have done so far, and it's very true to life. I think 'The White Bitch' would do Lynd very well, or else the *Manchester Guardian*. That's the kind of tripe the public likes, they call it literature, and sure, be Jasus, I am ready to believe them if they pay me for believing them. I mean the 'Bitch', not 'The Salted Goat'. I like the latter and have read it ten times.

By the way McCarthy rejected 'Beauty'. He said it was all wrong. That chap McCarthy is pretty bum when one comes to size him up.

Sincerely yrs
Liam O'Flaherty

[1] Robert Wilson Lynd, or 'Y.Y.', who wrote regularly in the *Daily News*.

---

38. HRHRC ALS to Edward Garnett
North Crawley,
Newport Pagnell   Saturday n.d. [? September, 1923]

My Dearest Friend,
    Got your letter this morning and had a delightful breakfast digesting all the news. I am very interested in Mr. McNamara. I have heard of those McNamaras, they are a well known Galway family with numerous branches, a clan in fact, though largely gone into the shop-keeping and lawyer business. I should be tickled to death to meet him. I should therefore be honoured if you could put me up for the night and meet him in the evening. My girl and I will come around to tea at four o'clock to your place. Then I will convey her to her sister, with whom she will stay the night, and

return to you. Then we can talk for hours. I haven't had a talk since I saw you last. I am so much in ... [unfinished]

---

39. HRHRC ALS to Edward Garnett

[no address]   Monday morning n.d. [? early September, 1923]

My Dearest Friend,

Just got your card. Enclosed find 'Spring' and first part of 'Summer'. You will have to strike out a few phrases – one in 'Spring' at least. I have no time to read it now myself. I am staying now at Quaker Farm as my other landlady and landlord went on holiday. I'll be glad to shift from here on the lst of October. I will write again.

Liam

---

40. HRHRC ALS to Edward Garnett

North Crawley,
Newport Pagnell   Tuesday [n.d], September, 1923

My Dearest Friend,

I got your letter on Saturday re. 'Salted Goat' etc. Sorry it missed fire. We shall have to try again some time. I reread the crowd sketch and could make nothing of it either. I am afraid I couldn't go back to either of them, unless I can get the spirit first shot I can never get it again. You don't like Lynd. All these fellows are no good. They are too mean and suspicious, but one must not expect manna in the desert, even though Moses got it.

Say, I sent you 'Spring' and 'Summer' of *The Black Soul* last Thursday by registered post. Did you get it? I am just finishing 'Autumn', probably tomorrow. I am glad or sorry, lonely after it and overjoyed at having finished it. It's the only thing worth-while I have done so far, and it's not worth much. I am now brooding over 'Chaos'. That chap De[sic] is a fine character. He wore a most peculiar kind of coat that was typical of his anarchical disposition.

I am going down to Chinnor on Monday.

My lady will follow me on the following Thursday. If convenient I would be pleased if you would do me the honour of meeting us both on Wednesday Oct. 3rd in town. We are getting on very well now and I am really enjoying life – love, and the prospect of starting 'Chaos' soon, although I suppose the melancholy that pursues the actual writing of a work will crowd into my consciousness as soon as I stick my fingers into the plasma to create the living structure.

Had a letter from Mrs Coppard this morning. She enclosed a note from Edward J. O'Brien as follows, 'Tell O'Flaherty that he is a fine artist.' Very nice indeed. The chap might be useful if he were not a sincere Catholic. I suppose *Thy Neighbour's Wife* will make him say, 'The man is a disgrace to the faith of his fathers.' But the word *artist* is encouraging, especially when used by an Irish American.

My brother wants me to come to the U.S. in Spring to go on a speaking tour on the Irish question at forty dollars a week and fees and expenses from the Workers' Party. What do you think of the proposition? My opinions on the Irish question would disgrace any party including myself, and speaking to a mob is boring unless one wants to play with them to the danger of public peace. Yet $40 a week and good hotels? What do you think of it? He liked *Thy Neighbour's Wife*, in fact he said it was 'refreshing and interesting and far superior to any of the muck that the Irish novelist turns out'. But I fancy he liked it because it is a satire on the priests, against whom he has very bitter prejudices. For myself, I am disgusted with the damn thing by now. I wonder when Cape is going to publish it?

I have not heard from the *Manchester Guardian*, McCarthy had me shorten 'The Black Mare' five hundred words, I expect him to print it this week. He had to hold it up waiting for space, so he thought it would be better shortened to save time.[1]

Is your Hudson book coming out shortly? And David's new book?[2] My girl was delighted with *Lady into Fox*. She was specially intrigued with the grapes episode. She asked me so many questions about David that I took extra pains to assure her that he is very devoted to his wife, and that he is a man of absolutely unassailable virtue. I will have to take extra pains with 'Chaos' in order to prove that ....

I read Conrad's 'An outpost of progress' yesterday. It is a wonderful story. Conrad's personality attains greater and greater force the more one reads of his work. Damn it, I think 'The Outpost' is pretty hard to beat. I couldn't come near it anyway, more's the pity, although I have tried several times to portray those emotions and failed. Even in *The Black Soul* I failed to portray them. Looking back now I find that the Stranger was wrapt in a mist on many things, a mist that Conrad could dispell with a wave of his inimitable cheroot. But Lucifer got the can tied to him for thinking himself as clever a little boy as Jehovah. He should have been content with making mud pies a little longer. One has to make the mud pies first before tackling the bridge across a vast river.

Autumn is very melancholy down here. One needs music in Autumn. That, I suppose, is the reason why primitive people are so fond of music. My girl doesn't play at all badly on the piano. I am going to get a violin for her so that she may learn to play. Then I can create while she plays, get an access to the depths of melancholic joy and prowl around knocking ideas about and banging on the walls of deep caverns with heavy instruments. Great thoughts are buried in deep caverns where the dropping of water from a roof makes a sound as distinct as thunder before the breaking of a summer storm. I could swear that the sound of the wind through the trees now is the noise of the surf on the strand at Kilmurvey. Perhaps it is an echo of it. Perhaps.

Liam O'Flaherty

[1] Published in the *New Statesman*, 3 November 1923.

[2] Refers to Edward Garnett's Hudson anthology. David Garnett's next novel was *A Man in the Zoo*, London: Chatto and Windus, 1924.

---

41. HRHRC ALS to Edward Garnett
North Crawley,
Newport Pagnell   n.d. [? end September 1923]

My Dearest Friend,
   I lost the original ending and I had to do this from memory. I think it's fairly correct. There are a few phrases that I think are new to it, and I don't take them to O'Daly's cottage, but you said that that scene in O'Daly's cottage was a shade banal – on a lower level. To my mind I think this ending keeps up the tension to the last, or as nearly as we can get it.[1]
   I saw that old Lady Morrell.[2] Not our sort, but more or less interesting, possibly less.
   I am going to begin an opening for 'Chaos' now. I have already torn up twenty of them. It's frightfully difficult. I have no inspiration – that is emotional impetus – compared to that with which I began *The Black Soul*. I'm afraid that London is a much better place to conceive a thing than the country. ... [unfinished]

[1] Refers to *The Black Soul*.

[2] Lady Ottoline Morrell, famous hostess and patron to the arts, lived in Bloomsbury and entertained a large circle of writers such as Virgina Woolf, D.H. Lawrence, Aldous Huxley, T.S. Eliot and the Sitwells. She would now have been in her fifties. For more about her see Claire Tomalin's *Katherine Mansfield: A Secret Life*, London: Viking, 1987, pp.51-2.

---

42. HRHRC ALS
Chop Cherry, Chimnor, Oxon   2 October, 1923

Dear Mr. Cape,
   I received six copies of *Thy Neighbour's Wife* and a copy of *Now & Then* yesterday. I think the wrapper of the book is splendid – wonderful effect. I wonder whether the wrapper paragraph is going to get us into trouble.[1] I see the *Evening Standard* has exhausted all its pothouse humour in an endeavour to kill it. Very silly, if I knew who wrote that in the *Evening Standard* I'd give him the soundest thrashing he ever got in his life.
   I am installed in Mrs Coppard's cottage – came in yesterday. Finished

The Black Soul on Sunday and began 'Chaos' last night. Nice place this, although the roof of my shack is so low that perforce I will have to take my ideas from the gutter instead of from the sky.

Sincerely yrs

Liam O'Flaherty

[1] The blurb on the book jacket read: '*Thy Neighbour's Wife* is an attempt to write a book about life in the Aran Islands from the point of view of a native. It was written for two reasons. In the first place because Synge wrote a book about one of those islands that irritated me, in as much as he failed to get the personal touch. It was written in the second place as a courageous attempt to save the Irish novel from the debauched condition of being a political pamphlet or a religious controversy, or worst of all, a literary facsimile of the third-rate music hall comedies that draw alcoholic laughter from an audience of very low intelligence. It does not attempt to preach anything. It merely endeavours to be a faithful picture of life as I have seen it. And it has failed absolutely unless its first paragraph can arouse a laugh in even the most melancholy breast.'

---

43. HRHRC ALS to Edward Garnett

Chop Cherry, Chinnor   6 October, 1923

My Dearest Friend,

   Well, we have dug in here quite comfortably, except for the one disconcerting factor of the non-arrival of Cape's cheque this morning, which fact, of course, will be remedied in the course of a few days. We are quite happy. The cottage, which at first appeared tiny to me, is now assuming the dimensions of perfective contentment which {comes?} neither great nor small but fitting like an epigram. I feel at home. There is a certain feeling of satisfaction, apart from love, a feeling of having reached a comfortable cave in a primeval forest, whence the hunter may issue at his whim in search of prey, and to which he may retire to rest or nurse his wounds or dream or just laze. The emotions, if stripped of the fantastic trimmings of vanity, are very simple and not so far removed from the first principles of life as one thinks in the hollow splendour of civilisation. Borrow says he went to shoe horses after writing his first books. He had good judgment. I am washing dishes and building fires. If I had a donkey and cat I surmise I would go and collect old cans and bottles. May the devil devour London and all its works and pomps.

   Still, instead of collecting pots and pans or shoeing horses, it is very interesting to sit down here in Chinnor and scheme. Let us say that Borrow, to satiate his passion for pleasure, luxury and debauch, wrote a book. We have written one. Let us say that Borrow, in order to satisfy his creative impulse, shoed horses. We are going to poke fun at the public by trying to persuade them to read our works. It's about as ultimately useful as shoeing horses. Since neither Borrow nor myself, nor any other literary individual, is a whit of use to the world except as a tolerated ornament. Gladstone cut down trees. He also cut down individuals in battle. And the sea wrecks ships. What is positive except motion? As long as one enjoys life without getting his neighbour rushing around with a noose to hang him, he is doing well and he is a clever man.

Tell me, would you do us the honour of coming down to Chinnor for the weekend of October 22nd? You could stay at the Inn next door. It's a six hundred year old place and Cromwell slept there. Since Cromwell was one of the few Englishmen who were the heroes of my youth, I respect the place. We should love to take you around these hills and discourse amiably on diverse matters. Please say you'll come, and I will be soft as soft.

I hope you have forgotten my instability of Wednesday? I was very tired that day and it hurt me no end. I nearly had a breakdown. It's a cursed thing this neurasthenia but I'm lucky it's not worse, especially in youth. But I am sure, dearest friend, that you will forgive me.

With best love
Liam

---

44. HRHRC ALS to Edward Garnett
Chop Cherry, Chinnor   12 October, 1923

My Dearest Friend,

I got your letter this moment, with two notices of T.N's.W. [*Thy Neighbour's Wife*] enclosed. The *Times Literary Supplement* was very decent about it and the *Observer* one I had seen already together with a still meaner one from the *Sunday Times*.

Both the *Observer* and the *Sunday Times* gave me an itching sensation in my left hand, but I suppose many a man with more merit than myself (and you are among the number) have been treated far more viciously. the *Daily News* review I rather like. Mr. Lynd was obviously maddened by the book and still more maddened by the 'blurb', so much the better. We can expect no mercy from that type of literary courtesan. And a man that can be thrust under cover by the first shot from a mean and treacherous enemy had better quit the battle immediately. I fear that the book is murdered in its birth. Well, if it is it died fighting anyway. I suppose McCarthy will join the pack as soon as he thinks it safe. We'll have the laugh on them yet, upon my soul we will!

In a way, I think it's better that it was not well received. For a man of my temperament (we shan't say weaknesses) immediate success might be suicidal. The strength of *The Black Soul* was born of hunger and the appreciation of a solitary friend. What more is necessary to a man than a friend? If the mob would only put down their money they could spit and curse at a distance as much as they liked. I don't want their applause but I want their money, so that I need not go into the world any more but stay hidden away somewhere debauching on literature and the conversation of people who think.

Cape has asked me to write a five hundred words sketch of my life for *Now & Then* for publicity. I will send it to you to avoid the mistakes of the 'blurb'. This is the worst feature of publicity, Cape wants to publish it under the heading 'About Myself'. That tastes of Horatio Bottomley, or Hall Caine or some such reptile. It reminds me too of Davies and the *Daily Mail*. But one must not be too fastidious. Once a man stands before the footlights he might as well expose his underwear at once as dally with his shoe strings. This ogre the public is merciless. It refuses to ask 'what did he write?' but lasciviously enquires into the colour of the author's pyjamas.

I have not begun 'Chaos' yet. I am writing a weak sketch about a black bullock. Last night I had an experience in the manner of Tchekov's conception of the Black Monk. I dreamt I was being drowned by the orders of Nicholai {?} as an intellectual spy, the manner of my drowning so clear that I must make a sketch of it.

Yrs
Liam O'Flaherty

P.S. Please tell Cape to cut up this any way he likes (that is, if you pass it).

---

45. HRHRC ALS to Edward Garnett
Chop Cherry, Chinnor   16 October, 1923

My Dearest Friend,

Got your letter and 'Autumn' just now. Your criticisms of the end of 'Autumn' are, I think, quite correct, though candidly any ending that we could give it other than the real one must be artificial. I saw the Stranger die in the conception of the thing and trying to make him live must be, to use Gen. Rathcroghan's language, a 'bollux of a business'. I have felt it all along. The emotion through the whole piece works evenly enough, rising gradually to the climax, and when the climax comes it's like putting the lid back on a furnace. At one moment you hear the [?} roar, at the next you hear a distant simmering sound, as if the furnace lost courage and cooled down before the roaring burst it, as it should artistically have done. Granted that this is so, anything we may do with the fellow after Red John's death is puerile. Say, on the other hand that he died in a death grip with Red John, with the peasants watching on top, with the wind, sea, sun, air, etc., changing, clashing, moving, with the soul of the whole piece contracting into an intense moment of fierce, beautiful, endless, immaterial, melancholy sadness. Then Little Mary casting herself down, a shriek from the peasants and the curtain – 'The Black Soul was dead'.

That is the way I saw it, but as you say, we can't afford it yet, which is the very devil. Because we can't afford that I think your way is the best. (But

I should like a copy written in my 'cream' way.) (All rot.)

I will do my best with the revision and send it to you when finished.

I am working at the conception of 'Chaos'. Haven't touched it yet. I got up at 2 a.m. one morning and wrote a page, but it was all rhetoric of the worst kind. I have changed the plan in my mind considerably. I am now taking most of the characters from the gutter, and the action will deal solely with the Rotunda affair and the two months leading up to it. Nationalism will not come into it.[1] That will permit it a greater universality. I have the plot almost complete now. That is, of course, there is no plot, but I have the theory of the thing complete. Whenever it will be published, if I write it as I contemplate – God help me, because no side will praise it. So help me Crom Dubh.[2]

That Morrell woman has asked me over, to tea I suppose, next Thursday. I don't think I can write here as well as in London, but I fancy it's squeamishness. When a thing is growing within a man has all kinds of vapours. And one gets very tired.

If you will allow me to say so, I fancy you are wrong about Red John and the knife. I know, probably, more about madmen than you do. You see, I had an opportunity of studying them for six months or so, from the point of view of a native. Now take Tchekov's 'Ward No. 6' and you will find that a generalisation about madmen is necessarily hopeless. In fact I would go so far as to say that about the only thing that is characteristic of a madman is lack of concentration, except in a state of coma. In a state of coma he is harmless. He will only do things mechanically, but when he is trying to put into execution the outcome of an active obsession – that is, killing an enemy – he is (to my mind) more like a wild beast than a man. If you disturb a cat watching a mouse he will run away. But if you try to disturb him when he has got the mouse in his jaws you will fail. I have seen a madman stropping a razor (he was supposed to be discharged the following day), laughing and chattering cheerfully, and then suddenly cutting his throat. He had looked at the edge to test it and mechanically drew it across his throat. His mind was not watching his hands because it was disturbed. But I could talk about this better than write about it. And I suppose even if we did talk about it for a year or so, we would discover nothing.

At the moment I feel pretty hopeless about life. I am afraid I will never again write anything but 'Black Souls', but then Gogol was an unhappy man, and who can say that unhappiness is not happiness in the extreme? But that is a violent truism, almost as false as the meanderings of the most impudent Jew who ever earned a dishonest notoriety by inventing platitudes.

Did I tell you that a man wrote to me claiming to be the head of the O'Flahertys. I would, I think, gain a certain amount of publicity by bringing an action against him if I had the money. Ha, ha! His cousin is in the

Museum. He himself belongs to the Eclectic Club, so to speak.

With love
Liam O'Flaherty

[1] In January 1922, just after the formation of the Irish Free State, O'Flaherty, with a few unemployed dockers, seized the Dublin Rotunda building and raised a red flag over it. They held the building for three days. Afterwards, to avoid arrest, O'Flaherty fled to Cork.

[2] Crom Dubh (Dark Crom) a powerful god in Celtic mythology, who needed to be propitiated.

---

46. HRHRC ALS to Edward Garnett
Chop Cherry, Chinnor   18 October, 1923

My Dearest Friend,

I got your note this morning. I am enclosing a letter I received from a Mr. Burke.[1] Do you think you should send him 'Three Lambs'? I think so, or perhaps two sketches. I wrote and told him you would send him 'Three Lambs'. Excuse me for causing you all this trouble but causing trouble is a mania with me, and you are very kind. I suppose the chap is all right since Cape recommended him.

I shall be glad to see you in November. My wife[2] is going away next Wednesday and she will be away for three weeks so I will be all alone. Coppard was over to see me yesterday. He flattered me re. *Neighbour's Wife* but I could see he didn't think much of it. Not a bad fellow though. [J.B.] Priestley of the *Daily News* is living near here now, so there is quite a colony of literary people. I am getting into working order again and will finish *The Black Soul* as quickly as possible.

Liam

[1] The same date O'Flaherty wrote to Mr. Burke promising him a short story for his projected magazine the *Troubadour*. He tells Burke that E. Garnett has all his unsold MSS and that he has suggested Garnett should send him 'Three Lambs', and perhaps another sketch.

[2] 'Wife' is here a manner of speech

---

47. HRHRC ALS to Edward Garnett
Chop Cherry, Chinnor   19 October, 1923

My Dearest Friend,

I cannot express my joy on receiving your letter this morning. There is no other man, other than yourself, whom I would like to appreciate *Thy Neighbour's Wife* more than David. This is bad grammar I think, and I think also that it badly expresses my feelings on the matter. But, my dear friend, it tastes to me so sweet, this fruit of struggle, hope, agony, misery, despondency and enthusiasm that I am beside myself. I had not expected it. I had felt certain that you, through your kindness and foresight, had praised the book in the hope that you could enthuse me to write something worth while.

Now I have a respect for the book and I had begun to hate and despise it. But even in this moment of softness towards my fellow men, which always comes after a word of kindness, I cannot forget the peculiar conduct of McCarthy. It is unexplainable that as a gentleman he should on the one hand promise to review the book himself, and on the other intend to give it to some scoundrel, undoubtedly biased against it. What is the man? Because it strikes [me] that the only [thing] left to a man nowadays is his word, and if that is worthless a man himself is worthless. Still, he very probably has reasons which, if we knew them, might exonerate him, but I fail to understand him. He's a damn sight more mad than I am, to say the least of it.

Mortimer's interest is excellent news. The man has attracted me for a long time, both by the piquancy of his writing and his attitude towards literature. Would you kindly tell David that I am very grateful indeed to him for all he has done for me in this matter.

If you manage to put over the *B.S.* on the *Dial* we are well away. But that would be too good to be true, then I wouldn't have to go to the United States, damn it. By God, I don't deserve all my luck but the devil is good and you're a damn sight better than the best devil that ever revolted against the monotony of heaven.

I will be eager to get Turgenev and I forgot, writing to you yesterday, to accept your offer of *Romany Rye*. My girl and I are reading *The Bible in Spain* now and [Hudson's] *Green Mansions*. I must have a long talk to you about 'Chaos' before I get down to it. It will be very difficult. The characters at the present time are all walking around Dublin with their hands in their pockets, eager to get to work on destruction, but the hero is in a workhouse suffering from {rash?} and I can't possibly locate him outside it. But I can't set out from a workhouse, can I?

Liam

---

48. HRHRC ALS to Edward Garnett

Chop Cherry, Chinnor   Wednesday n.d. [? end October, 1923]

My Dearest Friend,

I received your letters and two books, Turgenev's *Fathers & Sons* and Borrow's *Romany Rye*. I began *Fathers & Sons* toute suite. Can't say I am deeply impressed so far. But I have a rather bad nervous breakdown – began yesterday and is worse today – dizziness and an inclination to drop my head to the ground, forward. It's bad. However, we shall scrape through none the worse I expect.

In the meantime, Yrs,
Liam O'F

---

49. HRHRC ALS to Edward Garnett
Chop Cherry, Chinnor   2 November, 1923

My Dearest Friend,

Damn it, I wrote to you over a week ago saying I was dying, or pretty near it, and I thought when I didn't hear from you that you must be dead yourself. 'Oh well,' I said to myself, 'Garnett has at last been devoured by his enemies.' And lo! there you are, as hearty as ever. And lo! here am I as scoundrelly and fit as ever. And lo! there are Bullett and Mortimer exalting their pettifogging personalities at the expense of the blood and sweat of our intellectual loins. It's enough to turn a man into a Tchichikov. But let us hie to Holland where the just are rewarded. This is indeed a subtle counter-attack on your part, inciting the Dutch who are the bulwark of the anti-Papist movement against poor Fr. O'Reilly and the curate. Don't deny it, Sir. I thank you. Damn it, you'll make me famous before you finish and then well, and then, of course, well and then, Bullett and Mortimer and Sylvia Lynd[1] will immediately discover that *Thy Neighbour's Wife* is a great book, etc. *ad multam nauseam* or, to use the Irish expression, 'enough to make a dog turn on his vomit'.

I read *Fathers & Sons* and I say 'hats off to Turgenev'. It's a masterpiece among masterpieces. When we meet we will talk about it.

About my girl. She's gone home, for how long I know not. No, we did not get on very well together. The devil and I would make good bedmates. Still, I am in love with her yet, but I wish I had never met her. Now look here, I offer to act on your advice in the matter. I asked her to stay at home until Xmas, with duplicity because I wished to ... well, what should I do? In keeping with honour, what's that said Bazarov? I suppose in the end I will do what I please. *Enfin*, it is a matter to be discussed *tête-à-tête*, and for that purpose next Thursday I can get to town and back for four pounds and seven shillings. May I have a talk to you then? We could discuss various things. Tell me?

By the way, I hear the socialists are buying *The Neighbour's Wife*. You never know, we might sell two thousand copies before next June, in spite of the reviewers. Although if I could live otherwise I would rather the book didn't sell very well. It's a bad book that sells very well as a first book.

I had a very nice letter from David. He's a good fellow, damn it. I have begun 'Chaos', not much of a beginning, but I couldn't find a good beginning for it. It's not like *The Black Soul* at all. Tell me, may I see you next Thursday or not?

Liam O'Flaherty

[1] Wife of Robert Wilson Lynd, cf. She was a book reviewer.

50. HRHRC ALS to Edward Garnett
Chop Cherry, Chinnor   9 November, 1923

My Dearest Friend,

I scrapped all 'Chaos' completely. Am writing now after the fashion of *Thy Neighbour's Wife*. I have the book all mapped out to cover about three weeks or so June/July, the Four Courts Rising. I began at breakfast at 9 o'clock this morning. It's now 1 o'clock and I have written three thousand words. I intend to have written six thousand words before I go to bed. It's going as easy as *Thy Neighbour's Wife*.

I can't tell you how grateful I am to you for yesterday's criticism. I am acting on a three plank programme, no rhetoric, no philosophy and no bias. Rather negative but salutary. Finnegan's public house is my starting ground and I am making the blighters tell lies about one another to a third party. I have done two men and am now doing our friend Maurice Fitzsimmons, of whom 'nobody can make either head or tail', as Finnegan told his wife one night in bed. 'He's not with us I fear, and yet it's hard to say he's agin us.' Long life to them. It's a great laugh.

                                                                        Liam

---

51. HRHRC ALS to Edward Garnett
Chop Cherry, Chinnor   n.d. [? mid November 1923]

My Dearest Friend,

I just got back from London a few hours ago. I stayed with my friend Stroud to hear the election results.[1] I am very glad I did for the following reasons.

We were down in Piccadilly Circus about 2 a.m. standing apart from a crowd, when a man came up to me and saluted, and, by Jove, he turned out to be a school mate of mine, a Dr. Hallissey. I last saw him in 1918, and he had doctors with him, with whom I was at school also, fellows I had not seen since 1912. But the peculiar thing about this, i.e. the reason for which I mentioned the occurrence, is the effect the meeting had upon me.

Here were three men, typical of the Irish present day middle classes, well educated, of good parentage and in prosperous circumstances, and yet their outlook on life and their general mentality was just about equal to that of a well-to-do artisan in England. Taking away that charm of manner which is innate in an Irishman (myself excepted), they were as coarse and vulgar as peasants, and I felt a shrinking from them as if I had met an undesirable person at a public function. And it was only then that I remembered how morose and distant and bitterly hostile I had been to them at school and to the people in general afterwards. Without a doubt the mass of the Irish people are still without an atom of intellectual culture (in the abstract). And further it is only by contact and experience, never by thought or reading. That is what makes the modern English intellectual so boring. He never meets his opposites, since there are hardly any in his own class.

This chap Hallissey, a decent fellow, is practising in Poplar and asked me to come to see him. One or two of his friends are in the Irish F.G. cabinet and he is desirous that I should allow him to write to them on my behalf with a view to getting some short stories, etc. done in Irish for the Department of Education. Naturally I demurred. I would never be able to bring myself to praise God, which is necessary; that is, even if I did get the work, which is very, very doubtful. Strangely enough too I learned from him that the original of the hero of the now discarded 'Chaos' is on the run (that is Dr. O'Connor, in real life his name is {?}) with the Republican forces, so that I prophesied his future correctly. I had intended though to have him die of pneumonia in a dugout on the hillside, and it seems that he persists in living. But as he will not come to life in a literary sense it does not matter. But it is peculiar all the same.

I had an interesting letter from a man named Gregory about *Thy Neighbour's Wife*. He had just finished reading it and liked it and says he must recommend it to a friend with whom he once tramped in Connemara and Aran, in the days of the Land League War, 1882 or so. He lives in Harrogate. Must be an old man now. I must write to him.

I am very tired. All day yesterday I wandered about London planning out a new format for 'Chaos'. It seemed to be very much alive, emotional, and direct from the heart. I developed it powerfully from the first chapter to the last. But today it seems weak, uninspiring and fatuous. Perhaps it is because I didn't sleep last night. I rather fancy you would like this plot better than the other. But it would be so tragic as to be almost unbearable. And yet perfectly true to life. Perhaps it may stay with me. My wife is not back yet.

With best regards
L.O'F

P.S. I read Lynd on your [W.H.] 'Hudson's Letters'. I didn't like the review at all. It seemed insincere and journalistic. All of the letters that I have read I like immensely. But what an old scoundrel Hudson was about the war. He was an old man. L.O'F.

[1] The General Election took place 15 November, 1923.

---

52. HRHRC ALS to Edward Garnett
Chop Cherry, Chinnor   22 November, 1923

My Dearest Friend,
    Thanks so much for your letter of this morning, and I also thank you in

anticipation for parcel. In the latter portion of thanks my wife shares heartily.

I am enclosing 'Black Bullock' for *The Nation*. I don't know if it's any good but it seems to be all right. I am sending the new 'Salted Goat' to the *Adelphi*. I have written another one I like called 'Benedicamus Domino' and I am going to try the *English Review* with it. I am sending out a batch of ten today, England and America, some might stick. Hectic activity.

I would not be on my own in New York, even if I didn't go on a speaking tour. My brother could get me a journalistic job on one of the Communist or Socialist newspapers I fancy. I would rake in about forty dollars a week, maintain my privacy and have plenty of time to write. Whereas on a speaking tour I might get unenviable publicity. But that is all in the air. I dislike the whole business. I have a most healthy dislike to all forms of 'regular' activity and as I can hardly ever remain of the same opinion on any political matter for more than a week at a time, writing for a propaganda newspaper becomes fraught with grave danger. But one never knows which way the tide is going to turn between now and next April. I have been looking up the American publications and I find that most of them only accept drivel similar to our publications. Of course, those that do print literature pay awfully well.

I have not made much progress with 'Chaos' since. In fact I have hardly touched it. These blasted sketches have been occupying my time. So far it is not at all to my liking, but it might get better as it develops.

This cold weather is wonderful. We had snow yesterday, the first I have seen for a long time, and I ran out in the morning in my pyjamas and began to fling snowballs at everything in sight. By Jove, cold, frosty weather makes one content with life. And yet it is a melancholy kind of contentment altogether different from the peace that a warm summer morning brings, when the birds are singing. This weather reminds me of Aran.

I sent a book to father and I got an acknowledgement from my sister Delia yesterday.

She said that she forgave me for writing the book and also for my love affair. John Carmody, who came back from the U.S. a Socialist, is now reading the book in Aran and enjoying it immensely, evidently pleased with his fame (his real name is Pat Mullen). He reads it to the men of Kilronan in Mulligan's public house. I bet that the Aran peasants will like it, in spite of Bullett's prediction to the contrary.[1]

Tell me, will you fix up that paragraph for Cape about the B.S.? I would be very grateful if you would because I don't know from Adam what to write. We mustn't make any foolish 'arrogant' gestures, because I want the B.S. to be as classical as possible. I wonder will Cape like it? I don't suppose he will. Anyhow they will like it in Ireland, the young intellectuals.

I will send you 'Benedicamus Domino' when I get it typed. My wife likes it best of all I have written.

I say, that chap {?} was a genius, I am enjoying his book immensely. Poor fellow, it's a pity he had such a sad end. It strikes me that he had some of Tchekov's genius, spontaneous similarity, not the faked similarity that seems current in this country since your wife's translation. Of course none of these imitators would admit that they were inspired in style by Mrs Garnett. For example, I saw the proofs of a story at A.E. Coppard's but last week. The damn thing was obviously a reprint with variations of a Tchekovian elegy on a flighty woman, with background of a doctor husband and stupid female servants instead of peasants. But, my God, what a fake was there. Such a fake that Hutchinson's magazine accepted the story.

I guess I will come to town the week after next, that is next Wednesday week. Could I see you on that day? Well, with best regards from wife and myself,

Yrs sincerely
Liam O'Flaherty

[1] Gerald Bullett, reviewer in the *Daily News*.

---

53. HRHRC ALS to Edward Garnett
Chop Cherry, Chinnor   28 November, 1923

My Dearest Friend,

Your box arrived last night and we had huge excitement in Chop Cherry. We opened it after doing a war dance and then we feasted riotously. Then we sang a hymn of thanks to the donor. It was really delightful of you and I don't know what to say. My wife said, 'He's an angel.' 'No,' I said, 'he's a gentleman.' By the way, that honey is unbeatable. May your posterity prosper.

Have we to congratulate David on another prize or is it the same prize? I saw his name mentioned in *Now & Then* yesterday in connection with a prize, but I can't make out whether it's the Hawthorne or a fresh one. By Jove, won't his enemies feel happy about it if it's a new one. The last one inspired Murry to dedicate a few pages of the *Adelphi* to a denunciation of *Lady into Fox*. After all there must be some intelligence left in the English literary world, in spite of these dolorous secondrate idiots who are astride the press like whores waylaying a sailor returned from a long voyage. 'Come into my parlour, sailor,' said the whore. 'If you don't I'll get you blackjacked by my fancy man. And, of course, if you do come in you'll get ruined anyway.' 'Toady unto us,' say the secondraters, 'or if you don't we'll flagellate you and even if you do toady unto us you'll only get the rind of the bacon.' I hope David's second book has not lost any of its vim.

By Jove, this is great weather for work. We are at it hot and heavy. I have written a sketch about my wife and her little girl. I think it very amusing and my wife thinks it pathetic. Now that is amusing. My wife does not like Bazarov. She prefers Arcady and thinks Pavel Petrovitch a futile fop. She says she thinks Tchekov small beer compared to Turgenev. In that I disagree with her. I also pointed out that Turgenev preferred Bazarov to Arcady, but she refuses to believe it. I have given up all hope of ever writing a book equal to *Fathers and Sons*. Now that is something in the nature of an admission.

'Chaos' is beginning to preen itself like a young cock that is just becoming conscious of his spurs and his fine comb when he looks into a clear pool of water. I am greatly excited to see what you think of it. It's funny, but I can't imagine a thing being all right now unless you pass favourable judgment on it. 'The Cow's Death' always lives fresh in my mind on account of your congratulations when I wrote it. But I rather fancy it made me too conceited at the time.

I don't think Rowland Kenney is anyway near Lawson,[1] for instance. Still, I imagine his stories are very true to life. But somehow he strikes me as coming very near it and not getting there. It's the very devil to deal with that type of character, because their life and outlook on life is tragic in the extreme, covered with a maudlin jollity that is only skin deep. Kenney to my fancy was too obsessed with the popular 'cultivated' concept of the working man as a character, resembling Bainesfather's 'Old Bill'.[2] In other words the British lowest strata workingman is the devil of a type to handle from the point of view of art. What struck me in Tchekov's story 'Peasants' was the marvellous power that Tchekov had in giving us reams of the peasants' history and outlook in life and habits, by the mere statment,'their shoulders knocked together as they walked'. Damn it, I think that there is more poetry and literature in a slight action of that kind than in violent dialogue or clever portraiture, from a long distance. I can't do it myself so I know.

Well, here's luck and many thanks for the box.

With best regards
From Liam

[1] Both Australian writers.

[2] A cartoonist.

---

54. HRHRC ALS to Edward Garnett
Chop Cherry, Chinnor   30 November, 1923

My Dearest Friend,

Received your letters and cuttings from *M.G.* yesterday. Yes, I will be at Cape's place at 1.45 p.m. on Wednesday next.

By Jove, that *M.G.* reviewer discovered a new brick to throw at me. He said to himself, 'all the other chaps abused him for this and this, now I'll abuse him for the publisher's note of his life'.

I am glad they published 'The Rockfish'. It is awfully good of you to sell all these sketches to the *Guardian* for me. If I sent them they would pop them back next post.

I will bring 'Chaos' and sketches with me on Wednesday.

Until then, with affection
L.O'F

---

55. HRHRC ALS to Edward Garnett
Chop Cherry, Chinnor   n.d. [? early December 1923]

My Dearest Friend,

The enclosed note from 'AE' is interesting as a proof of my support of 'The Kill'. You cannot deny that 'AE' is the mildest of men.[1]

Mrs Casey's letter was very ferocious. It was a dunning letter.[2]

My girl has not come back yet. Can't say what is the matter. I didn't hear from her since Monday, a letter written last Saturday. Whether she has deserted me or not I can't say. If she has life is going to be very miserable.

I have ten thousand words of 'Chaos' done. Can't say I like it. I'll do the first few chapters and give them to you to read. I don't think the first chapter would be sufficient. Anyhow I have plenty of time. I rewrote 'The Salted Goat' and I finished 'The Black Bullock' and 'Two Dogs', so I have been busy.

Some blighter called the P.E.N. Club invited me to become a member. I wrote to say I would but they promptly invited me to pay a guinea. So I guess I will call the deal off. Anyway, what's the good of belonging to a blooming club when one lives in Chinnor. And I should only increase the number of my enemies.

I must pull myself together now and go to work. It's the only way to hide from worries and difficulties. Thank God for 'Chaos'. The last scene I imagine will be good. But it's a deuce of a time to wait for the last scene.

Yrs affect.
Liam O'Flaherty

[1] AE is George Russell, editor of the *Irish Statesman*.
[2] Mrs Casey, O'Flaherty's previous landlady, mother of his ex-lover Miss Casey.

---

56. HRHRC ALS to Edward Garnett
Chop Cherry, Chinnor   10 December, 1923

My Dearest Friend,

My wife[1] has come back and we had a talk about things. As a result of this talk I am writing to you. She suggested that she should try and get some kind of a job in town as I can't write here, and she finds it pretty dull and we could not live in London on my income. If you would possibly know of anywhere she could get a job of any sort could you tell me? I know it's a tall order trying to find an employer in this chaotic state of affairs, but there is a possibility that you might casually hear of something going around. I guess some form of clerical work would be most suitable. Or shall I say, like the chap advertising in an American news-paper, 'young woman desires to travel. Willing to accompany a corpse'.

With apologies for being an absolute nuisance,

Yrs
Liam O'Flaherty

[1] i.e. current companion

---

57. HRHRC ALS to Edward Garnett
Chop Cherry, Chinnor   12 December, 1923

My Dearest Friend,

I am very sorry to hear that you were suffering from the 'flu, that's bad. I hope you are better? The 'flu is the devil. And David got his head broken. What the devil does he mean by getting into these street fights. I hope he is not badly hurt? Anyhow, if he was in a fight I bet he made himself felt. He has got the neck and shoulders of a fighter.

Thanks so much for keeping your eye [open] for anything that might suit my wife, and Miss Heath also.

By the way, if you could not find 'The Black Bullock' sketch let me know and I will send the other copy to the *M.G.* I have a copy here.

The *Spectator* published 'Two Dogs' and the *Weekly Westminster* 'Tidy Tim's Donkey'. I didn't hear from Murry yet.

At present I am vegetating. Can't do a stroke. I heard my sister died last week of consumption.[1]

I hope you will get that blasted cold out of your bones soon. I think hot rum going to bed is good, though in Aran they use hot potheen instead, and chicken broth and gruel.

With tenderest sympathies

Yrs, Liam O'Flaherty

[1] O'Flaherty was born the ninth of ten children and the second son.

---

58. HRHRC ALS to Edward Garnett
Chop Cherry, Chinnor   21 December, 1923

My Dearest Friend,

Thank you for your letter of this morning, plus enclosures re. job for my wife. It's very good of Miss Heath. Please thank her for me. My wife will get after the place. Whether she will be able to fill it I doubt.

I have been down with the 'flu for the past week but I am better now. At least I think it was the 'flu, but my head was very bad and I thought I was going potty. Too much worry I imagine, about my writing. I guess I have been going the pace too much, though I find that I have done nothing for the past three months excepting a few sketches.

I was up in town last Friday and I caught a cold I imagine. {?} wired me to come up to meet him on urgent business. The business turned out to be two hundred thousand rifles plus ammunition that he wanted to sell to the Irish. I could have manslaughtered him, the scoundrel. Cape had asked me for a jacket for *The Black Soul*, so I gave him one. I expect you have seen it.

The Troubadour has failed before it started, so our 'Three Lambs' are still motherless.[1] I asked for their return.

I trust your cold is better? I expect to be able to get to work shortly now. My wife is going home on Saturday for a fortnight so I'll settle down to it.

Best wishes for Xmas

Yrs. affec.
Liam O'Flaherty

[1] See footnote to letter dated 18th October, 1923.

---

59. HRHRC ALS to Edward Garnett
Chop Cherry, Chinnor   24 December, 1923

My Dearest Friend,

Very many thanks for your present. You are really too kind to me. I will never forget you for these kindnesses of a personal nature, apart from your kindness to me as a writer which is beyond all valuation.

My wife went after that job but there was nothing in it, sixty pounds a year, part-time, repulsive woman, etc. She has now gone home for a fortnight and I am beginning the life adventures of Michael Rathcroghan. It will be a cross between Borrow and Gogol and I feel enthusiastic about it. There is plenty of scope and it can be artistic, which a personal diary could not be, as you say. In fact it might be the best of my work if I pull it off. It begins with leaving the army. Vol. I will deal with rambling over the world, and Vol. II will deal with Rathcroghan's activities in Ireland, Rotunda, raising an army, intrigues, love affairs, etc. No writer ever had such an opportunity, certainly neither Gogol, Dickens or Borrow had such opportunities. But of course their genius was not in need of opportunities.

About 'Chaos', I feel that it is a work better left alone. I find an antipathy towards it and one cannot approach a work with antipathy. I think I exhausted the *emotion* of 'Chaos' in *The Black Soul*.

I read a very scurrilous attack on you in the *Sunday Times* by a man called Gosse.[1] It pained me very much. It is terrible that such creatures should be able to get into print in an English newspaper, especially with the name of Gosse. I wonder what Hudson would have said had he read that review? Poor fellow. I will bring you the 'Letters' the next time I am in town, or else I will mail them if you require them now?

Affectionately
Liam O'Flaherty

P.S. I got the *M.G.* cheque.

[1] Sir Edmund William Gosse, influential critic of the day.

---

60. HRHRC ALS to Edward Garnett
Chop Cherry, Chinnor   27 December, 1923

My Dearest Friend,

You overwhelm me with gifts and I have no means of retaliation except with the blunt weapons of thanks. And indeed it is but natural that they should be blunt, being used so often against your generosity and kindness. The Conrad I received and have already finished. Yesterday I wrote three thousand words of Rathcroghan and read 'A Smile of Fortune' and 'The Secret Sharer', both after splitting my left eyebrow with a piece of wood will be a memorable day with me, the day of my discovery of that miracle of genius 'The Secret Sharer'. It carried me spellbound from the second page to the last word (the first page I thought bombast). It's wonderful. Reading 'A Smile of Fortune' immediately afterwards I felt a delicious tingling sensation in the brain, as one feels when taking a rest after a battle. He should have put 'The Secret Sharer' first in the book. What a wonderful genius is Conrad! I am very grateful indeed to you for having given me that book.

It is a jolly good thing Xmas is over. It was exceedingly uncomfortable sitting apart as it were at a carousal, while all the rest made merry, barbarously it is true, but still made money. Poor Rathcroghan consoled me, but this morning reviewing his exploits he seems to be a buffoon and worthless. And in all probability he is. But as he has commenced his adventures I will follow him to the end, whatever happens.

Now at the time approaches towards the birth of *The Black Soul*, I am getting excited, wondering what will happen to that product of our joint endeavours. I suppose the gadflies will sting it more than they stung *Thy Neighbour's Wife*, but that does not matter. Those two first pages are worth something, I am sure of that. And if there are two good pages in a book it was worth writing.

There is a man here called [J.B.] Priestley and I went to visit him on invitation, a most unbearable ruffian, one of Lynd's gang. He reads for Lane, he reviews for seven newspapers, he has a contract for five books of essays, and then he is going to write a comic novel. He tells me he writes a daily quota of two thousand words, week in week out. 'It's quite simple,' he said, 'to the practised hand. Lynd can do three thousand.' Gerald Bullett is his next door neighbour.[1] I don't think I'll go to see him again. In the name of the devil is there anybody worthwhile talking to?

Affect. yrs
Liam O'Flaherty

[1] Journalist and reviewer.

---

61. HRHRC ALS to Edward Garnett
Chop Cherry, Chinnor   31 December, 1923

My Dearest Friend,

I received your very welcome letter Saturday night. I had begun to believe that you disapproved altogether of *The Black Soul* and I was cheered immensely to hear that after all there is some good in it. Things have been so very black with me recently that I needed that little encouragement. (As the Irish has it) praise youth and it will respond, blame old age and it will fail.

I agree with you that 'contrasts' are necessary but to my mind it's too late for any meddling with the MS now. I can never change the conception of anything. The first throw of the dice brings me victory or defeat. As the Irish have always failed in battle – by the impetuosity of their attack that over-reached itself and didn't allow of the reformation of their forces to meet that deadly counter-attack on their exposed flank.

Personally I have no hope of the success of *The Black Soul* in this country, from a publisher's point of view, or even from the point of view of the 'cream' of the intellectual class. It is a book for the Irish and the Irish to whom it would appeal are too few and too powerless to count. I knew very well before I began it that it would be so. Do you remember I said the first day I met you, 'I want to make enough money on *Thy Neighbour's Wife* to publish *The Black Soul* at my own expense.'

I've just finished my first short story [sic] and sent it out to be typed. I am very proud of it but you won't like it I am sure. It's a twenty thousand story done in three thousand words. A bank robber murders his mistress's husband and gets murdered by his mistress who goes mad. Whole scene in a brothel in Dublin. I call it 'Atonement'. If you think well of it, I am going to develop it into twenty thousand words and head the book of short stories and sketches with it.

I saw a paragraph in the *Daily News* about David's next book.[1] I am greatly excited about it. Between the two of us I think David is going to become a 'big gun'. I congratulate you on your paternity. Of course the gadflies will do their best to draw his blood, but it's a peculiar characteristic of these gadflies that they only attack the defenceless. After all it's great fun.

My wife didn't come back yet and it's still very lonely. I haven't spoken to a soul for four days. The country in winter without a sea near at hand is the most desolate thing on earth. I shall be glad indeed when I feel the earth move again in Spring.

Yrs. affec.
Liam

[1] *A Man in the Zoo* , London: Chatto and Windus, 1924.

---

62. HRHRC ALS to Edward Garnett
Chop Cherry, Chinnor   8 January, 1924

My Dearest Friend,

I received your letter on Saturday and I would have replied sooner to wish you many happy returns of your birthday, but I have been {up?} to the neck in a deal of trouble concerning my wife. Damnable trouble. I don't think I have had a solitary hour's sleep for four days. She is back here now.

I am enclosing 'Atonement' in MS. I have sent a copy to the *London Magazine*. The *M.G.* returned 'The Black Bullock'.

I am unable to write, so please excuse short note.

Affec. yrs., Liam O'F

---

63. HRHRC ALS to Edward Garnett
Chop Cherry, Chinnor   12 January, 1924

My Dearest Friend,

Thanks very much for your letter and the {bromides ?} enclosed. I am feeling better now thanks. In fact I have been writing this morning. I am starting another thing now called 'Lamara'. I suppose I will hang onto it for a fortnight and then drop it.

I am coming into town on Wednesday to secure an agent for my sketches, etc. They are getting on my nerves and I fancy it would be far cheaper in the long run to pay an agent ten percent for selling them, if he did sell any. I hope to see you when I am in town.

I didn't hear anything about *The Black Soul* yet. I met the Priestleys again. Went there with my wife. More about them when I see you on Wednesday.

With affectionate regards
Liam O'Flaherty

---

64. HRHRC ALS to Edward Garnett
Chop Cherry, Chinnor   23 January, 1924

My Dearest Friend,

My wife has come back so I am quite happy. She has brought her little girl with her. Yes, I think you are quite right about going to the U.S. I am not going on my brother's talking match. The terms are not suitable. He wanted me to talk as the Workers' Party ordered me to talk. But we have decided to transfer entirely to New York next April, that is emigrate in *toto*. I will have 'Chaos' finished by then and therefore have fulfilled my agreement with Cape, that is if he accepts the book. In any case I will have fulfilled my promise.

I have finished another sketch and I am sending five out today to be typed. I have also sent 'The First Flight' to the American *Delineator*. By the way do you think it would be a good idea for me to get an agent or are agents any good? I suppose not. I guess it would be better to steer on my own, for all the work I have for the market.

Yes, I quite agree with you that 'Chaos' will not be popular. But dash it, I remember telling you in the Café De l'Etoile that I was writing it, not for the public but for the sake of itself. If you think I did it well that is all I want. I myself am satisfied with it. I often recite passages of it by heart and find great comfort. Far more comfort than I would get from reading the *Daily News* praise of tripe. What the hell is the difference. Neither will 'Chaos' sell, though it's not as good as the *B.S.*, or near it. But when I get to the U.S. I am going to give art the blind eye and steer towards the dollars for a few years. If I can't locate them, well and good. To the devil with them. But of one thing I am certain, that is, that I am going to make some money on *Thy Neighbour's Wife* in U.S., when I can get it handled in a business- like manner. Of course I would far rather go to the Sahara desert than U.S. but the scourge of economic necessity is stronger than any will o' the wisp of the intellect. If I were on my own I could do as I liked – probably would go before the mast next Spring to recuperate my strength and get a little kick out of life, and a little rest, after slaving at writing for a year. But the lesser of two evils is always better than tackling the two evils in rotation, that is, leaving my love is a greater evil than going to the U.S. and carrying on the writing.

When I am coming to town next I will take all your books with me in a suitcase. That will be in about three weeks' time.

I will never forget all your kindness to me, my dear friend. You are the only one that ever did anything for me that made life less difficult to live, spiritually and materially too. But the material existence is never as important as the spiritual. A man who feels at peace with his intellectual self-respect can be happy on a dunghill.

Yrs. affec., Liam O'Flaherty

P.S. What [do] you think of this para. from *B.S.* to drive the reviewers off their heads.

'I have found a greater God than God. I have found him in the roar of the sea against the cliffs of Inverara, and in the storm winds that lash its rainswept crags.'

---

65. HRHRC ALS to Edward Garnett
Chop Cherry, Chinnor   24 January, 1924

My Dearest Friend,
     This is 'The Wave'. I am sending it to you for your opinion of it because

it took me two days to do it and I don't [know] whether it's good, or bad, or middling.

I find I have your book of Hudson's letters here yet, so I will post it to you. I forgot to bring it with me last Wednesday.

I hope you are well in this very trying weather.

Yours ever,
Liam O'Flaherty

---

66. HRHRC ALS to Edward Garnett
Chop Cherry, Chinnor   26 January, 1924

My Dearest Friend,

I am very glad you liked 'The Wave', very glad indeed. It cost such an immense effort to write it, but I think I would rather try the *Spectator* with it than the *Manchester Guardian*. None of these young men who review books read the *Manchester Guardian*, the Bulletts, etc., but they read these bloomin' 'Reviews'. If Armstrong doesn't take [it], well, the *M.G.* might. So if you sent it back to me I would {mail ?} it, or give it me on Wednesday when I meet you at this 'lunch for the purpose of meeting Mrs Rickard'.

I am very ill so I think I will have to see a doctor when in town. This fellow here says my stomach is surrounding my heart, dilated stomach. So naturally I have not much energy. It's a damnable state of affairs when a man begins to crock up. It's one thing today and another thing tomorrow.

Some blasted photographer also wrote to me asking for a complimentary sitting, so I will hike along to them and be at Charlotte St. at 1.30.

Until then, yours affect.
Liam O'Flaherty

---

67. HRHRC ALS to Edward Garnett
Chop Cherry, Chinnor   [? end January, 1924]

My Dearest Friend,

I found the dentist all right. He said it would cost twelve guineas. He took a rough mould and I am coming up on Tuesday to get another mould. He also scraped the remaining teeth for me. He said they were coated with corruption that was poisoning my stomach.

I am ever so grateful to you for sending me to him and getting these teeth for me. I trust that getting them in will restore my vitality so that I may be able to work in order to pay my rather alarming debt to you. For the moment please accept my very heartfelt thanks.

Failing to discover Armstrong I sold 'The Wave' to McCarthy. He also gave me a book to review. It's a queer book called *Three Tibetan Mysteries*.[1]

I like it. The style is wonderful and appeals strongly to me. There is a queer magical swinging rhythm like the sea murmuring running through it.

This is a glorious day and I feel better. I hope you too are enjoying the sun.

With best affection
Yours Liam O'F

[1]*Three Tibetan Mystery Plays* (trans. H.I. Woolf) London: Routledge, 1924. No review by O'Flaherty of this book appeared in the *New Statesman*.

---

68. HRHRC ALS to Edward Garnett
Chop Cherry, Chinnor   n.d. [? end January, 1924]

My Dearest Friend,

I received your letter on Saturday and as you insist on being a Tchertof Hanov about my debt I suppose we shall have to find some other means of paying it. We shall eagerly expect you on Saturday at 2.00 p.m., in time for lunch.

Lady into Fox came yesterday. I spent the day with A.E. Coppard. It was fun listening to them talk. David beat us all at chess. It rained all day but in spite of that talking was incessant. Talk, I fancy, is better even than whiskey.

My health is improving and I can eat with greater freedom. I am also writing more. Very poor stuff though. It seems to me that I am merely passing the time until I get home and begin 'Chaos'. However, one sketch 'A Shilling' – Clayton wrote to me and asked [me] to let him know when and where it might be published so that he might procure a printed copy. I am sending the sketch to the *M.G.*,[1] so that if they print it and you happen to see a copy you might give it to Clayton. I will be in Ireland and I won't see it. I think this man Clayton must be a dear fellow, not because he wants to get a copy of *my* sketch, but because he wants to get a printed copy of a sketch.[2]

More anon, I am looking forward to seeing you on Saturday.

Yours affec.
Liam O'F

[1]Published the *Manchester Guardian*, 28 March, 1924.

[2] This maybe the Douglas Clayton who typed for O'Flaherty. See letter of 28 June, 1924.

---

69. HRHRC ALS to Edward Garnett
Chop Cherry, Chinnor   3 February, 1924

My Dearest Friend,

Be happy with me, I am definitely going to Aran on March 10th. I had a wonderful letter from my sister this morning asking me to come. Already I feel that all my nervous worry and sickness has vanished and that I see life again normally, beautifully, with a summer breeze dragging itself lazily over a voluptuous green sea.

The dentist will fit my teeth next Tuesday. I hope they are right because I am so anxious to get them in. I am as excited as a little schoolboy going to go for a holiday, counting the days, etc. I think I will become a tramp next summer and go around Ireland, loafing and begging and stealing. The wanderlust is seizing me fearfully. I become lustful for life. 'Chaos' will be a funny book written with this psychology. I am going to write it in Aran.

No *Black Soul* yet, I do wish it would come.

> Best wishes and affection
> From Liam O'F

---

70. HRHRC ALS to Edward Garnett
Chop Cherry, Chinnor   6 February, 1924

My Dearest Friend,

I couldn't come up to the dentist yesterday because I got a bad nervous stroke on Sunday which kept me prostrate until this afternoon. It's an awful nuisance, you know. I can do nothing. I can't think, or write, or feel cheerful. Afraid to eat anything. All that sort of thing. Tchekov could write a good story about me. I have decided to go home to the Aran Islands at the end of this month. My wife will go home. After a month in Aran, if I get better, I will come to Dublin and send for my wife. Such are the arrangements. It's a shocking thing to be knocked out. Frightfully boring and dull. Dull for oneself and immeasurably boring for those with whom one comes in contact.

The worst of it is I have a long short story I want to write and it worries me. Figure for yourself the title, 'Tired of Life'. It won't let me alone and I can't write it. Well, well!

Cape sent me his Spring list this morning. It appears to me to be a very good one. Wells, Sherwood Anderson, etc. I am eager to read *The Sea* by Kellermann.[1] I hope you will be so kind as to lend me a copy? Though I fancy Cape's adv. of it is rather vulgar.

I keep dreaming of Aran until I get quite excited. Like a little boy. The birds sing and it seems to me that I am in Aran listening to them, singing there among the ivy-covered rocks. But I can't hear the sea. After all one cannot live a long time away from the sea. Gorki's story 'Malva' has ended by irritating me. That man Gorki does not really understand nature. His talk of the sea and the sand and the waves and the sun in 'Malva' strike me like eating a dish of seamoss pudding with too much sugar in it. But you don't understand. Well, one does not use sugar with seamoss pudding. Without sugar it is strong, salt, ferocious. With sugar it is sickly, like a whore's kiss.

I expect the proofs of *The Black Soul* in a day or two. May I have your formal permission to dedicate the book to you? Would you permit this dedication: 'To Edward Garnett, in gratitude for his invaluable friendship'. Please tell me. You see, you are an awful man, and I am afraid to irritate you.[2]

Blackbirds and thrushes are singing everywhere but there are no robins about. And I like robins best. They seem to me to be the most artistic in their movements. And I prefer beauty of movement to beauty of sound. Let sound be wild, fierce, melancholy, abandoned, awe-inspiring, but let movement be gentle, soothing, sinuous, sweet. What nonsense I am writing! I must be very bad. I will probably be coming up next Tuesday to that dentist if I am better.

Liam O'Flaherty

[1] Bernhard Kellermann, *The Sea* (trans. Sasha Best) New York: R. M.McBride; London: Cape, 1924.

[2] The dedication was simply 'to EDWARD GARNETT'.

---

71. HRHRC ALS to Edward Garnett
Chop Cherry, Chinnor 9 February, 1924

My Dearest Friend,

I am very sorry indeed to hear that you are ill. I suppose it's the 'flu again. Isn't it a curse. Everybody has it. I hope you are staying in bed?

I will drop in at one o'clock on Tuesday. I think I am a little better now, though the head is a bit dizzy still. However, I have at last found my novel out of the 'turmoil'. I see it now. I have it. But I'm not going to touch it until I reach Aran.

This is shocking weather, rain and mist. The birds are gone away again somewhere, and they are too sad to sing. I myself am not sad, I am going home.

Liam O'Flaherty

---

72. HRHRC TLS
12 South Circular Road, Portobello, Dublin n.d. [? 8 March, 1924]

My Dearest Friend,

Well, here I am among the barbarian Irish once more. I really mean it. Since I came back I frankly have confessed to myself that we are still merged to a great extent in barbarism from the point of view of culture. Fortunately, however, culture is only a very small part of civilisation and it is really delightful to be back. The streets are dirty. Everybody is badly dressed, impudent, contemptuous and surly, and yet there is a freshness about even the dirt of the streets and the surliness of the man from whom one buys a tram ticket that is immeasurably preferable to the smug politeness and devilish immovability of the Londoner and the Englishman at large. I was talking to a man this morning who, after denouncing the country, its politics and everything in general for a long time, said at last with a wistful smile, 'Ah, but after all there is no other country like it. Man alive, but it moves. Upon my soul it does. It moves all the time.' That is the genius of the place. It is art in real life. There is the freshness of a tale by Tchekov in an ordinary scene in the street that surprises one. The very first hour after my arrival in Dublin I noticed it. I walked away from the railway station at Westland Row after leaving my kit in the office. It was seven o'clock in the morning and very cold, biting and dry. I walked along looking at the closed shops, the silent streets, the huge policemen standing at corners looking into the roadway and thinking of when they would be relieved for breakfast, and of what they drank the day before, and I felt a strange exhilaration as if I had drunk some whiskey. I felt strangely drunk. It was like looking through a microscope at things while under the influence of some pain or drug.

Then I came to O'Connell Street, wide, clean with towering statues that were menacing and aggressive in their silence and the coldness of the still air about them. At the Pillar[1] a little crowd had gathered. I reached it. A tramcar that should have started five minutes before was still there. Its passengers and the driver and the inspector of trams and two policemen and some newsboys, and four applewomen, were gaping at a woman who danced around cursing somebody. The woman was drunk. She was dressed in a tattered black hat that was too big for her, and a tattered black shawl that was also too big, and trailed along the ground at the back. She was a young woman made old by drink and whoring, but there was a monstrous vitality and terrific tragedy in her movements, her shrill voice, her drunken gestures, the despairing look in her eyes as she gaped at nothing, and cursed God and her husband who had beaten her the night before, and then went away to sleep with Mary Keegan of Moore Street. And everybody looked on without a smile, listening to her with as great respect and attention as they would give the president of the country.

I met Russell and got on very well with him. I am going to see him on Sunday night and meet Stephens the writer[2]. Russell will introduce me to the lot of them. I have met more people within 24 hours than I have met while I was in England. A commissioner of police, a schoolteacher, a business man, a man who runs fake companies, a revolutionary on the run, a priest. Damn it, man, this is where I get in touch with life. All sorts of copy. No danger of getting stale here.

I will write you all the news when I get settled down. You will excuse this vulgar note therefore. I have about twenty letters to write to change addresses and all that, and I have to type that story.

[Added in ALS] I started the madness story. I wrote half of it coming over on the boat. Drop me a line please.

Yrs. affectionately
Liam O'Flaherty

P.S. I read this note and thought that you would think it cold and arrogant. Please don't. It's meant to be affectionate, but we Irish, you understand, do not believe in wearing our heart on our sleeve. So if I talk about myself and did not ask about your health and Miss Heath's health, you will understand. I refrained from doing so simply because well, damned if I understand why I don't do the things other people do. L.O.F.

[1] The statue of Anna Livia Plurabelle has replaced Nelson Pillar in O'Connell Street.

[2] James Stephens, best known for *The Crock of Gold*, 1912.

---

73. HRHRC TLS to Edward Garnett
12 South Circular Road, Portobello,
Dublin   10 March, 1924

My Dearest Friend,

Let me see now where do we begin. Yes, the best place to begin is with a description of my visit to George Russell yesterday evening. He keeps open house on Sunday nights and about twenty people gathered there, people connected with art and literature. Stephens the novelist was there, a nice fellow enough, but rather proud of himself, denunciatory of the Russians, and very much of the pattern of Robert Lynd, Squire and those people. We got on well however, which I effected by keeping my mouth shut and agreeing with him on every point, even to the extent of saying that Tchekov is very much overrated. Then there was a Professor Curtis, expansive, voluble, a writer of ten guinea reviews for the American Press and a thoroughly hearty fellow. We talked about the Aran Islands. Then there was Professor Curtis's wife, a very pretty young woman, fifteen years younger than the professor. She has just written a pretty novel, she writes short stories and she made violent eyes at me.[1] I walked back to Dublin with her while the professor followed with another young genius, who combines great personal beauty, a taste in dress, a practice at the Irish bar with a taste for dabbling in literature. He reviews books. The lady told me all about her life since the year of her birth, including a description of her private life, her love affairs and her propensity for falling in love with every interesting person she met. She would be very valuable to Tchekov.

For the rest there were American journalists, Indian, an hereditary saint travelling in Ireland (why I don't know) and young poets and women of an indiscriminate type, who just seemed to be connected with the men, like all Irish woman just seem to be in public, unless they are very pretty like the professor's wife.

They had all read my book, but none offered to say it was good or bad. One young poet said he liked my stories and hoped that I would collect them and give up novel writing for short story writing and that was all. Still, I got on far better than I expected. But there is absolutely nothing doing from a remunerative point of view in the literary field. I must seek elsewhere for a job. They are a pack of scoundrels anyway. I met numbers of people who were asking about my book, but they wanted to borrow a copy. There is not a single copy offered for sale in Dublin. Several people told me they wanted to buy it and couldn't get a copy. I see David's *Lady into Fox* on sale here at Combridge's in Grafton Street.

I have decided to approach Curtis Brown with a view to getting them to act as my agent for short stories and sketches. The ten percent I would have to pay them is less than the worry of hunting around myself, and they might get me a few pounds more for them. I decided not to sell that 'Going into Exile' thing here. The country is not worth anything. They don't read, damn them.

It's great fun coming into contact with life again after being so long cooped up with books and silence. Everywhere I am meeting people and talking, talking, talking and watching, watching, watching. It's great fun. I have all sorts of types here in Dublin. One can get peasant types here as fresh as in Connemara.

There is a fine play running at the Abbey Theatre by a man called Sean O'Casey. He is a friend of mine and I went up this morning to see him. I found him dressed in a suit of dungarees sweeping out a hall where workmen gamble at night. That is his occupation. Fine chap. He is about forty and a nervous wreck like myself. He said he locks himself in at night and then feels happy and very often is afraid to stretch his legs in bed lest he might suffocate. He is also losing his eyesight. We talked about Tchekov and Eugene O'Neill for a long time. He is an artist, unlike the other bastard writers I met here. The play is a fine thing. It is called *Juno and the Paycock*. A fine piece of realistic work but in my own opinion he spoils it with tragedy. However, he naively asked me had I made much money on my novel and was dumbfounded when I told him I hadn't. He thought that one had only to write a novel and be rich, unlike writing a drama which only plunges one deeper into poverty. Poor devil.

It is very nice here but I am as far removed from the flesh pots as I was in London I fear. However, I am laying [in] a store of impressions and I am living. It appears that we are going to have another revolution here. Some generals are in revolt. Everybody is in a panic. President Cosgrave couldn't get a hearing yesterday at a public meeting. The whole audience hounded him off the platform.

Please send me all the news. Somehow I am more interested in London now than in Ireland. How is Miss Heath? I hope you are well.

Yrs affectionately
Liam O'Flaherty

P.S. I didn't see Yeats yet.

[1] Edmund Curtis had just published *A History of Mediaeval Ireland*, 1923. (His wife wrote under her maiden name of Margaret Barrington.)

---

74. HRHRC TLS to Edward Garnett
12 South Circular Road, Portobello, Dublin   12 March, 1924

My Dearest Friend,

Thanks so very much for your very encouraging letter which I have just received. You are very kind, but I am afraid that you are too flattering. That is, about my sketches. However, flattery is as nourishing as cod liver oil and malt, so the more I receive of it the better I like it. I thrive on it. See, I have written half of the enclosed sketch within the hour on the strength of it. I hope you will like this sketch. It's the one we were talking about in your flat the evening I left. I twisted the plot to suit myself. If you remember I think I told you the story is a true one, but in the interest of art, I must state here that there is not an atom of truth in the whole thing. It's a pure fabrication. What a scoundrel I am! But then I told you before not to believe anything I say.

I am going to write a sketch called 'The Storm' next. You remember I tried it once before in Chelsea. Now I am going to tackle it from a different angle and perhaps I may succeed. I read your review of Morley Roberts in the *Nation*.[1] I liked it. It was something altogether different to the tripe the other critics write. When one writes from the heart it always carried the hallmark of genuineness.

I have not been anywhere since but writing this sketch and getting my work in order. I walk about the streets a lot and stand at street corners and talk to the proletariat.

You see I know nearly everybody in this town who is of any interest from the point of view of thought. I don't mean people of importance but revolutionaries and queer people of all sorts. It is peculiar the effect of talking a lot about old times, and it's a peculiar thing too that although these bums, hoboes and tramps and manual workers know that I am a novelist, an educated man and of a different social standing to themselves by birth, etc., yet they do not take the least notice of it. They come up, clap me on the back and offer me woodbine cigarettes. It's fine. You don't find this aristocratic democracy outside Ireland. Among the bourgeois nations, they talk about equality but they don't practise it. We talk about dictatorships, we denounce the vote, the majority rule, etc. and yet we practise democracy.

We are a funny people. Not but that we have our bourgeois people too, but we spit on them.

I think my sister is coming up to see me. I will try and go down to Aran shortly for a week or so. I hear my father can still walk three miles to a funeral and back. He's eighty. My own health is improving wonderfully now. My cheeks are gaining their old dominant look. I don't mean the cheeks, of course, but the eyes. 'Damn him,' said Edward Garnett.

With best affection

Liam O'Flaherty

[1] Vol. 34, No. 23, 8 March, 1924, p.800 of *W.H. Hudson: a portrait*.

---

75. HRHRC TLS to Edward Garnett
12 South Circular Road, Portobello, Dublin   14 March, 1924

My Dearest Friend,

I just got your letter. Why are you so incredulous about literary agents? If the blighters were not of some use they would not exist, since in capitalist society only those institutions that are useful for making money exist. I simply must have an agent, so one is as good as another. These damn short stories have been the cause of more worry to me during the past year than the whole of the great war. Now I am rid of that worry. I have packed them all off to Curtis Brown. He will make a poor hand of them unless he can sell more of them than I sold. At the same time, since I have no contract with him I can sell to my own papers anything that's suitable. James Stephens told me that the only way to get anything for a story was through an agent. He himself never got more than five pounds for a story until he got one. So he said anyway.

I am glad Fannie Hurst is going strong in England.[1] By Jove, the Americans are going to put Cape on the pig's back. I am glad. I saw a review of *Thy Neighbour's Wife* the other day in the *Daily Telegraph*. It took that chap a good time to make up his mind about the book. But it was not a bad review so I forgive him.

After all we didn't have a revolution here and everything is very quiet. The weather is delightful and everything is very nice. Dublin would be a delightful place to live if one had a nice house on the outskirts and a fixed income. It's ideal in every other way except the financial way. I met the editor of the *Dublin Magazine*[2] and he likes my writing very much. He happens to be a Republican, of course. I think I may give him 'Going into Exile', but the blighter has no money and he can only pay about a guinea a thousand. I could sell everything I will write for the next two years in Dublin within twenty four hours, but all I could get would be a guinea a thousand. They pay for politics in this country but they refuse to pay for literature, unless it is political literature. Russell gave me some books to review and I fancy that in about a month's time, or so, I will be able to rake up enough here and there to keep me in rations. I am trying to get somewhere outside Dublin to live, so as to bring my wife over here, but so far I have been unsuccessful. I am writing a story called 'The Storm'. That's the lot.

One of the books I got to review was *The Forest Giant* by a Frenchman,[3] one of Cape's books. I think the first chapter is quite good. But then the fellow gave up the idea of writing about nature pure and simple, and began to tell us all about the origin of every damn thing in the world. Still, it's the only decent thing I have come across for a long time. I went out for a walk this morning to go to Phoenix Park. Fell into a brown study and got mixed up in the slums of the Coombe. Wandered around two hours before I could get out. My God, it's a sordid place! The most debased types of manhood that I have ever seen stood at corners. Numbers of them knew me and nodded, and some raised their caps. I suppose they remember me since the Rotunda incident. Last Sunday I went down to Liberty Hall and got a great reception from some of the gunmen there. They are all out of jail now and only one of my crowd got killed.

Yrs
Liam O'F

[1] Fannie Hurst's novel *Lummox*, New York: Harpers 1923: London: Cape, 1924.

[2] In MS 15.588 *NLD* (J.S. Starkey papers) there is a short note from AE to Seumas O'Sullivan, editor of the *Dublin Magazine*, introducing Liam O'Flaherty.

[3] Adrien Le Corbeau.

---

76. HRHRC TLS to Edward Garnett
12 South Circular Road, Portobello, Dublin   18 March, 1924

My Dearest Friend,

I'm awfully sorry but I have sent that 'A Day's Madness' to the agent so that *The Yorkshire Post* man, if he does take it, can't have it. At least the agent people would accuse me of sharp practice if he did take it. Anyway it is probable he won't take it. Anyhow, thanks very much for your great kindness in sending it there and soliciting that lady's favour on my behalf. You are very kind. I sold 'Going into Exile' to the *Dublin Magazine*. It will appear in the April number. They pay hardly anything but it's good propaganda here. Priestley is doing *The Black Soul* for the May number of *Mercury* but Bullett could not get it for the Times Literary. It was asked for shortly after Xmas by somebody else.[1]

I am doing a fine story now called 'Peasant Love', but alas it is such as will never, I'm afraid, see the light in a magazine. They will say, 'My God, what savages!' Still, it's the strongest thing I have done yet. It will be about ten thousand words. It's really a novel but I am getting it into that compass. I have six thousand words done. As soon as it's done I will send it to you.

I have finished a three thousand word sketch called 'The Landing', and I have done two newspaper articles, one of which appeared in the *Daily Herald* yesterday, so that you can see I am not wasting my time.[2] I also have an idea for a three act comedy. This place is all right for writing and I am getting very fit. So that on the whole I am pulling the devil by the tail.

Work, work, work, one keeps working and doing the same thing over and over in another dress and one says to oneself, 'Ha, I'm a great fellow, why doesn't everybody take off their hats to me.' It holds good of me and of you and of all of us. We are all very silly, life is very silly and yet it's all great sport. In Ireland, where nearly everybody takes himself seriously, it is very easy for a writer to see the silly side of himself. In England you all take yourselves seriously, all the time. That's what's the matter with England. The trouble with us in Ireland is that we have a sense of humour, now and again we see how ridiculous we are, and we go and make fools of ourselves, in shame of ourselves. Pretty sound and intricate reasoning that, apropos of nothing.

My head is swimming with writing too much, so I am going out for a walk. I will write you a long letter tomorrow with all the tittle tattle of life in Dublin.

Yours
Liam O'Flaherty

[1] This review (unsigned in the *TLS*) appeared 1 May, 1924, and was good apart from a criticism of 'violent bloodshot imagery' of nature 'too indicative of an impatient and rapid pen'.

[2] 'A dramatist in overalls', about Sean O'Casey.

---

77. HRHRC TLS to Edward Garnett
12 South Circular Road, Portobello, Dublin   21 March, 1924

My Dearest Friend,

I got your letter this morning and the Tchekov book. Thanks so much for the book. I was delighted to get it. Now I have several of them and I can take one down every time I want to get bucked up. I have nearly finished *Woman's Kingdom* already. Yes, it's splendid stuff. I am enclosing a sketch of my own, 'The Landing'. I hope you will like it. I didn't like it when I was doing it but now I think it's not bad. Maybe you might think it good enough for the collection of sketches. This 'Peasant Love' is, I am afraid, going to develop into a novel. I don't think I could do it under forty thousand words, so I am going to let it develop itself. The stuff is strong enough for a novel, but I am afraid that the movement of the style is too curt in the way I have begun it, to suit a novel. Still, that might be a delusion. The style I am using now is new to me. I didn't use it in either of the other two novels, only in the sketches and it strikes me as being too curt. If you would be kind enough to read the first few chapters I would like to send them to you and then you might tell me what you think of it. Please write and say that you would do me the favour of reading them for me?

I suppose you will think me an utter savage when I say that I have just written to Mrs Morris to say that I am breaking off all connection with her. Still, if a man is a low fellow, or a heartless rascal it is mere hypocrisy for him to try and hide the fact of his rascality.

How did I arrive at this decision? Well, I had intended to do so before I came to Ireland, because of my troubles last winter. Here I became luke-warm on the subject and then I fell in love with another woman, not very much, but just enough to let me feel that women still existed for me and that it was useless for me to try and hold on through a sense of false honour to a woman I had grown to hate. So I still am a scoundrel, in spite of your prediction that I was slowly becoming civilised.

The lady who is unfortunate enough to have conceived an affection for me here is also married and lives with her husband very dutifully. She belongs to an old Norman family, dark haired, shrewd, very cultured and very passionate in a cold, feline kind of way. She is one of the most sought after beauties in Dublin, but she does not enthuse me, at least not very much. But she is good copy. At the moment her husband is away in England attending some affair or other, and tomorrow the two of us are going to tramp out into the country. Today I am working hard at 'Peasant Love', so as to make up for the waste of a day tomorrow.

I don't go out at all now. I work all day. I got fed up talking to people. They are just as boring here as in England. I mean the literary people. I went to their club one night and I got disgusted with them. Anyway, one wastes too much time going about visiting people. It's surprising what a hole it makes in a day's work and then one comes home late at night bored, and tired, and enraged with that manuscript that has not grown a single line since the day before. One says getting into bed, 'What a stupid chap Moore has become, and his wife has got pimples all over her forehead.' Damn the life! I have been trying to get a little cottage outside Dublin, but I am giving up the endeavour. I work all right in this garret. I feel healthy and therefore I think I should stay here for some time. Also I think I require a deeper insight into the habits of both the town proletariat and the city and the business classes. Please write soon. I am very lonely for you. It is more than a fortnight since I saw you.

Liam O'Flaherty

---

78. HRHRC TLS to Edward Garnett
12 South Circular Road, Portobello, Dublin   n.d. [? March, 1924]

My Dearest Friend,
    I received your letter and read it carefully and I am sure that I extracted

all the juice from its contents. Rather bitter most of it, considering the nature of some of the advice that you gave me from time to time, both as regards my late wife and as regards women in general. However, I feel quite sure that you wrote in no spirit of bitterness or squeamishness or petty irritation. On the other hand I feel sure that you do not understand my character one bit, that is the 'personal' side of me. I feel equally sure that you understand the literary side of me very, very well and you like that side of me and that you like that side of me alone. However, I am glad you wrote that letter to me. It did me good.

Thanks so much for the nice things you said about 'The Landing' and about my writing. When anybody else praises my writing I feel suspicious and somehow discouraged, but when you praise it I feel overjoyed and confident. I enclose another little sketch that might be suitable for the book of sketches, 'The Blackbird'. I wrote it about a blackbird I saw in St. Stephen's Green. I am still working at 'Peasant Love' and have done about twelve thousand words. I am eagerly awaiting the arrival of *The Black Soul*. The American edition of *Thy Neighbour's Wife* reached me. It's very pretty.

I don't know what I am going to do about my wife. But one thing I shall not do is live with her again. I can see the difference since I came over here. She can have all the money I ever earn beyond the payment of my debts and my board and lodging, but I am not going to live with her. She damn near killed me.

Liam O'Flaherty

---

79. HRHRC TLS to Edward Garnett
12 South Circular Road, Portobello, Dublin   30 March, 1924

My Dearest Friend,

I received your letter yesterday. Thanks very much for appreciation of 'The Blackbird'. I felt that it was right and I am very glad that you think it is also. But somehow I get no pleasure from writing those short sketches now. They seem to advance according to a formula and it's like doing a day's work that you have been doing for a long time every day. The uncertainty of achieving anything alone makes literature pleasurable. Therefore 'Peasant Love' is of interest to me. Please read it at once and return it as I am very anxious to know whether it is worth my while continuing it or whether it's a lot of tripe.

I am finishing my first Dublin story and I will send it to you on Monday – local copy.

I am trying to get some place where I can be comfortable and work during the summer, but I cannot do so, so far. Dublin is a horrid place for diggings, but it's a great place for doing work. Here I can do three thousand words a day, and I am getting fat. But I better not crow until you tell me whether the words are good or bad.

I cannot write until I hear from you about 'Peasant Love'.

[unsigned]

---

80. HRHRC TLS to Edward Garnett
12 South Circular Road, Portobello, Dublin   3 April, 1924

My Dearest Friend,

Thanks so much for criticism of 'Peasant Love' which I received this morning. About style, I disagree with you. There will be written on the tombstones of most of the young English writers of talent: 'Here might have lain a genius, were he not cut off in his youth by the mania of style.'

Damn it man, I have no style. I don't want any style. I refuse to have a style. I have no time for style. I think style is artificial and vulgar. If a man is lucky enough to have a natural gift for saying things in a pretty manner, good luck to him. If he has not that natural gift he is a fool if he sidetracks his creative energy in an attempt to cultivate it. Them be my sentiments and I suppose they are quite wrong but because they are mine, the devil from hell with all his jesuitic guile could not persuade me to change them.

This is all rot and I don't know why I wrote because I wrote it this morning and now it is night. The fact is that I am irritated. My book is not come out from the hatching pen of Jonathan Cape, and I don't know what the devil he is doing with it. If it doesn't come out within the next few days I will go mad or something. What on earth is he doing with it? I have the population of Dublin in a whiteheat of excitement about it, and if it is delayed much longer the damn thing will fizzle out and they will say, 'Oh, that chap O'Flaherty is a bore.'

I am going to begin writing 'Peasant Love' again tomorrow. I have it all planned out. I have a great plot torn from life and I am going to put all our village at home into it. It won't be as good as *The Black Soul* but it will be hands down better than *Thy Neighbour's Wife*. The young bloods here rather liked *Thy Neighbour's Wife*, the followers of James Joyce, but they are a very, very small clique and they have no power. The power among the literary people is wielded by AE and Lennox Robinson, and they have the government behind them. I have won AE over to my side, but when he finds out what a scoundrel I have been he will dump me I believe. In about another month, however, I will have formed a powerful clique of my own and I am going to lick the bunch of them. O'Sullivan of the *Dublin Magazine* likes my writing and accepted three stories, one of them 'Going into Exile', but he is an enemy of AE's political views so he is cold except on the matter of accepting good stories for a bad magazine. I have secured the Jewish proprietor of the Irish Bookshop, a good man. And I have secured the wife of Professor Curtis, which is, of course, the most important conquest! Now you see that I don't make as many enemies here as I did in London. I have avoided all the Yeats's and the Stephens's, etc. They are no good at all. Therefore *The Black Soul*, unless anything untoward happens, should go well here. Which means, I suppose, that about ten copies of it will be sold in Dublin and five in the rest of Ireland. However ....

How is everybody in London and what is everybody doing? I go around and get all sorts of copy here but I never hear anything of what is happening in the civilised world, which is of course across the channel. When is David's book coming out, and how is *Lummox* selling? I am going to review David's book for the *Irish Statesman* if he sends a copy there.

With best regards and wishes that Shaw's abortion on Joan of Arc did not cause your digestion a permanent ill,[1]

Yours
Liam O'Flaherty

P.S. [ALS] Please send 'Fishing' and 'A Day's Madness', I want to sell them. L.O'F.

[1] 'Saint Joan' was first produced at the New Theatre, London, 26 March, 1924.

---

81. HRHRC TLS to Edward Garnett
12 South Circular Road, Portobello, Dublin   7 April, 1924

My Dearest Friend,

Here is a story by a friend of mine, a young woman, which I think is very good, because it's very true to life. She knows these damn people better than I do because, I suppose, she is a woman. I would like to know what you think of it as literature, so I hope you will be kind enough to read it. She has also written a novel which is very good and original, but unfortunately she had sent it to Dodd or somebody before I saw it. Otherwise I would have asked her to send it to you. Maybe something could be made of this woman as a writer. I shall be very eager to hear what you think of her story.

I also enclose a story of my own, which you might find good enough for the book of sketches, although it strikes me as being very weak. I would not send it to you for the purpose of including it but I thought it would be a good lark sticking a story of that kind among the others. I hope you will let it be included if not on its merits as literature, at least on its merits as a joke.

I am reviewing Wells' book for the *Statesman*. I think it's a wonderful piece of work, apart from the pages of dreary propaganda in it. Have you read it? I think the two scenes, Fanny's running away, and the father's death and the funeral constitute the finest thing I have ever read anywhere for simplicity and power.[1]

I can't do any work these days. I am in a state of too great excitement about my book.

With best affection
Liam O'F

[1] The review of Wells' *The Dream* appeared in the *Irish Statesman* 19 April, 1924.

---

82. HRHRC TLS to Edward Garnett
12 South Circular Road, Portobello, Dublin   11 April, 1924

My Dearest Friend,

I am disappointed about the date of publication of *The Black Soul* but we shall hope for the best.

Thanks very much for criticism of Mrs Curtis's story. I am glad that you think she has talent. Her novel is really interesting and I hope to send a copy of the MS to Cape in a few days. If it comes along your way will you read it sympathetically? She herself is very interesting too, though a trifle conceited and parochial on account of her environment, being the little marvel of the literary circle here, a parcel of old women, AE, Stephens, her husband Professor Curtis and the Yeats family, and others whom you would not recognise by their names. I fancy that she would become something really good if she had proper intellectual associates. But then there is only one Edward Garnett.

I am enclosing a story which is a new departure in method and in style, to a lesser extent. I wonder what you will think of it? I call it a flippant story. Whether I have succeeded in hiding its flippancy sufficiently under a cloak of art, I don't know. I would rather like this method if it could be developed into anything worth while. But one is always looking for new methods and one is never satisfied. I will rewrite that other sketch. No, there is no need to send back the sketches. How many of them are missing now from your collection? I have sent out 'The Tramp' and 'Going into Exile' and a few others but I will send them on. 'Going into Exile' will be published tomorrow in the *Dublin Magazine* and I will send a copy.

I have recast the novel I was beginning and am calling it 'The Curse'. I think it's stronger. It will give me the same opportunities in this manner that *The Black Soul* gave me. But in this case I will have to treat a whole family with the disease from which the Stranger was suffering. A family thinks they are under a curse and the curse falls on them because they think it is falling. In other words they all go mad, thinking they are cursed by an old widow whom they robbed of her land. The first chapter is the same as in the first edition, except for some slight changes of style, method and treatment of two characters. It appeals to me in this way more than in the other way. The whole thing in a novel is to get the spiritual ecstasy necessary to carry one's belief in the subject right to the end. Unless one keeps drunk one gets bored and disillusioned. In any case one gets disillusioned, but if there is always a supply of the drug of exaltation one can drink when one gets tired.

People accept me here now without a murmur. I am reputed to be very popular in the Arts Club. Of course I never go near the place myself, for diplomatic reasons, but my spies report that I am spoken of favourably, even by rank supporters of the government and of the church. If *The Black Soul* is not annihilated by the dark brethren, the two of us will shortly have a castle somewhere in Clare or Connemara. If we don't have a castle we can have a cabin anyway! Tell me when you are coming over here. I wonder could you come over during the Taillteann Games. It should be very exciting. Or maybe you wouldn't like the crowds?

My best respects to Miss Heath and David

Affectionately
Liam O'Flaherty

---

83. HRHRC TLS to Edward Garnett
12 South Circular Road, Portobello, Dublin   27 April, 1924

My Dearest Friend,

I must begin by an apology. I have been down to the Aran Islands and for that reason I have not replied to your letters before now. I have just come back, refreshed in mind and very weak in body owing to a cold I managed to secure while crossing the bay in an open boat in a violent gale. We were eight hours at sea. However, I am back and recovering.

I am sorry that Mrs Curtis's novel was not good enough. You must forgive me for having put you to the trouble of reading it. You must also forgive me for not reviewing David's book for the *Irish Statesman*. I felt it would be an impertinence on my part to review it after I had read it. I went and bought a copy instead. I think it is magnificent. My own book *The Black Soul* is very likely to be most favourably received here. AE is most enthusiastic about it and says that it is the greatest thing ever written by an Irishman! He is, I understand, reviewing it in the *Irish Statesman*, his own paper. What he says about it will carry great weight here. It is possible, of course, that if it is a great success in Ireland I may be able to sell twenty copies! The Irish Bookshop got a dozen copies of *A Man in the Zoo* this morning and they are already gone, that is at lunch time today. So that the two dozen people in Dublin who buy books have obviously been enamoured of *Lady into Fox*.

I have worked out my scheme for 'The Curse' completely and am satisfied with it. I have also worked out a rough scheme for 'Chaos' which is to succeed it. They are two pathological novels, both concerned with the perpetration of a crime, with a difference in the nature of the crime. In 'The

Curse' the crime will be that of a son who attempts incest on his sister and then finishes by murdering his father as the result of a curse which is implied. That is, the family gradually begin to believe that they are accursed. Scene, Aran Islands, as in 'Peasant Love'; background, the life of the village and all the impressions I got on my visit. By the way, the descriptions in *The Black Soul* of the sea and the crags and nature are all correct. I recognised the island from the picture I had drawn of it in the book. Especially in Spring when the larks sing. Otherwise my visit home was very melancholy and the only way I could see my way out of going mad was by pretending to myself that nothing mattered to me in life but literature.

My brother has been writing to me again asking me to go out to him, but I don't think I will go. My subsidy from Cape expires on the last week in May and after that I am on my own hook. I don't suppose I would be able to support myself by writing either in this country or in England unless the miracle happens of *The Black Soul* being a success. So that I have to marry a rich woman or take a hike for myself. Taking a hike would be more to my liking were it not for these two novels I want to write. But I may be able to write them and hike. But of course if one hiked what would be the meaning of writing novels? When one lives a vigorous life all one's energies go into the act of living. It is only when one does not live that one tries to create life. Brilliant idea, don't you think, like all my ideas?

Short stories have lost all interest for me. I brought back several with me, but they don't interest me and I don't want to write them. Big ideas devour little ones, like dominant men, while big ideas are awake and casting about them the little ideas have got to hide or just bow their heads and say, 'Yes sir'.

Yours affec.
Liam O'Flaherty

---

84. HRHRC TLS to Edward Garnett
Hell Fire Club, Rathfarnham, Co. Dublin   n.d. [? April, 1924]

My Dearest Friend,

I am sending you these sketches. I think there are two others, which are at present in the *Irish Statesman* office on consideration, 'Fishing' and 'A Day's Madness'. I will let you have them as soon as I get them. If there are any others that you have not got please let me know.

Bullett wrote to say he was enthusiastic about *The Black Soul*. He is doing it for The *Daily News*. He sent in the review and asked the editor not to cut it, but of course the editor is Robert Lynd, so that he may cut it.

I have been ill since I came back from the Aran Islands, but I hope to get better as soon as I get to the mountains. I am shifting tomorrow to the above address, a farmhouse near the ruins of the old eighteenth century club. I get board and room there for thirty bob a week. I think the address sounds very appropriate for the author of *The Black Soul*. They will say, 'The Priests soon put their curse on him.'

I got a note from my late wife yesterday saying that she was coming over here next week. What for I know not. I could not make out from the note whether she threatens to blow my brains out or whether she wants a divorce and is going to deliberately use me as a means thereto.[1] Her letters during the past two months would have disappointed you sincerely. The strangest thing about you is your absolute ignorance of women's characters and yet you must have known very many.

I expect to go ahead with my novel now. I am going to try and sell it serially and for film. I think it would work well on the films at least.

Yrs affectionately
Liam O'Flaherty

[1] The only grounds for divorce at this time were desertion or adultery. As Liam was not married to this woman he means she wishes to cite him as co-respondent to obtain a *decree nisi* from her estranged husband.

---

85. HRHRC TLS to Edward Garnett
Hell Fire Club, Rathfarnham   n.d. [? April, 1924]

My Dearest Friend,

I just received your letter and 'The Tramp'. The poor tramp is tramping some. I will try and put him in better dress before we present him to the British public, which we know quite well will examine his dress very closely. I think the order of your selection is excellent and I am quite enthusiastic about the collection now. I fancy it will be a good seller, unless a few of our more literary pieces will prejudice them. But you have sandwiched the 'literary' pieces well and they may escape. The other two or three sketches that you have not got are with the *Irish Statesman* and I will let you have them as they are published. I will send you a typed copy of 'The Bladder'. There is another little sketch too which I sent to the *Manchester Guardian* the other day which may be quite good for the collection instead of 'Matchmaking'. How much time is there for these things to be handed in? And do you wish to have the book dedicated to you? I asked you before but you would not reply either in the negative or the affirmative.

Now, I have laid aside 'The Curse' until next year and I am doing a novel about Dublin revolutionary life, my own experiences. It is very difficult but I am so full of it that it is forcing itself out. I have two chapters done. Of course it's very crude but I am doing a rough estimate first and then am going to go over it again, as I did with *The Black Soul*. If I don't get shot when it's published, if it is published, I will be lucky. I am calling it 'Chaos'. I have asked Cape to continue subsidising me until the end of September, when I will have the first draft finished. I don't want to be disturbed by any journalism until then. It's very hard and it takes all the energy out of me, but I have a beautiful place here to work, up on the side of a mountain. This morning I tramped away into a wilderness of moor and bog on the mountain tops. Lovely! And yet Dublin is only five miles away. Is it any wonder that men have died for Ireland? She is so beautiful that one wishes to die looking at her. It's just like listening to music or seeing a wonderfully beautiful woman, whom one knows one can never have for oneself completely. At least I never saw a woman of that description and under those circumstances, but I can fancy what it would be like after your description of Duse.

The Black Soul is selling well in Dublin. That is, a dozen copies have been sold by the Irish Bookshop, and the people who have read it have commented favourably on it. They are all important people. Of course it will be anathema to the average Irishman and to all Catholics. But strangely enough all these Catholics who are enemies of mine before they meet me, become staunch supporters after they have met me. Since I have been to the Aran Islands I am very popular there, so my sister tells me. I was only a week there, but the news spread all over Connaught. I bet if they knew of my coming they would ambush me and have me shot. I am safe enough here though, among Dublin people. You see, nobody knows here what following I have and with whom I am connected. The point is that I am connected with no organisation now, and have no following but that is all to the good. Nobody can betray me if I have no following and nobody can tell what is the strength of my following. I am generally reputed to be a Communist. AE strongly supports me, so that people are afraid to say anything against me. However, as soon as I get the first draft of my novel finished I am going to leave here and live among cultured people again. I should like to have a talk to you. Maybe I can live in London next winter.

Yours
Liam O'Flaherty

---

86. HRHRC TLS to Edward Garnett
Hell Fire Club, Rathfarnham   n.d. [? April, 1924.

My Dearest Friend,
    Just got your letter. I really don't know whether a cheap edition of *Spring Sowing* would sell in Ireland. You see, there are three stories or four there that would spoil it, 'Benedicamus Domino', 'Josephine', 'Beauty' and 'Three Lambs', and it is questionable whether there are sufficient half crowns in Ireland. I haven't got the missing sketches yet and won't have them I think for a fortnight or so. I will do 'The Tramp' and send it on.
    But I am working so hard at my novel that I am not very much interested

in anything else. I don't want to write anything about the artistic conception of it, lest I may confuse myself. But I am working three plots into a trilogy of different starting points, culminating at the same psychological point and then breaking in the different directions, determined by the different natures of the three characters; one civilised, one a gunman revenging his brother and uncivilised, another an ambitious and unscrupulous gunman defending himself against the husband of a woman he has seduced. The action takes twenty hours or so in the present year. Of course, as in *Thy Neighbour's Wife* this intensification of different aspects of life is merely in order to allow myself plenty of room for portraying as wide a slice of life as possible. I am going to make the canvas as vast as possible. If Cape is doubtful about it well and good. I take it that in that case I am at liberty to make arrangements elsewhere? He can't say that I didn't ask him.

The Black Soul should sell in England judging by the papers that are reviewing it well, the *Evening News* and the *Daily Express* and some Scotch paper. The 'intellectual'(?) papers are trouncing it, but of course that might have been expected. I fancy now that it could have been made a good pornographic proposition, handled as such in advertising, etc. Now, however, that it is launched as a literary gem it will have to stay as such. Anyhow I pat myself on the back. I licked all these swine here into a cocked hat. I wound them all round my fingers. I got AE to give me a thundering review. I got all the old women to praise me. Now that I have fooled them all I am telling these damned intellectuals what I think of them in choice scurrilous language. I have gathered a group of faithful followers about me and am starting a monthly paper called *Tomorrow*,[1] to which, by the way, I shall expect you, on pain of losing your immortal soul, to contribute. This paper is supported by voluntary contributions from the backers. Nothing paid, etc. If we get it out it should succeed because there is a Jew on the committee. Of course I use it merely as a platform for myself.

With best wishes

Liam O'F

[1] Two issues of *Tomorrow* appeared in August and September, 1924. The address of the manager was Roebuck House, Clonskeagh. Besides O'Flaherty's 'A Red Petticoat' contributors included Lennox Robinson, W.B. Yeats, F.R. Higgins, Joseph Campbell, H. Stuart (i.e. Francis Stuart), Cecil Salkeld, Maud Gonne, Margaret Barrington and others. L. Robinson's story 'The Madonna of Slieve Dun' was considered blasphemous and the periodical folded.

---

87. HRHRC TLS to Edward Garnett
Hell Fire Club, Rathfarnham   n.d. [? April, 1924]

My Dearest Friend,

I just got your letter. I also received a letter from Cape saying he would subsidise me until the end of September. I can see your hand in this as in everything else. How can I thank you, my friend? Your friend on the

Yorkshire Evening Post, I think you told me about a lady friend of yours on that paper, gave me a great review for the *B.S.* So that after all we didn't do badly. All the provincial reviews were good.

Dash it all I can't get this happy family story or the elopement. I have a little sketch called 'The Dawn' and another with AE called 'A Day's Madness' and that is all. 'A Life for a Life' is not finished yet. I will bring it along on Tuesday evening next. I will arrive at your place at six thirty. Then we can talk.

I gave David's two books to read to two ladies who are staying in a cottage near here. The following evening I went to visit them and they rushed at me, talking at the rate of a mile a minute. 'Charming' 'Delightful' 'Magnificent'! David would really like to have heard them. Especially as they are both very beautiful and intelligent women. Every single person who read *The Man in the Zoo* here was enraptured. They keep asking me to describe David and they refuse to believe that he is such a man, why I know not. Women are very queer, and I must confess that I do not understand them very well.

Now that I am secure for four months I feel delighted. After I have seen you and have got an outline of the work I should do, I'll come here like an ancient Gaelic warrior going to make an inroad against a Firbolg settlement. I have a great stunt for the dedication of *Spring Sowing*, if you allow it. It would be a great stunt. But I'll tell you about it.

With affectionate regards
Liam O'Flaherty

P.S. [ALS] This is what Curtis Brown, my agent, said of 'The Doctor's Visit': 'I am truly thrilled by your power to make a story so live as to make it seem to the reader as if the events were actually happening before his eyes.'

---

88. HRHRC TLS to Edward Garnett
Hell Fire Club, Rathfarnham   2 May, 1924

My Dearest Friend,

I just received your very melancholy letter. Damn it, the curse under which you English people struggle along in life is the curse of pessimism. Of course the *Times Literary Supplement* would make anybody melancholy. When I read that review yesterday I offered a prayer to the devil in thanks because my father and mother had been Irishmen, note the bull. However, here is a better review from an Irishman. He is the only man in Ireland whom everybody regards as the greatest man in Ireland, so that the review counts as something worthwhile. Whereas a review from some ridiculous pup of an undergraduate on the staff of the supplement, or the *Spectator* or the *New Statesman* doesn't cut any ice.

I have been reading your son's book ever since and at last I can say to myself that I firmly believe in David. I believe in him as one believes in Turgenev or in Dostoievsky. I think *A Man in the Zoo* is worth ten thousand *Ladies into Foxes. Lady into Fox* was exceedingly pretty art but I would never take off my hat to it. I would take off my hat to *A Man in the Zoo.* That's a great thing about the tiger ... 'up and down, up and down, up and down, etc.'

As far as my future is concerned don't bother about me. I will live and I will write if I have anything to write, so it will be all right. There are numbers of Americans coming over here in August, and I will get some money from them. Also after another few months I will be sufficiently well known in Ireland to spend my time at various houses in mediaeval fashion. Having no sense of honour that will be all right. I don't suppose Cape will sell a thousand copies of *The Black Soul*, but blast him he will make a little reputation on it, so that he will lose nothing. If he wants to make money on me quick tell him to publish that book of short stories. They go into rhapsodies here about my short stories but they refuse to discuss *Thy Neighbour's Wife.* I have had letters from every publisher in Dublin asking for a collection of short stories, after the publication of 'Going into Exile' in the *Dublin Magazine.* One clever blighter of a north of Ireland literary agent suggested that he and I should go fifty-fifty on the publication of a book. Talk about Americans. They are not in it. Unfortunately nobody in Ireland has enough money to pay more than a pound for a story of two thousand words. And they know nothing at all about the difference between, let us say, a sketch like 'The Rockfish' and 'Selling Pigs'. Of course they would consider 'Selling Pigs' much superior.

I am very interested in 'The Curse'. Very probably Cape will refuse to publish it but he can go to the devil. And your forecast of its reception by the public is also probably correct. But one writes as one sees or else one is a mountebank. You yourself were principally the cause of my becoming a puritan in art, instead of becoming an artist who is subtle enough to accept what the best people think proper and artistically refined in his own age. I will write in future for the satisfaction of my own soul, since that to me is the most important thing in this world, or in the next either. I have reluctantly but finally given up all hope either of being great before I die, or of ever making enough money even to pay my debts.

Tell me the sketches that you have not got and I will send them to you. You can fire them into Cape as soon as you like. I fancy they will do very well as they are. Unless you are kind enough to make corrections of misprints and that sort of thing. And I beg your permission to dedicate *Spring Sowing* to you also.[1]

With affection, Liam O'F

[1] The book was dedicated to Margaret Barrington.

89. HRHRC TLS to Edward Garnett
Hell Fire Club, Rathfarnham   n.d. [? May, 1924]

My Dearest Friend,

Herewith 'The Bladder', 'The Tramp' and a new story 'Colic'. Please put 'Colic' in the collection.[1] It will be popular in Ireland among the people that buy books. I am also writing 'A Pot of Gold' which will be good for the collection, and I will let you have 'A Rat Trap' as soon as the *Manchester Guardian* print it. I fancy that all my recent work will bear the mark of the Irish influence and that they are better in the collection than the previous human ones, which had a certain artificial influence. This is purely theoretical, but I fancy that I am in closer touch here with life and am writing with greater discrimination and greater difficulty of admitting a thing as finished, which after all is, I suppose, a proof that one is more critical.

I will send you 'Wolf Lanigan's Death' and 'A Day's Madness'. I won't send 'Fishing' as I think it's not good enough, as you say. The other two stories are in AE's office, but I am going into town in a few days' time and will get the office typist to copy them out for me.

The other day a man paid me a great compliment. He said that the only two people who seemed to be able to get the Russian 'picture' knack into their writing were Conrad and myself. Puffed up by such a combination of names, I said proudly: 'Ah yes, but Conrad and myself studied under the same master.' And the man said when I told him who the master was, 'There ye are, what did I tell you. Wasn't I right?'

For me life is very lonely here without you. It seems nobody else is in any way deeply interesting. You see one has a devilish hero worship for a man one allows to throw one's manuscript in the fire. During the past month when I was in agonies trying to find the right way out for my novel, I said to myself: 'Now, if Edward Garnett were here he would tell me in half an hour what I should do and the way would be clear.' But maybe it's good for me to have to begin to do these things myself. Although I would like very much if you would be so kind as to read the characters for me and give your judgment.[2]

'The Wren's Nest' and 'The Landing' have been printed last week and in this country 'The Hook' was printed,[3] so that as a short story writer I am becoming quite a little success. Maybe, after all, that I will be able to support myself by writing short stories. The agent is trying to sell some for me in U.S. but they said it would be difficult because the stories 'have a literary flavour'. What do you think of that? I am sending 'Colic' to the *Yorkshire Evening Post* where you advised me to try. I am sending it to the Literary Editor since I do not know your friend's name. 'The Wild Sow' was most unpopular in this country. Everybody expressed surprise that I could have written such a coarse and vulgar thing. The Irish national animal, the pig, is not popular in print. Inferiority complex again.

With best affection

Liam

[1] *Spring Sowing* 1924.

[2] Refers to *The Informer* which, according to a note held by Aberdeen University Library (Ref. CH Pre O'F), O'Flaherty states he began while at the Hell Fire Club.

[3] 'The Hook', the *Dublin Magazine*, 1 May; 'The Wren's Nest', the *New Leader*, 9th May; 'The Landing', *TP & Cassell's Weekly*, 24 May.

---

90. HRHRC TLS to Edward Garnett
Hell Fire Club, Rathfarnham   n.d. [? May, 1924]

My Dearest Friend,

I wrote this this morning and am sending it to you for the collection because I think it's worth putting in, instead of some of the other mournful ones like 'A Day's Madness' that I have got. But I leave it to your own discretion to decide whether it's good enough or not.

Do you think the ending is weak? I fancy it was impossible to get a dramatic ending under the circumstances. You see, it's an incident from life, and these incidents from life are generally more difficult from the point of view of good art than purely imaginative pieces. These are the three stories I brought back from the Aran Islands: 'Colic', 'The Rat Trap' and 'A Pot of Gold'. There is another, 'Begging', but it's serious and it does not enthuse in the present mood which is humorous.

Hoping that you enjoy the best of health and that you are happy.

Yours affectionately

Liam O'Flaherty

---

91. HRHRC TLS to Edward Garnett
Hell Fire Club, Rathfarnham   23 May, 1924

My Dearest Friend,

I just received your letter and another from Cape rejecting my proposals. I was on the point of writing to him myself cancelling the proposal so that it is as it should be in this best of all possible worlds. However, I am vexed that you rejected 'Colic' from the collection. I think you should include it. In fact, I must have it included as I consider it an excellent humorous story. You have a prejudice against humorous stories. Here is one, however, which you will like. It's tragic enough and I think it's lovely. It nearly killed me to write it, and I was just recovering from the effects when I read a review of *The Black Soul* in the *Irish Times* and almost had a complete collapse. Bullett gave me a good show in the *Daily News* and Gerald Gould in last Sunday's *Observer* gave me a good notice as a short story writer. So that after all the world is not too unkind. The only people who are really unkind are these syphilitic Oxford people. May they be double poxed, but then they are too thin-blooded to run the risk of getting the pox. I crack my fingers at them and in a short while I will make them lick my dust. After I have spat in the dust.

I have a beautiful short story on hand but I am too exhausted to write it. I have begun it. It's glorious!. What a delight it is to be able to write. When I have a writing mood I forget everything and every unpleasant person and thing that can meet with me.

I have not decided what to do, but I feel free, now that I am rid of my entanglements with Cape, etc. Naturally as he is not interested in another novel there is no reason why I should worry myself with the remainder of that semi-contract with him, so that I can do what I like now. But I will always cherish your kindness to me, and I will never forget that you taught me the major part of everything I know about the actual art of writing. Not to mention your encouragement when I badly needed it, and your sympathy and your assistance in the more material sense. This latter I hope some day to repay, but that is by the way.

As far as Cape is concerned he has made a good bargain, so that there is no good whiskey spilt in the gutter to be lapped by the rabble. I know that both these novels will sell on the strength of my short stories. My short stories will be popular but for myself these two novels will stand out as far greater and of more spiritual importance than anything I may do. So that Cape will get his money back.

I will probably come over to London shortly to see Curtis Brown about the sale of short stories, and I want to get things fixed up too with Cape re. *Spring Sowing*, the American edition of *Thy Neighbour's Wife*, etc. May I see you? Now I have to sit down and think what I am to do. America or not America, that is the question. And the world is an oyster for General Rathcroghan.

> With affectionate regards
> From Liam O'Flaherty [typed signature]

---

92. HRHRC TLS to Edward Garnett
Hell Fire Club, Rathfarnham   n.d. [? May,1924]

My Dearest Friend,

I got your letter this morning and I was delighted that you liked 'The Doctor's Visit'. Hurrah! I feel so glad that I was right about it. You know I never believe anybody's verdict about a story until you have said yes.

Well, damn the British public. The British public is all right. It's only the Oxford 'feeling' that has the poor public by the throat. Anyway I am an Irish writer and I have merely to make my living by the British public. The Irish *love* that kind of writing. 'Wolf Lanigan's Death', which is a damn sight more Russian than either *The Black Soul* or 'The Doctor's Visit', has been going the rounds of Dublin in manuscript. Miss [Susan] Mitchell, assistant editor of the *[Irish] Statesman* was taking it around and she is the mildest and most cultured of women – a puritan at that. And everybody here loves *The Black Soul*, except, of course, the people who correspond to the Nonconformist Snuffle on this side of the channel, to wit the *Irish Times* people and the clergy. But, good Lord, I am delighted with the reviews of *The Black Soul*. If Cape sells it in the proper channels it should sell well. Of course, if he sells it to the intellectual public it won't sell at all. Neither will it sell without advertisement. A thing that hits the people in the scruple stomach must be pushed or it will die anyway. It's a gamble of course, but then nobody ever made anything big without gambling. The man who tries consciously or otherwise to please people won't reap any substantial or lasting success. To him who dares ....

I am coming to London next Tuesday June 2nd, so that I will see you then and have a talk. There are various things upon which I want to get your advice if you are kind enough to give it to me. And I am coming to live in London from the beginning of July. I want to work up a boost for *Spring Sowing*. I have done very good work here during the three months I have been here. And by Jove, in spite of your predictions, or contentions rather, that I antagonise people, the only reviews of *The Black Soul* which were worth a curse were procured by me, AE's review and Bullett's, which I enclose. There is still another to come, Priestley's in the *Mercury*. I am going to try and get a job in London. T.P.[1] might be able to do something for me. Curtis Brown is my agent and I am going to try and work him up too. They write to me very enthusiastically about my short stories and predict a very successful future as soon as the market learns to 'palate' my stuff, whatever that means.

I am going ahead with my Dublin story. I am calling it *The Vendetta* now. It will, I fancy, only reach thirty or forty thousand words, less if I can help it, as I want it to be a serial. It should appeal as a shocker, thriller I mean, to the public that reads detective stories and murder stories.

Yours
Liam O'Flaherty

[1] Thomas Power O'Connor founder of *T.P.'s Weekly* (1902) which became *TP & Cassell's Weekly*.

93. HRHRC ALS to Edward Garnett
Town Farm, Aldbury, Nr. Tring, Herts   28 June, 1924

My Dearest Friend,

I have come over to England as you can plainly see. I am staying in a delightful farmhouse here, where it is delightful to work. The food is better than in Ireland and nobody can disturb me. I am up to my neck in the creation of a monstrous character called 'Gypo' Nolan – an Informer. I am calling the novel *The Informer* in his honour. He is a wonderful character and quite original, nobody has touched him. Not popular though.

In Tring I saw the grave of one Joseph Garnett aged ninety-eight, and I said to myself that the Garnetts must be a long lived family.

I expect you are back from Wales by this and I trust that you have had an excellent holiday.

My best respects to Miss Heath and to yourself.

Sincere affection from
Liam O'Flaherty

The typing of O'Flaherty's manuscripts during 1923/24 was done by Douglas Clayton of 54 Birdhurst Road, South Croydon. Two copies of *Spring Sowing* cost four shillings and ninepence. Postage was charged on accounts under ten shillings. O'Flaherty wrote to Clayton on 3 July, 1924, telling him of his return from Ireland. (Source SIUL)

---

94. HRHRC ALS to Edward Garnett
Town Farm, Aldbury   7 July, 1924

My Dearest Friend,

So glad to get your letter this morning and to hear you had a good time in Wales. It's very depressing to hear that Miss Heath's holiday was spoilt by rheumatism. She is so kind and gentle. I hate to think of her being ill, while a ruffian like myself, I won't say you, gets off scot free!

Congratulations on having begun to write your play. I feel very intrigued with the subject matter, but are not five doctors too many? I mean for you to handle. I am sure the lady could manage twenty.

Apropos of my lady, I may see you on Wednesday at the Café and talk about her. I will be in town and will try to get there sometime while you are there with Cape. Maybe you will have time to come and have tea with me afterwards?

I am going ahead very well with *The Informer*. Nothing that I have written so far has taken such a hold over me, although the book will be by no means as beautiful as *The Black Soul*, but even in its present state it's far stronger. This fellow Gypo is a regular monster and I love him. Poor fellow, I've got to kill him at the end. I have twenty thousand words done now, about one third or so of the whole thing. It would make a good German film, but would be, I fancy, too rough for presentation to a public that protested against steer-roping at Wembley. However, it may sell a thousand copies or so in book form.

I am getting fat here, so I'm glad I came. Everybody was highly indignant at my leaving Dublin and reverting to England. AE wrote for an explanation, so I wrote back and said that I had reliable information that the Republicans had discovered that I was writing *The Informer* and intended stealing the MSS when completed.

It's like living in a wilderness here. One never sees anybody and one does not read the newspapers. There is nothing for it but Gypo before lunch, Gypo after lunch and Gypo in the evening. There isn't even a river to distract and the women are uncommonly ugly. Why, I might almost become virtuous here. But the other day I went to visit a friend at Gerrard's Cross and ... Well, well now, I can see you straining your ears to listen so I won't tell you.

With affectionate regards to yourself and hoping that Miss Heath is quite recovered from her rheumatism.

I remain
Sincerely yours
Liam O'Flaherty

---

95. HRHRC ALS to Edward Garnett
Town Farm, Aldbury   9 July, 1924

My Dearest Friend,

I am sending you a copy of Mrs Curtis's sketch to read and a copy of 'A Thrush Leaves Home' (by myself) to read.

When are you coming down to see me? I understood you to say yesterday that you would come to see me, please come soon.

I am trying to catch the post, Yours
Liam O'F

---

96. HRHRC ALS to Edward Garnett
Town Farm, Aldbury   16 July, 1924

My Dearest Friend,

Thanks so much for sending M.B.'s sketch and for the nice things you said about it. She bids me tell you that you are the ... well, well now, I won't tell you what she said, but I am sure that you have made another conquest – very probably the 2597th.

For my part I was delighted 'The Thrush' was to your liking. Yes, I hope I have a special facility for writing nature sketches, because I would have to be very stupid unless your valuable instruction produced some fruit in me.

I got the proofs of *Spring Sowing* today. They appear good in print, and I think the order is excellent. Do you think we should expect success this time, or further denunciation?

How is your play going? I have already arranged in my mind all the details of your first night, including your speech, which will include a tirade against the disturbance caused by Irish hooligans between the acts. These hooligans will be provided by me, and also a band of respectable people to thrash them and throw them out. Then we might have a journalist hired, an honest fellow if we could get one, to rush down to his office with a description of the affair, and there you are, headlines next day, Edward Garnett Play, scene of faction fight, great speech by Garnett, libel action threatened against author by Irish Free State, etc!

My novel is proceeding apace. I have the poor hero on the point of making a fool of himself with the woman. It can't be helped. I like the book as far as it's gone.

I'm so glad to hear that you are coming down to see us. We are leaving here in a fortnight's time, so could you come before then? Remember me to Miss Heath, and tell her that I like all the Miss Heaths because they are all charming, but that I am very grateful to her for liking even some of the O'Flahertys.

We are having a glorious time here, in bed at 10 p.m. and rising at 9 a.m., swimming in a reservoir, walking in a wood, and I'm writing 'Gypo' while M.B. – who is very lazy – reads Conrad and Tchekov. Today, however, I have conscripted her to correct proofs. She has corrected 'Three Lambs' four times, I mean read it.

Well, hurry up and come down here to see us. Could you bring Miss Heath? Please.

Yours affectionately\
Liam O'Flaherty

---

97. HRHRC ALS to Edward Garnett\
Town Farm, Aldbury   28 July, 1924

My Dearest Friend,

I was very disappointed to hear this morning that we would not see you on Tuesday. However, let us hope that we will see you in Dorset in September.

I don't understand your reference to burnt boats exactly. I never burn any boats myself, I just use anybody's boats. In fact, I never burnt a boat. I won't say I haven't burnt houses though.

Just heard from Mrs Wallis now. We are going to take her cottage, but we can have it only until l6th August, so that my address from next Thursday will be East Chaldon, Dorset.

I have done two nature sketches since, one about hens and one about a conger eel. I will send you the one about the conger eel when Clayton sends it back, I like it.

I read a glorious thing by D.H. Lawrence in the *Adelphi* of this month called 'The Dance of the Sprouting Corn', it's a fine thing, spoilt by the last paragraph. Murry will ruin him, Murry and Jesus Christ.

I am fearfully bored waiting to set out for Dorset, not bored exactly but restless.[1] I promised that I would not touch *The Informer* until I arrived in Dorset and there doesn't seem to be anything else to do in Aldbury. Sketches, after all, don't constitute an intellectual meal. My Gypo always parades before my mind with ponderous movement, scowling, shaking his tremendous head, yelling now and again. I really will weep when I kill the beautiful monstrosity.

I haven't heard a single word from Dublin since I left. I don't write to anybody there anyway. Mrs Curtis gets letters from there though, and she tells me that the whole of Dublin is agog with the story of our elopement. It must be very pleasant for them. It's surprising what an interest some people take in other people's affairs. I suppose it's lack of personality. I hear that there has been an enormous queue for the past two months at East-bourne waiting to see the hut where the murder was committed, paying a shilling each too. If you want definite proof for my contention that the English are still far more uncivilised, barbaric and savage than the Irish, read the front page of yesterday's *News of the World*, which has a circulation of three million.[2]

Yours affec.

Liam O'Flaherty

[1] By 30 July, O'Flaherty has moved to East Chaldon, for Clayton writes and tells him how to get in touch with the B.B.C. to broadcast some of his stories.

[2] Headline: 'Shilling Chamber Of Horror'. People paid 1/- to view the scene of Emily Kaye's murder and mutilation by Patrick Mahon (each shilling taxed two pennies.). P. Mahon, ex-Dartmoor two years before for attack on woman, got a five year sentence. His wife told her friends her husband was in hospital with war wounds during his incarceration. Mahon, a handsome and charming philanderer, was fascinating to women. His wife remained loyal to him.

---

98. HRHRC ALS to Edward Garnett

c/o Mrs Wallis, East Chaldon, Nr. Dorchester, Dorset   3 August, 1924

My Dearest Friend,

We have landed in East Chaldon, got here on Saturday and we find it a beautiful place, although the weather is beastly and Middleton Murry is believed to have arrived here this morning, in a 'little motor car'. The natives have a great respect for him. Our landlady says he is 'head of the newspapers and supposed to have something to do with putting Kruschen salts into the papers'. I have seen Powys and he looks awfully nice.[1] There are tourists in Lulworth Cove, but I had a nice swim there and an hour's rowing. While I was in the water swimming, an army officer hailed me from a boat, a chap I hadn't met for eight years, and he cried: 'Congratulations on your delightful book *The Black Soul*, which I have just had the pleasure of reading.' Needless to say I was amazed, a most amazing adventure in an out of the way place like that.

The cycle ride from Aldbury was glorious. We did fifty-three miles a day and Mrs Curtis, though indisposed all the way, cycled like an athlete – great backbone. I was very sorry when we finished up at East Chaldon. My 'tramp' instincts had just come to life after three days, and I wanted to go on for weeks. The stretch from Salisbury to Blandford – twenty-two miles – across downs and moors, was glorious, not a house or a village and hardly any damn motor cars.

I am sending you 'The Conger Eel' sketch, which Mrs Curtis and myself like very much, amd another called 'The Jealous Hens'. I hope they will both amuse you and that you will comment favourably on them, so that I may be encouraged to write more.

I am looking forward to seeing you in Dorset with great excitement.

With best love
Liam O'F

[1] Theodore Francis Powys, writer, East Chaldon forms the background to most of his writing.

---

99. HRHRC ALS to Edward Garnett
East Chaldon, Dorset   8 August, 1924

My Dearest Friend,

So glad you liked the sketches, thanks for the kind things you say about them.

Isn't it awful about Conrad's death? So you were right about his dying if he didn't take exercise, well, he was lucky. He had done his work before he died and posterity will rank him among the masters, even if the clever ones of this generation don't give him that honour. Who are his executors? I suppose yourself and [Cunninghame] Graham.[1]

We are having a great time here, down on the beach at Ringstead every day from morning until night. I never was as happy in my life, and my work is going splendidly. After we leave Mrs Wallis I think we are going to live in a tent which Mrs Curtis has succeeded in borrowing from Miss Powys. It would be very nice if we got good weather to do so. I figure on finishing the first draft of *The Informer* by the end of this month.

How is your play getting on? You must have it nearly finished by now. When are you coming to Dorset?

If you think I am a conger eel you are mistaken. I am quite like a mackerel now, in a net and yet not in a net either. Point of fact, I have been frightfully lucky in meeting Mrs Curtis. She just suits me and we are devilishly in love. Our tastes are similar and our faults, defects, vices, etc., are identical, so that neither of us notices these things in the other. We have been living together now for six weeks and it seems like a day, or a thousand years for that matter. In a word, Sir, I am a lucky devil.

By the way, Clayton wrote saying that it would be a good idea for me to broadcast my nature sketches. He says they would go well, some of them. Supposing when *Spring Sowing* has appeared 'The Rockfish' and 'His First Flight' were broadcast with the name of the book, wouldn't it be damn good? I wonder would you mention the matter to Cape next time you are having lunch with him. I don't know anything about these broadcasting people myself. Whether Clayton has anything to do with them or not I don't know.

Powys is a delightful chap. Haven't met as cultured and well mannered a gentleman as he is for a long time. It's a veritable pleasure to talk to him. Fine type of Englishman – from Wales I suppose.

I was very interested to hear Colonel Lawrence is down near here. Yes, that accounts for 'the black soul' being in Dorset. Still, it's an amazing thing that there should be even one copy let loose among a number of soldiers.

With best affection and kindest regards to Miss Heath.

I am, yours
Liam O'Flaherty

[1] Conrad's wife Jessie and son Borys inherited his copyright.

---

100. HRCRC ALS to Edward Garnett
5 Perham Road, London W14   n.d. Sunday [early September, 1924]

My Dearest Friend,

The above is my address. It's in West Kensington near the tube station. I got two rooms there, a bedsitting room and a kitchen at the top of a house.

I finished *The Informer* today in Regents Park. It is a great load off my chest but I'm very sad. I had grown so fond of that poor devil of an informer. Both Mrs Curtis and myself think *The Informer* is a great book. I think I will have it rewritten in another month. I wonder, will you prefer it to the *B.S.*?

I have just written letters to several editors asking for work. I hope some of them respond. I wrote a note to T.P. O'Connor, and I find his full titles, in spite of abbreviations, cover the front of an envelope. What an amazing farce is journalism, the man never said an intelligent or original thing in his life, and they load him with titles. In Russia, according to Turgenev, they were not so kind to their buffoons. Here, damn it, such is the idiocy of those in charge of affairs, that they fail to distinguish between the buffoon and the man of talent .... I always become morbidly philosophical when looking for work.

I am going to write a short story about a priest, another about marine firemen in the tropics, and another about goats.

Liam O'F

---

101. HRHRC ALS to Edward Garnett
5 Perham Road, W14   8 September, 1924

My Dearest Friend,

Thanks so much for the invitation. We will arrive at seven o'clock on Wednesday at your place.

I am installed in my new quarters but I have not begun to work yet, rewriting my novel. I am waiting for the arrival of a typewriter I have hired. I fancy it will save time and money if I type it out as I rewrite it. In that way I will have it ready for the market in another month.

On Wednesday night I hope you will read us that love passage from 'Barbara's Case'.

With love
Liam O'F

---

102. HRHRC TLS to Edward Garnett
5 Perham Road, W14   18 September, 1924

My Dearest Friend,

Thanks so much for your kind letter. I will eagerly await Miss Heath's letter. I do hope you will be able to get away from town for a few days at least. Did you hear anything yet about 'Barbara's Case'? I suppose not.

I am working hard at *The Informer*. I hope to have it ready for your judgement in another three weeks or so. When you get it I want you to judge it not so much for what it is by itself, as for what I have set [out] to make and what I have succeeded in making. The mob can judge it for what it is. They never know anyway. They bring all sorts of eccentric things into the scales, morals, god, politics, etc. But in your criticism of 'Fathers and Children' [sic], I was greatly struck by the clarity with which you probed the very initial dreams of the author and their subsequent materialisation in the finished creation. It is on these lines, following from an initial dream, through its changing fortunes as other circumstances mould and redirect it, to a conclusion in a way unexpected from such beginnings, that I have tried to build *The Informer*. I have envisaged a brutal, immensely strong, stupid character, a man built by nature to be a tool for evil-minded intelligence. The style is brutal at that stage, without finesse, without deviation, without any sweetness, short and curt like a police report. Then, as other characters appear on the scene the character of the man changes gradually. Elements of cunning, of fear, of struggle that is born of thought, appear in him. The style changes to suit this, almost imperceptibly. More and more characters appear. The character is no longer brutal. Sympathy veers around and stands in the balance, for him or against him. He is now a soul in torment, struggling with evil influences. At this point the style becomes definitely sympathetic, lengthens itself out, softens, strikes a note of joy in the eternity of nature. Scenes of horror and sin present themselves.

Then with gathering speed the Informer is enmeshed by his enemies. His vast strength crumbles up, overwhelmed by the gathering waves of inconquerable intelligence. He stands alone, without the guidance of a mind to succour him, seeking an outlet for his useless strength, finding that it is no longer strength but a helpless thing, a target for the beings that press around to harass it. Intelligence, evil intelligence, is dominant and supreme, civilisation conquers the first beginnings of man upwards.

Then the Informer makes a last effort to escape. Here the style completely changes and becomes like a wild storm, cascading, abandoned, poetic. From there it rises rapidly to a climax at this point ....

'Shapeless figures dancing on tremendous stilts, on the brink of an abyss to the sound of rocks being tumbled about below, in the darkness, everything immense and dark and resounding, everything without shape or meaning, gloom and preponderance, yawning, yawning abysses full of frozen fog, cliffs gliding away when touched leaving no foundation, an endless wandering through space, through screaming winds and ... crash.'

After that I strike a note of pity and finish on it. This is what I have tried to do. See what success I have had. I don't know myself, but I have hopes.

Yours very affectionately
Liam O'Flaherty

---

103. HRHRC TLS to Edward Garnett

5 Perham Road, W14   n.d. Wednesday [end September, 1924]

My Dearest Friend,

I was delighted to receive a copy of the [W.H.] *Hudson Anthology* [edited by Edward Garnett] today from you. No praise of mine would be at all adequate to express the real pleasure that it gave me, even by glancing over the pages. Mrs Curtis read me the passage about the lady grasshopper during breakfast. It is wonderful. I myself was particularly glad that you had included the description of the passage of the birds from *Green Man-*

sions. It will indeed be a boon to those lovers of Hudson who cannot afford to buy all his books. You are to be congratulated. Together with my congratulations I offer my thanks for having sent me a copy.

I had the pleasure of receiving a delightful letter from Miss Heath in acknowledgement of a book I sent her. I treasure the letter very much, because she said nice things about my sketches and I think she is a good judge.

We are leaving here on Monday. The landlady ordered us out. Some reason or other, probably because we are poor. We intend going down the country to a cottage. It's cheaper and more healthy and one runs as good a chance of getting work by being out of London as by being in London. I saw Lynd. He was a wash-out, so was Caradoc Evans.[1] Cape thought that it would be no use going near Garvin, so that my chances of employment narrow down to the *Weekly Westminster* and [Leonard] Woolf. I have not seen Woolf yet. I put up a proposition to the *W. W.* and they are considering it. Tomlinson is the literary editor of it. I offered to do them a light descriptive article, six hundred words or so, each week. Might get two guineas for it. There are hopes.

In the meantime I am slogging away at *The Informer*. He is a consolation anyway. Damn this journalistic business. I would much rather get a gun and a blind lamp and go out at night to fill some bourgeois full of lead and appropriate his role without the asking, rather than commit the indecent crime of writing piffle for a few coppers. The modern cult of slim-fingered highwayism as opposed to the good old style of filibustering highhandedness, is to my mind a degeneration. Of course you prefer the civilised 'cult'. But I think we are coming to another wave of primitivism. I feel it. This culture is dead and the fresh uncultured 'phase' will need some mouthpieces before long that have a sting in their talk. They cannot be long satisfied with the Wellses and the Gorkis. Then we will come into our own and make everybody jump, though we might possibly be dead before that happens. Very possibly this revolutionary wave will pass through a whole generation, simmering and cavorting in its own trough, before it rolls cliffward. Then I will be left with an audience of about a hundred intellectuals who appreciate my 'art', so-called and don't appreciate my 'impetus' because it is foreign to them.

I won a victory at last over Middleton Murry. He took a sketch about a butterfly. Why he did so I don't know, maybe he doesn't know himself.

Yours affectionately
Liam O'Flaherty

[1] Caradoc Evans, satirical Welsh writer of short stories, had also just brought out a play *Taffy*, which caused a stir.

104. HRHRC ALS to Edward Garnett
Sunny Bank Cottage   [postcard postmarked] 26 September, 1924
Great Milton, Oxon

My Dearest Friend,

The above is my new address. Your suggestion as to finding work I have noted, but as far as the Irish Boundary is concerned I don't see any chance. Should war break out in Ireland that is another affair. Anyway I'm not going to do anything until I finish with 'Gypo'. I feel pretty confident that I have got something in him to put me off the penny a line market. All I have seen of Fleet St. makes me feel I would rather live starving than push myself into an early grave at that line of work. I'd rather go into the workhouse. I have written a heavy novel in three months. I don't feel like it. If the *W.W.* doesn't come to scratch and if I can't raise any money on Gypo, well, there might be a war in Ireland.

Liam O'F

---

105. HRHRC ALS to Edward Garnett
Sunny Bank Cottage, Great Milton, Oxon   4 October, 1924

My Dearest Friend,

Would you do me the favour of coming down to visit me for next weekend October 11/12th? I want to consult you about the end of *The Informer*. I would be greatly honoured and obliged if you would be so kind as to come. We have a spare bedroom at the cottage and you would be as comfortable as we could make you. Please let me know.

Allow me to congratulate you on the remarkable success of your new book. I felt so glad reading the *Sunday Times* review, especially when I noted that Gosse happened to be having a holiday. I remember his scoundrelly attack on you last year. My own book has had a rather shabby reception, but that was to be expected.

I sold 'The Foolish Butterfly' and 'The Conger Eel' to the *Dial*, so that makes a double sale for each of these two sketches, here and in the U.S.

This countryside is rather nice, and we are very happy here. If we can make ends meet it will be glorious all winter. The Gods are good and Mrs Curtis is an absolute angel. She is just the one woman in the world for me. Her husband paid us a visit last Saturday, just before we left London. He wanted her to go back to him and hummed and hawed about the impossibility of getting a divorce, but I believe he will do so when he sees us back in Dublin next Spring. I told him we were going to come back there and he was astounded that I should have such a lack of feeling for him. Finally I got him to agree to a divorce should Margaret still wish to live with me after another six months. So there the matter stands. He's rather a decent man, though frightfully nervous and conscious of his own importance.

Well, I hope to see you next Saturday. If you can't come down I will take the MS up some day the following week. I will have it finished by then, but I should like your advice before I write the last thousand words on a certain point. So, if you can at all, come down.

With sincerest regards to Miss Heath from Mrs Curtis and myself.

To yourself, my best love
From your Liam O'Flaherty

---

106. HRHRC TLS to Edward Garnett
Sunny Bank Cottage, Great Milton, Oxon   n.d. [mid October 1924]

My Dearest Friend,

I have been rushing work on *The Informer*, so I didn't write. I am finishing it today. I will be bringing the manuscript to town next Thursday and I am eagerly availing myself of your invitation to lunch. May I arrive about one o'clock? Unless warned not to do so I will.

The reviews of my book were not bad but I don't suppose the sales are any better. However, we will talk about that. I have a lot of things to talk about. The *Hudson Anthology* is an endless pleasure, we read passages over and over again every day.

I have done an excellent story about the goats I told you about. I will begin the sea story now. The priests have faded from my mind. There is another germinating about a spider and a centipede.

Yours for ever
Liam

107.
To the Editor of the *Irish Statesman*,[1]   18 October, 1924
Great Milton, Oxon

Dear Sir,

In your issue of October 4th I read an essay on 'Leaders of Indian Nationalism', an essay that aroused in me an intense interest. The vitality and force and passion and stinging truth of that essay, the surging rhythm of the prose, the ferocity of expression, caused me to cry out before I was half-way through; 'Bravo, Ireland! In no other country could there be life enough, passion enough, force, virile force enough to write this.' It was a praise of peace, of gentle forbearance, of quiet culture. What matter? In literature it is the method and the manner that counts, the manner of expressing the passion that is within the heart.

The essayist deplored the lack of culture in Ireland, the proneness of our young men to settle their quarrels at the pistol point. He compares this state of affairs with the age-long culture of India that enabled Mahatma Gandhi to impose a doctrine of passive resistance to injury upon a countless people. He upholds the latter people. He upholds the latter culture. It is superior, he says. Doubtless it is.

But the human race has not advanced from savagery to culture on the feeble crutches of philosophy. What epics have there been written about the disputations of scholars? Did Homer write of philosophy or of the hunting of wild boars and the savage wars waged around stone-walled cities? Did Shakespeare live in the days of twenty percent interest on oil stocks and the loathsome mouthings of Ramsay MacDonalds at Geneva about Leagues of Nations that are based on fraud, corruption, and the usury of slim-fingered, cultured bankers? Did he not live in the days when piratical adventurers carried the standards of Britain across the oceans and the continents? Did he not live in the days when his race was emerging, with bloodshot eyes, lean, hungry, virile, savage, from the savagery of feudalism into the struggle for Empire?

In Ireland, to my mind, we have reached that point in the progress of our race, the point which marked the appearance of Shakespeare in English literature. Let us not be ashamed that gunshots are heard in our streets. Let us rather be glad. For force is, after all, the opposite of sluggishness. It is an intensity of movement, of motion? And motion is the opposite of death. India is cultured. It is an age-long culture. It is a culture of sweet, beautiful words and of slim fingers, slim, long, aristocratic fingers that are effete and on their death-bed. It is a ghostly culture, the culture of dead men walking the earth, crying out in a wilderness peopled with ghosts. Beauty and peace, sweet, melancholy peace.

But ours is the wild tumult of the unchained storm, the tumult of the army on the march, clashing its cymbals, rioting with excess of energy. Need we be ashamed of it?

Yours faithfully
Liam O'Flaherty[2]

[1] Published in Vol 3, No.6, 18th October 1924, the *Irish Statesman* under the heading of 'National Energy'.

[2] Beneath this letter AE, as editor, adds a long comment beginning 'Dear Liam,' he disagrees with O'Flaherty and ends, 'We have seen the foam on the jaws of our wild boars for some years, and rather wish they would go asleep.' In the issue of 1 November Austin Clarke and F.R. Higgins write a reply to O'Flaherty's letter headed 'Art And Energy', to which the editor adds a further comment and asks the writers to develop their ideas on an artist's use of language.

---

108. HRHRC ALS
Sunny Bank Cottage, Great Milton, Oxon   16 November, 1924

Dear Mr. Spohn,

Thanks so very much for your delightful letter. It is so encouraging to get an appreciation from such a distance, and especially pleasurable from an American, because to my mind the Americans are rapidly becoming the leaders in the patronage of literature and art. Doubtless this view is very unpopular among the intellectual Americans themselves. You are very fond of running yourselves down, I notice, but a comparison of American 'art' periodicals with corresponding British ones easily gives victory to the former. The British, to my mind, are too insular. They lack the breadth of vision which is possible only among a people that is not too deeply rooted in the prejudices of the past.

I am sending you a signed copy of my collection of short stories, *Spring Sowing*. I hope you will like it. It had a big success here from a critical point of view, but it did not sell. Short stories will not sell in book form and the ordinary individual fights shy of the real stuff, here as well as with you.

However, making a career of literature is strikingly similar to making a career as a real estate agent or a purveyor of cigars. You have to get your stuff advertised for some time before you begin to sell. And when you think the time is ripe to begin the sale you must come across with something heavy. I expect to do that next February with *The Informer*, my next novel. I can guarantee you that there is going to be some fun when it appears. Cape is going to go the whole hog on it and I hope he is lucky. I have taken an extraordinary character as a hero in a Bolshevik spy drama in Dublin, a character resembling in a sense 'the hairy ape' or 'the thinker'. He informs on a comrade and the Revolutionary Organisation tracks him to his death. The whole novel occupies eight hours. I think it is probable that Boni & Liveright will print it in New York simultaneously with Cape, and possibly the Talbot Press in Dublin, so as to obviate overlapping in the effect.

As to manuscripts, I have disposed of the manuscripts of *Thy Neighbour's Wife* and *The Black Soul*. I still have the manuscripts of some of my short stories and of *The Informer*. I trust to hear from you soon again and permit me again to thank you for your kind appreciation.

I remain
Yours very sincerely
Liam O'Flaherty

P.S. I am going to take a house outside Dublin next Spring, and I hope that you will do me the honour of calling any time you visit Europe.

———————

109. HRHRC ALS to Edward Garnett
Sunny Bank Cottage, Great Milton, Oxon   19 November, 1924

My Dearest Friend and Gargantuan Godfather,

I thank you so much for sending me a copy of the first volume of Rabelais, which I received this morning, just after rising from my bed – eight days down with the cursed 'flu.

On rising, along with your Rabelais, I was greeted with a pleasant surprise, a dual one in fact. I had a request – per Reuter – from a New Zealand fellow to reprint 'The Conger Eel', for {thirty shillings ?}. He has wriggled to New Zealand, the devil! I also had a letter from the *Weekly Westminster* to say they would accept a weekly contribution from me at one guinea per four hundred and fifty words, that's about two guineas a week. Open your bottle and have a little drink, dear friend. We are coming out of the wood. The two of us will drink a quantity of champagne before many years are passed.

I would like it very much indeed if you wrote an article for the *American Saturday Review*. It would be great, and I think that an article coming from you would put me across in America. It would be a pleasure anyway to knock these bloody Irish Catholic crawthumpers on the head. They hate me. Let's get hold of Panurge's oar and when they try to crawl on board the ship, knock them off again, and when they cry for mercy let us jeer at them. And when they offer their friendship later on, we can say, 'We don't mind if you pay us well enough.' Mrs Colum, according to Mrs Curtis, is a little schoolmistress who has no sense of decency whatever. According to Mrs Curtis, she (Mrs Colum) simply uses men to get on.

Now, you scoundrel, I know very well you will generalise from this and muse considerably and then giggle to yourself, and then do all sorts of things and finally make up your mind in a peculiar fashion, i.e. you will shake your head twice vertically, and after that you will have another drink. Although, upon my dishonour, I am in doubt after all as to what will have happened within your subtle brain.

The *Nation* rejected 'The Flood'. I was afraid to reread it, but I can quite see now that your criticism of it was correct. It was more interesting as an example of what can come out of O'Flaherty's brain when he is getting a neurasthenic fit. Just so, I sent it to the *Dublin Magazine*.

I was pleased to read David's story in the *Nation*. I thought it very subtle and elegant, I mean the one about the horse – Old Prince. I think he is becoming much more individual in his style and in his approach to life. A great improvement, if I may say so. But why does he lash himself down to a negation of emotion? How cruel! In another couple of years he will let loose that passion that undoubtedly is latent in him.

How is Miss Heath? Give her my compliments. When are you coming down again, or are you coming down before we go to Ireland? We are coming to town next Thursday week. Perhaps we will see you then. Don't work too hard at your MSS.

Yours
Liam O'F

P.S. An American millionaire called Spohn, not spaun, wrote to know had I any manuscripts to sell! L.O'F.

---

110. HRHRC ALS to Edward Garnett
Sunny Bank Cottage, Great Milton, Oxon   28 November, 1924

My Dearest Friend,

I have [not] been very well and I am only just out of bed, so I couldn't come today. Can you extend your invitation to next Thursday? I am so sorry to have missed today, as you say Miss Heath was to be there. Mrs Curtis and myself would love to see her before we go to Ireland.

We are leaving for Ireland on 20th Dec. We got a house at Rush, in north Co. Dublin, for one pound a week. We hope to have you and Miss Heath there for Easter. It's right on the sea.

I am very weak, stomach attack, so you'll excuse the short note.

Liam O'F

---

111. HRHRC ALS to Edward Garnett
Sunny Bank Cottage, Great Milton, Oxon   12 December, 1924

My Dearest Friend,

I received your note and enclosed letter today. I am very sorry indeed that you have been troubled in this way on my account. Please try to forgive me. Miss Casey wanted to say that she is going to sue me legally for the money I owe her mother. That will be interesting.

I enjoyed my first book of Rabelais very much indeed. It's the greatest book I ever read. I will send them back to you before I leave, but as soon as I get home I am going to buy a Rabelais on the instalment plan. It's wonderful, magnificent. Thanks so much for lending them.

I greatly admire your review in the *Nation* this week, it was very good indeed. That fellow deserves much worse than you gave him.[1]

We are leaving here for Ireland on 19th. I am so glad to get away as my health has got very bad here. I am getting better now, but my stomach is very weak. Mrs Curtis has been an angel of kindness to me. Believe me, I didn't think a woman could be so good. I do believe she will make a decent fellow of me yet.

I am writing nothing at all. I can't write. I am fagged out by *The Informer*, but 'Chaos' is looming up big and I will probably tackle it next Autumn. I am expecting a big access of energy and strength from the sea air at Rush, so that I will probably do some stories there. Did you see a review of *Spring Sowing* in the *Bookman's Journal*? It might interest you.

I am sorry I won't be able to come to see you before going to Ireland. I had hoped to see you and Miss Heath, but I am relying so much on you both coming to Ireland to see us at Easter. You must come and see the people in Dublin. They will amuse you. Give my best respects to Miss Heath and to yourself.

> Dearest affection from
> Liam O'Flaherty

[1] Garnett's review in Vol. 36, No. 10, 6 December, 1924, pp. 366 & 368, was of Ford Madox Ford's *Joseph Conrad: a personal remembrance*. Garnett had introduced these two men to each other. He found Ford's account embellished with 'fantastic inventions', and factually inaccurate.

---

112. HRHRC ALS to Edward Garnett
Sunny Bank Cottage, Great Milton, Oxon   16 December, 1924

My Dearest Friend,

Thanks so much for the volume of Gorki. I am enamoured of it exceedingly. Only another three days here and then Ireland. I can neither eat nor sleep with excitement, thinking of it, so that it's really bad for my health. I am more like a bag of loose disjointed bones than a human being, but while I am alive I kick.

I heard from my brother yesterday. He told me that *Thy Neighbour's Wife* is beginning to cause a big sensation among Irish American radicals, but that the publisher has done absolutely nothing for it. However, as long as a public begins to form itself for me it doesn't matter. He says people are going around 'boosting' it, intellectuals not workmen. I can get no account from Cape, although I have written several times about it, as to what returns Boni & Liveright have made. It's far more important for me to have a publisher in New York than to have a publisher here. *The Black Soul* should come as a stunner to American intellectual radicals, but of course they might understand *Thy Neighbour's Wife* better.

I am able to do nothing but a weekly sketch for the *W.W.* I am writing piffle for them as I think they would appreciate it more than literature. If I could only get another little job like that I would be safe, that is unless I break down altogether this time, but I think I will pull around the corner when I get to Ireland. Neurasthenia is a curiously 'lively' disease.

We will probably have our divorce next summer so that we can get married, that will be more convenient.

Give my tenderest regards to Miss Heath and to yourself. I can wish you nothing better than a good book, and a good appetite.

> Yrs
> Liam O'F

---

113. HRHRC ALS to Edward Garnett
c/o Miss Nealon's, 16 Upper Mount St., Dublin n.d. [early January, 1925]

My Dearest Friend,

I am in a very low condition here and absolutely friendless – everybody has turned against me. I have no money. Would you ask Cape to purchase the copyrights of my four books for whatever he can give.

Yrs, Liam O'Flaherty

---

114. HRHRC ALS to Edward Garnett
16 Upper Mount St., Dublin   9 January, 1925

My Dearest Friend,

I cannot thank you sufficiently for your letter and your cheque for ten pounds. Very probably you will save my life this time again. I may get round the corner, but I felt so helpless and alone that I was near giving up the struggle. Now I feel inclined to fight on. It is only when one is ill that one can distinguish one's friends from the creatures who speak fair words.

Margaret is very good to me, but she is pretty nearly fagged out too. The church has organised a general vendetta against us here, but, by Christ, if I get on my feet again I am going to lick them all. I want to get strong enough to write 'Chaos', that will be my revenge. Just two years of life is all I want.

Yours lovingly, Liam O'F

---

115. HRHRC ALS to Edward Garnett
16 Upper Mount St., Dublin   17 January, 1925

My Dearest Friend,

I think I am beginning to pull around again. I am {facing?} up to a world in which I find myself snowed under with debt, with a shattered constitution and as many friends as a bailiff in the west of Ireland. Nevertheless I agree with Dr. Pangloss that this is ... etc.

Many thanks for the Rabelais. It was a welcome arrival. I have laughed already over it. If I ever get out of this difficulty I will blame you and Rabelais. I have appealed to my sister for funds. If she fails me I am damned.[1]

As soon as I am able I will write you a long letter of thanks for your inestimable kindness.

Remember me to Miss Heath,

With best love
Liam O'F

¹12 January 1925 letter from J.M. Barrie to Edward Garnett suggests that Garnett should ask
E.V. Lucas to get a grant for O'Flaherty from the Royal Literary Fund 'always very open to
good causes'. (Source HRHRC)

---

116. HRHRC ALS to Edward Garnett
16 Upper Mount St., Dublin   20 January, 1925

My Dearest Friend,

I am writing to say that I am slightly better physically. I am up and I
have been out. I am very weak and I can walk only about two hundred
yards. My mind is very low. I cannot sleep without drugs. However, I
am going to the country tomorrow and the doctor promises great things
as a result. He is an excellent doctor. I am going to write about him when
I get well. But he says I cannot work for six months, so he has to wait for
the honour.

Scoundrel, mountebank, buffoon, idiot, lying, deceitful, double- dealing,
slandering, calumniating rogue, immoral and degraded offscouring of a
degenerate people – hear, hear, I can hear all my enemies chanting about
me and I don't give a damn. My dear fellow, may they be devoured by the
archdevil's itch, without a broken bottle within a thousand leagues to
scratch their ulcerated haunches.

Troth, I have a few supporters from a literary point of view. 'The
Conger Eel' was loudly acclaimed here, which to me is more comforting
than all the medicine that doctors can pour into my belly with a bull's
horn. Margaret met O'Neill yesterday – [Eoin MacNeill] the Education
Minister – and he was very enthusiastic about *The Black Soul*. All that
have read *The Informer* say it is much inferior to *The Black Soul*. I
believe it myself now.

I want to write you a whole lot, but it gives me a pain in the stomach to
write anything coherent, so forgive the drivel. I heard from my sister, she
promises help, but I greatly fear a determined attempt to get me back into
the arms of the Church. There is a very wide movement against me among
the clergy, but of course they would be glad of a conversion, especially as
there is a terrific battle raging at the present time about Catholic literature
and immoral literature. Lennox Robinson has been hounded off the
Carnegie Trust by the combined churches – Jesuits and Church of Ireland.
But he's a poor fish. They'll have a bastardly job to get me under. I rather
think of getting converted – publicly – for a few months, get commissioned
to write a book, confessions, and produce 'Chaos', good joke. However, the
thing is to get better first and then we shall see.

I feel that *The Informer* is going to be a failure in England. Cape did not
take my advice about it. He is going to publish it as a literary book, and not
a sensational one. Reviews = 'It's a pity that Mr. O'Flaherty can't give us
something as good as *B.Soul*, none of the beauty, the high moral tone, the

chaste simplicity of that remarkable book are visible in *The Informer*,' sales = 747 copies.

> Yrs and be damned to it
> Liam O'Flaherty

P.S. I had meant to write this letter thanking you for your kindness to me, but what could I write that would be adequate? You know what I feel about you in my heart, dear friend, and the warmth of my heart, I hope, will always counteract the cold crudity of my expressions towards you.

> With best regards to Miss Heath
> Liam

---

117. HRHRC ALS to Edward Garnett
St. Valerie, Dargle Road, Bray, Co. Wicklow   29 January, 1925

My Dearest Friend,

It seems an age since I wrote to you, forgive me. I am in that stage of recovery when my brain seems on the verge of disintegration and any mental effort threatens me with immediate and dire insanity. But I am recovering, I will live and be damned to everybody.

First, let me thank you for the heroic deeds you are performing for me. Really, my dearest friend, I don't know what I have done to deserve all this consideration from you. I know I have been a dreadful worry and nuisance to you since I met you, but the more I worry you and the more trouble I cause you, the more you exert yourself on my behalf, instead of growing to hate me, as any ordinary mortal would do. I do verily believe I was done for this time, had you not come to my assistance. I was surrounded by a great wall of enmity that pressed in upon my soul. I was alone and it seemed that this time I had overreached myself. My exhausted body was not able to succour my sick brain. And in those circumstances the consciousness that you were abroad, working ceaselessly for me, came like a great cool healing draught, and I said: 'He is indeed a friend.' And I pictured you in your typical posture with one leg thrust forward, making a curious gesture aloft with your right hand, and looking at the ground, musing. But enough, the best way I can thank you is by getting well quickly and writing some great thing that I can dedicate to you. It need not be great, but it must be beautiful.

I am in the country now, among the Wicklow mountains. The weather is bad but I am getting better. My stomach is now comparatively good, but my kidneys are still bad, and my eyes are {?}, but my brain is beginning to get quite normal. Just occasionally I notice subconscious suicidal tendencies, but they are quite subconscious. As soon as I notice them they disappear.

They sent back the form again for some other formality. I fulfilled it and returned it. I didn't get a letter from AE for the reason that he wouldn't write one for me. I am cast out here, it remains to be seen who will be cast out last.

I will write again as soon as I mend. I am mending every day now. I had a good sleep last night – six hours – first sleep for a month, that is, a normal sleep.

Tell Miss Heath that I think a lot of her and that it does me great good to think of her – it soothes.

With best love, Yrs
Liam O'Flaherty

P.S. I enclose letters to Galsworthy and Lucas. Isn't Galsworthy a gentleman? Undoubtedly one of your generation.[1] L.O'F.

[1] This refers to the application for a grant to the Royal Literary Fund.

---

118. HRHRC ALS to Edward Garnett
St. Valerie, Dargle Road, Bray   31 January, 1925

My Dearest Friend,

Just got your letter and the book *La Revolte des Anges* Anatole France. I received cheque for fifty-five pounds yesterday from you, a multiplicity of thanks for all these favours. I was especially pleased with your letter of this morning. Yes, I will imitate 'The Conger Eel' and sink to the bottom to recuperate. I can do so as a result of your kindness.

This morning I am much better, nearly like my old self again. I am beginning to feel fit and ready to intrigue and plot against the whole multitude of my enemies. I have also discovered a very beautiful idea about a wolfhound lurking down in my soul. We will give birth to it next May or so. It's a great sign of returning health when a healthy creative power reawakens. I mean by a healthy creative power, one tending towards the creation of a gentle, beautiful thing.

These are the last days of winter and I am so proud that *The Black Soul* was right about them. In the beginning of 'Spring' you find: 'For three days storm driven rain fell furiously on Inverara.' We have had that for the past three days.

I am so eager to see you and Miss Heath again. I hope you will come over to Co. Wicklow this year? It's the most beautiful place on the earth for those who love nature, at times even more beautiful than Aran. Let us hope *The Informer* will terrify everybody into giving me ten thousand or so, then we can buy a house here and live a devil of a long time talking, eating, sleeping, walking about on the mountains, discussing Rabelais and writing beautiful things. Miss Heath could paint a mountain every morning and a stream in the afternoon when the sun plays on them.

Mrs Curtis is delighted that Miss Heath is going to write to her. I pictured you throwing twopence to the fiddlers and we laughed. Then Mrs Curtis told me how you gave money to all the tramps you met on the Oxford road when you were in Great Milton. I am happy this morning, I hope you too are happy?

With best love, Liam O'F

---

119. HRHRC ALS to Edward Garnett
St. Valerie, Dargle Road, Bray   12 February, 1925

My Dearest Friend,

I am writing again to thank you. The Royal Literary Fund sent me this morning a cheque for two hundred pounds. When the cheque arrived both Margaret and myself were overcome and we immediately said: 'What a good friend E.G. is,' for clearly understand, my dearest friend, that I owe this good fortune entirely to you, as indeed I owe everything to you since I began to write. You should be very, very happy, if only my wishes could make you happy, but I know you are always happy.

Now everything is rosy and the heart sings and the mind dreams of conquests, of beautiful rhythms and splendid epics. Out of the darkness we are coming once more into the wonderful light of creative energy. My body is getting stronger every day and all around me the earth and the sky and the very air is calling to me, and I want to sing, not in words but in the deep-sounding thoughts that rumble in the soul, forming into concrete images, like the primeval earth arose out of chaos – that's the word.

We shall be looking forward now for the time of your arrival here. We are trying to get a little house on the mountains. I think we'll get it too, although they are chary of trusting ex-revolutionaries with houses, especially as they are not quite sure about the ex. It would be very good for me to get a little house. It would have a stabilising effect on my character and it would be cheaper and healthier.

I am too excited to write. Oh, by the way, *Blackwood's* wrote asking for a story. Have you been talking to them? I sent them 'The Wild Goat's Kid' and said that you had thought well of it. I thought of sending it to you first but I decided not to bother you. I am sure you are working very hard and it seems that you do more of my work than I do myself.

With best love to you and Miss Heath

Yrs, Liam O'F

---

120. HRHRC ALS to Edward Garnett
St. Valerie, Dargle Road, Bray   16 February, 1925

My Dearest Friend,

I was heart-broken this morning to hear that you are ill. You really must take a rest before it gets serious. That's what happened to me, I kept on working too long and then I had to pay the piper. The devil is not paid in full yet. But I am confident that your powerful constitution and your force of character will toss aside this danger like a blow from a raindrop. Still, you must rest. I suggest that you come over to our mountain as soon as the weather gets on.

We have secured a little house on a mountain side. I think it's the highest house in Co. Wicklow, and therefore in Ireland. At the back, a hundred yards away, there is a tiny round boss, a young mountain, a delicious climb before breakfast to whet the appetite. To the right the Sugar Loaf rises to a stately point, with a sumptuous stretch of flank and graceful shoulders, like a Japanese picture. To the left stretches Glencree, with huge snowclad mountains bordering it irregularly. To the front, the land falls away to the sea. The Rocky Valley and the Dargle Gorge are within two miles and the most beautiful scenery in the world is all around. It is difficult to say which is more wonderful, the music of the many birds or the never ending gurgle of the cascading brooks and the deep, angry roar of the Dargle jumping down its gorges, beneath a canopy of serried trees. I think you would like it, let us say, from April. Until then the weather would be too damp, but, I declare to Christ, if this place would not make a man fit and able to enjoy life he should commit suicide.

We are buying some furniture secondhand and we expect to take possession next week. I am very excited about it, and so is Margaret. We have a lot of work to do in it, and about it, as it is in poor condition now, but that will do us both good, painting, digging and tinkering about. We will have everything shipshape by the time you and Miss Heath arrive. There are eight rooms, four bedrooms, a sitting room, a dining room, kitchen and scullery and we pay forty pounds a year for the first year. In this country everybody is a robber just now.

You seemed to be despondent when you wrote my letter and of course it's no wonder. But it sounds inconceivable to me that you should be borne down by any illness. When I told Margaret you were ill she said: 'You needn't worry about him, he'll live to a hundred and thirty and witness the erection of a monument to the author of *The Black Soul* in the quadrangle of Maynooth College.' 'Yes,' said I, 'and he will speak from the same platform as the Cardinal then officiating in the see of Armagh, but while he is making his speech, explaining that Liam O'Flaherty, in writing *The Black Soul*, really meant the Holy Mother Church when he wrote "nature", the said Liam O'Flaherty will rise from his grave and yell 'Damn it, don't go back on me, you were my accomplice in writing the said book.'

I am most anxious to have you over here because I want to discuss 'Chaos' with you, I want to dedicate 'Chaos' to you because I think you will like it. So I want to talk about it with you. Isn't it damn ridiculous that artists are not allowed a clean bill of health as a compensation for the insults of the mob. There was a scurrilous article in the *Irish Independent* about me which made me sore. It accused me of seeking notoriety by writing for porno-graphic papers. It meant the *Adelphi*, in which I had a story 'The Outcast'. Wouldn't Middleton Murry love to be called pornographic!

L.O'F

P.S. When is *The Informer* going to be published, I wonder? With best wishes for a speedy recovery from your illness from Margaret and myself, and our most tender regards to Miss Heath, from L.O.F.

---

121. HRHRC ALS to Edward Garnett
St. Valerie, Dargle Road, Bray   20 February, 1925

My Dearest Friend,

Thanks ever so much for the copy of *Letters from Hudson* which I received this morning. Reading the Preface and rereading the Introduction filled me with the curious and poignant joy that your writing gives me, your critical writing. You are undoubtedly a great critical genius and it is a grave shame that you do not spend all your days writing criticism instead of reading ridiculous MSS for Cape. Damn it, why can't I put a bestseller on the market and make a few thousand so that we could end our days in great happiness writing beautiful things and slashing the critics. I enjoyed your hammer blows at that loathsome creature the Lit. Ed. of the *Sunday Times*. Well done! As-suredly I will treasure this book as much as the *Hudson Anthology* and I love the *Hudson Anthology* almost as much as *The Black Soul*. I think your quotations from reviews was a masterly stroke. My dearest friend, these vulgar fellows have no sense of self respect. They will probably be glad of the publicity. You can't fight a low fellow. One can only glare at him and pass on. You have glared.

Margaret will write and send you a map of our new location. We expect to move in there next week, early. I am looking forward to happy times there tramping the mountains and writing stories. I have a beautiful thing in mind which I am going to call 'A Fisherman's Love'. This morning, after a bad and sleepless night, I was depressed, lying awake in bed, watching the dawn creep across the side of the great Sugar Loaf and I wrote a sentence which greatly cheered me. This is from the end of the story: 'The sparkle of the brine drops on the oarblades in the sunlight was like the shimmering of pearls; and the many sounds of the green-breasted waves rolling gently on the low shores made a symphony purer and sweeter than the music of kings.'

Tell me, do you like it? It would be interesting for me to find out what effect – detrimental? – my illness has had on my brain. I am glad you are not depressed. I knew you were too strong to worry. Only poor devils like myself, who are nervous wrecks, are bowed down before every wind. I am, however, getting better. I don't think I will ever regain my former health, but I will get strong enough to write and that is all I demand of the sea, and of the mountain, and of the soft-throated blackbirds that sing each morning outside my window.

So long
Liam O'F

---

122. HRHRC ALS to Edward Garnett
Ballybawn House, Kilmacanogue, Co. Wicklow   8 March, 1925

My Dearest Friend,

I don't think I have written to you since I moved to the mountains. Well, I have arrived among them. They are very beautiful but the house is anything but beautiful or comfortable. In fact, it is so ugly that it hurts to approach it, even if one shuts one's eyes one can see its ugliness. However, we have only taken it for nine months so that there is no harm done, and we have made our room look pretty by painting it all over.

Margaret's sister is staying with us, and there are charming people in the neighbourhood, so that we are not lonely. One lady has kindly offered me the shooting of thirty acres of timber and the fishing of her little bit of river, so that Margaret and myself will be self-supporting as soon as the season commences. Margaret is good with a freshwater rod, and hunting is just my calling in life, but we have to wait a month or so yet for these delights.

By the way, this lady – Miss Briscoe – lets half her house to summer visitors, so if you know of any nice people who are looking for such accommodation you might tell them it's a good thing. She supplies a maid with the apartments, I think five rooms or so, with a separate kitchen. It's the most glorious situation imaginable in full view of the Powerscourt waterfall. I believe I am going to get well here, though I am still very groggy in the matter of nerves and stomach.

Howard tells me that the date of publication of *The Informer* is still uncertain. To my mind this is unfortunate. I doubt the advisability of publishing it at all this year as he has not done so already. But I have to say nothing, I owe them money. Still, he destroyed the chances of *The Black Soul* last year by holding on to it until people were reading summer books. And *The Informer* is more a winter book than *The Black Soul*, but perhaps he has other plans that I know nothing about. I would have been very irritated a few months ago, but I am afraid my interest in my books has dwindled considerably of late. Here I never hear anything and I never see anybody in the literary or artistic sense, and I fancy I'm much the better for it. The peasants around here are genial, kindly and intelligent. One could fancy they were a different species entirely from the yokels of Great Milton. I saw a youngster coming from Mass yesterday wearing a green cap, a blue and white waistcoat, a huge Tara brooch stuck in a pink tie, a bright grey coat, blue/green knee breeches, bright yellow leggings and black boots. Can you

imagine him? Beats Gainsborough's 'Blue Boy', shows 'the powerful imagination of the Irish race'.

Today we are going over to Glencree to see some friends. There's a little
group of artists and writers living over there.

> With love to Miss Heath and yourself from Margaret and myself
>
> Liam O'F

---

123. HRHRC ALS to Edward Garnett
Ballybawn House, Kilmacanogue   23 March, 1925

My Dearest Friend,

I delayed writing to you because I was waiting to hear from Cape. I heard
from him yesterday and I am greatly disturbed by his communication, i.e.
about the arrangements he has made for *The Informer*. I gather that he is not
going to publish it this year, and in that case I look upon the business as
damned fraudulent. I agreed to let him have fifty percent of the American
proceeds on the condition that he published the book this month and
advertised it heavily. Now he apparently does not intend to publish the
book until next year, which means that he is getting forty percent of the
American profits for nothing (that is over and above the agent's ten percent
commission). I considered that his advertising it heavily here this Spring was
worth fifty percent gross of the profits of the book's sales in America, because
I calculated that since, very probably, he would not sell more than two
thousand copies in England even with heavy advertising, he was entitled to a
chance of regaining his expenditure. The arrangements he has made with
Knopf are good and sound but unless Cape publishes this month, or as soon
as possible in April, I lose on the bargain. Do you get my point? I don't think
that I will ever sell in England, but I think that I could make a big enough name
in England to put me over in America. If he published and advertised *The
Informer* this Spring I imagine that would have been effected. Unless this can
be arranged I am giving the whole business up as a bad job.

I am not going to write to Cape until I hear from you what you think
about the affair.

About other matters, we have been having rather an exciting time. Margaret's sister Adelaide is now living with us permanently. She ran away from
home because her father wanted to take her to Canada with him. There was
the devil to pay, but he heard such accounts about my past that he was afraid
to follow her. Now he has gone away to Canada with his wife, and Adelaide
stays with us. As she is without any means Margaret and she are setting up a
'tearooms' in this house, giving teas to tourists. Crowds of people come up to
see the mountains in summer, so they will probably make the thing pay.
Margaret will cook, Adelaide will serve, and I will be on the premises armed
with a monstrous axe to club the bourgeoisie if they become impertinent or fail

to pay their bills. I hope we make some money on the business because it seems there is very little hope of making money any other way.

Margaret's divorce is coming through in June or November. We expect a writ one of these days. However, we shall not be able to get married before another year. Please let me know the approximate date of your and Miss Heath's arrival so that I can make arrangements.

I am very unsettled about that damn book, but perhaps things will turn out for the best. It's a very hard life, writing literature. The temptation to scoop in easy money by writing for the magazines and the public will probably be too strong for me this year. I'd never put myself in danger of death writing another *Informer* unless I reap something tangible. As it is I am pretty crocky but improving gradually.

I will be very anxious to hear your advice.

With best love from Margaret and myself to you and Miss Heath,
From Liam O'Flaherty

---

124. HRHRC ALS to Edward Garnett
Ballybawn House, Kilmacanogue   1 May, 1925

My Dearest Friend,

I am greatly put out at not receiving an answer to my last letter. Have I offended you or are you ill? If I have offended you please forgive me, and if you are ill you know how sorry I am, but if you have just said: 'Devil take that scoundrelly O'Flaherty, I won't write to him again,' then it's just simply horrid of you.

This is the 1st May and you promised to come over on 18th or so, and we are expecting you. I expect to have my gun by then and we have fishing rods so we can have good sport. Further, I have my novel formulated and we could drag it out. There are other things we could discuss. Do please write and tell me what's in your mind.[1]

With love to Miss Heath and yourself, Liam

[1] An undated letter from Topsy i.e Margaret Barrington, to Violet and Theodore Powys mentions Garnett's visit. 'He and Liam argued day and night as usual.' O'Flaherty had been ordered to rest until June, quit smoking and give up his nightly bottle of wine, and now Liam 'had never been so well since he was a sailor'. (Source HRHRC)

---

125. HRHRC TLS to Harold E. Monro[1]
Ballybawn House, Kilmacanogue   18 May, 1925

Dear Mr. Monro,

Thanks ever so much for your letter and the very nice things you said about 'The Foolish Butterfly', I liked it very much myself and I spent a lot of time over it, so your appreciation was very pleasant indeed.

In answer to your very kind request for a story I am sending a little one called 'The Lost Thrush'. I am afraid it's not nearly as good as 'The Foolish Butterfly' and I wouldn't send it if I had anything better, but perhaps you would be good enough to like it.[2] I am sorry that Middleton Murry already published the 'Butterfly' in England in his own magazine the *Adelphi*. I have been ill for the past six months and have written nothing until this.

With best wishes for the success of the *Chapbook*.

I remain

Yours sincerely

Liam O'Flaherty

[1] Founder of the Poetry Bookshop and *Poetry Review* who had written to O'Flaherty c/o of the *Dial* New York, admiring his work, his ability to concentrate on essential details and his condensation of language. He asked for a contribution to his next *Chapbook* to be published by Cape for the Poetry Bookshop. He needs a twelve thousand word story, payment three guineas per thousand words.

[2] 11 June, 1925 a letter from Monro accepts this story, though he finds it inferior to 'The Foolish Butterfly'.

---

126. To the Editor of the *Irish Statesman*[1]

Ballybawn House, Kilmacanogue

Dear Sir,

I was interested in Mr. P. McCartan's letter in a recent issue and in your reply to that letter.[2] He criticises your paper because in your view of the Academy Exhibition you overlook a young artist, whose merits a French critic was clever enough to detect. You reply that your business is to notice the work of genius or rather what you think best, irrespective of whether the best is by a known or unknown artist.

I think you are both right, but the state of affairs in this country is not at all right as far as art is concerned. The *Irish Statesman*, you might have replied, is not very much concerned with Irish art, or, to speak more broadly, with Irish culture. It is concerned almost entirely with parish politics, with rambling discourses on things that might appeal to well-fed middle men who like to appear broad-minded, interested mildly in ideas that have been carefully predigested before being offered to their bourgeois palates. In fact, sir, your contents are in the habit of undergoing a mental process somewhat similar to the creamery process of separating the cream from the milk.

Mr. P. McCartan wants the cream, because, seemingly, he is interested in Ireland, and perhaps wants to build up a national culture. I agree with him, and I think the time is ripe to make a beginning. But we must begin at home. In art, in literature, in architecture, in general culture, we are submerged beneath the rotting mound of British traditions, traditions which have their spiders' legs in the columns of the *Irish Statesman* as securely as they have them in the illiterate columns of the Irish Republican organ from Suffolk St.[3]

Can Mr. P. McCartan and others like him do something to establish a national review of Irish art and literature and general culture, a newspaper that would make a stirring appeal to the younger generation? The younger generation is tired of bravado and politicians and mountebanks. The younger generation alone can decide whether in twenty years' time we will be still a nation of bigoted and intolerant people or whether we are going to build up a civilisation distinctly our own, a civilisation and culture that will make us a force in Europe.

I don't for a moment claim that your paper is not doing good work. But I do claim that it is not Irish, that it is not national, and that it is not representative in any respect of the cultural forces, in all spheres, that are trying to find room for birth in this country at present.

Yours faithfully
Liam O'Flaherty

[1] Published Vol. 4, No. l5, 20 June, 1925, under heading 'A View of Irish Culture'.

[2] P. McCartan's letter had been published 6 June. In it he criticises the *Irish Statesman* for not undertaking general criticism of art and literature, 'the notices of the exhibits at the Royal Irish Academy last year and this year were almost as stereotyped as those in the daily Press'.

[3] This may refer to Frank Ryan's four page monthly *An t-Oglach*.

---

127. HRHRC ALS to Edward Garnett
Ballybawn House, Kilmacanogue   [? end June, 1925]

My Dearest Friend,

Thanks so much for your letter, and forgive me for not replying immediately, but I am up to my neck in a piece of work, the nature of which I am not going to disclose to you until I mail the result to you in about a month's time. I've done several short stories and sold one already. I feel quite well now again, and ready to bear the strain of the twenty thousand pounds or so I'm going to make on *The Informer*.

O'Casey's address is 422 North Circular Road, Dublin.[1] I didn't see him since. I believe he's still writing something. Charley receives letters from him. We had great times here since with Charley's friends and everybody's friends. He gave a birthday teaparty here and some of my gunman friends in Dublin heard I was giving one and several of them turned up, in varying stages of disreputability. The Superintendent of Police found two of them in Bray sleeping on the beach and drove them up here in his car. It was great fun.

Well, back to work, eight days at it now and finished in another eight.

Love to Miss Heath and yourself
Liam

---

128. HRHRC ALS to Edward Garnett

Ballybawn House, Kilmacanogue   14 July, 1925

My Dearest Friend,

Got your letter yesterday. Thanks for sending me cutting from M.G. Yes, how clearly you understand my work, or rather how clearly we both measure it now. For myself I said too that 'this story is just a good second-rate story', 'The Library', but damn it all, that's the sort of work that the mob likes best. They buy that sort while they reject the first rate. I enclose an interesting letter from the *New Leader* which will explain my meaning. A pack of foul and degenerate scoundrels!

I had a nice note from Murry yesterday. I sent him a little translation of a beautiful thing by Padraig Ó Conaire and he's going to print it.[1] He is a good man and his countrymen are treating him very badly. I am also sending you two sketches in my first best style, to show you that I am still writing in that style, as done in the technique of 'Blood Lust', with the range cast more remote to get the degree of coldness that is necessary to liquidate the coarseness of the action; the other done in the technique of 'The Cow's Death', but I am afraid we must never hope to equal that first breaking of the virgin soil. Still, I like 'Exactly' immensely, would you please criticise it as strictly as possible for me, especially the last fifty words or so, which I imagine have slipped too rapidly towards a rather mediocre climax. But then, at a distant range, so to speak, one could not get a close-up climax without spoiling the feeling of coldness. What do you think? I am very anxious to hear your verdict, because if you pass on this method I intend to use it a lot in my new novel.

About the novel, I have definitely decided to baptise it *Marching Men*. I have it worked out now to the last detail and am holding it back in order that it may become as concrete as possible in its essence and detail before touching the first word. This is Topsy's advice. In the meantime I am going to put up a barrage of short stories for the appearance of *The Informer*, in the W.W., the *M.G.*, *T.P*'s, the *Adelphi*, the *Nation*, the *Calendar* , the *New Leader* and if possible *Blackwood's*, the *Dial*, and the *Atlantic Monthly* who wrote to me on Cape's recommendation for a story. In a week or so I will send you the completed sketch of *Marching Men*, theme, action, style, movement, etc. I suggest that its length, owing to the vast mass of copy and necessary detail, should be considerably longer than *Thy Neighbour's Wife*. What do you think? The action length is twenty-four hours. I suppose I won't need to present the MS to Cape before next May?

How about a collection of short stories for next Spring in England? Would you talk to Cape about it? I think it would be a good idea to solidify any reputation *The Informer* makes with the second best populace? Then we can crack all their heads with *Marching Men*.

That piece I was telling you about was an Irish play. I finished it but I have no time now to translate it into English, as I am throwing it to the wolves, i.e. the Irish Drama League. Let them produce it if they like. If not, I'll translate. It's not a good play in the ordinary sense, but it's a good piece of writing and I fancy you would like it. But at the moment the job is short stories, short stories, short stories. I have done ten in three weeks and I have about thirteen more to do.

Topsy says to send her love to Miss Heath and you, I also. We hope to see you in Autumn if and when we are going abroad. Remember me to Cape and tell him that I am becoming daily more confident of *The Informer*.

Liam

[1] 'The Agony of the World', the *Adelphi* III (4), September,1925, pp. 258-260.

---

129. HRHRC TLS to Edward Garnett
Ballybawn House, Kilmacanogue   'July sometime', 1925

My Dearest Friend,

Thanks awfully for your letter of criticism of my two sketches. I have carefully studied all the points you made and I hope that I will be able to correct exactly to your liking. For the moment I am putting it aside with the criticisms. I have done another sketch which I am sending you to examine. I am really a heartless fellow because there is a fault I think in it, which Salkeld[1] and myself detected and I want to make sure it is a fault. I mean that I think the end is too abrupt. For the rest, I think myself that the sketch is perfect. Now why is the end bad? This is very important for me to find out, because if I do understand it and master that fault, I imagine that I am master of that length of sketch, in that method. I hope you will like the theme and the treatment.

I have done a few other things but they are inferior. I have tried my novel several times but I have put it aside again. I think the time is not ripe for it. I must get abroad first and *The Informer* must make its appearance first, because really if that does not succeed financially I am simply going to write novels like *The Black Soul* in future and not ones that might sell. What the devil good is there writing to pay off your debts if the stuff is not marketable? One might as well write for the love of the thing. My short stories fill that instinct.

I didn't hear about that play yet. As soon as I get hold of the manuscript again I'm going to rattle it off into English and send it to you. It's fine stuff I think, but as a play I am doubtful about it. Poetic plays hardly ever sell well. Even Synge's *Deirdre*, which is the most beautiful thing he wrote, acts badly.

I translated 'The Cow's Death' into Irish and it appeared last week in the organ of the Gaelic League, with a leading article acclaiming it in gorgeous rhetoric, the greatest story ever written and the rise of a new poet who would make Irish, etc., etc.[2] Very good, two days later the report of the divorce of Curtis versus Curtis and O'Flaherty appeared in the papers. I wonder what ...

By the way I wrote this sketch 'Poor People' in Irish first and then translated it into English. The whole thing, both the original and the translation occupies exactly an hour and three quarters. Now that is curious, but it may merely mean that the method was new and therefore sufficiently interesting to excite my energy.

O'Casey, Salkeld and myself are trying to start a small club or society or whatever you call it, where we can meet and discuss things. We feel that we should get together and interchange our ideas so as to knock the corners off one another's brains and see whether we have anything in us. We are to hold our first meeting next Sunday, collect a little money and hire a room for meetings. I think it would be very good for us and protect us against the old fogies, like Yeats and AE and the rest.

What's doing in London? When is David's book appearing? I suppose *The Informer* will be out in September? Any new books of importance coming out? I feel in a wilderness here away from everything – no irritants. By the way, we have got a cottage in Glencree, in a little clump of trees, with a fairy wood and old burial place, a magic well and all the other accoutrements of a truly Irish settlement. My address will be Lackandarra, Glencree after next October. That's a beautiful address, isn't it? It means 'the lake of oaks in the Horseshoe Glen'.

I sometimes long for the Fitzroy St. district, and the enthusiasm of that period when I wrote *The Black Soul* and 'The Cow's Death' and met you first. Really that is the greatest romance of my life and will be unfortunately. If one could only write like that again. But there is an old Irish proverb: 'The sandlark cannot have both beaches at the one time.'

> My tenderest regards to Miss Heath and to yourself all my love
> From Liam

[1] Cecil Ffrench Salkeld, an artist.

[2] 'Bás Na Bó', *Fainne an Lae*, 18 July, 1925, p5.

———————

130. NLD(MS 10,864 (9) F.R. Higgins papers) to F.R. Higgins[1]
[no address]   n.d.[end July, 1925]

A Chara,

We're starting that club I was talking to you about and we're holding the first meeting to elect a committee etc. next Sunday week, August 2nd, at 39 St. Stephen's Green at 6.30 p.m.

We have about fifteen people to be present and I do hope that you will come along and bring one pound, first year's subscription. I'm trying to get in touch with Leventhal. O'Casey, Salkeld, Fallon, myself and yourself, if you come, will be so-to-speak conveners.

As soon as you come back write to me and tell me if you are on.

With best love
Liam O'Flaherty

[1] Frederick Robert Higgins was a poet, 1896-1941.

---

131. HRHRC TLS to Edward Garnett
Ballybawn House, Kilmacanogue   31 July, 1925

My Dearest Friend,

Just got your delightful letter. I am inclined not to agree with you about the sketch, except on the point that the struggle should have been made more evident between his desire to stay with his child and the necessity to go to work. But unfortunately in real life in Aran there is no such struggle. The people accept necessity without any resistance, and there is only a dull mourning and rebellion of the heart. It's curious. I don't think I exert any judgement whatsoever in my writing at the moment of writing, but seem to be impelled by the Aran Islanders themselves, who cry out dumbly to me to give expression to them. And of course that has the drawback of all instinctive writing, that it appears to be unfinished, just like a natural landscape. You don't know where to put an end to it, or it sometimes ends where it shouldn't end. Still, it is well for the lame to be conscious of their infirmities.

I have been working steadily at my novel in spite of my lamentations. I imagine I have already written twenty thousand words, and yet there is not a word to the good yet. I am groping for a beginning and I hope I am getting nearer to it. In fact, I have written exactly twenty-three beginnings and burned them all. Now I am beginning to see that it's a monstrous subject, which perhaps I have not sufficient genius to tackle, or to succeed with, because of course a senseless fellow like me would tackle anything. Damn it, it's a cursed thing that you are so far away, because I can't write about characters. I can only talk about them or create them. This woman Sheila Joyce is a wonderful character, and her father is no less wonderful. They are quite different now from the beginnings of them we were discussing a few months ago. The name Joyce is changed from the Hynes, and the novel at present is entitled *Ramon Mór*. Mark you, the only difficulty now is the beginning. I have the body of the thing worked out completely and I could write the end very easily just at this minute. The end should be good, about ten thousand words describing the last few hours of Lord Clonmore's and Sheila's lives, ending with the appearance of the father. Running counter to the decadent, immoral and passionate (in the sexual sense) story of Clonmore and

Sheila I will have another couple of characters, Dominie Cooke and a lady unknown (who will probably be Topsy) thinkers and lovers in the natural sense, and around them the whole process of Irish life of the present day, with its foolish parochial nationalism, bigotry, ideals, meanness, etc.

If I can write this I will be a great man.

I have two more novels ready to write, *Chaos* that I told you about, and a terrific story of Aran island life, called *The Curse*. Not the incest motive that I thought of last year, but another natural motive, the psychological study of a reprobate old man's fear of an old woman's curse, but that's a long way off.

Why the hell are you not living near me? There's nobody else in this world that cares a damn about my work except you, and you are in London. My sister is here now.

By the way, look out for a little sketch in the *Manchester Guardian* called 'Milking Time'. Topsy is not feeling very well, but she said she was going to write to you and ask for the loan of Lady Murasaki's book, a lady whom she appears to know very well from her poetry, though I never heard of her,[1] and thanks ever so much for the Italian novel. It's really too good of you to send it because I love that man's writing. I think he is really very great, and if not one of the masters at least very near them. His lyric power is equal to Turgenev's I think, but of course as far as I have read his stuff, his understanding of life is not so acute. Maybe he is more like Gorki, but I haven't read this book yet. It's a godsend. I read nothing now but Joyce and Dostoievsky and Gogol.

Miss Heath promised a letter and we are both waiting for it, so she mustn't disappoint us.

With love to you both from

Liam

[1] Shikibu Murasaki, *The Tale of Genji*, (trans. Arthur Waley), London: Allen & Unwin, 1925.

---

132. HRHRC TLS to Edward Garnett
Ballybawn House, Kilmacanogue   10 August, 1925

My Dearest Friend,

Topsy has had a dreadful accident, she fell off a bicycle going down a hill and had a double fracture to her shoulder and several other things, together with a severe shock. She is now in hospital waiting for an X-ray. She has been there since Saturday and they are only ready to operate on her today. What a country! So you see, the poor girl has had a time, and we all are in a terrible state.

She asked me to write to you to ask for some books to read. Send them to me and I will give them to her. I don't know yet whether she will have to stay in hospital or whether we can move her home after the doctors have spliced the shoulder up. I hope we can, then we could seize Dr. Ryan and keep him on the premises with a supply of whiskey until she got all right.

At present I can't sleep or do anything, not to mention working.

The doctors tell me she will be a month on her back but that she won't suffer any ill effects from it afterwards. Forgive this short note, as I have to rush into Dublin now to see her and get her some things.

With love to you and Miss Heath
From Liam

---

133. HRHRC TLS to Edward Garnett
Ballybawn House, Kilmacanogue   13 August, 1925

My Dearest Friend,

Thanks so much for your letter and for the books. The Murasaki novel arrived, followed by your other two. Thanks also for your offer of a loan, but I have written to Cape asking for a remittance of the advance which he agreed last February to give me on *The Informer*, so that will be all right. Topsy is fixed up now, and I'm transferring her from the hospital to here tomorrow evening. Then I am engaging Dr. Ryan to look after her. That will be cheaper for me because added to the hospital expense there is the whole time wasted running in and out of Dublin, all day every day so that I can get no work done. But it doesn't matter as long as she is all right.

Mrs Barrington, her mother, is with her now, staying here in Dublin and my sister is expected to arrive from Belfast today, so that we are pretty full up. But Topsy is writing to you and she will tell you all about it. What do you think though, her father has joined the Roman Catholic church. Isn't that extraordinary?

I would have been well on in my novel now were it not for this accident. As it is I have one chapter done and four others ready in my head. I will go straight on next week, when Topsy is at home. I have done nothing for a week of course. The proprietor of the *M.G.*, Mr. Scott, wrote saying he liked 'The Library' and asked for more stories like it. Of course I answered the blighter by suggesting that I should tender a series of articles about Ireland, but I don't suppose he'll bite at that.

I am mixed up and don't know what I want to write about so please excuse me. I wrote a good story last week called 'Civil War' and sent it to *Blackwood's*, I haven't got another copy or I would send it to you.

With love
Liam

134. HRHRC ALS to [Esther Archer] the editor of *New Coterie*, London
Ballybawn House, Kilmacanogue   20 August, 1925

Dear Sir,

Thanks for your letter, I highly appreciate the favour of your asking me
for a contribution for the first number of the *New Coterie*, I enclose a short
story 'Civil War' which might possibly interest you. Would you be so kind
as to let me have your decision as soon as possible, as to acceptance or
rejection, rate of payment, etc.

I do hope your quarterly will be a success.

Yours very sincerely
Liam O'Flaherty

---

135. HRHRC TLS to Edward Garnett
Ballybawn House, Kilmacanogue   6 September, 1925

My Dearest Friend,

We don't know what has happened to you and we are wondering
whether you have gone away on a holiday, or whether your wife is ill or
what it is? I hope that you yourself are not ill, but I'm sure you are not.
Please do drop us a note when you get this.

Topsy is well again and she has your books parcelled up ready to return,
but as this place is so far away from a parcel office it may be days before
she sends them, as she is pretty hopeless in these matters. I enjoyed the
modern Japanese novel immensely and Murasaki was certainly amusing,
but I agree with Murry in saying that it's not as great as it's claimed to be.

David's new book must be out shortly now,[1] the seventeenth I believe?
Several ladies here are in a great state of mind as to whether they will be
able to get first editions or not, especially as the Irish Bookshop is gone bang
now, and there is nowhere special to order a copy. I see Wells' novel will
be out the same day but there is no mention of *The Informer*. He will probably
sneak in, drunk and disorderly, behind the crowd of them. Then he will
utter a piercing yell and terrify all the dear ladies. I hope they don't send
him into quad.

I have done a number of stories since, one of which I am particularly fond
of called 'The Tent.' It's about tinkers, a tinker and his two wives. I shall
soon have my new collection completed. Cape says he will bring it out in
Spring, on condition that my new novel follows it six months later. I am
waiting to hear the result of *The Informer* before I decide which novel I am
going to write, or rather the form of the new novel. If *The Informer* does not
catch on, I am going to give the serious novel a slip for once and write
Michael Rathcroghan. If *The Informer* does catch on I will, of course, write
Ramon Mór. Either form would, however, deal with present social conditions,

questions etc., but the former would be humorous and the latter tragic.

O'Casey dropped out of the Club project, but we have it under way all the same. We are holding the inaugural meeting on Saturday next and I believe we will succeed very well. It is our intention to draw in everybody interested in culture of any description in Dublin and form a nucleus of an organisation to resist the encroachment of the clergy, at the same time encouraging the appearance of new writers, etc. Everybody is very enthusiastic so far, but we have to keep out Yeats, Senator Gogarty, etc., who want to have their finger in every pie and make a mess of it.

O'Casey is getting more and more popular. They played *Juno and the Paycock* for a fortnight last month and every seat was booked every night with an overflow clamouring to get in. I am sure they could run it, even in Dublin, for six months to a full house. They are now playing *The Gunman* (O'Casey) and Chekov's *Proposal*. O'Casey's new play will be on in October I think, or November at the latest. I hear it's better than *Juno*. I do hope you will be able to come over for a few days to see it.

I don't think we will be able to get away for the winter but we might come to London in October for a week. There is a return ticket for two pounds something. Love to you and Miss Heath and please write soon. Would you like to read 'The Tent'?

Liam

[1] *The Sailor's Return*, London: Cape 1925.

---

136. NLD (MS 10,864 (9) F.R. Higgins papers) ALS to F. R. Higgins
[No address]   n.d. (? early Autumn, 1925)

Dear Féardorcha,

Here is a proof copy of my new book [*The Informer*], will you read it and give me your opinion, but I put you on your word of honour not to show it to anyone, or discuss it except generally before publication. Would you bring it along when you are coming down with Mac next week.

Love to your wife and I'll give yourself a drink when you come.

Liam

---

137. TCD (MS 10,171/10,38-9) ALS to Mrs Joseph [Nancy] Campbell
Ballybawn House, Kilmacanogue   21 August, 1925

Dear Mrs Campbell,

Enclosed you will find the signed agreement.[1] As to land – I don't know. The only reason I would take it is to prevent the Macs from being near the place. But no doubt they will want it again next year. If not I should think it would be very easy to get at least thirty pounds again.

We are trying to start a club in which you might be interested. Do you go into Dublin at all? If you do happen to be in town next Saturday I could tell you about it. If not later. Frank Higgins, the Salkelds, etc., are trying to organise it with me.

Hoping you are very well, I remain,

Yours

Liam O'Flaherty

[1] The Agreement is dated 22 August, 1925, and witnessed by Louis V. Ryan. It is for the letting of Joseph Campbell the poet's Lackandarragh house for two years to O'Flaherty at a rent of twenty pounds per annum payable half-early from 1 October in advance. There are to be no structural alterations, trees cut in yard or haggard. Campbell is responsible for rates, taxes and repairs to cottage and outhouses. Campbell had left for New York, not to return for fourteen years.

---

138. HRHRC ALS to Edward Garnett

Ballybawn House, Kilmacanogue   21 September, 1925

My Dearest Friend,

Thanks very much for *The Sailor's Return* and *Suspense*, I have read the former and half of the latter. The first book, to my mind, is much superior to the second and I have no hesitation in saying that as a writer David will undoubtedly have his place in English literature, whereas I cannot persuade myself that Conrad will have. He doesn't wear very well. I was not at all pleased to renew my acquaintance with him. Why? I don't know, but it's just that he can't tell a story without making a song about it. Now for *The Sailor's Return*, in places I became extremely enthusiastic and in places I said: 'Oh, damn this bloody fellow!' That's exactly what I felt. There are descriptions and scenes which are absolutely magnificent, pages 49-52 and the 'dance with the following ride to the sea'. There are other places where the recital becomes boring – why I don't know. But on the whole I place it above the other two books. *Lady into Fox* is more beautiful and more simple but *The Sailor's Return* has got more bone and marrow. It succeeds in getting an atmosphere of actual life. Where it fails in this latter aspect is that the reality of life is not sufficiently comprehensive owing, in my opinion, to lack of contact with people. Outside of Tulip and the Sailor the people who are drawn in are seen through a lorgnette. To my mind they should not be brought in at all but suggested. The drama should have been intensified by narrowing the canvas. This would bring out the central characters more sharply, make them larger and more comprehensive and give a feeling of universality which is now lacking. One character painted in full is more efficacious than ten characters sketched. Of course ten characters in full would be much better as in Tolstoi and Dostoievsky.

But really I think David must be congratulated. I didn't think he had the guts to write that and I feel for the first time sympathy and kinship with him. *The Sailor's Return* is the best book by an English author produced within the last five years, and I think that David will go far if he drops his Puss in Boots, his silly preoccupation with the coterie attitude towards life, and a trace of the Oxford manner. You have every reason to be proud of your son and let me tell you, of your daughter-in-law, her drawing is magnificent. Even Salkeld admitted that it was the best woodcut he had ever seen. Not a word to David about my criticism of his book.

I will probably come over to London next Friday evening. As you will be out for the weekend I will see you sometime on Monday next, or maybe I might prowl in on Friday night, you never know! I am coming over about *The Informer* for certain reasons. Topsy is coming with me.

Love to you and Miss Heath
Liam

P.S. Topsy wants to say that she loved the christening of Sambo, and that she was delighted with *The Sailor's Return* entirely. You see what I told you was quite true, these ladies are prejudiced in his favour. Evidently he has inherited some of your attraction, my dear fellow. Liam.

---

139. HRHRC TLS to Edward Garnett
Ballybawn House, Kilmacanogue   30 September, 1925

My Dearest Friend,

Forgive me for not writing, but I have been suffering from a fit of melancholy during the past week which has left me incapable of doing anything. I haven't written a solitary word for three weeks. Last night I started again and immediately wrote three thousand words of my new novel, so expect that I am over the bloody fit of melancholy. I am really sorry that I didn't get to London. I would have only for this spiritual catastrophe, but the pleasure is only delayed and I will set out as soon as we have changed our digs. I am sending you a copy of *The Informer*. I have seen some reviews of the book. They were rather good and perhaps we might sell a few copies over the usual five hundred this time. But it is hard to say I suppose. People get into the habit of not buying my books and they stick to it.

I am attuned perfectly to my new novel and I think it's safe. I intended to finish my collection of short stories before starting it, but I found myself absolutely bankrupt of short stories and I decided there was no use marking time, but that it was best to carry on with the longer work. Anyway, I fancy I will have the collection ready for the Spring list as there are only about twenty thousand words to write. It should be very nice and a bit stronger than the first.

I would like to know how David's book is going? Forgive this short note.

Yrs

Liam O'Flaherty

---

140. HRHRC TLS to Edward Garnett

Ballybawn House, Kilmacanogue   5 October, 1925

My Dearest Friend,

God damnit, God damnit, God damnit, what are you vexed about? Your letter was so sharp that I felt inclined to shave myself with it, instead of with that razor which I lent you last Spring and with which you scarred your face so badly that old Nevinson looked at you very curiously that day in the Bonne Bouche, as if he were saying to himself: 'My God, poor old Garnett has got himself into bad company and he looks like reverting to the native.' There you are, the young generation speaks its mind out crudely about the last generation, and the last generation, instead of smiling serenely from the height of its knowledge, rushes down amidst the fledglings with its shirt sleeves rolled up, armed with all the delicate fighting instruments of its superior wisdom. Fie, fie, sir! I am sending back *Suspense*. The ayes have it. It's a rule and so ordered.

I am afraid that *The Informer* has come a commercial cropper, therefore, unlike *Suspense*, the dogs have it. It's a calamity and so ordered by the beloved public. *Arceo profanum vulgus* but the bloody vulgus keeps its money in its pocket and I have to gnaw a bone and sit on my mountain waiting for the coming winter with terror in my heart.

I am writing my new novel at an amazing pace. Amidst my new characters, who are glorious men and women God bless them, I feel quite happy and I tell you I am going to give them a devil own's time before I am done with them.

I feel very happy because Miss Heath liked *The Informer*. I was afraid to send her a copy because I thought that it was too rough for her. But now I will hasten to send her one. I gave a copy to another lady here whom I thought would represent the less intelligent public as she reads Hutchinson, the fellow who wrote *If Winter Comes* and that sort of thing. The book terrified her but she sat up all night until she read it, and she loved Gypo. Therefore undoubtedly the public is not going to read it, because women only buy something they can read in public and not in bed. In bed they prefer to experiment on the heroes of their romances in a more actual manner and could any modern young woman experiment in that fashion on my poor hero? No.

I don't think we will be able to come to London at all now. The last dregs of our finances will be expended on those bones which we will have to gnaw in Glencree in winter. And you can, if you like, form a picture of me stalking snails, toads and frogs with my long single-barrelled gun on the mountains. But Topsy tells me to send you both her love and to say that she faces this coming catastrophe with all the pristine valour of her ancestry. Things might in fact be very interesting here this winter as we have started a club with which we are going to wake up Dublin. I have succeeded in gathering all the intellectuals into one club and that in itself should cause such an uproar that the government will have to call out the troops to save the last remnants of the ladies' hair and of the men's whiskey.

The ruffian, you say, he appears to be in a good humour. So I am. Take out a bottle of that good Madeira you drink now and again, and have a drink to my health and kiss Miss Heath's hand for me.

With love from
Liam

P.S. Did you like 'The Tent'? It appeared in *The Calendar of Modern Letters*, [II, October, 1925, pp.104-111].

---

141. HRHRC TLS to Edward Garnett
Lackan, Enniskerry, Co. Wicklow   Tuesday n.d. [early October, 1925]

My Dearest Friend,

Thanks for your letter. I am very sorry to hear from Miss Heath that you are not feeling very well. Under these circumstances you will be glad to hear that we are coming to London next Friday, Topsy and myself, to buck you up. We will stay for a week. We will put up at an hotel in Bloomsbury somewhere I think. Anyhow we will call in to see you two as soon as possible. I will haul along the amount of my novel that I have written for your inspection. This novel is a stop-gap to fill in the time before I start on 'Johnny Hynes' which will not be until next year. I have decided to hold it back because it will be my most important work, and I want to be as strong as possible before tackling it. But we will discuss all these things when I see you. We are moving tomorrow to Lackan, and there is desperate excitement packing up. In the midst of this excitement I am typing away. Every review of *The Informer* is better than the former. Every soul that read the book loved Gypo, so I think that I have at least created a good character, if nothing else. It's very cheering anyway, for a poor man, to think that people think well of him. Like hell!

No sir, our club will not be a Pangloss club. On the other hand it will be a Candide club. We are going to try our hand not only at Pope's daughters but at running Jesuits through the body if we can buy up a few specimens.

With love
Liam

---

142. HRHRC TLS to Miss Esther Archer
Lackan, Enniskerry, Co. Wicklow   8 October, 1925

Dear Miss Archer,

About getting out a hundred signed copies of my short story 'Civil War',
I would be delighted to sign them for you at that rate, that is ten pounds
(£10) for the lot. I suppose you would get them out presently because the
story would appear in book form next Spring. I hope the *New Coterie* will
be a success.

Remember me to all the boys and if you see Stroud or Kirwan or Bishop
or Budgeon[1] remember me to them especially. If I can raise the money I will
come to London shortly and see whether they have all died of drink yet or
not.

It's very good of you to boost my stuff, as the Americans say. With very
best wishes for your success in business and in love, I remain,

Yours very sincerely
Liam O'Flaherty

[1] These are all London friends. Their favourite pub was The Plough, Museum Street, WC1.

---

143. HRHRC ALS postcard to Edward Garnett
Lackan, Enniskerry, Co. Wicklow   n.d. [October 1925]

My Dearest Friend,

De profundis clamo ad te Garnett, Garnett preserve me. Here I am stuck
again. Moving our goods to Glencree we had a chapter of accidents. I nearly
killed myself by upsetting a cart, a horse and myself, crossing a bog. Topsy
caught a cold and our furniture had to stay on the road all night – so London
is off. Great story – O'Flaherty trying to get to London – Damn it! Will we
ever get there? I doubt it. We are here in the wilderness, there is a mile of
sheeptrack between us and the nearest lane to anywhere. Mountains encir-
cle us, there are fairy woods, etc., and Topsy has got a cold. However, next
Friday we may travel, I say may. In the meantime I have resigned myself
{ four words?}.

With love to you and Miss Heath
Liam

---

144. HRHRC ALS to Edward Garnett
Lackan, Enniskerry, Co. Wicklow   n.d. [mid October, 1925]

My Dearest Friend,

Why don't you write to me? I always feel when you don't write that I
have committed some crime, that I have insulted you in some infernal way,
or that you are ill and saying: 'That fellow O'Flaherty is killing me.' What

on earth is the matter with you? I expect you were vexed because I didn't come to London but really I couldn't. One long {succession?} of troubles for the past three months and the terrific necessity to keep writing at a break-neck pace, for I have the memory of last winter always before my mind, and I must make some provision for this one. As it is we will be hard pressed but I think we will tide it, if I don't fall ill. But I really believe you know when you are ill. Topsy and I talk about you every day and every post we expect a letter from you. Topsy says she owes you a letter but she has to work so hard here that the poor girl can do nothing but play patience. I am writing four stories a week here. I will have my new collection finished by Xmas. I am going to have hundred percent first rate stories I hope, forty-five thousand [words] now and all first rate. Of course, I expect you will condemn half of them, but then nothing would satisfy you. I am doing a story now which I think you will really like, but do write and tell me the news.

The Informer caused a terrific ruction here among the clergy, and the bourgeois nationalists. At last I have got under their hides. But curiously enough all the ladies loved Gypo. The scoundrel AE denounced it in his paper while in private (in his own salon) he said it was as good as Dostoievsky.[1] But I'll beat the bastard. We have started a club and we are well under way with it. One of its principal objects is to fight the Catholic Truth Society. Here, we are rushing for the bus to Dublin. We have to cross a bog and walk five miles. Goodbye, and write soon.

Love to Miss Heath and you from Topsy and myself
Liam[2]

[1] *The Irish Statesman* review was 10th October, 1925.

[2] A postscript from Topsy explains that she has had a bad cough and could not be left alone with Charlie, so they missed the cheap excursion to London. The weather is atrocious.

---

145. HRHRC ALS to Edward Garnett

5 Upper Leeson Street, Dublin   21 November, 1925

My Dearest Friend,

Many thanks for your letter. I am sending you on the material for *The Tent*, Perhaps there are some stories that you will reject. If possible don't send the manuscript to the printer before the end of December. By that time I will have more stories for you to choose from. Some of the ones I am sending you I could reject myself. Others, which are first rate are not to hand at the moment but they are included in the list.

I am now translating my play into English. They are very excited about it in Dublin, the Gaelic crowd. O'Loughlin, who is going to produce it, is exceptionally enthusiastic.[1] I am sending the English version to an agent in London. I wonder would you care to see it?

I am getting very tired with work and there doesn't [seem] to be any hope of getting any money. This cursed strike is holding up *The Informer*. Well! We have to live on hope.

I saw O'Casey yesterday. He offered to lend me five pounds as the result of his success. Very naive! He's a character. He is going to leave his slum now and come to live in Clare St. among the bourgeoisie – well, well! The Irish, of course, couldn't turn him into a middle class man but once he touched the sweets of London, ah ha!

With love to you and Miss Heath,
Liam

[1] Géaroid O Lochlainn, Irish Drama League, produced the play *Dorchadas* (Darkness) in Dublin in 1925.

---

146. HRHRC ALS to Esther Archer
5 Upper Leeson St., Dublin   19 December, 1925

Dear Comrade,

Thanks so much for your letter and five guineas. I want to thank you also for your kindness in propagating the sale of my books. You are very kind. I tried various shops here for *New Coterie* but not a single shop in Dublin sells literary magazines. The priests have the whole country collared. However, we'll soon change that.

I won't be in London for Xmas, but sometime after Xmas I'm coming over to meet an American comrade and then I'll see you, January or February. I hope the magazine is selling and that you will be able to get rid of the booklets.[1]

Yours ever
Liam O'Flaherty

[1] A limited edition of 'Civil War' published by E. Archer, 1 November, 1925.

---

147. HRHRC ALS to Edward Garnett
5 Upper Leeson St., Dublin   18 January, 1926

My Dearest Friend,

Now that the whole business of *The Tent* is settled let us in the name of God resume amicable relations. Not that my feelings towards you have not been all this time those of the deepest love, but I have felt that you are vexed with me, and in fact rather violent. I have insisted on *The Tent* being the title story because I felt I was right. I felt it had a particular significance which I wanted to give to the volume. It may be a failure as a story but my aim was not a failure.

Well now, do you agree that the two of us write a foreword to the book? You will denounce 'The Tent' and I will defend it. As short as possible. I think it would be very good and do us both justice. As you are responsible for my art I feel I owe it to you, and as I am your pupil I feel you owe it to me. Please approach Cape on the matter if you are agreeable.

I am halfway through *The Firebrand*. I think it's going satisfactorily; that is, I have it well in hand so far. I began at the end of *The Informer* and am trying to carry the emotional feeling higher, spiritualising the action, which of course is rather obscure. The main character, the Firebrand, is an intelligent Gypo, a human being who is hounded but knows why he is hounded, and has deliberately chosen to be hounded because he is driven by a force within him to his own doom – also rather obscure. I'm no good at explaining things.

I am coming to London soon if I can get some money. I have a few things to show you if I come, among them a short story I have written recently called 'The Child of God'. We are very well, but just waiting for Spring when we can go to the country again.

Would you mind asking Miss Heath to let me dedicate *The Tent* to her. You understand I would ask her personally, but I feel that you could do it with more delicacy.[1] Thanks. When I arrive, if I arrive, we will discuss everything. I am eager to know whether you will recognise 'Johnny Hynes', so I will bring along the portion of *The Firebrand* I have written. I am nearly certain of getting the money so I will arrive. I sold a story to *Eve*!! at least my agent sold it, 'The Tyrant' it was called. Not much good, I expect that's why they took it.

I hope your health is good, with best love from Topsy and myself.

Liam

[1] *The Tent* was dedicated to Topsy. Garnett disliked 'The Tent' short story and called it a fake.

148. HRHRC TLS to Edward Garnett
5 Upper Leeson St., Dublin   24 January, 1926

My Dearest Friend,

I was rather relieved by your last letter, because I have been so violently oppressed for the past month by your quarrel with me, that I felt very sad about the whole thing. And indeed if I had explained the real nature of my desire to have that story used as the title one, I am sure you would have understood and not quarrelled with me. The fact is that I used it as the title story in the hope that it might sell the book and enable me to sell stories to magazines, for the reason that it is absolutely necessary for me to get some money in the next few months. Topsy is going to become a mother and we have no money. I was never as hard pressed as I am now, as I can't write stories while I am working at my novel and I can get very little advance on my contract, and *The Informer* has been a failure. I don't see the faintest ray of hope anywhere, so, in that case my interest in 'pure art' and such trivial matters is not very great. I write my stories as I have to write them, perhaps unfortunately. But I have never written a word yet with my eye on the market. So that it's immaterial to me, once I have written the stories, in what rotation they are handed to the public, whether the good shall be first or last. But it is of vast importance to me, that my wife, whom I love more than the delectation of the literary public, shall not be in need of the best medical attention.

My curse on publishers, editors and the public. To the deepest pit of hell with them. I have a lovely story on hand and I have to rush it off at such a speed, in order to get back to my short stories for some money, that I'm afraid it's going to come a cropper. It won't be as good as it would be otherwise if I could spend an extra month at it. I'm writing about four thousand words a day steadily. Topsy is good enough to praise it, and as long as it pleases her I feel contented.

We won't be able to come to London at all now, unless something very extraordinary happens. As far as I can make out Cape is a scoundrel, because I found in last October's accounts that he was cheating me (whether intentionally or not I don't know). I engaged an agent to make my contracts with him and look to the accounts, and Cape is howling now. That's the worse of being under an obligation to anybody. However, next year we are going to make thousands. What on earth would we do with them? Anyway, this is always the leanest time of the year and I would be quite contented myself, but it's devilish when you have somebody you love very much, who never grumbles and never pretends to be worried about anything, but does everything to please you and make you happy. Then you praise God, that after all there is one woman who is an angel. As you have a friend yourself who is also an angel you will understand me.

How I would love to have you with me for a whole week to quarrel with.

And please don't make any resignation of your position as literary uncle, for no matter if you never read another word of mine, and indeed that would be a relief to you I am sure, I will always write now as if you were about to read it – Topsy and you. For I always believe that you care for me myself, apart from my work, and that is what pleases me and makes me feel tender towards you.

I felt I must make this explanation to you in order to clear the whole business. Forgive me if you wish, and if you do not I shall still love you, because I never forgive an enemy, and I never forget a gentleman. It was my father's only religious belief.

> Salutations to Miss Heath and to yourself my deepest love
> Liam

---

149. SLUL (Folio V 36) ALS to Esther Archer
5 Upper Leeson St., Dublin   29 January, 1926

Dear Comrade,

I am writing to my agent, Mr. A.D. Peters, about another story for you, one called 'Blackmail'. It's a little better than 'The Terrorist' and perhaps the two of them would pass in a booklet? I hope you get it in time. If not, we'll have to pass up the idea of a reproduction this number because my new collection of short stories [*The Tent*] is appearing this Spring, and these stories will all be included. How did you get on with 'Civil War'?

I think I will get to London in three weeks' time or so, unless I die in the meantime. Met a little fellow here called Hilliard who met Lahr in London. Do tell me all the news? With best wishes for longevity, etc.

> From
> Liam O'Flaherty

---

150. HRHRC ALS to Esther Archer
5 Upper Leeson St., Dublin   2 February, 1926

Dear Comrade,

Ta-ta for your letter. Yes, that arrangement will be quite all right unless you get 'Blackmail'. I thank you also for Powys' story, it was very good but not as good as the one in *New Coterie* which was magnificent.[1] You didn't do too badly at all with the magazine and I should think, if you keep up the standard you will make good. After all, its advertisements' payment keep a magazine off the debt side, not sales, and your sales were astonishingly good, in spite of the high standard.

I am eagerly looking forward to my visit to London. I have a short play which I will bring to show you. You might like to use it for the next number of

New Coterie, and then issue it as a booklet. It would go very well. It's the best thing I've done. I like your idea immensely of getting things out in this manner. It's the only way to escape the public and make the bourgeoisie pay.

Heigh! So all these chaps are getting married. I wonder who Bishop married? Being a woman of strong character of course you have escaped. You are quite right, a woman can afford to do without marriage but a man is a weak-kneed animal and he must have somebody to put his tie on straight. I hardly ever wear a tie myself but still –

Hoping to see you soon,
L. O'Flaherty

[1] 'The Bride' by T.F. Powys was published in *The New Coterie*, 4, Autumn 1926. Esther Archer, from the Progressive Bookshop, 14 Red Lion Passage, Holborn, published O'Flaherty's stories 'Civil War' (1925), 'The Terrorist' (1926), 'A Child of God' (1927), also his play *Darkness* (1926). Her magazine ran for six numbers and published work by D.H. Lawrence, Gerald Bullett, Rhys Davies, translated poetry, art reproduction from Eric Kennington, Stanley Spencer, Augustus John and Cecil Salkeld, among others.

---

151. HRHRC TLS to A.D. Peters, literary agent
5 Upper Leeson St., Dublin   12 February, 1926

Dear Peters,
    Enclosed you will find a letter from the editor of the *Popular Magazine*, New York. I am sending him on three short stories, 'The Stolen Ass', 'The Library', and 'Idle Gossip'. The first two have already appeared in the *Manchester Guardian*, the third has not yet been printed, although purchased months ago by the *New Leader*. I have asked him to communicate with you respecting these stories.
    I will be in London next week with *The Firebrand*.[1] Probably call to your office on Saturday morning, if not on Friday. Probably on Friday, anyway I can ring you up. In the meantime if there is any other story you've got you might think suitable for this 'guy', you could hurl it along, with a stick of chewing gum pasted on it. But I fancy these three would be enough until you hear from him again.

Best wishes from,
Yours sincerely
Liam O'Flaherty

[1] The first title of *Mr Gilhooley*.

---

152. To the Editor of the *Irish Statesman*[1]
.   15 February, 1926

Dear Sir,
    Permit me to protest in your columns against Mr. Yeats's demonstration

in the Abbey Theatre on Thursday last. The protest by those who objected to the play (*The Plough and the Stars*) was undoubtedly in bad taste, but nobody loses anything by it, least of all the author, who gained a good advertisement. But the protest by Mr. Yeats, against the protest of the audience, was an insult to the people of this country. I feel that I am personally justified in protesting against his protest because the manner in which they have received my own work (and in all probability the manner in which they *will* receive my work) defends me from the accusations of appealing to the gallery. Allow me to review the position.

In my opinion *The Plough and the Stars* is a bad play. It would be quite in order for an audience to hiss it as a bad play. It was, however, a boorish thing to hiss it because the opinions expressed by the author injured the feelings of the audience. Every man has a right to his opinions. Mr. O'Casey has a right to his opinions. He has a perfect right to protest himself against this treatment of his work by the audience. But Mr. Yeats had positively no right to strut forward and cry with joy that the people of this country had 'been cut to the bone'. Our people have their faults. It is a good thing that artists should point out these faults. But it is not a good thing that pompous fools should boast that we have been 'cut to the bone'.

I say *we*, because I too was cut to the bone. I am not a Nationalist in the political sense. But I am an admirer of any man who has the courage to die for an ideal. And I think the most glorious gesture in the history of our country was the gesture of those who died in 1916. No great artist in any country in the world refused to give credit, to glorify men who died likewise. Even Tolstoy, the great pacifist, bowed down before the courage of the Cossacks and of their brigand enemies (even brigands) who died with their death-song on their lips. I bow down before the courage of Pearse and Connolly and their comrades. I did not have the honour to fight with them. But I 'am cut to the bone' because an Irish writer did not, unfortunately, do them justice. I do not blame O'Casey. I believe him to be a sincere man. But I am sorry to see him defended by a man who rose to fame on the shoulders of those men who stirred this country to fervent enthusiasm for ideals in the last generation. What does it matter to us whether these ideals were practical? No ideal is practical, but all ideals are the mothers of great poetry, and it is only from the womb of an ideal that a great race, or a great literature, or a great art can spring.

I am not 'cut to the bone' because the play was not anti-English. I fervently admire the English race. I envy the English race for their greatness, for their bravery, for the great men they have produced. I envy their Cromwells, their Shakespeares, their Shelleys, their Darwins, their count-less heroes who have struggled for the English ideal, whether it be a Wat Tyler or a Frobisher, a Clive or a William Morris. The great poetry of life is the struggle of brave men. And the contemptible thing in life is the strutting of pompous people who spit at the justified anger of enthusiasts. 'Let him who is without sin cast the first stone.'

Sir, I am of Gaelic stock. My ancestors came into this country sword in hand, as conquerors, as the Danes came and the Normans and the English. To conquer is the right of the strong. We who conquered once have been in turn conquered. I acclaim our conquerors. But now the conquered and the conquerors are one. And out of their seed another race has sprung. We are all brothers. All but those who turn their backs on their people and cry, spitting, that they 'have been cut to the bone'. It was not so that McCracken cried, or Tone, or Emmet, or even the great Parnell.

Finally, I do not believe in political nationalism. I do not believe in Empires. The human race has advanced considerably since the time of Daithi and even since the time of Napoleon. I believe in the political union of the human race, in the ideal of human brotherhood. But there always will be strife and struggle. Soon perhaps that strife will be intellectual competition. But it is certain that always people born in one place will love that place and try to make it pre-eminent by the achievements of its people. And always brave men will love the weak and struggle with them. And always poets will side with the weak against the strong, and not with the strong against the weak and ignorant. And always great men will not become embittered, even as Synge did not become embittered, but smiled gently like a Christ at those who reviled him.

Yours faithfully
Liam O'Flaherty

[1]Published Vol. 5, No. 24, 20 February, 1926, under the heading 'The Plough and the Stars'. AE (editor of *The Irish Statesman*) in a letter to Seán O'Faolain in Spring, 1926, called O'Flaherty 'a genius when he imagines and creates and a goose, a delightful goose, when he thinks and reasons'. He believes O'Flaherty to be clever but intellectually immature. 'If he keeps his genius he may do something big', in the meantime he is a 'most likeable companion'. *Letters from AE*, sel. & ed. Alan Denison, London, New York & Toronto, 1961.

---

153. HRHRC ALS to Edward Garnett
31 Torrington Square, Bloomsbury, London   8 March, 1926

Dearest Scoundrel,

The marriage will take place at 14 Bloomsbury St. Monday next at 12 o'clock (noon), so be there with Miss Heath.

The title of my next novel is *Bawdy Daniel* or *The Widow's Bastard*.

Yours with love from Topsy and myself to you both
Liam O'F

P.S. The scene is my native village, the main elements will be blasphemy, buffoonry and nature description. It's a good story and Mistral will be put in his proper place, so will Rabelais.

Now be sure and turn up. We depend on you. To hell with the famous. I'm quite sober, but this Bawdy Daniel is a great fellow.

---

154. HRHRC ALS to Edward Garnett
Lackan, Enniskerry, Co. Wicklow   15 March, 1926

My Dearest Friend,

We have arrived safely in our glen. It's beautiful here. Spring has arrived. We fished today and yesterday I shot a woodcock. It was very thin. Our cat got caught in a trap while we were away. My goats are vagrants over the glen, and I have not recovered them yet. There are all sorts of intrigues in Dublin and the Radical Club is in a state of civil war, but it's very quiet here. Daffodils are out and numberless tits sing in the morning (or do tits sing?) Something sings anyway, and I see the tits. I am afraid my goats are not in kid, damn the buck, he was impotent I discover now. Unless they found another buck after my departure I'm ruined.

Ech! It's very pleasant after London, although I did enjoy Tchekov and poor old Shakespeare – good fellows both of them. And you, you scoundrel, were as witty as ever. Still, it is nice to cultivate one's garden, even though one hires Charley Doyle to do the digging. Topsy is very happy and we both hope you are happy and enjoying your poker games with the Americans, or has Miss Heath brought you back to grace again? New novel entitled: *Poker and Herbal Tobacco* or *The Fall of Edward Garnett* (special Knightsbridge Edition on Japan paper, a hundred signed copies).

It's eight o'clock and we are going to bed. I have already written a story about a fat rabbit and now I'm writing one called 'Tobacco' tomorrow.

We have not yet framed our marriage licence but we are going to do so, then we'll offer it to the National Gallery. Do write and abuse me. No provocation? All right, to h ... Oh! by the way, we have great fun with your wedding present to Topsy – wonderful. She giggles all day at them.

                                                                                   Liam

---

15 March, O'Flaherty also wrote to A.D. Peters giving him his new address, and apologising for not coming to his home 'that night in London', but his brother had turned up from Chicago. (Source HRHRC)

---

155. HRHRC ALS to Esther Archer
Lackan, Enniskerry, Co. Wicklow   20 March, 1926

Dear Comrade,

I am sending the play *Darkness* under separate cover.[1] Thanks for the copies of 'The Terrorist', you may use the play under those terms but if possible try and get it acted before printing it, so that I would not lose the dramatic rights. One act read in a drawing room would be sufficient I believe. Not that I expect it will ever be acted, but it's better to make sure, and it was a big stage success here in Irish.[2]

I am sure the drawing is all right, and it's very nice of Mr. Roberts to want to paint me.[3] With best wishes from my wife and myself,

Yours
Liam O'Flaherty

---

[1] *Darkness* was performed at Roberts' studio on 27 April, 1926 with the following cast: Mary (Miss R. Dornan); Daniel (K.S. Bhat); Bridget (Mrs Roberts); Margaret (Marthe Goldberg); Brian (Rhys Davies). The dialogue in the play is good, but its mood is one of unrelieved gloom, and it is obvious long before the end that Daniel will murder his brother Brian.

[2] A copy of the limited one hundred copy edition of 'The Terrorist' was sent by O'Flaherty to Edward Garnett marked; 'With affectionate regards, Commandant Liam O'Flaherty, Standard Bearer of the Catholic Truth Society, Procurer of "Fairies" for his Holiness the Pope.' (HRHRC)

[3] William Roberts did an excellent charcoal sketch of O'Flaherty for the frontispiece of the *New Coterie*, Summer, 1926.

On 20 March, O'Flaherty wrote to A.D. Peters offering him 'Child of God' for *Georgian Stories*, an annual anthology, but Peters replied that it was too long. (source HRHRC)

---

156. NLW TLS to Jonathan Cape
Lackan, Enniskerry, Co. Wicklow   7 April, 1926

Dear Cape

I have re-read *The Firebrand* and I am of the opinion that we had better hold it up for a year or perhaps two. I quite agree with Garnett that it would have to be re-written, but the point is this. Would any re-writing make it possible for us to put it on the market at this moment? At least before the Healy book comes out?[1]

Let me know what you think?

I am very depressed about it all but what can one do. I did my best but it appears that one makes mistakes now and again. I think perhaps that if I put this manuscript away for a year I could have a clearer conception of it.

Yours very sincerely
Liam O'Flaherty.

[1] *The Life of Tim Healy*, London: Cape, New York: Harcourt Brace, 1927.

---

157. NLW TLS to Jonathan Cape
Lackan, Enniskerry, Co. Wicklow   n.d. [April 1926]

Dear Cape

Please send me copies of Ussher's poems and of that African book by Hans somebody or other.

When is *The Tent* coming out? Curse the strike.[1] I am going ahead splendidly with *Gilhooley*. This is the goods, much better than *The Informer*. Hope it continues so. I think you can be sure it will be ready for September 1st, though it may be much longer than *The Informer*. It is straight art, so there is not much difficulty of the sort that attaches to complicated theoretical work. Hurry up with that *Tent*.

My African Neighbours is the title of that book.[2] I may get some copy out of it. Anything else on your list that is literature? The Ussher book promises to be exciting.[3] My wife and I are anxious to read it.

With best wishes
Liam O'Flaherty

[1] The General Strike lasted from 3 April to 13 May, 1926.

[2] Hans Couden Hove, *My African Neighbours: Man, and Beast in Nyasaland*, London: Cape, 1926.

[3] Percy Arland Ussher translated Merriman's *The Midnight Court* (with a preface by W.B. Yeats) in 1926.

---

158. HRHRC ALS to Edward Garnett
Lackan, Enniskerry, Co. Wicklow   Tuesday n.d. [13 April, 1926]

My Dearest Friend,

I am now a father. Topsy became a mother last Saturday morning,[1] the third member of the family is a daughter called Margaret (nicknamed Bunty). We forthwith call on you to become godfather. The mother and the daughter are quite well. The mother is deliriously happy and the father looking at the mother, with the first joy of motherhood making her eyes wonderful, feels very proud.

The daughter, of course, is indifferent to her parents. Undoubtedly an O'Flaherty's daughter therefore. Physically she is the image of her mother, but I am afraid that she is born with my temper and restlessness. God help her suitors! Therefore, O benign Edward, stretch forth your spiritual hand to her so that I may murmur in her tiny ears: 'You mustn't scream, Edward Garnett is your godfather. Please don't disturb him.'[2]

This baby is so sensitive that when a man, whom I know is not a gentleman, entered the room she shuddered in her sleep.

Thanks for your criticism of *The Firebrand*, I have not been able to write to you before now about it on account of my affairs, but I wrote to Cape. He has probably told you. I feel you are quite right and that you would be even more severe were it not that you did not wish to wound my feelings. I re-read it and found it all very confused. Confused – that's it exactly. I have put it away.

My friends here are very sanguine about *The Tent*. I gave them a proof copy to read. They all liked 'The Wild Goat's Kid' best. I am eagerly awaiting its appearance.[2]

Give my love to Miss Heath and to yourself. My thanks and most affectionate love,

Liam

[1] 10 April, 1926. The baby was one month premature.

[2] 20 April, 1926, Topsy wrote to Edward Garnett from St. Monica's Home, 16 Lower Mount St., Dublin, thanking him for the silver mug he had sent the baby as her godfather. The baby, though small, is plump and healthy with thick dark hair. Topsy will be back home by 1st May and looks forward to meeting Liam's brother for a week's visit upon his return from Moscow, en route to the U.S. She is delighted that Sean O'Casey, after all his struggles, has won the Hawthornden Prize for *Juno and the Paycock*, a fine play, but she thinks he will not return to Ireland for some time.

---

159. HRHRC ALS to Charles Lahr[1]
Lackan, Enniskerry, Co. Wicklow   21 April, 1926

Dear Lahr,

Enclosed you will find two dozen copies of drawings signed by me. Glad you are printing *Darkness* in the *New Coterie*, and I am sure I'll be delighted to have you put the drawing as a frontispiece. I like it very much and so do my friends. I think it's frightfully good.

I met Leventhal over here the other day.

I hope everything is going well with you. Just had a daughter, I mean my wife just had a daughter, so my affairs are in a chaotic state at the moment.

Best wishes to Miss Archer and yourself,

Yours sincerely
Liam O'Flaherty

P.S. Give my compliments to Roberts and say I thank him for the splendid work he did.

[1] Charles Lahr was owner of the Progressive Bookshop in Holborn, from which Esther Archer published the *New Coterie* edited by the Czech poet Paul Selver. Lahr published one or two under-the-counter items for the officially disgraced D.H. Lawrence, and found collectors for the MSS of needy writers, including Sir Louis Sterling, head of HMV gramophone company. Rhys Davies in his *Print of a Hare's Foot, an autobiographical beginning*, (Heinemann 1969) describes Lahr's wife as 'a shrewd, book-loving Jewess, [who] cut through his rhetorical flightiness, sentimentalities and business generosities with the same realistic common-sense as my mother possessed' (p.114). Lahr had a basement room with a sofa where writers could sleep overnight. H.E. Bates met the first writers there who did not want to do anything else,

and Davies describes O'Flaherty as 'Irish to his insurgent bones'. Lahr paid Davies for three stories he published with a twelve volume set of Maupassant's short stories.

---

160. TCD ALS n.d. to AE at the *Irish Statesman.*
Lackan, Enniskerry, Co. Wicklow   n.d. [end April, 1926]

Dear AE,

Please offer my congratulations to the author of the poem '*Aodh Ruadh O'Domhnuaill*' which appears in your current issue. I think it is very fine indeed. The author is unmistakably a poet. I hope he is Irish and that you will encourage him. It's so utterly different from the abortions that the rest of your poetasters produce (pardon my bluntness). My wife joins me in offering congratulation.

> With best love
> Yours Liam O'Flaherty

P.S. Do please let me know who he is?[1]

[1] A note dated 4 May, 1926, from AE to 'My Dear M'Greevey' forwarded O'Flaherty's letter, saying he has revealed M'Greevey's identity to O'Flaherty. [TCD] This was Thomas MacGreevy who in 1934 published a book of poems but who will be chiefly remembered as friend of James Joyce, art critic and Director of the National Gallery, Dublin 1950-64.

---

161. HRHRC TLS to A.D. Peters
Lackan, Enniskerry, Co. Wicklow   11 May, 1926

Dear Peters,

Got your letter this morning after its strike wanderings. Glad to hear you sold 'Tobacco'. I have no photographs at all. Cape has got several which he gives out to editors. *T.P.'s* have borrowed ones from him on several occasions, so I should think they could get one this time.[1]

I am sending you a story, an intellectual one more or less. I have not written anything for a long time but I will start in a day or two and I will note your suggestion about stories like 'The Tyrant'. I have a good one in mind about a professor, so I will write it and send it to you next week, if the strike is over and the mails are running. We have received one mail from England during the last ten days.

You must be having a rather embarassing time.

> Yours very sincerely
> Liam O'Flaherty

1 'An Ounce of Tobacco', *T.P's Weekly*, 8 October, 1927.

---

162. HRHRC TLS to Edward Garnett
Lackan, Enniskerry, Co. Wicklow   15 May, 1926

My Dearest Friend,

Now that the strike is over, perhaps it is possible that the Empire will once more be able to carry a letter from me to you. It seems such a long time since the last time that affairs were normal. My dear fellow, I fancy you always hitherto despised the power of the Bolshevist idea. There you have it. The Muscovite has allies all over the world and unless he founds the greatest Empire the world has ever seen, the Russians are worse even than Tolstoy's conception of the Germans, who never conquered anybody but one another.

About ourselves. We are back in Lackan, Topsy, Bunty, Bunty's silver mug which her godfather sent her (for which I thank him here) and myself. After a fortnight of hailstones and many other unpleasant things, the weather has suddenly become fine and we are happy. I have written a good story about a professor and I am beginning a short novel which Cape is going to produce in November if God is kind, about the length of *The Informer*. I will send you the first two chapters if you would care to see them and give me your opinion of them. The subject is simple and sympathetic. Not in any way complicated but on the other hand not very ambitious. I feel in good fettle for writing, and as Tchekov's character in 'An Anonymous Story', I feel that my philosophy of life is changing or has changed since the birth of my daughter. I feel very conservative, or rather revolutionary conservative. I have made an alliance with AE, so to speak, against Yeats and his spiritual family. As AE controls a newspaper we shall probably drive Yeats out of the country.

Of course you will take this last announcement with a grain of salt, or a herbal cigarette, but the fact remains that I have at last to support the government in power as the only bulwark against the encroachments of the church. That is the explanation of my alliance with AE. AE of course supports the government, he is a Fascist, because he fears that if the mob gets into power by manoeuvring the electorate, they would make short shrift of him as a pagan. So the two of us are going to make war on democracy, priests and all these other evils. This is going to be a delightful country, now that we have Germans to make electricity for us.

The snipe have gone from the glen. But there is a bittern which does a noise at night, not unpleasant and very romantic. Pigeons have appeared about to nest. There are innumerable rabbits. One little bird, of which I don't know the tribe, comes into the kitchen for food and a thrush is nesting in a hawthorn bush at the gate, four yards from the door. The hawthorn bush is just like a speckled cauliflower now. I have planted a row of peas and a ridge of lettuces in the haggard but the goats walk over them on purpose.

Goats, of course, have returned. Contrary to expectations they proved fertile. The Swiss had three kids and the unicorn had two. It was a very interesting study, the unicorn, being a bastard goat and a proletarian, concealed her maternity almost to the day of birth. The other goat, however, being of good family, was not at all able to look after herself. In a state of nature she would have fallen prey easily to wolves and other wild beasts. For three days before kidding she could hardly walk and her womb had dilated so considerably that her fundaments dropped, as Rabelais would say. I had to perform the function of a midwife for her. What was my astonishment to find that she had three kids, a phenomenal performance among goats. When I presented the third kid to her, she was so exhausted with travail that she refused to recognise it or lick the birth slime. So I had to murder it barbarously with a stone. While the Swiss goat was kidding the other goat took positively no notice. The Swiss goat controlled her emotions perfectly, uttering no sound but rooting up the ground savagely. After giving birth to the first kid she rooted the earth (it was in a shed where peat had been stored), careless of the fact that she was tossing her screaming kid about with her hoofs. She had no feeling at all for her offspring and in a state of nature both she and they would have died. The kids from want of motherly care, and the mother from want of somebody to milk her.

The vulgar goat, however, was quite different. She screamed giving birth. But as soon as she had given birth, she arose quite smartly, warded me off savagely with her horns, licked her kid and almost immediately forced it to feed. She is a wonderful character but a hopeless milker. I shot her kids and in revenge she is deliberately withholding her milk, so that very probably she will go dry in a fortnight unless she changes her mind and decides to behave herself. I think she is a most unhappy animal for she wails at times for no reason in the world. Possibly she is infected with the Bolshevist idea.

We have a maid, fifteen years old. She and wife are already on a footing of intimacy. I fancy my wife has told her I am a terrible fellow and that spurs her on to work, while at the same time she won't run away, lest she might leave my poor wife to my mercy. All this is very interesting. I have nicknamed the girl 'organised labour'.

> With love to you and Miss Heath
> from Topsy, Bunty and myself
> Liam

---

1 May, 1926, O'Flaherty wrote to Peters sending him a photograph of himself as a private soldier, 'rather fatter and more idiotic' and one drawing which makes him look drunk. He tells Peters he does not like seeing his face in print.

21 May, 1926, Peters wrote to O'Flaherty suggesting that he should make his stories less episodic and try and work them up to a definite climax. (Source HRHRC).

---

163. NWUL TLS to Edward Garnett
Lackan, Enniskerry, Co. Wicklow   16 June, 1926

My Dearest Friend,

After all, I didn't send on the chapters of *Mr Gilhooley*. I decided to finish it first, for the reason that at the end of each chapter I realise you could offer no criticism of what had transpired except a purely technical one. It's just a story, so constructed that the drama does not come until the very end.

We are living in absolute seclusion for the past month. We have a notice on our gate: 'Visitors forbidden, by order'. We allow only exceptional people to visit us, people we could not keep away even with a notice, like the Countess Markievicz and Captain White. Topsy is getting fat and I am getting red in the face. I have sown two rows of peas and some lettuces and yes, by Jove, radishes that are already quite good. The goats have become thieves. They are now a perfect menace. They dash into the kitchen or the sitting room and devour everything. They have eaten several loaves of homemade bread, a packet of cigarettes and a sponge. Even if I beat them they like it, because they love me and they know I love them. So they are just as rascally as ever, after I have beaten them. I must tie them to a stake but it seems such a cruelty, not to the goats but to myself. The goats, tied to a stake, would scream all day, knowing that I would be uncomfortable listening to them. They *are* scoundrels.

Well, well, what is happening in the world of letters? One never hears. I get press cuttings about *The Tent*, some of which are quite good and others quite bad.[1] The English literary coteries seem to be ranging themselves into partisans, some praising me far more than I am worth, others going into hysterics with savage and ferocious hatred. L.P. Hartley and H.C.H., our old friend on the *Manchester Guardian*, belong to this latter crowd. Good luck to them! I am sure their digestion is as bad as mine was a few years ago. One gets so bored with these people who fight behind a newspaper. I expect they inherited these tricks from their ancestors.

Our baby is becoming quite a character. She is thriving remarkably well. We are now feeding her on goat's milk. She doesn't cry very much but still ... Topsy finds it very hard.

This country is falling every day more and more into the clutches of the church. People are beginning to be alarmed. There are processions of devotees through the streets every Sunday and there are constant rumours of repressive legislation against any sort of freedom of thought. However, in this glen it seems incredible. It is probably the end of the church. All dying organisations become diseased, and it serves a useful purpose because one notices a remarkable freedom of thought here which is absent in other countries. The Irish are a damnably intelligent people now. It's extraordinary, they are comparatively uninformed, at least compared to the educated class in England and Germany – as uninformed as the French, yet even a peasant in the glen is more subtle than many editors of English newspapers. It is because they are young, as a race, I suppose. And the struggle for existence is so great.

I must get away. Every day the brain assimilates a mass of copy which threatens to block up the selective cells. I must get away. Where? What do you think? We will probably run around the west a little in late Summer and then wipe our feet at Kingston Pier. Whither? What do you suggest?

> With best love ... I say, I have caught four trout with a line
> Liam

P.S. I saw a story in *Now and Then* by a man called [H.E.] Bates. Very, very promising – who is he, do you know? Has he published anything? I should think he has read Tchekov and has a delicate constitution, but very, very good. L.O'F.

---

[1] The *Irish Statesman* (26 June, 1926, p.445) reviewed *The Tent* noting humour as O'Flaherty's strong point, but disliked 'The Sensualist' and 'The Tent'. 'As humour grows in the same soil as tenderness O'Flaherty finds his true way in stories like 'The Wild Goat's Kid', 'The Lost Thrush' and 'Mother and Son'.'

---

164. NYUF ALS to Herbert Devine[1]
Lackan, Enniskerry, Co. Wicklow   23 June, 1926

Dear Devine,

God blast it! You're a good fellow. I drink your health, or at least I will when I get to a pub. Thanks very much for the six guineas, which I think is far more than the bloody story was worth.

However, I worked my kidneys dry on 'model 3'.[2] I hope it will please you. The one called 'Birth' is the best story I've done yet. I am enclosing both stories. Read 'The Fairy Goose' with one eye on a biblical parable; the old pagan legend of good versus evil, upon which all religious cults are based, fear versus love of course is the Christian one. Fear God and love one another. Sounds ridiculous because you can't honourably love one person through fear of another. However, the fact remains that the poor little goose got the worst of it. The goose, of course, represents love, the priest fear. It's a *true* story.

P.S. My wife is delighted you wrote for stories because she had been nagging at me for six weeks to write a story and I consistently refused.

But of course in face of your request I couldn't refuse further. Wives are the very devil. You see, I'm writing two blasted books at the same time, a cursed novel and a biography. I hate writing novels, and the biography makes me vomit. I hope to get to London some time in August and we'll have a bottle of beer together. Good luck to you, L.O.F.

L.O'Flaherty

[1] Editor of the *Humanist*, journal of the British Humane Society, published March 1924-August, 1927.

[2] 'The Black Cat', The *Humanist*, July, 1926. pp 237-39.

---

165. NLW ALS to Jonathan Cape
Lackan, Enniskerry, Co. Wicklow   22 June, 1926

Dear Cape

Salutations. The editor of the *Humanist* wants a photo for a review in the July number of his journal. As the *Humanist* people are very well-to-do and fond of animals, you should let them have one, Kenworthy, Galsworthy, Arbuthnot Lane and those people run it. Please send them one if you can. Ech! What blessed people! Gordon Selfridge is one of them. It would be better for him to do away with his bargain basement than to try and cure donkeys of piles on their shoulders. However, do let them have a photograph if you have one.

Judging by the *Morning Post* review of *The Tent* I think the reviewers swallowed my contention and rejected your and Garnett's. I hope you are selling a few copies?

By the way, don't you think it would be a good idea if I made a trip to the U.S. next winter for three or four months? My brother passed through here last Summer on his way home and he suggested that it might do good. I could see a few people and I think I would make a better impression on Irish Americans than on the native Irish. What do you think? Do you think it is advisable? You won't by any chance be going there yourself this winter? I really think we should make a little effort to collar the American market pretty soon. I have to clear out of Ireland anyway for a year or so because I can't stick this blasted Papish despotism for any length of time. My curse on Cromwell for not having been a little more intelligent in his biblical arguments. Tell me what you think, and forgive me for troubling you.

Yours
Liam O'Flaherty

---

166. NLD (MS 26,743) TLS to Percy H. Muir[1]
Lackan, Enniskerry, Co. Wicklow   30 June, 1926

Dear Sir,

Thanks for your letter. I don't think there are any other publications under my name other than these you mention. It is very good of you to note my books in your catalogue and if you would tell me what to write in the shape of a prefatory note I'll gladly do so.

I think I disposed of the manuscript of two of my books and of the other two books I have nothing. The first two – at the time I wrote them I was under the impression, perhaps rightly, that they were worthless, so I burned the manuscripts when I had finished with them. The only thing I keep are the manuscripts of my literary short stories. If your client would care to purchase these I would be willing to part with them.

Thanking you once more for your kind interest in my work, I remain, yours very sincerely,

Liam O'Flaherty

[1] Of Dulau & Co. Ltd., London, booksellers, then in Margaret St. W1 but moved in 1927 to 32 Old Bond St.

---

167. NYUF ALS to Herbert Devine
Lackan, Enniskerry, Co. Wicklow   3 July, 1926

Dear Devine,

You are too kind! You have a gentle soul and I thank you very much indeed for your review of my book. May your life be the happier for your kindness. I tell you that a man like myself, who is always denounced as violent, brutal, etc., appreciates these things.

Well! I think your magazine is first rate. It's much superior to Nash's and in fact superior in interest to anything I see coming out of England at the moment. I think you will go far with it and you certainly deserve it. I am glad you have Kenworthy writing for you. That is a thoroughly good man, every ounce of him a gentleman. Even my own little story looked good to me in print, except that the ending was slovenly and technically very bad. I made it too hurried, but the illustrations added fifty percent to it. Give my compliments to the artist.

Toto said you were coming over here shortly. I hope to see you when you come. I am living very quietly here and I see nobody hardly, but soon I will stir out. My wife sends you her best regards and thanks. The little one is now making 'noises'.

Yours sincerely
Liam O'Flaherty

---

168. HRHRC TLS to Charles Lahr
Lackan, Enniskerry, Co. Wicklow   3 July, 1926

Dear Lahr,

Thanks for your letter and enclosed money. I have a story called 'The Child of God' in MS which I would be willing to sell, that is the manuscript. I would not take anything under five pounds for it, as it's the best thing I've done, seven thousand words long. If your client wishes to buy it he would have to guarantee to keep it private for some time as it's not printed yet. I intend to baptise a volume with it very probably, *'pour épater le pape'*.

I will be delighted to get T.F's drawing. That was a damn fine story 'Feed My Swine' – my wife and I love Powys' work and thought that the best thing he has done yet. I think he is by far the best man writing in England today. You must make him drunk when you go down and give him my love. I have a story which I am going to write which would probably suit you, if I can get it written. Whether I can write it or not I don't know yet.

That damn fellow Kirwan sold *Thy Neighbour's Wife* in typescript. I left a portion of the typescript in his digs, as far as I can remember, or he took it with him. Anyway I never knew anything about it. I am certain I had no manuscript of it. If he got a shilling for it good luck to him.

With best regards to the Archer part of the firm and to yourself.

Yours sincerely
Liam O'Flaherty

---

169. NLD (MS 26,743) ALS to P.H. Muir
Lackan, Enniskerry, Wicklow   3 July, 1926

Dear Mr. Muir,

Forgive me for addressing you as 'Modern Department' but your signature was beyond me. I'll send that biographical note within a few days. In the meantime if your client wishes to have short story MSS here is the list and the price:-

'The Tent'
'The Wild Goat's Kid'
'Charity' all for twenty pounds
'The Wounded Cormorant'
'The Inquisition'
'Stoney Batter'

These include my best short stories. If the price is too small your client can, of course, add a little. If too big, I can still keep the MSS, so it will be satisfactory in both cases. I have also the MS of a three-act play *Darkness* which I would be willing to sell for fifteen pounds. It is written in Gaelic originally by me. I afterwards translated it into English. The Gaelic MS would be, of course, merely a curiosity for your client.[1]

Yours sincerely
Liam O'Flaherty

[1] O'Flaherty wrote to P.H. Muir again later in the month sending the MSS promised, and also offering the MS of 'Civil War' for sale. 'Conger Eel' and 'The Foolish Butterfly' MSS are already sold. He says he is moving shortly 'so the less I cart around with me the better'.

---

170. HRHRC ALS to Edward Garnett
Lackan, Enniskerry, Co. Wicklow   21 July, 1926

My Dearest Friend,

Please forgive my delay in answering your letter. I had written, we had no envelopes, the letter got lost. So I am writing again.

I will be coming to London on 3rd August, next Tuesday week. Will you be in London then? I am taking over the MS of *Mr Gilhooley*. As I intend going to the U.S. this Autumn, I'd like to see you very much before I go.

I have been working very hard on this MS. Now that I have it nearly finished I think it's not as bad as I thought it was. It is undoubtedly not first rate, but perhaps it will pass. But you will see for yourself. Anyway, I'll be very glad to write the last word.

I had an American lady here to see me, a woman called Erlanger (wife of the man who makes B.V.D. underwear). She runs a little theatre in New York, presumably for fun. So when she heard we were going to the U.S. she invited us to her estate in New Jersey, where she declares she will look after us. She has arranged with Topsy to organise lectures for me in New York, see editors and do all sorts of things. It seems I must go through with it, as Topsy declares we must get some money. In that case, old friend, be of good cheer, I won't have to take that trip to Spain and you'll get paid my bad debts, or your bad debts, to be more correct.

However, it's going to be a very extraordinary business. Can you imagine me lecturing to American women?

My fellow countrymen have attacked my last book more violently than any of the previous ones. Still, I love them all. I think it's very healthy to be attacked. It makes me more remote. Do you think American applause would have a bad effect on my art? I think not, there is a limit to the susceptibilities, even of an author.

Tell me, do you see O'Casey at all? I must look him up when I get to London. It will be good to see people again, though it's very salutary for the mind living in this delightful wilderness. I have become quite hardy this Summer. I find it very soothing to stand naked in a sandy pool, up to the waist in the water when there is a full sun. Have you ever tried it? Hardly anybody comes and people are becoming very indignant because they say we have become churlish; but it's curious that when I was hospitable and invited visitors they managed to be very {?}. I like middle class people less, the more I know of them. That is, a certain type of middle class person. There are others of course.

You will be pleased to hear I wrote another good sketch called 'Birth' about the birth of a calf. Topsy and I claim that it's as good as 'The Cow's Death'. This is an idyll though, perhaps lacking the power of tragedy. I am eagerly looking forward to the drunken pleasure of writing more sketches when I finish my novel.

How are Miss Heath's prisoners?[1] And I hope she is enjoying all the happiness and health that she deserves. You too, my foster father.

We have Charley with us and there are various parleys in progress between the four surviving members of the Barrington family. The father is delivering releases from his retreat in the South of France. Mrs Barrington is, I think, coming to Lackan to look after Pegeen while we are away.

My goats are still prospering but our relations have become subdued for the past month. They realise I am busy with my novel and they do not press their affections. Alas! There are nettles growing round the door and Charley is busy since he returned cutting down the wilderness. I'm afraid Topsy and I are hopeless people.

I have various things to tell you when we meet, so I trust your health will be good? Perhaps we might go somewhere and share a bottle.

With best love to you both, from all of us
Liam

[1] Miss Heath was a prison visitor.

---

171. SLUL (Folio V 36) TLS to Charles Lahr
Lackan, Enniskerry, Co. Wicklow   10 August, 1926

Dear Lahr,

Sorry to have left before Sunday, but I got a note from my wife to say that an American lady wanted to see me on her way back from the Aran Islands, so I had to rush back on Saturday morning. However, I hope to go through London in the beginning of October when I am going to the U.S. and I'll see that picture.

I'll send those manuscripts on to you. I think there are four or five altogether of the last stories I wrote, and I am writing a good one which you might like for the *New Coterie*. I am going down to Cork tomorrow and when I get back I'll write the story and send on the manuscripts.

By the way, that little story you gave me is very good. That boy is a writer, no cod about it. He's sincere, which is the main point. I enjoyed the story immensely. If somebody taught him how to write properlyhe'd do something big perhaps. Make him write.

With best wishes
Yours sincerely
Liam O'Flaherty

---

172. HRHRC TLS to A.D. Peters
Lackan, Enniskerry, Co. Wicklow   20 August [1926]

Dear Peters,

I enclose proofs of *The Tent*. As you already know from Cape, the manuscript of *The Firebrand* has been withdrawn by me and a new manuscript *Mr Gilhooley* has been substituted. I have written Cape to change the agreement with your help, so that *The Firebrand* agreement will become the agreement for the new manuscript. There is no need to send on the terms for my approval as there will be no change in terms, and I believe no signature required. At least I think not.

I intend going to the U.S. next month or in October, so would you send me copies of the stories you have. Perhaps I might be able to sell them in America.

Yours very sincerely
Liam O'Flaherty

---

173. HRHRC ALS to Edward Garnett
Lackan, Enniskerry, Co. Wicklow   21 August, 1926

My Dearest Friend,

Please pardon my delay in writing to thank you for your hospitality during my visit to London. I have been extremely busy and disturbed. Topsy and I went to Cork for a week and since my return I have been taken up with matters dealing with the biography I am writing. My curse on the foul thing.[1]

I read *Two Sisters* [H.E. Bates] and I think it's splendid work, beautifully written and delicately handled. Unless something unforeseen happens that boy will do big things yet. Unfortunately, although I went personally to AE to get it for review, he told me it had been done already, so it seems the book has been published for some time. I spoke to as many of my friends as I met about it, and some said they would get it. I think women would like it very much if Cape found some means of getting it into their hands.[2]

I am enclosing that sketch I told you about, 'Birth'. Would you return it as I have no other copy. The *Dial* rejected it and said they were sorry I had not sent them something like 'A thrush Leaves Home'! An odious woman called Marianne Moore is now editing the *Dial*. I gave those MSS to Muir and he is negotiating with a client, who is at present in France and will return early in September.

Nothing strange is happening in Lackan. Everything is partaking of the dullness which exudes forth from this foul book I am writing. It will do me at least one good, however, it will forever cure me of all belief in politicians, politics, nationalism, imperialism, communism, the Pope, religion, Gods, devils, reformers, revolutions, stable governments, conservatives and the mob. In other words it will burnish the mirror of my intellect, so that pure art will find there a clearer reflection of her beauty.

We heard from Mrs Erlanger. She is eagerly awaiting our arrival in the United States. Topsy is negotiating with her father for payment on account of my legacy, and when this materialises (if it does) we set forth, to open the American oyster with our blackthorn sticks – or rather, since such weapons lack the subtlety of the rapier, to bludgeon the thing. I trust it hides a pearl.

AE's paper is becoming very amusing. You should subscribe to it. Or would you like me to send you any copy that is particularly amusing? At times it is excellent reading, much superior to papers like the *Nation* or the *Spectator*, though of course it lacks their erudition and their balance. AE, however, has a most pernicious influence on the budding young writers who are beginning to show their heads. He sends them contemplating their mystic navels, instead of contemplating something more interesting. The extraordinary man is a profound realist and sceptic in his editorial pages – elsewhere he is a mystic, a bounder and a fool. So are we all – all honourable scoundrels.

Ech! My dear fellow, this is a great country. I was staying in Cork with a friend of Topsy's, a man of the landowning class, *ci-devant*, married to an aristocratic woman (*ci-devant*). They are both excellent citizens, now labouring at the farming profession. They are both Royalist, Unionist and extremely reactionary in mentality. Yet they are the only efficient, progressive citizens in the district. Their neighbours are all republican nationalists, who love Ireland but refuse to work for it and let weeds smother their land. This *ci-devant* family hate the Irish nation, but they are doing their level best to build it. They are loyal to the Irish government, while the Republican Nationalists all round, although they love Ireland, are intent on the overthrow of the government. I have not yet written the story. Cork is a wonderful place. Still, we were glad to return to Dublin. One feels oneself becoming a Corkman and an Irish imperialist, even after a week there. Those fellows the Corkmen will swarm over Europe unless something is done. I received the impression there of a field, pregnant with seed on a soft, warm Irish Spring day, bursting forth, pushing upwards with irresistible force, a fierce, ruthless, ambitious people. At the railway stations we saw peasants watching the train with hungry, menacing faces. We shut the windows.

With love

Liam

[1] *The Life of Tim Healy* (Governor-General of the Irish Free State) was published, Cape (London) and Harcourt Brace (New York) in 1927. The book is an excuse for a historical survey of Ireland 1850's to 1920's, very ironic, sometimes deliberately scandalising, but contains much sound opinion. It was O'Flaherty's only attempt at non-fiction.

[2] Bates was another Garnett protegé, and this his first novel.

In a letter from Topsy to Edward Garnett, dated 22 August, she says she is pleased Garnett likes *Mr Gilhooley*. She would like to introduce Garnett to Bill Gleeson at their 'little paper shop' who is the Bill Hanrahan of the story; 'he and his two brothers are most remarkable in their own way, gunmen and heavy drinkers, one kindly, the other brutal.' The visit to Cork was to the family of Topsy's goddaughter. They had some nice drives there and went out to Gougane Barra lake and to the sixth century hermitage of St. Finbar, patron saint of Cork. She reports on the development of 'Pegeen Liam' who now has an imperious frown and is 'a regular little Napoleon'. 'Liam burst his gun and nearly burst himself, so he has no way of amusing himself. I'm afraid he is working too hard.' [Source HRHRC]

---

174. HRHRC ALS to Charles Lahr
Lackan, Enniskerry, Co. Wicklow   27 August, 1926

Dear Lahr,

Thanks awfully for cheque and for copies of T.F. Powys' drawing. They were both splendid. Still I wish you had taken your commission for selling the MSS. Of course I will be delighted to sign any books you like for you, but look out for the first edition of my new novel *Mr Gilhooley*, it's likely to go right out immediately as far as I hear.

I am afraid I have no other MS left, except a portion of a funny novel I once began to write and gave up writing.[1]

The Powys drawing is wonderful, really great work. It should draw attention to the new number. By the way, I haven't got any story, but my agent has several of mine which he has not sold. His name is A.D. Peters, 20-21 Essex St., Strand WC2. I'll write to him today to send you one.

I'll probably pass through London on my way to the U.S. so I'll see you then. I'm working like the very devil on the Tim Healy life I'm doing now in an attempt to get it done in six weeks. I've another fortnight to go. Some life!

With affectionate regards to Miss Archer, yourself and all the fellahs.

Yours

Liam O'Flaherty

[1] Probably *The Adventures of General Rathcroghan*.

---

175. To the Editor of the *Irish Statesman*[1]
Enniskerry   21 August, 1926

Most Honoured Sir,

I hope that you will allow me to make a protest in your most estimable newspaper against a very gross violation of the liberty of the Press in this country. I am a writer of books. These books are offered for public sale by my publishers in various countries, including Ireland, my native country. A copy of each book is sent for review to newspapers that are considered by my publishers to be important. The usual procedure in civilised countries, with reference to the review copies, is to send the books to reviewers and to publish the opinions of the reviewers thereon, with, occasionally, a certain curtailment. In this country, at least with regard to my books, a different method is adopted.

A friend of mine told me recently that he was approached by an employee of a prominent Dublin newspaper and asked whether he was willing to review a book of mine. My friend answered in the affirmative. 'Will you attack it?' said the newspaper employee. My friend answered that he would not promise to attack it unless he considered that it deserved condemnation from an artistic point of view. 'That's no good to us,' said the newspaper employee, 'The policy of our newspaper is to attack everything he writes.' And the newspaper employee left my friend, in order to find, as he said, somebody who was willing to attack the book before he had read it. As it happened, he found nobody willing to do so, so he had to attack it himself.

Most Honoured Sir, I think this is a very gross and petty form of tyranny. The newspaper in question is a violent opponent of Soviet Russia, so that its method of supporting the freedom of the Press cannot be copied from the methods which are supposed to be used in Russia. On the other hand, these methods of regulating the freedom of the Press can hardly be sponsored by our Government. Although I belonged a few years ago to a minority that waged war against the Government, I have since received nothing but courteous treatment from the Government of the Free State. I can hardly believe, indeed it is impossible to believe, that the Government which I now respect as a good and efficient administrator of the law current in most civilised European countries can be responsible for this. Who, then, is responsible? Is there a mysterious and secret organisation ruling the Press in this country, in fact ruling the Government of this country, over the heads of the honourable and upright citizens that form the Government? As a member of a very small, free-thinking minority I tremble at the thought. In the old days, before we became a component and free part of the British Empire, when we were ruled by a group of conspirators that lived in Dublin Castle, I belonged to the persecuted majority. Now, alas! it seems that I belong to the persecuted minority.

Most Honoured Sir, permit me to remain,

Very sincerely yours
Liam O'Flaherty

(Dear Correspondent, do not worry. Nobody attaches any importance to the literary criticisms in the papers you refer to. Every Irish writer of repute made his name without their assistance, and in almost every case, in face of open attack by them .... If they approved of you wholeheartedly, it would be almost evidence to us that you were not worth reading. – Ed.*I.S.*)

[1] Published in Vol. 6, No. 26, 4 September 1926, p.711 under heading 'Literary Criticism in Ireland'.

---

176. NLD(MS 26,743) ALS to P.H. Muir
Lackan, Enniskerry, Co. Wicklow   25 September, 1926

Dear Muir,

Thanks for your letter. 'The White Bitch' story was not published in book form but it was printed in the *Weekly Westminster*. It's a second rate sketch and very slight, but if the American wants to print it I don't see why he shouldn't. However, wouldn't it be better to give him a good story of a greater length? I'll write one if he likes. What about *The Black Soul* MS? If you get any offer for it sell it because I'm very hard up for dough just now and I'd like to get some. I intended to come to London for the winter but owing to a wife and a baby I have to stay in Ireland. I am taking a flat near Dublin into which I am going to install my family in a fortnight's time. When that's done I am coming to London for a week or a fortnight on business. My new book will be published on October 21st. I'll go to the U.S. for a few months, probably in January and I'd like to meet your friend then. In any case I'll see you and drink your health over a glass of beer when I get to London. At present I'm loafing, having finished *The Life of Tim Healy*.

Do let me know if you can get rid of that MS.[1]

With best regards to your wife and yourself
Yours
Liam O'Flaherty

[1] On 15 October, O'Flaherty writes again to Muir from Hazelbrook, Kimmage Road, Terenure, saying that they will have to call off their plan to bring out a booklet, for it would be a breach of contract, so he returns Muir's cheque for ten pounds. It is his own fault for not having made enquiries in time. Muir evidently replies with another suggestion, as the next letter indicates. [Source NLD]

177. NLD (MS 26,743) TLS to P.H. Muir
Hazelbrook, Kimmage Road, Terenure, Dublin   20 October, 1926

Dear Muir,

Perhaps if you got in touch with Cape he might agree to the proposal. I can't see that it would do him any harm. Try him anyway.

I'm glad you liked *Mr Gilhooley* and I'm sorry that you think it won't sell, but I never expected it to become a bestseller. Still, it might sell as well as *The Informer*. I like it myself very much but I think *The Informer* was more romantic.

I got a note from the Phoenix Bookshop in New York asking for a long manuscript, so if you have any you might sell it to them. I have none.

With kindest regards to your wife and yourself, I remain,

Very sincerely yours
Liam O'Flaherty

------

178. HRHRC TLS to Herbert Devine
Hazelbrook, Kimmage Road, Terenure, Dublin   20 October, 1926

Dear Devine,

Just got your letter. I'd like the hero pictured standing on a large rock, at dawn, in the glen, with the sun breaking over the mountains that surround the glen on all sides. On the rock with him are two goats, one hornless, one with one horn. The hero has his hands stretched out towards the rising sun and his face is illuminated with a suggestion of a halo around his head. There is a difficulty about his head, because in the beginning of the story he is clean shaven, while later on, as he increases in sanctity, he grows a beard and long hair. But he is golden headed, with a long pale face. The ordinary individual would say he had the face of a fanatic or of a lunatic; but to the discerning mind it would be obvious that he had the face of a saint. He is about thirty years of age, tall and slim. He wears a linen smock that reaches to his hips and is bound about the waist with a leather belt, well tanned. Any sort of trousers will do him and his feet are bare. He wears no hat of course.

Birds should fly around his head and settle about his person in various attitudes. Various other animals stand around the rock, in attitudes of curiosity. Such is the man. You might put a red-roofed cottage surrounded with trees, nettles, etc. in the background if you think fit, and also a suggestion of peasants sleeping in their cabins instead of being busy with their work at that hour of the morning.

As to the title, I am still stuck with *The Wilderness*. I may get out of this and on to a better title later on. As to the advertisement, I think the word 'astounding' might be too strong for the *Literary Supplement* people. This ad. might do:

> We beg to announce that we have secured the serial rights of Liam O'Flaherty's new novel and we intend to begin it in our January number. In this novel Mr. O'Flaherty deals with a new tendency that is manifesting itself in a certain section of the Irish intellectual class. This class consider that Ireland is going to save western civilisation by presenting a new conception of religion to the human race. A new order of saints is being formed and the remote valleys of Ireland are likely to become as interesting to the decline and fall of western civilisation as the deserts of Africa were to the Roman Empire following the advent of Christianity. In this novel Mr. O'Flaherty draws a serious and convincing psychological picture of the first Irish saint of the twentieth century. He claims that whatever resemblance his hero bears to Saint Francis of Assisi is purely a coincidence.

You may do what you like with this suggestion but it is the sum total of my intentions.

Now about private affairs. I'd surely be delighted to meet Woodville and more delighted still to meet his wife. Here's to my next visit to London. We are settled in here now and I can soon get to work. I am thinking out my novel at present and in about a fortnight's time I'll begin on the first part. Mrs Cogley's Cabarets are going strong. My wife and myself were at the last one and it was very crowded. Dublin is becoming quite lively. Did you meet the naval commander's wife yet and if so what luck? I envy you in London with all the attractions of that mighty place. However, I think it's easier work here. *Mr Gilhooley* is coming out tomorrow and I hope it sells a few copies. I think it will get a good press anyway.

Here's good luck to you and great success for your paper.

Yours sincerely
Liam O'Flaherty

---

179. HRHRC ALS to Herbert Devine
Hazelbrook, Kimmage Road, Terenure   30 October, 1926

Dear Devine,

Just got your magazine. I think the number is very good and I was very intrigued with the announcement. I hope that the MS will come up to scratch. I have it worked out and I think it will be all right. By Jove! you'll soon be a very big {hit?} in London, which you undoubtedly deserve. The list of your contributors becomes more and more aristocratic every month. What with Commanders' wives and the Lyceum Club your atmosphere is becoming practically unapproachable. Ah, those Jesuits! They still have a big kick in them.

I have not begun to write yet but I fancy I shall soon do so. I'm not going to tell you the plot in order that it may surprise you. I don't know what's going to happen to *Mr Gilhooley*. I fancy the reviewers are terrified of him. I'm sending you a copy to get your opinion of the book. There was a bad review in the *Spectator*, but I got a very enthusiastic letter from some man in Chester about the book. So it goes.

We might come to London somewhere about Xmas and have some fun. This flat is rather comfortable, but the weather is very cold and there is no coal. Damn the Empire![1]

I was intrigued to see Madame Erleigh on your list this month.

Yours

Liam O'Flaherty

[1] The coal miners' strike lasted long after the rest of the General Strike had been called off.

---

180. HRHRC ALS to Edward Garnett
Hazelbrook, Kimmage Road, Terenure   1 November, 1926

My Dearest Friend,

I am sending you a copy of *Mr Gilhooley*. I am afraid it's going to get an extremely bad reception. Indeed, I am beginning to despair of ever getting any sale for my work and it is bitterly disappointing. Added to the racial prejudice there is in England against an Irish writer there is the added prejudice of puritanism and unless one becomes both a buffoon and a charlatan there does not seem any possibility of overcoming these two prejudices. Next year I'll very probably have to emigrate either to America or Russia. Russia would be infinitely preferable were it not for the difference in language. My father used to say that it was better to be a devil than a small boy, but I fancy either is better than being an Irishman – or perhaps an Indian – or let us say an Egyptian. We'll omit the Russians as they have had the extreme consolation of shedding a considerable volume of their enemies' blood.

On the whole the world is treating me in a very unkindly fashion at the moment. We moved into this flat and a few days after our arrival Miss Bavington was delivered of a child. What an experience! The hapless girl concealed her condition through the fear (as she alleged) that we would turn her into the streets. As a result we were suddenly aroused at midnight last Monday to find her in travail! Even then she said it was the cramps and it was not until I had gone for the doctor that she told my wife. As luck would have it the doctor was a Republican friend of mine and a member of the Gaelic League Executive, and he managed the affair excellently for us. We got the child into a nursing home next day and the mother is now recovering. But last week has been a nightmare. Of course I don't suppose it's the end of the affair, as she refuses to let us know the father – if indeed she knows herself. I suppose I'll have to provide for it, as she doesn't seem to have any interest in it. Poor little baby! What a cruel and merciless state of society this is that vents its hatred on the newborn. Christ! to hear its little cries and to realise that all through its life it will have to meet contempt and oppression for no fault of its own. Human beings are in many ways far more foul than the so-called lower animals. Eh? All this supposed tenderness is largely humbug and is exercised only when it is profitable.

Poor Topsy is dreadfully upset, so am I. And yet, on Tuesday evening, the day the child was born, I had invited a number of friends to spend the evening. They came and we had a gay conversation. Russell told funny stories and we all laughed. However, I thought they'd never leave, or that something might happen which would place the poor girl at their mercy. So far we have managed to save her from scandal, but I wonder ...

I suppose David's book will be published shortly? I read Coppard's short stories and they impressed me very favourably, although they are very melancholy. Not like Tchekov's melancholy though. I am reading considerably now, but I can't stand these modern writers, and one gets to the end of the older writers. Hudson is always beautiful. I can read him over and over again for the beauty of his prose and the marvellous power of exact observation. My wife did not like [C.M.] Doughty and she thinks Hudson superior to him. Of course she is slightly prejudiced against all English prose except that of Sterne and our only intellectual quarrels are about her over-rating of French literature.

I am not writing at all now, although I have a load to write – no energy I suppose. I have to do a serial for a magazine and it's detestable to have to write something definitely in a definite time. I fancy it won't be any good.

By the way, I read your novel *The Paradox Club* a few weeks ago and I intended writing to you about it.[1] My friend McManus[2] got it for his first edition library and he lent it to me. I think the first chapter was very, very beautiful, especially the description of the little child stealing the fruit. Then you seemed to turn it into an essay. Why the devil didn't you write it all like the first chapter? I can frankly tell you that I was enchanted with the first chapter. I was so enthusiastic when I had finished reading it that I wanted to write to you at once. Then I thought you might not be pleased, as you have no respect for my judgment. I wish I could write English in such a subtle way.

> With love to you and Miss Heath
> from Liam

P.S. If you had lived in Ireland instead of living in England you would have become the father of Irish literature, instead of waiting till your death in England to get due recognition of your genius. I say damn the English bourgeoisie!

[1] Garnett's didactic first novel on a socialist theme, published T. Fisher Unwin, 1888. Just after its publication Ernest Rhys first met J.M. Dent (bookbinder/publisher) in Garnett's rooms at Gray's Inn, and from this meeting grew the Everyman Library series, its first volume being Boswell's *Life of Samuel Johnson*, see Rhys's autobiography, *Everyman Remembers* (1931).

[2] Presumably the M.J. McManus to whom O'Flaherty dedicated his *The Life of Tim Healy*. This may be Michael Joseph McManus (b. 1888) who became literary editor of *Irish Press* from its foundation in 1931.

---

181. SLUL (Folio V 36) ALS to Charles Lahr
Hazelbrook, Kimmage Road, Terenure   2 November, 1926

Dear Lahr,

I am sending on signed booklets and two copies of *Mr Gilhooley* signed. Thanks for the Powys booklet and the *New Coterie*. The *Coterie* was very, very good, easily the best number. I haven't it all read yet, but I read [Rhys] Davies' story and it's very good. He's coming on splendidly. Powys' story is not up to scratch although the material is good. On the whole it's a splendid number, splendid.[1]

Yes, I'll sign those bally things for five pounds certainly. I'm glad your friend liked Gilhooley. I'm afraid he's going to get a bad press. Curiously enough all the Dublin bookshops are placarding him, although they boycotted my other books as obscene! What on earth is the idea?

How is your wife, and has the expected one arrived yet? My family is well, although the baby is teething and very cross.

With affectionate regards
Yours
Liam O'Flaherty

[1] The Davies story was 'Mrs Evans Number Six', and T.F. Powys contributed 'The Bride'.

---

182. HRHRC ALS to Edward Garnett
Hazelbrook, Kimmage Road, Terenure   7 November, 1926

My Dearest Friend,

For Christ's sake answer Gould's review of *Mr Gilhooley*, it's full of holes. Sting him if you love me. I feel like travelling to London by express to give him a horsewhipping but I doubt if the fellow is worth it. He is evidently getting afflicted with what Cunninghame Graham called the 'Nonconformist Snuffle'. He is also obviously illiterate, the Latin tag is proof of that. We mustn't let him get away with it scot free.

I was enraptured by your praise of the biography. It did me no end of good to hear you liked it. Thanks dear friend. Please apologise to Miss Heath for Topsy's failure to acknowledge the necklace. She was so dreadfully upset by Charley's affair. I am writing to Miss Heath tomorrow.

In haste, Liam

183. NLW TLS to Jonathan Cape
Hazelbrook, Kimmage Road, Terenure   9 November, 1926

Dear Cape,

What are you going to do with *The Life of Tim Healy*? I wrote asking you to get a copy typed but you did not reply. Would you let Curtis Brown have it to get a copy typed or return it to me because it's important that Doran get his copy in time. It is well on in November now. I know I should have done this myself before sending it on to Brown, but I never do anything right. Do let me know what is to be done. It's a damn nuisance, I'm sick of it.

I see *Gilhooley* is getting an awful hiding. [1] Is it selling at all? I had hoped that they would ban it in the Free State but for some reason or other all the Dublin bookshops are placarding it in their windows. I have counted almost a dozen copies in the shops and I believe four copies have been sold. Why not advertise it in the Pink Un as a shocker?[2]

Yours sincerely
Liam O'Flaherty.

P.S. [Bertram] Rota sends me a catalogue in which copies of *Thy Neighbour's Wife* (First ed.) are quoted at Fifteen shillings! Is it not still in its first edition?

[1] The *Irish Statesman*, 27 November 1926, pp.279-80 reviewed *Mr Gilhooley* as follows: 'I do not know of any contemporary writer of fiction who can realise for us with such vivid emotional power the agony or blind gropings of an individual ... I feel sick and shaken after reading *The Informer* and *Mr Gilhooley* because I have been absorbed into and identified with souls in agony .... His tale of the informer is a pure identification of the writer with his subject, so is his tale of Mr. Gilhooley.'

[2] According to an article written in the *Irish Times* 8 September, 1984, page 7, just after O'Flaherty's death, his Gilhooley (along with images from Joyce, Synge and others) both figured in a window commissioned from the artist Harry Clarke for presentation to the Geneva League of Nations. This window was never presented.

In an undated note to Peters of this period O'Flaherty wrote: 'I am returning the account for *Mr Gilhooley*. If Cape hadn't finished the damn book it would have done well, however, there is slight hope for it yet.' For *Mr Gilhooley* O'Flaherty got fifteen percent on the first five thousand (five percent more than for his previous work). On his next novel Peters tells him he should get fifteen percent on the first two thousand five hundred copies sold, twenty percent up to ten thousand and twenty-five percent thereafter. (HRHRC)

---

184. NLD (MS 26,743) ALS to P.H. Muir
Hazelbrook, Kimmage Road, Terenure   3 December, 1926

Dear Muir,

Thanks awfully for the catalogue.[1] Really you make me blush with praise. I thank you very much indeed for your kindness, because that boost will do me no end of good. My wife is also very grateful to you. What a magnificent collection of books. When I get rich, if I ever do, I'll collect books, just to look at them.

I got your letter this morning. Yes, I still have the MS of *Gilhooley*. I am trying to get my wife to come to London for a few days before Xmas, and we'll bring the MS along to you. You can put it in your drawer so that if a customer comes along you can negotiate. Cape got terrified of the book. Now he wants me to revise the second edition. Harcourt is doing it in America, and he also wants it revised. I don't like it, but I expect I'll have to make considerable alterations or take it off the market, as Cape refuses to get out the second edition unexpurgated. As it is, the first edition was considerably expurgated as compared with the original draft, so there won't be much left of it by the time it is a few years in print if the public goes on becoming more and more finicky. It's an awful world.

I am now writing the life of a saint and I expect they'll object to that just as much. It's being serialised in the *Humanist*. I really don't believe they'll give *The Informer* the prize, the squirearchy were very indignant at the recommendation. I believe they will exert all their influence to reverse the judgement.[2]

Unless my wife backs out we'll get to London within the next fortnight. It's terribly cold here and I get nearly frozen watching Rugby matches, which is my main occupation, other than writing. Give my regards to your wife. I suppose your charming German cousin-in-law has left you long ago.

Yours affectionately
Liam O'Flaherty

[1] A copy of the draft of P.H. Muir's notes about O'Flaherty for the readers of his catalogue, is appended to this letter.

[2] *The Informer* won the James Tait Black Memorial Prize 1926.

---

185. NLW TLS to Jonathan Cape
Hazelbrook, Kimmage Road, Terenure   14 December, 1926

Dear Cape,

I had a letter from Moscow from a man called Ochremenko, who informs me that *The Informer* is already published there, while *Spring Sowing* and *The Tent* are in process of publication. No mention of the word royalties occurs in the letter. I fancy it is forbidden.

However, the following passage occurred in the letter: 'I should be much obliged to you if you would ask your publishers (Jonathan Cape) to send me the book *Pandora Lifts the Lid* by Christopher Morley and Don Marquis. If he publishes any humorous stories please ask him to add two or three books of humour to the above mentioned book. The cost of the books I will remit to you or to the publisher when I get the books.'

The address is: Peter Ochremenko, Kropotkin Street, Chisti Pereulok 6, Apartment 26, Moscow 34, U.S.S.R. He says all parcels should be registered. (Don't blame me if you send the books and don't get the money.)

I hear very amusing news here. The Royal Irish Academy are thinking of establishing an Académie de Belles Lettres on the French plan.[1] They asked Shaw to be President. He agreed provided they did not exclude Joyce, Robinson and myself. Now there is hell to play in Dublin in scholastic circles, because they are put to shame if they refuse and if they accept they are in for trouble. It's amusing to find Robinson in the same boat as James Joyce and myself.

Yours sincerely

Liam O'Flaherty

[1] The Irish Academy of Letters was established in 1932 with W.B. Yeats and G.B. Shaw as leading lights.

---

186. NYUF TLS to Herbert Devine
Hazelbrook, Kimmage Road, Terenure   2 January, 1927

Dear Devine,

Thanks for your letter and the copies of the *Humanist*. The story was very nice, I'll send the second instalment along in a few days.[1] I'm coming over to London on February 12th for the football match, and I fancy I'll have the whole novel finished by then. This instalment is a little better than the first. I hope your readers will be pleased. You certainly advertised it very well.

Excuse these few words as I'm busy typing the instalment and finishing it off. I'm pressed after all the disturbance of Xmas.

With best wishes for success and happiness in your new home. Best regards to C.J. and secretary and all the staff.

Yours sincerely
Liam O'Flaherty

[1] *The Wilderness* was serialised in the *Humanist* in six monthly instalments from January-June, 1927, but not published as a novel until 1978 by Wolfhound Press, Dublin: and as a 'lost novel of the twenties' by Dodd, Mead & Co, New York, 1987.

---

187. HRHRC TLS to Charles Lahr
Hazelbrook, Kimmage Road, Terenure   8 January, 1927

Dear Lahr,

I received the proof sheets of 'The Child of God' today.[1] I arranged to sign twenty-five copies for five pounds. Now you offer to give me four pounds ten for forty-five copies. I'll sign forty-five copies for ten pounds, or twenty-five copies for five pounds. If either is unsatisfactory I'll return the sheets *toute suite* unsigned. That's not business.

As for Roberts of Newcastle,[2] please tell him that I'll complete the manuscript with great pleasure for thirty pounds, approximately half the remainder of what the manuscript is worth to me now, if I had it. He got it for a song through the idiocy of my friend and if the American from Chicago (I know the man) wishes to have it completed he has got to pay for it.

C'est ça.

Yours very sincerely
Liam O'Flaherty

[1] Refers to the limited edition printed by Archer, 1926.

[2] Arthur Roberts, dealer in rare books of 46 Handyside's Arcade, Newcastle-upon-Tyne, to whom O'Flaherty wrote a three line letter on 4 February saying he would buy back the MS of

The Informer or finish it for thirty pounds. The MS was sold by Roberts to Walter Hill in the U.S. who had found some pages missing. There are a few letters from Hill to Roberts. As the original price was too low O'Flaherty knows he can re-sell the MS for more. Presumably Hill in the end kept the incomplete MS. (Source McMU) SIUL have a previous letter dated 13 January, 1926, to Arthur Roberts in which O'Flaherty first, but at greater length, mentions this matter.

---

188. NLD TLS to P.H. Muir
Hazelbrook, Kimmage Road, Terenure   13 January, 1927

Dear Muir,

Very sorry but I have been very very busy and still am. If the manuscript is unsatisfactory, I shall be delighted to return you the sum I received for it. If, on the other hand, you wish me to rewrite the missing portion, I shall try to do so at the earliest convenience, if you tell me what is missing. I was certainly under the impression that there was nothing missing. In fact, I thought there was a duplicate of quite a large part of the copy. However, let me know and I'll meet your request, whichever you prefer. I'm fearfully hard pressed with the *Humanist* copy, as I got behindhand at Xmas and I want to get it off my stocks as soon as possible.

Hoping life is progressing favourably? I hope to get to London for the match, but at this rate it's becoming doubtful. Further a gunman out of *Gilhooley* is visiting the public houses with a revolver with which he claims he is going to murder me in cold blood. Additional busy-ness!

Yours very sincerely
Liam O'Flaherty

---

189. SLUL (Folio V 36) TLS to Charles Lahr
Hazelbrook, Kimmage Road, Terenure   17 January, 1927

Dear Lahr,

I got your letter, your money and I sent on the sheets signed. For all of which, O Lord I thank Thee. I also received Davies' book for which I thank you both very much.[1] I have not had time to read it yet, but I'll write Davies a note when I do. My wife is reading the stories and likes them very much. I am frightfully busy with this depressing thing in the *Humanist* I have half done.

Good luck,

Yours, Liam O' Flaherty

[1] Rhys Davies, *The Song of Songs and other stories*, London: E. Archer, 1927 (a hundred copies).

---

190. HRHRC ALS to Edward Garnett
Hazelbrook, Kimmage Road, Terenure   17 January, 1927

My Dearest Friend,

I am sending you the booklets produced by Archer under separate cover.

Forgive the delay in writing. I am suffering from my winter apathy and I am writing the unfortunate serial for the *Humanist*. I don't think it's much good, except as 'pretty' prose and I am afraid that my wife has the same opinion of it, so I'm not sending it to you until it's finished; then we can argue about printing it. I don't think I'll try a serial again on the instalment system, and I'm also afraid that I'll lose a type by this. But that does not matter. Winter is always barren, so it's good winter quarters' exercise. I have now three thousand words done.

My dear friend, I am again in danger in two ways. I am in danger of becoming popular in Dublin society (major danger), and there is a gunman after me. The gunman is ex-Captain Gleeson and he claims to be Hanrahan from *Mr Gilhooley*. I don't think he's very dangerous except to the extent of terrifying my wife, but if I have to wing him I might be inconvenienced considerably. The other danger is much more pressing, as I find myself gradually surrounded by a stream of useless people. But of course I'll get away from them in Spring.

I showed the MS of *The Life of Tim Healy* to a friend, who is chief of the I.R.A. and strangely enough he was delighted with it and guaranteed that if it were suppressed his whole organisation would assist in smuggling it into the country. Another strange character who had just returned from France and Spain after taking part in the Catalonian conspiracy, also read it, and was very flattering about it. This man, Commandant O' –, has about thirty wounds in his body and was a leader in the civil war on the republican side, yet he is an enthusiastic admirer of Tchekov, Turgenev and Strindberg and talked to me about them for a few hours. He is now studying medicine, trying to introduce books into the Irish countryside and, as far as I can gather, preparing for another revolution. Yes, sir, we have Elizabethan conditions, even though we haven't got any Shakespeare. Anyhow, *Tim Healy* seems likely to go. A republican officer said to me after reading the MS: 'Well you know, I rather like the old boy now after reading the book. I sincerely admire the man's courage, and it's written in a very fair spirit. But don't you think the English will be wild?' 'Oh, no,' I said, 'On the contrary, my English friends were afraid that the Irish would be wild.' 'Oh well,' he said with a shrug, 'The mob always howls. There is nothing for the mob in any country but stern suppression.' So that in this world nothing is certain.

I attended a very extraordinary gathering a few nights ago. Captain White gave a ball at a ruined mansion near Rathfarnham on the mountain-side. He invited the country people from the neighbourhood and about a hundred of his friends from town. There were lousy tramps and very important government officials, intellectuals, bourgeoisie, peasants, servants, etc., all together. White himself having forbidden his guests to come in evening clothes, appeared immaculately dressed, swallow-tailed and, I believe, perfumed. Then, in the middle of the whole thing, he made a speech, the counterpart of which you might find in Dostoievsky's *Possessed* at the governor's ball. The wind howled, there was snow and motor cars broke down. I never saw anything like it. He himself, you know, is a landowner, so that giving a ball in a deserted mansion was rather interesting.

Opinion is very divided about my last book, but many like it much better than *The Informer*. I don't see Cape producing that second edition after getting me to bowdlerise the book.

Pegeen is getting on splendidly and Charley[1] is now learning shorthand and typewriting. Topsy goes to the Cabaret on Saturdays and is enjoying herself immensely. I myself am solaced by Rugby football and a concertina. I believe my brother is appearing here again soon from some quarter of the globe, so I am thinking of leaving here for some quarter of the globe.

I am anxious to see David's book, it should be out now shouldn't it?

Topsy sends you and Miss Heath her love and I am sure the noises Pegeen makes mean something to the same effect, but we cannot yet decode her messages.

I hope they don't start another beastly war over China. Last night I saw a very fine actor in *Emperor Jones* [Eugene O'Neil] at the Abbey, a man called Rutherford Mayne. He was really superb and got a tremendous ovation. The play itself I thought rather disappointing and a trifle melodramatic, though very powerful.

Yours

Liam

[1] O'Flaherty's name for his wife's sister.

---

191. HRHRC TLS to A.D. Peters
Hazelbrook, Kimmage Road, Terenure   26 January, 1927

Dear Peters,

Please note that the above is my new address.

I think that's a jolly good offer for the second serial rights of *The Tent* and you certainly should close with it. The second serial rights have not been sold in any of the stories and none of them are on offer – in fact I have never heard of such things as second serial rights in a book of short stories. Thanks very much.[1]

I am just writing the novel for the *Humanist* by instalments and won't have it finished until the end of next month. If you think there is a possibility of placing it serially in America I'll send it along when finished, or if you like I'll send you all I've done? Though I'm doubtful about its serialisation value over there.

I haven't written a single story since. When I've finished this novel business I'm going to write some and send them along. I have a few to write but I have to keep writing this thing from week to week and I never get time to do them. However, I think there is no great hurry, as whatever hope I have of a market will come in about three months when *Tim Healy* appears. Have you tried *Vogue* with that sketch 'The Invitation'?

With best wishes from
Liam O'Flaherty

[1] The second serial rights offer was from the editor of *The Golden Book*, two hundred dollars for the right to select stories from *The Tent*, probably three or four stories, payment twenty dollars per thousand words and if the total comes to more than two hundred dollars the editor will pay the balance. (Source: A.D. Peters files at HRHRC)

---

192. HRHRC ALS to Edward Garnett
Hazelbrook, Kimmage Road, Terenure   22 February, 1927

My Dearest Friend,

I am awfully sorry I was unable to see you when in London, especially as I heard from Nelly that you had been ill. Under the circumstances I felt it inadvisable, in the interests of my family, to get rid of a previous engagement with Devine. Like every Irishman of his class and generation, he is very touchy on the matter of his dignity, (he's marked down). A most exalted number of personages attached themselves to us in the course of the evening in Fleet St. There is room for another Shakespeare in that street, or rather, since the interesting ones are Irish and Scotch, an Irish writer might feast royally there with a novel called 'In Exile' or 'The Exiles', or some such title.

I was greatly cheered by your letter and your present to Pegeen was a most charming one. She has chewed two of the dolls but we are saving 'Karamarov and the Bear' until she is able to appreciate them more.

I am coming near the end of my serial. Soon I'll send it along to see can we make anything of it for the press. I have my doubts and I'm afraid my wife thinks the {?} is not altogether happy, but I'm not oppressed by the prospect of failure as I have very interesting pieces ready for work. These are 'Barbara Hynes' and our old friend General Michael Rathcroghan, who is nearing birth under the title of *The Parasite*. I have a whole army of types and characters and incidents under mobilisation orders on these two fronts. I think I'll tackle Barbara first, as she suffered an abortive birth in *The Firebrand*. I think that should be fairly good. I made a bad mistake in the first attempt and I am very grateful to you for having arrested it. Hynes himself should have been the pivot, as the representative good type, whereas the character formerly known as Michael Joyce should be robbed of his mysticism. I have disembowelled the idea of mysticism in the thing I'm doing now, so I think I'm fairly safe.

Miss Heath told me you didn't like [David Garnett's] *Go She Must*. We, on the contrary, liked it immensely. The beginning and end were I think masterly, and evoked unbounded artistic enthusiasm in me – especially the delineation of the parson's character, most subtle and delicate. However, I would have centred the story around the parson and pursued him relentlessly to the death. I didn't think the girl was worthy of a central place as her type is rather too universal. That parson is fundamentally English. I saw one in every village I was in. I like them. Recently I read a natural history book by one of them that lived in the eighteenth century, a chap called [Gilbert] White – very good indeed.

Talking of natural history, I am becoming more and more enamoured of [W.H.] Hudson. What beauty of expression. He has just that curiously indefinable method of approach to a situation which is the true and necessary quality of the highest art. It seems that each word is made to be reflected in clear ice. I take him up at random and read any time during the day. It is as refreshing as the smell of wild heather or watching a slow old man cut virgin soil in Spring. What pleasure you must get from the work, having been a personal friend of his. As a rule I am a poor reader, but there are some writers – hell! I must be becoming an Anglo-Saxon, or an old man. Do you remember the character in Tchekov whose ideas were undergoing a change?

I am afraid that Cape are getting more and more nervous about *Tim Healy*. It's a pity if they don't print it, but possibly a libel action might do them serious injury. I'm not very interested financially in the English edition, still, it would be amusing to see it in print. However, when Cape returns he may be more courageous than Wren Howard.

People are starting a number of little theatres here in Dublin now, but there seem to be more little theatres than little dramatists. I fancy drama should appear before a theatre to house it. Still, the activity is a good sign. Wives of new bourgeois ministers, officials, etc., are very eager to become leaders of culture, and it's very amusing. Man here last night trying to get some money for his theatre. He is a Quaker – started the Irish Volunteers and nearly got shot for treason later by the I.R.A. – curious character. Now he'll probably get shot by order of the Inquisition.[1] It's a very curious community this. A schoolmate was also in last night, a sort of dilettante solicitor. His grandfather was a parson and now his family is one of the leading Dublin Catholic families. This fellow was telling me that our Minister of Education, who started the evil literature campaign, and is the chief leader of the Catholic Truth Society, is a confirmed agnostic and cynic. He eats one pound of beef per day and privately ridicules God, the Pope, himself, Ireland and his wife's uncomfortable virtue. I have him marked down.

My brother's wife was over here from the U.S. She tells me that my brother is coming over again this Spring, so I fancy that I had better clear out somewhere. I am afraid all my relatives still look askance at me.

I may come over in May to broadcast. They wanted me to broadcast in Belfast but I refused to set foot in that filthy boorish town. Then I refused to broadcast anywhere. My wife insists that it would be a good advertisement. So I may have to go for Pegeen's sake, or for the sake of my creditors.

I believe *Jew Suss* is a fine book. I am having a copy sent me. Have you read it? I got *The Shooting Party* but I thought it was not entirely up to scratch. When is the Lawrence book coming out?[2] Nothing at all is being written here as far as I can see. People are only interested in the theatre, frivolous wretches.

Well, good luck and good health.

Love from all, Liam

P.S. Tell Bates to send a story to the *Humanist*. The proprietor is interested in his work. As the proprietor is a millionaire it might be useful. They might use his new novel as a serial. Tell him not to forget to call on Devine, the editor, at his office and mention me. Don't forget. Liam.

[1] Probably Bulmer Hobson.

[2] Leon Feuchtwanger, *Jew Süss* (trans. Willa & Edwin Muir), London: Secker, 1926. A. Chekov, *The Shooting Party* (trans. A.E. Chamot), London: Stanley Paul, 1926. Lawrence's novel was *Lady Chatterley's Lover*, to be published privately in Florence, 1928.

---

193. HRHRC TLS to A.D. Peters
Hazelbrook, Kimmage Road, Terenure 26 February, 1927

Dear Peters,

All right then, I'll write a bawdy story for the *New Decameron*, it will be called 'The Sinners'. I'll send it along within the week.

Did you get copies of the *Humanist* that were sent to you containing some of the serial? I expect you got them but that your opinion of the story is about the same as my own, and you preferred to say nothing.

Cheerio.

Yours sincerely, Liam O'Flaherty

P.S. Cape's secretary sent me a note re. some Colonial paper that wanted second serial rights of some story. I told her to write you. Would you fix it up, and collect the money. L.O'F.

---

194. NLD (MS 26,743) ALS to P.H. Muir
Hazelbrook, Kimmage Road, Terenure 1 March, 1927

Dear Muir,

Thanks for the cheque which I promptly lost at Baldoyle on exceptionally poor horses. Not all, but most of it. It's exciting your moving to Bond St. – congratulations, sounds big anyway.

Sorry your client got an apopleptic fit over the price of *The Wilderness*, I hope he recovers. Anyway one always gets three strokes before death. Let's have another – tell him I want a hundred and fifty pounds for it now as I have changed my mind. Third stroke ... tell him I have almost closed with an offer of ninety pounds.

Don't know when I come to London again, possibly never.

With best wishes,

Yours sincerely
Liam O'Flaherty

---

195. NLD (MS 26,743) TLS to P.H. Muir
Hazelbrook, Kimmage Road, Terenure   7 March, 1927

Dear Muir,

Enclosed you will find the two MSS 'The Mountain Tavern' and 'The Sinner'. They are real manuscripts so I will await cheque for fifteen jimmies with equanimity. Do read 'The Sinner' and tell me what you think of it.

About *The Wilderness*, hadn't your client better wait till I have finished it? I want a big price for this MS as I expect it to arouse considerable interest on the question of divine blasphemy and the end of it conceals the pea. Also, it will be a trifle prettier than my other manuscripts. At the moment I think one hundred and twenty-five pounds is my price. Does your client want an offer of it at that price? If so I am willing to let him have the instalments so far finished as a security. I have fifty thousand words finished.

I am having a great success in Russia and wonderful to relate they are going to pay me for my books. What do you think of that? I can soon pay for Guinness with good roubles!

Cheerio,

Yours sincerely
Liam O'Flaherty

---

196. To the Editor of the *Irish Statesman*[1]

19 March, 1927

Dear Sir,

Allow me to protest against the speech made the other day in the Free State Senate by Dr. Oliver St. John Gogarty. He referred to the West of Ireland as decadent. The West of Ireland is very poor, but not decadent. Its poverty largely results from the facilities with which the English conquerors of this country were able to induce the inhabitants of the Pale to accept bribes and positions of importance. Invariably these placemen referred to their less amenable or less lucky fellow-countrymen as decadent or aboriginal.

I am not quite sure, but I am almost positive that not one single character in *Ulysses* comes from the West of Ireland.

Yours faithfully
Liam O'Flaherty

1 Published Vol. 8, No. 2, p.37, under the heading 'The Gaeltacht'.

---

197. NLD (MS 26,743) TLS to P.H. Muir
Hazelbrook, Kimmage Road, Terenure   24 March, 1927

Dear Muir,

Michael Davitt began life as a factory hand somewhere in Lancashire. He lost his arm in an accident, became a Fenian and a dynamiter and was sent to jail for a long term. After his release he organised the Land League in Ireland and became associated with Parnell. He was the principal figure, next to Parnell, in Irish politics during the Parnellite period. He had extreme views on social questions and was an ardent supporter of Land Nationalisation. He went into the English parliament as an Irish nationalist. He went on a visit to Russia, in order, I believe, to study the movement there. On the occasion of the Parnellite split he opposed Parnell. That seems to have finished him, as he never attained any prominence afterwards until his death.

I take it that Moore was not quite right in claiming him to be the most courageous man in Ireland. He was a type a little similar to James Larkin, an undoubtedly sincere man, a great public orator, but not gifted with a great degree of political intelligence. He was a peasant and a Catholic.

There is a life of Michael Davitt called *Chief and Tribune.*[1] I don't remember the author but if I remember to ask MacManus I'll tell you. However, this little note might be sufficient.

Thanks very much for your interest in *The Wilderness*. I'll hold on to it until I hear that you cannot effect a sale. It's nearly finished now. It's a very extraordinary book and I'm afraid that the *Humanist* is going to baulk at the end of it.

Yours ever
Liam O'Flaherty

P.S. In the private records of the British Secret Service Davitt is blue pencilled during that period as the most dangerous conspirator in Ireland. Davitt came from the same county as George Moore – County Mayo. L.O'F.

[1] M.M. O'Hara, *Chief & Tribune: Parnell & Davitt*, Dublin & London, 1919.

---

198. SLUL (Folio V 35) ALS to Charles Lahr
Hazelbrook, Kimmage Road, Terenure   n.d. [? late March, 1927]

Dear Lahr,

Sorry for not having answered your last letter and acknowledged receipt
of magazines. I was trying to finish my book and have not written any letters
for a fortnight. Having finished it I now write.

Congratulations on the birth of your daughter. May she never bring
disgrace on the family, as they say in Ireland. You have chosen a pretty
name, especially as she has black hair and blue eyes.[1] I hope your wife is
very well? Please give her our compliments.

Thanks very much for sending me the Bates booklet. It's very good. I
hope he gets that novel of his serialised with Devine. It would put some
money in his pockets and do him a little good in the matter of publicity.

I think that number of the magazine was very good excepting a few of
the short stories, including my own in this latter category. The Salkeld oil
came out rather badly.[2] It's a fine picture that.

I'll be in London for the B.B.C. on April 30th or so, so I'll drop into the
shop. Cheerio, best love to everybody and to the little girl in particular.

                                                              Yours
                                                              L.O'F

[1] Lahr's daughter was named Oonagh. the *New Coterie*, No. 5, Spring 1927, contained
O'Flaherty's story 'The Child of God' and a reproduction of Cecil Salkeld's painting 'The
Builders'.

---

199. HRHRC TLS to Herbert Devine
Hazelbrook, Kimmage Road, Terenure   25 March, 1927

Dear Devine,

I enclose the second last instalment of *The Wilderness*. I'll send the
concluding instalment along shortly. The last instalment will be something
in the neighbourhood of fifteen thousand words. As I am not certain of the
length I'll send it along in plenty of time so that you won't be put out about
space. I trust you will find it satisfactory.

I think they forgot in the office to send along the cheque for this month.
You might remind them.

I hope you are keeping fit and prosperous? I'm feeling very well myself
but I'm getting a trifle tired, so I'm going on a holiday when I have finished
with *The Wilderness*.

Did you have any luck on the Lincoln and National? Best regards to
everybody.[1]

                                                              Yours ever
                                                              Liam

[1]HRHRC has an ALS note headed 'Prey' by Liam O'Flaherty.
I herewith give this manuscript to Topsy, in consideration of four pounds sterling given to me by her for the purpose of gambling on race horses at Naas. Signed: Liam O'Flaherty, Hazelbrook, Kimmage Road, Terenure, March 26th, 1927. P.S. One fourth of this sum to be put on 'Easy Virtue' in my own interest, one fourth on 'Take Notice' in her interest. Damnation to the bookmakers. L.O'F.

---

200. HRHRC ALS to A.D. Peters
[no address]   n.d. [April, 1927]

Dear Peters,

Get in tough with this chap.[1] This is a good thing I believe, if you land it. I'm going to write a novel, beginning next August about racing. It'll be very popular stuff and good I think, title *They're Off*, dealing with betting, horses, etc., all on the race course, booking offices, etc. You might keep it in mind and if any chance for serialising it occurs in the meantime you might mention it. I have written a note to Hamilton today mentioning the fact, so if you meet or talk over the 'phone you might bring the matter up.

Yours sincerely
Liam O'Flaherty

[1] A note written at the foot of a letter dated 4 April, 1927, to O'Flaherty from James Hamilton, in charge of *Harper's Magazine* London Office who had in the past met O'Flaherty at Jonathan Cape's. Hamilton says T.B. Wells, New York editor of the magazine, expressed great interest in O'Flaherty's short stories. Garnett has now suggested that Hamilton should write and ask for stories from four to six thousand words long or so. Will he keep them in mind for the future, if he has no stories available now.

---

201. HRHRC ALS to A.D. Peters
Hazelbrook, Kimmage Road, Terenure   7 May, 1927

Dear Peters,

I think it is better to let the editor of *Georgian Stories* pick out anything he likes from anything I have published, as I have nothing else at present.

I called to see you when I was in London but you happened to be out.

I have not yet decided whether I am going to publish my novel *The Wilderness*, so I can't make any arrangements about it. In any case it requires a good deal of re-writing before it would be fit for publication.

Yours very sincerely
Liam O'Flaherty

---

202. NWUL ALS to Edward Garnett
Hazelbrook, Kimmage Road, Terenure   9 May, 1927

My Dearest Friend,[1]

That man O'Donnell is sending along his MS. I gave him a note for you to include with it, so you'll recognise it as the one I told you about. There may be some meat in it.[2]

I have not got hold of the complete print of *The Wilderness* yet, when I do I'll send it to you. I don't know whether Cape would want to print it in the Autumn or not. He's bringing out the *Healy* book on June 8th or so, so everything is fixed up at last.

I'm still loafing. The weather is beautiful here and I continually remind myself of Turgenev's saying that leisure is the goal of an artist's ambition. Warding off hunger with a handful of coppers. The only drawback in life now is our presence in the city away from the complete solitude of our glen. I'm tired of seeing faces and hearing voices and whenever Spring comes it becomes so apparent to me that no life is worth a candle but one of constant wandering – like a tramp.

Yesterday we went to the mountains to visit a friend who has had a new baby. Her husband, the painter Keating, told me a funny story about one of the Aran Islands he had visited. It is the most primitive of them. He said there were two botanists there at the time and an islander said of them: 'They're very queer people. The women, she has a big knife with her all the time. Only for that, we'd follow them among the rocks and take their money off them.' Keating thought that this proved the complete savagery of the islanders, but the fool should have known that the islander was merely playing in his mind with the idea of robbing these people among the rocks and then fleeing from justice over the ocean in his curragh. A playboy in fact who would never kill his father but would always boast of having done so. Keating is, of course, a fool and a Roman Catholic. I remember a native of that island – they are all amusing scoundrels – telling me how they made fun of him.

I have been reading T.E. Lawrence with great interest and pleasure. While I don't think he is anywhere near [C.M.] Doughty, he is undoubtedly very big. He could go in with the Elizabethans as a man of action and with {?} as a writer. A curious train of thought is aroused by the appearance of this type in the English social organism. It seems to be both a sign of the further growth of this vast organism and also a sympton of its decay. Perhaps if the artistic impulse in Lawrence had been more nicely balanced by his ambitions as a soldier he would have made himself the master of the Empire. Undoubtedly some other Lawrence will in the near future – I wonder? A splendid fellow and a thorough gentleman who despises inferior types without being a snob in any sense. It's a pity the type is not sufficiently prevalent to form a ruling class. But their individual vanity would preclude any lengthy cohesion. You remember the role of Coriolanus in early Rome and in a lesser sense, very remote of course – oh damn, I forget the Greek's name – the man {who himself was a lover?} with Socrates at the banquet. Lawrence is like both of them. What a beautiful beast is man. Like a choice flower he grows in a myriad shapes and each perfect form gives pleasure to the discerning eye.

I was very interested in the subsidiary characters, especially the Irish generals and admirals. The choleric redheaded man is wonderful.[3]

My books are now going to be translated into Japanese by a professor in the university of {Yamakota [sic]} or some such place. They are already translating it into Russian so I am becoming a person of some little consequence, though of very little wealth.

I am sorry we are not going to have the pleasure of seeing you here this Summer.

Oh! I met a most charming young Russian emigré woman yesterday. An English officer helped her to escape from the Crimea. She married him and they live here. The officer is of middle age, a nice fellow but a trifle dull. She is just like the lady who ate the radish and got ill in Tchekov's story – a rather pert kitten.

Well, well! When am I going to write something again? The mountain brooks sing sweetly now and in the evening it is pleasant to watch tourists {?} from the mountains, but the {magic?} of nature has no voice for me.

With best love from us all to you and to Nellie.

Liam

[1] This letter is an example of O'Flaherty's smallest handwriting, and is hard to decipher.

[2] Peadar O'Donnell, whose first novel *Islanders* was published by Cape in 1928 with an introduction by Robert Lynd.

[3] T.E. Lawrence, *Seven Pillars of Wisdom* was privately printed in 1926, published for general circulation by Cape in 1935.

---

203. NLW ALS to Jonathan Cape
Hazelbrook, Kimmage Road, Terenure   19 May 1927

Dear Cape,

If you have done nothing yet about the German translation of *The Informer* I wish you'd let Frau Sternemann do it, she is a very good translator and places a number of my short stories in German magazines.[1] You see, if we could get the book on the market there it might have a chance of getting filmed.

Yours sincerely
Liam O'Flaherty

[1] Heinrich Hauser did this translation.

---

204. HRHRC TLS to Charles Lahr
Hazelbrook, Kimmage Road, Terenure   23 May, 1927

This is an S.O.S. We have an overdraft on the bank and no money so I am sending along the MS of *The Wilderness*. See can you sell it at any price, it does not matter what provided it's money.

Yours in haste
Liam O'Flaherty

---

205. HRHRC TLS to A.D. Peters
Hazelbrook, Kimmage Road, Terenure   23 May, 1927

Dear Peters,

Thanks for your two letters. Yes, I should accept the *Criterion*'s offer.[1] I don't think there will be any difficulty about getting the two stories placed in America at any time, as they have often published for me there after publication in England. I am returning the proofs of 'Prey'.

I am going to begin my novel and will send along the first chapters when I have written them. The *Healy* book is coming out next week and if it makes the stir which I expect there may be a good market in America for stuff shortly.[2]

Thanking you for your work on my behalf,

Yours very sincerely
Liam O'Flaherty

[1] This was for *Monthly Criterion* to publish 'The Mountain Tavern' in August, 1927, for two guineas per thousand words. *Outlook* had accepted 'Prey'.

[2] The MS of *The Life of Tim Healy* is at HRHRC. The book was dedicated to 'My fellow-worker M.J. McManus.' O'Flaherty lists twenty-two books he consulted (ten of which are about Parnell), including T.M. Healy's *Why Ireland is not Free*.

---

206. NWUL ALS to Edward Garnett
Hazelbrook, Kimmage Road, Terenure   30 May, 1927

My Dearest Friend,

I was delighted to get your enthusiastic note about Peadar O'Donnell's book *Islanders*, now I feel sure that it is all right. I have not been able to get in touch with him yet, as he had to go to Donegal on Saturday morning about the case of some peasant that beat a bailiff, or something like that. But he is coming back tomorrow and you can picture how delighted he will be. The publication of the book can't be so much to him as your praise, as they all regard you as the only Englishmen (?) whose opinion is worth while.

About the introduction, I wonder would AE be suitable? He has been out of touch so long with things in general and the younger generation that

I'm afraid he would not do. He is also very prejudiced against republicans, of whom O'Donnell is the principal intellectual leader. If we could get you to do the introduction it would be different. You have a big reputation here and nobody is prejudiced against you. Anyhow, *nous verrons*. The book will undoubtedly have a big sale in Ireland, at least two thousand. Tell Cape that, the chap has already published a poorish novel which sold fifteen hundred copies here.[1] The Talbot Press wanted to print *Islanders* but they are outrageously vulgar people and they must not get a work of art.

Last week I met your brother here. He is very like you but I missed the fire in the eye. He was going on a tour, I believe down to his mother's country.[2] I suppose you are getting ready for Wales now? I intend going to Aran for a few days to see my father, then perhaps Topsy and I may go for a holiday somewhere. I am unable to do any work owing to the Healy book coming out. I hope it will be all right. There is a prospect of a big sale here, but I remember what Mahaffy said. Cape is advertising it well.

Nothing interesting is happening in this country, except that a swarm of bees have settled in a lion's mouth over our door. They are making honey there. 'Out of the strong, etc.'

Pegeen is able to stand up now and is showing signs of great character. She is a very amusing baby, just like her Mother. Topsy is very well but is terribly afraid of getting too fat. Owing to Pegeen we are not able to roam around so much. I expect we'll have to play tennis or some such nonsense.

Most honourable father in literature, I am reading nothing, neither is Topsy. It's becoming dreadful. What is going to become of us? We have both become equally wise and equally barbarous. I have attained her level of wisdom, and she my level of barbarism. Now we are both equally stupid, but neither has any {nerves?} so there is a recompense. Charley is going strong.

Dublin is crawling back to its old life prior to the revolution, so it seems there is going to be another revolution perhaps in fifteen years time. The young republicans are talking of stamping out the illiterate barbarism of their predecessors by making each battalion area a cultural cell instead of a centre of active operation. Talk, talk, says you, but intelligent and well-meaning talk is better than apathy or fanaticism of an efficient kind. At the moment there is a beastly election on. I have been lucky so far in not having seen a single election meeting.

I hope you and Miss Heath are going to have a glorious holiday in Wales and that it does not rain while you are there, and that you come back living furiously. Hoping to see you soon again, with love from all of us,

Yours, Liam

[1] *Storm*, Dublin: Talbot 1925.

[2] Edward Garnett (b.1868) had two brothers, Robert (b.1866) and Arthur (b.1881). His mother was from Ireland.

207. HRHRC ALS to Charles Lahr
Hazelbrook, Kimmage Road, Terenure   30 May, 1927

Dear Lahr,

Thanks very much for your expedition in disposing of the MS and the cheque. Just saved my bacon. As you prefer it I will send along a MS for yourself. I am delighted to hear your daughter and wife are getting along well. The baby is now over the worst part of her life.

My Healy book will be published here on Wednesday next and in London on June 9th. I am expecting a splash but it may fizzle out, I don't know. It all depends on how people take it. It's more or less Communist and anti-Imperialist, so they may all rise in a body against it.[1]

I am afraid Bates dallied too much with the *Humanist*, he probably will miss it now. It's unfortunate as the ready money could have helped him. Money, money, would it be Christ who invented it?

I have written nothing since I saw you last and it seems I never will again. Bloody awful, hanging around doing nothing. If this lasts much longer I'll be out in the streets again organising a revolution. Writing is the only outlet for my energies.

With best love from both of us,

Yours
Liam O'F

[1] NLD T.M. Healy papers MS 23,275 is a letter from T.M. Healy to Max Beaverbrook, dated 19 April, 1927, in which Healy says: ... I send you the advertisement of which I told you of my 'Life' by some O'Flaherty, dated 19 March, 1927, by Jonathan Cape in *John O'London's Weekly* price twelve shillings and six pence. I am cheered to think the fools believe that anyone would give twelve and six for a book about me, by a man I had never heard of, but from enquiries I have made it may entitle me to place myself in a posture of defence, by a genuine narration .... I offer no opinion as to whether this O'Flaherty is sufficiently malodorous, such obstacles should be regarded as overcome.'

---

208. HRHRC ALS to Edward Garnett
Hazelbrook, Kimmage Road, Terenure   7 June, 1927

My Dearest Friend,

Tell me what you think of 'The Mountain Tavern'? I am sending also a little sketch called 'Prey' of which I am fond. I think the Tavern is good, though the end is a trifle abrupt. I would be thankful for some criticism.

Hope you are enjoying your holiday? I am still as dry as a stripper cow. Topsy and Pegeen are grand,[1 & 2]

Yours
Liam

[1] 14 June, 1927, Topsy wrote to Garnett during O'Flaherty's absence in Aran, where he went

for six days. She writes: 'He is very gloomy at present and says that he's completely tired and stale, so I hope his trip to Aran will do him good. Then, if I can get any money together I'm taking him up to Co. Donegal where he never was, and where I come from. We are thinking of going to Aranmore Island off Burtonport, where it is quiet and there are fewer enthusiasts learning the Irish language.' She reminds Garnett that Peadar O'Donnell was schoolmaster there, 'I'm sure you would love Peadar O'Donnell. He is a beautiful, gentle creature, who talks ferociously – a regular Donegal man, small and thin, though he's smaller than most of them.' The Russian translation of *The Informer* has just arrived. (Source HRHRC)

[2] Topsy also wrote an undated letter to P.H. Muir during O'Flaherty's absence to say how delighted they would be if he came over. She recommends two small hotels as there is no room in their flat. (Source NLD MS 26,743)

---

209. HRHRC ALS to Edward Garnett
Hazelbrook, Kimmage Road, Terenure   17 June 1927

My Dearest Friend,

Thanks awfully for your letter. I am glad you liked the sketches and that you preferred 'Prey' to the other one, because I feel that 'what is good in itself', should be better than what is good largely by artifice, i.e. as a result of applied intelligence, what is commonly and erroneously regarded as the true expression of art. The harder the rock the longer it lasts. The more primitive the stock the longer it takes to become over-refined by civilisation, and conscious art is always over-refined. The modern short story or sketch seems to have become a poem, and where ideas and images attain lordship over poetry it ceases to be elemental and universal. I think a child would like 'Prey', but not 'The Mountain Tavern'.

I am still very empty and melancholy. It seems that I am never going to write again, or see any happiness in the world. I went down to the Aran Islands for a few days and I was gloriously alive for three days, alone by the sea, fishing rockfish. Then I came here again and I am again so melancholy as before. I don't read, I don't think joyously or even with bitter strength. There is nothing. It's extraordinary. Have I written too much and become stale? I'm not ill, neither do I feel fit. I feel like a tired stockbroker, without his money-complacency.

Cape has accepted O'Donnell's book and it's going to be published next Autumn. It was very good of you to get Cape to publish it. I hope it gets a good reception, and I think it will.

My own book seems to have been a failure, but that does not matter very much as the results of its success, financially, would not materialise for a year or so. It seems that the only country that regards my work favourably is Russia, and Russia is very poor. I may go to live there later on.

It was splendid in Aran. The island has the character and personality of a mute God. One is awed in its presence, breathing its air. Over it broods an overwhelming sense of great, noble tragedy. The Greeks would have liked it. The people are sadly inferior to the island itself. But the sea birds are almost worthy of it. The great cormorants thrilled me. And while fishing on the brink of a rock, a great bull seal rose from the sea in front of me. He looked at me with brutal, drunken eyes and then dived. Father says they have nests there in caves.

When I was going away an unshaved publican came down to the pier and, boarding the steamer, kissed my hand and asked me to write a story about him and his public house, even though I gave him 'a cutting up'.

A schoolmaster there has built an enormous wall around his school and in the yard he has planted various trees. I saw him there {?} in the moonlight. A man of ideas, or a madman, or both. The mute God collects his dues from them all. I saw many things there and yet I am mute and queer.

Give my love to Miss Heath. Topsy and Pegeen are well. We may go away somewhere soon, perhaps to Connemara.

With love from
Liam

---

210. NLW ALS to Jonathan Cape
Hazelbrook, Kimmage Road, Terenure   21 June, 1927

Dear Cape,

Thanks for your letter and the enclosed press-cuttings. I read Ervine's review. Could anything be done with it? It's a pity he did not review the book in some less remote paper than *Time and Tide*. How is the book selling? Or is it selling at all? On the whole I think the reviews were not bad. It certainly got plenty of notice. I am afraid the price is too big in Ireland and AE let me down badly.[1]

I am glad you are publishing O'Donnell's book. He is the coming man in this country. But don't get AE to write the preface, that would ruin him in Ireland. Why not get Lynd? O'Donnell will sell between two thousand and three thousand copies here at five shillings. If Lynd introduces it you might very well sell another thousand copies in England – possibly. I think you will be quite safe in gambling on O'Donnell's future. He is the very best of them here. He is very popular nationally and he has got plenty in him. His experience sounds like a Buffalo Bill serial. He has another novel well on the way, and from what I have read of it it's far more promising than *Islanders*.

Yours
Liam O'Flaherty

[1] The book review of *The Life of Tim Healy* was printed in the *Irish Statesman* of 4 June, 1927, pp. 310, 312. The reviewer finds O'Flaherty a novelist of genius 'with that strange power

of giving birth to characters which belongs to the storyteller', but doubts whether he has the talent or patience to be a biographer for O'Flaherty lacks the analytic mind. 'I think he began the life in a harum-scarum mood, intending to make all kinds of reckless observations about his subject, about Irish society and politics, and after a while he dropped that impish mentality becoming almost seriously interested in Irish politics.' The book contains no viciousness about the Governor-General, but does not do the subject justice, for none of Healy's oratory is quoted. 'If Liam O'Flaherty had allowed the artist in himself to dominate he would have found out and exhibited that core of genius in the man he writes about,' The reviewer thinks O'Flaherty is too young, too absorbed with his own generation. He wishes O'Flaherty had written a novel about Healy with facts invented but the character retained. 'Of course the book is readable. No young man of ability can write a reckless volume, hitting out at established powers without interesting us,' but he should stick to his fiction.

---

211. HRHRC ALS to Edward Garnett
Hazelbrook, Kimmage Road, Terenure   23 June, 1927

My Dearest Friend,

Just got your letter and enclosed letter – which I return. Damn it, you have had the advantage over me, in so far as you have been able to get drunk. When I feel melancholy I can't drink. Then some instinct within me compels me to refrain from every bodily or mental activity that is not absolutely necessary. I eat, I sleep, I sit and wait, like a wounded animal.

I read the letters from the man with the crude name. However, if I had the means of transporting my family at the moment, nothing would prevent me from going to the ends of the earth. In America I intend, if I get there, to become a journalist, a political scoundrel, a sharper of the worst kind, and an utterly unscrupulous individual. The failure of Irish literature in the U.S. is a tribute to us.

I am sending you a Russian translation of *The Informer* as a curiosity. I imagine it is a curiosity.

I hope you get O'Donnell's book published in U.S. That man Huebsch is a fool. O'Donnell will sell in the U.S. He has an organisation behind him there. He is a sort of hero at the moment and heroes sell like patent medecine.

I think we are going away somewhere shortly into the country. Well, drink another bottle of Chablis to me and let us curse the world. Shortly I may begin to write again.

With love from all
Liam

(Later) Topsy and I have decided that it is best to emigrate to the United States. That may mean the end of me as an artist – indeed it probably will. However, we are going when we get our fares. There is no hope here, and

the strongest man may break his skull dashing it against an iron wall. I have
a sufficiency of contradiction in my nature to fight any influence and
perhaps I may survive America, though it's very doubtful. Now France
would be better but France is as bad as here.

Well anyway – my love to you both,

Yours, Liam

---

212. HRHRC ALS to Charles Lahr

Hazelbrook, Kimmage Road, Terenure   23 June, 1927

Dear Lahr,

Sorry not to have acknowledged your letter and receipt of cheque, but I
have been down to the Aran Islands until a day or two ago and since then
I am feeling ill. The world in general is treating me badly and I am rather
fed up. I have a notebook which I want to send to you as a souvenir, when
I summon up the energy to mail it.

How are you getting on – wife and family? I am writing nothing.

With best wishes,

Yours
Liam O'Flaherty

---

213. SLUL (Folio V 36) ALS to Charles Lahr

c/o Mrs Boyle, Glen House, Arranmore, Burtonport, Co. Donegal
n.d. (early July, 1927)

Dear Lahr,

My agent A.D. Peters, 20-21 Essex St., Strand, has a story called 'The
Sinner'. Tell him I told you to have it.

Don't, on any account, print anything which I have not sent out for
printing myself. Anything which I think worth printing I print it myself. I
don't remember what 'Fear' is, but I expect it's very bad. Anyway, don't
print it.

I hope your wife and baby are going strong. We are living here on a
remote island. I fish.

Yours
Liam O'Flaherty

---

214. HRHRC ALS to Edward Garnett

Glen House, Arranmore, Burtonport, Co. Donegal   7 July, 1927

My Dearest Friend,

Here we are on the west coast of Donegal, in a charming little cottage, kept by a charming woman for twenty five shillings a week each – Topsy and myself. The baby is thrown in I believe. The sea is within a stone's throw of the end of the lawn. There is a lawn, as this place was once owned by a very small landowner, some sprat among landowners, who was driven out by the people. The people, having driven him out, are charming, quiet, hospitable, peaceful, small in stature, with dull intellects. The island scenery is fine, though not so good as my own island. Peadar O'Donnell, author of *Islanders*, taught here in one of the schools. I have tried to catch a rockfish without success, but I have caught one flounder – a sort of rough plaice. So there you are. I am getting a colour and a ferocious appetite. My mind is asleep and I feel that it's a time to cultivate one's garden unless the effort is too great. At least I incline to the view that human happiness consists of living on an island watching people cultivate their gardens.

You said something – a long time ago – about writing a guide book. My dearest friend, that's dangerous. Tourists might find this place, and places like it. Nobody has found this place yet. It is glorious to think that few strangers have looked on the brave, strong legs of these peasant women walking on the bog, and one can look for a whole day at a crab gallivanting in his pool without being disturbed by a human being.

I say, this letter is a trifle maudlin. I have eaten a blood pudding for the first time. It's a Donegal delicacy and don't ask me what it's made of. Well, well. There's meat here, but where is the energy to kill and dress it? Why write? Yes, good sir, but some day one has to go back and provide for Pegeen's future and pay those creditors, bless their souls, a few shillings in the pound. Back then, we shall come, some day, when the cold Atlantic whistles the approach of winter and with loins like Rabelais, we'll write.

By the way, before I left Dublin I wrote a great story called 'Red Barbara'. Did I tell you about it? Yes, it's a good one, about the beautiful widow of Feeney the fisherman. She refused to conceive of a weaver. I sent it on request to a French paper called *Commerce*. Here, I should think it's impossible to write. One looks, watches, smells, thinks, listens, ponders, eats, sleeps, hech! What about it? We have not paid our rent in Dublin. The good Miss {Ford?} can constrain on our carpet, chairs (secondhand), typewriter and kitchen stove. There is also a gramophone and pictures by Salkeld. Let her restrain, or is it constrain? What do you think?

Love to Miss Heath and yourself. I'm getting fat already.

Liam

---

215. HRHRC ALS to Edward Garnett
Glen House, Arranmore, Burtonport, Co. Donegal   12 July, 1927

My Dearest Friend,
    It is awfully good of you to send me the Barnum book.[1] I find it delicious.

I shan't throw it into the sea after finishing it. It's the sort of book I like. I got by the same post for re-reading, *The Brothers Karamazov*. I'm reading Barnum greedily and admiring our friend the visionary Mahomet of the Steppes. Any other old book like Barnum that is hurled at you and you feel would desecrate your choice shelves, float it in my direction and I'll bless you. Then perhaps some future critic in the *Spectator* will talk not of third rate novels, but third rate lives of charlatans as in Hudson's case. Long may the small fry curdle the shore froth with their writhing.

Topsy has put by the French book you sent her for night reading, I believe, while I am away fishing with the schoolmaster and the curate, and she has snatched Barnum from me.

Life here is glorious. The rockfish are scarce owing to trammel nets, but I have caught a few big ones. I row out to a black weed-covered rock at low tide and caught some there with sand bugs. Topsy has come too but has not caught one yet, as she insists on pottering about admiring weeds, starfish and sea urchins. She has also procured an assegai and spears crabs in holes, in her knickers.

I caught a great conger eel, a ferocious brute who looked so majestic and fierce that I managed to extract the hook without cutting his jaws too much and then let him slip back into the sea. Mackerel have come here a few nights ago, we captured about sixty. I find the stem of a clay pipe is most fetching in these parts for mackerel. It's good sport rowing about, watching the gannets bite at them and then bearing down on the gannets. There are trout here too in lakes in the centre of the island. The natives fish them with 'otters', curious contrivances of wood with a line attached. A small boy is going to teach Topsy how to use an 'otter', and he is making her a present of one. Personally I detest fishing in fresh water. The sea or nothing.

I am promised a day shooting seals and lobster fishing next Tuesday north of the island. I am going with some fishermen in a motor boat. They tell me we may get a bottle of rum from a French smuggler and have a good day of it. I fancy I'll have to pay for the rum.

The good princess[2] bought 'Red Barbara' and paid me twenty pounds for it. I fancy though that she didn't like it. She asks me to send her my next animal story. You'll like 'Red Barbara' when I get a copy to send you. Anyway, we can live here for six weeks on 'Red Barbara'.

There are quite a few characters here. One a schoolmaster who married a fishing girl and is drinking himself into a deplorable condition. The curate is a curious phenomena. A drunken priest turned up on a holiday from the mainland. He drank eight bottles of whiskey in three days and invited the whole island to visit him. We had some funny experiences with him. The postman is also curious. He had a wandering fanatic called Lutet to stay with him last year and he has imbibed most of the fanatic's strange religion.

The postman is a cunning fellow. He can smell whiskey a mile off. The other night he and the drunken schoolmaster were drinking, the postman made the schoolmaster go on his knees and swear to be faithful to Ireland. This was in relation to the murder of Kevin O'Higgins.[3]

By the way, I am thinking of a novel called *The Assassin*. It sounds good and strong. I'll probably write it this Autumn, but not just yet.

Life here is simpler than in my island. The people are less intelligent, and they have practically no imagination. Their speech is abrupt, considered, and very realist. They are more straightforward, more kindly and less astute than my people. My people of the south are all born aristocrats with all the vices of aristocracy and some of its virtues, by virtue of the {imported?} element from pirates, military brigands, saints, political refugees, etc. There are no ruins here, no churches, forts or works of art as in my island. It is a serf of a place. Nobody ever fought a battle here, but it's got its own particular quality – a very fine one.

How I ramble along! It's Sunday and the girls swim in the afternoon. I must go and watch them. It is too sultry to write or be more than a hundred yards from the shore. It is a pity you are not here to talk and wander about with. However, you are now a confirmed Roman and it would be difficult to drag you too far away from the centre of life. Some day soon I'll knock at your door in Chelsea and we'll talk far into the night with the blinds drawn and I'll see what new pictures you've got and whether you still have a bottle of wine in your hospitable cellar.

Best love to Miss Heath and yourself, from Topsy, Pegeen and myself. Us five and no more, Amen. The Kerry Protestant's prayer.

Yours
Liam O'F

P.S. There is an island near here where the natives formerly lived by making poteen. They are fine fellows and much superior in physique and character to the other islanders. Now, however, they have become law abiding and I expect they'll degenerate.

[1] *Barnum's Own Story: the autography of P.T. Barnum,* ed. Waldo R. Browne, New York: Viking Press, 1927.

[2] Princess Marguerite de Bassiano, Villa Romaine, av. Douglas Haig, Versailles, who ran *Commerce*. O'Flaherty also sent her 'Invitations' and 'The Letter'.

[3] Kevin O'Higgins, Minister for Justice, whose murder seems to have inspired O'Flaherty to write *The Assassin*.

---

216. NWUL ALS to Edward Garnett
Hazelbrook (or on the road there)   2 August, 1927

My Dearest Friend,
       We are leaving our island. Topsy had to go back to meet Mrs Rudmose

Brown[1] and I decided to accompany her because three English visitors have arrived. They are decent people but they are a group of rather strange people and unable to become one with the place, so it's impossible to stay.

Thanks so much for the books. I say, *The Son of the Bond Woman*[2] is first rate. Really first rate, as far as I have gone. It's good of you to have sent it, many thanks. The other books are also amazing, but this one is good. What lads those Spaniards were, and how sane a country life makes a man, sane and savage. It seems they go together, unless one is a Roman or an English-man. What then? Sane and ...? *Nescio quid*.

About my novel! I have it planned out. I think the idea and method are good, very good. It marks a change in as far as the character travels to London. You remember I suggested to Bates at your flat that certain aspects of London called out for description – the gaping mouths of the tubes. Well, my character ends there in secret exile. The assassin disappears, not into a canal, like Gilhooley, or spewing his life-blood in a church like Gypo, but, sodden with drink, you see him emerging from a public house with a harlot on his arm. The harlot buys a Union Jack from a flag seller and sticks it in his coat lapel. He looks at it, the once hated emblem of foreign imperialism. He fumbles at it with his drunken fingers. His lips twitched, but he did not pluck it out.[3]

It's a good psychological study, intense action, mystery and surprise. I think it should be good. After various castings about I have pitched on, I think, the most central type of revolutionary for the role of assassin, and have taken an ear as his distinguishing mark. A listening ear, slightly prominent.

Mr. Barnum-Cape seems quite interested in it. I will send it along chapter by chapter when I begin. But your Michael McDara is too romantic a man for an assassin, and I think Barney Merlick would be a better name.

Best love from all of us, Liam

[1] Rudmose Brown was a French scholar at Trinity College, Dublin and a friend of Beckett, Leventhal and MacGreevy

[2] Probably Geoffrey Uther Ellis, *The Bondwoman*, London: Duckworth, 1927.

[3] In fact *The Assassin* ends with McDara on the train from Liverpool to London.

---

217. NLD (MS 26,743) ALS to P.H. Muir

[no address]   n.d. [envelope postmark 8 August, 1927]

Dear Muir,

Here you are at last. Very sorry to hear about your wife. I hope you have better news by now. These things have got to be borne, dear boy. I know.

With affectionate regards,

Yours, Liam O'Flaherty

---

218. NWUL ALS to Edward Garnett

Hazelbrook, Kimmage Road, Terenure   29 August, 1927

My Dearest Friend,

I have just come back from the Aran Islands. I had a great time down there, and I brought back a good story called 'The Oar'[1]. I have not begun my novel yet, and I don't know when I am going to begin as it seems impossible to start a novel in a room with Pegeen screaming around the floor, and everybody dashing in and out. I have nowhere to work and in the middle of a sentence I may have to answer the grocer boy. This is shocking. In Aran, though, I was alone and thought a lot while I fished. It was great.

My novel sounds good, very stark and sombre. It's an extraordinary business. The only danger is that it might bear too close a resemblance to the O'Higgins business, and I suspect that the fellows who did that are now ruling this country with the support of the British government. Very brutal and inconceivable things happen in politics, and our hapless people never seem to be able to get rid of this terrible {?} that presses on them, the Church, the English ruling class and the Secret Society.

I may be in London within the next fortnight and have a talk with you. An American wants me to sign some books for him and he's paying my expenses back and forth. That will be handy for I want to talk to you. I'll bring 'The Oar' and we'll read it. It's good.

Topsy and Pegeen send their love to you and Miss Heath. Pegeen is now a tremendous girl, like a firebrand {three words?} with Topsy's face.

Liam

[1] The MS of 'The Oar' at HRHRC is marked 'Written in Gortnacapall, Aran Islands, August 14-15th, 1927'.

---

219. NLD (MS 26,743) ALS to P.H. Muir

Hazelbrook, Kimmage Road, Terenure   29 August, 1927

Dear Muir,

I am ever so sorry to have messed up our correspondence. I have just got both your letters on my return from the West of Ireland yesterday. I was out on the Islands there, moving around and my mail followed me. In one place there was only one mail a week. However, here I am now. And I expect it's too late for your holiday. Could you manage to postpone it until September 15th-22nd? There is a Civic Week or Carnival on in Dublin and it will be good fun.

If that man, for Bruce Rogers, sends me the money I'll come to London any time during the next fortnight to sign those things.

With best wishes
Yours
Liam O'Flaherty

---

220. To the Editor of the *Irish Statesman*[1]

Dear Sir,

The whole thing is a shocking scandal; this humbug called art criticism and the tyranny exercised in Dublin over the respectable art of painting by imbeciles and dishonest persons.

This morning I read a review in a daily newspaper of an exhibition of paintings held in the School of Art in honour of Civic Week. So I went this afternoon to look at the exhibition. I am not a painter, but I know a horse's spine when I pass my hand along it. The exhibition, which was supposed to represent modern Irish art, and which was highly praised by the reviewer was really a dreadful collection of daubs. Some of them were clever, others amusing; others might pass for the scrawling of my baby daughter. *Nash's Magazine* buys much better illustrations. There was no art there, and whatever there was there was neither Irish nor modern. It was just muck.

All but one picture; one that was not mentioned by the reviewer. That was a picture by Cecil Salkeld, depicting a scene in a pawn shop. The picture is undoubtedly a work of genius, and it is very seldom that a painting is a work of genius nowadays, when genius carefully avoids an art that is patronised mostly by parish priests and municipal galleries.

Now there is the scandal. There is an artist who is producing first rate work, and the critics pass him by with contempt, either through jealousy, imbecility or just that casualness that seems to be Original Sin of Dublin intellectuals. I suppose the man is too poor or too foolish to clear out of the country and go abroad where he is sure to gain speedy recognition. But one may be sure that if he does go abroad, gains fame and fortune and returns here, he will be hailed by the same critics that pass him by at present in favour of fifth rate photographers.

Why is this the only country in the world where an artist must be fifth rate if he is to gain recognition from his own people? In letters it is different, because the man of letters has a voice, and he can raise it to the four winds to heaven. But the painter is dumb, and generally a crazy fellow whom nobody pities until he has died of hunger. It's tough cheese.

Could nothing be done though to massacre the Dublin art critics?[2]

Yours faithfully
Liam O'Flaherty

1 Published 1 October, 1927, p.83 under the heading of 'Art Criticism'.

2 Y.O., an art critic, appends a note to this letter. He thinks O'Flaherty praises the work of Salkeld because his pictures come close to the novelist, for Salkeld is a storyteller in paint. 'Artists have other ideals than those of the novelist. If they had not there would be no necessity for picture exhibitions at all. To "know a horse's spine" when he passes his hand upon it has never before been advanced as evidence of aesthetic competence.'

---

221. BOM ALS to A.D. Peters
Hazelbrook, Kimmage Road, Terenure   11 October, 1927

Dear Peters,

Thanks for your cheque, which was much larger than I thought was due to me.

I am sorry to say that I have not begun that novel yet, and I don't know when I am going to begin it. I have been off writing for months and unless I can begin soon it looks bad for my chances of survival. However –

Yours very sincerely
Liam O'Flaherty

---

222. HRHRC ALS to Edward Garnett
Hazelbrook, Kimmage Road, Terenure   11 October, 1927

My Dearest Friend,

I enclose a most interesting advertisement from this morning's paper. I hope it amuses you. It's mostly all directed against Yeats, Lennox Robinson, Joyce and myself, under the pretence of being directed against Sunday newspapers. That's what I like. I must write a story about sodomy in Irish seminaries as a fitting reply.

Allow me to thank you for the most enjoyable evening that Topsy and myself spent at your house. I can't remember when I enjoyed myself so much. And I don't remember ever seeing you look so well or talk so well. No, my dear father-in-Christ, I don't want anything, not even ten shillings(!).[1]

I can't write even yet. I am beginning to curse the *Humanist*, I must have spent my year's energy on that cursed serial which came to nothing. Not that I lack material. I have the seeds of a dozen novels, but they won't begin. So it's best to leave them till they do begin. Life is long, and hunger assuredly our end, either way.

I say, I am beginning [to dislike?] these blasted priests more than is good for a human being. I am afraid there is no hope for the Irish people as a result of them. They have corrupted everything. So it seems in Dublin, and yet when one goes to the islands or the mountains hope again grows. But is it not too late? We are too far behind Europe, and the black horde is firmly entrenched against the assaults of knowledge. A kingdom for a Rabelais.

Have you got that typescript of 'The Oar', or did you send it away somewhere? I forget what I did with it, but I sort of remember that I left it with you to send to somebody.

Pegeen is wonderful and she sends you most charming kisses, and to Miss Heath too. Topsy and I add our more clumsy affection,

From Liam

[1] Volume two of H.E. Bates' autobiography, *The Blossoming World* (1971) p.52 he mentions that in July 1927 (but this date must be wrong) he went to E. Garnett's house in Pond Place. The only other guest was Liam O'Flaherty, and after supper both men witnessed Garnett's Will. O'Flaherty also told Bates about Charles Lahr's bookshop, of which Bates then gives a description as 'little more than a cubicle 12' x 8', walls lined with books, paintings and drawings. Its owner turned out to be Lahr, a German who had left his native village near Kreuznach in the Rhineland before 1914. Charley Lahr went barefoot a lot, a familiar figure in London's book world for fifty years. Very energetic, he cycled, ran or walked London in search of books.' Lahr had a phenomenal devotion to writers and painters, a good nose for first editions in Farringdon Road market, ran the *New Coterie*. His authors had no contracts, were paid in dribs and drabs of cash, or in books.

---

223. HRHRC ALS to A.D. Peters

Hazelbrook, Kimmage Road, Terenure   n.d. [? October, 1927]

Dear Peters,

I enclose two sketches 'The Stream' and 'Little White Dog'. I also enclose a note from the *Manchester Guardian*. Send them 'Little White Dog'. It's a little over the length but as there is no dialogue it will just fill a thousand word space. You see they offer five guineas. Is that enough?[1] I am sending two copies of this as I think the Americans would like it. It's the sort of work people like as it doesn't make them feel unpleasant. See can you do anything with 'The Stream'. I am afraid it's unsaleable and not much value, except from a literary point of view.

I am writing another animal story which I will mail in a few days.

Yours sincerely
Liam O'Flaherty

P.S. Many thanks for your very kind letter.

[1] The normal payment was three guineas per thousand words.

---

224. HRHRC ALS to A.D. Peters

Hazelbrook, Kimmage Road, Terenure   29 October, 1927

Dear Peters,

I'm sorry but *The Informer* and *Mr Gilhooley* have already been translated into German. Kammerer, or some such name, is publishing them. *The Informer* I think this Autumn.[1] My books have also been taken up by a {?} firm and will begin to appear in Spring. Cape sold these rights early this year.

I am enclosing a short story 'The Strange Disease' which I think rather funny. Tell me when you have enough, all you can handle.

Yours sincerely
Liam O'Flaherty

P.S. The *Manchester Guardian* has already printed 'Little White Dog'. [24 October, 1927]

[1] A.D. Peters sold the German rights of *The Black Soul* to Knaur Nachf. Verlag, of Berlin for forty pounds, and of *The Informer* for forty pounds. Cape had previously sold German volume (not serial) rights to Kamerer Verlag, who took their cut having serialised *The Informer* in the *Frankfurt Zeitung* (end 1927). O'Flaherty sold German rights of *Mr Gilhooley* to 'A German lady' without telling Peters or Cape. (Source A.D. Peters files, HRHRC)

---

225. HRHRC ALS to A.D. Peters
Hazelbrook, Kimmage, Road, Terenure   3 November, 1927

Dear Peters,

I am awfully sorry about that story 'The Strange Disease',[1] but the fact is I haven't got another copy. I have only a first draft of the MS and it's nothing like the story. I couldn't write it again. Could you get a copy typed and charge it to my account?

I am just going to begin my novel *The Assassin*, but I doubt if it's going to be seriable. Glad you like the story. Funny thing about it is that it's a true story, all except a few touches in the relating. A priest who lived in that district, rather a nice fellow, told it me.

Yours sincerely
Liam O'Flaherty

[1] 'The Strange Disease' was sold 7 November to *The Bermondsey Book* (ed. Frederick Heath) quarterly, and was published in Spring 1928.

---

226. SLUL ALS to Charles Lahr
Hazelbrook, Kimmage Road, Terenure   {?} November, 1927

Dear Lahr,

Thanks very much for the charming photograph of your daughter. She is surprisingly big and fat. Really a fine tribute to both of you. Give my compliments to your wife.

About the MSS, I have several short story MSS. The best of them is 'The Oar'. This is, I think, the best short story I have written so far. It's not published in English yet, but I sold it to a French journal. It's about two thousand words long. I couldn't sell it for less than ten pounds. I have others which are not so good, except one, 'The Alien Skull' which I like.[1] That is about two thousand five hundred words and the price is seven pounds.

Thirdly, an animal story 'Little White Dog', costing five pounds. Hear, hear! If your friend wants to buy an MS as a speculation 'The Oar' is, I think, the only one that will have market value. If any of my work ever has market value, which I doubt.

I'm completely sick of life. I can't write and I'm approaching bankruptcy and I'm thinking of giving up writing altogether and taking to journalism. But I'm afraid I'm no good at anything. It is bloody miserable. I'm thinking of coming to London to look for work as a literary journalist, but that is rather a forlorn proposition. Who the devil would give me any work?

I got Davies's book, and I wrote a review for the *Irish Statesman*.[2] They would only allow five hundred words. I was disappointed with the book but I tried to make the criticism as spectacular as possible, because even though the book has horrifying faults, Davies is undoubtedly a coming man and he has lots of good qualities. He won't like my review, but it may draw attention to the book, here at least. He must learn that although life is miserable, art is beautiful, and even the most miserable and disgusting life is made beautiful by art. Even syphilitic sores, for which he has a penchant, if described properly, have divine significance. But what is the use?

Life here is disgusting. I expect London is equally disgusting, but people think there which makes all the difference. Here they gabble.

Yours
Liam O'Flaherty

[1] 'The Alien Skull' was sold to the *Criterion* for six guineas. The MSS of this story and of 'The Oar' are now in the HRHRC collection.

[2] The Davies review mentioned was never published.

---

227. JR ALS to May O'Callaghan[1]
Hazelbrook, Kimmage Road, Terenure   8 November, 1927

Dear O.C.,

For Christ's sake try and get those bastards to send me some money, otherwise I'm coming over next February or March to blow up the Yossisdat premises and to abduct all the mistresses of the Commissars. I'm really very hard up as a result of going to Paris. Tell them it's not bleedin' well fair to use a man's work and then not pay him for it.

I'm writing like hell and feeling like hell too. Hope you are feeling like gin and ginger. Everybody here is just the same – rotten.

Yours,
until we are both properly roasted in hell,
L.O'F

[1] A friend in London.

---

228. JR ALS to May O'Callaghan
Hazelbrook, Kimmage Road, Terenure   11 November, 1927

Dear O.C.,

Just got your wire. I wrote to you in Moscow yesterday. You'll probably get the note when you get back. In it I threatened to blow up Yossisdat unless they sent me some money. To be quite candid I think they are a cheap lot of swine and a bloody lot of four-flushers. As a sane workman I'm not interested in anything publicly connected with my work except in selling my labour power at the highest possible wage. If they publish and use my work without paying me for it, well then they can do so and be damned to them, but I'm not going to thank them for it. I'm not a small boy or a woman and I'm not interested in seeing either my face, or my name, in the newspapers.

All the same, I thank you for your kindness and I wish you all luck and happiness but I am *bloody hard up*, and I feel sore about being fooled by a lot of lowdown Jews and lousy swine.[1]

Yours, Liam O'Flaherty

[1] He refers to Russian translation rights.

---

229. HRHRC ALS to A.D. Peters
Hazelbrook, Kimmage Road, Terenure   11 November, 1927

Dear Peters,

Thanks for the cheque. I wish you would take up that matter of *The Informer*. I think we should be able to get something for it. This scoundrel Hauser probably told the *Frankfurt Zeitung* that he had bought the rights from me. I'm going to look for Hauser. If he's in this country – well![1]

Thanks awfully for finding out about the man. Am working hard at my novel.

Yours sincerely
Liam O'Flaherty

P.S. I haven't got a copy of 'The Sinner'. I hope it's not lost as we'll need it for a collection which I'll probably get out next Autumn if my novel is in time for late Spring. Yours L.O'F.[2]

[1] Heinrich Hauser then lived in Limerick. In 1930 O'Flaherty wrote an introduction to his novel *Bitter Water* (translated from German by Patrick Kirwan). Hauser later became a Nationalist Socialist and returned to Germany. See *Shame the Devil* by Liam O'Flaherty p.135.

[2] In reply to this A.D. Peters says he will get a copy of 'The Sinner' from America, and get some money for him for serialisation of *The Informer*. On 9 November O'Flaherty sent 'Red Barbara' to Peters, saying he needed money urgently, and 'Gilhooley has been sold in Germany'. Peters replied to this – 'to whom? Cape knows nothing about it.' There is a long correspondence in the Peters files about the German rights of various books.

230. HRHRC ALS to A.D. Peters
Hazelbrook, Kimmage Road, Terenure   12 November, 1927

Dear Peters,

I think you should wait another month before going to Cape about *The Assassin*. I want to be quite sure that it's coming off, although I'm certain it's far the best thing I've begun yet. But I think you should at least have half the MS in your hand. I don't think you can make the contract any different from *Gilhooley*. At least he is entitled to the same contract by the agreement I made with him for all my work until 1929. But you could get busy with it in other ways. Finally I'll need some money at Xmas, and it's about then I should like to get any advance we're going to get.

Glad you sold 'The Strange Disease'.

About the German rights of *Gilhooley*. The lady who translated my short stories into German bought the rights of *The Informer*, but owing to some difficulty with Cape lost them, and so asked for *Gilhooley* instead, which I gave her.[1]

Do you handle the sale of MSS? I have seven short MSS which I want to put on the market. I don't know whether there is any demand for my stuff at present, but I have sold all my past work at from five to ten pounds per short story MS. If you care to handle them for me, I'll send them along and you could lock them up for me until an offer turns up. I fancy you could make a better bargain than I could.

Yours, Liam O'Flaherty

[1] Josephine Sternemann.

---

231. HRHRC ALS to A.D. Peters
Hazelbrook, Kimmage Road, Terenure   n.d. [? November, 1927]

Dear Peters,

I enclose a note from *Transition*.[1] Give them 'The Sinner' if they agree to pay five pounds for it. Or if you can't sell 'The Fall of Joseph Timmins' give it them also for the same money.

I think it's quite hopeless serialising any of my novels in this country. But when I do write another I'll send you along the first 1,000 words. But the point is that there wouldn't be time to serialise it as it would go to print about as soon as it's finished.

Yours sincerely
Liam O'Flaherty

[1] In reply to a 24 October request from *Transition*, 40 rue Fabert, Paris 7, (eds. Eugene Jolas and Elliott Paul); 'through the kindness of Miss Sylvia Beach' Jolas asked for an O'Flaherty story, payment thirty francs per page. No O'Flaherty story was published 1927, or in 1928 when this magazine became a quarterly.

232. NWUL ALS to Edward Garnett
Hazelbrook, Kimmage Road, Terenure   22 November, 1927

My Dearest Friend,

Why in the name of God don't you drop me a line? I need a letter from you badly. I'm working very hard, sometimes from nine till eight. And yet I have only four chapters of *The Assassin* done. I have done and redone these four chapters. Three are typed. Would you be your most charming and charitable self and read them for me?

I'm going to prove that Welsh prince of yours is wrong – the mountaineer. He claims that an assassin is a normal person. My contention is that the complex of assassination is the result of temporary insanity and that the reaction, in a certain general type, leads to normality. In other words that intellectual and moral despair produces the complex of assassination.

I am trying to follow out your plan of giving a comprehensive view of the political background. But as usual I am pressed for time. I have to be done by the end of January. If this is a failure, I'm afraid I'm ruined for good.

The other day Gordon Campbell, I think you may remember him (he is now secretary to the Ministry of Industry and Commerce), offered to show me how to make two thousand pounds a year. His idea was a letter of introduction to Arnold Bennett. What do you think of that? I would have knocked him down had I not been in his own house.

I was very amused to see in a collector's prospectus the other day that your father, yourself and David are quoted one after the other. When will David's son Richard be added to the list?

Damn it all, do write me a note. Love to Miss Heath,

Yours sweating blood
Liam O'F

---

233. HRHRC ALS to Edward Garnett
Hazelbrook, Kimmage Road, Terenure   28 November, 1927

My Dearest Friend,

Thanks very much for your kind criticism of *The Assassin*. I don't know how I could have embarked on such a blunder. Now, of course, I see it plainly, but only after you pointed it out. I see further, to the cause of the blunder. The assassin was wrong in the first place and in the second place I was trying, for the purposes of the market, to write seventy thousand words about a story that should only run to about forty thousand words. That was the cause of the disaster.

I think I am going to try it again, though in the way I am circumstanced I may be forced to chuck writing for a time and take up journalism. The fact of having a family is a terrible danger of leading me into errors of this sort, and I think it is better to leave writing alone altogether rather than try to make a living out of it. You understand what I mean. However, as I said, I am going to have another shot at it. But then will Cape consent to publish a story of such length? What does that matter, says you? Perhaps it would serialise at that length, though I doubt if the matter would be tame enough for any public.

In any case, I am very grateful to you for having saved me from perpetrating this atrocity. I am never again going to try to write anything a certain length. What I must do here, I see, is to create a definite type of human being, to wit an assassin, not to give a picture of the forces that led to the assassination of somebody or other, which is merely a matter of very local and very ephemeral interest.

Yours with love
Liam O'Flaherty

---

234. HRHRC ALS to A.D. Peters
Hazelbrook, Kimmage Road, Terenure   2 December, 1927

Dear Peters,

Thanks very much for selling *The Black Soul*, that's bully! I am enclosing the signed contracts. I notice that *The Informer* serial rights are not sold, so in that case the *Frankfurt Zeitung* can have no right to them.

The *M.G.* sent me a cheque for five guineas. You can charge the commission to my account instead of my sending you the cheque. I am enclosing six MSS. I am in communication with some collectors as to their sale – in fact only yesterday I had a request for one. I'll send the offers on to you and you can deal with them. The story entitled 'The Oar' is important and is worth ten pounds, no less. 'The Alien Skull' is worth seven pounds, the 'Little White Dog' is worth five pounds. For the rest, what you can get, but not less than five pounds for any. More, of course, if you can.

'The Oar' is now offered on the serial market, as it's my best story I have been holding it back for re-reading. Make two typewritten copies and kindly charge to my account. I think either the *Spectator* or the *Nation* would like it, but its principal value is in the sale of the MS.[1]

I'm having great difficulties with my novel and I am beginning all over again, after getting half way. It's the very devil of a story, but it's going to be good whenever I get it finished.

[Unsigned]

[1] 'The Oar' was published in *Outlook*, 14 January, 1928.

---

235. NWUL ALS to Edward Garnett
Hazelbrook, Kimmage Road, Terenure   12 December, 1927

My Dearest Friend,

I expect I have to thank you for Cape's kind work in letting me have a hundred pounds advance on *The Assassin*. Here's to your good health, sir! I wish you thirty years of good wine, good conversation and merry thoughts.

I have done thirty thousand words since. I've written those chapters you suggested re-writing and added others. I think it's better now, though that second chapter is still weak. I am following out your instructions and perhaps I'll get through with it all right. Anyway, I have divested myself of coat and waistcoat and am at it night and day. Fifty cigarettes a day ... my wife says the ferocity of the narrative will terrify the readers. Perhaps we could tone it down a bit later.

I think the best thing I could do now is to make a complete draft of it and send it on to you. Or shall I send you what I've done? No, I think I'll go through with it and then re-write it after you have criticised it. You are really too kind to an undeserving person. Here's to your health!

Liam

---

236. To the Editor of the *Irish Statesman*[1]

Dear Sir,

Una McC. Dix, whoever she is, is a very foolish person. Otherwise she would not draw my attention to her existence in the manner she has done in your current issue. Because now, as the Governor-General said, I am going to find out all about her and for the same reason as His Excellency.

Apart from that, in order to prevent more gadflies from worrying this labouring horse (I am quoting Tchekov), I am going to tell the lady why I don't write in Irish. Even though her name is Dix and therefore more likely to be interested in my reasons for not writing in the language of her ancestors.

I have written in Irish. I wrote in Irish when I was sixteen. I won a gold medal from an organisation in Philadelphia for some Irish prose at that age, and procured a holiday, as far as I can remember, for the whole of Rockwell as a result. Yes, and a leading article from the *Tipperary Nationalist*. That was a few years before the great war. I wonder was Una McC. Dix at that time interested in the Irish language?

When I began to write professionally I was no longer interested in the Irish language from a political point of view. I was more interested in politics and in the Irish people. I felt, in my young arrogance, that some ideas which I had picked up around the world might be useful to the Irish people, and I chose the best language for presenting these ideas to my people. As the people spoke English I naturally wrote in English. If I wrote in Irish they would not be able to read the stuff. And, of course, as the editor kindly remarked, no printer in Ireland would print the stuff, either in Irish or in English.

Two years later I became less interested in politics and in the regeneration of the Irish people, intellectually; having come to the conclusion that my people were too hopelessly sunk in intellectual barbarism to be capable of being saved by a single man. The Shannon Scheme appeared to me to be more capable of doing the job. So I was seized, like George Moore, with a sudden desire to use the Irish language as a medium of expression. I wrote a few short stories for the Gaelic League organ. They printed them and sent me three copies of the issue in which they were printed. Then I consulted Padraig Ó Conaire and we decided that drama was the best means of starting a new literature in Irish. I became fearfully enthusiastic. The two of us went to Dublin and entered a hall where some fellows were holding a Gaeltacht Commission. We put our scheme before them for a travelling theatre and so on. I guaranteed to write ten plays. They thought we were mad and, indeed, took very little interest in us. In fact, I could see by their looks and their conversation that they considered us immoral persons.

However, I was undaunted. I wrote a play and gave it to Géaroid Ó Lochlainn. He liked it and got the Gaelic Drama League to produce it. That was not easy. Because some horrifying Christians from the Education Department threatened fire and brimstone if they staged my work, on the grounds that I was an immoral person. In fact, I believe, they had to pack the hall with detectives in order to prevent the Gaelic Christians from throwing my unfortunate play to the lions.

Although the theatre was packed, which rarely happens for these Gaelic plays, I was never paid for the production.

Here is the joke. The only remuneration I received for this play was from an English Socialist who dislikes Irish and everything connected with nationalism of any sort in any place. He paid me twenty five pounds for the Gaelic manuscript, i.e. for my handwriting.

I naturally swore that I would never write another word in Irish. If I do write in Irish I'll take good care not to publish it and place it at the mercy of these sows.

I don't write for money. If I wanted to write for money I could be a rich man now. I am a good craftsman and I am cunning enough to understand the various follies of mankind and womankind. In fact, if I ever get so hard up that I'll lose my self respect, I'll start a religious paper in the Irish language and make a fortune on it.

I write to please myself and two friends. One is my wife and the other is Mr. Edward Garnett. I don't write for Una McC. Dix, and for that reason

I'd be pleased if she refrained from drawing my attention to her existence. Because I just love writing about gadflies.

Liam O'Flaherty

P.S. In answer to Messrs. Chambers and Colum, permit me to say that English was the first language I spoke. My father forbade us speaking Irish. At the age of seven I revolted against Father and forced everybody in the house to speak Irish. Finally, allow me to say that I think Colum and other fellows like him are humbugs. If he is interested in Irish and in Ireland why doesn't he stay in Ireland, learn the language and write in it? All the best Irish patriots live in America[2]

L.O'F

[1] Published 17 December, 1927, p.348, under the heading 'Writing in Gaelic'.

[2] A commentary on the background to this letter is to be found in the *Irish Times*, 22 November, 1984, Tomás de Bhaldraithe, 'Ó Flaitheartaigh agus léirmheastóirí eile' [O'Flaherty and other reviewers].

237. NWUL ALS to Edward Garnett
Hazelbrook, Kimmage Road, Terenure   n.d. [early January, 1928]

Dear Maecenas Garnett,[1]

   Here is the manuscript. I hope it's not the last straw and that you recover
from it. Pass it on to Cape, with either your curse or your blessing. As I have
only the copy I am sending you, you can destroy it by throwing it into the
fire, if you feel the world should be saved from it.

[unsigned]

[1] Maecenas, patron to both Virgil and Horace, himself a turgid prose writer, but O'Flaherty
means the title as a compliment.

---

238. NWUL ALS to Edward Garnett
Hazelbrook, Kimmage Road, Terenure   24 January, 1928

My Dearest Friend,

   Thanks ever so much for your kind letter and the kind things you say
about *The Assassin*. I really was quite in despair about it. Now that it has
found favour in your mind I feel more friendly towards it.

   But what's to be done about the bad chapter? I consulted my wife and
she suggested that I ask you to cut out the last chapter as you recommend,
and let the rest go. For this reason, I am so exhausted mentally with writing
the story that if I tackled these other chapters I'd only mess them up still
more. And I might come over later and ask you to go over the proofs with
me. If you could find time and patience we might do a little patching. Of
course if you think it's absolutely necessary that I rewrite these chapters, I
must obey like a faithful apprentice. But O Lord, spare my wife! What do
you say? Could we compromise on the excision of the last chapter and let
it go to Cape? Then touch up the proofs? I'd be fresh then.

   As it is, I am more than surprised that you liked it at all, because it's very
patchy owing to the difficulty of fitting in this dreadful Kitty, who does not
really belong except as a tool. And a woman is never satisfied with being a
tool. Anyhow, I hope the English part of your nature will agree to this
compromise, although I remember your advice about *The Informer*. If I had
acted fully on it, it would have improved the book fifty percent. In this case
also, if I had the strength at present to rewrite these chapters, the same
improvement would result . But I'm afraid I have not. Therefore I hope you
understand that it is not through any feeling of vanity or conger eelishness
that I am trying to avoid it, but simply for purely physical reasons. Even
from the disjointedness of this letter, you can see what a state I am in. I

should be thanking my stars that I have escaped writing another abortion like *The Firebrand* [the original title of *Mr Gilhooley*].

You remember last year you suggested a humorous *Tourist's Guide to Ireland*, I am now thinking of doing it when I have had a rest. We are going to live in the country near Arklow next week. We got a cottage there for fifteen pounds a year. It's near the sea and the vale of Avoca. It will be very nice and quiet as it's fifty miles from Dublin. We'll be safe from our friends except on weekends.

I have a big scheme for a novel which I want to discuss with you when I meet you again, although I am afraid that I am yet too raw to tackle anything important. My failure to do justice to *The Assassin* showed me my failings. I have yet to finish my apprenticeship, which indeed is very pleasant, as the world would be very empty if I didn't have you to advise me, and more especially I always think of you when I am writing and wonder: 'Now, what would Edward think of this?'

Topsy and Pegeen send you and Miss Heath their love. I hope Miss Heath is well and happy? Have you yet decided whether you are coming over to Ireland this summer? I am sorry not to have been able to come with the MS but we couldn't afford it.

Thanking you ever so much.

Yours with love
Liam

---

239. HRHRC ALS to A.D. Peters
Hazelbrook, Kimmage Road, Terenure [? 28] January, 1928

Dear Peters,

I delayed writing because I had an altercation with Cape over various matters, relative to a contract which I signed with him some years ago. I cannot go into the matter fully, in justice to Cape, who has done me favours in the past, so I must let it pass at the risk of, as you put it, 'disturbing our good relations'.

The whole affair is so messed up that I can neither make head nor tail of it, but I know that the contract expires March 1929. I can also gather that I'll benefit very little by the American and English rights of my first four books.

The upshot of the business is, so far as *The Assassin* is concerned that I had to sign a contract with Cape. I don't know yet whether he is going to print the book or whether it's fit to be printed. If you are prepared to overlook the matter, for my part I am prepared to guarantee that you are to look after all my work without exception after that date I mention, March 1929. I assure you it would be more to my interest in the present instance also, but from a point of honour I can't explain the matter fully.

If you negotiate the film rights of *The Informer* don't consult Cape.[1] He may claim fifty percent of my proceeds. If there is a sale and he claims fifty percent, I am going to fight him for it, as I think I find an error in reckoning, intentional or otherwise, in his accounts for another book. Please excuse this disjointed letter. I'm rather upset.

Yours sincerely
Liam O'Flaherty

[1] Already in 1927 there was interest in the film rights of *The Informer*. In 1928 exclusive option was granted to Rudolf Kaemmerer Verlag, Berlin from 24 January to 20 February for a minimum of five hundred pounds, extended to 10 March, but nothing came of this.
In fact Cape claimed a two hundred pound share of the film option, not fifty percent. There was much correspondence between Cape and Peters on financial and legal arrangements. O'Flaherty did not agree that the remittance of part of his liability to Cape should depend on his signing another agreement with Cape for an option on two novels and one volume of short stories. O'Flaherty left the whole entanglement to Peters.

---

240. NWUL ALS to Edward Garnett
Hazelbrook, Kimmage Road, Terenure   27 January, 1928

My Dearest Friend,

I fear that you are disgusted with me about *The Assassin*, but I'm hanged if I could do anything better with it. But to tell the truth I felt that from the moment McDara left Tumulty's room the last time that something strange had happened and there was no necessity to go farther. I feel there should be a very powerful ending but it should be on a low note, considering that the highest actual note was reached at the assassination. It should drivel away from there, but it didn't. So it's a fearful mess-up, and I don't know what'll become of it. Your cutting of the last two chapters certainly strikes me as excellent and may save it, but I'm afraid, even at that, it's shaky. I must try again. I see where I came a cropper, taking it too close to life. One should create from the very root. From the moment I began to write instinctively it was all right. That is, I only saw the actual assassination, with its balancing atmosphere, and did not see the general environment. So the general environment, chapters 11-12 and 23-24 was wrong.[1] But will the other critics see this? Let's hope they are the duffers I think they are.

I'm sorry the thing is not good, because I hoped you would allow me to dedicate it to you. Damn it, that may be a stroke of genius, ending it in the train. What do you think? Or did you just feel that it was merely the best possible way of mending a bad puncture?

Yours
Liam

[1] The book ends after chapter 22 in the Holyhead/London train.

---

241. JR ALS to May O'Callaghan

Sea View Cottage, Coolboy, Arklow, Co. Wicklow   29 January, 1928

Dear O.C.,

Many thanks for your letter and money order for fifteen guineas. I didn't get the other twenty-five pounds which were sent on, but I got the ten guineas which you sent previously. I was under the impression that the bank would acknowledge the arrival of myself to cash the telegraph order. Then, of course, I intended every day to write and did not. I was writing a story and in very bad state of concentration, so I was afraid to write lest you might think my letter was still more deranged than my previous ones to Serge Dinamov. However, I have finished the damn thing now and we are going down to Arklow to live.

If you have a few days to spare, come over and spend them with us. We could put you up and would be very glad to see you again. I think it is not as long a journey as from London to Dublin. You could go by Fishguard and Rosslare. I could in fact drive down to Rosslare and meet the boat. If you are staying in London some time I believe there is an excursion from London to Dublin on Feb. 11th for a very small sum, I think 22/6 return. Do tell me whether you could come over. I have a little book of three stories of mine which has recently been published in a private edition. I'd like to give it to you, so will I send it or will you be coming over?[1]

My new book will, I think, be published towards the end of May. It's not much good I fear, and I don't think it would suit the Russian market as they would probably consider it reactionary. It's called *The Assassin*. *The Informer* may be filmed in Germany. I'm negotiating at the moment about it with some people in Berlin.

What is to be done about that money that went astray? Or how was it sent on, by registered post?

O'Donnell's book *Islanders* has been published and it's having an excellent press. You may have seen it by this? I think it would be a very good thing if the government locked him up for a few years and made him write instead of playing at tin soldiers to the danger of the community, and no reasonable good for the spreading of civilisation.

Nothing very interesting has happened here since you left. Topsy and Pegeen are very fit and well. We're moving tomorrow morning, so we are in a flurry.

Do write,
Liam O'F

---

1 *Red Barbara & Other Stories*, (New York: Crosby Gaige, London: Faber & Gwyer, 1928) included 'The Mountain Tavern', 'Prey' and 'The Oar', illustrations by Cecil Salkeld.

---

242. HRHRC ALS to A.D. Peters
Sea View Cottage, Coolboy   5 February, 1928

Dear Peters,

I received the German copies of *The Informer* yesterday. It looks awfully good but I don't think the translation is very good. When I get a copy of *The Assassin* I'd like you to get in touch with Frau Sternemann of Hamburg for the translation of it. She has written to me offering fifty pounds for the German rights of it; but perhaps we could do better if *The Informer* is a success. I sent her an indefinite reply, so that you can do as you think fit. It might go as a serial, which would pay better I should think. I didn't hear from Cape yet about it, but I believe Garnett sent it in with a positive recommendation.

About your letter – if you send on a contract as you suggested I'll sign it with pleasure from March 1929.

I'm settled now in a very remote place, miles from anywhere. It's very quiet and I may be able to plan something good. I want to write a really good novel, something quiet, restrained and lyrical, like a short story. I'm getting bored with stories of town and slum life.

Yours very sincerely
Liam O'Flaherty

---

243. HRHRC ALS to Edward Garnett
Sea View Cottage, Coolboy   6 February, 1928

My Dearest Friend,

Thanks for your note. It is good to hear you speak so well of the second half of *The Assassin*. Unless you lodge any serious objection I'm going to dedicate it to you, just for the sake of that second part and also for the very considerable responsibility you have for the finished product. Somehow I feel the same about it as about *The Black Soul*, which we wrote together and which is the most artistic thing I wrote, even though nobody appreciates it. So, unless you write to say you object I'm going to dedicate *The Assassin* to you, just simply 'To Edward Garnett'.[1] Please allow me to do so, it would make me feel somehow that you are still fond of me, as of a disciple who did not get *too* vain of his feathers, after leaving the nest for his first flight.

The *Frankfurt Zeitung* are serialising *The Informer*, but I benefit nothing financially from it, owing, I believe, to some mistake on Cape's part. Perhaps it will do good some other way; and it's a moral encouragement anyway. The German edition has reached me (of *The Informer*), and I'm sending you a copy as a curiosity. I think the translation is bad and just as much expurgated as the Russian edition.

It's very nice here in the country. It's very quiet, near a little fishing town

(Arklow) with a hinterland of magnificent mountain scenery. I think it's a good place for the soul and I'm dreaming of a big fellow called Ramon Mór, whom I believe I'm going to work on next. He is going to be an epic, though tragic, figure and I'm going to place him in my native island. The Irish Shylock, of whom we spoke at Ballybawn, but he'll be big and not at all a mean figure, unless he is judged by the standards of a suburban Socialist who subscribes to the *New Statesman*. However, I'm only walking around him as yet, having a look at his clothes, listening to his muttered speech and the way he sniffs at things. It's very pleasant, like contemplating a beautiful horse and wondering what it would be like to be mounted on it, in the middle of a prairie.

Yes, it's good to be away from 'the bloody troop' – I amend Shelley. There is a patch of ground here to be dug and the birds seem glad that I have returned to them. Even the bare trees that one passes have a great dignity and that silence which is like the friendship of great minds. And how nice it is to watch evening fall, just like a blanket that a mother tucks about a child.

> Topsy and Pegeen send you and Miss Heath their love, and I also
>
> Liam

[1] *The Assassin* is dedicated 'To my creditors'.

---

244. JR ALS to May O'Callaghan
Sea View Cottage, Coolboy   20 February, 1928

Dear O.C.,

Hello! Thanks very much for the Dreiser.[1] I'm sorry I missed you that night. I went down all right but the train was just gone – the guide was wrong. I'm glad you enjoyed Miss {?} and Jack {Brennan?} and *The Shadow of the Gunman*. I believe O'Casey's new play will be out shortly.

I got another letter from Dinamov. He wants the MS of my new novel for some literary magazine of foreign literature. I must get a copy of the MS and send it to him. I wish I had somebody to do these things for me. I think he had better deal with my agent and then everything would be all right. What do you think? I wonder if you have nothing to do, would you see my agent and put him in touch with Dinamov? What an extraordinary thing to ask! Never mind, I'm potty. I must go and see my agent. But would the Russians deal with my agent? I must go everywhere and see about everything.

I've planted a whole lot of things including strawberries, and quite a lot is done in the garden plot. Did you leave a scarf behind when you were here? There is a strange one here and we don't know who owns it. Serge Dinamov tells me you wrote an article about me. What on earth did you do that for? All right! I'll write a story about you. Do you know you have an uncle in Arklow who is rolling in money and is very old? So a shopkeeper told us. She recognised you and asked who you were. You should have made up to the uncle and seized his money.

Yours
Liam O'F

P.S. Just finished Dreiser's book. It's very fine indeed, thanks for sending it to me. Parts of it are first rate stuff and the whole thing stands out.

L.O'F

[1] Probably Theodore Dreiser's *Dreiser Looks at Russia*, London: Constable 1928.

---

245. HRHRC TLS to A.D. Peters
Sea View Cottage, Coolboy   12 March, 1928

Dear Peters,

I enclose a letter from the *North American Review* asking for a contribution or two. I don't think we have anything for them have we? I'll try and write something. Could you suggest anything? I suppose a story about American life would be more suitable.

I am also sending along a proof copy of my novel. You could try it on that German paper.

Yours sincerely [unsigned]

P.S. ALS You have a story of mine called 'Red Barbara'. Let the *North American Review* have it, together with 'The Strange Disease'. That will probably give them a moral colic. Any other you think they might like, 'The Oar' or 'The Mountain Tavern'. Sorry I can't come over for the match.[1]

L.O'F

[1] They had planned to go to a rugby match together.

---

246. JR ALS to May O'Callaghan
Sea View Cottage, Coolboy   12 March, 1928

Dear O.C.,

I am sending you the MS of *The Assassin* for the U.S.S.R. Please tell them when you send it on that I want the MS returned, as it is worth about fifty pounds. If you don't think they'd [like] the story return the MS to me, as it's worth more than the problematic remuneration for its serial publication in Russia. You see, I can't get a copy made as I have no handwritten copy. If there is a copy of a typescript [that] has no market value. Of course if they would only deal with my agent it would be an easy matter, but *c'est ça*. Please let me know you receive the MS.[1]

We are all quite well. The records arrived in small pieces.

Yours

Liam O'Flaherty

[1] Evidently O'Callaghan received the MS back, for later in 1928 O'Flaherty sold it. A letter from O'Callaghan of 2 April 1928, mentions that she sent the MS registered to Russia. Dinamov says he will return the original after translation. *The Assassin* was to be published in a new foreign journal *Vestnik*, and her impression of the novel would appear in the May 1928 issue. 'The Mountain Tavern' had appeared in the April issue. She thinks two thirds of this novel 'the best writing you ever did', and O'Flaherty has excelled himself in vivid description. She also tells O'Flaherty about Piscater, a Communist in Berlin who had taken a big theatre there to produce 'revolutionary stuff', for which *The Informer* might be suitable if Piscater dramatised it, should O'Flaherty agree. (Source JR)

---

247. HRHRC ALS to A.D. Peters

Sea View Cottage, Coolboy   n.d. [? March, 1928]

Dear Peters,

   Twenty pounds is all right provided he does not require me to sign any copies and that he pays on receipt of MS.[1] If he agrees to this I could write a story of five thousand words or so within a month.

Yours sincerely

Liam O'Flaherty

P.S. By the way, there was an American who wanted a story, a bookseller from San Francisco named Leone Gilber of the firm of Gilber & Lilienthal. Don't know his address. If you think it worthwhile you might get in touch with him, I don't know whether it is worthwhile as Americans are rather fishy in my opinion.

L.O'F

[1] Refers to M. Marrot of 54 Bloomsbury Square, London WC1.

---

248. HRHRC ALS to A.D. Peters

Sea View Cottage, Coolboy   8 March, 1928

Dear Peters,

   I enclose a letter from Frau Sternemann, who has been translating some of my stories into German for the past few years, without I'm afraid reaping much benefit for herself.[1] You see by the letter that she makes an offer for *The Assassin*. If you find it suitable please let her have it, ten percent of the serial rights seems rather little though. But I am sure she would agree to any terms you suggest as she is a woman of good family and extremely honest.

Yours sincerely

Liam O'Flaherty

Frau Dr. Josephine Sternemann, Hochkamp bei Hamburg, wrote 23 March about translating *The Assassin* but she refused upon reading it, finding it not as powerful as *The Informer* or *Mr. Gilhooley*.

---

249. JR ALS to May O'Callaghan
Sea View Cottage, Coolboy   3 April, 1928

Dear O.C.,

Just got your letter. You'll excuse my previous note because I have been for the past fortnight in a state of temporary insanity owing to creating a new work and to the fact that everything has gone wrong. First the film business came a cropper. Then those blood-sucking American millionaires refused payment on the de luxe booklet of *Red Barbara*.[1] I have four large parcels of sheets which I have refused to sign and they are threatening me by cable. But I'll kick their bloody guts if I get hold of them. Then the proof copy which my agent sent to Berlin for the serial rights of *The Assassin* to the labour paper, has got lost in the post, and having just had a violent quarrel with my scoundrel of a counter-revolutionary publisher, Jonathan Cape, I can get no other. But I am getting my wife to write for me, so to speak with her baby in her arms. It's bloody awful. If there were only open war or something, one could go away quietly and polish off a few of these rotters. However, Oh, yes – even the damned motor car failed me, because it's practically a rattle box, just now when I'm trying to sell it.

However, I fancy something is bound to turn up. I've worked out this Ramon Mór business, which is a good thing. It's a very big novel and if I can pull it off I'll have done something good. Will I though – I doubt it.

In any case thanks for your good work, and do write to your friend about *The Informer*[O'Flaherty's letter of 12 March]. *The Assassin* would make a better play though, but it's immaterial which. That sounds a fairly civilised country – I mean Germany. This country is a horror. One can smell priests even on a calm day, and that even worse abortion the little country bourgeoisie, with a terrible rotting manure of brutalised peasantry, upon which this two-headed buzzard feeds.

Yes, get back to Russia, for it seems there is nothing for Western Europe but the sword of Michael, or perhaps some new avenging spirit of the Steppes – the golden whore of youth emptying the chalice of her lust among the ruins of this depravity.

Well! Cheerio, tomorrow perhaps or next week, I'll begin to write again and forget all my worries. Or we might set off somewhere. Old Bill Prestige (72) took strychnine and died. He was the only honest man in this district. Of course he was a Protestant, so the local priests are more convinced than ever that God is secreted from the Pope's genital.[2]

Yours
L.O'F

[1] The American limited edition was six hundred copies.

[2] From the state of his handwriting O'Flaherty was very upset when he wrote this letter.

---

250. HRHRC TLS to A.D. Peters
Sea View Cottage, Coolboy   6 April, 1928

Dear Peters,

My wife got a copy of the proofs from Cape, so I am sending it along. She could only get one, as there were no more. But I expect to get sheets next week. I think you had better send this copy to Frau Sternemann and close with her for fifty pounds, for the book rights. She can translate it and negotiate with those labour people, etc., for the serial rights. Do this because I need some money just now.

About those two stories, they are free of course. Harper's never published any story for me. At least they never paid for it if they did. Cape has no right to any story in *The Tent*, other, of course, than the British Empire book rights.

---

251. HRHRC to A.D. Peters
Sea View Cottage, Coolboy   15 April, 1928

Dear Peters,

I have begun to write a comic or satirical guide to Ireland for tourists. It's really a satire on priests, politicians, publicans, peasants and geniuses, with chapters describing the various amusements and pleasure resorts. I'll have it done in about a month. I think it's very, very funny. I'll send you along in a couple of days the first forty pages or so, and you'll see whether there is any chance of serialising it. I doubt if there is, but on the strength of the forty pages you may be able to go ahead with the sale of the book rights. I'd like to get it published in July or so if that is possible, for the tourist season. I think you had better approach Cape first, as I am under contract to offer him everything until March next. However, you may think it's advisable to offer it for publication. This is to advise you that I am sending it along shortly.

The title of the book is Ireland and it will be about sixty thousand words long.

Yours very sincerely
Liam O'Flaherty

[26 April, T.S. Eliot wrote to A.D. Peters returning 'The Alien Skull', which he liked, in favour of 'The Letter' which he liked even more and published in *Criterion*, June 1928.]

252. JR TLS to May O'Callaghan
Sea View Cottage, Coolboy   27 April, 1928

Dear O.C.,

Thanks for the magazine, which of course I could not read, farther than noticing that there was an article about myself. I presume this is the article you wrote?[1] I should feel flattered. No doubt when I become prosperous I'll gloat over these outward signs of my own importance. At the moment an overdraft of thirteen pounds is a great deterrent. Every day we wait for the post and find nothing. People have even stopped writing to me. Did you ever notice that when you are hard up everything seems to combine in order to produce an atmosphere of perfect blackness? I went to see Peadar O'Donnell and found him in even worse condition. He had also just been arrested and released, and was feeling very blue. So it's a comfort to have a companion in adversity.

How are you getting on? I believe the weather in London is very fine, whereas it is still winter here. Without any disrespect to yourself, the County of Wicklow in its southern parts is the most awful territory I ever had the misfortune to live in.

I began a scurrilous book about Ireland, but I have got bored with it. It's like whipping a dead horse trying to stir up this country. The papishes are bringing out a new weekly paper called the *Standard*, presumably to make war on Mexico. I say, the Russians have to buck up or they'll be put in the halfpenny place by the Mexicans, at least in the columns of *The Irish Independent*. With best wishes,

                                                                       L.O'F

[1] This would be the Moscow magazine *Vestnik* – see Letter 246, 12 March, 1928.

---

253. HRHRC TLS to A.D. Peters
Sea View Cottage, Coolboy   1 May, 1928

Dear Peters,

I think you are right about that book on Ireland. It would probably do me more harm than good, so I'll stop it. Send back that portion some time.[1] I'll go on writing stories. I'm going to wait to see how *The Assassin* sells before I begin my new novel, as I have two to write and it depends on my luck with this one as to which of the new ones I'm going to tackle first.[2]

                                                          Yours very sincerely
                                                          Liam O'Flaherty

[1] 3 May, Peters returned the MS of what later became *A Tourist's Guide to Ireland*, saying he was glad O'Flaherty had decided not to publish it.

[2] 11 May, O'Flaherty was at the National Hotel, Bloomsbury, to discuss the German translation rights of *The Assassin* and the film rights of *The Informer*, an option on which he was willing to

sell for not less than five hundred pounds. The representative of Knaur Nachf. Verlag of Berlin (a literary agency) was told that the Society of Authors was making a stand against the outright sale of foreign rights in English books. In future any amount paid for rights must be an advance on royalties. A.D. Peters pushed Knaur's terms up for *The Assassin*. They paid an advance of fifty pounds per twelve thousand copies and two thirds of the serial rights. H. Hauser was told to contact Knaur and ask for the job of translating *The Assassin*. (Source, A.D. Peters files, HRHRC)

---

254. JR ALS to May O'Callaghan
Sea View Cottage, Coolboy   n.d. May [? 1928]

Dear O.C.,

Thanks for your letter. Well! I hope the Russians do pay me something, either in June or sometime some month. I fell out of my car the other night, breaking the car and my ribs, so it would be very pleasant if the Russians paid either for the car or for my ribs.

My book has had a bad time, so I've nothing to hope for in that direction. I don't suppose it will even sell one edition, which leaves me more in debt than ever, as I've drawn royalties on two editions last November.

There is nothing of interest here but my broken ribs.

Yours, Liam O'Flaherty

---

255. HRHRC ALS to A.D. Peters
Sea View Cottage, Coolboy   1 June, 1928

Dear Peters,

I am returning signed contract for Swedish *Informer*. That's bully of you. I think they are excellent terms. About the German rights of *The Assassin*, if you have not yet made any contract I think you might give it to Hauser, who did *The Informer*. He's over here now and he'd agree to any contract you draw up. He's a very good fellow and well known in Germany. I fancy it would be good business to let him do it. But just as you please.

I got a very cheeky letter from Curtis Brown saying you were not looking after my business properly, and suggesting that he should do it. I take it this man Joseph is not an Englishman. Would you mind dropping him a note to say that if he wants to make any enquiries he should write to you in the first instance.[1]

I'll send you the address of the Frenchman, Louis Postif, who is translating *Mr Gilhooley* and *The Assassin*. See if you can make a contract and get a few pounds out of him.[2]

I'm going to hold up all my writing until March 31st next so as to evade Cape's contract. By that time I hope to have MS of two novels ready. In the meantime I think we'll get out of a volume of short stories.

Yours sincerely
Liam O'Flaherty

[1] Michael Joseph the publisher, whose letter of 22 May, suggesting that he might generate more interest in O'Flaherty's work, is tactfully worded.

[2] On 15 May, Louis Postif of Les Charmettes, par Arnonville-les-Gonesse (S. et O.), wrote a long and effusive letter upon which O'Flaherty scribbled, 'Could you look up this chap and see if the French pay in other commerce than politeness?' The French version of *The Informer (Le Denonciateur)* appeared in *Revue Hebdomadaire* and *The Assassin* later in the same revue.

---

256. SLUL (Folio [SL] V 36 (viii)) ALS to Charles Lahr
Sea View Cottage, Coolboy   n.d [? June, 1928]

Dear Charles,

Does that bloke really want the manuscript of *The Assassin*? I didn't hear from him about it. I expect the blighter doesn't want it anyway. How's the kid and is there any news of consequence? Do drop me a line. I nearly killed myself last Monday coming home from Baldoyle Races. I drove the car into a ditch and broke some ribs, but I was lucky to escape. With the help of a sergeant in the C.I.D. and an American Jew, whom I met, both drunk, coming from a country whorehouse, I set her on her feet again and drove home. Damned awful experience.

Give my regards to Davies if you see him. Do you know did Cape get out that special edition of *The Assassin* yet? The fearful Jesuit is not pushing the thing at all, curse him.

Well! Cheerio old cock! Could you find out whether that man wants the MS. I've got to pay for this broken car, not including my ribs.

Yours
Liam O'Flaherty

---

257. HRHRC TLS to A.D. Peters
Sea View Cottage, Coolboy   15 June, 1928

Dear Peters,

I have just come back from the Aran Islands, so you will excuse my delay in answering your letters. There are only two mails a week down there.

First, I thank you for selling *The Assassin* in Germany at such a good price. I was with Hauser down in Aran and I told him about this. He said he would get the translation from Knaur as soon as he got back, sometime next week. This Hauser is an excellent fellow, and is a sort of literary editor on the *Frankfurt Zeitung* and is a real live wire in the American sense. He said he would try to interest Ulstein in getting a volume of my short stories printed there. I think that would benefit my literary reputation a lot in Germany.[1]

Do just as you please about the O'Brien anthology. He's a tight fellow and is sure to stick to his extra two guineas, so perhaps you might accept the three guineas.[2] I'll sit down and write the story for Elkin Matthews.[3]

Archer went to Foyles about the MS of *The Assassin*, so they sent me an enquiry. I asked them for sixty pounds this morning. When I get a reply, if they accept this sum, I'll send their letter on to you, saying you have the MS. Then you hold them up for a few days until I have the MS written out. I'll send you the MS as soon as it is finished and you collect the money from Foyles.

The Frenchman Postif has no contract for *Mr Gilhooley* and *The Assassin*. I have dug up the Curtis Brown letter and am sending it to you.

With best wishes

Yours

Liam O'Flaherty

[1] Knaur wrote to A.D. Peters 11 June apologising for not taking Hauser as translator of *The Assassin*, as the work had already been given to Mr. Fein (translator of Sinclair Lewis into German). (Source A.D. Peters files, HRHRC)

[2] For the annual 'Best Short Stories' volumes edited by E.J. O'Brien, Peters had asked five guineas for 'The Oar', whereas O'Brien offered three guineas for British and American publication, and refused to give more.

[3] Elkin Matthews had asked O'Flaherty to write a story for a fee of twenty guineas.

---

258. JR ALS to May O'Callaghan
Sea View Cottage, Coolboy   n.d. [mid June, 1928]

Dear O.C.,

Sorry for not thanking you for the book sooner but I was down in the Aran Islands with a friend making a film. *The Diary of a Communist Schoolboy* is splendid work.[1] True book, best book I've read for some time, so healthy and damned sane, and everything so hopeful and different from this blasted decadent outlook in Western Europe. Fine, it made me feel happy. If Kostya {Rialstrof?} is really a type that is growing and not a Turgenevian creation of the author's that should grow, then Russia may feel content. The other book by {?} I thought poor stuff. I read a chapter only. Drat these English socialists, they haven't enough blood in them to feed the germs of syphilis.

By the way, will you be in London in August? My sister is going over there for a holiday and I thought it would be nice for her if she could meet you. She is very holy and very nervous, but a very good fellow. Do let me know.

This friend of mine, a German, wanted a plane to fly over Dublin to take film stuff and he went to Fitzgerald, Minister of Defence, for an army one. Fitz became violently indignant when he heard I was going up in an army plane. 'On no account,' he said. My friend asked why, 'I don't like him,' said Fitz. 'Why?' 'Because he's in close communication with Russia. We're watching him very carefully.' Did you ever hear the like of it? And then he said, (this King's Minister): 'And I don't like an Irishman who joined the

English army.' Even better, a Bolshevist, and an Imperialist at the same time. I feel like Jekyll and Hyde, but am hated as both.

Yours
L.O'F

[1] By N. Ognyov (trans. A. Werth), London: Gollancz, 1928.

---

259. SLUL (Folio [SL] V36 (viii)) ALS to Charles Lahr
Sea View Cottage, Coolboy   26 June, 1928

Dear Charlie,

Thanks for your letter and for your kindness in helping me to get rid of the MS. I think Bloch is going to take it. At least he said so by telegram and offered to pay my price of fifty quid. That's bravo. I sent him the MS. Foyles offered thirty, so I didn't reply. It was very good of you and I sha'n't forget it, old cock.

Say, I've written a most extraordinary story called 'Patsa' for the new magazine that is going to be produced by the Fanfrolico Press, I doubt if they can print it.[1] If they do they'll be locked up without a doubt. But it's bloody good, and it's true. It's the first Rabelaisian story I've written and it's true, every word of it. Ask Stephenson[2] to let you have a read of the typescript. Tell him I told you to read it. It will make you laugh.

I am glad you have the kid back. If you get it into the country it will surprise you how it will improve. Of course this summer is awful, but the sea air is always good. You should get it away as soon as possible.

We'll be coming to London the end of September and I think I'll go to lecture in America the 1st of January. I'll probably be put in jail before the end of the lectures.

Did you read *The Diary of a Communist Schoolboy*? It's damn good I think. Remember me to your wife and to Davies. I'll look forward to seeing him in September. It's very dull here now.

Yours
Liam

[1] The *London Aphrodite* published 'Patsa or the Belly of Gold' in its first issue, August, 1928.

[2] The Fanfrolico Press, also The Mandrake Press (P.R. Stephensen) were at 5 Bloomsbury Square, WC1.

---

260. SIUL ALS to James B. Pond[1]
Sea View Cottage, Coolboy   26 July, 1928

Dear Sir,

My publisher Mr. Brace has written me that you would kindly arrange a lecture tour for me in America, beginning January 1st, 1929. I should be very pleased if you'd do so. I have been wanting to get to America for a long time. Of course I was there before but not in the capacity of lecturer.

If you agree to manage a tour would you kindly send me full particulars as to terms and anything else that might be useful, for instance, whether it would be useful to publish a book in America coinciding with my arrival there? And whether you have any idea as to what form the lectures should take? I think I have some new matter dealing with an outlook on Irish peasant life which is significant of the new generation since the origin of the Free State.

As I want very badly to make some money I am quite prepared to do anything short of murdering somebody.

Trusting to hear from you soon, permit me to remain,

Yours very sincerely
Liam O'Flaherty

[1] Addressed to 25 West 43rd St., New York.

---

261. HRHRC TLS to A.D. Peters
[No address, London]   n.d. [end September, 1928]

Dear Peters,

Sorry I could not get to see you today. I am leaving for France in the morning. Please hold any correspondence until I send you my address from Nice, or wherever it is my wife is taking me.[1]

The Baroness de Hueck will get in touch with you about the lecture tour in America.[2] I rather think you should sign me on if you satisfy yourself that everything is correct. Personally I like her very much indeed, and I am anxious in any case to do a lecture tour in America, beginning next October. That should be the date of publication of *The House of Gold*, and I am determined to get there with this book. I think a lecture tour would be the real thing. So be nice to the Baroness.

I suppose you'll send the Cape contract along. I expect to arrive in the south of France in about a week's time. I don't expect there is any great hurry with it.

Well, cheerio, until I see you again and please give my best regards and compliments to your wife and thank her in my name for her hospitality. Thanking you also for your kindness and your excellent management of my affairs. I remain,

Yours, Liam O'Flaherty

[1] While in London the O'Flaherty's stayed at 43 Guilford St. WCl and were invited home by A.D. Peters. There had that summer been some confusion between Curtis Brown and A.D. Peters over the French translation rights to Louis Postif. Curtis Brown, acting on behalf of Cape to whom O'Flaherty had sold his rights, had arranged a contract with Librarie Stock, and an option on his future work. The advance on this (half of two thousand francs) against royalties of six percent to six thousand, ten percent thereafter, had been paid to O'Flaherty. Postif had

also sold the French serial rights for one thousand francs (to be shared between Cape and the author). A friend of Postif's, Paul Dottin, made a special study of O'Flaherty to add to his fame in France, and his article was published in *Gringoire*.

On 20 August, 1928, British International Pictures Ltd. had acquired film rights of *The Informer* for eight years for seven hundred and fifty pounds, fifty percent down and fifty percent on production. With these various payments O'Flaherty could therefore now afford to travel.

[2] On 18 September Cape had written asking Peters if O'Flaherty would be willing to go on a lecture tour to America. The Baroness C. de Hueck, staying at White Hall, Bloomsbury Sq., WC1 while in London, ran a lecture bureau. O'Flaherty would go under the auspices of Leigh Emmerich. Her terms were not generous, and Peters, who was wary of the Baroness, proposed to settle nothing until he arrived in New York.

---

262. HRHRC ALS to A.D. Peters
Hôtel Beau-Séjour, La Colle sur Loup, Alpes Maritimes[1]
                                                n.d. Monday [October, 1928]

Dear Peters,

I am returning the contract signed. I think it is excellent and I thank you very much for putting it through. I'll try to get the remainder of the stories written by the end of December. I'll probably be able to do so as this place is excellent for work. I've already done twelve thousand words of my novel.

I note what you say about the Baroness and her lecture bureau. Of course I had no thought of committing myself to anything personally. I leave it entirely in your hands. Whatever arrangements you make will be entirely satisfactory to me.

I wish you every good luck on your American trip. Please convey my best regards to your wife.

                                                Yours sincerely
                                                Liam O'Flaherty

P.S. I read with pleasure in the *Observer* that Roughead[2] was easily the best forward in the London Scottish this season. Congratulate him for me.

[1] The MS of 'The Stone' (at HRHRC) is marked with the above address, dated 12 October 1928.
[2] W. N.Roughead on Peters' staff is a keen rugby player.

---

263. HRHRC TLS to A.D. Peters
Hôtel Beau Séjour   19 October, 1928

Dear Peters,

Do please let the Irish police have the serial rights of *Spring Sowing*. It is very important for me that they should print the stories in view of the Censorship Bill that is now being passed by the Irish Government, and which is largely directed against me by the Church. My friends in the police force are obviously making a gesture in order to show that the police do not regard my work as in any way immoral or contrary to the best interests of public morality. This would ensure the continued circulation of my work in Ireland.[1]

I don't know what they might be expected to pay, but perhaps something like twenty-five or thirty pounds. If you have a story called 'The Fall of Joseph Timmins' still on hand, perhaps you might send it to the Fanfrolico magazine, *The London Aphrodite* for their next number.[2]

With best wishes,

Yours sincerely
Liam O'Flaherty

---

[1] *Garda Review*, Dublin, offered a reprint of *Spring Sowing* stories for twenty five pounds outright (this was reduced to ten pounds at O'Flaherty's request on 1 November, 1928).

[2] This story first appeared in *The Mountain Tavern* collection.

---

264. HRHRC TLS to W.N. Roughead
Hôtel Beau Séjour   n.d. [mid November, 1928]

Dear Roughead,

I just sent off a cablegram to Peters accepting the lecture tour. That's very good.[1]

I am sending on the manuscripts for the book of short stories, with a list enclosed giving the title of the volume and the order in which the stories are to be printed. There are still two stories missing, 'The Alien Skull' and 'The Sinner'. I think 'The Alien Skull' is with *The Tatler* so perhaps you could enclose it in the package.[2] I don't know where 'The Sinner' is. If it can't be found, better send on the package to Cape without it.

Any money that reaches the office for me between now and March, I would like you to hold for me until I turn up in London.

With best wishes,

Yours very sincerely
Liam O'Flaherty

---

[1] On 7 November, Peters had written to O'Flaherty telling him that the Leigh Emmerich Lecture Bureau of 11 West 42nd St., New York City, could offer a guarantee of three hundred pounds and steam and rail fares for a tour to begin in November 1929 or January 1930. Peters advised acceptance (the letter is from Roughead), with payment based on forty percent of lecture fees to O'Flaherty up to seven thousand dollars and fifty percent thereafter. O'Flaherty accepted these terms. (Source A.D. Peters files HRHRC)

[2] O'Flaherty often failed to keep copies of his work. The *Tatler* printed 'The Alien Skull' 29 January, 1929 and paid twenty guineas for it.

265. HRHRC TLS to W.N. Roughead
Hôtel Beau-Séjour   24 November, 1928

Dear Roughead,

Thanks for your letter. I am writing a story for the *People* and will send it along in a few days.

I enclose a note from Germany. You will notice that it refers to a letter from Neue Deutche Verlag. I have not received that letter. Perhaps they wrote direct to your office. In any case you might communicate with them as to the possibilities of their publishing my volumes of short stories, and perhaps the serialisation of my new novel next Spring. They are labour people, and I believe difficult in the matter of money. However ... Their address is, Neuer Deutcher Verlag, Berlin W8.

Please thank Peters for me on account of having sold the volume of short stories to Brace. I am working hard on my novel, which promises well.

By the way, I don't know whether you are aware that the Fanfrolico Press owe you money for 'Red Barbara' which they printed in the *London Aphrodite*. They printed the story in their last issue. I have a sort of idea that you might be confused about their having paid me before, owing to their printing a former story which I sent to them direct. If so, get after them, as they also are a bit fishy.[1]

Yours sincerely, [unsigned]

[1]SLUL has an undated letter from this address from Topsy to Esther Archer written during what is evidently the grape harvest. In it she says: 'Liam is now engrossed with his new novel. He goes forth every day with his manuscript under his arm to write up in the pinewoods.' They had seen Sylvia Beach while in Paris. James Joyce was ill and could see no one. Miss Beach wanted to meet Rhys Davies.

In his autobiography *Print of a Hare's Foot* (1969) p. 131 (late in 1928) W.H. Davies describes how he 'took a bus to La Colle, a village lying on the road to Vence, where high-strung Liam O'Flaherty sat writing a novel under a fig tree in the garden of an inn, living there with his patient Irish wife.'

---

266. HRHRC TLS to A.D. Peters
Hôtel Beau-Séjour   5 December, 1928

Dear Peters,

I enclose the signed contracts. Thanks very much for putting them through, especially the contract for the short stories which I did not at all expect. The lecture tour sounds exciting.

I am re-writing the first part of my new novel. The part is now almost complete, about one hundred pages. I'll send it along to you if you think you might be able to serialise it, but I doubt very much whether in its completed form it would serialise, as the end will be too strong. In any case, I'll send the complete first part along. You can get a copy made and send my typescript back, as I may make further minor alterations in the text when I have it all finished.

In any case I'll be interested to hear what you think of it, as far as it has gone. I hope you feel fit after your American trip. My family and myself are all in the pink of condition.

With best wishes for yourself and your family, I remain,

Yours very sincerely, Liam O'Flaherty

In December 1928, Cape refused 'Patsa or the Belly of Gold' as 'too fierce' to include in *The Mountain Tavern* collection, this is conveyed in a letter from G. Wren Howard dated 15 December. It is interesting to note that 'The Ditch', printed for the first time in this collection, has a variant seven page MS in HRHRC. In the printed version Mick drowns the newborn baby of Maggie, made pregnant by him, and is given three years penal servitude. In the MS Mick leaves Maggie in the ditch before the child is born and goes back to the farm to stable and feed his horse and himself.

In November 1928, O'Flaherty was asked to write a true-life story for the *People* for fifteen guineas per thousand words. He sent this to Odhams Press via Peters on 3 December. It was published, cut and with a changed title, in *John Bull*, 13 July, 1929, pp.20-21 'Cashiered, the drama of the barefooted Englishman – Liam O'Flaherty's real life story'.

---

267. HRHRC TLS to A.D. Peters
Hôtel Beau-Séjour   24 December, 1928

Dear Peters,

Thanks for your note with reference to the volume of short stories. Tell Cape he can either print or omit 'Patsa' just as he pleases, that's his business.[1] As far as I am concerned the volume is complete. I add nothing to it.

Thanks for your charming Xmas card. As it's too late now to wish a happy Xmas, my wife joins with me in wishing you and your wife and family a very happy New Year

Yours very sincerely
Liam O'Flaherty

[1] HRHRC has the MS of a different 'Patsa', six pages unfinished. This Patsa used to beat his wife to make her fart. It ends with a description of how Patsa used to exploit tourists to get money out of them. The original title of *The Mountain Tavern* was *The Painted Woman*, changed by Cape.

268. HRHRC TLS to A.D. Peters
National Hotel, Upper Bedford Place, Russell Square, London[1]

n.d. Thursday, (? end January, 1929)

Dear Peters,

Thanks very much for the cheque for £22.10. I'm awfully sorry to have created such a lot of worry for you about it. I'll send the other cheque back to you when it comes from France. I never knew we had run out of money until my wife told me that our account was overdrawn; so there you are. I think I can persuade the film people to pay up the remainder of the money and that will put me right.[2]

My novel is going splendidly but it's becoming rather terrible. It will frighten the life out of people. Has Roughead managed to get tickets for the match? I tried the *Daily Mail* man I know, but apparently there's nothing doing in that quarter.

Yours
Liam O'Flaherty

[1] O'Flaherty remained at this hotel during February while finishing his novel, and returned to Wicklow suddenly 12 March. On 7 February Mrs Lily Anne Coppard, of Chop Cherry, Chinnor (A.E. Coppard's wife) was paid £6.9.0. for typing *The House of Gold*.

[2] By 28 February, 1929 the cast for the film of *The Informer* had been mentioned in the press. The British International Films production began end February and was due to be released for showing a year later. The second half of the seven hundred and fifty pound option was received 31 August, 1929.

---

269. HRHRC TLS to A.D. Peters
Sea View Cottage, Coolboy   14 March, 1929

Dear Peters,

I am awfully sorry our visit to Elstree did not come off. I telephoned to Mycroft and he told me that Robinson did not want to have anybody around just now, as he was shooting scenes in small rooms and that I should wait until he was shooting the big street scenes in about a fortnight's time. I decided therefore to come home at once and if possible make another trip to London in about a month's time to have a look at the show. Should you like to go down to Elstree in the meantime, my friend Miss Iris Barry would be delighted to take you down there. If you phone her any day about midday she could arrange it for you. She is a very decent soul, and a much more amusing companion that I would be.

Please send me along the original typescript of my novel when you get it complete.

Please convey my apologies to your wife for being unable to join her party last Saturday night. My affairs here at home were in rather alarming disorder and I had to come home at once.

With very best regards

Yours sincerely
Liam O'Flaherty

---

270 HRHRC TLS to A.D. Peters
Sea View Cottage, Coolboy   27 March, 1929

Dear Peters,

I enclose the article for the *Daily Chronicle*.[1] It's not much good but I hope it will do. I'm rather empty after the effort on my novel and I can't write.

I enclose two letters I got. If the Fanfrolico people want to reprint 'The Fight' they may do so, I suppose, but I daresay they'll pay nothing.

Yours sincerely
Liam O'Flaherty

P.S. May I remind you that Cape's half yearly settlement of royalties is on April 1st, he should owe me something.

[1] 'What brings Happiness to Me' commissioned by the *Daily Chronicle*, was printed 5 June, 1929, p.8, as 'From Flag-Fall to Winning Post'. It also appeared in the *Liverpool Post*. The ten guinea fee was paid by August. In the article O'Flaherty says he finds happiness most easily in excitement that drives out the memory of the past, the memory of all his good comrades killed in the war. The rest of the article is about the race course.

---

271. HRHRC TLS to A.D. Peters
The Old Schoolhouse,
St. Valerie, Dargle Road, Bray, Co. Wicklow   29 March, 1929

Dear Peters,

The above is my new address. I'll get it shortened later. I have now got a lovely cottage with bath and electric light ten miles from Dublin in glorious mountainy country. I hope perhaps that you and your wife may be able to wander over this way in Summer for a few days.

Listen – I am selling *The Tourist's Guide to Ireland* to the Mandrake Press. It's about eighteen thousand words and they offer me fifty pounds down and fifteen percent royalty on all copies sold over three thousand. I think that's fine. Would you put the deal through, collect the fifty pounds, deduct what I owe you and send me the remainder? I remember you advised me against publishing it as it might injure me in Ireland, but I have come to the conclusion that the time is now ripe for publishing it this Summer, owing to local politics and that it will, on the contrary, do me a lot of good.

I am terribly glad you like *The House of Gold*. You wait till you read *Rathcroghan* which is going to be my first humorous novel. I'll begin it when I have rested sufficiently.

Cheerio! Best regards to your family, and keep lowering good beer. There's nothing like it. Tell Roughead I have not forgotten that I owe him ten bob. I'll send it next week to him. Damn Scotland.

Yours
Liam O'Flaherty

[Liam sent Peters a separate note of the same date telling him to let Louis Postif have all his French translation rights.]

---

272. HRHRC ALS to A.D. Peters
The Old Schoolhouse, St. Valerie   8 April, 1929

Dear Peters,

I enclose the signed contract for *The Tourist's Guide to Ireland*. About those lectures, if you could arrange with either party for a visit at the same time, September or October next, I should like it. The following are tentative subjects for my lectures:

1. The Art of enjoying life.
2. Geniuses whom I have met.
3. Why Ireland is the greatest country in the world.[1]

Yours sincerely
Liam O'Flaherty

P.S. Excuse this abrupt note, my daughter has got hold of my trouser leg and she is hauling me from my chair. L.O'F.

[1] On 6 April, Peters' letter to O'Flaherty, which crossed with this, told him that the lecture tour bureau company had disbanded, so his U.S. tour was cancelled. A new lecture contract was later made with Celebrities Management Inc. of 11 West 42nd St. New York City (with Emmerich as President), but in the end this too was cancelled.

---

273. HRHRC TLS to A.D. Peters
The Old Schoolhouse, St. Valerie   n.d. [early April, 1929]

Dear Peters,

Awfully sorry not to have sent an acknowledgment of that cheque for *The House of Gold* sooner. I thought I had and then realised I had not. I was very busy with some good copy which brought me around the country.

I trust you enjoyed immensely your trip to Eastern Europe. I bet you feel fresh and enlightened after it. Shortly I'll send along a story called 'The Black Mastiff' for the *Radio Times* and one called 'Pay on South Pole' which you may be able to sell to *Nash's Magazine*. I am going to make a definite assault on *Nash's* this Summer. I think it's about time.

Cheerio, hope you find time to have a look at Ireland during the Summer. I am told that Lya de Putti may come over here shortly to see the fellows. We are all going into training. Oh, yes! Tell Emmerich that his date will suit me admirably. I mean about the lectures. Thanks very much for all your good work on my behalf.

Yours sincerely
Liam O'Flaherty

[13 April, O'Flaherty wrote an unsigned note to Peters, asking him to sell the *Radio Times* the longest possible story, perhaps 'Spring Sowing'. He is beginning his Rathcroghan novel, and is hard up. Peters sent him copies of the reviews of *The Mountain Tavern* from the *Spectator*, the *New Statesman* and the *Evening Standard*.]

---

274. HRHRC ALS to A.D. Peters
The Old Schoolhouse, St. Valerie   18 April, 1929

Dear Peters,

Thanks for cheque and note. I got a note from Howard [of Cape] to say my book of stories was selling very well. That's nice. By the way, if you can raise any money for me please do, because I am trying to liquidate the cost of my removal and Punchestown.

Did you really go to Buda-pesth? And where the devil is it? Silly man! You should come to Dublin instead. As an American said to me at Punchestown, 'This place is too good to be true.'

Yours
Liam O'F

---

275. HRHRC TLS to A.D. Peters
The Old Schoolhouse, St. Valerie   25 May, 1929

Dear Peters,

Please forgive me for not turning up to see you at the appointed time last week and for not thanking you for the loan of ten pounds. As a matter of fact I was on the most preternatural skite and have only just recovered from it. *C'est ça*, I do not feel like talking about it. It was worse than the war.

I enclose a document which I signed and which you are to send on to Pinker, telling him to pay you any money that comes due to me from this awful business. Some fellow called Elsner[1] wrote to me a few years ago saying he had dramatised *Mr Gilhooley*, and sent a contract from Pinker, his agent, which he asked me to sign.[2] This is the result. He sent me a copy of the play, which I considered pretty awful and which I did not acknowledge, but as it has gone this far, let it go ahead. One's reputation cannot be ruined in America, as they don't know good from bad. And we at least get fifty pounds. I enclose Pinker's letter.

Did that German dramatisation business fall through and is there any news of the German rights of *The House of Gold*?

With best wishes and apologies

Yours sincerely
Liam O'Flaherty

P.S. I think the contract for this Gilhooley play is fifty/fifty between Elsner and myself. Yes, that's it.

P.P.S. It appears this came from Pinker's London office by the stamp.

[1] Frank Elsner dramatised *Mr Gilhooley*, May 1922.

[2] Eric Pinker, son of New York literary agent James B. Pinker (died 1922), who had nurtured Joseph Conrad. A.D. Peters replied to this letter on 28 May. He does not much care for the play agreement, seeing the dramatisation is a bad one. Also does O'Flaherty realise he has signed away seventy-five percent of the film rights, the producers to have fifty percent and dramatist twemty-five percent. Peters has not yet come to terms with the German people over *The Informer* film rights, but American agents are negotiating with them. Peters sent a cheque for £44.1.11 on 30 May from Eric Pinker, staying at Talbot House, Arundel St.,WC2. O'Flaherty's agreement with Elsner had been made before Peters took over O'Flaherty's affairs, and a copy of it was later sent him by Pinker.

---

276. HRHRC TLS to A.D. Peters
The Old Schoolhouse, St. Valerie   31 May, 1929

Dear Peters,

Thanks very much for your cheque which was very welcome.[1] Are *John Bull's* going to publish that other story I wonder, and the article I wrote for the *Daily Chronicle*? Did they take it?[2]

I have written nothing yet, but I am getting into fighting condition. I have my novel planned out but cannot get a title for it. When I get the title I may begin. I think it will be more publicly interesting than my others, as there is racing, football, theatres and so to speak civilised life in it. I don't know, though, whether I'll be able to have it finished before I go to America. Perhaps I should.

With best wishes

Yours sincerely
Liam O'Flaherty

P.S. Since I wrote this letter, I wrote the enclosed sketch which I think funny, though true. Sell it somewhere if you can. L.O'F.

P.P.S. Thanks for the Pinker cheque. You forgot to deduct your commission, which you must debit or whatever it is, from my next cheque. L.O'F.

[1] *The Mountain Tavern* was published in the U.S. on 16 May and O'Flaherty got two hundred and fifty dollars advance on royalties. Harcourt, Brace & Co. also took *The House of Gold*.

[2] 'Cashiered – The drama of the bare-footed Englishman. A real life story' was published in *John Bull*, XLVI (No. 1204) 13 July, 1929, pp20-21

---

277. HRHRC TLS to A.D. Peters
The Old Schoolhouse, St. Valerie   18 June, 1929

Dear Peters,

Thanks very much for selling the sketch for that enormous sum of money. It's preposterous, but sad, that people pay money for a poor thing and refuse to print something that's good.[1]

I got the proofs of *The House of Gold* from Cape. I'm correcting two sets. I expect Brace will want the other. I'll send them along as soon as I have them corrected. I'll have my new novel done, I think, before I go to America.

They have now finished the film so I suppose they should pay up.[2]

With affectionate regards
Yours
Liam O'Flaherty

[1] 11 June, 1929 *The Tatler* was sent a story, 'Fifty-Fifty' by Peters, and accepted it on 13 June, for fifteen guineas, first British serial rights. The only story they published was 'Pay on Cruiser', 30 October, 1929.

[2] O'Flaherty has forgotten that no further payment is due from the film of *The Informer* until the film is released.

---

278. HRHRC TLS to A.D. Peters
The Old Schoolhouse, St. Valerie   27 June, 1929

Dear Peters,

I think the best thing to do with the proofs of *The House of Gold* is to let Cape do what he likes with them in the matter in question. The error originated with the typist, who did not put in the heading for the third part 'Nemesis'. Of course, it looks funny to me without the third part, but it will mean nothing to the public, who won't notice whether there are three or two parts. It would be better now without any Part heading.[1] But I certainly could not omit any lines. I think the firm of Cape is exceedingly mean and stingy.

Tell him that I prefer to have *all* the half titles cut out, rather than have two without the third. If it costs money to do that, let him keep the two half titles and omit the third which I inserted into the proofs. Also, when you are sending him the proofs you might tell him that he should try to get the book published about the middle of August if possible, because the film of

The Informer is being shown in September and the attention attracted by the film would not do my novel any good if it appeared about that time.

There is likely to be another Civil War about my *Tourist's Guide to Ireland*.

Yours
Liam O'Flaherty

[1] *The House of Gold* was published with three parts, 'Passion', 'Disintegration' and 'Nemesis'.

---

279. HRHRC TLS to A.D. Peters
The Old Schoolhouse, St. Valerie   2 July, 1929

Dear Peters,

I enclose a letter from the *Forum*.[1] I have written to him to say that you would send on a story or two as soon as I have them written. As far as I know you have nothing to send him at the moment, or would he take 'Fifty-Fifty' after the *Tatler* had bought it? I suppose not. I'll probably have two stories written within the week. I hope he pays on acceptance if he buys them, as these Americans are so crooked.

I am going great guns with my new comic novel. I hope it pans out all right. It's called *Rathcroghan*.

Yours
Liam O'Flaherty

P.S. [ALS] We are going to throw a great party in September for the trade show of *The Informer*. I hope you are both in town for it. L.O'F.

[1] The *Forum* (ed, Henry Goddard Leach), 441 Lexington Avenue, New York, offered two hundred dollars for the first serial rights of a two thousand word story up to 15 September.

On 5 July O'Flaherty sent Peters a story, 'Pay on Cancer', saying he would send another story in a few days. This is the 'Pay On Cruiser' published in the *Tatler*.

---

280. HRHRC TLS to Douglas Clayton.
The Old Schoolhouse, St. Valerie   10 July, 1929

Thanks for your letter. I am sending you the manuscript of a story called 'The Mermaid'. I am also sending you the typescript of my new novel *The House of Gold* and the typescript of a curious little sketch which I wrote years ago, but never published, 'The Flood'.[1] I am sorry I have no trace at all of the Tim Healy script. I probably burned it. Perhaps the American might like the other typescripts?

I have also the manuscript of the new book I brought out recently (or rather booklet), a thing called *A Tourist's Guide to Ireland*. It's about twenty thousand words. It might probably be of interest as it's most likely to be the first book banned under the Irish Censorship Bill.

It's very kind of you to write to me about these things. As to the price of the typescripts and MSS, I have no idea. I certainly shall not quarrel with anything I can get for them.

Permit me to remain

Yours very sincerely
Liam O'Flaherty

[1] In fact published twice in 1925, as O'Flaherty later realises.

---

281. HRHRC TLS to A.D. Peters
The Old Schoolhouse, St. Valerie   n.d. Wednesday [? early July, 1929]

Dear Peters,

I enclose a story 'The Mermaid' for the *Forum*. I'll send you two more within the next few days. If we sell to the *Forum* does it mean that we also sell first English serial rights? I also enclose a letter from the editor of the *Boston Herald*.

If you don't think this a popular story don't send it to the *Forum*. I have one about a horse which I'll write tomorrow that will be more popular. Still, they'll buy several, so we had better send them as many as possible. If they buy any at all?[1]

Yours
Liam O'Flaherty

P.S. [ALS] My new racehorse, in the story of course, is called Cancer, by Indigestion, out of Canned Meat.[2]

By the way, I got a letter from Emmerich asking me to extend my lecture tour for a month in order to go to California, where there have been a number of demands for my lectures. I lost the letter and don't know his address. Would you write and say I'll stay another month, by all means, or send me his address and I'll write myself. L.O'F.

[1] 8 July O'Flaherty sent Peters 'The Modest Virgin' and 'The Flood'. Peters liked 'The Mermaid' and sent it to the *Forum* who refused it. On 26 October, 1929, it was published by *John O'London's Weekly*.

[2] This is evidently Cruiser by Indigestion out of Canned Meat in 'Pay On Cruiser'. There is another horse mentioned in this story, Gripes, by Cramp out of Lobster Patty!

---

282. HRHRC ALS to Douglas Clayton
The Old Schoolhouse, St. Valerie   26 July, 1929

Dear Clayton,

Thanks very much for disposing of the MS at such a fearfully good price. I am returning the signed page and when I return from London, where I am going for the weekend, I'll root out *A Tourist's Guide to Ireland* MS and send it to you and perhaps you would be so kind as to allow some foolish person to waste good money on that too. One of the very few good things that God has done is the creation of Americans, I mean in this sense – or without sense.

Thanks awfully. Oh! I say, I think I sent you a note to say that 'The Flood', that little sketch, was published already in a magazine, the *Dublin Magazine*, about six years ago!

Permit me to sign myself

Yours very sincerely
Liam O'Flaherty

O'Flaherty had written to Clayton two days previously saying he had no other MSS to sell. He had sold them all for loose cash. On 27 July John Huston and S. Jaffe cabled about dramatising *The Assassin*. They wanted a six months' option with a five hundred dollar advance, but later withdrew lacking backers.

On 10 August O'Flaherty wrote hopefully to Peters, 'This American dramatisation mania sounds lucrative and bless them, so badly needed. Thanks very much.'

---

283. HRHRC TLS to A.D. Peters
The Old Schoolhouse, St. Valerie   n.d. [? August, 1929]

Dear Peters,

I just got a letter from my friend Heinrich Hauser. He says he can get the best publisher in Berlin for *The House of Gold* and that he will translate it himself.[1] This is very good, so if you can get a copy of the proofs from Cape send it along to him, as soon as possible, at: Berlin W10, 79 Kaiserin Augustastrasse.

Yours sincerely
Liam O'Flaherty

P.S. I have lain down everything and am writing a war novel. Will have it done in two months. Great excitement. Probable title *The Bombers* or *Bombs*.

[1] There was much correspondence during 1929 between Peters and various translation rights applicants for German, French, Dutch, Spanish, Italian, Swedish, Czech and Polish rights, etc.

---

284. HRHRC ALS to A.D. Peters
The Old Schoolhouse, St. Valerie   18 August, 1929

Dear Peters,

I enclose signed contract for Dutch translation of *The Informer* and a letter that came from Ernest Rhys.[1] I suppose 'The Mermaid' would do for him if you think he should have a story.

I'll probably turn up in London at the end of this week to work. I can't work here as people won't let me alone. I'm writing a war story called *The Murder of Corporal Williams*.[2] I've boiled it down to about thirty thousand words or I hope less, and I think it will be very strong and interesting. I fancy I could do it in a month in some back room, as I feel just about miserable enough now to get on with it. I have an idea that such a story, published at a short price, might turn out to be lucrative; as the motif will work out almost similar to that in *The Informer*, but even in a smaller compass and without unnecessary detail, and with a wider appeal – less local. A good title I think too, suggestive of detective work within.

If I turn up I'll come in for a pow-wow and a glass of beer unless you're too busy.

Yours
Liam O'F

[1] Ernest Rhys was collecting stories for a volume of previously uncollected work from different countries. O'Flaherty was at the National Hotel in London by 22 August. 'The Mermaid' was not used, as Rhys's fee was very low, so he took the already published 'Going into Exile' for this anthology, *Tales from Far and Near*.

[2] The Corporal Williams story, finally titled *The Return of the Brute*, was being written for Mandrake Press, against a royalty of one hundred pounds, half paid in advance of publication.

---

285. HRHRC ALS to A.D. Peters
The Old Schoolhouse, St. Valerie   12 October, 1929

Dear Peters,

I enclose a contract with Fischer Verlag which I signed when in Berlin.[1] You will see that I received from them fifty pounds thirty on *The House of Gold* and twenty as part payment on the next one they produce. I think the contract is all right except that they insisted on fifty fifty for second serial rights. In any case that holds good only for *The House of Gold* and it's not a serialising proposition. Hauser had great trouble in getting the *Frankfurter Zeitung* to take it. They will begin serialising it in January. Fischer will publish *The House of Gold* in March or so, and will probably publish *The Return of the Brute* sometime before Xmas.[2] They seem to be an excellent firm. Please deduct your commission on fifty pounds from my credit, and send the remainder of the American money on to me.

I came through Paris on the way back and I was told there that *Mr Gilhooley* was being a great success there. I heard also that a man called Titus, who runs a magazine called *This Quarter* wants to bring out a limited edition (five hundred signed copies) of a story about three thousand words, for which he might pay one hundred pounds. Ernest Hemingway told me. I wonder could you get in touch with Titus, and try to sell him 'The Mermaid' on those conditions. His address is Edward W. Titus, 4 rue Delambre, Montparnasse, Paris. There is also the story 'Patsa' that was published in the Fanfrolico *London Aphrodite* which might suit him. A hundred pounds would be useful.

Please get rid of Cape. He's doing nothing whatsoever to push my work.

Yours
Liam O'Flaherty

[1] O'Flaherty seems to have spent most of September in London, either at 14 Guilford St. WCl (c/o Miss Barry) or at the National Hotel, Bloomsbury. A letter from his wife to Peters dated 2 October says O'Flaherty tells her he is off to Berlin. By 14 October he was back in Ireland.

[2] *The House of Gold* was published 23 September. O'Flaherty got £62.10. in advance royalties, and on 24 September five hundred dollars from Harcourt Brace, as advance on the U.S. edition.

---

286. HRHRC TLS to A.D. Peters
The Old Schoolhouse, St. Valerie   24 October, 1929

Dear Peters,

Thanks very much for your cheque and for the news that you sold the Tauchnitz rights of two books.[1] I am enclosing the Spanish contract. A chap asked me for your address. He wanted to have *The Informer* translated into German. I told him to write to you. The Portuguese Consul here also wants to translate it into Portuguese, but I think these countries are not worth while bothering about. I enclose also a letter from some Boston magazine.

I believe the film of *The Informer* was a frost.[2] I hope to be able to come to London before I go to America in order to have a talk to you. I didn't hear from Emmerich yet about the date, etc.

Hoping you and your wife and family are very fit and happy

Yours
Liam O'Flaherty

[1] *The Mountain Tavern* was sold for twenty five pounds and *The House of Gold* for thirty pounds to Tauchnitz (Peters' letter of 22 October to O'Flaherty).

[2] *The Informer* film was shown 21 October, 1929. Peters sent O'Flaherty two tickets. There was no trade showing of the film.

For the rest of 1929 the following details can be gleaned:

l9 November Harcourt, Brace & Co. accepted *The Return of the Brute*.

19 November, *Everyman* arranged that O'Flaherty should write a series of ten articles of three thousand words each, weekly, for ninety pounds (British serial rights) to start from 5 December, the more biographical the better, and this seems to have started his

autobiographical writing of what eventually became *Two Years*.

20 November his article on boxing 'What the Big Fight Did to Me' was published in the *Daily Express*, fee eight guineas.

20 November, O'Flaherty at 73 Finchley Road, London NW3 and on 29 November his wife gave Peters as a referee to open a bank account.

2 December, Victor Gollancz wrote to A.D. Peters enquiring about O'Flaherty's previous sales.

By December 1929 Peters tells Cape O'Flaherty is writing *Two Years of My Life* and will they take it in lieu of a volume of short stories. Cape agrees on 5 December, but O'Flaherty tells Peter he will demand an advance of not less than two hundred and fifty pounds, and the book should be ready by February 1930. Cape defer their decision until they have seen the first twenty to thirty thousand words, as it is likely to be more than a hundred thousand words long. Meantime Gollancz proposes terms to O'Flaherty. Cape is distressed about the sale to Tauchnitz, as this edition kills English editions on the Continent. An author is bound to lose if he appears in a Tauchnitz edition and it might also affect the sales in reprints such as the Travellers' Library (letter of 10 December, 1929).

1930

There are no letters extant from O'Flaherty in January, 1930. Frank Elsner was now dramatising *Mr Gilhooley*. It was passed by J.B. Pinker, Inc. of New York, to Jed Harris, theatre manager on 24 January. Peters in a 27 January letter to O'Flaherty sent him a hundred and twenty-five dollars, his half share of the advance on royalties. When the play was staged in New York later that year, *Bookman* 72.297 November, 1930, called it a play about 'the bankruptcy of the flesh, sin shot with remorse' though well acted. On 22 January *The Ecstasy of Angus* was sent to the Aquila Press (Mrs Henderson) by Peters and accepted. As there was some delay in drawing up the agreement, however, O'Flaherty accepted Joiner & Steele's 1931 edition (three hundred and fifty signed copies). (HRHRC A.D. Peters files)

---

287. HRHRC TLS to A.D. Peters.
Hôtel Ste Anne, Martigues, Bouche Du Rhône, France

n.d. [? February, 1930]

Dear Peters,

Thanks very much for sending me that money by wire[1] and please accept my apologies for troubling you, and also for running away to France, but the truth is that I could not possibly work in London. I got mixed up with such a crowd of drinkers. I am working at a great pace here, writing about four thousand words a day. I'll have the book done practically on scheduled time. I'll send you the end of the manuscript at the beginning of next week. I still have that Harcourt, Brace contract and will send it along signed, or unsigned, when I hear from you.

I hope to stay here for a few months and get on with my novel, as soon as I get finished with this autobiography and perhaps write some short stories also. This is an incredibly dull place. Never come here except to see me the next time you come south. It's quite near Marseilles though, only an hour on the bus. I hate foreigners and foreign countries, but it's good for work as there is nothing else to do. Roy Campbell lives here and has become quite an inhabitant, being accepted generally by the fishermen as an eccentric Englishman, etc. He belongs to the local team for the *jeux nautiques* and I believe does a spot of bullfighting in the season.[2]

Please tell Roughead that I quite enjoyed Ireland's victory over Scotland, and give my best regards to your wife. Keep on the beer and forget everything else. The women here are unapproachable and the beer is bad, so I am on the water wagon in both senses.

I am afraid I am being very satirical about Americans. One must tell the truth at all costs. Cheerio,

With best wishes
From Liam O'Flaherty

[1] At the end of February O'Flaherty wired Peters urgently to send him money. He had received a thousand dollar advance on *Two Years* from Harcourt, Brace.

[2] Roy Campbell, 1901-1957, South African born poet, who in *Broken Records – Reminiscences* (Boldiswood, London, 1934), p. 167, mentions that except for Wyndham Lewis and Liam O'Flaherty he avoided literary contacts and found most writers affected.

---

288. HRHRC TLS to A.D. Peters

Hôtel Ste Anne, Martigues   6 March, 1930

Dear Peters,

Thanks for your letter. I am enclosing the completed MS of my life. I will try to write some short stories before I begin my novel. At the moment I can't think of any, but as I have time on my hands I may do a few in a week.

I was greatly excited to see you got another hundred out of Harcourt. I am amused by Postif saying that *The Return of the Brute* is the best of my work. It's bad enough suffering from the regular literary critics without having to suffer from foreign translators.

These Mandrake people are damnable. Tell them to pay up or you'll take the manuscript away from them, that will leave them down ten pounds. They'd rather pay than lose a tenner. To think that I wasted a whole month writing that story and then be badgered about with it. Curse Bloomsbury. I feel like joining the United Empire Party, though that sounds a bit Bloomsburyish too.

My wife and family are coming along here from Nice next week and as my brain seems to function well here, I think I'll stay a few months. The peaceful, soft nature of the place might help to tone down my new book, although the stuff I have written here seems to be as wild as ever.

Everyman directed their cheque to me at your office and it was sent on unopened. It amounted to £37.16. for the month of February. Please charge commission to my account and send them a copy of the final part of the MS.

With best regards

Yours
Liam O'Flaherty

[7 March, O'Flaherty sent Charles Lahr a postcard telling him more or less the same as he had told Peters, and ending 'I think I should stay away until people have forgotten about me.']

---

289. HRHRC ALS to A.D. Peters

Hôtel Ste Anne, Martigues   8 March, 1930

Dear Peters,

I enclose a blurb for *Two Years*. I think these blurbs are usually perfectly ridiculous and useless, so I enclose a particularly useless and ridiculous one, to remind Howard that a little advertisement is infinitely superior to any sort of blurb.[1] Dear, dear! I do hope he does something with this book, which I have written almost solely for the purpose of making money.

I can think of no short stories except pot boilers, so I may write a few of the latter. I am beginning my novel, under the rather odd title of *The Tower of Ivory*. It's going to have practically a happy ending. That is lucky as happy endings must have become fashionable again. My novel stops like a fashionable novel. I hope it doesn't 'run green'.

Have a couple of bob each way on Kilbuck in the Grand National if it runs.

Yours
Liam O'F

[1] From Peters' reply dated 11 March the blurb was too outrageous to use.

---

290. HRHRC ALS to A.D. Peters
Hôtel Ste Anne, Martigues   13 March, 1930

Dear Peters,

I enclose the cheque I received from *Everyman* for £37.16. Would you do me the favour of cashing it and sending me the money, as I have no bank account here and it's troublesome getting a cheque cashed. I'll send along two stories when I have finished them.

Hoping everything is going splendidly with you. The weather is quite good here during the day, but it's extremely cold at night and it's extremely dull both day and night. Sorry to trouble you with this cheque.

Yours sincerely
Liam O'Flaherty

By 27 March O'Flaherty is back at the National Hotel, Upper Bedford Place, Bloomsbury. Peters writes to say *The Informer* film has been banned in the Irish Free State and several papers have rung up asking for an interview.

30 March the *Daily Herald* under 'Irish author hits back' explained that O'Flaherty believed the real objection to the film was that it showed the deplorable living conditions of Ireland's slum dwellers.

In Peter Alexander's critical biography *Roy Campbell* (Oxford U.P. 1982), he gleans from letters written by Campbell to Laurens van der Post and Enslin du Plessis in April/May 1930, that Campbell and O'Flaherty went to Dublin together to watch the Springboks play rugby, and it was only through the intervention of Senator Oliver Gogarty that they avoided arrest after a series of drunken escapades.

24 April, A.D. Peters wrote to Horace Liveright, Georgian House, Bury Street, SW1 to say he has just discovered that 'O'Flaherty sailed for Russia on Tuesday' and will not be back

for about a month. Meantime his wife and child remain in Martigues, address c/o Roy Campbell.

On 3 May, Topsy wrote to Peters. She is with the Campbells (this would be the Tour de Vallier farmhouse, two miles from Martigues), as she has no idea whether she can pay hotel bills or not, but the landlord in Ireland is dunning her for rent. Will any money come in this month – if so how much? Pegeen plays all day with Roy's children. O'Flaherty had wired her that he was going to Russia. Peters replied that as O'Flaherty had collected the money there would be no more due for several weeks, but there should be a hundred pounds by the end of the month, and he sent her twenty-five pounds in advance. Topsy had by now heard from Liam in Norway, asking her to correct the proofs of *Two Years* so she asks Peters to send them to her. Then on 15 May O'Flaherty wired from a P.O. Box address in Moscow, 'Send letters'.

The Return of the Brute (trans. Louis Postif) was published in *Monde* (ed. Henri Barbusse) on 29 May. *Le Réveil de la Brute* was the first English language war book translated into French, published by Stock early July, 1930.

---

291. SLUL (Folio V 36) ALS to Charles Lahr
Hotel d'Europe, Leningrad   8 May, 1930

Dear Charles,

Hello, you old son of a bitch. Here I am in Soviet Russia at last, having a hell of a time. I arrived here three days ago and am going tonight to Moscow.[1] I shall be in London in three weeks time. Please give any of my books you have in stock to the bearer of this letter, Dr. Chrypoff, and I'll settle with you when I get back.

I have received such extraordinary impressions since my arrival in Russia that I really don't know where I am, but I've some stuff to try [and write] when I get back and [it will] put Jesus Christ on the bum for good. Have a drink for me

Cheerio Charles
Liam O'Flaherty

[1] In *I went to Russia* O'Flaherty leaves Moscow on a Soviet ship on 23 April. The voyage is due to take twelve days, calling at Norway en route.

On 28 May, O'Flaherty wrote from Moscow asking for his wife's present address.

14 June, he wired Peters to send him thirty pounds at Hotel Coburg, Berlin and the rest (£31.16), to his wife.

On 17 June there was another wire to Peters to send thirty pounds to Koburgerhof, Berlin. By 20 June Topsy was in the South of France and O'Flaherty has returned from Moscow but has no fixed address.

On 23 June Topsy asks Peters if he knows where O'Flaherty is, as his letter from Berlin said he was moving to Paris. Pegeen is very ill and must be got away.

3 July, Peters wrote to O'Flaherty c/o P.R. Stephenson, Mandrake Press, 41 Museum St., WC1.

On 10 July Peters wired to O'Flaherty c/o Stephenson at his home address at Toys Hill, Brasted, Kent, asking him to call at the office to discuss important American business.

15 July, Peters wrote to O'Flaherty at Brasted, sending him his copies of *Two Years*, and a copy of an agreement with Mandrake for *The Situation is Such* (the first title of his Russian book). Harcourt, Brace snapped it up at once. Peters tried it for serialisation in *Everyman* (ed. H.L. Morrow), who refused it. *Colliers Magazine* also refused the Russian book.

By 23 July Topsy's address is c/o Mrs Ruth Wolfe, 47 Clanricarde Gardens, W2. Peters sent her six hundred pounds on O'Flaherty's instructions, and he also sent money to O'Flaherty, now back in France.

---

292. HRHRC ALS to A.D. Peters
Poste Restante, Concarneau, Finistére, France   28 July, 1930

Dear Peters,

I have arrived at this delectable place in Brittany and hired a flat in a tiny village by the sea's edge for two months. For instance, this morning I had merely to walk thirteen yards from my bed in order to take a dip in the tide. Splendid! It's really excellent and extremely quiet and the wine at the buvette across the road is excellent, at the price of three francs for a large bottle. I'm digging into work and I expect to get a monstrous lot done almost at once. But the curse of it is that the Corona [his typewriter] cast itself ... [rest of letter missing.]

In August 1930 *The Weekly Record* (Glasgow) took twenty thousand words of *Two Years* for fifty pounds. *The Informer* film with Putti and Hansen was released without much success because the speech synchronisation was so poor. The rights for this film had been sold in August 1928 for eight years.

---

293. HRHRC ALS to A.D. Peters
Poste Restante, Concarneau   5 September, 1930

Dear Peters,

I enclose German contract signed. Really it's a public scandal about that *Two Years*, I'm simply furious about it. Unless the librarians boycotted it I can see no explanation for its failure but Cape letting it drop. The bloody swine.

I had a letter from Mrs Graeme Ewing saying she wants me to do a book about boys. I told her I'd do it. I think it's a good idea which I can do easily if you can come to terms with her.

I'm leaving here in ten days or so, when I have finished two hundred pages of my Russian thing.

Yours, Liam O'F

---

294. HRHRC ALS to A.D. Peters
Poste, Restante, Concarneau   6 September, 1930

Dear Peters,

I am sending on pages 39-124 of *Lies about Russia*, which makes about half the book completed now. It's all typed and finished. You needn't get any copies. I am sending on two and keeping one. It will give you an idea what the book is like. I think it amusing, but I am rather tired of this sort of book and I shall be glad to get rid of it, as I want to settle down to my novel.

I am afraid the novel is shaping out as melancholy as my previous ones. I have finally decided to call it *Harry Romayne*. It is odd that I can be quite cheerful when writing about melancholy bastards like the Russians, and yet become tragic about individuals of my own creation. But I shall revenge myself on the uxorious Mahomet if I ever tackle him.

Two Years had a better reception at the hands of the critics than any book of mine so far, but Cape has remained stoically silent about it. Never mind, I even got a good review from the *Methodist Times*.

I think I shall move on to Paris about the 20th of this month.[1] My staying there for the winter depends entirely on my getting an apartment or a studio or some sort of shack to work in. Of course, I'd like to go to New York for a few weeks and shall try to do so when I finish with Russia if possible. It would do me a lot of good I should think, provided I refrained from antagonising the Americans by delivering lectures to them.

I feel rather lonesome for London and would like a game of billards, a pint at the Plough[2] and a steak at Simpsons. I see that great events are happening there, such as Roughead's becoming captain of London Scottish rugby team.

Well! Cheerio, best of luck

Yours, Liam O'F

[1] On 16 September, O'Flaherty moved to Hôtel Palais, D'Orsay, Paris and a little later to chez Mlle Lalaux, 9 rue Victor Considerant, Paris 14. By 2 October he was at the address given in the next letter.

[2] O'Flaherty's favourite London pub, in Museum Street, Bloomsbury.

---

295. HRHRC TLS to A.D. Peters
Hôtel de la Paix, 225 Boulevard Raspail, Paris 14
                                            n.d. Sunday [28 September, 1930]

Dear Peters,

Thanks for your letter. In rotation I am going to answer your enquiries as regards myself.

Paris seems to be looking fine, but I am seeing little of it and in any case most of the important people are not yet back from their holidays. I am trying to avoid people as much as possible for the moment, until I get well dug into my work.

My plans are to stay here for the winter. I have, I think, definitely given up the idea of going to America until Spring. If I begin again to move about my work will be further disorganised and I've done nothing but trash for a long time. I want to finish this Russian book, which is, I hope, the last piece of trash I'm ever going to do. I have begun my novel *Alice Romayne* and if this children's book comes off I'll have to do that too. So my work is cut out for at least six months. If Stephenson offers anything at all for the serial rights of the Russian stuff let him have it, as he is a good fellow and it would be useful in any case as an advertisement. But for goodness sake, try to get rid of Cape for my novel. I definitely think he is hopeless and we might do something with this book. It's about London life and less tense and terrifying than the former ones.[1]

Shortly I shall send you some of it. If it is at all possible let Gollancz have it if he wants it.

As regards money, I have none. There is still some in my bank in London but I want to leave it there in case I should come to town and want to cash a cheque. I can hear you howl, but experience teaches that writers only work when they are broke. Therefore the sooner they get broke the better. Send me what you have to my account. Please send it in notes and do come and see me here sometime in the Autumn.

It's getting shockingly cold, but good for work. Still, I'd rather be in London, but one knows too many people in that charming town and work suffers. I'm rather excited about this novel, but then one is always excited about every fresh thing one begins.

Best luck

Yours
Liam O'Flaherty

[1] This is the still unpublished novel finally entitled *Stack*. The 175 page MS is in HRHRC.

I Went to Russia was refused by *Scribner's, Forum, Harpers, Colliers, Atlantic Monthly* and *World's Work. New Republic* showed interest, but in the end only took an excerpt 'Red Ship' (published 23 September 1931).

On 28 October O'Flaherty sailed for New York on the *George Washington*. His address there was c/o Harcourt, Brace, 383 Madison Avenue.

On 17 November while in New York O'Flaherty signed a contract for *The Wild Swan* and got a four hundred and twenty-five dollar advance in cash.

On 26 November O'Flaherty sent a cable to Peters, 'Belloc is right, returning Saturday, Cheerio.'

On 28 November Carol Hill wrote to A.D. Peters: 'I thought American authors were temperamental, but at least they're practical and commercial. All artists appal me! ... O'Flaherty has been very sweet, however, except that he, and you should know it, is scrapping his Russian book ... He is going to tear the script in little pieces because he is afraid it will wound the feelings of his Russian friends.' (The MS of this book, with many false starts, is in NLD). She calls *The Wild Swan* contract a deed of charity in a later 9

December letter.

On 30 November Donald Brace wrote to Mrs Carol D. Hill of Ann Watkins, Inc. (the U.S. agent working with A.D. Peters) saying how amicable his talk with O'Flaherty had been.

On 15 December 'Patsa' was sold to Random House (sole rights until publication in the U.S. for three months) for one hundred dollars.

On 18 December Mandrake Press went into liquidation and O'Flaherty reclaimed his rights for *A Tourist's Guide to Ireland, The Return of the Brute, The Ecstasy of Angus,* and *The Machine God,* [an unknown work].

By 22 December, 1930 O'Flaherty's address is The Bungalow, Pheasant Hill, Hambledon, Henley-on-Thames. (Source, A.D. Peters files in HRHRC)

1931

296. HRHRC TLS to A.D. Peters
Poste Restante, Palma de Malloca, Spain   6 January, 1931

Dear Peters,

I enclose a short story called 'It was the Devil's Work'.[1] You see I have arrived in Majorca (the Spanish call it Mallorca) and have set to work. It's a delightful place. It seems dull, but the scenery is fine and the air is good and it's cheap. I'm jolly well fed here for a little under two pounds a week. The company, of course, is of the usual type of suburban Londoners evading the income tax. Jolly old ladies who drink too much and others who don't drink at all. I'm sure there are worse places. I stayed a few hours in Barcelona on my way. It seemed the wildest town I've ever struck. Nobody ever goes to bed and everything and everybody is exceedingly immoral. I shall go there for a small holiday when I finish my novel.

I saw the rugger match in Paris between Ireland and France. It was the most frightful exhibition I ever saw in my life. Oh dear! I expect it's the last match I'll see this year.

I hope you're fit and that everything is going well and that you may sell these stories, so that I can get some more dough sometime.

Yours
Liam

[ALS] Haven't got a damn penny.

[1] A longer first draft of this story, entitled 'The Good God', about the birth of a two-headed calf is in NLD (MS 16,973).

Among stories pushed by A.D. Peters in early 1931 are 'Three Husbands' (sent to George Blackwood); 'It Was the Devil's Work' and 'Proclamation' (sold to *John Bull* for Twenty-five guineas), and 'Lovers'. 'The Candle' (a lost story) was sent to Miss Carruth-Connolly of 135 East 34 St., New York, in response to Martin Coffin's wish to publish an O'Flaherty story for two hundred dollars, signed limited edition, not to be published for one year.

By 23 January O'Flaherty's address was 26 Redesdale St., Chelsea, SW3. Carol Hill liked 'Three Husbands' (letter of 7 February).

By March 1931 A.D. Peters were giving O'Flaherty five pounds a week, perhaps to stop him spending too much, but in April this rose to ten pounds and twenty pounds.

On 5 March Joiner & Steele took *The Ecstasy of Angus* for forty pounds, and someone named Alec McLachlan was typing the MS of *Stack*. A story, 'The Man Who Fell in Love with a Horse' was sent by Peters to the Amalgamated Press on 10 March, and to Carol Hill, who did not like it, but *Harpers* paid two hundred dollars for 'The Lovers', and 'Proclamation' was sold for one hundred and fifty dollars to the *Yale Review*.

On 25 March, 1931 O'Flaherty's address was 16 Trebovir Road, Earls Court, SW5, but by 1 May he was back at the Henley-on-Thames address. In May Harcourt, Brace offered to publish *I Went to Russia* against an advance of two hundred and fifty dollars.

On 20 May A.D. Peters told Cape that O'Flaherty was scrapping his *Alice Ronayne* (or *Stack*) novel and working on a new one to be ready end 1931.

By 26 May the title of this novel is mentioned as *Teresa Joyce* to be ready end August. Also in May Eveleigh Nash & Grayson published *I Went to Russia*, and O' Flaherty was at the launching party. This publisher was a new one, started up by Sir Henry and Lady Mulleneux Grayson of 66 Curzon Street, W1.

In June, 1931 Grasset, Paris took *The House of Gold* (trans. L. Postif), Fayard & Stock having refused it. On 19 June O'Flaherty is still at Henley-on-Thames, his wife being there too. Peters tells him *Ideas and Town Talk* has bought fifteen thousand words of *I Went to Russia* for three guineas per thousand, publication to begin in three weeks. The MS of 'Three Husbands' was destroyed by Ann Watkins, Inc. after being refused by nine American publications (26 June). The typescript of 'It Was the Devil's Work' was destroyed in the same way after refusal by seven U.S. journals. 'The Man Who Fell in Love with a Horse' was destroyed 30 June after rejection by seven U.S. journals. 'Spot', a dog story was sent to *The Sketch* by A.D. Peters (5 July, in response to a request for an animal story) but the editor, Captain Ingram, found it too childish to use.

In July O'Flaherty went to Aran.

---

297. HRHRC ALS to A.D. Peters

Kilronan, Aran Islands, Co. Galway, Ireland   25 July, 1931

Dear Peters,

Thanks awfully for wiring me that money. I found it fearfully expensive travelling to here, as we were four days on the road owing to steamship difficulties, and hotels are on the Dorchester, or the Berkeley scale. A room for the night may cost anything from a pound to thirty shillings. However, it's all right on this island and I've settled down to work in great style.

Please assure Howard at Cape that I'll have the MS of my novel delivered sometime towards the end of August, so that he can get it out this Autumn as promised.

I'm going to stay here some time as I find it very invigorating and full of copy, together with being very cheap if one lives *au naturel*. Still, the weather is frightful. If it's like this in England you're not getting much cricket.

I'm going to write some short stories here that will amuse you, especially one about a war between the two local priests, who trespass their cattle on one another's land at night.

Remember me to Roughead and your family,

Yours
Liam O'F

---

25 August, Topsy wrote to A.D. Peters from c/o A.J. Leventhal, 33 Upper Baggot St., Dublin, sending the typescript of the first half of Liam's new novel (*The Puritan*), the rest was to follow in a week or two.

25 August, Peters wired O'Flaherty on Aran, the *Sunday Dispatch* want him to write a series of fifteen hundred word articles on literary figures of today, payment fifteen to twenty guineas per article. O'Flaherty's wire in reply read: 'Mailing Shaw article with rest of novel today, thanks.' (Published as 'Saint Shaw', 8 November, 1931)

---

298. HRHRC ALS to A.D. Peters
Kilronan, Aran Islands   n.d. [end August, 1931]

Dear Peters,

I just sent off remainder of novel and an article on Shaw, by registered post. If the article is not the right sort I'd like to try another kind, as I'd like to do that series very much, even apart from the very handy lucre attached.

I think the novel is quite good. Please touch Howard for an advance on it.[1] I am again broke, my wife having made an expensive trip to Dublin in search of a flat for the winter. I've got lots of material here for short stories and am feeling very fit, sober and industrious. It was a very lucky thing for me in every way to come down here.

Best wishes
and thanks
Liam

---

[1] 22 September, 1931 O'Flaherty got an advance of seventy-five pounds from Cape on *Teresa Joyce* (renamed *The Puritan*).

---

299. HRHRC TLS to A.D. Peters
Kilronan, Aran Islands   12 September, 1931

Dear Peters,

I enclose Spanish contracts. I wrote a story for Steele but it's not good enough so I'm not sending it on. I simply can't write a short story good enough, so if I can't write one within the next six weeks I'll pay him back his thirty pounds. All the material I have dug up here I am incorporating into a novel, which I have already begun, in which the main characters are a schoolmaster and a priest. It's called *Skerrett*. I am anxious to get away from here to Dublin as soon as possible, so as to read up the account of a lawsuit in the National Library files of provincial newspapers. I imagine I'll deliver you the manuscript of this novel about the middle of January for publication in May or June. I am concentrating for the next couple of years on this type of work, the novel of about sixty or seventy thousand words. I'll get out about three a year. I have two more after this one ready to tackle.

This has been a great Summer here. I feel quite a different man after it. Things don't look very well in England from newspaper reports. I daresay the country will pull round in its usual manner. The arrival of Gandhi fills me with Rabelaisian humour. I must finish my Limerick about him.[1]

With best wishes

Yours
Liam O'F

[1] Arrived London 29 August to attend the second round table conference on India.

---

300. HRHRC ALS to A.D. Peters
4 Lower Fitzwilliam St., Dublin[1]   n.d. [end September, 1931]

Dear Peters,

The above is my new address. Thanks for sending on that draft for fifty pounds. I say, I'm getting worried about this novel *The Puritan*. What on earth does Cape mean? Is he going to have it out this Autumn? It's getting horribly late and it's very important that it should be out on this list. I'm pretty well fed up. He really doesn't give me a fair show with my work. And I'll need the money before Xmas. As far as I can see there is only two hundred and fifty dollars from Harcourt, one hundred and fifty dollars from the *Yale Review* and a few pounds from the Spaniards coming to me otherwise. This is a Christly life when one has no foresight! But then even the bankers have made a mess of it.

You heard nothing since about those *Sunday Dispatch* articles? I'll try to write some funny stories too. Misery! However, this novel I'm doing now amuses me.

Yours, Liam O'F

P.S. or rather S.O.S. The Government has taken my last copper for a two year old telephone bill under a threat of unjust imprisonment. As I must undoubtedly be saved (and without good reason) from an immediate and dastardly death by starvation, I suggest that failing your ability to advance me any more in consideration of the good and lawful moneys coming to me in the near future, that you offer me (not bodily but intellectually) to some other publisher. Failing everything, I shall drop *Skerrett* and join the Catholic Action Party.

L. O'F

[1] A wire dated 22 September to Peters gave his new address as above.

----

301. HRHRC ALS to A.D. Peters
4 Lower Fitzwilliam St., Dublin   n.d. [end September, 1931]

Dear Peters,

   Thanks awfully for your cheque and letter. I see I've made something on the fall of the pound. Cape told me they were not publishing *The Puritan* until January, so I'm dropping my new novel for the moment, as it won't be needed until next Autumn, I suppose, and I am writing short stories. I enclose one which seems funny to my distorted sense of humour.[1] I hope you discover some magazine that also believes it funny. It's wretched of the *Sunday Dispatch* not to want more of those articles. I fancy I have ideas too odd for the average newspaper.

   Things are getting awfully exciting in this country. I daresay they will be in England also this winter. Bad for our trade. Our local government looks like going up in powder. God have mercy on us all!

Yours
Liam O'F

[1] The story sent was 'Dismissed without Prejudice', now unknown. He also sent Peters 'A Night's Lodging'.

----

302. HRHRC TLS to A.D. Peters
4 Lower Fitzwilliam St., Dublin   n.d. [? early October, 1931]

Dear Peters,

   I received the typescript of my novel this morning but not the page proofs. Perhaps they'll arrive later, if you sent them in a separate parcel, or that you forgot to enclose them? Otherwise they were seized by the Government, which seems improbable. If I get them tonight I'll let you know. Things are rather queer here at the moment, and God only knows what's going to happen. If you hear that I have been imprisoned, shot, abducted or what not, don't be surprised.

Did you receive payment for the story I had in the *Yale Review*? If so, please send it to me.

Yours

Liam O'Flaherty

---

12 November, 1931 O'Flaherty was at the Raglan Hotel, Upper Bedford Place, WC1 and went to see Falk, editor of the *Sunday Dispatch* about the rest of his series of articles. The result of this was 'Are the Irish as Witty as Ever?' published 29 November, payment twenty-one pounds.

On 17 November he signed an agreement with Victor Gollancz for an anonymous novel to be entitled *My Amorous Adventures*, and received one hundred pounds in advance.

On 19 November O'Flaherty's address had changed to 21 York Buildings, Adelphi, WC2.

1932

303. HRHRC TLS to A.D. Peters
4 Lower Fitzwilliam St., Dublin   5 January, 1932

Dear Peters,

The above address will find me at present. I'm going into the mountains to stay at a chap's house and write. Please try to get Cape to bring out *The Puritan* as soon as possible this month.[1] And would you let me know whether Harcourt will pay the advance on this novel, or push it on to *Two Years*? Thanks ever so much for putting through that agreement with Gollancz. It has relieved me no end.

   With best wishes,

Yours

Liam O'Flaherty

[1] *The Puritan* was published 25 January and banned by the Irish Censorship Board. The advance Harcourt, Brace had given O'Flaherty for *The Wild Swan* was set off against his next book. The agreement with Victor Gollancz for *My Amorous Adventures* gave O'Flaherty twenty percent royalties. In addition to the advance, Gollancz sent thirty pounds a month for five months.

On 26 February, 1932, the *Manchester Guardian* published a letter from W.B. Yeats protesting against the banning of *The Puritan*, which he hailed as an Irish 'Tartuffe', and a satire on a movement which had produced the Censorship Board itself. Yeats praises O'Flaherty as a great novelist whose work should be influential and 'it is grotesque to call any portion of this novel obscene'. Perhaps as a result of this *The Puritan* was never listed on the Irish Register of Prohibited Publications.

---

304. HRHRC TLS to A.D. Peters[1]
4 Lower Fitzwilliam St., Dublin   n.d.

Dear Peters,

   I enclose a letter that reached me from Cape, by devious ways. Please tell him:

(a) that I'm waiting to see how *The Puritan* succeeds before making fresh agreements; (b) that I would sign a contract immediately for getting out an illustrated collection of nature stories already published ... advance as much as you can get, half to be paid on signing contract.

I think this is a good scheme. He'll sign the contract for the short stories and pay the advance in the hope of pleasing me. If the novel doesn't sell ten thousand copies, which it won't, I can always say I am disappointed and announce my marriage with Gollancz.

I'm getting on well with *Skerrett* and shall have it ready by the end of March for publication in May. Could you tell Gollancz not to put it in any list until we get this short story book contract signed with Cape, or until he refuses to sign and pay. I'm so pleased to worry Cape, as I think he's a shabby fellow.

Liam O'Flaherty

[1] In reply to a letter from Cape dated 8 January, 1932. Peters had difficulty 'keeping Cape at arm's length' and on 27 January told Howard that O'Flaherty had signed an agreement with Gollancz.

By early February O'Flaherty was in Wicklow, perhaps at the Royal Hotel, Glendalough, where Peters wired him some money, or staying with Francis and Iseult Stuart.

---

305. SIUL TLS to Francis Stuart
The Chequers Inn, Slaugham, Hayward's Heath, Sussex
14 February [1932]

Dear Francis,

Hello! You dear bawcock, it's nice writing to you. I have landed after various tribulations at this nice pub and have already dug into work and am getting my affairs in order, I hope. It's dark yet on the financial front, very dark, but there's a chance of getting onto the rails in the next furlong.

I had a lousy time in London. Ankaret was at her wildest and I found that things had gone no farther really. I ended up at Basil Murray's house near Ankaret's place on Saturday; left my kit there and was persuaded to stay for a week, as the Murrays were going to Cornwall. Then we all had lunch, Basil, Pauline, Ankaret, William and I. That was bad enough, but Elizabeth and Constance strolled in and they were pretty frosty. So I cogitated and decided to get out at once. After lunch I pretended to go back to Basil's house to work, and then cleared up to Vyvyan's and threw myself on his protection. He gave me an excellent dinner, excellent sherry, excellent claret and sound advice. I stayed with him Saturday night. In the morning he procured Enid, who drove me around the country in a fast car until we found this place. She was damned nice. Now I feel normal about everything. I love Ankaret more than anything in the world, but I'm determined to sit tight and lead my own life.[1]

I pay two and a half guineas a week here, all found. It's very comfortable and there's nobody else staying here. It's about thirty-five miles from London, just off the main Brighton road. If you are coming over, you might come and stay here for a bit. I feel good now, though a trifle disoriented yet.

Give my love to Iseult and thank her very much for her kindness to me at Laragh. Christ! I'm glad to be out of Ireland at the moment. It's too nerve wracking when one is in any sort of trouble. Already, I see my freedom looming in the distance. It's very nice. Do write to me Francis.

[ALS] I liked your review of *Lit. Supplement*,

Liam

[P.S.] Enid just rang up to say Vyvyan rang her at four this morning to say he was going away. Apparently very tight. He went to play golf yesterday with {?} and went on a binge, so God only knows what river he is in by now. People are much queerer even than I am.

Liam

[1] It has not been possible, even with the help of Francis Stuart's memory, to trace all persons mentioned in this letter. 'Basil' may refer to Basil Murray. 'Ankaret' was Lady Ankaret Howard. Enid Raphael was a lifelong friend of O'Flaherty's, who first lived in the family house in Hill Street, Mayfair, later in a Farm Street flat. Vyvyan Holland (b.1886) was the second son of Oscar Wilde. An impression of O'Flaherty in London is to be found in Stuart's autobiographical novel *Black List, Section H.* (S. Illinois University Press, 1971) pp.187-198, and in Stuart's article on O'Flaherty, 'Recollections of a Great Spirit', the *Irish Times*, 27 November, 1984, p.12.

---

306. SIUL ALS to Francis Stuart
The Chequers Inn, Slaugham   n.d. [? 26 February, 1932]

Dear Francis,

I was intensely amused by the cutting you sent me from the 'Ockwash Tabloid'. My candidate certainly looks in racing trim, although I am afraid she is a difficult filly to train for a race of this length. Five furlongs would be nearer her distance; only it's impossible to run her for any lucrative price over a short distance of ground, owing to the likelihood that the handicapper would not overlook her previous record in assigning her weight. In view of these considerations, which I am forced to take into account in spite of my notorious prejudices in the filly's favour, I'm casting my eye about for suitable second strings. Anything may happen, Your Excellency, and it's best to be prepared.

How are things in Laragh? And then, as Mr. {Thale?} would say, why Laragh? I could never understand why things go wrong. Why, for instance, all this trouble about distance which causes more interest in the Japanese elections than in the struggle at Shanghai between the Irish and the Pekingese. I always knew this craze for pets would end in disaster for the League of Nations, in spite of the fact that the French are making at the moment such a fine gesture of friendship towards Great Britain. Indeed, it's a tribute to the much maligned toleration of the noble race that they have not gone to war long ago on the question of Salkeld's defalcation concerning a certain consignment – you will notice the alliteration – of champagne, of doubtful quality though it may have been, but Leventhal liked it. Sent, you will remember, by our friend the Baron de Bouvier de Monteyvand'Armagnacde Cochonde Cock-and-Bull, on his mother's side. I had never much time for these spurious French titles myself, and I may say that Lulu showed tact in refusing to use his own: though it may very well have been through motives of economy when he began first of all to send cables, and then betting at Civility [Dublin bookmaker] that came later.

This is all very tiresome and doesn't seem to have much bearing on the question of Spanish finance, as far as I can see, but one gets nowhere nowadays in any sort of literary discussion, owing to American influence on taste. Nothing is more degrading, in my opinion, than the fulsome flattery showered on the late Edgar Wallace by deputations from literary societies from small American towns. But then, you will ask, are these towns really small, or is it merely another stunt to make us believe that Chicago is not as criminal as it is supposed to be.

God knows we have troubles enough of our own, and some to spare, if we weren't too damn hypocritical to admit that all this business about the Eucharistic Congress is merely eye-wash to distract public attention from the real evil, which is, in my opinion, entirely a question of the proper control of the basic industries, under some generous system of public supervision. This would give free scope to individual ambition, while at the same time, without undue hardship and without setting a premium on corrupt practices, would ensure the community at large being properly catered for.

My God! I was almost forgetting Lisbeta. But then ... where is she? Have you had any news of her?

> I have the honour, sir, to sign myself,
> Yours in *flagrante delicto*
> *Baranogdanoff (Count: retired)*

As this letter needs some interpretation, Francis Stuart kindly provided the following information: The first paragraph refers to girls as fillies. Cecil Salkeld was a heavy drinker. Leventhal a bookshop owner in London, friend of Samuel Beckett, who later moved to Paris. The long pseudo-French title refers to General Gombosh, Prime Minister of Hungary, about whom they had standing jokes. 'Lulu' was de Ruiz Loba, a rich young Spanish/American at Trinity College, Dublin, met while they were all gambling together. 'Lisbetta' was a fictional person, subject of another standing joke between them.

307. HRHRC ALS to Edward Garnett
The Chequers Inn, Slaugham   29 February, 1932

My Dearest Friend,

I daresay you have thought me a particularly low fellow for quite a long time now, but for me you have remained the finest man I have ever met, together with being the kindest and most joy-giving. I am writing to you after reading your introduction to S. O'Faolain's book. I think your fore-word is great, but that O'Faolain has little in him except a great deal of imitative cunning. Your introduction is so much stronger than he is, and your own work in *The Wind Knows the Earth*, or have I got the title wrong? is worth ten millions of it.[1]

I have been wanting to write to you ever since I wrote to you last, but I love you very much and I feel you don't think much of me any more, so I didn't.

In any case, permit me to thank you once again for all you have done for me and for the joy your existence gives me. You are the person in this dismal age of charlatans that makes literature appear a profession worthy of a gentleman.

Please believe me when I say that I am your most humble servant, admirer and friend. Would you tell Miss Heath that I hope to have the honour some time of kissing her hand.[2]

O'Flaherty

[1] Edward Garnett wrote nothing with this title. O'Flaherty is perhaps thinking of his prose-poem *Imaged World*. Seán O'Faolain's first book, published by Jonathan Cape, 1932, was *Midsummer Night Madness and Other Stories*.

[2] From the appearance of the script in this letter O'Flaherty was in a very emotional state when he penned it.

---

308. HRHRC ALS to Edward Garnett
The Chequers Inn, Slaugham   3 March, 1932

My Dearest Friend,

I can't tell you how delighted I was to get your letter and your book this morning. May I come to supper Wednesday or Friday of next week? I don't often come to London as I have cut myself off from everybody now, and am trying to do what I think is best for my work, i.e. to live without women. I have separated from my wife and there is talk of my being divorced, but I am not enthusiastic about that as it might put me in danger of remarriage. And what conclusions did our disreputable friend Panurge arrive at?

I say, it's fine being in touch with you again, although, to speak the truth, you have rarely been out of my mind since. I have gone through a lot during the last few years; so to speak, deliberately undergone a rather stupid cycle of experiences, to arrive at a clearer consciousness of what I want to do. Now, it's coats off, and to do it.

I am writing a novel called *Skerrett*. Perhaps if you feel very kindly towards me you might cast your eye over it. That would be wonderful, as I have had hardly any intellectual relationships since I last saw you. I don't make friends easily I am afraid; and in any case there are so few people who are worth knowing.

I've just started reading *The Breaking Point* during breakfast. I think the dialogue is magnificent. I like the phrase 'I daresay I am a scoundrel'. Good God! Do you think we are both scoundrels? How nice for me! God blast it, your play is keeping me from my work, to hell with you. Although these characters are civilised Englishmen you couldn't get this play across with English actors of the present day. That is the lousy thing about plays at the present time. You are an unlucky bastard with your work.[1]

[Unsigned] Part of this letter may be missing.

[1] 1931 Edward Garnett published his collected plays written 1906-1911. His first play, mentioned above by O'Flaherty, was refused a licence for its production by the Lord Chamberlain because it dealt with the fears of an unmarried pregnant girl. At the time it aroused anti-censorship agitation.

---

309. HRHRC TLS to A.D. Peters
The Chequers Inn, Slaugham   14 March, 1932

Dear Peters,

I enclose signed contract for Long.[see fn to Letter 312] Thanks awfully for getting this through for me. I don't know what I would really do without you. You are so kind and I give you such a lot of beastly trouble; much more than I am worth. But there you are ... I hope Mr. Long will go the hog on my new book. I feel it in my bones that I'll come through with it. I have about half of it done now, and expect to finish in another five weeks or so. Well, here's good luck and many thanks.

Yours ever, Liam O'Flaherty

---

310. HRHRC TLS to A.D. Peters
The Chequers Inn, Slaugham   n.d. Monday [Spring , 1932]

Dear Peters,

I have decided to stay on here. Please send me my manuscript here when it comes back from the typists. And please also send me the balance of the American money by cheque. I think I will stay here until I finish the novel. I hope you find time to read it and tell me what you think of it.[1]

Yours ever, L.O'F

[1] 4 April, 1932 O'Flaherty signed an agreement with The Albatross, Verlag, 37 rue Boulard, Paris 14, for an option on his next book after *Skerrett*.

311. SIUL TLS to Francis Stuart
The Chequers Inn, Slaugham   n.d. [Spring, 1932]

Dear Francis,

I think that review is great and should do you a lot of good; but don't let this sort of praise give you a swelled head, or influence you in any way in your work. It's the manner of your writing, the power and beauty of expression, insight into life, that matter to you as an artist and poet. Your opinions about western European civilisation, about Ireland or Christianity, or any other topical question [are] just as valueless as anybody else's, whether he be the Pope, or Einstein, or Stalin, or Mussolini, or your wife, or myself. All these things pass away and are forgotten and men will retain only beauties that are near permanent and immutable as anything can be on this changing earth ... things like 'Rough winds do shake the darling buds of May' and Papa Karamazov's lip like a bun hanging out the window waiting for Grushenka, or Yeat's 'loosening thighs'. I daresay you know that well enough yourself. In any case, three cheers, old boy and go to it. Now is the time to strike the iron. It's hot, get on before the price shortens. What news of Elizabeta?

I'm seeing mine today at Gatwick races, so I'm excited. I'm getting on with *Skerrett* too, although he's a tough proposition to handle. And otherwise I'm settling down with a great effort. It all looks unreal to me as yet and almost farcical; and at moments it requires a great effort to hold myself in hand. I'm glad the election has gone as it has. It's a sign at least that the people are struggling to their feet once more. Things look good on all fronts in fact. The information brought in by live prisoners is encouraging. You might send out a pigeon or two to reconnoitre. Come over soon.[1]

Liam O'F

P.S. [ALS] Stop Press. Elizabeta is, I hear, a zebra. Try one of the literary papers with a short sketch or essay. It does good to get among these periodicals when digging into the literary fortress. Send out all sorts of things just now. Be of good heart, Liam.

---

[1] The first paragraph, and the last line of this letter refer to Stuart's 1932 novel *Pigeon Irish*. The election mentioned had taken place the previous Autumn on 31 October and brought in a National Government under J. Ramsay MacDonald. By Autumn 1932 an estimated six to eight million people were living on the 'dole'.

---

312. HRHRC ALS to A.D. Peters
Benner's Hotel, Dingle, Co. Kerry   n.d. [? early May, 1932]

Dear Peters,

Please send Mr. Gollancz's cheque to me at the above address in notes, and any letters there are. I'm looking around here for a cottage but haven't found one yet. Amusing place, though quite as dead as the interior of Abyssinia. I'm going to write the tourist article for the *Fortnightly*, but personally I should warn all decent tourists against this country.[1]

Good luck
Liam

P.S. Have you sent *Skerrett* to America?

[1] He had been asked to write a three thousand word article for three guineas per thousand words. 'The Kingdom of Kerry' was published 30 June, 1932.

18 May, O'Flaherty had been at Castlecove, Killarney, and 19 May at Hotel Caraghlake, Kerry. Gollancz was worried about libel over *Skerrett* and enquired whether all the characters in it were now dead. Harcourt Brace were informed by Peters on 26 April that O'Flaherty had changed his U.S. agent to Ray Long & Richard R. Smith, Inc. of 12 East 41st St., New York. While in London 15 March, 1932, O'Flaherty signed an agreement at the Savoy Hotel with Long for his next novel. Long had sent him five hundred dollars (half the advance). *Skerrett* was sent to Long in early May. Meanwhile Margaret O'Flaherty was being sent money regularly by Peters. She still lived in Lower Fitzwilliam Street, Dublin.

---

313. HRHRC ALS to A.D. Peters
O'Connell's Railway Hotel, Cahirciveen, Co. Kerry   25 May, 1932

Dear Peters,

The above is a further address, at which you may swear. I have, as a matter of fact, covered in the past fortnight practically every yard of the Irish Free State and have at last found a tiny cottage near here where I am going to settle down for the Summer. It's an ideal place for me – completely wild and remote, overlooking the sea with a mountain behind it. I expect to do big work there and catch an enormous number of fish. This, my God, is the most astounding country in the world. I fail to understand why I never came to Kerry before. It is alive with material.

Gollancz has written to say he has sent on the proofs of *Skerrett*, so I daresay he'll have it out in a few weeks. Smart work. Would you ask him whether he would publish the new book I'm working on, *The Toper*, about November? So that I'll know whether to hurry with it.

When do you expect to get the remaining half of the American advance on *Skerrett*? When at least could you let me have some of it, as I want to get things for this cottage.

Well! This is a great life. I'm glad I found this place. Not Cahirciveen, but my cottage.

God Bless you

Yours in Jesus Christ
L.O'F

---

314. HRHRC ALS to A.D. Peters
O'Connell's Railway Hotel, Cahirciveen, Co. Kerry   [?] June, 1932

Dear Peters,

Sorry to appear so brusque and confused that night I met you in Jermyn Street, but I was on a somewhat secret mission – nothing to do with Mr. De Valera's affairs – and I felt sort of caught out, so to speak, that I shouldn't be in London at all, which, of course, I shouldn't. Nor did I go to see Gollancz the following day because I felt so muzzy and on edge that I was afraid I might muddle things instead of being any help. I gave the proofs to a friend to hand in. Apparently he's publishing the book at once. I have no great hopes of it as it's about the worst novel I've done. But one can never tell, 'the last shall be first', according to the hateful Christians.

Thanks for the cheque. When the money comes would you please send on the rest so that I can fortify myself for the Summer by warding off my dependants and getting done with it. I at least came to London at somebody else's expense and left the cheque at home, which consoles me. I like this thing I'm doing now much better than *Skerrett*. One manages to get every second or third novel right.

I'm reading *The Water Gypsies* [A.P. Herbert, 1930] which I think is a delightful book. I wish I could do one like it.

I wish many centuries during this rainy season.[1]

                                                                    Liam

[1] Presumably refers to cricket.

---

315. HRHRC TLS to A.D. Peters
O'Connell's Railway Hotel, Cahirciveen, Co. Kerry n.d. [early June, 1932]

Dear Peters,

I enclose the article for the *Fortnightly*. I don't know whether it is right or wrong, probably wrong, as I don't believe a word of it myself and I find it difficult to tell lies in print. In any case, offer it to them with my compliments.

I see Gollancz is not publishing *Skerrett* until the 11th July. Did the American advance for *Skerrett* arrive yet? If it has could you send me the balance? Hope you are feeling fit. Life is pretty good here.

                                                                    Yours
                                                                    Liam O'F

---

316. HRHRC TLS to A.D. Peters
West Kells, Cahirciveen, Co. Kerry   n.d. [end June, 1932]

Dear Peters,

Thanks awfully for sending me fifty pounds.[1] I have moved out to my cottage and am definitely settled down here until October. It's a grand place, five miles from the nearest pub and ten from the nearest village. I live alone, mostly on milk and eggs and whatever fish I can catch. My book is going on fine.

Wishing you every good luck and thanking you again, I remain

Yours sincerely
Liam O'F

[1] Flaherty received the remaining half of the U.S. advance on *Skerrett* at the end of June, less Peters' commission and payments made to his wife.

---

317. HRHRC ALS to A.D. Peters
O'Connell's Railway Hotel, Cahirciveen   n.d. [early July, 1932]

Dear Peters,

Thanks for cheque, etc. I've been in bed with bad attack of 'flu for ten days, so have been unable to correct American proofs. Will try to do them now and send them along.

Please collect new Gollancz advance and send it to me. The arrangement is that he pays forty pounds a month advance on my next novel, upon publication of *Skerrett*.[1]

Best luck
Liam O'F

[1] On the novel to follow *Skerrett* Gollancz paid monthly instalments of £41.13.4. Margaret O'Flaherty's address was now c/o Leventhal, 59 Upper Leeson Street, Dublin. On 21 July she sent a wire for money to Peters, saying Pegeen was ill.

---

318. SIUL ALS to Francis Stuart
The Chequers, Fingest, Henley-on-Thames   n.d. [postmark 21 July, 1932]

Dear Francis,

Have arrived here since yesterday, and have already got a nice little cottage, furnished, until the middle of September, where I'm installing myself with Pegeen and a village maid, I hope, if I can get one. Pegeen is really a scream. She's delighted with herself. The faithful Enid [Raphael] met the train and drove us down here. I didn't see anybody else in London as I came straight through. Cecil [Salkeld] was on the train, en route, I should think for Bucharest, very drunk and utterly impossible, so I passed on. He's hopeless.

All this is in great haste and incoherent, Francis. I'll write you a sane letter later. But I feel fine and very happy and am going to write a great book about the Civil War in Kerry. Let's stir them up. Which brings me to *The Coloured Dome*.[1] I haven't finished it yet. (Pegeen doesn't allow much reading until I have her parked in the cottage), but all I have read is really very beautiful. In language and poetry it's a great advance on the Puritan

Pigeons.[2] Until I have finished it I can't say anything about the story or the philosophic content, but it thrills me. As in fact all your work does. It's so beautiful, but then you have really a very beautiful soul. O.K. Chief, lay off the bolony!

I'm writing a letter to my wife in care of you. I don't know where else to address a letter to her. Try and give her the letter, if she doesn't turn up at Laragh. I don't know what to make of her. She's almost as difficult as myself. However, to hell! I think Paulina is awfully well done. Yes ducky, really fine.

I got a letter from Ankaret. She'll be all right. The English don't stagger, you know, neither do the Irish, some of them.

I say, this is a funny letter, but I'm so excited about my new book. It's like falling in love without the jealousy.

Kiss Iseult's hand for me and thank her for telling me what to do. She will understand. She is a fine woman, Iseult, which is odd, as beautiful women are generally pretty lousy bitches. I want to go on writing to you, but ... later, later! If you take off for a day or two over this side, come and see me, it's near London.

                                                                        Liam

P.S. Concerto is not running. Cockpen might do it.

[1] Francis Stuart tells us about his novel *The Coloured Dome* (1932) in his autobiography *Things to Live For* (1934). Francis himself is the hero of the novel, named Garry Delea, and a friend Paulina Caddell is the model for the character Clarice Morrisey. In real life Paulina was married to Robert, who smuggled arms from Russia to the Irish Republicans and was killed in the Spanish Civil War. Paulina later went to Australia with a Dr. O'Toole, whom she married. There are a number of anecdotes about O'Flaherty in *Things to Live For* connected with their mutual interest in horse racing. Another relates how, just after O'Flaherty had finished writing *Skerrett*, they met in Galway. Stuart remarks on the curious contradictions in his friend O'Flaherty's character, how he moves from heavy drinking and betting to putting all his money in a church box. For Irishmen, Stuart says, London was then like an enormous race-course. 'How is Lisbeta?', which appears so often in their correspondence, is a joke from Stuart's friend Billy Weller who telephoned London from a Dublin pub pretending Lisbeta was a horse. In fact Elisabeth is a Paris flame of Stuart's with whom he had a rather spiritual type of affinity.

[2] *Pigeon Irish*, London: Gollancz 1932. Stuart's previous novel published six months before.

---

319. HRHRC TLS to A.D. Peters
16 rue Denfert Rochereau, Paris 5   31 August, 1932

Dear Peters,

I enclose a short story called 'The God Among Sparrows'. I have arranged with Drawbell of the *Sunday Chronicle* to do a series of six articles for sixty pounds. I have done four of them. He is beginning to print them next week I think. Would you please ring him some time and say to send payment to you.[1]

If Gollancz enquires about my new novel *The Martyr* tell him I have half of it done and that it will be ready by November 1st, as arranged.

I have a good place here and am doing a hell of a lot of work, plus excellent other things.

Yours sincerely
Liam O'Flaherty

P.S. [ALS] I see that *Everybody's Weekly* are printing some stories of mine. Do you know anything about it? L.O'F.[2]

[1] The *Sunday Chronicle* (Manchester) (Allied Newspapers Ltd.) paid forty pounds for a series of articles 'My grouses in Life', but the only one they printed was 'Snobs', 6 November, 1932, p.10 illustrated with O'Flaherty's photograph.

[2] 'The Wild Goat's Kid' and 'The Funk' (changed title of 'The Wing Three-quarter') at three pounds each.

O'Flaherty had written to Peters in mid August, giving his new address, and telling him that Hauser wished to translate *Skerrett* into German.

---

320. SIUL TLS to Francis Stuart
Kilronan, Aran Islands   6 October, 1932

Dear Francis,

What's all this racket about Yeats's Academy?[1] Some one was telling me he started one. How is your colt getting on? Showing any signs? I'll pick up Lord Abbadie[2] some day and we'll go and have a look at it. Abbadie might be persuaded to take it over if the animal is no good. We could make him drunk or something; though I believe the old boy is feeling the pinch at the moment and might be a bit tight, in the less interesting meaning of the word.

How are things, Francis? Any fresh cuties on the horizon, said the count, lapsing into the Ockwash patois. Personally, I am living a monastic life. No cigarettes, no drink, no women, nothing but work. I shall have finished *The Martyr* in a fortnight. He looks like going to the post a worthy candidate for classic honours, though just a shade too rough in the muscle. My family is in London. Did I tell you I was thinking of buying an old watch tower on this island. Well, I am, if I get the tower first of all and then the money to buy and repair it. We shall all live in towers and castle presently. I'm staying down here vaguely, indefinitely. I like it very much for work. I feel in harmony with the people. But to be idle ... *sais pas*, until I get my tower, if and when. Went to Paris for a fortnight with a girl I met here and got fed up with her. I give them up. It's much better to live alone and be immoral now and again, so to speak ... to stand five or six times a year, for about a week at a time.

If you are at Laragh, give my best regards to your family and drop me a line if you're bored some time and have nothing to do. Any news of Lizbeta? I'm afraid we might as well give up the chase as hopeless.

Liam

[1] The inaugural meeting of W.B. Yeats' Irish Academy was held 18 September, 1932, in the The Peacock Theatre. O'Flaherty accepted membership but did not attend the meeting.

[2] In Stuart's novel *The Coloured Dome* (p.202) O'Flaherty is the man the protagonist meets in Dave Arigho's pub, just back from the races with Abbadie and two girls. 'Lord Abbadie, a low fellow but he's plenty of money, and I'm Seumas Arrochar.' O'Flaherty (otherwise Seumas) is described as 'an Irish novelist with vivid blue eyes – a sensuous, energetic character, fond of horses, life and women, who is one of nature's rebels'. At the end of this episode Seumas suddenly remembers he has to be in Bucharest the next night, hails a taxi and disappears. This is the only appearance of the character Seumas in the novel.

---

321. HRHRC TLS to A.D. Peters
Kilronan, Aran Islands   12 October, 1932

Dear Peters,

Thanks for sending me that money by wire to Galway. I have returned to my island a sadder and more frustrated man and yet thanking the devil I didn't go any farther than Galway. I heard from Gollancz that he sent *The Martyr* to the printer, so I expect the proofs any day. I am now going to write some short stories.

Does Ray Long take *The Martyr* according to contract or do you merely submit it to him?[1]

Yours sincerely
Liam O'F

[1] On 9 October O'Flaherty had written to Peters, 'Please send me the Cape returns for this half year to have a look at them. My novel *The Martyr* is great, I think. I've done it this time. Shall send it along in a fortnight's time. Good cheer.'

---

322. HRHRC TLS to A.D. Peters
Kilronan, Aran Islands   23 October, 1932

Dear Peters,

Thanks for the Gollancz money which I received. You didn't send on the Cape returns, but it doesn't matter. Don't bother. Please send me the money in notes when it comes in next week. I am finishing my novel in about six days time and am sending it direct to Gollancz as I promised to let him have it by lst November, so there is no time to make a copy. He can get it printed at once and thus give us a copy for Ray Long. It looks good to me. I wonder is that *Sunday Chronicle* man waiting for me to do the last two articles of that series I promised him or not? [unfinished, no signature]

Carol Hill (of Ann Watkins, Inc. New York) had by October 1932 formed her own literary agency (with Peters) Hill & Peters, 24 West 40th St., New York. She was not then aware that O'Flaherty had moved from Harcourt, Brace to Long & Smith. On December 7, 1932 she wrote to Peters that Long & Smith were likely to go bankrupt soon. Under the contract Ray Long is entitled to see each novel MS before coming to a decision. *Skerrett* sold poorly in the U.S.

On 10 November O'Flaherty was at the Railway Hotel, Galway.

O'Flaherty's *The Wild Swan* (with 'It Was the Devil's Work' and 'Unclean'), was published in 1932 as *Furnival Book No. 10* by Joiner & Steele, and also appeared in *The Furnival Book of Short Stories* (1932) pp.245-271.

Gollancz published *The Martyr*, 16 January, 1933. Long & Smith, New York refused *The Martyr* as *Skerrett* had only sold five hundred copies in the U.S. and withdrew their option on O'Flaherty's next book, to the relief of A.D. Peters and Carol Hill. During the publication of his novel O'Flaherty stayed at 17 Sydney Street, SW3. *The Martyr* was then sold to Macmillan for one thousand dollars (half at once), with royalties of ten percent up to three thousand and an option on the next novel.

On 24 February, 1933, O'Flaherty was back in London at the National Hotel, Upper Bedford Place, WC1.

By 6 March he had moved to Madrid and wired for money to be sent to Paseo del Prado 32.

On 13 March another wire came from Toledo.

By 14 March *The Martyr* had sold almost five thousand copies. Peters heard from O'Flaherty in Spain (letter missing) that he was starting a new novel to be called *Famine*.

---

323. HRHRC ALS to A.D. Peters
Hotel Maravilla, Toledo, Spain   n.d. [mid March, 1933]

Dear Peters,

Here I have landed. Thanks for wiring me that money last Wednesday, and also for the very kind letter you wrote me about my book *The Martyr*. I hope you are fit again now, and that your holiday put your back into a proper shape, fit to tackle the usual human vices, although one is better without them.

This is quite a nice place, very dull and peaceful. I have decided to try and write my book here. I am about the only foreigner in the town at the moment, and as I speak no Spanish I'm having a monastic time. When I learn more of the language I'm going to move out into a village. Living is cheap. I pay about thirty-five shillings a week for my hotel, but it's not very good living. Excepting the sherry one would have to be a hog to drink any of their liquor.

When my monthly revenue from Gollancz reaches you, would you please send a cheque for twenty pounds to Mrs Margaret O'Flaherty, The Walk, Park Gate, East Finchley, N2. Send the remainder to me here, plus any other money you may get, as I've spent all my dough trying to find some place I like.

I'm tempted to write a funny book about Spain like the Russian one, but [unfinished]

By 11 April, 1933 O'Flaherty is at 8 Walpole Street, London SW3. He then moved to Sennen Cove Hotel, Cornwall, and sent two notes to Peters from there, one requesting money and the other signed 'Yours in an overcoat'; also the following letter to Victor Gollancz.

---

324. VG ALS to Victor Gollancz
Sennen Cove Hotel, Sennen Cove, Cornwall   21 April, 1933

Dear Gollancz,

I don't know what to make of *A Plebeian's Progress*, [Frank Tilsley]. It's not the sort of thing that interests me at the moment as I am a hundred years behind the time and deep in *Famine*, so my opinion is worthless. But the impression I got was an imitation mixture of Wells and Dreiser, without the personality of either. However! As I said before, my opinion is worthless at the moment.

I am hoping to do big things with *Famine*. I don't expect to finish it before September. I have found an excellent place to work here and am going to move later, I think, to an island off the coast of Donegal.

I want to thank you once more for your kindness to me; for without your help I wouldn't be able to do this book until it was perhaps too late.

Yours sincerely
Liam O'Flaherty

On 15 May, O'Flaherty wired Peters for money from Hôtel des Arcades, Dieppe. On 17 May, he asked for money from the National Hotel, Bloomsbury, and for money to be sent his wife. In May 1933 the *Evening Standard* took 'The Wild Swan' for ten guineas.

On 29 May O'Flaherty was at 138 Fellowes Road, NW3 but on 28 June back at the National Hotel.

On 3 July he wired for mail from Concarneau.

---

325. HRHRC ALS to A.D. Peters
Poste Restante, Concarneau, France   n.d. [early July, 1933]

Dear Peters,

Please tell Gollancz that I cannot get my novel finished before December. It was wrong so I tore it up. Now I am doing a volume of short stories, which will be ready for publishing by the end of August. Please ask Cape does he want this volume. [1]If he does I want fifty pounds now and fifty pounds on handing in finished manuscript. Title of collection is *The Grey House*. If Cape does not want it, offer it to Gollancz on same terms. Please let me know as soon as possible what happens.

Yours, Liam O'Flaherty

P.S. *The Grey House* will consist of twelve Irish peasant sketches, length seventy-two thousand.

[1] O'Flaherty was still tied to Cape for an option on a short story volume which carried an advance of fifty pounds. Peters tells him he will try to persuade Cape to pay more, or forego the option in Gollancz's favour. Cape say they will decide when they see the MS. They do not like the title.

326. HRHRC ALS to A.D. Peters
Poste Restante, Concarneau					n.d. [July, 1933]

Dear Peters,

An alternative title for my book will be *The Caress*. There are thirteen stories and the MS will be complete by 20th August. But I think it's lousy to get merely an advance of fifty pounds as I lose the chance of selling the serial rights. And I have no money whatsoever at the moment. Well, well! However ... tell Howard to go ahead. He could get it out in October. Try and get some money out of him.

Yours
Liam O'F

P.S. I think *The Caress* would be a good title, although it's rather a wild story but the best I've done for a long time I think. L.O'F

A note to A.D. Peters dated 27 July from Concarneau says: 'Please forward to Mrs O'Flaherty any money that falls due to me. I'm through with writing. Cheerio.'

---

327. HRHRC ALS to A.D. Peters
Poste Restante, Concarneau					29 July, 1933

Dear Peters,

I wrote you yesterday a note which you must find rather odd, but I felt in a frightful mood and rather like committing suicide. However, having slept on the idea I have changed my mind. One must carry on, as one has responsibilities. Why, God only knows. One should be like Jean-Jacques Rousseau and let one's children go to the workhouse.

Can you persuade any editor to let me do some articles at any price? I must find some means of tiding over the present. I see no point in wasting time over this short story book, considering I would gain hardly enough to pay for the typing. So I'm going on with my novel *Famine*. Damn the thing, I had fifty thousand words written and had to scrap them. I am writing to Gollancz about it. Please see can you do something about articles. Pound of the *Express* might take some. Could you give him a ring and say I'm — what? Anything!

Yours ever
Liam O'Flaherty

---

328. ALS VG to Victor Gollancz
Poste Restante, Concarneau, Finistère, France					29 July, 1933

Dear Gollancz,

I don't know what to say about *Glory*, [Francis Stuart]. Really, it's a bit

too mad to tell the truth. Please say if you like 'What magnificent extrava-
gance'! but I think it's just insanity.

I am bordering on the same state myself, after writing fifty thousand
words of *Famine* I had to scrap the whole and reconstruct, and now I'm in
a devil of a way. Broke and pestered by people who for some damn reason
depend on me. I don't suppose there is any use in asking you to advance
me any more money in instalments on any sort of contract you like? But if
something doesn't happen I'm *foutu*!!! It will take me at least another three
months to finish it, unless I jump off one of the local rocks. Have you any
influence with any editor who would let me do articles or reviews to tide
me over the intervening space?

Sorry to be behind time, but unless I blow up I'll let you have a good
thing by December.

Yours
Liam O'Flaherty

---

329. HRHRC ALS to A.D. Peters
Poste Restante, Concarneau   n.d. Wednesday [early August, 1933]

Dear Peters,

Thanks awfully for your letter. It cheered me up no end. You are quite
right. It's no good thinking the game is lost before the final whistle. As a
matter of fact, I'm slogging away cheerfully and when I get my head above
water again I'm going to stay there. I've played the fool for the past year,
got in with a bad set, but I've dumped them all and feel full of ideas. Only
this cussed business of money! I don't think it would be any good moving.
In the first place I came here to get away from people that were worrying
me, and to return to England as yet might be suicidal. In the second place
I'm dead broke and couldn't move if I wanted to.

I'll send along the complete manuscript of a book of short stories within
three weeks. We might sell some of them, though the subjects are doubtful.
I have no typewriter and am writing them in large notebooks, so I can't send
them piecemeal.

Would the *Express* take my description of a bullfight in Madrid? I'll
write several articles and send them to you. Young Harmsworth of the
Daily Mail wanted me to write for the *Mail* some month ago. I don't know
what he wanted, as I didn't feel like doing it at the time and didn't go to
see him. Now, however, I would write advertisements for brothels. This
is a son of a bitch of a position to get into.

I do think I had better stay here as I'm in a working fit and it would cost
as much to get to London as it would to live here for a fortnight.

Well! Thanks awfully for your letter. I hope you had a good time in Capri
and are feeling fit? I'm feeling very fit myself, as far as health is concerned,

and after all that's something. When one thinks of all who have consumption, syphilis and the pecularities of the young man of Devizes.

Yours ever

Liam

On 17 August Liam moved to Hôtel de la Poste, Pont Avon, Finistère.

He sold 'A Field of Young Corn' to *John O'London's Weekly* for twelve guineas (printed 29 September).

By 6 September, 1933, he is back at National Hotel, Bloomsbury. He sent Peters two stories, 'Day Dream' (sold to *John O'London's Weekly* for ten guineas), and 'Parabellum', a greyhound racing story criticised as inaccurate by the *Evening Standard*, who took it for twelve guineas after O'Flaherty had amended it, but in the end published 'Civil War' 11 September, 1933.

22 September, 1933, O'Flaherty was at 61 Oakley Street, SW3. At this time he signed an agreement with Grayson & Grayson for a book of reminiscences.

On 29 September O'Flaherty had moved to New Inn, Send, Woking, Surrey. Margaret O'Flaherty was usually sent an allowance of twenty pounds monthly by Peters.

Victor Gollancz wrote to Peters 2 November asking why he had not been offered the autobiographical volume, to be entitled *Shame the Devil*, mentioned in the *News Chronicle* that day. Peters told Gollancz that O'Flaherty proposed calling the reminiscences *Trinc* and it would not necessarily be autobiographical, if it is Gollancz is entitled to it under contract.

7 November, O' Flaherty is at Hotel Lutetia, Boulevard Raspail, Paris, and Peters tell O'Flaherty that if *Shame the Devil* is described as reminiscences and not autobiography Gollancz will not be bothered. The limited edition of *Shame the Devil* had a page of the original typescript inserted inside the front cover.

On 1 December O'Flaherty was at 48 Ebury Street, London W1 and his brother Tom had arrived from Boston (via Ireland). He discussed the U.S. lecture tour contract with W. Colston Leigh, Inc. of 521 5th Avenue, New York, which gave O'Flaherty forty-five percent of gross takings up to three thousand dollars then fifty percent, with a minimum guarantee of eighty-five dollars per week for not less than eight weeks, and two hundred and fifty dollars towards the fare, one hundred and twenty-five dollars on arrival and one hundred and twenty-five dollars before leaving, five lectures each week if necessary and all rail fares paid. O'Flaherty agreed to go on this tour and the first lecture was planned for February 1935. The flyer for the tour of 'Liam O'Flaherty, famous Irish novelist' was produced end 1933.

At short notice O'Flaherty wrote an article on General Duffy's Christmas for Allied Newspapers, and took it to A.D. Peters' office 20 December for a fee of seven guineas, and he agreed to write a series of 'Mustard and Cress' articles for the *Sunday Referee* for ten guineas weekly. These four articles appeared on 31 December 1933, 7, 14 and 21 January, 1934 on page 7 of the newspaper.

1934

There is little correspondence available from O'Flaherty in 1934, but it is possible to trace his approximate movements during this year. On 30 January he was at the National Hotel, Bloomsbury, when *Shame the Devil* was published. He received twenty-five percent royalties on the one hundred copy limited edition at one guinea each.

---

330. HRHRC TLS to A.D. Peters
219 King's Road, Chelsea, London   6 March, 1934

Dear Peters,

I enclose contract for lecture tour. I find I cannot for the life of me write out synopses of my lectures at this moment, so if he must have synopses the thing has got to fall through. I can only write out the lectures, which I could send to him later.

The subjects I have chosen are:
1. The art of enjoying life.
2. The influence of Ireland in modern literature.
3. The Aristocracy of the future.
4. Is Europe doomed as the centre of world culture?

Yours ever, Liam O'Flaherty

---

331. HRHRC TLS to A.D. Peters
Royal Hotel, Glendalough, Co. Wicklow   n.d. Thursday [end April, 1934]

Dear Peters,

With reference to Miss Hill's letter,[1] (which seemed to be needlessly impertinent,) I would like to point out that it is most unlikely any Catholic organisation in America would ask me to lecture, since I have been excommunicated by the Pope and denounced as a menace to that particular form of bunkum which is known as the Catholic religion. In any case, I refuse to give any lectures whatsoever, unless I am allowed to say what I please; as it is now too late in the day to toady to anybody. Under the circumstances they can call the whole business off, or not, just as they please.

I am very anxious about what is happening to my book *Shame the Devil*, in America, and whether or not Macmillan are going to print it.[2] Have you heard any news about it? It is an urgent matter with me at the moment as I have run out of money.

Yours sincerely, Liam O'Flaherty

[1] This letter from Carol Hill says she has heard about O'Flaherty's reputation *vis-à-vis* the Roman Catholic Church. Will Peters talk to him firmly and solemnly before he comes over. She thinks he will do a good job for his own reputation's sake.

[2] A.D. Peters warned O'Flaherty that Macmillan, New York, were likely to reject *Shame the Devil*, and they did.

By end April O'Flaherty had sailed for New York, and in Carol Hill's letter to Peters of 4 May she has met him there, en route to Hollywood. He promised her to send *Famine* by the first week in October, and expected to be back in New York early in December to lunch with Macmillan and work out a cooperative plan of lecture-selling for *Famine*.

O'Flaherty was still trying to sell the film rights of *The Informer* in Hollywood. *Shame the Devil* did not attract any U.S. publisher. During O'Flaherty's absence without address all his royalties were sent to his wife, now at 83 Fitzjohn's Avenue, London NW3. Peters had not seen Mrs O'Flaherty for some time and knew nothing about her financial position.

12 July, 1934, Carol Hill sent A.D. Peters O'Flaherty's Hollywood address, 8118 Sunset Boulevard. He did two weeks' work at Paramount and wrote a filmscript. He was also writing short stories such as 'Blood' (later entitled 'All Things Come of Age' (published *Esquire*, January 1935), and 'The Accident' published for two hundred dollars in *New York Herald Tribune*. Enid Raphael was now forwarding O'Flaherty's mail from her address at 38 Hill Street, Mayfair. Meantime Mrs O'Flaherty had moved to 52 Parliament Hill, Hampstead.

---

332. HRHRC TLS to Carol Hill
73 Humphrey Road,
Montecito, Santa Barbara
California   30 August, 1934

Dear Carol Hill,

The above is my address for the next few months. I have not heard any more about the lectures on the west coast. Unless anything definite has been arranged I'd just as soon not do them, as I want to do a lot of writing from now until Christmas. I daresay the ones in the East would be the only ones to turn out in any way lucrative.

Do you think you could sell any short stories or articles for me in New York? I daresay that articles about Hollywood are a drug by now, but I have seen rather interesting things in California that I should like to write about from the point of view of a foreign visitor – if you think there is any market for articles of that description from my pen.

Had a poorish time in Hollywood, but did on the whole enjoy it, rather. I certainly feel rejuvenated and quite a different person altogether from the wretched fed-up person who left London four months ago.

Would you let me know as soon as possible whether you think you could sell any stories or articles for me?

  Permit me to remain

Yours very sincerely

Liam O'Flaherty

---

11 October, Peters wrote to O'Flaherty at the above address saying he had not heard from him since he went to America. Twenty-five pounds had been paid to his wife, which cleared his account. He has signed an Agreement with Cape for a florin edition of *The Assassin*.

---

333. HRHRC TLS to Carol Hill
73 Humphrey Street, Montecito, California   n.d. [end October, 1934]

Dear Carol Hill,

  I am leaving Los Angeles for New York on Tuesday night and will arrive in New York on Saturday, so don't send any more letters or etc. here. Will look you up when I get to New York. All the best. I finally sold *The Informer* to R.K.O. so am taking off from the region of Hollywood, having effected my purpose, which was more than Caesar did in England on his first trip.

Yours

Liam O'Flaherty

---

31 December, 1934, Carol Hill cabled A.D. Peters, 'O'Flaherty apparently defaulting lecture contract having left New York without O'Flaherty here, sorry cannot help'. It is mentioned in F.A. Lea's *The Life of Middleton Murry* (London, Methuen, 1959) p.205, that on New Year's Day 1935 a bewildered New York audience, expecting to hear Liam O'Flaherty on 'The Art of Enjoying Life' were treated instead to a very seasick John Middleton Murry speaking on 'The Agony of John Keats'!

Catherine H. Tailer told the editor that she first met O'Flaherty at a fancy dress party in Santa Barbara in 1934, a few months after her divorce. From now on Kitty Tailer was to be O'Flaherty's most regular companion.

O'Flaherty did not leave the U.S. at the end of 1934 as he had originally planned to do. On 5 March, 1935, Carol Hill wrote to him at Hotel Seville, Madison Avenue & 29th St. New York, to say that out of the two hundred dollar fee for 'The Accident' she is withholding $172.86 to pay Colston Leigh's claims against the cancellation of O'Flaherty's lecture tour, although the money cannot be paid to Leigh until the Courts have decided.

On 29 March, O'Flaherty cabled Peters: 'Wire all money my credit to Great Northern Hotel, West 57th St'. Eighty pounds was sent.

5 June, 1935, Carol Hill wrote to A.D. Peters saying that she had just had a very difficult half hour with 'your friend Liam O'Flaherty' who wants to get out of his Macmillan contract, for an agent in Hollywood had told him he could get a far larger advance from another publisher. She continues: 'I am also under the impression that if O'Flaherty washes

this contract up he will vanish into the deep blue, probably signing a contract with some fool publisher and generally making a mess of the situation. He is sailing on the 14th for England and will be seeing you immediately, I believe. You may be able to handle him. The man's attitude and everything about him basically irritates me so much that all I can really do is be extremely cross and hardboiled with him, and I don't think he particularly relishes this.' (HRHRC)

---

334. IUL ALS to John Ford
Hotel Windsor,
100 West 58th Street, New York   n.d. Monday [postmark 3 June, 1935]

My Dear Jack,

Please forgive me for dashing off the way I did without saying goodbye properly, but I felt it was the best way, considering you were working and I wanted to get back home myself to put *Famine* on the stocks. I'm going to Galway next week and then out to Aran for a few months, until about September. Maybe though, I might stay instead at Lettermullan, about twenty miles west of Spiddal. Any case, somewhere around that territory. I think *Famine* is going to be great, and you need never feel ashamed, I assure you, that it's dedicated to you. I'm going to hammer out every word from the depths of my soul.

Well Jack, I'm very glad I came out to Hollywood. Looking back now, it's been a marvellous year and I thank you very much for all your kindness, particularly for *The Informer*, but perhaps most of all for yourself. During the past year I have learned to admire you as the great man you are. If I have gone away three thousand miles to say so, that is the Irish way. We are a strange and complicated people, but by Christ, that's our own business.

This will be my address until Friday week. After that: Kilronan, Aran Islands, Co. Galway. Sorry I'm not going with you on the *Araner*, but I'll time a few pints of stout at Daly's of Kilronan or Lydon's with you, and you drinking down the highways of the western seas under the awning of your great white sail. May God go with you, Jack, and with everyone belonging to you.

Is mise le grádh mór
Liam

---

4 July, 1935, Peters wrote to O'Flaherty at 91 Oakley St. SW3 sending him copies of the agreement for *The Puritan* to sign. O'Flaherty changed the contract more in his own favour since he now had a reputation in Hollywood. Chester Erskin (an American dramatist) through the agent Eric S. Pinker & Adrienne Morrison Inc. of New York, had dramatised *The Puritan* before Peters could corner O'Flaherty to sign a contract, though he had agreed to the dramatisation in principle by cable 17 June, 1935. Colston Leigh sued O'Flaherty for

$380.99 on the cancelled lecture tour plus interests, costs and disbursements.

In early July (n.d.) O'Flaherty wrote a note to Peters from Hôtel des Sables Blancs, Beuzec, Concarneau, saying 'I am here to finish *Hollywood Cemetery*', and 5 July Peters replied asking for the first half of this new novel, perhaps for serial rights.

---

335. SIUL ALS to Francis Stuart
Hôtel des Sables Blancs,
Beuzec, Concarneau, Finistère   n.d. [postmark 13 July, 1935]

Dear Francis,

Looks a likely venue for preparing a useful animal. For what, though, as they say in the Dominions? The regulars are not yet in evidence, though there is a fair sprinkling of holiday makers in the silver ring, feeding the lesser fry among the layers. My candidate travelled well, but have not yet stripped him. Expect to do so this afternoon, weather and other circumstances permitting. Hope to see you later, as they say, when we might clock him over the full distance, prior to slipping him with confidence. Anything I can do with regard to training quarters locally on your behalf, will receive my closest consideration and eager cooperation at your request. Stabling moderate in price, in spite of tariff.

Any information from headquarters would be welcome, especially about such another one as Jocanda (won easily), with a view to minor coup to relieve momentary embarrassment. Also address of Eccentric c., who I believe on information received, has been cast in his box at the Marxian training quarters. Worried about rumour that he has been scratched from all engagements under our rule.

Yours respectfully
Liam (late Bill. G. lst I.G.) No. 2 boy)[1]

[1] Francis Stuart can put no particular interpretation on this letter! Kitty Tailer told the editor that she, her sister, and her two sons (who were usually with their father) spent a month with O'Flaherty in a Brittany hotel in the Summer of 1935.

Peters wrote to Victor Gollancz 19 July regarding *Hollywood Cemetery* taking the place of *Famine* on O'Flaherty's contract. Gollancz replies that he wants to publish *Famine* too and has quite a nice advance country subscription list. Eric S. Pinker Inc. wrote 26 July that Erskin would accept O'Flaherty's altered terms for the dramatisation of *The Puritan*. The play would be a powerful psychological study and a copy would be sent to O'Flaherty shortly.

On 6 August O'Flaherty had moved to Hôtel de la Belle Etoile, Le Cabellon, par Concarneau. He cabled Peters for money, but there was nothing for him. By end August *Hollywood Cemetery* had been typed and sent to Peters, O'Flaherty is now at Royal Court Hotel, Sloane Square, and shortly moves to Hans Crescent Hotel, Knightsbridge, SWl. Gollancz is worried about the outspokenness of *Hollywood Cemetery* (a letter to O'Flaherty dated 2 September), and in a letter to Peters Gollancz describes O'Flaherty's heated reaction to this suggestion. Gollancz had paid two hundred and fifty pounds advance for O'Flaherty's next novel, under the agreement of January 1932, outstanding since June 1933, and had been announcing *Famine* (the third book under the Gollancz contract). O'Flaherty appreciated Gollancz's forbearance and said so, telling Gollancz 'an author does not expect a publisher to be a gentleman, but you have been'. Three alternatives remain, 1. the book is toned down, 2. O'Flaherty publishes elsewhere but still owes Gollancz his next novel, 3. O'Flaherty publishes elsewhere in modified form. (Source A.D. Peters files, HRHRC).

In September, 1935, *Hollywood Cemetery* was sent to Carol Hill, then returned at O'Flaherty's request for revision.

By 21 September, O'Flaherty's address was the Red Lion Hotel, Henley.

By 26 September, Gollancz had received the revised *Hollywood Cemetery*, read by Norman Collins. It is now all right, and will be published.

By 18 October O'Flaherty had moved to a rented farmhouse with Kitty Tailer, Moyleen Farm, Marlow, Bucks, where they expect to stay for he uses die-stamped writing paper for the first time. *Hollywood Cemetery* was published 18 November, 1935. See George Jefferson's *Liam O'Flaherty: A Descriptive Bibliography of His Works*, pp. 47-48 for more about this novel.

---

336. SIUL ALS to Francis Stuart
Written on headed paper fromThe Gargoyle Club,
69 Dean St. W.l. and marked 'my address is:
Moyleen Farm,
Marlow, Bucks'   Tuesday lunch [postmark 19 November, 1935]

Dear Francis,

Here I am at the Gargoyle once more (not likely to get among the money I'm afraid) with the most charming and beautiful lady, who is passionately addicted to your works (B ... lie what?) and would adore to know you (rather true E.N.). I feel that you two would really become friends, Francis, and therefore I wish you would write a note to Mrs Elizabeth Nicholls, The Priory Mill, Tonbridge, Kent.

When are you coming over (Yes, when? E.N.). Watch out for Clear Diamond about January or late December.

                                                                    Liam

---

337. SIUL TLS to Francis Stuart
Moyleen Farm,
Marlow, Bucks   n.d. Thursday [postmark 28 November, 1935]

Dear Francis,

Thanks for your letter. I am longing to see you again and to sit with you somewhere in Dublin, or similar and talk and drink. As they say, the old times back again. Christmas! What? I'll certainly come over and we might pick one or two unexpected ones, at a shade over, at the Foxrock venue on 26th.[1] There is a lot to be said, but I feel that I'm not the individual to say it in a letter. I'm hopeless at it. However!

Catherine and I are rusticating at Marlow. I'm working on *Famine* in a more or less desultory fashion. I'm like an old colonel with it, you know, one of those fellows who spend their declining years writing a preposterous history of their East African or Northern Frontier campaign as a subaltern. I live in the period mostly, but hate to make any progress with the novel, lest the public might hear about it and spoil my pleasure. I'm afraid I'm at last getting old and uninteresting. Vain statement! As if one were at some glorious period, now become legendary, an interesting figure.

Why the hell didn't you go to America? I felt that it was the moment for you. Or have you some hidden and Goemboesian plan about the invasion of the Jazz Spangled Dollarland (a miserable pun in the best gossip-column tradition, a neck, two lengths, third behind *Daily Express* standards)? I'm afraid your *Angel of Pity* got about the same treatment as my Hollywood shocker, except from a different point of view. They attacked me most foully and said about your book, to use Rupert's words[2] that it was rather odd. We should worry. One of these days we shall knock them. As [Patrick] Kirwan says, the opposition is paltry.

But more anon. Were you mystified by my note from the Gargoyle? An awfully nice girl asked me to have lunch with her, or she with me, I forget which, and she started in at a rousing pace gallop to tell me how much she wanted to know you, but was timid of making an epistolary approach. So I said at once: 'Waiter! A sheet of paper.' I hope you have written to her.

Kirwan is now running a typist and turning out serials and stories and what not. At least he was a few weeks ago. He stayed down here with Brian Hurst for a day or two and was very full of plans for conquering the fortresses of fame and fortune. Harold I have not seen for months.[3] I feel somehow that we are drifting apart, but I hope it is only temporary. In fact I see nobody as I hardly go into London. Enid telephones now and again. She has been to Berlin, Vienna and Budapest where she made a great impression by her knowledge of the General's money borrowing episode.[4]

Your friend Miss Haslip is, I hear, going to Mexico. Robert Caddell I saw, with his Marcia and former wife, Paulina, who is now Mrs O'Toole it seems. And that man Davidson. One feels that a marvellous life is going on quite near, but that it is just as well to pay no attention to it.[5]

I am longing for Ireland. When I have finished my book I am coming back ... I think ... More likely it will be Martinique or Ecuador. The chasing season, which for some unaccountable reason you don't like much, has started and I have had several enjoyable days at Hawthorn Hill, Sandown and elsewhere. I expect to go to Kempton tomorrow. John Beary trains near here. Why not come over for a few days. We are here until February and there's lots of room in most comfortable surroundings, including hard tennis court, and jigsaw puzzles. However, I detest the English countryside.

Dear Francis, are you working? I hope you are. Because you seem to be in a great productive mood at the moment and you should keep it up. I'll be over around Christmas unless you turn up here in the meantime. I've had a lean period for cash for some time now, but I expect to be out of it any day now. They are putting on *The Puritan* as a play in January in New York, and I might get a few bob out of it.[6] Bloody Cape is trying to sue me for money over the film rights of *The Informer* and refuses to pay my royalties. These publishers!

Do write again, Francis

With love, Liam

[1] Leopardstown Races, 26 December.

[2] Rupert Grayson, publisher of both *Shame the Devil* and Stuart's 1935 novel *Angel of Pity*.

[3] Patrick Kirwan was man about town, close friend to Grayson, German translator and a minor writer. O'Flaherty had shared rooms with him ten years before. Brian Hurst was film producer of Synge's *Riders to the Sea*. Harold Stroud lived off a private income, drank at The Plough regularly and was a Marxist.

[4] Enid Raphael . General Gombös (or Gombosh), Prime Minister of Hungary.

[5] Joan Haslip had written a book on Parnell, and novels. Norris Davidson still lives in Wicklow, and Francis Stuart (to whom the editor is indebted for all this information) ran into him in 1987 after twenty years.

[6] At the Belmont Theater, 23 January, 1936.

---

338. HRHRC ALS to A.D. Peters
Moyleen Farm, Marlow, Bucks   11 December, 1935

Dear Peters,

Do what you can about the Cape business and thanks for your work in the matter. I feel miserable about putting you to all this trouble.

I don't think I want to give him *Famine*. I expect big things from it and I feel confident that it will have more success than *The Informer*, so I want some publisher who is not as slippery as Mr. Cape has proved himself to be. Except for Mr. Gollancz's yellow wrappers I think he is the best of them, but I don't want you to make any contract until you have seen the MS yourself and decide what is best to do with it. If we should happen to have a good thing this time, there is no point in getting it tied up for the sake of getting out of a momentary difficulty.

Thanks awfully, old man, and do please forgive me for putting you to all this bother.

Yours, Liam O'Flaherty

Peters told O'Flaherty he had a good case against Cape but litigation would be expensive, and not worth it. Cape have offered a settlement of the dispute and renounced claim to a share of the film rights. Peters tells O'Flaherty that the dispute is due to a misunderstanding, and neither side is to blame. Peters' commission on the film rights of *The Informer* came to fifty pounds as O'Flaherty got just over two thousand five hundred dollars. Peters agrees to take his commission in instalments to help O'Flaherty's shortage of money, and sends him a contract for the Norwegian translation of *The Informer*.

1936

339. HRHRC ALS to A.D. Peters
Moyleen Farm, Marlow, Bucks   24 January, 1936

Dear Peters,

I am off to Martinique for two months. Please [send] to Mrs O'Flaherty, 68 Parliament Hill, Hampstead, any money that comes in for me in the meantime. I shall come back with *Famine*.

I'll send you my address from Martinique in case there should be anything important.[1]

Best wishes

From
Liam O'Flaherty

[1] In fact they went to Jamaica, so Kitty Tailer told the editor. She went first and O'Flaherty followed, then her mother became ill and she had to go back to New York. By end February *Hollywood Cemetery* had been rejected by seven American publishers. The following letter was presumably sent in before O'Flaherty left.

------

340. To the Editor of the *New Statesman and Nation*[1]

Sir,

As an Irishman resident in England, I felt deeply grateful to you for publishing Mr. Carter's splendid article on De Valera's work in the southern part of Ireland under his control.[2] It was a fine appreciation of a statesman who has done more than anybody since Parnell to remove from his fellow countrymen the characteristics of serfdom, bred by centuries of feudalism. The letter which you publish in your present issue from Mr. W.P.C. of Dublin, a letter which its author did not think worthy of his full signature, rivals in idiocy a recent article by a conservative Irish senator in the tabloid Tory press.

This extraordinary Irish Socialist finds fault with our President for imposing an import duty on tea and butter. As we produce more butter in

Ireland than we need, an import duty on that commodity cannot affect the poor, while the consumption of tea has done more damage to the bodies and minds of the Irish poor than the exaction of Irish landlords in the past. A tax of five shillings a pound on that nerve-wrecking foul beverage would be more to my liking.

Furthermore, he claims that a community of peasant proprietors is a force of ignorance, reaction and superstition. France is such a community, without being ignorant, reactionary or superstitious; at least far less so than Germany, or the U.S.A., which are both organised on the basis of large-scale production of food and industrial commodities.

I do not belong to De Valera's school of political thought, I believe that the U.S.S.R. claim the allegiance of every civilised person in the world today. However, I believe at the same time, that any Irishman who fails to appreciate the magnificent work being done by President De Valera is an enemy of his country.

Thanking you and Mr. Carter for your courtesy towards a much maligned but noble statesman.

Yours faithfully
Liam O'Flaherty

[1] Published 8 February, 1936, under the heading of 'Irish Housekeeping', Vol. XI (259) New Series.

[2] This is in response to W. Horsfall Carter's article in praise of De Valera's economic policy, published 18 January, 1936, pp.73-74. W.H.C.'s letter was derogatory. He wrote that 'Irish Ireland' appealed to the primitive tribal instincts also glorified in Germany and Italy.

---

30 March, O'Flaherty cabled Peters 'Please send mail to N.Y. office.' By this date Mrs O'Flaherty's address was 51 Belsize Lane, London, NW 3.

On 2 April, Carol Hill sent A.D. Peters a long letter after what she describes as a 'very interesting and indeed amusing luncheon'. She says O'Flaherty has an interesting mind and can be engaging and amenable when he wants to be. She was taking two-thirds of *Famine* away with her to read over the weekend. O'Flaherty wishes Random House to have the book. Hill agrees with this for Random House have a tolerant editor who will be able to cope with the difficult author. Peters has suggested Viking Press as first choice. She wishes that Peters could read the novel for 'so few Americans, if any, are in a position to really criticize and have full appreciation of an Irish novel'.

On 13 April, Carol Hill wrote to A.D. Peters saying the first two hundred and ninety-two pages of *Famine* are very moving and good. She offered it to Viking Press, who rejected it, then to Random House.

On 14 May, she wrote again saying that O'Flaherty had disappeared having sent 'a very attractive girl, duly draped in silver foxes, to collect his MSS which he said he wanted to do some work on. His mail was accumulating. A cable had come from Walter Kane in Los

Angeles 'We have an assignment for you to start immediately. Will you return at once.'

On 19 May Liam's brother Tom diedaged forty-seven in Aran, of heart failure, which may explain the hiatus here.

On 23 June, Peters discovered that O'Flaherty was working for Walter Kane, and his address was c/o Columbia Pictures Corporation.

On 20 August, O'Flaherty cabled Peters, 'Please send mail to Hotel Guetharia, Guethary, Basses Pyrenées.'

---

341. HRHRC TLS to W.N. Roughead
Hotel Guetharia, Guethary, Basses Pyrenées, France   1 September, 1936

Dear Roughie,

I enclose the two agreements which I have signed.[1] I am rewriting *Famine* which will be finished towards the end of October, at which time I am returning to London with it. I shall be glad to have done with it, as it has nearly broken my heart. I hope it's worth something after all this trouble.

Could you send me an account of whatever I have earned since the end of January, and whether you received anything for an edition of *The Informer*, a film edition, which appeared in America?

It's very exciting down here near the Spanish frontier, where there has been a battle going on for the possession of San Sebastian between the rival Spanish factions for the past week or two. One can see the two armies distinctly from the French side. The French farmers charge a penny to let you into their fields and sixpence more to look through a telescope. Good show.

Give my best regards to Peters and to yourself all the best

Yours sincerely, Liam

[1] The agreements are for the Czech and Hungarian volume rights of *Hollywood Cemetery*.

---

342. HRHRC TLS to W.N. Roughead
Hotel Guetharia, Guethary, Basses Pyrenées   17 September, 1936

Dear Roughead,

Thanks for the accounts. I am returning your cheque for thirty pounds. Would you please send the total of seventy-four pounds sixteen and threepence to Mrs O'Flaherty. I am moving away from here on Saturday to get a bit farther away from the Spanish war, so please don't send me any mail, until I give you a new address.

By the way, would you enquire from Mrs Hill about that American screen edition of *The Informer*?

All the best

Yours, Liam

On 30 September an O'Flaherty to Peters cable read: 'Send mail to Hotel Lutetia, Bd. Raspail, Paris.'

10 October, Zeppo Marx sent a cable to O'Flaherty c/o Peters: 'Will you return here to do a screenplay of the *Road Back* by Erik Remarque? Contact R.C. Sherriff London, he will give you script to read and rewrite. Cable immediately salary and when you can leave – regards.'

On 13 October, another cable read: 'Deal off, letter follows, Zepmarx'. Kitty Tailer could throw no light on what this assignment might have been. John Ford had paid poorly for the rights of *The Informer* which grossed a huge amount. To her knowledge O'Flaherty did no work for Zeppo Marx but they used to talk Yiddish and Gaelic to each other as a joke, and got on well.

The completed MS of *Famine* was sent to Carol Hill by A.D. Peters 3 November. It was rejected by Random House as too gloomy. Max Perkins of Scribners also found it too harrowing.

6 November, the owner of a Knightsbridge flat applied to A.D. Peters for a reference on behalf of Catherine O'Flaherty [sic] staying at the Cadogan Hotel. Shortly after this O'Flaherty's address became 6 Hans Crescent, SW1. The agreement for *Famine* was signed with Victor Gollancz on 23 November. Their reader, L.A.G. Strong, praised it highly though he would have preferred a shorter book.

---

343. HRHRC TLS to W.N. Roughead
Royal Hotel, Glendalough, Co. Wicklow   30 November, 1936

Dear Roughead,

I enclose a short story 'The Beggars' and under separate cover two other stories called 'Prayer' and 'The Wedding'. I think they are good stories and you might be able to find a market for them in England.

Do you think the world is ever going to become sane again? I am glad Peters is back from the war.

Yours sincerely
Liam O'Flaherty

P.S. Thanks for cheque. I have sent these stories to America myself. L.O'F.

On 23 December, Carol Hill was told to destroy the typescript of *Famine*. It had been rejected by Simon & Schuster, who found it too depressing.

1937 – 1945

From 1937 on there are many letters from O'Flaherty to Mrs C.H. Tailer (Kitty), so many that a selection has been made to cover the period up to the early 1970s. O'Flaherty also sent Kitty frequent cablegrams, signing himself 'Liam', 'O'Flaherty', 'Reilly', 'Barbare', 'Pee', 'Bill', 'Pidge'. His letters to Kitty also have various signatures. Kitty had two young sons when they first met, and later other family responsibilities. She travelled frequently. O'Flaherty occasionally went with her, but for the most part remained in Dublin during his later years.

11 January, 1937, *Famine* was published by Victor Gollancz and O'Flaherty got an advance of two hundred and fifty pounds.

On 18 January O'Flaherty cabled Peters: 'Wire sales *Famine* to Knickerbocker Hotel, Hollywood.'

By 19 January three thousand copies had been sold.

On 20 February 'C.T.' sent a note asking that all mail should be kept as O'Flaherty was returning to New York shortly. In February 1937 Random House accepted *Famine* for U.S. publication.

Kitty's copy of *Famine* bears the following handwritten dedication: 'This is Kitty's book. In Memory of Jamaica, Marlow, Martinique, Greenwich Village, Guéthary, Paris, where we wrote it, from Reilly.'

---

344. KT ALS to Kitty Tailer
Part of letter on headed paper of Hotel Lutétia, 43 Boulevard Raspail,
Paris   Wednesday night p.m. Paris 26 March, 1937

Darling Sweetie Pie,

I am on my way back from Dublin – bound for Paris. Dublin was too frightfully melancholy, and I just didn't feel there was any point to staying there. A kind of slime was seeping through the streets, it drizzled, the people looked miserably poor, impolite, unhappy. The influence of Catholic Fascism was everywhere, and I had the feeling of being in a dead city. Maybe it was the sudden change from the terrific vitality and the wealth of New York, but there it is. At the moment I am determined to apply for citizenship in U.S.A. and settle down in the west. 'How long will this last?' says Kitty.

Oh darling, I love you so! I am exhausted with sleepless travelling and I am only half conscious, but I am aware that you are now my whole life and that I would be utterly lost without you. I got your lovely telegram in London. Aren't I lucky that you love me in return, because I am too fond of you to live without you.

I shouldn't write now as I am silly for lack of sleep. I couldn't sleep on the *Normandie* on account of the nervous exhaustion of listening to politics at meals and in the smoking room all day, to Esther, Chester and their friend, an English Socialist lady, {...}, what a woman! That bloody Supreme Court is out of luck if it has to deal with many like Esther. Otherwise it was not a bad crossing, though dull and dreary, since I was going from you instead of coming to you like last time. I think we had better get a divorce for me in Reno and get married and live on the American Continent, than run back and forth like this, don't you?

I saw nobody in London except a fellow called Charley Ashleigh. It sounded dull. I had a Turkish bath there and that was all. I am going to start writing as soon as I get to Paris. I think I'll write a book about America. That sort of thing.

What sort of thing? I forget, I am going to write short stories. You see I am *'installé'* on the *6ème* at the Lutétia. I have had a good sleep. I am beginning to write and things look good. It's very nice here, like coming back home. Have read {...}, *L'Humanité*, *Herald Tribune*, and *Le Temps*. The journey from Dublin to here was frightful, such a crowd coming to Paris for Easter! Now I can wait for you in peace. Hope I'll have a lot of little things written in the meantime. I suddenly have an ache to write little sketches. (Darling, I love you).

It's going to be awfully long until you come but I shall put up with it better than last year, because I feel better in mind, now that I am a sober man and we are nearer to one another. I think we should get married in America though. Think about it and tell me what you decide. Seems to me the simplest way out. Also, America is the best place for me to earn a living and Europe does not look like having a peaceful future. I have outgrown Ireland. This time I couldn't see any difference between them and the English.

What do you think of the National result? I picked second and third, while my Cooleen could have won were it not for a loose horse getting in her way (clever Reilly).

I have a funny article for *Herald Tribune* which I will send you and you will offer it to the Literary Editor, name of Ryan I think, or O'Sullivan.

Sounds odd being back here after our journey to Hollywood (or rather Santa Anita). Hope it bears fruit. Didn't hear much about *Famine* in either London or Dublin, but I had the feeling it did not raise a tidal wave in either the Thames or Liffey. I don't think anything could. Perhaps Hollywood has, after all, taken the place of literature in the human mind. If so let's get in on it. There is no point in struggling against *fact*, is there, sweet?

This letter, duck, is mad and pertains somewhat to the outpourings of an *énergumène*. However! I am full of love and yearning for you, little darling and I am enthusiastic, optimistic and *enfoutiste*. I must write to Peters and get some information about *Famine* and those short stories.

Take care of yourself, loveliness. I get frights about something happening to you. I believe Chester is in Paris but I sha'n't see him. I have become antisocial. Are you having a lively time? I hope you do a lot of seeing people as it's good for you. It's bad for my nerves I think.

Well, sweet one, I'll write a few words again with that article the day after tomorrow.

Love, love, love
Pidge

---

345. HRHRC to A.D. Peters
Hotel Lutétia, Paris   n.d.[received 31 March, 1937]

Dear Peters,

Sorry I missed you going through London. I had a look at Dublin, found it uninhabitable as far as I am concerned, and came over here. I intend to spend some months writing short stories and sketches here. I failed to sell *Famine* for the moment in Hollywood, as Mrs Hill failed to get it published in America, with the result that I had nothing to go on. However, I think I have sown the ground pretty well.

I asked Miss Stephens to find out about the collection of short stories which Cape intended to bring out. Would you tell me what happened to it? Also how *Famine* has sold? With best wishes to you and Roughead, I remain,

Yours
Liam O'F

---

23 March O'Flaherty had been at the Ivanhoe Hotel, Harcourt Street, Dublin. Peters replied to this letter that the sales of *Famine* were 4,750. As Edward Garnett had died [on February 19, 1937, aged sixty-nine] could Rupert Hart-Davis, now adviser to Cape, be selector for O'Flaherty's collected volume of stories? O'Flaherty agreed to this, and *The Short Stories of Liam O'Flaherty*, consisting of fifty-eight stories chosen from his first three collections, was published 11 November, 1937.

---

346. HRHRC TLS to W.N. Roughead
Hotel Lutétia, Paris   10 April, 1937

Dear Roughie,

I am prepared to do the articles for the *Graphic* at ten guineas an article, commissioned and payment on delivery for the lot. Not on any other conditions.[1]

Could you please tell me:

a. If the film rights in *Mr Gilhooley* are free. I ask this because I may do it after *The Puritan* here in France, at a much better bargain. A play of *Mr*

Gilhooley was produced in New York. Does that entail any rights for a film version of the novel?[2]

b. When is Cape bringing out my short stories?

Hope Peters is not very sick and hope to see you around Derby time when I am coming over.

Yours ever

Liam

[1]The *Sunday Graphic* had asked O'Flaherty to write twelve sixteen-hundred word articles on prominent living Irishmen for use in their Irish edition. He was to send a list of chosen people first, payment one hundred pounds. This offer was later cut to eight articles at ten guineas each, and the first of four names agreed to were De Valera, William Cosgrave, John McCormack and General O'Duffy.

[2]*Mr Gilhooley* film rights were clear for France. Peters wrote to Louis Postif on 10 April that O'Flaherty was supervising the filming of *The Puritan* (with Jean Louis Barrault, Viviane Romance and Pierre Fresnay in the leading roles). Postif had done the film script. The French press gave O'Flaherty some attention.

1 May, 1937, *Les Nouvelles Littéraires* carried a long article by Jeanine Delpech '*Aux courses avec O'Flaherty, révolutionnaire Irlandais romancier et cinéaste.*' For this writer O'Flaherty '*incarne l'âme Irlandais*', and has an ardent imagination bordering on '*la folie*'. She dissects his contradictory character with great perceptiveness. The producer of *Le Puritain* was Jeff Musso from Marseilles, who had helped in Hollywood with the filming of *The Informer*. O'Flaherty told both Delpech and Georges Blond, who wrote about him in *Candide*, that he had a Breton grandmother (Her surname was Nez). In another article by Jean Rollot in *Le Journal de Paris* 13 July, 1937, O'Flaherty gave a description of *The Puritan*. This article, entitled '*La légende et les vérités de Liam O'Flaherty*', contains an amusing anecdote about a bistro worker of magnificent Celtic physique whom O'Flaherty had met in Brittany.

By 24 May, 1937, O'Flaherty had moved to Hotel Gallia, 63 rue Pierre Charron, Champs Elysées.

On 1 July, Carol Hill cabled A.D. Peters to say that *Famine*, published by Random House, had been selected by the Literary Guild with a guaranteed sale of forty thousand copies, payment four thousand and eight hundred dollars and six thousand dollars if the sales go up to fifty thousand. This novel had been rejected as too depressing, harrowing or gloomy by Scribners, Simon & Schuster, Knopf, Little Brown, Reynal & Hitcock, and Houghton Mifflin. O'Flaherty was asked to write an article on the ideas behind *Famine* for *Wings*, the Literary Guild journal, in a letter dated 8 July, 1937, from John Beecroft. *Famine* was also the choice of Great Britain's Readers' Union, for one hundred and fifty pounds.

In August, 1937, it is evident that Kitty had crossed the Atlantic in the *Queen Mary* and O'Flaherty, after a holiday on Aran with Pegeen, joined her in Paris.

By 11 November he was back at the Hans Crescent Hotel, London, en route to New York where he arrived by the end of that month.

14 December O'Flaherty left for Cuba. At Christmas he sent Kitty a cable to the Colony Club, New York, 'Season greetings, love and lotus leaves from Reilly.'

Through the files of A.D. Peters and cables to Kitty, the movements of O'Flaherty can be traced. In early March he was in Paris.

By March 16 he was at the National Hotel, Upper Bedford Place, Bloomsbury, and sent Peters some stories. Peters writes back: 'New stories sound grand, all except "Moonlight", and should sell well.'

By end March O'Flaherty anxiously awaits the arrival of Kitty on SS *Normandie* from New York. Upon her arrival they go to Cannes. Peters told Carol Hill in an 8 April letter that O'Flaherty had stopped drinking on his fortieth birthday (in August 1936) and so far had stuck to it. Carol Hill now has her own agency at 22 East 40th St., New York. Not knowing this O'Flaherty went to another agent called Chambrun. Mrs O'Flaherty is still being sent money to 51 Belsize Park. The short stories 'Brosnan', 'Rum', 'The Bath' and 'The Mouse' are of this period.

On 3 May, O'Flaherty cabled that his mail should go to Les Lézardières, Anthéor par Agay, Var.

---

347. HRHRC TLS to W.N. Roughead.
Les Lézardières, Anthéor par Agay, Var, France
n.d. [received 1 May, 1938]

Dear Roughie,

Thanks for the accounts and for sending the money to Mrs O'Flaherty. Please keep what you have in hand until I return.

Could you please tell me about income tax? I have received a form from the authorities and I don't know to what tax I am liable, as I am not a resident of Great Britain and am subject to income tax in the Irish Free State, or Eire rather, being a citizen of that part of the country. Do you know am I subject to taxation on what I earn in England? Is there some new law to that effect?

If so, could you please tell me, from your books, what I have earned in England during the year ending April 5th, 1937? Thanking you for your trouble, [1]

Yours sincerely
Liam O'Flaherty

[1]Roughead explained the income tax regulations and the forms to O'Flaherty who left this French address end June and cabled A.D. Peters to keep his mail. He now moved to Hotel Prince de Galles, Avenue George V, Paris, but before doing so sent the following letter from France.

---

348. HRHRC ALS to W.N. Roughead
Anthéor, Var   6 May 1938

Dear Roughie,

  You were away when I called at the office before leaving. I asked Peters
to send some money that was due, amounting to about one hundred
pounds, to Mrs O'Flaherty. Could you tell me if it has been sent to her?

  Also those stories. This chap Chambrun has already sold two of them
and has sent the rest out all over the place, so I can't take them from him
naturally. So would you try to sell them in England? Also, could you send
me Cape's bi-yearly reports as I'm interested to see how my book of short
stories sold.

  I went to see that man who made a film of *The Puritan*. He told me it was
a failure and that there was no money to come from it. I am inclined not to
believe him, but I have no means of finding out, or have I?

  Hope you've had a good holiday and are feeling fit. My new book, *Black
Wedding*, sounds very promising.

Yours
Liam O'Flaherty

On 29 July Margaret O'Flaherty wrote to Roughead from Farrington House, Ticknock,
Sandyford, Co. Dublin. Pegeen is in Ireland with her and they are to meet O'Flaherty at
Kingsbridge Station. She does not know his address. Another cable shows that O'Flaherty
was in Aran early August, presumably with Pegeen, as the following letter would indicate.

---

349. KT to Kitty Tailer
Great Southern Hotel, Galway   n.d., Wednesday

Darling Kitty,

  Am feeling very miserable and disappointed with everything ....

  Don't think I want to live in Ireland or England any more. I feel farther
and farther away — hostile to the people's point of view and rather eager
to plunge the land into revolution against priest craft. It's too frightful, all
those black insects crawling about, and that atmosphere of dark hostility
they leave in their trail.

  Well, well, Kitty, it may be the climate! Let's stick to the sun and the healthy
attitude towards life of Maurice Thorez with the cowboys of Nevada.

  This morning I took Pegeen for a drive through Connemara a hundred and
twenty miles. It's so beautiful in the mountains. Passing Michael Killanin's
house, the driver said: 'An Englishman named Lord Killanin lives there.' 'But
he's Irish,' I said. 'Well!' said the driver, 'In a class of a way he is. He's like the
English factories they have in Ireland now. The site is Irish but the capital is
English. A good natured man though, a fine Englishman.' 'But he was born here,'

I said, 'and all his people for hundreds of years. If he's not Irish who is?' 'We are,' said the driver. There was no reasoning with him, neither would he believe that I was Irish. The point is that the priests have persuaded them that all non-Catholics are foreigners. It's now a completely Fascist country.

It would be fun if Marlene Dietrich does the film. We could at least get the five hundred pounds! I saw Mrs Palmer for a moment. She was going up to Dublin to the horse show, full of social chit chat. Very provincial but still good looking. Another chap called Davidson, you met him once at the Café Royal, is staying at the hotel, with a motor boat on the Corrib. I feel very lost without you and shall be glad to get to Aran for a fortnight. All this makes me unhappy. I don't suppose I'll be able to write a word. However, it stirs one up and one is better for it afterwards. The thing in life is to feel and go on feeling more and more acutely. Thus one gets a wider comprehension of reality. As Crowley said, 'one lives in a lie' by avoiding disturbing contacts, until one might reach the Marie Antoinette stage of telling the hungry to eat cake instead of bread.

Saw people loading a turf boat out near Cashla. Saw a fair and sheep being put on a lorry, also a man driving a resisting sheep. Several old women, a band playing to a crowd on the green at Galway. A row of twelve nuns sitting in a boat. Had a long conversation with a Benedictine priest who liked me and gave me a packet of cigarettes. I roused him against the secular clergy. He agreed with my suggestion that they should be abolished. He was a Walloon, a tribe of Belgians starting a monastery in Ireland. Ireland is being invaded by ever greater masses of priests and nuns. Nuns are now going into the hotel business. They'll soon be running hostels, that will be the end.

Pay no attention to this dreary letter, sweetheart. I miss you and Campesino and have no idea what is happening in the great world. I want to belong to the great world. Harry Clifton was right, I have outgrown Ireland. Perhaps it wouldn't be so desolate with you. I wonder? I found London quite cheerful and kindly.

Pegeen is much fatter and quite pretty, but looks sad. I find the majority of people here very ugly, excepting the men I saw in Connemara. The women are invariably ugly. What must people have looked like in the Middle Ages? Compared to Californian youth these people look ghoulish. *Les nerveux n'aiment jamais l'endroit où ils se trouvent. C'est une maladie bien établi, tu sais.*

Goodbye, adorable one. I love you no longer as something outside of myself but as part of myself. That is why my letter is like a soliloquy. I kiss your feet, dearest,

Liam

On 22 August O'Flaherty sent his address to A.D. Peters as, la Résidence d'Haicabia, rte de Corniche de Saint Jean de Luz, Hendaye.

On 6 September he wrote saying sorry to change his address yet again but he had now taken a permanent place in Paris and was to move there at the end of the month. He wrote from another address in St. Jean de Luz, as the next letter shows.

---

350. HRHRC TLS to W.N. Roughead
Villa Betty Baita, Quartier Aice-Errota,
St. Jean de Luz, Hendaye   10 September, 1938

Dear Roughead,
About that libel action, here is the information they require.[1]
(a) I have no permanent address.
(b) In writing the story I had no particular hotel in mind and only used the name of the town of Wexford because it was the distance from Dublin required by the plot.
(c) I have no information whatsoever about Wexford or its hotels. My sole idea in the story was to describe a typical country hotel and I did not ascribe any characteristic to this particular hotel in the story which could not be ascribed to scores of hotels of a similar kind all over the country. Reference to my book *A Tourist's Guide to Ireland* would prove that it was a faithful description of the pleasant and easy-going hotels which are one of the main charms of our Irish countryside. I had no intention whatsoever of being malicious about these charms, and am very disappointed that anybody should think otherwise.
(d) I did get a letter from a solicitor in Wexford, but thought it was a joke; or if not a joke, certainly a very unmannerly way of thanking the patriotic efforts of a writer to draw attention to a small town which enjoys an obscurity altogether unwarranted by its old world attractiveness.

                                                          Yours sincerely
                                                          Liam O'Flaherty

[1] When O'Flaherty's story 'The Bath' was published in *Britannia & Eve* (1938) a Wexford solicitor issued a writ for libel on behalf of Black's Hotel. The story 'Galway Bay' was also written about this time.

September (n.d.) there was a note to A.D. Peters from O'Flaherty: 'Don't send more mail. Coming back owing to Mr. Hitler's doubtful behaviour. Hoping we don't have to eat plum and apple jam once again. Yours, L.O'F. But on 15 October, 1938, his address is: 38 Quai Louis Blériot, Paris 61, according to a cable asking for his mail.

On 22 December, 1938, O'Flaherty cabled Kitty that he was sailing for New York, and wrote her the following letter.

---

351. KT ALS to Kitty Tailer
South Western Hotel, Southampton   p.m. 22 December, 1938

Darling Kitty,

Here I am in Southampton waiting for the *Rotterdam* to turn up, which it does not do, at least so far. The man keeps coming in and saying that it will be another hour late, so I am writing you a little letter.

I am so glad to have got out of London. It was dreadful weather and I *did* get a bad cold at Hurst Park. However, my cold is getting better now. I saw Pegeen and got her a pair of small skis and ski boots and sticks and socks and *imperméable* gloves and a pipe to play, so she is going off to Haute Savoie with her mother to learn how to ski .... Pegeen looks marvellous.

I'm in a queer mood, but I love you very much, Kitty. What does that mean? Being in a queer mood but loving you very much. Rather empty in my other self, and full in the self that is part of you. In the train coming down I felt remorse of conscience for not having been very nice to you lately. But it's not *me*, Kitty. It's not *me*.

It's nice writing to you, darling. I may write 'The Sun' after all At least I am going to write something shortly. I didn't ring up the bank about Musso. I felt that was pointless as there was nothing to be done about his not honouring the cheque. Kitty, something big is going to happen. I feel it. Not in Cuba though.

Situation in Europe looks better. Franco is breaking up and the Irish are getting ready to – MARCH. Craigavon had to arrest a lot of them in Belfast today. The English expect to be at war within a year. Duff Cooper and Eden are coming back into the Cabinet. France looks safe for the moment, or a decade, and Quai Louis Blériot will probably flourish to the extent of its lease.

I kiss your feet, darling, I think of you always
Liam

1939

From A.D. Peters' files in HRHRC and cables to Kitty the following information emerges for 1939. O'Flaherty went to the Plaza and then the Presidente Hotels, Havana, on 3 January, 1939.

By 24 February he was back in Paris. Kitty joined him there in early March.

In late May he was briefly in London, evidently alone, for he wired Kitty from the Euston Hotel to tell her he had won a hundred pounds on Blue Peter. Kitty and he went to St. Jean de Luz that year. After war broke out on 3 September he wrote to A.D. Peters from the Washington Hotel, Curzon Street, London W1, no doubt en route to Ireland from where he later wrote to Roughead.

---

352. IUL to John Ford
38 Quai Louis Blériot, Paris   15 March, 1939

My Dear Jack,

I am sure you were rather astonished at receiving my wire, but it was difficult to explain in such short space what was on hand. A film company which has just done *Louise*, with that singer Grace Moore, wanted to do *Famine*. As I did not particularly want to have it done in French, and wanted them to do *The Martyr* instead, which could easily be transposed to any country, I said that you were the only person that could do *Famine*, which is true. Then they asked me to wire you to come and do it. They were prepared to put by twelve million francs for the costs and give you complete control over the production, story, etc. I knew perfectly well that you were filled up for this year, but now the sons of bitches are thinking I am holding out on them and refuse to do *The Martyr* instead, saying they want '*un grand sujet*'. Jews are funny people. This company, however, is very little Jewish, as the King of Belgium seems to have put up most of the money, and they are somewhat Fascist.

It would have been fun if you could have come. They would have got out the whole town to welcome you, but I am glad you didn't. If you ever do the story it should be in Ireland, I think, with as many Irish actors as possible.

Kitty and I are going over to the Grand National next week and then on to Dublin for a week or so, as I want to do some research work in the library for *Land*. I don't think we Irish are very popular at the moment in England, owing to the activities of 'the boys'. Is there any chance of your coming over this year? You talked about doing *The Quiet Man* when I saw you, or have you dropped the idea? It was marvellous meeting you in New York. I certainly did enjoy the days you spent in that hotel, sitting around and talking. Kitty told me that *Stage Coach* got a great reception in New York. A journalist here asked me what you were doing and I said *Stage Coach*. 'Ha!' he said, 'That would be in the genre of *The Iron Horse*. Is it as good as *The Iron Horse*? I said it was far better. 'Then,' he said, 'it's a great film.' They still show your *Lost Patrol* here which they think is your best work.

How is your nephew doing since he reached the coast? Has he gone fishing on the *Araner*? Do write and tell me the news about all the fellows. Kitty told me that Dudley Nicholls is writing a play. What next? For myself, I intend to get down to the writing of *Land* sometime this year. It's almost ready now. Another of my stories is being done on the screen here next month, with an actor called Rainu. It might be quite good. I wish you could take a trip over here sometime this year.

What do you advise me to do about *Famine*? Do you think Hollywood would let you do it? And if not should I let this fellow Feder do it in French? Excuse this rambling letter, Jack. It's practically the first one I have written in years, except to my daughter. I'm going to see her next week and try and persuade my wife to divorce me at the same time. *Quelle vie*! Jesus!

I hope to see you soon. It did me such a lot of good meeting you in New York. This is an empty bloody world, Jack, with such a few people in it and they are scattered. They that have eyes to see and ears to hear are scarce, old son. Well! God damn it, all my love to you.

Liam

---

353. HRHRC TLS to W.N. Roughead
Royal Hotel, Glendalough, Co. Wicklow   18 November, 1939

Dear Roughead,

Could you send me the statements of my publishers for this half year? And also any money that may be due to me. I have written some short stories and would like to know whether there is any market for such work at the moment, or has everything dried up in the short story line? Would you please let me know whether it's worth sending them to you? Hoping you are holding out well, and that Peters is fit,

Yours sincerely
Liam O'Flaherty

The Royal Hotel told A.D. Peters in early 1941 that O'Flaherty had left them a year before, leaving no address. By February 1941 his mail forwarded c/o American Express, Liverpool, was returned and he was thought to be in Mexico, but he seems to have spent most of the period 1940-1945 in the United States. From this period a few facts emerge and there are some letters to Kitty Tailer.

In June 1940 there is a cable from Liam (in Los Angeles) to Kitty (in New York).

On 16 February, 1941, O'Flaherty's lecture 'Hands Off Ireland' was given in New York City Town Hall. A copy was obtained via the British Council by Stanley Unwin who told G. Wren Howard at Cape, who told Victor Gollancz, that O'Flaherty was engaged in dangerous anti-British propaganda in the United States J.F. Kennedy, junior, was present at this lecture. The lecture will eventually be published with O'Flaherty's collected prose.

Kitty Tailer told the editor that in 1942 O'Flaherty sent money urgently needed for medical expenses for Pegeen. They spent two winters near Phoenix, Arizona. *Land* was written partly in New Canaan, Connecticut, in a house they rented. Here, for the first time, O'Flaherty had the use of a secretary and dictated some of his writing.

O'Flaherty also undertook a Hollywood project during the war, to write the script of *How Green Was My Valley* with Dudley Nicholls, but they did not get on and O'Flaherty pulled out half way through: Zanuck (the producer) refused to pay, and O'Flaherty held him up with a property pistol for the money!

In 1944 (n.d.) there is a note from Laura Harding (Kitty's sister who had an apartment at 400 East 49th Street, New York) saying please forward mail for O'Flaherty to R.F.D.I. New Canaan, instead of to the apartment.

11 April, 1944, Mrs O'Flaherty's address was Kilmacabe House, Leap, Co. Cork. She wrote to A.D. Peters asking for O'Flaherty's address. There was no money in O'Flaherty's account and such royalties as arrived were paid direct to the Inland Revenue to clear off taxes that should have been deducted when he became resident abroad. Roughead was now in the Royal Navy, another staff member in the army in India. A.D. Peters replied that O'Flaherty's address was c/o Jacques Chambrun Inc., 745 5th Avenue, New York City, as he still seemed incapable of remaining in one place for more than three months. Mrs. O'Flaherty was receiving some money from the U.S. at this period.

The following five letters to Kitty are from these war years.

---

354. KT ALS to Kitty Tailer
The Lombardy, 111 East 56th Street, New York 22
'Communiqué No. 2, Lombardy Tract'
[Kitty is in Chatham, Massachusetts]   p.m. 31 August, 1944

Dearest Kitty,
    Yesterday I met Pat O'Connor in the street and I had dinner with him

and his wife. He is quite an amusing character. He is now a wrestler and expects to become world champion in that peculiar profession. He and his wife are rather worried about how to spend the large amount of money – about one million dollars – they expect to win during an incredibly short time. It is just like the two thousand dollars we spent at Palm Beach next [sic] winter on the lucre derived from an *Unforgettable Character*. Both he and his really beautiful wife are very happy owing to their fantastic prospects. He has already won ten obscure victories in small towns (*dans les environs*)....

We had a super excellent dinner at a place called the San Remo, about the best I have had in this country, unless one includes the Tampa Spanish Chicken Joint. We had minestrone, steak and ice cream. *And bread*, what bread! It's a saloon where one also eats. O'Connor says that it is unfortunately becoming fashionable. The word fashionable used in connection with any conceivable change in the social standing of San Remo is quite as ridiculous as O'Connor's hopes of becoming world wrestling champion. I think these Greenwich Village people play with the idea that they have created a Parisian atmosphere in that sordid precinct of New York. (I maintain that the baseball parks and Belmont racecourse are the only things Parisian there.)

Kitty, this is rather an impersonal chat, almost frivolous, but you asked me to tell you what I did with my evenings. That was quite an amusing evening.

Even so, I don't like New York. For the life of me I don't know why. Even the Trotsky papers are no longer amusing.

I have as yet been able to write nothing, although the typewriter functions perfectly.

Well, the war in Europe seems to be coming to an end, all the people say so. And as Clemenceau said: '*Les fous ont toujours raison.*'

Darling, there is no more ink in this pot. As you say, I miss you terribly. I say, I feel like a lost puppy without my Kitty.

Yours
Me

---

355. KT TLS
New York   Friday morning [p.m. 1 September, 1944]

Dearest Kitty,

By right I shouldn't write to you at all, since I have not yet received tale of tidings of you since you went north. It is a poetic vengeance that I, who never write letters, should be slighted in this manner on the solitary occasion that I reverse this custom.

There is nothing good to report. I feel very gloomy and inclined to abandon the sort of life I am now living. The only deterrent is that I see no means of assuming any other way of living. I am tired of trying to write my novel and being unable to make any progress with it. I am also very tired of writing in English. I would like to spend the remainder of my life writing in Gaelic, not because I want to produce a work of consequence in that [language], but simply that writing in Gaelic would give me pleasure. I really am a whore when I write in English, no matter how I try to gild the lily with pretensions to art structures, etc. In the Anglo-Saxon world literature is a form of commerce. I am tired, tired, tired of the Anglo-Saxon world, whether writing in it, or being millionaire in it, or a general, or a dishwasher, or King of England, President of the United States of North America. I am forty-eight and I am bored with everything I have seen beyond the frontiers of County Galway. Even within County Galway a great deal is remote and unworthy of attention.

I went to bed at six thirty last night and slept until four. I got up at six and had to walk to 46th Street for breakfast. Then I went back to bed in my clothes and read the papers. There was a good photograph on the front page of the daily news (enclosed).[1] You will note that the pro-German girl seems to be an approach-worthy blonde, whereas the patriot women are skinny and ugly. Heaven is for the virtuous, but the conqueror's bed is for the beautiful. At the same time it is worth noting that a prudent conqueror would make provision for the sexual appetites of the skinny and ugly among the conquered women. [The rest of the letter is missing]

[1] The enclosed press photo shows a scene in the South of France in which the women mentioned confront each other. The caption mentions that the U.S. 1 Army has crossed the Meuse.

---

356. KT TLS
New York   p.m. 2 September, 1944

Darling Kitty,

I got two most beautiful letters from you yesterday shortly after sending you a particularly gloomy missive which, I hope, did not injure your digestion, or darken your view on life. I was very glad to hear from you, especially as you said you still love me. I need you to love me.

Yesterday I worked all day, peculiarly enough, after writing to the effect that I had finished writing for good. Today also I am writing, so I have no time for gloomy thoughts. The man on the radio just said that Patton had entered Germany and all sorts of others, normally things which do not interest me in the least at this moment.

I am terribly glad you are coming back on Wednesday. This is a bore, still I do think it's probably easier to work here than in New Canaan. That is such an incredibly dull neighbourhood. There is another marvellous photo of branded French women in the daily news today. I'm not sending it to you because it's cruel and rather beastly.

I was amused at your story of the Dutch woman. I had seen a picture of her and her children in a paper. It must be infuriating to you, sacrificing some of your good American men for this fat creature's property recovery. Your Roosevelt certainly has a lot to answer for.

I like the Lombardy. As you say, it's clean. This room in particular is very cheerful and I can sun myself on the little balcony. But the little radio has static here. There are enormous radio stations sticking up from the tops of buildings all round.

Darling sweetie pie, I hope you are having a wonderful holiday, because you certainly need it after having been with me so long without respite. I must be an awful person used as permanent company. However, I love you and that should count for something.

Dear me, it's only half past noon and I'm tired already. Wonder should I go to the bleachers at the Yankee Stadium this afternoon. It's beautifully warm but it's Saturday, so it would be crowded. I don't know, but I probably will. I'm tired writing. I love you sweetheart, with kisses,

Liam

---

357. KT ALS to Kitty Tailer
The Lombardy, 111 East 56th St., New York City

p.m. 3 September, 1944

Dearest Kitty,

They put ink in my well and I have discovered how to make my typewriter go again when it stops. So things are not so bad. I also got your telegram. I heard you ring at eleven this morning, but I never dreamed it could be you, so I didn't answer. I thought it might be O'Connor and didn't want to be disturbed at my work. I am working very well here now (X fingers).

Even so, there is bad news. I went to Belmont to see this Pavot, the crack two year old. The result is that I have not paid my room rent and yet I have only eight dollars for food until Wednesday. Somehow I don't feel depressed because I'm working. When one is working it is nice to have no money. It's questionable whether a writer should ever have any money. Yes ... for occasional debauch.

If this spurt lasts long enough I may finish my novel by the end of the year. My God! What a relief it will be to see the end of it. And what loneliness! I'm fond of Lettice and Raoul. Today I got fond of Michael too. Barbara is just a whore I think.[1]

Lunchtime I went into a tiny place where I remembered eating eight years ago. Then I got soup, Yankee pot roast with vegetables (enormous helping), apple pie, bread and butter ad lib, coffee, for thirty-five cents. Today I paid fifty cents for pot roast, bad stuff, with two small pieces of German fries and one slice of rye bread, plus a tiny slab of dyed margarine. A glass of milk and a piece of apple pie brought my check to seventy cents. If I had soup the price would be eighty-five cents. That makes the inflation about one hundred and thirty percent without allowing for portions being almost halved. The *real* restaurant inflation is about two hundred and fifty percent. What the hell!

Thanks for your lovely telegram and thanks for being lovely. I love you and am today feeling happy. I hope to have finished Barbara and the groom by the time you come.

Yours

Me

[1]The characters referred to are from *Land*, published by Victor Gollancz, London; Random House, New York, 1946.

---

358. KT ALS to Kitty Tailer
Hotel Pennsylvania, West Palm Beach, Florida   p.m. 24 December, 1945

Dearest Sweetie Pie,

Just several small words to tell you that I love you very, very much, that I got your telegram from Jacksonville, that I am going to the races today, that I am longing for your return and counting the hours thereto, that the weather here is still bad, that this is the stolen pencil, and – believe it or not – that President Camachi of Mexico has given the National Prize to Alfonso Reyes for his book *Criticism of the Athenian Age*.

Imagine Truman giving an American writer a prize for such a kind of book?

However, my *primpeallán*, I long for you with all my fingers and toes. God be with you,

Me

1946, O'Flaherty was still in the U.S. On 25 March, A.D. Peters wrote to Harold Matson, (now O'Flaherty's agent) 30 Rockefeller Plaza, New York , asking O'Flaherty to write to him about *Land*. This novel was due to be published by Random House. From 1 May Mrs Catharine H. Tailer took over the management of the literary property of Liam O'Flaherty and acted on his behalf with full power of attorney, as she writes and tells A.D. Peters. In this letter Brian Hurst is granted a one year option at one hundred pounds on the film rights to *Famine*, with a purchase price of five thousand pounds. Arrangement for the publication of *Land* had already been made with Victor Gollancz, and there is a query about income tax. A.D. Peters replied that under his contract the agency of *Land* is his right.

By 4 July, 1946, there is £149.7.8. in the O'Flaherty account with Peters, after paying the income tax he had owed.

5 July, Kitty announces her arrival in London early August, and she met A.D. Peters 12 August. Peters then wrote to Gollancz that he would act as agent for *Land* and the remaining novels under the *Famine* contract of 23 November, 1936.

---

359. HRHRC TLS to A.D. Peters
Gresham Hotel, Dublin   5 September 1946

Dear Peters,

Thanks for your cheque for £283.10.8 which I received. As I intend to reside permanently here now, I'll take whatever steps are necessary for remission of the tax.

Hope you are keeping well? I myself am more or less above water. Give my regards to Roughead. Hope to be in London towards the end of the year.

Yours sincerely
Liam O'Flaherty

Peters had already told O'Flaherty that money might not be sent to the U.S. because of exchange control. On 10 September Brian Hurst, of 9 Kinnerton Studios, SW1, took a year's exclusive option on the *Famine* film rights.

---

360. HRHRC TLS to A.D. Peters
Gresham Hotel, Dublin   22 September 1946

Dear Peters,

I got your note this morning about the rights to my books published by Gollancz. Here is what I would like you to do, if possible.

I want to retain the following titles of all I have published so far, and to have them republished by a single publisher:

Novels – *The Informer, The Black Soul, The Puritan, Skerrett, Famine, Land, Insurrection* (in preparation and to be submitted next July).

Short stories – volume of short stories published by Cape in 1937 and volume to be submitted next month.[1]

Miscellaneous – *Two Years*.

If Gollancz wishes to make a proposal of contract for all these titles, well and good, in spite of his yellow jackets and mediocre advertising. If not, I am given to understand that the Pilot Press might be interested to make one.

There was no question in my mind about going to an Irish publisher, either in whole or in part, or *pro tem*. I merely want to point out, on information from my friends, that certain London firms evade paper shortages by printing in Dublin, under certain circumstances (at least, such circuitous methods were suggested to me by people connected with the Pilot Press, or friends of theirs).

I take it that the other titles, which I do not wish to have republished owing to their immaturity, would still remain valid for purposes of film and dramatic rights? And what do you think of the possibility of getting some such publishing deal in the U.S? I'm afraid I've got a very poor market in the U.S. though, but one never knows in that extremely changeable community.

In any case, there is no particular hurry about this business. I hope to be in London by November, by which time you may have had an opportunity to explore the possibilities.

Yours sincerely
Liam O'Flaherty

[1] O'Flaherty seems to have forgotten that he had sold the copyrights of *The Informer* and all the short stories in the 1937 collection to Jonathan Cape.

---

361. HRHRC TLS to A.D. Peters
Gresham Hotel, Dublin   30 September 1946

Dear Peters,

With reference to Pilot Press enquiry, you are correct in supposing we should offer the short stories to Gollancz first of all and to Pilot Press, or similar, only in case of rejection by Gollancz.[1]

The republication of my novel *Famine* in the immediate future, and *Skerrett*, is what I really want. I am certain they would have a big sale while this left wing tendency lasts (if it is not already somewhat late in the day). I think Gollancz is as good as any, if he cares to cooperate ....

All the best
Liam

[1] He refers here to the new collection of stories, *Two Lovely Beasts*, Gollancz 1948.

---

362. HRHRC ALS to W.N. Roughead
Gresham Hotel, Dublin   n.d. [received 3 October 1946]

Dear Roughie,

Thanks for your note. I have not had any communication with Postif for years – don't know if he is still alive.

Any publisher that wishes may do *Famine* in France for advance royalty of fifty pounds or twenty-five thousand francs. Don't care who translates it, as they all seem equally bad.

Yours
Liam

---

363. HRHRC TLS to W.N.Roughead
Gresham Hotel, Dublin   29 November, 1946

Dear Roughie,

Thank you for your letters of the 19th and 22nd. First of all, with regard to Cape, I don't think I'll bother reclaiming the rights in *Thy Neighbour's Wife* and *The Assassin*, since I have no intention of having either of them re-printed, I don't see why I should give Cape fourteen plus of my all-too-scarce pounds. I'm sorry he has decided to republish *The Informer* and the short stories. He must have some very unpraiseworthy reason for wanting to do so.

As regards the film rights of *Famine*, I don't quite understand the rather peculiar proposals put forward by Sistrom-Hurst. I gather, however, that they are making an offer to buy the rights for two thousand pounds, provided I do a treatment *gratis*. I have no particular desire to do a treatment. However, I might do one if they pay five hundred pounds over and above the two thousand. In other words, I'm willing to let them have the film rights for two thousand five hundred pounds cash and would do a treatment for that sum.

It must be understood, however, that I would want the total amount before I sign the contract. That Sistrom belongs to the Cape ilk, if I remember rightly. Do you think it's advisable to hold out for a percentage of the profits?

Yours ever
Liam O'Flaherty

---

364. HRHRC TLS to W.N. Roughead
Gresham Hotel, Dublin   14 December, 1946

Dear Roughie,

Please send all further communications for two months to Hotel Lutétia,

Boulevard Raspail, Paris, where I am going to be domiciled for good or ill.

As Sistrom has evidently refused to accept my offer it does not hold any further and I again revert to my demand for five thousand sterling for film rights of *Famine*.

I want to know if Gollancz intends to publish *Famine* and *Skerrett* in a new edition. If not, I want the rights, as I want to bring them out myself. I have lost a great deal of money by not having these two books in print during the past four years. Furthermore, would you kindly ask Jonathan Cape to omit the dedication from the new edition of *The Informer* that he contemplates publishing.[1]

Mrs C.H. Tailer is taking you some short stories that I have written recently. I hope you may be able to find an outlet for them. I also would like you to send to my Paris address your cheque for any money due to me.

Yours ever
Liam O'Flaherty

[1] The dedication was 'My beloved Margareteen'.

O'Flaherty must also have been in Paris, probably with Kitty after her arrival in August, for an interview with Jeanine Delpech entitled '*Liam O'Flaherty nous dit ...*' was published 19 September, 1946, in *Nouvelles Littéraires*, as well as a sketch of him by Roger Wild and the short story '*Le Joueur de flûte*'.

Delpech had last seen O'Flaherty seven years before at the Auteuil racecourse. She asked him now about his opinion of the United States. He replied with typical exaggeration: 'I am not made for factory life. Hollywood has become a factory. After three months of forced labour there I had a nervous breakdown which lasted for three years. As a citizen of a non-belligerent country I could not even return to Ireland. I was classified as a neutral. Me neutral!' As for America: 'It is a country where there are no aristocrats because money is so respected. An aristocrat has no need to be rich, he can live, toothless and alone in a forest. The aristocrat is a man who does not fear death. One cannot fear death when so many ancestors await you in the tomb. In Ireland sand and other infiltrations quickly rot coffins. When they bury a family member they lean over the prepared ditch and recognise grandfather with his short leg, and uncle's big head. They know they will be welcomed and will have marvellous tales to tell you. The O'Flahertys were kings from the fifth to the eighth centuries, then the O'Connors took over.' Asked whether Ireland continued to inspire him he replied: 'At this moment I am writing a book on the 1916 rebellion, so I walk around Dublin looking for role models.' Have you time to read? Delpech next asked. 'Yes, *Paris-Turf* each morning. I work in the morning, in the afternoons I go to the races.'

1947

From now on Kitty Tailer dealt with O'Flaherty's business correspondence. 4 January, 1947, she wrote from c/o American Express, Paris, about the reversion of rights of *Skerrett* and *Famine* made by Gollancz.

1 February, 1947, there is a short ALS note from O'Flaherty to Margaret Stephens at A.D. Peters, will she send fifty pounds from his account to his wife at a Co. Cork address.

By 23 March, O'Flaherty's address was Gresham Hotel, Dublin.

On 1 May, he sent M. Stephens four stories from 564 Park Avenue, New York. He was now working on the stories for the *Two Lovely Beasts* collection. O'Flaherty proposed this title, his alternative choice being *Galway Bay*.

Stories written during or shortly before this period include 'The Challenge', 'The Flute Player', 'The Seal', 'The Beggars', 'The Parting', 'The Eviction', 'Grey Seagull', 'The Old Woman', 'The Tide' and 'Keep Faith' (withdrawn from publication).

On 17 November, Kitty sent one more story from Paris. O'Flaherty was there but she was returning to New York for a few weeks. This was 'The Hawk', first published in the *Evening News* with 'some of the more pointed details of the mating habits of the birds cut out'. While Kitty was away O'Flaherty sent a telegram to Gollancz asking them to correct the proofs of *Two Lovely Beasts*, the agreement for this had been signed that Autumn.

Two Lovely Beasts was published by Gollancz in July 1948 and presumably O'Flaherty passed through London then.

On 8 July, he wired Peters to send money and his mail to the Royal Hotel, Glendalough.

24 September, 1948, Kitty wrote to Peters on O'Flaherty's behalf from Hotel Powers, 52 rue François 1er, Paris. On her way back from the U.S. earlier that year she had brought a food parcel for a member of Peters' staff, rationing still being strict in the U.K. of this period. In October 1948, Kitty wrote to A.D. Peters to tell him that O'Flaherty was not in Paris but would arrive 30 October for one week. In the meantime he wrote from Cannes.

365. VG ALS to Victor Gollancz

Poste Restante, Cannes, Alpes Maritimes, France   10 October 1948

My Dear Victor,

Many thanks for your letter of September 9th. I was very pleased with your advertising of my short stories and the good reviews the book received. I am finishing a novel called *Insurrection*. It will be ready by the end of December and submitted some time in January. It's at least of the same quality as the short stories in your collection, so I'm hoping it may receive the same treatment from the reviewers.

I was disappointed that you decided not to re-issue *Famine* and *Skerrett*. I am convinced that these two books would have a considerable sale in the British Isles at the present moment. *Famine* sold fifteen thousand copies at five hundred francs of an edition brought out last February by an obscure firm called Editions de Flore here in France, and *Skerrett* is being published this Fall by three different countries. However, I daresay you know your own business best.

Hope to see you when I come to London in April.

Yours sincerely
Liam O'Flaherty

---

366. HRHRC ALS to A.D. Peters

Poste Restante, Cannes   2 December 1948

My Dear Peters,

I am glad Gollancz is going to reissue *Famine*. I don't know where he got the idea that it was reissued in the south of France. Here they only print pornographic books as far as I know. Nothing has been done to *Famine* since he relinquished the rights; except, of course, the French translation that Editions de Flore brought out last January. No reprints, no editions of any sort in the English language. It has been out of print in America for twelve years.

Insurrection will not reach you until the end of January. My daughter is coming to visit me here after Christmas and she will take the MS back with her on January 30th. I don't see how a reprint could conflict with the publication of a new novel, provided there is a space of a few months.

Yours ever
Liam O'Flaherty

1949

In 1949, O'Flaherty's movements can be traced through an undated typed 'account of my whereabouts' subsequently sent A.D. Peters which covered the period 1949-1952. In 1949 he was in France April-June, Ireland in July, France in August, Ireland September-October, France November-December.

---

367. IUL ALS to Montgomery Evans

(As from) Great Southern Hotel, Galway   15 October 1949

My Dear Monty,

Well! Your letter of September 6th certainly brought back nostalgic memories of the old days – or the good old days to describe them correctly. I am here at Cannes at the moment, on the French coast, but return to Galway on Tuesday. I hope to hear from you further there. Funny this, it was only a few days ago I was telling a chap about your 'coup' on the Eclipse Stakes at Sandown Park. Remember that day? Your sitting down on the wet concrete in Tattersall's Ring with a handful of bookmaker's chits on Caerleon. I bet you don't!

I got a previous letter from you during the war while I was in the U.S. but lost your address and was unable to answer. In any case you were on active service at the time, moving about the Pacific. Well, what a life! You're luckier than I am in being with the woman of your choice. I am now wandering about, a lonely man, carrying the torch for someone who is in New York.

As you know I spent a lot of time *chez toi* since I saw you last – Hollywood, New England, New York, Florida, Cuba, Mexico, etc. Certainly wouldn't regard it as a personal injustice to get back there again. Indeed, I would give quite a lot to get back for the opening of the baseball season next Spring (as far as I remember you prefer football). It would be wonderful to sit down and chew the rag with you for a while, although I now eschew heavy potations and addict myself to Coca Cola.

I see little of London these days. It's like a morgue, although it's picking up a little. Passing through there three weeks ago it seemed quite cheerful on the surface. The imperial glitter and the feeling of security is gone, however. The Fitzroy was crowded with frightful pansies. The Café Royal was inedible and all the old crowd gone. The only part I really liked was the Swiss Cottage area where my friend Harold Stroud, now trembling under the internal weight of alcohol, still protects three pubs from the necessity of declaring themselves sotrupt. Stulick's Eiffel Tower is now run despicably by a Greek, Ma Lewis's place is still open, or so they say, but merely a barely perceptible chink.

My dear fellow, forgive this hasty note, I am just breaking camp here. Do write me to Galway and love to your wife, the three dogs and seven cats. Hope your drink book is signed and sealed by now.

Liam O'Flaherty

For 1950 O'Flaherty lists his whereabouts as January/February in Ireland, March/August in France, September/October in Ireland, November/December in France. In between he also made short trips of a few days to Spain, Switzerland and London. In France he moved between Paris and a rented flat in Cannes, sometimes with Kitty, sometimes on his own.

Liam and Kitty are mentioned in Madeleine Stuart's *Manna in the Morning – a Memoir 1940-1958* (Raven Arts Press, Dublin: Colin Smythe, Bucks, 1984) pp. 90-93. Francis Stuart's diary for March 29, 1950, is quoted: 'Dinner with Liam O'Flaherty and Kitty on Saturday and an evening at the Flore and the Dôme. A strange meeting again after ten years. Much laughter and talk of old times and friends, but some echo of sadness beneath it. He told me that he and Kitty were no longer living together. They were to lunch yesterday and left for London in the evening, Liam en route for Aran and Kitty to America.'

On June 29 Madeleine describes how O'Flaherty came to lunch in their little attic overlooking Montmartre, 'Liam shone in a role I had never before known him: the storyteller. It was as if he had opened a magic suitcase full of wondrous tales, credible or incredible, they were sheer magic. I was spellbound.' O'Flaherty was now living in a small hotel, less expensive than the Lutétia where he had previously stayed with Kitty. Madeleine, Francis, and Liam, Kitty remained friends, and in his old age she used to visit him, and get him to sing 'Lili Marlene' in English, then in Irish. A photograph of Liam and Kitty together in Paris in 1950 appears in Madeleine's memoir. O'Flaherty was gambling a good deal at this time.

In May 1950 O'Flaherty signed the agreement for *Insurrection* with Gollancz, staying at 10 Hanover Square, W1. The previous month he had delivered the MS. This novel later appeared in braille, and did well in the U.S.

For 1951 O'Flaherty lists his movements as January/February in France, March/April in Ireland, May/June in France, July in Ireland, August in France, September/December in London. An unknown story 'The Peacock's Dance' was returned by the *Evening News*, and 'The Enchanted Water' sold to *Chamber's Journal*. O'Flaherty's London address on 29 October was 5 Culford Gardens, SW3, but the previous month he had been at 20 Chesham Place, SW1 where Kitty often stayed. The only 1951 letter is a short one to Margaret Stephens (A.D. Peters) written from Paris on 1 June about *Insurrection*.

According to O'Flaherty's account, sent to A.D. Peters for tax purposes, during 1952 he was in London January/March, and in Ireland April/September. In April 1952 O'Flaherty took a lease on 9 Court Flats, Wilton Place, Dublin, which was to remain his home base for the rest of his life.

---

368. HRHRC TLS to John Montgomery of A.D. Peters
9 Court Flats, Wilton Place, Dublin 2   13 August 1952

Dear Montgomery,

Please note that the above is my permanent address. By chance I went around to the American Express and found a note from you saying *House-wife* magazine wants to buy a five thousand word story for one hundred pounds. I think I have an idea for the kind of story suitable for such people and will send you a hundred word synopsis in two days' time.[1]

Hoping it will be the right sort of thing for them, I remain

Yours sincerely
Liam O'Flaherty

[1] 18 August, Liam sent in a synopsis of 'Black Sheep's Daughter'. He was asked by *Housewife* to change to first person narration, concentrate mainly on the character of Charlotte, and condense the account of several deaths and past history so that the opening was not too gloomy.

---

369. HRHRC TLS to John Montgomery
9 Court Flats, Wilton Place, Dublin   4 September, 1952

Dear Mr. Montgomery,

Thank you for the synopsis and for getting *Housewife* to commission the story, which I now proceed to write according to instructions, i.e. I'll make the groom relate the story and concentrate mainly on Charlotte. It's my first essay in literary prostitution and I trust that my advanced years won't hinder my giving the customer complete satisfaction.

I don't know what they mean by awaiting 'American release' as I'm writing this story solely for them. Can you sell the story for me in America? I wish you would, if you could. It would be fun whoring on two such widely detached fronts simultaneously.

I have three short stories written and am having them typed, after which I'll present them to you. You might also tell Gollancz, is that right? that my new novel *The Gamblers* will be ready for publication in March.

Yours sincerely
Liam O'Flaherty

---

370. HRHRC TLS to Margaret Stephens (at A.D. Peters)
9 Court Flats, Wilton Place, Dublin, 2   10 September, 1952

Dear Margaret,

I'll have the manuscript by the end of March, at which date I'll deliver it into your hands. As for publication, of course that's another matter. It seems so far, in any case, there might be a good chance of serialising this story; but of course one never knows. Certainly, there are masses of people other than myself interested in the gee-gees. My interest, I can assure you, has been largely professional and is now waning. Even so, it would require a large sale of the book to enable me to recoup my losses.

I enclose dates for the Income Tax people. I'm terribly sorry, dear, to

subject you to all this annoyance and am very grateful for your kindness in
dealing with it. Poor Margaret! Perhaps I'll stand you a few drinks next
Summer on I'lle du Levant. I'm not being flippant either.

Yours sincerely [unsigned]

P.S. [ALS] Montgomery's *Housewife* story will be ready next Monday or so
and am getting the other three typed at present.[1]

[1] In late September (n.d) O'Flaherty sent Montgomery 'The Mirror', 'The Fanatic' and 'The Post
Office' for serialisation in English. Of the last he says: 'I think it's quite funny. At least it makes
me laugh. The *Housewife* story will follow shortly.' This was published in April 1953.

---

371. HRHRC TLS to Margaret Stephens
9 Court Flats, Wilton Place, Dublin, 2   8 December, 1952

Dear Margaret,
I'm afraid that I must be, once more, an awful bore. The income tax
people, Eire, have requested me to give them a detailed account of my
earnings from April 1st, 1951 to April 1st, 1952. Would you kindly send me
the list of all the money and its source, paid out to me by your office during
that period? So sorry to trouble you again about this wretched business.

I'm sorry, too, that I am bound in your opinion to let Chambrun handle
the American rights of *The Gamblers*. I am going to try to get rid of him,
however. Since I have no contract with him I don't really see why he should
be entitled to handle it. In the meantime, I am going 'right along with it' as
the Americans say. I hope it is really as good as I hope.

By the way, what happened to that story I did for *Housewife*? Were they
pleased or horrified or what?[1]

Yours sincerely
Liam O'Flaherty

[1] Receiving no immediate reply, on 29 December O'Flaherty wrote to Montgomery at A. D.
Peters enquiring after his story, and repeating the income tax query.

1953

372. HRHRC TLS to Margaret Stephens
9 Court Flats, Wilton Place, Dublin 2   13 April 1953

Dear Margaret,
Thanks awfully for sending on that money. About Mr. Gollancz's enquiry. I really don't know what to say. The novel is not yet finished, since
it is longer than I thought it would be, or rather it is taking me longer to
write than I thought it would. What with loss of energy in this extraordinary

climate, etc. I doubt very much now if I can get it done befor end of July. I am gambling all on the success of *The Gamblers*, so that I don't want to hurry it. If Victor wants to announce it on those terms, that is getting the manuscript in early August, let him go ahead. If not, then not, I don't really care. Either the thing is what I hope it is, in which case there is no hurry, or it's not what I feel certain it is. Then it doesn't matter when a poor thing is produced. I have about seventy thousand words done and there are another thirty thousand to do. I expect to be in London sometime early in May, when I hope to see you and talk about it. So far I have been unable to do anything about Chambrun, except that I have washed my hands of him. However, there is always that contract he made with Little Brown, blast it.

Thanking you again, Margaret, for warding off the landlord.

I remain –

Yours sincerely, Liam

According to a letter from Mrs Tailer to A.D. Peters, O'Flaherty was ill in the early Summer of 1953. He had a burst duodenal ulcer and Kitty was sent for. His sister Delia's son, Breandán ÓhEithir, also helped.

1954

373. HRHRC ALS to A.D. Peters
9 Court Flats, Wilton Place, Dublin 2   n.d. [received 11 January, 1954]

Dear Peters,

Glad to hear from you and sorry that Victor G. is again badgering me about *The Gamblers*. I really got a haemorrhage and nearly died last year trying to hurry it along. Unless I have a relapse, which I sincerely hope not, it will be ready in June. He can have two hundred pages in March if he really wants to see what it's like. I am rewriting the whole thing. Really, I'm pinning all my hopes of success on this final effort and I don't want to let it go hurriedly, as I have done with many previous novels.

Yours ever, Liam

P.S. I hope your team gives the All Blacks a good game, ours didn't, L.O'F.[1]

[1] All Blacks is the New Zealand rugby team.

21 October 1954, O'Flaherty was at 20 Chesham Place, SW1 where John Montgomery sent him a contract for work on the script of a film *A Grand Man*. His engagement was for fourteen days from 18 October, and included a fee, Dublin fares, taxis and expenses. The production was by Group Film Productions of Arthur Rank, Pinewood Studios, Iver Heath, Bucks. According to Kitty Tailer, O'Flaherty began work on this script but never completed it.

1955 - 1957

June 1955, *The Gamblers* was still unfinished. O'Flaherty seems to have remained in Dublin for the major part of this year.

In May 1956, John Guillermin paid one hundred pounds for a twelve month option on the world film rights of *Insurrection* against a purchase price of twenty-five thousand dollars.

In May 1957, Guillermin, from a London address, paid A.D. Peters a further one hundred pounds to extend the option. Various translations of O'Flaherty's novels appeared this year, such as a Dutch pocket book edition of *Skerrett*, a Serbo-Croat translation of *The Informer*, a German *Das Schwarze Tod (Famine)* and a Danish *Hollywood Cemetery. The Gamblers* remained on the Gollancz list.

In 1957 a one act version of *The Informer* by John McGreevey was published in Chicago by the Dramatic Publishing Company.

Late 1950s

The following selection of letters, some undated, show the kind of life O'Flaherty was leading during the late 1950s when he wrote frequently to Kitty Tailer. They also show the variations in his moods and the sometimes precarious state of his physical and mental health.

---

374. KT TLS to Kitty Tailer
[from Dublin]   n.d. 'Derby Day 2 p.m.' [1955]

Darling Kitty,

I got your letter on Monday and I was waiting to see if Miss Stephens would send on the Certificates before replying, but they have not come so far. There seems to be some Indian sign on everything connected with this cursed Income Tax affair. However, it's best not to worry about it too much. Why should one? Presently I shall listen to the Derby running and find out if my horse is going to win. More interesting.

I am not, unfortunately, getting any farther ahead with my novel. Just stuck in the same place. No incentive. My nerves are too near the surface and rebel at the least exertion. They hear everything and find no rest, so that there is no driving force.

I do hope you have splendid weather and peace of mind in the south. It should be good there now. We still have winter. The flies, which showed their horrid faces in April, have all died or disappeared into hiding places. Yet there is a dull sun nearly every day.

I received the underwear and the soups, most of which I have already consumed. Thank you. I lead the same sort of life as before; a weird solitude broken occasionally by unpleasant contacts with undesired human beings, *ça commence vraiment à me taper sur les nerfs.* I am trying to read Lucretius *De Rerum Natura*, which just goes to show. Have just finished re-reading 'To the Finland Station'. This story of Marx, Engels, Bakunin, Lenin and Trotsky begins to become sad, rather like the Europe I barely remember; that of the Danube waltz and the young Hussar officers with their jackets hanging from one shoulder, and the ladies with long swishing dresses. All things of that *fin de siècle* have become so nostalgic, but most of all the common belief in an ultimate utopia! Now it seems to us disillusioned people THAT THE UTOPIA WAS THEN. *Comme c'est drôle, n'est ce pas?*

4 p.m. *Daemon n'était pas là. Il n'était nulle part. Voilà, encore une fois, on était foutu d'avance ....* [the horse he backed in the Derby has come nowhere!]

6 p.m. Just got a pretty card from you in Geneva. Didn't know they had horses in the Gauguin country. Oh well! I'll direct this to Sainte Maxime, or is it Saint Maxime. No, surely it's feminine! Funny thing about this horse

that won the Derby, one called Phil Drake that I saw run second by a neck at Longchamps, I said to myself: 'That there Phil Drake is going to win the Derby, if he runs in it.' That's enough now, that's enough![1]

I certainly will let you know right away if forms arrive from Margaret. What I would much prefer to let you know is that I could write again. It's really beginning to drive me off my rocker, this business of being permanently frustrated. I feel like one of those Russian characters I have just been reading about, they kept hanging themselves while waiting for the revolution. Of course, when the revolution came the survivors were hanged in any case by Stalin. So there is really no chance for the *'exaltés'*, is there? Poor darling people, they get their reward *en passant*, but when paid they still expect more, rather, when they have 'spent' their spiritual boodle of ecstasy they keep on expecting to get more, but there just ain't any more after a certain time. Just old age and loneliness or ... what a wonderful generation Dostoievsky had to *'décrire'*! A whole nation of lunatics. The Bishop of Galway recently referred to Karl Marx as an obscure German Jew. I was going to reply by saying that he was far less obscure than the Jew on which the Bishop is 'living'. Indeed, of all the Jews in history Marx is undoubtedly the least 'obscure'. He certainly documented both his life and his ideas with appalling truculence.

Oh well Kitty, one must get on with life somehow! I sent Laura a cable just to show that I had not forgotten her simply because I didn't write. A cable is always somehow more impressive, as if it were *'d'urgence'*, don't you think so? Please go on writing to me often, darling Kitty, and please get brown in the face by lying down somewhere in the sun and not keep rushing madly about the place. Surely there must be some beach somewhere where you could lie down for a day or two. God bless you in any case.

Me, I'll just start typing again until it is time to lie down on my wretched bed,

Goodbye now

P.S. The phrase 'shake it up, Mac' is, after all a racing term long in use. In racing the 'shake up' is when the horses deploy in the straight and begin to 'make their run'. So the guy must have undoubtedly been a railbird. All my deepest love, Liam.

[1] Phil Drake won the 1955 Derby.

---

375. KT TLS to Kitty Tailer
[from Dublin]   n.d.

Darling Kitty Pie,

Yesterday I got your delightful letter announcing your return to Paris or its environs. How wonderful! I may hear you on the telephone and I do hope the sun did finally get 'bulk', I mean depth, but I suddenly thought of the ludicrous word 'bulk' in connection with a cure for constipation!

Personally I am on edge to such an extent with tension, through exasperating boredom, that my glance could give a hairy man a clean shave. So I can hardly get anything done. I almost shed tears when I think of the horrible waste of time, when there is so little time left. Darling Kitty, you know damn well I don't want a *house* in the south. I want a *shack minimum* or a room, just a tiny shelter of the most primitive and inexpensive sort. However, nothing will ever happen for me, nothing. It's now too late. Yet I do so want to get away from this constant irritation.

Wow! Why are you coming to England? Do you have to see the doctor again, or is it the tailor? I hate England quite as much as I hate Ireland. It's just the ugly cut of the houses I think. *Tout ça m'énerve*. The weather here remains the same. Yesterday it was so cold that they had to turn on the heat again. Quirke said his wife had to get up in the middle of the night and go for a walk around the square. Today it's warm for the moment. Later, of course, it will freeze again. It's all very jolly, like Evelyn Waugh's icy cold day in June.

I'm still at the Madrid chapter introducing Mrs McNiece. It should have been done a fortnight ago. Quirke promised to hang the horse when he does the flat today with Mike. My stool is still chez Danker. Can you imagine the boy did not call last week for my laundry because I was out. That too is in the hall. *Tu vois*? In this chapter there is such a poisonous temptation to put in 'odd characters', present at the McNiece party, but I must not slip into that sort of thing. It would be still worse than horse racing. One must just go on with the bare *minimum*, my new word obviously. I can't wait to hear from you over the telephone. I have completely lost touch with everybody now except you. The cocoon has become so small that there is barely room for myself to turn round. That is why I feel so irritated. When it gets still small, *c'est la morte*.

I noted on the back of your envelope that B12 is on its way, that sounds exciting! Maybe its atomic power, I mean its cargo of vitamins, will do the trick and enable me to get something done in spite of this irritation.

Do try to see the Chinese Opera in Paris if it's still there. It's probably gone by now though. The Grande Semaine will have terminated itself by the time you arrive and then ... Deauville and the '*gars du batiment*' will start drilling in obscure streets and all one sees are exposed pipes and huge trenches.

I am trying to interest myself in baseball again, having lost all interest in horse racing. I found some more Maupassant short stories that I had not read. Funny thing, most of them were just *précis* of characters he had developed in his more ambitious work. The bugger sold *everything* like a true Normand. There is just so much seed in one's sack, I suppose.

Dearest Kitty, forgive this irritated scrawl, I have been six hours this morning trying to do one paragraph without success. Can you imagine? It's all there but I'm all a jingle-jangle. I need a long, long walk. How lovely it is to feel utterly tired and utterly relaxed after a long walk alone, walking along absolutely flat ground so that one can walk almost completely asleep and without conscious effort. I must be on the verge of going mad. Perhaps these few words of protest will help to keep the wolf of madness from my brain.

Au revoir et à bientôt, Kitty dear. It will be so wonderful to hear your voice, as I hang on the edge of this desolate pit where a voice cries in the depths: 'Thy feet shall not walk by the ...' It's too hard to finish the variation. In any case, darling, I am longing ever so hard to hear you again.

All my love
Liam

---

376. KT TLS to Kitty Tailer
[from Dublin]   n.d. 'Wednesday noon'

Darling Kitty Pie,

This is just a hurried note to say that I am sorry for my delay in answering your last letter. I keeled over about five days ago as a result of working too hard. I am almost better now but still averse to the typewriter. So I am taking two or three more days off. *Do not worry*, I am very happy and confident. It's just that my motor boils over and I've got to let it cool off. The final blow was my eating a whole small chicken in rage at getting tired. I grilled it in a lot of butter. Well, well, I love what I am doing so much that it's hard to stop! It's foolish, though, to try and keep to a schedule ....

To go on to more serious matters. Everything is going fine in the flat, except that the new saucepan keeps boiling over unless I turn down the heat very low, which I always forget to do. I see nobody and I have given up visiting pubs. Good thing, you say! My Sunday visit to Croke Park is enough contact with humanity. Last Sunday was terrific, even though I was barely able to endure the excitement owing to my tummy. Next Sunday I shall be fit and well for the bigger show between Dublin and Mayo.[1] 'Fit and well' reminds me that I met Martin Hemphill's man while fetching my milk yesterday morning. He said Martin has been at death's door for some time, so I sent a telegram saying: 'I hope you will soon be able to face the starter once again, fit and well.'

The news about the McKenna woman is amusing. Laura[2] does know odd people! I wonder should she involve herself with a lot of pansies and lesbians! *ça pue, pas vrai*? Also, I have mixed feelings about Miss McKenna. On second thoughts I am convinced that she 'set' those pansies onto me at her dressing room. Later, while we were in a restaurant having a snack, she made a remark that told me she is an enemy. However, *c'est pas mon affaire, heureusement.*

Connie Neenan never turned up, so I cannot ask him anything further about Miss McGuire of Chicago. Let's forget all those people. *The gamblers are the only people that count* and you may now rest assured that 'they'll be up there', foot loose and fancy free, like the cruise prospectus of long ago. Remember? Yes, I am promising myself another visit to the West Indies with the resultant booty. Want to come, babe?

Darling, I have never felt so happy in my life. I get afraid sometimes that there may be a drug in those vitamin pills, otherwise how could I feel so exalted all of a sudden? *The Informer* and *Famine*, my only two efforts that achieved some sort of technical success, gave me no such ecstasy. What sort of a kick does Frances get out of those things? I really think I'm going to quit taking them. I have a horror of drugs except tea and burgundy wine. *Vive le Beaujolais!* I hope my next bottle will be after I hand in the manuscript to Kitty. Then *I shall not listen to reason. Armed with cases of bufox I shall really go to town.* Do you know that Jack McNiece once beat his wife when under the influence. How awful! I have pretty things for you to read, Kitty, when you return, so please hurry. Since you seemed to like Peter, I did work on him since. He comes out the best of the lot I think.

Listen, sweetheart, I shall write a long letter after tomorrow. For the moment I dare not risk writing any more. Goodbye my love, goodbye on paper but not in my heart which always throbs for you; little naked feet trotting around the carpet on their heels while you open and shut drawers and write things in notebooks. I like that best.

Liam

[1] 1955 GAA football semi-final

[2] Laura was Kitty's sister.

---

377. KT TLS to Kitty Tailer
[from Dublin]   n.d.

Darling Sweetie Pie,

I am getting confused now about you, because I have put a tiny bit of your outer person in that peculiar Juliette McBride. Not peculiar to me, of course, but to others I expect. Myself, I love her and have just finished describing her as she was before 'dull-footed time', the fellow that 'plucks the keen teeth from the fierce tiger's jaws', had drawn the dark shroud of death over her beauty.

Well, I am sorry for being so sleepy last night. I just couldn't keep my eyes open for a long time while waiting for you to call. Yet afterwards I had to get up and do some work, being no longer able to sleep. These B12 pills are funny. I am very excited at the prospect of seeing you again in London next week. I do hope I have this chapter finished by then. Again I have the feeling of great things. In any case, I am certain that it is there, this good mine and that my *burro* and myself have finally settled down, after a lifetime of weary wandering, by the rich lode of which I had always dreamt.

I am going out now to have my jacket and pants cleaned and pressed for the journey. I really do look disreputable, but that is in keeping with Dublin, and I notice I have not been deliberately insulted by a member of the slovenly intellectual *canaille* since I have abandoned my pretty stick and the various other irritating reminder of the gay world outside this enclave of sordid failure, and rain and morbid worship of a dead Jew. Hurrah! I really am not worried at all, or annoyed, by the Stock people. I don't know why I dwelt on it so irritably. It's just that I'm so anxious to get my novel finished and begin life once more in some sort of abundance.

The Indian Summer of O'Flaherty. Let's hope it's not rainy, certainly it won't be silent. Galsworthy and his 'silent footsteps in the grass' as descriptive of Indian Summer. An O'Flaherty of my sort is not silent, *il est bavard de temps en temps* ....

Kitty sweetheart, this is merely a note. I haven't got a drop of words left in me after this morning's work. I have been a week working on this complicated arrangement of introduction to this vital conversation between Gerald and his mother, ending with his putting a hand into her bag .... All I can say is that I love you always and you only, comrade of the unfathomable me. Shy wanderer that I could never spansel or hold, or even cheer when present with the gay frenzy of fulfilment. However, there are many planes of consciousness and some works of art can only be seen and loved in their fullness at a distance. When close at hand the highest mountain is a mere slope.

Allons, allons! It must really be the B12s that are at work. I must not take another for several days. Goodbye now, sweetheart, to next week and let us for a little while ride once more to heaven, or hand in hand to hell.

Liam, *l'orgueilleux*

---

378. KT TLS to Kitty Tailer
[from Dublin]   n.d. 'Sunday 8 a.m.'

Darling Kitty Pie,

I got your letter from Stamford last night and I now beg to report that I am almost back on my 'good mental feet' again. I expect to resume operations on *The Gamblers* at 5 a.m. tomorrow. The issue remained ominously in doubt for a few days, but is now definitely in my favour. I am rather inclined to believe that de-alcoholisation was responsible. No safety valve through which to let off steam in this dreary town .... However, there is Croke Park to which I am going this afternoon for my weekly 'shouting in the afternoon'. Yesterday I also went to Baldoyle and won three pounds ten. As a result I feel *en forme* again. A bit rocky in the forehead yet, but definitely *en forme*. I do hope you did not get too disturbed by my letter, but it was better all the same to tell the truth, in case the issue went against me.

.... I really must be alone unless I have the people I want. Zoe turned up with a carton of King Size Chesterfields on my birthday. Very nice. Her brother also rang. Have not seen either since.

The flat was very lucky to have me laid up. The kitchen and bathroom have been scrubbed, the remainder hoovered and dusted. The stove is bright and shining. Even the flies have been put to death by a wet zinc rag. I paid the bill from Phillips and whatever. Also, I also committed a *bêtise* by losing the form returned signed by the income tax man, the one I was to forward to England. Where is it? Down the chute by mistake? What now, Kitty? Should I report the loss? I know not and refuse to occupy my terrified mind with such things.

I do not believe Laura is happy in her many undertakings, she is just showing off, as she has always been very jealous of you and wants to persuade you that her own life is really more full. Poor Laura! She is so attractive and so mean, nobody should be mean to little Kitty who is too kind to everybody. I hope your trip to Bill's up-country hick town is a success. Alas! the Bosox look like being out of the Pennant. Last night I listened to a game they played with Cleveland in Boston and it looks like the end of the Beantowners. If Cleveland wins the American league pennant you must put ten dollars on Brooklyn for me in the world series. Ten dollars, get it? If lost I'll give you three thousand six hundred francs out of my French *Informer* money. I hope you have news of Garrity by now?[1] I'd like to see those new little stories in print. How small short stories are compared to a novel. Old Garnett always said so too. They can only be perfect, but not majestic.

If I get any more of these spells and am delayed beyond May as a result, I shall have saved enough money to carry on. This month I saved fifty pounds. Next month I hope seventy. Alas, I don't make much progress with the script. It's all so exciting to me that I try to make it all as perfect as I can. Yet in the end, I suppose, it will be just another effort. In any case, darling, *afuero todo el mundo*.

Liam

[1] Devin A. Garrity whose *Liam O'Flaherty: Selected Stories* was published 1958, New York: Signet books.

---

379. KT TLS to Kitty Tailer
[from Dublin]   n.d. 'Thursday'

Darling Kitty,

Just got your letter, which said you are not coming over until next year. So right away I decided to go over to Paris for a few days, since I consider it imperative that I must not get bogged down now and into a barren mood. The change, as always, will set me going again, and nowhere else but France can do that. So would you please send *half* next month's allowance to Amex by wire when you get this? I'm leaving here on Saturday morning and will stay at the Lutétia, if there is a room. Even if not, I shall call there for mail. So would you please cable me when you get this at the Lutétia? Excuse this rush but I know myself and just must get out before I get a worse fit of depression. I can get ten thousand francs from the bank and that will do me until I get some more. The return fare I can pay here, as I have saved a lot of money this month and last. *Voilá*, already I feel better. Am looking forward to my return and resuming work with a fresh mind.

I am delighted to hear you are not in an air pocket and that you had the little girl with you for a few days at Laura's place, but could not understand why you did not dispense a kiss without further thought to the aforesaid Laura? Or has she turned against me? Seeing so many Irish people, off and on, she is probably by now as changeable as we are. Yet I am Irish myself and *unchangeable*. Or is it just that Japanese smile which stayed on radiantly even when they were trying to make arrangements about my burial? I mean is my unchangeability merely superficial? I think not.

Last night I was unable to listen to the baseball game, not being very intelligent. In order to be fresh I had a sleep in the afternoon and drank tea for the evening meal, so that I did not get to sleep until late. It must have been the weather that prevented them broadcasting, because even from Germany and Tangiers the AFN and Voice of America were indistinct. Then of course the goddam Russians keep on trying to blast the Voice of America. I howled and cursed and became violently anti-Communist for a while. Later I got the result from Munich, six five in favour of the Yankees, so I says to myself: 'I couldn't back a winner in a million years.' Still, the Brooks may pull their socks up. They've got the bench, as they say in the trade.

I must visit Enghien casino while in Paris, if it's open and if I can get out there. I believe there is a bus, but is a dinner jacket necessary? However, since all casinos are the same, maybe that's not necessary. I am giving so much to this book that I hope it's well-bred enough to be good in appreciation of my efforts. However, are books gentlemen?

Darling Kitty, I think you should stay put until the beginning of the year since that is what you feel you should do. I would feel guilty of influencing you in the wrong way. Do stay, because I'll go along on an even keel for another two or three months after my return. Just send that dough right away by cable to Amexco. Thirty thousand will be enough, or perhaps forty thousand.

Goodbye now, Kitty. I am going down to Aer Lingus for my ticket. Awreddy [sic] I feel het up and exalted.

Liam

380. KT TLS to Kitty Tailer
[from Dublin]   n.d. 'Saturday'

Darling Kitty,

Since I got back here last night and today I feel better for the first time since I left. In fact, I was ill the whole time in Paris, in mind and body. It was one of those journeys into hell, when one decides that all is lost and one longs for death while hating annihilation, when one halts at the corner of a street and finds oneself utterly incapable of going backwards or forwards and one just stares into nothing. Otherwise I met new people that were interesting and old acquaintances that were pleasant to meet again. *En somme*, however, I gained nothing of what I wanted,which was to walk from Cannes to La Napoule every day for a week. Furthermore, I got an insight into the littleness of my talent, a very bad thing under the circumstances. Even so I am determined to go on with my novel tomorrow or Monday. There is nothing for the old ass to do but to plunge forward and thereby avoid the stick.

I feel glad, in a way, to be back here. It is at least a cave in which to hide. Summer has finally gone and the wind is blowing strongly outside my window, yet it's not cold. I put on a jersey going out and it felt too much ....

I found the translation of *Famine* waiting for me.[1] They seem to be much more friendly than the French, judging by their preface, although they do not understand a word of what I have been trying to do in my writing. For the reason, I suppose, that I lacked the power to make myself clear. When one is good even a child that is *mentalement faible* can understand. This phrase I got from a waiter in a little café, after having brought a ham sandwich and a glass of milk. As I remarked on the great size of the mustard pot he brought, the man shrugged his shoulders genially and said: '*Evidemment, ce n'est pas un moutardier pour les économiquement faibles.*' In Paris one comes across gems in most unexpected places and hardly ever in places where people pay great sums of money to hear them, theatres, etc.

With this war in Morocco a plethora of new words have entered into ordinary conversation, like '*bled*', '*toubib*', '*goumier*' '*barraca*' etc. A poet called Pierre Reverdy, remarking that he tried the Catholic Church at one time, shrugged his shoulders and said: '*C'est an goum, comme un autre,*' whatever he meant! The *goum*, of course, is a Moroccan miltary formation. This Reverdy is Juliette Muller's new lover, a queer fellow of great talent. All the aristocrats and their *poules de luxe* have fled the Montalmebert. Grasset is dying there of cancer. The Portuguese have all gone but one. A new horde of Brazilians were arriving when I left. The Lutétia had no rooms to let and a new doorway is all done in glass and chromium and Emile has a brilliant fieldmarshal's uniform like Tito. There is also a plague of Germans. On the plane coming back an Irish nurse from Portlaoghaise [sic] was announcing in a loud voice that she would consent, in order to live in

France, to sell her soul. This created a scandal among the passengers ....

I found a letter from Pegeen in which there was a delightful description of her cat at play. She really has a delicate talent. Maybe some day she will write well, about cats, squirrels and such creatures. Like myself she instinctively dislikes human beings.

In this week's issue of *Time* magazine there is a long description of President Eisenhower's bowel movements, given because the nation is 'vitally interested in bowel movements', so the doctor said .... A cat scratches earth over its excrement and even in the act of defecating looks ever so graceful and charming.

I was unable to write any of 'The Blemish' in Paris.

Love from
Liam

[1] Italian translation *Fame (Stanis la Bruna)*, Firenze: Parenti, 1949. Why did it take so long for O'Flaherty to receive this?

---

381. KT TLS to Kitty Tailer
[from Dublin]   p.m. 15 September, 1957

Dearest Kitty,

I received your letter last night and for the life of me I cannot understand how you could possibly have considered my last letter either cheerful or hopeful. In any case, I have been ill for some time and am not yet quite recovered. Shocking indigestion and consequent depression. At a given moment I thought my ulcer was going to have some more fun, as of my experience a few years ago, the symptoms were the same.

It was a bore going to Paris under those circumstances, yet I have a few good memories of the trip and in any case *I did get out of Dublin for a few days*. *Ce sacré Dublin*! It's so unhealthy to hate the chief town of one's own country so much and so constantly. In fact, I hate the whole island and its population with a few exceptions. I'm like Bill Gaunt of Hull, my remaining ambition is to get away and never meet anybody that hails from here.

Enough of that. As I said in my last 'cheerful' letter, I love it here and I'm so, so happy. Well! My money is all gone once more. Are you going to send me some more or do I face extinction? *Je m'en fous éperdument*! Yes, I'm writing the episode of Isabelle slowly. She has sloping shoulders with fixed dark eyes that glitter. However, her hair is the most outstanding aspect of the bitch. Everybody, I suppose, has his idea of what a Grushenka should be like. Mine is Isabelle, wicked, heartless and fascinating. But is she any more wicked or heartless than our friend Gerald? Impossible! I do wish I had seen the last of her, although it begins to be sad, the idea of getting to the end of this effort that is bound to be my last. *C'est beau quand-même, ce cri de coeur nostalgique*.

You know damn well I don't write to Irma, or to anybody else. As for Syria, I couldn't careless what happens there. Don't you remember my telling you some months ago what would happen there? Yet you had a cocky conviction at the time that your stupid people in the State Department were clever with their stupid Eisenhower policy and their doling out dollars like Christmas turkeys to the poor Arabs. *Quels cons frisés!* Excuse me, I feel so goddam bitter, I could almost bite myself like a mad dog. Presently I shall begin to write like Céline.

I met a fellow at Dupont's on the Place de la Bastille, that was very charming, an engineer. When we exchanged names on parting, he was most flattering in his appreciation of my work. Of course, I accepted his invitation to dinner and never appeared, simply because I decided to go home the following morning. Since my return a young Frenchman from Bordeaux turned up and was equally charming. He is only twenty and yet so mature and brilliant that I never noticed the great difference in our ages. Can you imagine, his name is Bouchard, like my butler. He said he had never heard of Ireland until he read *Le Mouchard* in the Club Français du Livre edition. Then he got so excited that he decided to come here for his vacation. Poor French! As I was leaving the Gare des Invalides I met a French women from Maroc with her little daughter of four, emigrating to Canada. '*C'est fini pour nous en Afrique,*' she said sadly. Her little daughter was so gay and charming and kept giving me *cacaouettes*. On reaching home I found a number of them in my jacket pocket, where she had stuffed them unknown to me.

I am glad Laura likes the stick. I was afraid she would be annoyed by my curious message. Is she coming to Europe? I guess not, or you would have said so. In any case, the idea of her going to live in Ireland, quarantine or no quarantine, is appalling. Good God! the whole world is at her disposition, excepting Red China and Grey Russia. It looked grey and sombre to me in any case.

Yesterday I saw Francis Stuart and his wife in the street, together with Zoe and Peter Marron. For a moment I was tempted to go up and speak to them. Then I sneaked round a corner. After all, we have nothing in common.

Well Kitty, I expect this is a poor effort, but I love you all the same.

Avec tout mon coeur
Liam

---

382. KT TLS to Kitty Tailer
[from Dublin]   p.m. 24 September, 1957

Dearest Kitty,

Thank you for the cable and the letter and sorry that you were cast down by the bitterness of my last epistle. After all, it's damn hard for me to write cheerfully when I feel the opposite. However, one always begins again and one has begun once more ... What could a doctor do about my ailment and its cure, it would be like telling a hungry man that he needs food. The poor sod might get so annoyed that he would hang for the murder of his informant. No, I have conceived a much better plan, the philosophy of the Irish constable who was up for seduction and could not borrow money to bribe her father. 'Have it yourself or do without it,' so pissed off to Australia. I have no intention of trying to do any such thing. What I mean is, one should take measures to satisfy one's own wants without external help, or else stew in one's own juice. I have decided to take those measures and already the decision has lessened the pain in my chest. Frankly, a strong dose of milk of magnesia also had something to do with it ....

I am on the verge of meeting Isabelle. It's very exciting. She is so real and sensual that the acrid taste of her passionate sweat makes me shudder. Please don't imagine that I shall treat her with coarseness on that account. *Motif sensuel*! Would that I had more energy!

There is a terrific storm this morning, that is pleasant. I hate summer in this country. Winter gives it a little dignity and one gets buoyed up by dreams of flight to a Lotus Land, 'where it is always afternoon and the poppy hangs in sleep over the heated ledge' and no moronic savage shouts insults as one passes. How I hate their baboon laughter! Yet what matters is to finish this gloriously satisfying *cri de coeur* .... Shall I be able to finish? Each fragment of the cursed thing is so entire in its emotion that each small stone in the structure must be cut and polished to the nth degree. In the end, no doubt, nobody will see the bottle in the snow. I refer to Chekov's reaction to the reception of one of his major short stories. 'Nobody saw the bottle in the snow,' he whispered sadly. In other words, only the artist himself can see the cunning ....

Hell! I must go out and get food in spite of the storm. Lucky I have those rubber boots and the new fur lined inner shoes and my old coat. But my caps are all gone. I caught a slight cold at Croke Park last Sunday. Indeed, the excitement also did me a lot of harm. But that mob ecstasy is my only pleasure. What horror though, to see their urine issue in a flood from the *pissoir*. Yet there was something splendidly Rabelaisian in the remark of the big fellow that shouted, 'With so many mighty cocks turned on full pelt you could almost drown the whole city in the stinking flood.'

Did you write to Irma for me? She must be back in Paris by now. Maybe I'll send her a note. In any case, I was right not to go to that place on the hill. I hate hills. Maybe I'll walk along that flat stretch from Cannes to La Napoule before Christmas. Jesus! My ulcer is growing great guns again. What the hell can I eat? I'm so tired of steamed fish. I'll try a chop I think. Of course it would be a good idea to stop smoking, but I could write nothing. So ... dear me, I hope you don't find this letter equally melancholy, because I don't feel melancholy right now. Not while the good cloth is growing slowly in the loom.

Le Monde has an astounding article about an 'anti-party faction', to use the Russian phrase, that threatens to cause a civil war within the Jesuit Order. The Pope addressed them in Latin and said they must 'obey the party line' without question. Otherwise, they'll be sent to Siberia. Be wonderful if it happened! *Le Monde* was also very good about the *coup d'état* in Thailand. They got away with three billion American dollars and now their newspapers have cartoons of J.F. Dulles in a high top hat, with the dollar sign on the front in gold. What fun for the American taxpayer! The poor deluded sod!

All my love Kitty,
and please forgive my nonsense
Liam

---

383. KT TLS to Kitty Tailer
[from Dublin]   p.m. 9 October, 1957

Dearest Kitty,

Thanks ever so much for the cable, the letter and the fric. Thanks too for saying that you are coming in November. I hope you'll be as steadfast in that purpose as the northern star, or the Russian satellite that keeps going round and round.

I've been ill ever since, this time with Asiatic 'flu, however, it's now getting better owing to an amazing spell of good weather that makes everybody say, 'Why couldn't it happen in summer?' Who cares, the important things is that the sun is shining and, as you have once remarked, even Dublin looks almost gay when the sun shines. The insane baboons become happy louts and the moronic savages hide in awe, with their blinds drawn, cowering over their dying fires, waiting for the return of mist and rain to feed their joy-in-misery.

Alas! Lying in bed I was unable to work, so that my Isabelle still awaits her birth. But there she is, 'standing 'neath the lamp-light, by the barrack gate ...' However, I hope you don't expect too much from her, no more do I. Let her serve her purpose, which is merely secondary ....

Pegeen wrote to say that she had just read *Skerrett*, and said nice things about it. She is even slower than myself.

Well, Kitty, I'm glad to hear that the bubbly is flowing in streams *dans* Les New Jersey. Fancy Dorothea getting married! I liked her. Why can't Laura get herself tubed? A new bladder should be easy. I daresay there is no talk of her coming to Europe. If you stayed put, of course, she'd take off at once. It's handy having a contradiction of oneself.

As you see, I am on edge with desire to write and for that reason I bitterly regret being here and not somewhere else, somewhere to walk and have food cooked for me. Oh well! I heard one game of the World Series and the man at Munich mumbled something last night about Milwaukee being three-two ahead. I couldn't hear exactly owing to interference. He said there would be a game tonight. What do you know? You remember I picked Milwaukee early on and stuck to them. The game I heard sounded like good pitching by Burdette.

Everybody here is talking about the Russian satellite and the Catholic newspapers seem to be very worried. 'Why doesn't his Holiness speak?' I heard a woman say in a shop. The French say they are going to launch a *'Président du Conseil'*. Since these early satellites don't return it might be a good idea if they launched *all* politicians into the *'néant'*. How do you suppose they are still able to keep the franc so stable? Judging by *Le Monde* they've had it good and proper. Apparently their atrocities in Algeria are utterly, utterly appalling. Yet people go on talking about Little Rock.[1] It's so comforting to sparrows, reeking with their own dirt and littleness, to find a speck of dust on the eagle's wing. Good old Eagle! Why not stop giving money to ungrateful foreigners and launch a proper satellite, with a battalion of leather-necks on board, to make the Russians stop boasting. Better idea would be to put Eleanor Roosevelt on board. 'My first day on the moon' would make good reading.

Kitty, don't forget to bring me a lot of that thick paper and some good ribbons. I must buy a new ribbon one of these days. What a queer life I lead. A dreary kind of hermit, getting madder an' madder every day. Met Kavanagh yesterday morning on my first trip out. 'I'm going to emigrate,' he said, clasping his sides with his apelike arms. 'Where?' I said excitedly, hoping he was in earnest. 'To the fuckin' moon,' he said. 'So I wouldn't have to see Brendan Behan any more. It's my only chance to die happy.'

The Irish horse, Gladness, was defeated in the Prix de l'Arc de Triomph. It's looked upon as a national disaster. 'Ah, the poor creature didn't have the early foot,' I heard an old man say. He was in rags and scratching his shoulder blades against the wall of a closed tavern.

All my love, Kitty darling, and thanks ever so much. *Siempre y fuera todo el mundo.*

Liam

[1] Little Rock, Arkansas. After serious riots, desegration of schools had taken place.

384. KT TLS to Kitty Tailer
[from Dublin]   p.m. 1 November, 1957

Dearest Kitty,

I got your cable this morning, which said you intend to arrive sixth of next month and for me to write or cable you on my arrival in France. Previously you had cabled to say you had sent money to my bank. It has not arrived and I now have about three pounds left, so naturally going to France is out of the question.

Indeed I no longer want to go as my mental state has deteriorated to the point where one place is as good as another for what remains to be done. A sombre prospect! I wish you would write to me. Pegeen writes shorter and shorter notes, they are like the guttering of a candle, which presently will cease to give any light at all. Last week there was a longish airmail letter in my box and for a moment I thought it was from you. Going up in the elevator, however, I saw it was a French stamp. A bad blow! Some fellow from Paris wanted to know the intellectual origins of the ideas that led to the writing of *The Martyr*. As if I knew by now!

I just received the second last number of *Le Monde*. The weather is beautiful, sharp and sunny. The fur on the collar of my coat is beginning to fall. I am reading a beautiful book called *Yankee Whalers*, also Negley Farson's *Way of a Transgressor*. I knew Farson well at one time and it seemed to me that his only transgression was a gross preoccupation with fornication. That sort of thing, surely, does not permit him to use such a grandiloquent title. Transgression worthy of the name is surely in the mind and not in the genital organs. Yet it is pleasant to read of Petersburg during the revolution from the point of view of the people that were dispossessed. Have you ever read it? Funny fellow Farson, apparently he has made himself an Englishmen and lives near O'Casey in Devonshire. What an appalling way to end one's life!

Do write to me, Kitty. I am clinging to life like a half-dislodged limpet and struggling desperately to regain the hold of my crushed shell on the rock. Surely there must be some means of finishing this book. If anything untoward should happen one hundred finished pages are in a yellow folder. After all, a wave might put an end at any moment to the limpet's vain efforts.

Kirwan turned up last Sunday with a crazy scheme for making television plays of Nat Gould's racing novels. On Monday he rang to say he was going back to London at once to conclude the deal. Have not heard a word since, just as I expected. The man looked on the point of death and the fear in his eyes was startling. He said Stroud's brother, whom he visited to borrow a copy of Shakespeare's sonnets, never goes out at all. How does he live? A loaf and a bottle of milk are left at his door from time to time. By now, of course, Harold must be totally disintegrated to the medical students.

I hope the wedding has been or will be very gay and a happy affair. Is Dorothea the girl I knew as a child? The one who had a crush on the tennis player? What a strange world the little children are going to inherit! I daresay nature will provide them with a mental carapace sufficiently strong to cope with Sputniks and voyages to the other planets. Judging by the extraordinary courage and endurance of the Yankee whalers, the youngsters must surely have inherited enough guts to stay the course. Especially the one that says, 'Wha's that?' 'That's Mars, darling on our port bow.'

I'm afraid I simply cannot write any more. Do send me a little word, darling.

All my love
Liam

---

385. KT TLS to Kitty Tailer
[from Dublin]   p.m. 10 November, 1957

Dearest Kitty,

Thanks for your letter which arrived last night. Yes, I got the fifty-three pounds you cabled to the bank, but the cheque in francs did not arrive and the sample copies of paper. The paper I need is called Esquire Bond and its size is continental quarto. I enclose a specimen sheet. All that is, however, theoretical the way I feel at the moment, the issue is extremely doubtful.

I have had frightful brain tension for about a month now and it's a constant struggle to maintain sanity. 'His upper forehead and his eyes ached terribly', yet there is no sign of unconsciously tapping the floor with alternate feet, or of thrusting daggers subconsciously. I am re-reading Chekov's 'Ward No. 6' at the moment and I find it a relief to study the gradual decline of Gromov into insanity. If the judgement cells remain intact, within their insulated chamber, one has a good chance. It took me a long time before, from 1918 to 1923 or so to beat the rap. No reason why I cannot do it again, in spite of diminution of physical energy. That is why, Kitty, I need exercise and why I should not have come back to Dublin from France last summer. Remember how ill I got? ... No indeed, I should not have come back.

I have to have more money as rent is to be paid and the other expenses. On top of all this, I believe they are really going to make *Insurrection*, but the bastards still do not contact me. They have pushed Guillermain out and somebody from Columbia has got it now, a producer. Kieran Moore rang yesterday from a 'flu bed and said he heard 'they are going through with

Insurrection, but he said they have put in a girl.'[1] I said: 'I don't care if they put in a syphilitic eunuch provided they pay me in American currency in notes of twenty dollars same as in the underworld, to Geneva, Switzerland.' He laughed. Later yesterday John Ryan, who has been somewhat unfriendly, rang up and took me with him to Leopardstown races and was very friendly. On the way out I learned why. He said: 'I believe you have another major film on the stocks?' 'Is that so?' I said. 'Why be cagey, Liam,' he said. 'I know all about it through Colonel D'Alton who is going to handle the technical end. Killanin is on it, too. Don't you think there would be a spot for my sister Kathleen in the cast? I hear you have a girl in it that would just suit her type.' 'Sure thing, John,' I said, 'leave it to me to do what I can.' So I can't understand why I heard nothing officially about all this, either from Peters or the man from Columbia. I suppose they are still at the promotion stage, or is the Irish Government raising objections? In the latter case the addition of Killanin and I believe the Jew Ellerman, or Eliman, of the Theatre Royal and of Colonel D'Alton of the Irish Army is a help. Jesus! It would just solve my problem right now, but you can imagine that it's no ⌊good⌋ for the pain in my upper forehead, all this waiting ....

Personally I could not care less what they do, I just want to finish my book 'before the axle breaks that keeps my brain in its rounds', to bowdlerise Mr. Yeats whom Paddy Kavanagh could 'do without'. In the meantime I am getting nowhere with McNiece.

Forgive me, Kitty, I must finish now. Please send that other part of the money by cable so I can pay the rent and the other bills, Topsy, telephone, electricity and have some left. I take those pills in the bottle for my head but they are no longer any good.

Love from this miserable fellow. How nice about the weddings.

Liam

[1] *Insurrection*, in the end was not filmed.

---

386. KT TLS to Kitty Tailer
Hotel des Negociants, Cannes   p.m. 17 December, 1957

Dearest Kitty,

Well, the Regina was closed, so I came back here. I don't see much difference except that I don't have a toilet, or a bathroom. However, there is a wash-bum, or as the man from St. Louis said so succinctly, equipment for anal sanitation. Wash-bum is much better. I feel that I may be able to do something now. I walked already as far as the Hotel Méditerranée and then back along the Croisette to the big hotel and enjoyed the sun without my heavy coat. Practically everywhere is closed, even the Coq Hardi, which reopens on Sunday.

Here the old women say there is *'du monde'* and the same dreary old people are about the place, but it's a comfortable feeling of not spending too much on habitation. Martin Hemph would agree from '*les profondeurs de l'enfer*' where his tongue is no doubt hanging out for a little table wine, poor sot. He was so jealous of any expenditure apart from drinking and betting. Yet the swine left eighty thousand pounds, ten of which were mine.

It's nice to be out of Dublin and equally so almost to be out of Paris, but it's a poignant loss to be without Kitty. Here begins another period of waiting for the aforesaid. Make a good subject and title, *Waiting for Kitty*, including the wrong side of the tracks at Palm Beach ....

As you see, I bought five hundred francs worth of paper and a bar of soap. I think I'll eat at the Lafayette, which is practically next door. I bought the *Herald* and could not make head or tail or what is going on. The Norwegians and even the English say no, no orchids for Ike, poor man.[1]

I slept and slept on the train, having the compartment to myself. The young man moved to another compartment. How nice that banqueting hall was at Gare de Lyon. I still see the inlaid lace and the multiplicity of chandeliers and gas stands. I do hope Munich is not too cold. I'll probably ring Irma round next Sunday or so. Maybe it would be better to call over there on Christmas day ....

That is all for the moment. I just wanted to get in touch with you again, so I'll say no more. You may be sure that I will do my very best to put a good foot forward and keep up with the pack in this back stretch. Rounding the final turn I might then be in a good position to make my effort '*en pleine piste et en bolide*'. Goodbye now, Kitty, and happy everything and don't think ill of me.

Yours
Liam

[1] Lester Pearson of Canada, not Eisenhower, has been given the Nobel Prize for Peace.

---

387. KT TLS to Kitty Tailer
from Dublin   May 27 [1958]

Darling Kitty,

I got your letter this morning, posted in Geneva, and yesterday a telegram saying you had arrived in Cannes. I sent one a while ago. Thanks awfully for the money, which the bank has received. The carpet has been put down and is really beautiful. The other things did not come yet. I have paid Feldman and the rates. No news yet of the Irish Estates bill. Now that you have paid dentist everything is OK for the moment.

Montgomery sent me a copy of a letter he sent to you about Foreman and Co. It appears they really are going to pay that five hundred! My story 'Bohunk' is almost finished and I really think I've got something veddy [sic] popular there. It's also very good I think, because not only the dog but the two men are very interesting and fully developed characters in that short space, which is something. Hope I'll proceed at the same rate and tempo with 'The Unique Passion'. Am sure I will, because my unpoisoned system is now able to think clearly and things are looking up on this front.

Am still worried about your being down there in the midst of things, but the Midi people don't fight very hard do they? Let's hope not in any case. I wish you had stayed in Geneva or gone into Italy, but I know there is no point in ever trying to turn you from whatever you have 'planned'. I fear there is going to be heavy trouble in France. The French are not illiterate Spaniards and they all know how to fight efficiently when their dander is really up.[1]

I put on that beautiful new *bleu marine* shirt today. It looks really swell. We have the first day of sunshine for a long time. I really am worried about you and cannot see how you can even think of taking the little children down there. Feeling is bound to run very high, no matter what happens.

Pegeen has chosen this moment to abandon her job and return to that frightful address she had before in Edge Street. That's her own affair. Cannot live other people's lives, let alone my own with any sort of sanity or success .....

Poor France! Lovely France! I still get *Le Monde* but I daresay that also will stop. How good of you to send me all those things, I mean Sartre's magazine too .... Rumour has it that Nice or Toulon are going to be occupied tomorrow and *'les masses travailleuses'* are coming out on general strike this afternoon. *Quelle barbe!* ...

God bless and protect you, in any case, dearest Kitty, but I daresay old Picot will wangle out of trouble.

All my love, darling
Liam

[1] France was on the point of civil war over Algeria.

In 1958 the option on film rights for *Insurrection* was passed to Carl Foreman for a fee of six thousand pounds paid in two instalments. In January John Montgomery of A.D. Peters writes to O'Flaherty in Dublin that the B.B.C. have bought TV rights in *The Informer*. Four Square publishers also brought out a paperback edition of *The Informer*. In April Montgomery writes to O'Flaherty at 20 Chesham Place, W1 about his Yugoslav royalties deposited in a Belgrade bank.

In May 1958 O'Flaherty wrote to Montgomery from Dublin that he is writing a story called 'Bohunk' for *Lilliput* for a fee of seventy-five guineas.

---

388. KT TLS to Kitty Tailer
[from Dublin]   p.m. 17 June, 1958

Dearest Kitty,

Just got your letter, after cable late last night. Poor darling! It looks as if you're having the kind of a 'time' I thought you would have. There's nothing for it now but to hold on grimly. Poor little Kitty, what a year! Maybe it will end up well.

Sorry for not writing. I've been ill, nerves and stomach. Seem to be getting back on an even keel again. Result is that 'Bohunk' is not yet finished, but it will be in the next few days. It's just odd, like everything I do nowadays. Yet it seems to have the quality of something beyond myself, at least beyond my miserable and paltry self. Is there really another self? Like the 'self' of those saucer men in which you believe. I am anxious to get on with McNiece and got to hate 'Bohunk' because of him. Maybe that's why I got ill. However, there it is. Oddly enough, just now I got a book from Peters and a note enclosed from Victor Gollancz. It's a novel he's bringing out with all drums beating and he wants me to send him a few words about it. He said: 'I keep thinking about your own novel and waiting for it year after year. For God's sake finish it before I die, because I am now sixty-seven.' What do you know about that? Probably I will finish it soon.

Pegeen .... is going to Titoland on the 22nd and I had to get my bank manager to certify my signature on that authorisation for touching the dinars. Hope that will do.

Hurrah! The divan cover and the chair cover and the red curtains and pillows from Strahan's are really *très chic* and I bought a little red table cover from the other room, and the little red ashtray (gift of my Finnish Jewess). The whole red symphony, together with the red papayas in the reproduction of the Tahiti man's picture, is really '*très fin*'. Have not yet got the bill, or the bill for the Irish Estates work. However, the money is there.

I have worked on the Madrid story (in my mind) and have rather thought of calling it 'Black Sheets'. It's very good now and will do it by easy stages while taking Mr. McNiece up to the theft. This 'Black Sheets' might be very good, as I created two excellent characters, same as in 'Bohunk'. It is a formula that I am now taking out of the mothballs ... however, all that appears tawdry and small compared to 'The Unique Passion'.

I feel lonely, of course, terribly lonely without you. The town is just as frightful as ever. Yet I have established greater power over myself and the horizon is beginning to show signs of dawn. In other words, the great weight shows signs of being lifted. If I could only get to the theft, this damned diamond necklace and the Little Father.

I do hope you are able to swim and lie in the sun. If you only had another servant to leave in the house while the Scotch girl went to the beach and let you lie in the sun a bit. Here there is only permanent rain. Always rain. Kirwan turned up and we made friends again. He seems attached to this new film company at Bray and had a cheque for four hundred and fifty pounds. What a strange and feckless character! Stewart is now living in Meath. I met Lord Glenavy (who has become appallingly provincial and *foutu*, poor man) and he said that he got a letter from Francis. 'At least,'

Gordon said, 'he happily avoids contact with the appalling middle class in Meath.' Poor Gordon, he himself has been devoured by them, body and soul, like undelousable lice.

Dearest Kitty, I do hope you send the stallions, if you manage to find time to copy them. I might be able to do something with them. I seem to have more force and buoyancy now, at least I will have, when my stomach gets back to normal. It's the food and the boredom. I just hate cooking and it's a torture to eat out. Please be cheered by this saddish letter. I'm not at all sad, only worried about your being worn out by the children and that slut of a Scotchwoman. There are a lot more things I want to say, but I can't remember them right now. I'll write again in a few days. In the meantime, dearest heart, all my love.

Liam

---

389. KT TLS to Kitty Tailer
[from Dublin]   p.m. 2 July, 1958

Dearest Kitty,

Thank you for sending me the typed story. I've read it and it needs a lot of reshaping, but there is quite a lot of power inherent in it. I'll make a good job this time. I've finished 'Bohunk' and am sending it off today. I'll make a copy of my own copy in a while, when I get over the disgust that a finished story inspires, and send it along to you. It's good and I hope commercial, but one never knows what that oaf Montgomery will manage to do with it. Do you know that he never collected Guillermin's share of that money? Are they in cahoots? I should have sued Foreman. I could easily have got a few thousand for 'abus de confiance'. In other words, he played the 'con' trick by announcing that he possessed a property that did not belong to him, i.e. the film rights in my novel. Of course, he was getting a cut from these Jews in Dublin that were trying to raise money for their new studio. Never mind, when one is broke two hundred and fifty pounds is all one can get apparently.

It's still raining and there's no sign of release from this appalling downpour that has lasted a month, except for two half days I think. One sees pictures in the English papers of sandbags protecting Dublin houses from the floods. However, their own weather ain't much better and Wimbledon tennis tournament has been deranged.

My nerves are all shot to pieces and I'm getting mortally afraid of going mad .... I don't know why you think 'Single Combat' is not a good title. The story is not so good that a title becomes vitally important. After all 'Boule de Suif' is not such a good title for a masterpiece, is it? And my story ain't no masterpiece. I wonder did you get the Goya book? There is a tiny edition that they have. I know I've got a Velasquez of that type. Of course it would be wonderful to see another bullfight or two, but the idea of going to Madrid horrifies me. All those nights in different hotels. '*Queremos dos habitaciones, un con baño...*' You know what I mean. Still, that journey over the mountains in the snow is nice in retrospect. Trouble is, that arrival was not so good. Apart from seeing the Velasquez pictures. That appalling hotel where the man said the next morning: '*Dondé marchan Ustedes?*' In other words, 'Where are yiz goin', you two?'

The Scotch girl sounds amusing with her bikini. Are there many people at Sainte Maxime? You sound to me like a person having a tough time. I daresay it's that kind of a year. However, maybe it's going to end well. I'm so looking forward to seeing you. When? This is already July. I must carry my clothes to the cleaners, as they all look quite frightful. Alas! This letter is not going to be two pages. I have been typing since before dawn and I just hate the sound of the machine at this moment. As a result ideas don't form themselves, either good or bad.

Can you imagine? I don't even know what won the Grand Prix last Sunday. I still get *Le Monde* and perhaps today's number will give me the result three days late. It still carries amusing news, in spite of the censorship. It turns out that Malraux, in spite of having been a revolutionary writer for years, is a worse censor than most. Malraux and Jacques Soustelle were both Communists at one time. It's the French routine, of course, to begin at the far left and end at the far right. Furthermore, it's natural and quite normal in my way of thinking. How awful if people travelled from right to left, prudish youth and debauched old age ain't pretty.

I keep thinking about Caldwell's character Ty Waldon: 'God's a big man. He doesn't mind as long as he gets his fair share.' You remember *God's Little Acre*?[1] I hear the film is being shown in America. I see that old Caldwell is really well-heeled now. He himself footed part of the production. I like to see a writer get into the money for a change. If I do myself, it will be at the age when Dreiser got it, sixty-four. The whores', he said, 'only gave me a piece of Jack when I had got myself stomach ulcers and hardening of the goddam arteries so bad I can neither eat, drink nor fuck.' The whores is right!

All my love, darling, and keep writing. I'll send you the MS soon.[2]

Liam

[1] Erskine Caldwell, *God's Little Acre* (1933).

[2] On 4 July O'Flaherty sent Kitty a cable: 'Long live fourth July, Fernande the sixth fleet and Kitty.'

---

390. KT TLS to Kitty Tailer
[from Dublin]   p.m. 9 July 1958

Dearest Kitty,

Thanks awfully for sending me that beautiful Goya book. I didn't recognise the picture among the examples given, but I think it's one of the Baron d'Erlanger's collection of *'Peintures Provenant de la Quinta del Sordo'*. The *'Pèlerinage à la Fontaine de San Isidro'* will do perfectly, or the *'Al Aquelarre'*, or the *'Deux Vieux mangeant la soupe'*. In any case, thanks a lot and I think 'Black Sheets' is going to be good.

In the meantime, however, I really must solve the problem of my life, which is the problem of getting somebody to look after me. Otherwise, I'll finally break up without being able to do anything further, at a moment when I'm at my best. *I simply can no longer cope with life on my own.* And certainly not with life in Dublin. The least things throws me off balance and I'm getting mortally afraid. For instance, this damn dog story is not yet completed really. I have not re-written the horse story, and I have merely touched up the opening of the Isabella episode in 'The Unique Passion'. I just hop about like an enraged flea from one thing to another. *Quoi faire?* If one knew ....

Kieran Moore is now at Greystones, after returning from Greece. He is still trying to sell *The Assassin* to Holden, and now he says that Aldrich would very much like to do *Insurrection*, if it's free. So I rang up Montgomery and asked if Guillermin has yet paid his two hundred and fifty. The silly little Montgomery got into a dither, to such an extent that I really believe he entered into some mean arrangement with Guillermin. So I said: 'I give you four days to collect. Otherwise I'll sell the property elsewhere.' I wonder will he be able to do so. In any case, it's all very disturbing. I told him that I'd send him the two stories, one for *Esquire* and the horses for *Lilliput*. After all, one would be lucky to get seventy-five pounds for them. Even so, I hate giving that little wretch anything. Why can't I have some efficient person I can trust, among other things.

This *'Deux Vieux mangeant la soupe'* is very beautiful and 'horribly' gay. That probably would be best, although I have not seen it at the Prado. The one I saw was still better, being a mass of distorted faces.

How are things going with you and when are you leaving there? The weather is now rainless and muggily hot here, dripping with humidity and spinelessness. What a Summer! Already it's well into July and nothing done really, except 'Bohunk'. *Voilà!* I am thinking of changing 'The Legacy' into 'The Foster Father'. In French *'Le Père Nourricier'* would sound better. That will be a 'horribly' gay story. Not gay really but innocently tragic.

Pegeen keeps sending me postcards and saying what a wonderful holiday. Apparently she is now beginning to live life in some other way and may finally do something, although she has too much of her mother in her really, to [do] anything. Is that disloyal? *Je ne crois pas.*

Perhaps, after all, the stallions are very good. I shall call them 'Mortal Combat'. I am sitting here bathed in sweat, so I must have a bath. Darling, forgive this poor disjointed outburst. There is nothing I want to do but 'The

Unique Passion'. I wish I had gone on with it after coming from London.

My teeth keep falling out again when I eat. Presently I [shall] swallow some of the damn things with my food. How is the Scottish girl's bikini? I have now come to the conclusion that de Gaulle is the Zionists' man, or rather the agent of the international Jewish banking fraternity. So there's going to be more trouble in France ....

I'm afraid I signed a contract from Peters giving MacLiammoir right to make a play of *The Informer*. Do you mind?

All my love
Liam

In October 1958, *Esquire* also refused 'Bohunk', saying it had wonderful background but was pointless and over-written. 'Bohunk' was also refused by *Argosy*, *Atlantic*, *Cavalier*, *Harper's*, and *Playboy* and in 1960 by *Blackwoods*. The story first appeared in print in *The Pedlar's Revenge* collection (Wolfhound Press, Dublin, 1976). In the same collection 'Mortal Combat' appears as 'Wild Stallions'.

In late 1958, Micheal MacLiammoir wrote to Louis Elliman at the Gaiety Theatre, Dublin, confirming his verbal agreement to produce his dramatisation of *The Informer* at the Olympia Theatre, Dublin, and the play was performed in Dublin for five weeks up to 13 December 1958. The script was dramatised straight from the novel with twenty-one scenes and sixty characters, MacLiammoir himself played Gypo, Maureen Potter and Dennis Brennan had principal roles. A review in the *Irish Times* of 11 November, 1958, called it a 'tremendous *tour-de-force*' up to the end of part one. The reviewer for The *Irish Press* on the same date wrote that the play was a challenge and a success, but he found it hard 'to warm up to those rather long drawn out passages in the first part', but the second part produced brilliant writing which made up for the boring passages. 'All told he has captured most of the quality of the O'Flaherty original.' By the end of five weeks, however, audiences tailed off and the play lost money.

---

391. KT TLS to Kitty Tailer
[from Dublin]   p.m. 16 November, 1958

Dearest Kitty,

I hope this gets to Cannes in time, as I don't remember your telling me how long you intend staying there. All goes well here in Dublin, as regards my walking and writing. The prospect of another little trip in January is a great release from tension.

The play at the Olympia shows faint signs of becoming a big success. In any case it has been retained for another week, and the papers, as in the case of the film, are recanting on their first rather cold appraisals. Last night the *Evening Herald* said. 'The theatrical event of the year.' Another said, 'a triumph!', another said, 'They're flocking to see *The Informer*'. Well, one never knows, we might get a piece of change out of the blasted thing. Still no trace of the contract. Bugger that fellow Montgomery, or whoever is responsible. All I need is the money safely lodged in my account, because I feel definitely on top of this novel at last. It certainly is very consoling to know that I can write just as well without stimulants. However, I'm making no promises to myself. If stimulants are necessary later on, then we shall take them and be damned ...

I went to Naas races yesterday and it cost me nothing. One of the races was very good and I had a conversation in the train with an old maid from north county Dublin. She talked about farming all the way, mostly the dairy business that 'gives you a handy cheque every fortnight and doesn't cost much for upkeep, even when you milk by hand as we do'. I told her about Andy Lord's experience with swine fever and how he lost the compensation for six hundred pigs, because the government man refused to come with his machine gun until the following morning. 'Aw', she said, 'If only Almighty God would lend me an atom bomb to kill them government men. But sure killing would be too good for them. Far better to geld them with a jagged knife.' A grand little woman!

There's a grand pavement all the way to Dollymount on the Howth Road and another one that stretches five miles along the Grand Canal towards the west. Next Saturday I'm going to walk to Leopardstown Races. That should be nice, if I do it there and back on a good day. So far the weather is really good and I don't feel the need of a thick coat. I'm afraid you're right about there being no good Burberry coats in Dublin ....

Dearest Kitty, I'm looking forward to your arrival, with or without the jam and the dates. The local dates ain't got what it takes, being full of hard rinds and kernels by the dozen. Have not yet started Pasternak's book, nor even finished my second detective. I fall asleep as soon as I hit the pillow these evenings. That is exactly how I like it. I keep thinking how nice a recorder would be, and some records of Mexican Malagueña. One day I went to the cinema to see a gun show and heard 'La Paloma' done with rock an' roll undertones. Believe it or not, it was swell! I'd love to have tangos and flamencos and malagueñas to play in my study. I'll get myself an outfit when that bastard Foreman and his lawyers come to camp with the mazuma.

Goodbye now, Kitty, and look after yourself well on the way back to Paris. No driving after dark.

With all my love
Liam

---

392. KT TLS to Kitty Tailer
[from Dublin]   p.m. 17 December, 1958

Darling Sweetie Pie,
Today I got the fric and your letter from the new hotel where you waited

for the boat. So I am writing to thank you on this new typewriter. Do you notice the difference of type? It's smaller and I like it much better, apart from saving beautiful paper. One gets over a hundred words more to the page. By the way, the correct description of aforesaid paper is, Sphinx typewriting paper, Macadam Bond, then there is 16B 8½ x 11-16 lb white. Got all that, baby doll? If not, I shall send you a sheet later. P.S. it also says on the sheets fifty percent rag content. I think that should be sufficient identification.

Now that crowns for conduit have been put in my passport, which is already made out, all I await is the monthly account from Peters. Then I twiddle my thumbs and start saying, 'Well, Bo, when shall it be?' In spite of everything I feel sure that Cannes is going to be my destination. How could I desert the '*Vannerie pour fleuristes*' or the back road? or the free W.C. by the main bus stop beyond the Mairie? Of course you say the weather may be bad for long walking this time of year, but what the hell! That soup at the Palace Brasserie is also attractive, and Cannes is the quietest town in winter. Just sweet bugger all!

Can't say I feel any different under these new circumstances. The weather here right now is too frightful for gaiety. I like my overcoat a lot, but I have taken to wearing an extra jersey and my raincoat during this rain, which has now lasted six days. Nothing happens otherwise, except that my teeth behave in a most extraordinary manner. One day they fit and one does not notice their presence. The next day they joggle and hurt and have to be put back in their glass like naughty children.

I didn't throw the Illinois fan letter down the chute, on the contrary I sent the woman a note. Unfortunately I had got tired of her by then and the note was very short. Even I myself could not make head or tail of it. However, it's written and mailed. I hope Laura doesn't throw this one down her trash-can before you lay hands on it.

I'll try to send that radiogram on tomorrow morning. I keep thinking you are in the *Queen Elizabeth*. That G.G. book on Havana was frightfully bad. What a bogus fellow Greene is, when you weigh the fellow in cold blood. He talked about seeing a bullfight 'one night in Madrid'. Of course, come to think of it, Hemingway refers to night-fighting in a short story, but only sand-lot stuff.

I notice in your letter that you have already become vague about the date of your return. That looks bad, for the date will lengthen, when procrastinating Kitty gets to work on it later. However, what's the difference between February and March in a big year? Certainly not if you sell something to those Signet people and we have a dollar or two to put on the Grand National, or the Grand Prix.

I like the Christmas card of Degas's horses. Good bloke that! Was there a river at that time at Longchamps? Of course there was, for a score of people were drowned in a thunderstorm while returning from a meeting in 1847, so they say .... Thank goodness *The Informer* has disappeared from the theatre and now there's a comforting silence once more. Denise and Jonathan Cape have sent me Christmas cards. They both went into the Canal, which now looks quite clean. Must be a shortage of illegitimate babies, cats and dogs ....

I got a good chicken at McCabe's and am reading an excellent book about Central African negroes. In other words, my lousy life goes on as before, with Dublin as appalling as ever. Not a word from the Marrons or from Francis. Kirwan is in London still and I hope he stays there, so I'm quite alone. There's a race meeting on Boxing Day and not a damn thing until then.

The grey sports jacket looks very grand in the mirror. I think I'll take it south. Do you really think you should drive to Georgia in that car? It's quite a way, is it not? Lovely trees on the way down and then the red earth, with mules on the horizon.

I wear a blanket round my shoulders when I go to work in the morning. It's great fun to walk around in it, too. Big Chief Piss in the Night. My God! that's awful rain and I've just noticed that it's twenty past one .... All my love, darling pie, *siempre! siempre! siempre!*

Liam

1959

393. KT TLS to Kitty Tailer
[from Dublin]   p.m. 3 January, 1959

Darling Kitty,

Well, I didn't go any farther than Paris, because I had an instinct against doing so. Just couldn't get myself to go on the plane or on a train, so I came back yesterday evening. Even so, I feel a lot better for the trip and it cost me far less, so all is well. Of course I could do with being in better health. *Mais, c'est l'hiver!* Paris was very amusing, what with the heavy and light money, etc ....

On my return I found a cheque from the office to the amount of three hundred and eighty pounds, being my share of the *Informer* money at the Olympia Theatre. Rather good? Apparently one gets five percent of the take. Not in New York, I don't suppose. Did I tell you they are putting it on in New York? At least Miss Stephens says so. I rang Montgomery before I left and the little bastard says that he has not got the money for *Insurrection*. He's just about as aggravating as drawing one's finger-nail along the surface of a smooth stone. However, I shall wait patiently until 25th January. If he hasn't got it by then, I'm going to get really angry.

Now I'm going to try once more to go ahead with my book before it drives me insane, or before I drop it for good .... There was a note from Zoe under my door when I returned, asking me to ring. I did so and she told me that her husband, poor girl, got radioactive on Christmas Island, while serving with some atomic bomb squadron of the navy. What appalling luck!

I sent you a cable before I left, and another last night, to say I'm back, both chez Laura. Hope you got them both, and that you have not written to Nice .... In a day or two I shall be back in routine. I have a horror of being alone. I felt that I would be less alone here than down there on the Côte d'Azur. Also there are some rugger matches and horse races coming up ... I stayed at the Pont Royal and everybody was very nice to me. It was only a tiny bit dearer than horrible Montalembert. They gave me the famous author treatment, which I found pleasant, as we all do, to use the words of Franklin Delano. The *cassière* told me a funny story about the *Bonjour Tristesse* woman Françoise Sagan, who comes there often. I won a few bob at Vincennes one day and took a taxi back to the Deux Magots and brought the chauffeur in for a drink. It was crowded and we talked 'horse' in a loud voice with '*voyou*' gestures, to the utter amazement of the gaga people there. A waiter then joined us and talked 'horses', using similar gestures, until the manager came up and sort of begged us to tone down the incipient riot. It was very funny. The chauffeur was a rare find ....

This novel must be finished this year, as you said, because I've reached the point of being about to get annoyed. Tolstoy said that the point of boredom was the one to be attained, in order to finish quickly.

I had another good conversation with a book huckster on the quays. We gestured about the place in great style, talking about Diderot and Voltaire. He knew Jonathan Swift's work very well and had made a study of Dublin as a result. It was funny to hear him talk about the various taverns of that period and recite the jail songs in his guttie accent. I brought back a dozen books. I also paid a visit to my Greek boy at the Louvre. He is still very beautiful and tragic.

It's very comforting not to worry about money any more. It has a steadying effect, I must say, on the nerves especially. This typewriter works awfully well, but I haven't taken the other one to be mended yet.

What gives over there in America? I mean on the family front. It seems ages since I heard from you, Kitty darling .... Did you see those Signet people? On second thoughts, I don't think there's much chance of selling them anything .... After all, the main thing is to finish my book, together with being the easiest thing to sell it's the most lucrative.

Please send me all the dope about your return, which is the next event on the programme. After all, you've been away several weeks now.

> All my love, dear heart
> Liam

---

394. KT TLS to Kitty Tailer
[from Dublin]   p.m. 17 January, 1959

Darling Kitty,

I got back from London last night and got your letter and postcard, so I daresay you are now arrived. I also got a bunch of cable forms from Western Union, so I presume the telegraph boy came with a cable in my absence and did not leave it.

The reason for my going to London was that damned contract for *Insurrection*. The Columbia people objected to the one I signed and insisted on trivial alterations. So I took off at once, last Sunday, with a new contract, determined to get the thing finished some way or other. Indeed, I had come to the conclusion that it was all a subtle scheme of torture. However, I made a strong diplomatic *démarche* at Peters' office, including seeing the old boy himself and buying Margaret Stephens several glasses of champagne at the Wine Tavern, and being nice to Montgomery. So maybe they will stir a foot a little.

I ended up by getting the impression they were not quite so hostile as they had been. The 'grumpiness', if such it was, lay at the head. In other words old Peters got the idea that I was deliberately cutting him. I must say, of course, that I never acknowledged his having read the adaptation of *The Informer*. All I need is to get that money, then I don't have to bother about anybody for sometime. I could also get out of here, a very necessary operation. I just can't cope with being alone any more, or with living in this climate.

I have hardly written a solitary word since the end of October. The business of living takes all my energy. Even that trip to London was a great relief. I used to walk up and down Sloane Street and revel in the cleanness of the shops and the elegance of the people that passed. At the same time, it was difficult to hold another attack of suicidal mania at bay. Now I feel better, but for how long?

Before leaving I got a notice to attend Court as a juror. On my return last night I rang Zoe. Sure enough, I was able to contact her. It was one of those days when her lunatic mother decided to answer the telephone. Then Zoe came and said she'd fix it for me. She still had some of the certificates she stole years ago from old Dr. Mackay's office. This morning at four, when I got up, I found a note under my door with the forged certificate which she had left while I slept. I'm sending it off to the Registrar in a registered letter with a polite note. Jesus! I hope it's all right. After all, *I couldn't condemn anybody*.

Thanks for going to Signet. I wish you would see them again on your return, since I feel the time is ripe to get some of my books before the cheap reading public. Maybe you could give the guy a really hard sell for *Famine* and *The Assassin* and *The Puritan* as well as the other two, *Mr Gilhooley* also.

I had another letter from that woman in Illinois, yards long. She sounds a bit insane but very shrewd and intelligent. She says that she has already organised a sort of O'Flaherty fan club among her fellow Campus people ... I prefer, really, to get my books into the drugstores and let them stand on their own merit.

.... I got the feeling England is completely *foutu*, like France, intellectually. America and Russia are the only live wires these days. Perhaps Germany has a little something too, but not much. I was very interested in the U.S. reaction to that horrid Armenian. I bet Dulles is furious that American businessmen can't be stampeded by his childish and vindictive fanaticism. With whom does he think he is dealing? After all, there is still a strong element in that country that have inherited the adventurous blood of the robber barons and the covered wagoners.

I stayed at twenty Chesham and found that the Pont Royal is now cheaper at this new rate .... On the whole, quality for quality, Paris is cheaper than London at all reckonings. It's cold here right now, I went round London shivering and I feel like a feeble old man. I hope that's the end of my labours on *Insurrection*. I told Montgomery they had to take or leave that last signature. He laughed and said I was becoming an 'avaricious author'. Son of a bitch! I didn't see Pegeen ....

I wish you'd hurry back. It seems such a pity not to get 'The Unique Passion' finished this year. It's really pretty as far as it has gone. I have rewritten it all on this new typewriter, which is a different size of type and it gave me a feeling of perfection and poise.

The frost is so severe all over the British Isles that all racing and football is cancelled. What are they going to do? The Irish, of course, would just drink themselves sodden if they were not so broke .... Hope you get some sun down there in Georgia. It's nice of Laura to accompany you back. All my love, darling and come soon.

Liam

---

395. KT TLS to Kitty Tailer
[from Dublin]   p.m. 23 February, 1959

Dearest Kitty,

I find it hard to write to you, indeed I have tried in vain several times, because I have finally gone over the precipice in thought. Not angrily, but sadly and without resistance. Neither do I believe that disappointment over *Insurrection* is really responsible. If they had bought the film rights, or rather paid for them, it would very likely have been the same. All roads come to an end and mine apparently has done so. What now? Having failed to get away from here and try some other way of life, while there was still time, there seems nothing to do but wait, as the bullock waits, for the final blow. It's equally true that I can do nothing personally about *that* either. As a matter of fact, all I have done is *wait* for a long time.

Sorry you got a bad cold and I do hope it's better by now. I really don't know why you don't stay in the sun since it does you most good and you have the means of doing so. February is nearly at an end. If you really come over in March perhaps I shall see you again. Though that, too, would be akin to embarrassment. Even so, one should tidy one's billet before leaving. Do say what your programme really is, I mean about your deplacement. We two have been so long meeting and parting, to meet again and part, that it has become a function of our life.

Sorry about this letter, Kitty. It really must end here because it does not get any more cheerful, and sad things should be as short as possible.

All my love
Liam

O'Flaherty received the remaining three thousand pounds for the world film rights of *Insurrection* in March, 1959.

---

396. KT TLS to Kitty Tailer
[from Dublin]   4 August, 1959

Dearest Kitty,

I enclose a letter from Margaret Stephens. Could you do anything to get these people off my neck? Life goes on in the same furtive and unreal way. I feel that my supply of energy is getting very low in the tank, but I forge ahead like an exhausted tortoise, inch by inch. I do hope you return in October, as you foretold. I need your help to finish this work. Even so, *mon petit pot*, it's all very exciting and wonderful. I have complete confidence in the result, which only a physical collapse can keep from ... what? I have got confused. In any case, this chapter has begun in a most promising fashion, with the Spanish war and the identification of Le Château de la Chimère, together with the preposterous attempt to raise bulls and horses for the arenas on the estate of Colonel Jean Lesieurin in the Camargue.

I've been up since three o'clock and it's now nine. I must go for a walk in the park and get food. Yet I hate to go out, since time is so limited and the effort is so enormous. I feel so sorry for Juliette McNiece and her crazy husband. How remote that world of theirs has become! ...

How jolly for you to watch the television while Krushchev is touring America. After all, it is a much more pleasant way to make war.

There are large holes in the elbows of my smoking jacket and I have thrown my tattered Madagascars down the chute. All that too is very pleasant.

How nice it was that day among the flowers at Tremblay! ... I hope the grandchildren are not going to be too much for the exhausted Kitty, together with the heat and virulent mosquitoes of Georgia. Is Laura going down there too? Or has she reneged on the expedition to Europe?

I have had no word as yet from the income tax people. In any case, I don't have to pay anything until January, which may be able to look after itself by the grace of some god or other. I have so many of them in this book. Clairvoyant and forlorn, abandoned, drunken and blasphemed. All very gay and immoral.

The Russian cigarettes are unsmokable. Why don't they import Chesterfields to steal the technique for making them? Somehow, I'd rather be American. How go the Giants? They were still in front last Saturday. God Almighty! I'll be sixty-three shortly. Like Dreiser I can say, if my book is a success, 'The bastards waited until I had an ulcer', however, he lived a long time on the proceeds of his *American Tragedy*. Well, Kitty, we're a queer pair but there is nothing we can do about it.

Here's my love to you, dear heart, and let us ride to heaven or hand in hand to hell, amazing the welkin with our broken staves.

                                                                                    Liam

Kitty Tailer was still dealing with O'Flaherty's literary affairs, and her addresses were c/o Colony Club, Park Avenue\62nd Street, New York City, or c/o American Express, rue Scribe, Paris. Her legal residence was with her sister Laura Harding, at Bayonet Farm, Holmdel, New Jersey. Laura also owned a shore house at Mantaloking, New Jersey.

---

397. KT TLS to Kitty Tailer
[from Dublin]   p.m. 4 September, 1959

Dearest Kitty,

Here's the letter I promised to write. Rather late, ain't it? However, I've not felt any too well ever since I spoke to you last Friday. Just not too good at all. I tried to put on too much pressure, I guess. One goes so far and then one has to stop. I long, and long, and long ever so much to get out of here. it's my own fault, of course, that I'm still here .... One bores a hole through the prison wall and then one fails to find sufficient initiative for making the break. I've finally become bitter and distrustful.

Really, Kitty, I've no news whatever ... No news from Peters' office and none from Pegeen either. It's still warm during the day, but at night one knows that winter is coming once more. In the newspapers I read talk of Rugby football clubs being readied for the coming season. Steeplechasing also ... the finals of the All Ireland hurling and football contests are being played. Over there, the World Series is on its way. Krushchev and Eisenhower. *Voilà!* the world seen through a glass darkly. My own part in the strange affair, the urge to finish what I'm doing and nothing more.

I was re-reading Druon's life of Alexander last night and came across a motto sculpted on a public monument at Biblos in Syria, 'Eat, drink and make love, all else is vanity.' It appears true to my mind .... Wonderful creature man! One day he will find a substitute for his penis and testicles. *Olé! los impotentes!* I long too for the music of La Guitarra.

I've got a new laundry called the Swastika. Now that Mrs Dreaper-Clements' husband does not drink any more she has him round the house all day, and looks more unhappy than before ... Remember that girl you met here called Prendreville? She sent me two bottles of Lafitte-Rothschild for my birthday. Zoe also left two packets of Kingsize Chesterfields on my doormat. I seem to get along better with women than with men, yet I make no effort to retain the friendship of either. After all, one must guard one's solitude and hate it, since it's merely a defence and an acknowledgement of one's weakness. Even so, I love life and wish that I could afford to live as I please.

I wonder is that *'Vannerie pour fleuristes'* doing well, on the road inland beyond La Bocca. It was always nice to watch them paint the baskets white as I walked past early in the morning. Why did I walk so fast? After all death will always wait for one. So why be afraid of being late? Forgive this boring letter, but it's the best I can do. I have been trying to write for days. Now it appears to me that cables say all there is to say, especially if one feels mean and spiteful, and one's bile is incurably vile.

Au revoir, Kitty
[unsigned]

---

398. KT TLS to Kitty Tailer
[from Dublin]   p.m. 17 September, 1959

Dearest Kitty,

I just got your cable, having already got your letter yesterday. Excuse me for having disturbed you by sending my cable, but I was in a particularly bad frame of mind. That is only natural under the circumstances, because the tension is very severe at the moment. My brain is working at full pitch and I have no protection against life, which has been doing its damnedest to throw me off balance. In any case, here is the situation. My book is finally going very well, though slowly as usual, but magnificently well, giving me those moments of ecstasy that are *everything* in an artist's life. However, the problem is again posed, *Comment finir sans argent?* I have no more *argent* and am just waiting to reach a decision as to what should be done.

Curiously enough the owners of this flat helped a little this morning by sending a letter to me to say that the rent is going to be raised, as from April next. If I disagree they are going to cancel my tenancy as from that date. Naturally I am going to say no, which gives me the excuse to leave. You will notice that I no longer take macabre and false decisions to throw down my hand, no madame! I'm determined to play out the hand that fortune served. Everything must be sacrificed for a unique passion. *Olé!*

Do you agree that the best thing to do would be to announce vacation of this flat in April and stay on until then, or until I reach the theft? Please let me know. Also, if you possibly can, come to see me soon, since this novel is, after all, your property, or rather my liquidation of a debt of honour. All I want personally, after that, is to finish my song *en beauté*. Do write at once, Kitty, to say how soon you can come, if at all. I must decide almost at once. Is all this clear? When one is speaking from a mountain top, one's voice becomes a confused murmur to those listening from the valley of ordinary life. After all, you continue to be my tigress and I'm destined to go on gripping until the end, bitter or otherwise. What makes it more difficult, of course, is that some or all of these difficult situations are deliberately fabricated, as you probably know by now. A remark you made in Paris this Summer led me to suppose that you do know. Probably more than I do myself. One must live what one writes, otherwise it's secondhand, no matter how brilliantly polished and repaired.

Do write to me at once, Kitty, or send another cable with advice, and forgive my not finishing this page .... Kitty I feel on top and to hell with everything. At the same time I need your help, spiritually. So I'm signalling the bull pen and calling you to the mound.

What a wonderful race in the National League! I'm still backing the Giants, although the Braves are making a brilliant stretch run. Tough luck on Krushchev to find a red hot struggle of that kind during his visit. What a crude fellow he is, boasting about his extremely vulgar success with the moon!

All my triumphant love, darling, *ex tenebris*
Liam

---

399. KT TLS to Kitty Tailer
[from Dublin]   30 September, 1959

Dearest Kitty,

Thank you ever so much for sending money. I have notified Irish Estates this morning that I surrender the flat on April 1st. Fortunately, it seems that Carl Foreman is going to do *Insurrection* after all, so I may get the necessary money to go and live in the Swiss mountains until this book is finished. You know, it might be the best energy-making climate for my type of system. In any case, I intend to give it a try, if all goes well in other respects.

At the moment, however, I still continue to live on the edge of things, although my mind is happily free from doubt, a most bright and happy-making state after all these years of uncertainty.

What gives with you, Kitty? I mean as regards your plans. I do hope you'll come over. The tax people have put me down for one thousand pounds, but I have no real intention of paying them anything at all. I'd rather take cyanide really. If you do come over next month, or in November, will you kindly bring another packet of that paper? It's so good.

I have more or less decided to publish *The Unique Passion* ie. *The Gamblers* under an assumed name. Personally, I have made so many enemies that it would be a handicap to go along with the old firm. In any case, a new name would be such an adventure, like being young and unknown once more. 'Alas! One can never regain the lost paradise of youth,' or taste once again that 'superb wine in which a slow and tasteless poison has been dipped'. My passport is good until August 1962, which gives me plenty of time, should I decide to become invalid with its expiry.

Really, Kitty, I don't believe that Laura is going to come over at all. She's even more efficient than yourself at the game of procrastination. Do please turn up this once, Kitty, because I want to give you the completed part of my manuscript, should my plans go wrong.

I expect America feels very quiet after the departure of Krushchev. Dear me! I have a horrid feeling that war between your country and the Soviet

Union is inevitable. His visit looks so much like the old Mongol habit of sending cunning ambassadors to dull the enemy into a feeling of security. However, I may be wrong and sincerely hope that I am. Yet how can one get rid of *general staffs*. Neither the American politicians or the Russian could very well do so. The lust for power is so strong in military people.

Do write at once, Kitty, and please do come as soon as possible. It's the last favour I ask. In the meantime, I am working as hard as possible, in spite of a heavy cold that has now lasted a fortnight. It makes one extremely weak. Even the brain becomes stupefied.

How exciting the struggle in the National League has been. I'm sorry the Giants got eliminated. Their pitching finally collapsed. God bless, Kitty, and let me hear from you, darling. An empty arena feels so menacing. There are two ways of drowning the future with the past. One of them does *not* produce 'the ecstasy of the eternal present'. I try hard, on that account, to maintain contact with the romantic past. 'The Lizard' still cries out to be written.

All my love, darling
Liam

---

400. KT TLS to Kitty Tailer Headed 'This is the sample of typing paper'
[from Dublin]   p.m. 28 October, 1959

Dearest Kitty,

Thanks for your letter and enclosure. I'm so glad you're sailing on the 11th November. I don't feel very well, but will survive until then no doubt, since it seems that I'm rotting very slowly and putting up an instinctive resistance of savage power against the ending of a life that has become a nightmare. Yet I'm still desperately anxious to finish my novel. It is also very odd that I feel completely [word missing] about its form and its merit. I'll stay here until you arrive and then, perhaps, you'll telephone me from Paris, or wherever else you land. How wonderful it would be to get away from here! Like my old ass, I long for a pleasant valley where there is silence.

Please don't get depressed by these remarks, I'm just tired and bewildered. Too bad Laura is not sailing with you. I feel you wanted her so much to do so. I have no news of any sort, except that Pegeen said in her last letter she is writing a novel, and going away for a week to Lancashire as an interpreter for a group of Russians.

Bad weather has now set in here, but it's more pleasant than the peculiar heat that was so humid and unhealthy. I seem to have lost contact with everybody. However, some walking in the sun would probably put me right for the final effort. For the first time I see daylight and the goal in sight. Have I really gone mad?

What is to be done with this furniture and all these things it cost you so much putting together? That too is depressing. I have the strange feeling of going back to the beginning inevitably, that appalling garret in Bloomsbury.

Apparently they are going to spend a lot of money on this film. According to them it is going to be the most expensive film ever made in the British Isles. I didn't hear who is going to play the lead. Couldn't care less apart from getting the remainder of the money. The other film seems to have gone down the drain. *Famine* has appeared in the paper edition. All three of them are shown in the little tobacco and paper shops around town. Gives me false impression of being a popular writer ....

I hope you don't change your mind about the boat, because that would be the end and I don't want to end just yet. Not until I find out what happens to Gerald McNiece. I have gone back over the first part and am putting it into very short chapters, each one like a scene in a film. It's very effective and makes it more understandable by the ignorant, just as in a newspaper article one must have only one idea clearly stated.

How long ago it is since we went off to Arizona in your little gold-plated car, and the old house at Jamaica where the swallows flew out in the evening over the calm sea. All that is very beautiful and what went before is becoming less and less important. *Olé!* That word is being made flesh and the dance is being unfolded to music that has assumed the dignity of eternal truth.

Goodbye now, Kitty, until we meet again, very gay I hope and confident of the frail shoot that must not wither in the first embrace of the sun.

Liam

In November 1959, A.D. Peters asked Michael Relph of Relph, Dearden whether there was any prospect of their filming *The Martyr*. He replied that there was too much prejudice against Irish civil war subjects, and the two hundred and fifty pounds option later expired.

It is evident from a letter postmarked 16 December that Kitty Tailer visited O'Flaherty in Dublin earlier that month. In the following letter she is evidently still in France.

At about this time Kitty bought the lease of a flat at 8 rue de la Paix, Paris.

---

401. KT TLS to Kitty Tailer
[from Dublin]   Boxing Day morning p.m. 1959

Dearest Kitty,

I don't know whether or not I promised to send you a cable for Xmas. If yes, I failed to do so. However, I sent 'the *niña*' one. Haven't been out of this flat, except to run across the bridge for food through the rain, since last Monday. Today, however, I'm happily going to Leopardstown through a hurricane with a paltry sum. If lost, I shall have to begin pawning things once more. Alas, I never learn, do I? Yet life appears rosy at the moment.

The rewriting is nearly finished and I proceed on January 1st, as intended, to carry on with Isabel. So far so good, what has begun so well must surely end in triumph.

I never heard a word from Pegeen since that card written in Hamburg. Could she have been secreted by the Russians? No doubt, like myself, she just forgot to show signs of life. Well, that's exactly what happened. I just rang her number and spoke to her and she sounded hoarse but alive. Said her second party of Russians were better than the others, etc ...

All I want is a pastrami sandwich, a cup of coffee, and not to be annoyed by any external things just now. *Afuera todo el mundo* except Kitty. Do hurry up and come back and tell me all about the villas on the Cap Ferrat, just at the angle near Beaulieu. Indeed, you might look see into the casino at Montecarlo and bet a thousand francs on number thirteen, if there is such a number. One croupier's face, minutely described, might also be indicative. Never mind the croupier but it would be nice to have a description of one villa, preferably white, *donnant sur la mer côté de Nice.*

How wonderful that Christmas is over and each day will be longer and presently one shall fling the garment of depression in the fire of Spring. Good old Fitzgerald! I bet he was a penniless drunken Irishman, who suffered the misfortune of becoming a posthumous hero to myriads to amorous school girls, who read his translation of a minor Persian poet that he dolled up into a genius. Poor old Fitz! I daresay he couldn't get a publisher by saying the poem was his own. So he had to invent an unknown selling-plater called Omar.

Zoe sent me two packets of Kingsize Chesters, Irene two bottles of Lafitte - Rothschild, Peg two cigars in metal containers. What do you know about betting number two on the card in the first race at Leopardstown this afternoon? Like hell I will, unless Blueville carries that number.

All my love, darling *querida niña*. Here we go into the wild blue yonder.

Liam

402. KT TLS to Kitty Tailer
[from Dublin]   p.m. 3 April, 1960

Darling Kitty,

I got your letter last night with the enclosure for which I thank you very much. I've had the flu for the past week and have been mostly in bed covered with neck pieces and sweaters, but the weather changed suddenly yesterday and I felt better and bought some beef which is now stewing, much to my delight. When I've eaten some I'll go to the G.P.O. and post this letter. However, I sent you a cable on Thursday lest you might worry.

What do you know? I went down to see Peter Marron before I got ill. As usual, he was not at home, but I peeked through the window of the back room where he works and saw a photo which seemed familiar. After long inspection I realised it was an enlarged snapshot of you and me, taken that night at the party. You remember the man came along a second time and snapped with his flash? It looked good of you and I've been meaning ever since to get in touch with him about it. What a cunning fellow! I bet he got the photographer along expressly.

I love *Le Monde*'s account of the K[rushchev] visit. Apparently it was a terrific success. He certainly won over *Le Monde* which was sneering at first.

Any news of Laura? This goddam cold has held me up but I feel ready to go ahead now. For the first time I feel sure the end is near. I got two copies of *Insurrection* from Yugoslavia, a de luxe edition with an inside photo and my signature underneath. The photo looks like a Jew and does not bear the slightest resemblance to me. There was a list of other books published by the firm, all old friends like Dzon Prisli (old J.B. Priestley) and E. Koldvel (he of *Tobacco Road*) and best of all Dzejn Osten (whom the English call Jane Austen I presume). All very gay, even E. Hemingvej, author of *Preko Reke iu Sumo*.

Darling, I am already looking forward eagerly to your arrival about 20th. Let's make a trip to Connemara and get some real sea air. Toddy O'Sullivan is going to build a five million dollar hotel here, two hundred and fifty rooms *mit bahnen* in every one, so Dublin ain't dead yet.

I love you very much and am so sorry you're not getting any sun. Maybe by now there is some ....

There seems to be a new man at Peters. He sold a short story, I forget the name, to an anthology for thirty pounds and said he was trying to sell 'Bohunk' in Australia. The guy is trying in any case, unlike that foul Montgomery who hated my guts for some reason. Maybe things will suddenly look up. Jesus! it's about time because they hardly ever looked so black.

All my love, sweetie pie, Liam

1 March, 1960, Liam O'Flaherty and Catharine Tailer signed a World Stage rights agreement
for *The Informer* with Mícheál MacLiammóir and Hilton Edwards of Dublin Gate Theatre
productions. As Jonathan Cape's rights over this novel did not include the US and its
dependencies, Harcourt, Brace (paperback Bantam) published a new edition of *The Informer*
in 1960.

---

403. KT TLS to Kitty Tailer
[from Dublin]   p.m. 3 May, 1960

Dearest Kitty,

Well, there you are again in Joysey [sic] after another voyage, which
included Kilkerrin *l'introuvable* [on the Connemara coast] and Manister [on
Aran] of the hair-shedding white horse and the croupier of Enghien les
Bains, with his undulating sliver of pale wood indifferently shifting cards
and multi-coloured chips from victory to defeat and from defeat to victory.
I too have returned to my strange illusion, timid but relentless, buoyed up
by craving for victory that has already begun to become vaguely apparent
on the far horizon and terribly afraid of defeat, which can only be the work
of my internal devil, the dark angel of weariness that whispers .... Never
mind, Kitty, the dice are cast and my hands are clutching the summit of the
wall.

God Damn it! I got a note from Margaret yesterday, asking me to do a
foreword for the Folio Edition of *The Informer*, whatever that is, for twenty-
five pounds. I daresay it must be done, only twelve hundred words. How
amusing to write one utterly opposed to the other. Yet it's a waste of time
or rather of writing energy.

How strange that meeting with Joyce![1]... Let these dogs lie for the
moment and howl in the dark night. We must go on in loneliness.

I met Clem, my neighbour, yesterday coming back from my morning trip
to the bridge. 'See anything?' he said. 'A colt by Nimbus out of Nigrette,' I
said. 'Good?,' Clem said. 'Very good,' I replied. 'The Gimcrack, no doubt,'
he said, 'will be his objective. The French would like to get a line on
Floribunda.' Queer language!

I paid the rates, or half of them, a moiety they call it, amounting to thirty
pounds. I hope to swim on the remainder until I see you again. Today I'm
going to have a beef stew, not as rich as the boeuf bourguignon I had before
leaving Paris. First of all I'm taking a bus to the Pillar, in order to post this
letter at the G.P.O.

Looks like the *guerre en Algerie* is going to go on. I have also sadly come
to the conclusion that Kennedy is a vain and self-seeking creature and that
Nixon would be better perhaps. There was an appalling article about
'Kennedy the man' in *Newsweek*. Of course an alliance between the Irish and
the Jews would let me out of encirclement at the crucial moment.

Give my love to dear Laura and say I am wearing her shirt while writing this note. And to yourself, dear heart, my different love, from the depths.

Liam

[1]Joyce Rathbone, O'Flaherty's daughter, see 24 May, 1975.

'The Post Office' was sold for thirty pounds to *Macmillan Winter Tales,* 12 May, 1960. World Distributors Ltd. Books (Manchester) asked for a paperback reprint of *Two Lovely Beasts* against an advance of one hundred and fifty pounds, and this was published April 1961 (Consul Books), but they refused *Land, The Martyr* and *Skerrett*. O'Flaherty wrote one of his now rare letters to Michael Sissons of A.D. Peters on 14 May, thanking him.

---

404. KT TLS to Kitty Tailer
[from Dublin to Paris]   p.m. 26 May, 1960

Dearest Kitty,

Hope this address is right, as your postmark was somewhat indistinct. In any case, Amexco is bound to get it. Thanks for the lettuce and your lovely long letter. I didn't hear from Margaret yet about that book I sent, so maybe it didn't get there. I do everything wrong.

Things are going along as usual, ever so slowly and stupidly dull in this horse-faced town. I'm looking forward to the 24th and a visit to Enghien Casino. Are they going to admit me in a grey sports jacket? In any case I can see the pool behind the casino, and Longchamps and read the *Paris Sports*.

I got a note from Pegeen yesterday saying, 'we missed you very much yesterday' that being Derby day, at which the French favourite, the widow Strassburger's Angers, broke his leg and got shot. As the hall porter at Chesham Place forecast, the race was won by Saint Paddy. However, I've lost interest in the affair by now.

The weather here is warm and fine. Makes one long for cool, clear, sea water. Probably the best place would be that Seagull's Rock at Manister. *Ça, c'est pour l'année prochaine.* I play records a lot. Today I bought fresh peas and broad beans also tomatoes, onions and a chicken for boiling tomorrow.

Is Denmark really beautiful? I heard the opposite .... Apparently Pegeen managed to get herself employed by the British Council. She leads people about London, people from all nations. What a peculiar [life] she fashioned for herself. Something may come of it, other than death of course.

How frightful! The fellow who lives across the way is quite tiny, crippled by infantile paralysis. Bad luck – this is really an appalling year in the matter of luck all round. Mr. K[rushchev] seems to have taken a violent dislike to Eisenhower. A low fellow, after all, that Ukrainian.

Dearest Kitty, I seem to be in a permanent state of excitement. I do wish that Isabel had reached her second casino and passed into the unknown, however, it should be fun while it lasts, this episode.

I'll try to remember the books before I leave. Excuse this ridiculous note, I should go for a long walk somewhere, but God only knows where I'd like. So goodbye for the moment, darling Kitty, and come back safely from the pig country. Or as you called it, the 'Maria here' country. Wonder what happened to her? All my love, darling, until we meet in Paris.

Liam

---

5 July, O'Flaherty wrote to Margaret Stephens of A.D. Peters, promising to send a twelve hundred word preface to the Folio edition of *The Informer*, against a fee of twenty-five guineas, by the end of July.

On 9 August, however, he sent a telegram to say he was ill and could not write the preface. In October 1960, he was offered thirty guineas by *Homes & Gardens* to write an article of fifteen to seventeen hundred words on 'I live in Ireland' for their 'I Live In' series. This commission also was never completed. Yet in a 12 July letter to Kitty he wrote 'How I hate this penury'. His now restricted energies were concentrated on the novel, *The Gamblers*, he was still struggling to write.

---

405. KT TLS to Kitty Tailer
[from Dublin]   p.m. 17 July, 1960

Dearest Kitty,

Thanks for your letter and the anniversary cable, about that night in Santa Barbara. How very far and near. Darling, you gave me the impression of being very tired and disoriented (I mean your letter). The only protection is to become increasingly remote and uninfluenced by the slings and arrows of the people that have been surpassed and made hostile by one's progress towards the light of comprehension ....

This chapter is easily the worst so far, but it gives signs now of being overwhelmed by the protracted violence of my attack. What a labour!

I note what you said about Kennedy, even so it would be fatal to back Nixon against him. All along I have regarded Kennedy as a necessary evil on the road to the destruction of the present system of government in U.S.A., whereas Nixon might very well mean annihilation of the country itself as a great power.

On s'en fout! All I want personally is to get out of here and get my book finished. First of all, though, I want September to come and bring me Kitty back again. I'm afraid that Margaret will have to whistle in vain for that *Informer* foreword. I hate the damn book so much by now that I couldn't write about it. *Tant pis*, I never sent a copy of *Land* to the other man either. I'm just at a very low level, Kitty, in respect of getting things done. The amount of energy gets less and less and has to be conserved for the 'main event'.

Well, darling, goodbye now and all my love and let's get back to barracks.
Tell Laura not to annoy Kitty with trivialities.

Liam

---

406. KT TLS to Kitty Tailer
[from Dublin]   24 July, 1960

Dearest Kitty,

Got your Wednesday's letter last night and note gratefully that you're
sending batteries [for his recorder] which I am to insert head first. Also am
forwarding copy of paper required. Also note that it's Michael Sissons who
wants *Land*, which you kindly offer to forward.

Alas! I have to add from my part of the front, that I've been ill ever since
I wrote to you last Sunday, that I am again without any pocket lettuce and
that Peters have sent none this month. Ill, my God I've been ill this time all
right. However, it's beginning to look as if I'm on the mend, although as
yet unable to eat anything but milk .... Looks possible that I'll never get this
damn thing done, even so I have not lost hope.

How are you going down, by Opel? I'll certainly write to our old and
very good friend, Ye King and Prince Hotel, if I'm still around, which I
certainly have no intention of not being.

Lots of fun at the moment in the Congo. As I get no papers except *Le
Monde*, which is always two days late, I try to listen to the radio which is
very amusing if you listen to Paris, Brussels, Moscow and Schenectady
altogether, more or less. These buck negroes are having quite a ball with
nuns, etc. according to some sources. One fellow claims they held a priest
tied to a stake and made him watch twenty nuns being raped several times,
by all ranks of the local Force Publique .... There is a very grave problem
involved, if the report is true. Should these nuns, if they become pregnant
as a result of being raped by negroes, produce and rear their children? or
should they abort? or should they give away into fosterage the newborn?
Let John XXIII work it out.

I'm going to head out now to post this note. I've shaved and bathed, so
I really don't look so bad, quite slim I must say, must have lost twelve or
fifteen pounds. Without stimulants, tea, meat, tobacco, alcohol, one feels
quite at peace, but extremely bucolic.

Being deprived of detectives, I've been reading Morgan, Maeterlinck and
a poor life of Tamerlane by a Frenchman. 'Lame Tim' was his name really,
I mean Timour Leng or Tamerlan or whatever. Not in the same class as the
old fellow, the great Ghenghiz, the O Chon O, or Ochon Oh, as they call
him in their lamentations in the wesht of eirland (consult *Famine* by
Liam O'Flaherty).

Why do the Mongols have such a fascination for me?

Do send me a little lettuce, Kitty, if you can, *autrement je suis foutu.*

Love
Liam

---

407. KT TLS to Kitty Tailer
[from Dublin]   p.m. 13 August, 1960

Dearest Little Kitty,

I just read your letter and am so oppressed to learn that you have gone and wounded yourself again, as if the eyes were not bad enough. Poor little crazy girl!

I do hope you have received the letter I sent to Holmdel last Tuesday. I told you in it that I had forgotten the Crown and Prince address. Dear me, it's too bad about Bill's affairs. Of course, you expected something like that to happen all along, but what can be done? Poor little one that cried! You remember the coats at Harrods? One of them was for her, *n'est ce pas?* Well, it was nice of Peter to come along and drive back with Ma. Smart boy, he never puts a foot wrong, even in the business of making children.

Well, darling, I wish I could cheer you up by reporting excellent conditions on this sector of our dual front. In fact things are good in a sense, that is with respect to my book. Financially they are at their very worst. The tax people are dunning me and have finally sent a menacing note, threatening dire things unless the remainder is paid within ten days. The only solution is flight, but how under these circumstances? ...

.... Come what may, Kitty, I shall finish this novel next year. And it's going to be good. After all, I always wanted to go out brilliantly, like a falling star ... I read Pegeen the Saint Cloud chapter and she was deeply moved, especially by the lecherous woman crossing the cobbled yard and the horses throwing up clods of earth that disintegrated in flight.

Olé Kitty darling. *Afuera todo el mundo.* I love you
Liam

---

408. KT TLS to Kitty Tailer
[from Dublin]   p.m. 24 August, 1960

Darling Kitty,

I imagine six morning, my time, would be a better time to call, except it means your staying up until half past one. However, please yourself. I shall be here at six and again at noon. Good Lord, by then I'll be sixty-four and my book not done yet. If you can get a La Paloma singing record that will be fine because I've got enough Guitarra records for my purpose. What I would like is a good Argentine tango record, principally La Cumparsita and Media Luz, not jazzed up things but the pure original. The Germans do them best. Also a record of Mexican Malagueñas. Enough of Pepe and the others, I've got all I want from them. In any case, La Paloma and the tango is much later.

What about Yugoslavia? That money is attractive under the circumstances. If one could get it and then come back to spend a month with it on the Riviera, which is the only place I like and that suits my present purpose ....

You said nothing about having recovered from the eye trouble and the foot wound? So you must have done so ....

As you said I have done nothing about the income tax notice. I met Peg Gallagher and she said I was a damned fool to give the correct return. 'Nobody does,' she said. Too late now. How about trying to get somebody to advance the twenty-seven hundred pounds for a discount? This money complication is getting me down and every ounce of energy counts, now that the final effort has arrived.

I suppose Laura shows no sign of coming over this year? In the end she'll probably travel in a space ship, as they'll be a commonplace mode of transport by then. Dear Kitty, I'm looking forward to talking to you, and more so to seeing you, as I'm not good on the telephone and it doesn't cure loneliness. *J'ai horreur d'être seul!* I met a delightful French women I hadn't seen for thirty-five years. She lives in Versailles. *'Vive le F.L.N.'* she cried out in exaltation. The French are delightful (when they are delightful). All my love, darling, and don't miss the boat whatever you do.

Liam

---

409. KT TLS to Kitty Tailer
[from Dublin]   p.m. 2 September, 1960

Darling Kitty,

For the life of me I can't remember whether I answered your letter, lettuce laden, that arrived on Monday last. If not, here is thanking you for same, with knobs on.

... I finally went out yesterday and drank four gins and then came back to bed.[1] Now the swelling of my stomach has gone down and the savage diarrhoeic pains have gone too, leaving me with that strange uncertain gaiety following deep coma, a dread rehearsal of annihilation. All that keeps back my book, but I'll still make the deadline of this time twelve months (or October rather), if my plans are not further disturbed.

I've got rooms at 20 Chesham for Monday 19th, and I'll be at Waterloo to meet the boat train, with or without Joyce's van.

What about this money in Yugoslavia? As time is running short I don't want to dash around on tours, Kitty. Yet the extra Jack is enticing. Indeed, it may become vital. We shall discuss all that. I've done nothing further about the tax man, but I'm all square otherwise, except that I need a jacket. I really do want to have a long at Montecarlo and that environment. *Alors! On y va*, by hook or by crook. How exciting it is to be in sight of victory.

'This morning at dawn, between the Dnieper and the Don, the Russian and German armies joined in battle.' There looks like being a glorious fight in the American League Pennant Race, but the Presidential race gets more and more disappointing. At the moment it looks as if Kennedy has sold out all along the line. His campaign 'intellect' now seems to be Walter Lipman. You know what that means? He made peace with Harry an' Eleanor and the rest of the gang. Poor America! However, as a Giant baseball fan once told me: 'Don't sell little ole America short, Liam, don't sell her short, son. She's still in the game with a favourite's chance.'[2]

All my love, darling, all my love
Liam

[1] Passage omitted. Accustomed to living alone a visit from Joyce, whom he had now met, and Pegeen had tired him.

[2] John F. Kennedy, elected President of the USA by a narrow margin on 9 November, was running against Richard Nixon.

410. KT TLS to Kitty Tailer
[from Dublin]   p.m. 3 January, 1961

Darling Sweetie Pie,

Well, here I am once more, back to barracks almost successfully, after a bit of a tussle with the results of my own cooking, in other words the demon indigestion. Seems to be conquered by now, as my wrists are beginning to 'get a little of their strength back', as Denny Dwyer would say. Am blasting my way through the end of that going south chapter, and my morale is fairly high, although an anxiety complex is a bit tiresome.

What do you know about the enclosed letter? I thought it would amuse you to learn the abject profundities of Musso's damned soul.

The papers have arrived this morning, so I am back on an even keel. My teeth are also giving satisfaction .... Many thanks once more, for that and everything else. Let's hope you will get your reward, here on earth and not wait for heaven which is a thousand to one proposition at the latest declaration of odds offered and taken.

Speaking of odds, Joyce rang to say that she had gone to Newbury races with a girl friend, so that I worry about having sent her on the evil path. She said Pegeen took her severely to task, thinking it was Angela, the girl upstairs, she had brought. On learning the identity of Joyce's companions she said: 'Oh well, it doesn't matter, she's already corrupted.' Seems Pegeen is a chip off the Kitty block in that respect. I wrote to her as you suggested and said sorry for being rude.

Dublin is just as appalling as before, but I shall struggle bravely to live '*ma vie intérieure*' without putting myself in harm's way by demanding the impossible from occult barbarians.

Irene came round with two bottles of Christmas burgundy (Clos Vougeot) and told me she had listened to a Kennedy broadcast. He made a bad impression on her. 'He sounded', she said, 'exactly like our own awful politicians, except that his accent was even worse. If Ireland could only give *that* to America for the New Year, it's a bad look out for our reputation, which was already bad.'

Great to-do here about Princess Margaret's visit to Ross Castle.[1] In spite of the newspapers, however, the populace paid far less attention than they would to the return of the Grand National winner of Irish origin. Excuse the sacrilege of comparing the princess to a God animal.

Thank Laura for mentioning me in her cable and give her my love, and to yourself all the best wishes for a terrific coming year, on which so much depends.

I think this damn strong tea I drink is largely responsible for my indigestion. In any case I'll figure things out. I got a note from Delia for Xmas.[2] She
now has a telephone. Can you imagine, Ulla sent me a card from the top of
Sweden! The one with the stove, the Inspector woman, sent me a Xmas cake,
which was very good but may have been partly to blame for my tummy.

Long live Kitty. All my love, darling, to do

Liam

[1] Princess Margaret had recently married Anthony Armstrong-Jones, whose family owned
Ross Castle.

[2] O'Flaherty's sister.

---

411. KT TLS to Kitty Tailer
[from Dublin]   p.m. 18 January, 1961

Dearest Little Kitty,

I was so glad to get your letter yesterday, because I had begun to worry
about not hearing from you. Furthermore, I am in the usual state of tension
when writing is difficult, although I am forging ahead by inches. What a
beastly life a tortoise must have!

I'm so sorry about Aunt Amie. It's wonderful for you to take the whole
burden on your frail shoulders. Really people take advantage of a gentle
and ever obliging person. They say to themselves smugly, 'Kitty loves
doing things for people, why deny her the pleasure?' Let's hope the place
you found won't go sour all of a sudden. Christ! How awful it is to be very
old and sick and dependent! I'm so afraid of that and so afraid of lacking
courage to call a halt.

When are you going south? At this rate you'll be a total wreck. Who is
little Catharine Harding? Is that Timmie's daughter? This tribe has now
become so large that I've lost track ....

Darling, life here is as horrid as usual. I try to live as much as possible in
my interminable novel, it's the only escape. The *Herald Tribune* is a great
help, so down to earth and dead pan .... I saw Behan but didn't quote
Shakespeare to him. He seems quite friendly and I'm rather sorry for the
poor devil. The fickle people are already beginning to refer to him as: 'Ah,
a decent poor man but an awful cod all the same.' Patrick Kavanagh, he the
poet, on the other hand, is now assuming the manners of a distinguished
literary gentleman. I actually saw him on Grafton Street, dressed reasonably
well and clean, raising his hat courteously and bowing to somebody that
passed. '*Un drôle, hein?*' I've been told that he now has a cheque book, which
he takes out solemnly now and again, in the bars he frequents, but without
making any attempt to draw money. Just stares with pen in hand absent
mindedly and then puts everything away once more untouched.

There's something the matter with my record player. Which is the place to get it fixed? Keep writing to me, Kitty, if you possibly can, because it cheers me up so much to get a little note from you.

This weather is appalling, yet I have not yet worn my balaclava. It's just that kind of weather .... I wish I could get as far as Montecarlo quickly before I forget that Russian's face and your old women with the rocks.

All my love, darling
Liam

During the late fifties and early sixties a fairly lively interest in O'Flaherty's work prevailed, with translations into languages such as Hindi and Vietnamese, requests for contributions to anthologies, school course books, broadcasts, reprints and productions for the blind. End January, 1961, Columbia Picture Corporation sent three thousand pounds for the film rights of *Insurrection*, as the balance of money from Open Road Films, Ltd. Evidently this money had not reached O'Flaherty when he wrote the following letter.

---

412. KT TLS to Kitty Tailer
[from Dublin]   p.m. 27 January, 1961

Dearest Kitty,

I deeply regret to announce that my sins have again caught up with me and that I am in dire straits. Unless some relief comes, my continued existence will be in doubt after a short number of days. In other words, I'm broke and my agent again failed to find me any money this month. So what's to be done?[1] There's no point in thinking of the Hill of Howth, which would mean defeat, a humiliating thought at this advanced stage of the game. Can you help? If so please let me know by telegram as my mental state is very precarious. How I got into this further pit is a long and tiresome story and I won't dwell on it here.

I hope you haven't left for the south before this appalling note arrives. Everything here is depressing as there's a flu epidemic, something akin to the horse fever that's spreading from Asia through the Middle East. In the ordinary way it might be a good idea to wipe out this population and start afresh, after allowing the island to become disinfected for a number of years. Owing to one's presence, however, one regrets the incident. I daresay that must have been Defoe's attitude to the Great London Plague.

Please forgive me once again, Kitty, for being such a blasted nuisance. I can't forgive myself, but I try to forget in order to finish what I have undertaken to do ... Curse that too! I always knew it was too much for my talent. Even so, the finished portion is passing strange (as they used to say in Defoe's time).

There's a howling wind, which I like under ordinary circumstances, but not now. Just now I have found a new depth, just been scooped out, I imagine by my dark angel.

All my love, darling
Liam

[1] In a subsequent letter, p.m. 15 February, 1961, he still complains of being 'littered with bills' including his tax bill, which was one for Sur-tax of £68-10-0. Does 'my sins have again caught up with me' mean he has been gambling again?

---

413. KT TLS to Kitty Tailer
[from Dublin]   p.m. 28 February, 1961

Dearest Kitty,

Terribly sorry not to have answered your letter until now, or thanked you for the mazuma, but I've been under the weather pretty bad, still am for that matter, just trying hard to keep from folding completely. Nothing definite, just the way I felt in twenty-four. Tough luck! Perhaps I won't make it after all. I'm getting nowhere, just beating my head steadily against the wall, which fails to crack. 'A severe pressure against the front wall of my forehead.' It sounds all right written, but not felt.

Please forgive this lament, darling, I do hope you are in better shape and that Aunt Amie's affairs are finally cleared up. So Laura finally took off somewhere.

Tomorrow it's going to be March. Did you say that you might come over then, or not? Damned if I can remember anything clearly. 'That one talent which is death to hide ...,' how paltry words are really! Never mind, Kitty, I'm certain to feel better in a day or two. In the meantime I send you all my miserable love and thanks again for your kindness.

Liam

---

414. KT TLS to Kitty Tailer
[from Dublin]   p.m. 9 July, 1961

Darling Kitty,

I got your letter from New York last night and noted that you had not received my reply to your previous one. Let's hope it arrived at Mantaloking, although I have strong doubts about the existence of that place. It's what the French call, with very appropriate heaviness, *'invraisemblable'*!

You seem doomed to follow the avocation of cook-housekeeper and not receive a greater reward than to be told, when you take your apron off and sit down for the customary *'brin de causette'*, *strike one*! It really is unfair. However, it was you yourself thought of the damned idea in the first place.

The Jews have finally got poor Louis Ferdinand Céline and boy they have gone to town with venomous glee covering the spiritual corpse with gelded fleabites. *Le Monde* hired three different kikes to wield the dagger. I heard of the death from Marron, who telephoned to say: 'They've got Céline.' Not that I could ever finish anything he wrote. Yet I must admit he was a far greater writer than Hemingway. Such is life! Connolly, in the London *Times* today describes the latter as a giant and I failed to find any mention of Céline. However, in Shakespeare's time Aretino was universally recognised as a literary giant, receiving a gold cross from François I and a cardinal's hat from the Pope, whereas the Warwickshire lad had to wait some two hundred years for European recognition and even in his own land his origin is still in doubt. They say Cervantes had to run a modest whorehouse for a living in his latter days, using his nearest female relatives as stock in trade. Poor old Céline! They kept his death secret for several days, then the bloodhounds got on the trail. Must try again to finish *Voyage au Bout de la Nuit*. Curious thing, I heard him read the manuscript (when he was still Docteur Destouches) in that peculiar cottage in the south of France, above La Colle sur Loup, where I also heard 'Little Father' denounce the Bolsheviks and describe how he fired a machine gun from an upper window in Moscow until there were no more bullets. His mistress sat there blind drunk with a big Borzoi dog, while the old man raved. I paid no attention, therefore, and angered the Swede, who stood to attention very rigidly, with his eyeglass glued to his eye socket. Aye, why should my own indifference find fault with the indifference of others? In any case, Little Father[1] was in his own right a greater man, although he really never wrote that little poem about 'The Stork'.

I must go out now and travel to the G.P.O. to post this letter, so you won't complain again. With all my love,

Liam

[1] Probably Maxim Gorky.

---

415. KT TLS to Kitty Tailer
[from Dublin]   p.m. 25 July, 1961

Darling,

Thank you ever so much for your letter and the lettuce. I sent you a cable and I hope you got it. My stomach trouble is gone and I am eating again, although my own meat can't be as good as the Washington stuff, because cooking has become an appalling torture for me. However, nothing I can say, I suppose, would stop you worrying which is due to a defect in one's own state. The effort to look after the children must have been extreme, although Thomas appears to be delightful and to have completely put his little sister out of the picture. Of course he has done so all along. I feel exactly as he does about light. So did Goethe, who kept hollering for *'mehr licht'* as he lay dying. 'There just ain't no more, old un,' his wife grumbled. 'I guess you've had all there is and the drug store is closed at this hour.' Or whatever did she say!

For Christ sake stop thinking about what is happening on the political front. Personally I don't think about it at all. The struggle to survive is too great. I have no news at all, and that is all to the good judging by experience. Now I just look forward to seeing you again towards the end of August.

I'm reading Richard Aldington's attack on Lawrence of Arabia. A horrible book but fascinating at the same time.[1] Apparently the author of *Bonjour Tristesse* has brought out another novel which *Le Monde* describes as *'très faible'*.[2]

I do hope Garrity does not track me down. Joyce rang me and said Margaret is still at her house and that there isn't much wrong with the girl. She took her, of course, to the horse races at Kempton Park. Peculiar! No further report from Pegeen who seems to be minding her own business manfully.

The Folio edition of *The Informer* has come out and the young man wrote me a nice letter saying he regretted my refusal to write the introduction. Apparently they got an Irish judge called McDonagh to write it, news that horrifies me with fear of another Garrity affair.[3] Oh well, so much has been done to *The Informer* that another little sting can't matter. I shan't read the intro when the copies arrive. As I said, the struggle to live is too hard. One must conserve every little atom for the main purpose.

Darling Kitty, I wonder what Thomas dreams about as he chews his food. I adore that. Have not been out of town since you left. I set off twice with the intention to go in the Portmarnock direction and turned back. Not even as far as the zoo have I gone. Just to the Nelson pillar, day after day. The circle becomes ever smaller.

All my love, darling, and be of good heart because I am.

Liam

[1] *Lawrence of Arabia: a biographical enquiry*, London: Collins, 1955.

[2] Françoise Sagan, *Les Merveilleux Nuages*.

[3] Devin A. Garrity of Devin-Adair, New York, published the American edition of *Two Lovely Beasts* in 1950, and a collection of O'Flaherty's short stories in 1956 over which there had been disagreement.

---

416. KT TLS to Kitty Tailer
[from Dublin]   p.m. 5 August, 1961

Darling Kitty, .

Thank you for the letter from your solitary stay at Mantaloking, within your rampart of poison ivy. You were probably depressed about affairs. I do hope the southern visit will come out all right and that it won't depress you still further. Personally I'm going through a continual series of depressions, each more severe than the previous one, but for me that is an old story. At the moment there is a spell of warmer weather and my zona is sort of defeated by it. If only I could get away from here I might be able to go ahead. I rush to my desk with a fury of creation hot within my bowels and then twenty minutes suffice to drag me down and bring back the pain in my ear. However, none of that now.

Padraig Concannon just telephoned after a lapse of about three years and invited me to go with him to Croke Park tomorrow for the Kerry-Down match. It was nice talking Irish to him. He's so charming and genuine.

I get no little letters from Pegeen. I spoke to Joyce on the telephone and Margaret is still with her. She had only an abscess on her spine, no tubercles or whatever they are. She has by now been to several race courses, including Royal Goodwood. What a lark life is! I wish I were young again to enjoy it, just as foolishly as I did before.

Dear Kitty, I'm delighted you got the Spill and Spell. I don't want anything else. The record player broke down again, but I don't want it right now. The only thing is La Paloma, it still moves me. The Folio *Informer* came and there is no introduction, thank goodness. The young man was decenter than Garrity and obviously paid and threw out the cripple McDonagh's attack. Behan is apparently back in Europe again, having been found wandering around Hoboken by his wife and put on a plane. They're making a film of his first play. Brian Hurst is filming *The Playboy* in Kerry, using Siobhán McKenna as the female lure and God knows how many pansies as the male ones. Kirwan is still here trying to con somebody into launching a television series about horse racing. The man is a total wreck. However, he told me how much he enjoyed reading 'The Post Office'. I thanked him and thought, 'Is this a bite or is he in earnest?' No, he didn't ask for anything.

This last year has been a total loss. Do you think I'll make it? Please don't miss that plane on the twenty-fifth, Kitty. All my love, darling,

Liam

---

417. KT TLS to Kitty Tailer
[from Dublin]   p.m. 17 August, 1961

Dearest Kitty,

Thanks ever so much for the lettuce which arrived last night. It was very thoughtful of you and forgive me for the letter which I addressed to Holmdel asking for some. I'm so sorry that things did not go well *là bas en* Georgia. However, things always look blacker on those occasions than they really are, especially in so far as the young are concerned. Nowadays society has gone far beyond the family and the individual gets caught up in the

general scheme of things soon after leaving the cradle. Indeed, I'm personally in favour of removing them from the care of almost always incompetent
parents as soon as they are weaned.

You remember my picture of the village where I was born? It served its
purpose very well, the idea of subtracting the little individuals from their
homes and teaching them to live together, using their young skill in
government and achievement of combined tasks.

I am looking forward to your coming with great joy. The tension is once
more almost unbearable.

Irma turned up yesterday with her young German lover, Peter the
sculptor. I bought them a drink at the Shelbourne and then escaped. They
were staying down at a place called Ashford in Wicklow, where the crook
McKenzie apparently has a house. They were going to tour Connemara in
Irma's car which Peter drives with German efficiency. She had a big story
about giving an exhibition of Madame Couve de Murville's painting next
November. I meanly whispered in her ear, 'And suppose the ministry has
fallen by then? Nobody is of less consequence than the wife of a former
minister, recently fallen.' She is going to stay until the 27th and I told her to
ring about the time of your arrival. We needn't answer the telephone if you
don't want to see her.

Behan has come back and told me in the street that he had met Marie
Tilyou at Coney island. She said, 'How is Liam? I'd love to see him again.'
You remember her?

Irma says that zona affects the brain. That was before I told her about the
possibility of Murville's fall. So it must have been something she heard and
not a deliberate bite. I really do believe it's right in any case.

I'll try to clean up the flat a bit before you come. It would be better if I
could write a few pages. Give my love to Laura and to yourself, dear Kitty,
my whole heart and soul.

                                                                                    Liam

---

418. KT TLS to Kitty Tailer
[from Dublin]   p.m. 23 September, 1961

Dearest Kitty,

I fulfilled your commission re Quirke [his caretaker] yesterday evening
and found him in great form, with his adoring wife by his bedside in a rather
dreary hospital which he appeared to adore. In any case they were both
very happy about a prosperous continuity of their mutual life.

Me *miserum*! What a lot of things one sacrifices in pursuit of the mysterious beauty that is really unattainable. The brightness of all brightnesses
that always vanishes when one comes too near.

Rain has begun this morning, so I'm glad I walked yesterday morning in glorious sunshine all the way to the end of the Great South Wall and back. That was good and the seashore did not look too forlorn. I saw great heaps of empty shells (sea-knives we call them in Gaelic) on the strand which stretched out naked even farther than at Saint Michel ....

I do hope all is going well in Lordland. Personally I have settled down to work and have not yet 'sunk back' into gloom, although that is undoubtedly hovering on the horizon in one of those appalling clouds.

Peter Marron telephoned last night and it appears that he is back again in Bray, so his mother must have recovered. I still did not see my way to making any reference to his sister's death, neither did I offer to see him. Poor man! he said Francis Stuart has now given up both horse racing and Jesus. What on earth has he got left apart from Gertruda[1] whom he brought back from Germany as '*apologia pro vita sua*', in other words a living proof that he had put away his love for Adolf Hitler and turned his face towards Israel?

Thank you again for that trip and for all the arenas and the journey back from Arles. I should have paid more attention to the road as I'm now travelling that way. Also for the proprietor of the tabac, where I saw the *soi-disant* Ricard salesman. You didn't know why I went back there twice, but he seemed ideal for one of the tavern-keepers on the day of Jack McNiece's death ....

Darling Kitty, I'm looking forward to seeing you in London next month. It's good that you're no longer so far away, although Messrs Boeing have murdered time, sleep too no doubt, but distance would be less pointed. I hope you don't get skeletal again, especially your little wrists. All my love,

Liam

[1] In fact Madeleine, baptised as Gertrude.

---

419. KT TLS to Kitty Tailer
[from Dublin]   p.m. 7 December, 1961

Dearest Kitty,

Thank you for the lettuce which arrived yesterday morning. I hope to post this today, although I've been '*enrhumé*' now for a week, badly since Saturday. That sounds a better word than 'flu. I suppose it originally meant 'in snuffles'. I didn't want to tell you on Saturday cos you sounded depressed a bit and worried. However, I insist on struggling to my work desk for a few words now and again, being in excellent spirits, together with being furious at loss of time.

Thank you for being interested in our friend Durham. After all we know him well, don't we? I hope I'll get him right. He's so rich one can't go wrong, except on the score of exaggeration, but then it's not his peculiar eccentricities that serve my purpose, just his character and face. A prop in other words, of the same calibre as Pierre, but more *distingué* and exotic and dramatic. There will be a good scene at Luigi's before the casino at Enghien. I am really more than optimistic right enough, in spite of the snuffles and the delay.

I'm waiting ardently for Monday week and a chance of getting rid of the snuffles down south. Let's hope it's not one of those winters with snow and tumbling mountainsides. At least there will always be a place to walk in the afternoons. What happiness! In any case, Kitty, I'm living my great times just now, as I always knew would happen .... I knew my end would be noble, like a falling star. I'm no longer afraid of my end, simply because I no longer think of it.

Thank you for putting me right about Israel. I've got the bitch spancelled now, tied down in her exact groove and unable to move therefrom ... I feel sure you're going to enjoy all these intricate machinations, darling.

What do you know! I got a letter from Stock saying they're going to pay me about two hundred pounds. Their bank has been ordered to forward the money through a Dublin bank. However, one will believe those foul Manhattan Indians when one sees their dough. It is apparently for a rag book of old Gypo brought out by Hachette in France *'et les pays d'outre mer'*. I was so surprised. I wonder how much do they *really* owe me?

I'm coming via Cork, darling, and will reach Le Bourget at about 1.30 p.m. December 18th. I'll give you the exact time later. In the meantime all my love and don't worry about my snuffles, because they'll be gone by then. I'm wearing all my heavy jerseys, neck pieces and three pairs of socks.

Liam

---

420. KT TLS to Kitty Tailer
[from Dublin]   p.m. 12 December, 1961

Darling Kitty,

Your letter just came and I'm glad things are going ahead with the apartment, no matter how slowly. Everything looks impossible at first to arrange. I would like you to meet me at Le Bourget if possible and drive down south next day, as it would help to arrive there in a car, since we have to find a place. How about that, sweetie pie?

It seems fitting under the circumstances to make that route once more with white wheels turning. It's all so exciting that I'm afraid at times .... My plane is supposed to get to Le Bourget at one-forty p.m. Damned if I know why they are going by Cork, except that it's hard to get passengers and they'll probably pick up some local Arab women or male crows. In any case Cork has a new airport. Of course the trip is made much longer, but I don't care. I'll be sitting there doing my games and going to land in France and meet Kitty. It's quite hard to wait peacefully for the big moment.

My cold is practically better, but I'm quite weak after it. The weather has now eased somewhat. I do hope I'll hold out until this is finished. I go on and on, don't I, darling?

Somebody is again looking for *The Assassin* for a film, but I don't think much of the prospect. The important thing is to get Foreman to pay. The Stock money didn't come yet, maybe not before I go. That will be a nuisance as I have to sign for it at the Bank of Ireland as before.

There's a lot of talk here about Cruise O'Brien and the scandal of his affair with Máire Mac Entee, the daughter of the present Minister of Health. The present population of Ireland is really beneath contempt, at least the bourgeoisie. They always hate people who try to give them 'the dignity of freedom', or just dignity *tout court*.

Kennedy seems to be handling affairs much better now, very well in so far as foreign affairs are concerned. Hurrah! Baseball will soon begin again and the players will go south to train. I went out to Lansdowne Road on Saturday and saw a wonderful Rugby match.

By the way the new hotel looks magnificent on its foundations. The first really big American operation in the country. Even the roots of the building smell of 'the big time'. Bechtel is the firm. Really a first class outfit by all appearances.[1] Poor old 'do it yourself' Sisk and McManamin[sic] are made to look so small and prehistoric. *Vive les Etats Unis!*

I'm reading a peculiar book about an airbase in Spain and the war between the airmen and the population. The American heroine is really attractive and quite a dish, both in body and in character. All my love until Monday, darling. *Please* be at Le Bourget airport.

Love
Liam

[1] The Intercontinental (now Jury's) Hotel.

---

421. KT TLS to Kitty Tailer
[from Dublin]   p.m. 25 February, 1962

Darling Kitty,

Thank you for the beautifully loving letter that I got yesterday evening on my return from Lansdowne Road, where I saw the Scottish team beat ours with brilliant ease. The only satisfaction was the cheer that rose when the news of France's victory over England at Colombes was announced by the Haut Parleur. '*Vive la France!*' a bearded man behind me cried with great emotion. '*La France eternelle!*' he continued and shook hands. I was on the point of saying, 'Tick, tick, tick, tock-tock!' Remember our broom bangs at the flats down below in Cannes?

I am writing this in haste, with a view to going up to the G.P.O.[1] and posting it forthwith, being ashamed of my failure to write earlier. I have such a hatred of letters. That wretched Lola has held me up, although she is very good, I think, as well as her husband Miguel, both bandits of course, but so polite and helpful to the story.

I am dying to know what sort of conversation you heard. *Le Monde* carried a large article on Israel's attempt to get into the Common Market. It's going to be damn common if they get in.

Yesterday, at Lansdowne Road, I heard a lot of young make savage remarks about Bobby Kennedy's invasion of Ireland. They were equally critical of the First Lady and the whole tribe. Oh well, one never knows how the cat will jump these days ....

I thought we had fixed April for my visit. Or had we? I don't want to spend a lot of money extravagantly, yet I must see you, Kitty. I just must. Why the big hotel on Quai D'Orsay? I thought we had quarrelled about the bill, but I don't suppose they'd mind. Yes, I must get over there. I think I'll send you a telegram before going out with this note. I had something to say which I now forget. *Quelle barbe!*

The weather is beastly cold but quite invigorating. The French tea is good, thank you. I'd love to see what gives in the flat. You must have a whale of time with notebooks. Isn't there a hotel opposite where I could stay, because you are sure to be around there the whole time.

The record player doesn't work at all, yet it looks so pretty and I can remember the sound of La Paloma, so it doesn't very much matter. Did you go to see Irma? By now she has probably become a Zionist again, so perhaps you had better keep away.

I see nobody so I have no news about local happenings .... My brain is blank and I can think of nothing to say. Please forgive me for knocking off, here and now. With all my love, darling, I simply must get out and breath air.

Liam

[1] O'Flaherty often mentions taking his letters to the G.P.O., though there was a letter box close to his flat, whereas the G.P.O. in O'Connell Street was more than a mile away.

---

422. KT TLS to Kitty Tailer
[from Dublin]   p.m. 9 March, 1962

Dearest Kitty,

I got my ticket yesterday afternoon for the plane leaving Dublin on Friday morning, the sixteenth, at 10.45 and arriving Le Bourget at 1.40 your time. If you are there in your car, we could take off and wander away somewhere. I thought we might kill two birds with one stone and go to Zurich, or wherever in Switzerland there are Russians buried in cemeteries beside American women. Yet that distance may be too far and the time of year inappropriate. Even so, I hate going anywhere without purpose and Switzerland, hateful as it is, is a momentary purpose.

I feel absolutely determined to buy another typewriter, since the present [one] is becoming insufferable. It never was any good, yet I am now committed to the type size, so I'll forage around for the same model, Smith Corona portable, but not defective. People here are so dishonest. They like to cheat in any sort of bargain, being so recently peasants.

.... I went out and got the *Irish Independent* but still don't know if there is racing today at Naas or not. There has been none in Ireland for some time now, owing to snow ... It's comforting to learn that some sporting affair at Cannes last Sunday was cancelled owing to bad weather ....

I went down to Bewley's and bought three pancakes, which I'm going to eat later with what is left of the Log Cabin. Ye gotta to keep warm this weather. I put all the blankets I could find on last night, in desperation. Have given up smoking again, so I feel rather confused in my thoughts. That's not unusual, says you. What I mean is, I'm dumber than usual.

That Peking book is not much good. Louise Lin Yu Tang is the writer. We should have known before we bought the book ... The pictures are beautiful but there is no history of Peking, which is what I hoped to get. What's the matter with trying to finish that book on Tibet, which I've been trying to do for ten years. Or I might try to finish my novel ... hush – Appalling thought! I've given up reading whodunits, they got unbearable, worse than westerns. You could shuffle the sheriffs and detectives around in the end, irrespective of the lot, or the place. I do believe the game is no longer worth the candle, but what can I do? It's the only game in town ....

Well, Kitty, it seems I have nothing more to say but to send you all my love and to repeat that I'll arrive Friday 16th instant at 1.40 p.m. your time, so please be there, at Le Bourget, and don't mind my being as sore as a skinned nose for want of a cigarette.

                                                                    Yours
                                                     Desperate Wade Mercer

----

423. KT TLS to Kitty Tailer
[from Dublin]   p.m. 28 March, 1962

Dearest Kitty,

I do hope you are getting better from the grippe. Curious thing, I myself got diarrhoea today, but I feel the worst is over and my spirits are up .... All morning I've being doing chores, stretching from my bank via the laundry to my rental firm. The goddam people in the laundry were frightful and in the ordinary way my loss of temper would have set me back considerably (if not into the Bailey or the Dolphin), however, this dual regime gives one reserves of strength.

I'm still in doubt as to whether I should have a small sum on Honeymoor, in the three-fifteen race at Lincoln. If it were at Lingfield there would be no doubt. The answer would be definitely no ....

Thanks ever so much, pie, for the lovely holiday and especially the South Western Passage, meaning the tidal crossing to Noirmoutier. I liked Paris too, going to the races every day, above all the day I spent in the *pelouse* at Saint Cloud. Also the man that picked on me at Enghien to maintain that *'ce con Briand est vendu'* – you remember? He kept rushing back and forth and shaking his fist in front of my eyes. *'Il a fait des conneries,'* he shouted in supreme rage. *'Il a fait les choses infestes derrière les tribunes.'*

Your thin wrists worry me, they look so weak. Yet they must have always looked like that. I do hope Laura is not going to change her mind, as I feel you are looking forward to her visit very much.

The weather here today is really appalling, drizzling rain and absolutely no air to breathe, everybody coughing and snuffling, cursing unkind Divine Providence for having created this island in the first place, obviously with bits and pieces that got mouldy somewhere in the back of God's store, shop soiled and got at by vermin in barrels or what not.

Perhaps I'll get up tomorrow at four o'clock in better spirits. The real reason for getting up early is that one cannot [see] the place at night, so one has the illusion of being somewhere else.

Listen Kitty, I just wanted to send you a word or two of thanks for the trip and to say that, like the character in Uncle Vanya, I shall go on to the end working for others, no matter what the end may be, like one of those roads that end nowhere owing to the politicians having spent all the money beforehand. Indeed, the do-it-yourself people were unable to complete their yard on that account. God knows what bookmaker got the yard money.

The two buns crumpled to pieces in my overcoat pocket, but I was able to get sliced brown bread from a little man in Parnell Street, together with milk and eggs. He even sent his son into a back room for a papier maché box to carry the stuff, including three cartons of milk.

I got a letter from Pegeen in which she talks about taking Japanese to schools, etc. She says Joyce is now teaching the children of the Czechoslovak ambassador to play the piano. Can you imagine? The Bolsheviks want their children to be just as dainty and proper as the Victorian bourgeois ....

Goodbye now, Kitty. I've decided to have a small sum on Honeymoor after all, in Kilmartin's shop across the bridge, and I have just time to post this farther down. God bless and cheer up and look after yourself and don't work too hard at the flat. Leave something for the next generation. All my love and thanks again, darling, for everything.

Liam

---

424. KT TLS to Kitty Tailer
[from Dublin]   p.m. 6 July, 1962

Dearest Kitty,

I got your letter last night and a cable this morning, for both of which I thank you kindly. Too bad that Peter, at least, was unable to meet you and that the trip was not particularly crowded with incident. In any case, you were going somewhere and that's what pleases you most.

My return to Dublin must have been the most appalling in my experience. By now, however, I have gloomily come back to a state of tolerant despair and am going ahead slowly with my work. In fact, I again suffer from the insane conviction that I may be able to finish the damned book. Otherwise everything goes on as usual, boring and sordid, viciously painful, like drawing one's fingernails along the surface of a smooth stone.

I did go to the Curragh, after all, to see *the big race* I felt it was sad and pathetic, the effort of this wretched little country, to get a place in the gambling sun, in competition with elegant people like the French and English, not to mention the enormously wealthy Americans. True enough everybody was boasting about so much money being spent, without a thought of the rotten canal near my flat, or the rotting pavements of this dying town, or the ragged fields over the countryside that lie untilled and unweeded, or the horde of young people that keep going away with their cheap suitcases every day. The Chinese, sitting around their bare table, sipping soup made from the scum that floats on village ponds, surely must be buoyed up to the starvation sticking point by noting the idiocy of the 'decadent west'.

It looks at the moment as if the Jews are going to fool the Algerians after all by splitting the F.L.N., as I could see clearly they were trying to do. It was apparently Honey Fitzgerald's crowd of Yids that pulled the trick and bought over Ben Khedda, just as Churchill bought Michael Collins in a similar coup. However, the issue is not yet decided and the great Emir Abdel Karim is returning to Morocco from Egypt, threatening to arm even the women 'as of old', in order to hurl the infidels into the sea. At least so the *Manchester Guardian* coldly foresees. Their lady correspondent was really delightful in her description of the traitorous Ben Khedda parade through Algiers. The vicious little woman, showing remarkable bitchy talent, dwelt almost entirely on the difficulty the wretched fellow had in keeping on his spectacles, which got blurred with heat and dust, fell off continually and finally got lost on the floor of the motor car in which he rode. Quite a clever girl![1]

It reminded me so vividly of a similar parade by the spectacled Arthur Griffith through O'Connell Street, with Michael Collins standing by his side, on their return from selling the Irish Revolution for a mess of sow belly and cabbage. The same ragged mob cheered and sang: 'Kevin Barry died for Ireland', then they packed their shabby suitcases and went to look for work in England to find notices on lodging house doors: 'No Irish or Negroes accepted'. Soup made from the scum of one's own ponds is far more dignifying.

Pegeen sent me a postcard from Paris and I gathered from her remarks that she was enjoying the town immensely .... I hope she doesn't join the Russian Orthodox nuns. In my opinion nothing is more depressing than faith in a dead god. Much better to spur one's proud charger hard and ride to hell.

It would be wonderful to get beyond Montecarlo and back to Paris before you return. Perhaps, who knows, the seed of creative energy may be germinating once more in my antique brain. I'll try hard in any case, spurred on by the desire to get at the main scene and give Little Father his new name, Alexander Nikiforich Ilin. I feel very lonely and lost without you as usual.

A man wrote from Washington University to say he was writing his doctoral thesis about my work. Funnily enough his name is Anthony Canedo.[2]

I did no more about the tax form and the man's insolent request that I should fill in a duplicate form.

I do hope everything is going well and that little Laura's tendon is mending. Don't work too hard. Can't remember when that wedding [is], or whether you'll be gone to Washington before this letter arrives. Look after yourself until we meet again for the tournament at Sète. All my deepest love, my darling Kitty.

Liam

[1] This passage, full of O'Flaherty hyperbole, refers of course to the French proclamation of independent Algeria (3 July), the new Prime Minister of which was Benyoussef Ben Khedda.

[2] Anthony Canedo's doctoral dissertation *Liam O'Flaherty: Introduction and Analysis*, University of Washington, 1965, was the first full-length study of O'Flaherty's work.

---

425. KT TLS to Kitty Tailer
[from Dublin]   p.m. 14 July, 1962

Darling Kitty,

I enclose your enclosure with my approval for the inclusion of 'The Pedlar's Revenge', glad you found it finally. One had quite forgotten that it was published by Ellery Queen.[1] I worked so hard writing the damn thing that losing it was a most unpleasant thought.

Thanks for your long letter from Holmdel. Why worry about the wheat being unneeded? After all its beauty is the end for which it was created. At least a field of wheat in all its golden bloom has often given me infinitely more pleasure than eating bread. A sated belly, says you, is a lying philosopher. I also enclose the letter from Egghead Toni Canedo, as you asked. Unfortunately, the poor fellow had the gift of ruffling my easily ruffled intellectual hair the wrong way and I was never once even tempted by the thought of answering. *A quoi bon?*

So the wedding is today and father sits at London airport with one of those last moment Pakistani immigrants (or was he a Trans-Himalayan Kirghiz peasant), grinning in insane ecstasy as they wordlessly touch their garments and gesticulate. *Bravo!* It is good, too, that we were right about Charlie's yacht bearing bonanza, rightly named in honour of the Main Street cretins whose Virgin fear made them sell and buy again. Although perhaps *Salve Lucrum* might have been a better title. 'Hail profit'! Remember? They found it written over a banker's door at Pompeii.

Dearest heart, I envy your journey to the steaming jungles of Georgia. The weather here remains appalling. Yet a barber said to me the other day, 'That little drop of rain last night was badly needed.' 'Thank God for it,' I said venomously, 'although it came a bit too late.' 'Ah yes,' he said, 'The ground is so scorched that we'd need a fortnight's downpour.' Only the senseless survive.

I got so melancholy that I set out to my bank that day for money to buy a record player, hoping that La Paloma would cheer me up, but I changed me mind on the way and I'm still melancholy. So now I am toying with the idea of getting those Switzer people to make me a suit, but that idea too is bound to be discarded, since all effort seems meaningless in these depths.

I got a letter from Pegeen about her trip to Paris. She seemed exalted by the subtle joys of that 'royal crown studded with the most gems of the human intellect'. How odd it is to watch the gradual change of another person's mind! If we could only shout in a commanding voice, 'Hurry up,

Pegeen!' the whole journey might be achieved in a few days or weeks ....

I feel muzzy having risen this morning at two. I think I'll walk to Baldoyle races and have tea with jam sandwiches in Mrs Walsh's tent. Maybe that would be too far. I'm afraid that I only like to walk from Cannes to la Napoule and around by Mandelieu and the Vannerie pour Fleuristes.

I found another book about the U.S. air force during the last war. It's hard to read, being one of those bloody stream of consciousness things à la James Joyce and Corncob Bill Faulkner, with ghastly sessions on dirty toilet seats and f—ing and s— strewn at random, like spittle dripping from an enraged idiot's mouth. However, this fellow Hershey has also read Balzac, or rather Priestley, giving technical details that might come in handy for a paragraph or two later.

That scene I wrote last winter at Cannes keeps maturing gloriously. It's now right up there and is, indeed, a field of golden wheat in its [own] right. The dance is also beginning to assume the proper shape. What an appalling way to live the last few years that should be spent in idle reverie! Opium, obviously, the heated ledge and the poppy hanging in sleep. Ay! how long ago it is since I worshipped the sated buck that horns his mate and the savage lioness ... to hell with this drivel!

I regret not having renewed the sub to *Le Monde*, they should be good on this affair in Algeria. The *Guardian* woman is letting me down badly. Even the *Herald* is far better. It's really beautiful, this march of Ben Bella into his native land, with his soldiers crying: 'Ya, Ya, Ben Bella!' Poor France. It was beautiful too when they were crying: *'Vive l'Empereur!'* from Arcola to Moscow. *'Allez-y, bande de couillons!'*

Hurry back Kitty, because it's very lonely here without you in the wilderness of thought. Well, here I go to post this letter at the G.P.O. Hope it gets there in time. All my love and *afuera todo el mundo*.

Liam

[1] 'The Pedlar's Revenge' had been published three times, *The Bell*, XVIII, June 1952, pp.148-161; *Collier's*, CXXXII, 25 July, 1953, pp.38-43; *Ellery Queen's Mystery Magazine*, VIII, November, 1956, pp.56-66.

---

426. KT TLS to Kitty Tailer
from Dublin.   p.m. 14 September, 1962

Dearest Sweetie Pie,

Here is a little note to thank you for the 'Haut Bois et Tambourine' and all the other memories, that lose their untoward characteristics at this distance and time, like all things do indeed when they are done in the company of one's beloved.

Here I am once more, dug in and determined to get beyond those chapters at all possible speed and without loss of rhythm. The weather is not bad at all as yet and it's cold enough already to kill all the flies.

I met Francis and his wife while coming out of the post office after paying my telephone bill. They gave me startling reports of Kirwan's behaviour. In fact he brought the police to poor Marron and made that hapless man fork out a sum of money. What for? Francis did not know. But Pat, the cunning crook, apparently persuaded the police that precious manuscripts had been stolen. Can you imagine? The fellow is undoubtedly insane by now. As long as one does not see him .... Now is the time, of course, for Marron to take the dive, if he ever can screw his stomach to that dire sticking [point], or perhaps, like our friend in the film, he by now finds suicide *'trop dangereux'*.

No other news of any sort. I did not yet contact Pegeen. My stomach has taken all this time to come round to scratch and this morning only was I able to get to work. I did, however, sleep all the hours I missed abroad. A diet of steamed plaice and potatoes seems most conducive. I also stopped smoking until this morning, when I was forced to capitulate, since whoever he is simply refused to sit down to the typewriter without his favourite weed.

I did like the little flat and I wish you would let them go ahead and take Paris tiles instead of those of Tourcoing, as I don't like the thought of your driving up there alone at times like these. *Le Monde* didn't begin yet, so I don't know what's going on, but somehow they are not times to wander the north roads alone in a car. I do hope Frances, *'la malade imaginaire'* won't let you down over the weekend. You looked so wonderful when you had all that sun on your lovely face, down below by the sea.

I am going out now to see *The Private Life of Walter Mitty* again, and to buy the *Herald Tribune*. The Giants have drawn level again and it's really a good finish in the National League. *Time* had all sorts of bright paragraphs this week about obscure places. I am already looking forward to London and long conversations with herself. Hope I don't break out in the meantime in search of conversation. It appears that Rugby football has begun, so I'll go to the matches and avoid the race course, which also happens on Saturdays.

Kitty darling, forgive me for having been so crotchety all the time I was in France. I really was very tense and unbearable, both to myself and to others. This typewriter seems to be working all right. Now goodbye, Sweetie Pie, and don't forget to ring on Tuesday morning. I feel better for having written you these few words, because I love you very much, miss you very much and worry about you very much. So all my dearest love, darling, *hasta luego* and *afuera todo el mundo*. I keep hearing the *haut bois* and drums and see the sweep of oars and the way the jousters spread their legs so wide at the moment of combat. I also taste that dreadful *vin blanc du pays* and the glasses of beer by the railroad. Ugh! All my love, again and again, sweet darling.

Liam

In 1962 the film rights of *Famine* were being discussed by A.D. Peters. Brian Desmond Hurst (who had filmed *The Playboy of the Western World*) offered five hundred pounds for a six months' option and a further fifteen hundred pounds if the option were taken up, and finally four thousand pounds when the film cleared its costs plus five percent of the profits. Later in 1962 a draft script of the screenplay was sent to two actors who might be involved.

For some twenty years, on and off, there had been discussion of filming *Famine*. Of all O'Flaherty's work, however, it is *The Informer* which has continued to excite the most dramatic interest, and in the sixties, though all radio and television rights on this novel were held by R.K.O.\Radio Pictures, O'Flaherty amended his agreement of March 1960 with Hilton Edwards and Mícheál MacLíammóir on the dramatic performing rights. There continued to be enquiries about dramatising or staging the novel. For example in 1965 Kermit Bloomgarden Productions of New York took an option on a musical play to be called *Gypo* for three thousand dollars the first year (half of which went to Edwards and MacLíammóir), two thousand dollars the second year, and one thousand dollars the third year. During 1965 cables went to and fro between Peters and the elusive O'Flaherty, finally traced in Cannes, and there was a long wrangle over the dramatic rights of *The Informer*.

---

427. KT TLS to Kitty Tailer
[from Dublin]   p.m. 13 March, 1963

Dearest Kitty Pie,

Here I am, beginning to write a letter as promised and cursing the facility with which I make promises and then have to keep my word, especially to you. As I get older the idea of putting finger to typewriter becomes more and more repulsive.

I managed to catch this grippe, or was it in France? But have stoked up copiously on that wonderful drug and put on underwear, *gilet de corps* is also used, if one is to go by the bloody Belgian Simenon. In any case, I am still waiting to go to work, as soon as I have finished this letter, although I did get up at four and went through all the preparations and then corycidin put me straight to sleep, almost before I got my second pair of pants off again. Now I feel much better.

To go on with the story. I paid all bills yesterday and sent off the income tax half gale in a letter franked by the bloody Tammany government. Then I paid Quirke five pounds. The son of a bitch almost grabbed it out of my hands (they only half cleaned the windows, he and blind Mick). Then I got mad and went over to Kilmartin's and put two pounds on Honour Bound in the first race at Cheltenham and got back my Mick and Quirk money plus one or two more pounds. So I don't feel so bad about the dirty windows and the fact that the swine left so many letters in my box without sending them on, so that the telephone people cut off my phone yesterday morning and I had to go to the place with my receipt to get it put on again, and told everybody in a loud voice what I thought of Irish politicians and of the horde of office rats living at the taxpayer's expense. It must have been good fun for any other taxpayer listening.

Then I got my hair cut and told the barber about having seen Berg riding at Cagnes sur Mer. Whereupon my barber yelled out to all the other barbers in the room (at the Maison Prost), 'Hey lads, Mr. O' saw young Berg riding in the South of France!'.... I bought and devoured a chicken with the rest of the money won on Honour Bound.

In spite of the grippe, which is really slight, I feel in great form and on an immeasurably more even keel than I have been for a quarter of a century. The Simenon I bought (or rather you bought) at the French airport is quite good. I must go ahead now without fiddling about and get off the Côte d'Azur with all possible speed. I mean this Simenon book has got a character a bit like Isabel, *la petite comtesse* somebody or other. Still, Simenon is such a poor writer he has no idea what constitutes an attractive woman in that milieu. He only understands people who run and frequent zincs and small bistros, etc, ... Did you start to read Maugham yet? ...

I read somewhere yesterday, *Daily Telegraph* I think, 'Relations between the Irish and ourselves have not been so good for the last seven hundred years.' As the saying goes, it takes a lot of trouble to know one's real friends. What do you know about that? Proper lot of bastards!

I do hope you have not lost your temper with the workmen again and worked yourself into a state, and wrung your hands in anguish. Thanks awfully for putting everything shipshape here. The smoking jacket is beautiful again, all mended like new, with a note on it, under where it says 'Harrods', 'Dry cleaning essential'.

I really do feel super confident, and it's an odd feeling for a bloke like me, so used to up and down jitters. This old man alcohol must be a four letter word ... he certainly gave me a lot of trouble while he was around. Must be a character like Kirwan ....

Those slum people next door, the Tourist Bureau building, have finally started to finish the backyard. At the moment I hear hammering inside the high wall they built ....

Dear Kitty, I hope this letter will do you for a long time, because it has left me plumb exhausted, out on my feet, everything from bursitis to barley horses. All my love, darling, and thanks a lot for everything, everything, everything.

Your Irish Liam

428. KT TLS to Kitty Tailer
from Panoramic La Croisette, Cannes   p.m. 8 May, 1962

Dearest Kitty,

The trip from London to here was wonderful, flying over the Alps. I never saw anything so beautiful as the snow-covered peaks, in streaks of black and white. It was really quite extraordinary and made me want to paint. I was also rather frightened at the difference between the next door peaks and the far away ravine bottoms just beyond.

It's wonderful being back in Cannes. I have really felt happy all the time since my arrival, even though I managed to catch a cold before leaving Dublin and it is bothering me a lot. However, I got up at four this morning and stayed out until nine walking. The concierge and his wife had the bed made for me and some food installed, so I paid off with fifty for good will right away. Saw the secretary this morning and she said a maid would come tomorrow at nine, so I'm all settled in again, so to speak.

They have *not* done much further to the croisette promenade except that cars can function back and forth. The trees also look quite settled down already. A man was hosing them at four-twenty as I passed the Carlton. The beach is finished and looks magnificent.

Right now at 2 p.m. quite a number of tall Germans, female, are doing nudism on the beach in front, yet I don't feel that Summer has arrived. Mrs Buddle's horse got short headed in the English two thousand Guineas yesterday. There was a good piece in *Time* magazine about the new oil Sheik of southern Arabia, very amusing poker faced writing.

I hope you are having everything your way chez Laura and that she's willing to do whatever you want her to do.

I bought a filet (quite mignon) on my way back this morning ... the filet was real food, but I'm afraid was not cooked properly by your correspondent – too fast, fast Willie ....

God, it's so nice to be here and not in Dublin. It really is a nice place, once you get used to looking on it as a real town and not a frigging brothel-cum-jag place. Don't seem to be many people around this house. Hope I can get a few pages done this time .... How often have we heard that song?

Well Kitty this is all the letter you're going to get this time, so make do dear heart, and accept all my deepest love.

                                                                Liam

---

429. KT TLS to Kitty Tailer
[from Dublin]   p.m. 4 August, 1963

Darling Kitty,

Here I am true to promise writing you a note and enclosing a queer cutting from the *Daily Express* of Laura's former boy friend, now in the news vaguely by marriage of sister to 'that turd Profumo'. Thanks ever so much for beautiful cable and kind unbelievable statement which I duplicate *de ma part*.

I feel in great form and am working away on this chapter which seems finally to be breaking up obediently into words. Let's hope this mood and condition of mind is a little [more] permanent than usual. You know how it is, Kitty? In any case, I didn't feel at all depressed coming back and the good weather still persists, although today is heavy and humid, but it's great not to wear a jersey at night in this country.

I bought a whole lot of food yesterday, since tomorrow also is a holiday. Have to slow up on eating in view of belly. Got a little off already. Am going today to Croke Park where Galway is playing Kerry at football. Hope it's not too bloody stuffy there. No money from Peters, just a letter from Montgomery wanting me to sign a Yugoslav contract for a new edition of *The Informer*. He says they are going to pay in future through the British-Yugoslav trade scheme. Maybe you could try to get paid through him for that amount for which you hold a note. The amount would come in handy right now for this impecunious individual. The rent and electricity bill amount jointly to thirty-two pounds, that makes less of a hole than I feared since the telephone bill was not there. It's funny writing about priceless sapphires and champagne under these sordid circumstances, however, that makes it all the more amusing ....

I do hope your trip goes well and that Georgia is going to surprise you by being far better than you expected. Indeed I'm not going to be surprised if Laura finally insists on sharing your return plane, in order to inspect the flat, now that it's nearing conclusion.

I do believe the trip to Paris did me a lot of good. I have a new lease on life. Ah dear! When I look around and see all the people that have made a success of things and cunningly built up fortifications against old age ... I don't know really that I have enough sense, even yet, to regret my folly ....

Darling Kitty, do hurry back. I so love to have you around, even as far away as Paris, somehow a prop is taken away when you cross the Atlantic. Even when they have Concordes that can do it in an hour?

I don't know but I suspect it's not going to make any difference.

The Giants looked good for a moment and then began to fade again. I guess that's the story on this year's baseball. I see they have folded the film industry out at Bray. What a lot of money the Irish government poured down the drain on that too! Stupid people, they could have made it pay with a little courage and less respect for their witch doctors. *Mais, je m'en fous.*

Do you remember the days of '*afuera todo el mundo*'? Well, I seem to be much better than I was. Was it Pegeen said that one gets less depressed as time goes on? *Olé*! It's nearly twelve and I must eat something before going to post this on my way to the football game. So dearest heart, dearest little heart, loveliest little Kitty heart, I must say goodbye and send you all my love to do with it what thou wilt. What futile language this thou business! God bless, Darling, and *à bientôt*.

Liam

---

430. KT TLS to Kitty Tailer
[from Dublin]   p.m. 22 August, 1963

Darling Kitty,

It was wonderful getting your cable because I was at my wit's end with worry owing to not having heard. Your letter came yesterday. Too bad the brouhaha got too much for you, as I was afraid it might. I do hope that the journey does not knock you out still further. Poor little Kitty, you do get involved in so many things, far beyond your strength. Well darling, it's exciting hearing about your return trip already, and I hope the kitchen will be ready when you get to rue de la Paix, otherwise it will be rue de la Bagarre, or will you just wring your hands and tearfully announce that you have been made an *'objet de ridicule'*? Personally I think both the bed and the kitchen will be ready, in which case you are practically installed and there will only be the pigeons to deal with severely.

I don't know about telephoning me on Wednesday 28th, that costs an awful lot of money, which is unfortunately necessary to maintain me alive. I have none at all left now. Could you send two hundred dollars right away for September? I only have the rent to pay during that month, the remaining pounds will be ample for my needs. This month was bad because I had everything to pay and Peters has again failed to find me anything. I daresay the people who pay are all away on holidays.

Some bastard just knocked on the door and gloomily handed me the enclosed as coming from Mr. Ryan of Bachelor's Walk. What the hell does that mean? I understood it was not due before October? Under these circumstances one finds it difficult to think or achieve anything. In fact one feels that Ward took the right way out, but then how could one even get enough sleeping pills?

I adore your descriptions of lunches with Laura at Barclay's pool .... The delightful Mr. Krushchev announced yesterday in Yugoslavia that 'Henry Ford was a great man'. Took the Russians a long time to get around to that idea. Might have saved themselves a lot of trouble to have learned that wisdom forty years ago!

I just read about Rome the whole time now, the Mediterranean area 2300 to 2000-1700 years ago. This morning early I read a delightful paragraph in Plutarch's life of Pompey about some ruffian in the Roman Forum who dumped a bucket of dung over the chief magistrate's head. That too reminded me of Mr. Krushchev who threatened to make the Albanian Ho-ha lick off the similar basket of dung hurled into Nikita's face. There must be something significant in a mystical sense about a hamper of that nature. I laughed and laughed thinking about what the Consul Clodius looked like after that douche!

I still keep forging ahead at a snail's pace. A mean and spiteful fellow, this Plutarch, a Greek writing about his Roman masters, in the way that an Irish nationalist would have written about the English round about Queen Victoria's reign.

I finally heard from Pegeen who has returned to [London], looking as she said, like a duck egg on account of sun freckles. I also got a card from Joyce saying Switzerland is a foul place without any horse racing.

You'd better make your plans about September when you arrive. I am not in a position even to make a minor suggestion. Have not been in such a precarious state for the longest time .... I read Xenephon's *Anabasis* again with great delight. I do wish there was something new to read. This cursed town is like a desert for a man interested in things of the mind solely. A cursed blasted desert, a rotting corpse that was once part of a dying Empire.

Goodbye now and I do hope you are in better health when you read this and I hope to see you very shortly, darling one.

Liam

---

431. KT TLS to Kitty Tailer
[from Dublin]   p.m. 16 October, 1963

Darling Kitty,

This is the Bread and Beaujolais note that I promised. I do feel better today, but not what you would call fighting fit, far from it. The various chores I had to do in the morning left me pretty low and I had to return to the couch, from which I have not arisen. Having warmed up the remainder of this morning's tea I'm trying to write to my darling to thank her for the beautiful holiday in France and even for the slag heaps, whose size was indeed impressive, and the pink plastic inlays on the corridor walls in the Arras hotel (where the little boy with two dogs refused to be seduced by Kitty and maintained a Nordic silence). Most of all I liked the beach at Le Touquet, in spite of being unable to plough over that beautiful sand for mile after mile. How lovely the sun was going down! All in red, all in red, he sank down into bed, down in the ocean where we could not see.

I bought a turbot and black sole and a nine shilling chicken, thus leaving the sirloin and chops for Friday, Saturday, Sunday. In any case I went out again and bought carrots, onions, dates, bananas, milk, potatoes, bacon and loaf of bread. So that I am now fortified and even if old man 'flu gives me a parting shot, out of sheer Semitic malice, I can lie quietly on my couch, all in red, all in red, on my old Clery's bed, utterly indifferent to the slings and arrows. However, I wish I could feel up to the point. I took a vitamin pill just now and don't feel any result. On the contrary, it hit me in the gizzard, a sort of ulcer nag ....

They go on calling Scott Fitzgerald a genius, I mean *Time* magazine. I wonder why? I got a letter from an Englishwoman named Josephine Bondy. She says: 'I have read *The Informer* several times, but am particularly keen to read 'The Rat Pit', 'Moleskin Joe' and some others, but particularly those three which several booksellers tell me are out of print.' Can you imagine? She thinks it disgusting that my books are not available through a library. After that let's have no qualms of conscience or of anything else about bringing out our novel under a *nom de plume*. Who wants to read a novel by the author of 'Moleskin Joe'?

I must write to Pegeen now, then I can begin tomorrow on an even keel. My sweetest darling pie, you have no idea how fond I am of you and how much I love you because you get more charming and irresistible every day, except that you are so thin that I worry about you breaking in pieces suddenly, especially going about on that ferocious Parisian *'transport en commun'* cheek by jowl with Spaniards that sleep in tanyards and bidonvilling Algerians ....

I do hope nothing further goes wrong and that all these people will finally agree not to make my beloved an object of ridicule, especially the bed woman as you rely on her ... I ain't much good at writing letters any longer, dear one. In fact, I ain't much good at writing, period. I hope you won't mind my ending the affair at this point, beloved, this 'flu has taken more out of me than is gentlemanly .... All my love, Kitty Pie, all my love, darling and keep your fingers crossed for me to go ahead and ahead, ahead and ahead the whole time, go right ahead, go right ahead.

Lunatic Ducky

---

432. KT TLS to Kitty Tailer
[from Dublin]   p.m. 10 November, 1963

Darling Kitty,

Here is the note I promised. The rain is coming down in torrents, as it has been doing for days, in order to prevent this ducky from breathing probably. Another plot by those people. I decided to let this typewriter slip as it willed, in order to show you they didn't clean it at all, and just for fun it hasn't slipped once so far, has it? Another plot!

I do hope you heard something good about the kitchen ... I'm just hanging on by the skin of my teeth to the hope of finishing this goddamned book, which I love so much in spite of everything. The impression of being encircled (and of the circle quickly becoming smaller) gets stronger every day. Yet when one boils it down to fact, the only adverse element is lack of money ... I am very pleased with that key chapter, before the dance. It was so hard to do and for a long time it appeared impossible to do, then finally it rummaged down somewhere and got its own *deus ex machina*. In any case, *ça y est maintenant* ....

I don't remember when you said you were going to London, but it won't be long before you ring on Thursday. I would like that magazine. I'm damned if I can [find] the copy I had, it's called *China Quarterly Review*. Would you look it up in the telephone book at twenty Chesham? I know the address is Oxford Street, but I've forgotten the number. I would like to get the past several numbers. They are very good, the chaps hired by whoever to write that stuff. Did you see in *Time* where Shanghai surgeons sewed on a severed hand and enabled the renewed hand to play ping pong! All that remains now is for the rejoined hand to win the world championship at ping pong. That will put Krushchev in his place and prove that He and not Mao is the foul dogmatist and modern revisionist.

I feel half dead and am beginning to have a sobering conviction that the other half is just beginning to have had enough, so how far am I going to get in this slow motion *'course contre la montre'*? Maybe not very far ....

Here goes, Kitty, this is the end of your note, all my love and *afuera todo el mundo*, without any sombre significance.

Liam

433. KT TLS Kitty Tailer
[from Dublin]   p.m. 5 March, 1964

Dearest Kitty Pie,

Here is the promised missive, let's hope it's gay. I have just about dug in again, having paid all outstanding bills and commitments, which leaves me enough to go on with – awful to end a sentence with a preposition.

They had no rain here for six weeks before my return. It has rained every hour, on the hour, since then .... Quirke, in spite of his beautiful letter, did nothing at all to the flat, as far as I can see. I didn't get that parcel of medicine from him yet, which he told me he was holding, when I paid him the two pounds for not cleaning the flat. He has become completely corrupt by now.

Mentally I have not quite settled down yet, not quite finished with my depression yet ... I do hope the painter, the carpenter and others are going ahead with your flat. You must be coming near the end of your tether by now ....

I saw Garech Browne in the street, accompanied by a choice gang of satellites, including one young Irish Lord and two English Lords, all happy and gay as if they had stepped out of Fielding's epoch. Garech is a card. He was wearing a bawneen in absolutely filthy condition. Young Gormanston, the Irish Lord, was immaculately dressed, simply because he has not got a single bean. *La vie est bien drôle, n'est ce pas?*

I want to thank you again for all your kindness, dear Kitty, especially for driving me back from the coast. Somehow I have a premonition that it was a farewell trip. I felt that the effort took a lot out of you and I was sorry to have subjected you to it.

I read in *Newsweek* what you told me about the Chinese bowing to the *femmes de chambres* and giving them huge tips. Seems the wrong thing to do, because once you start it you've got to keep it up and the day comes when, like the day Armand Sossian met Pepe Le Moko and decided that he couldn't possibly shake hands with the fellow ever again, so he made a deadly enemy, simply by going past with his head in the air.

Apparently Behan did not die. The taxi driver told me he was not hit. He merely hit the ground himself, 'And he loaded. After all, the unfortunate man had already hit everybody and everything else. The bloody road was all there was left to hit.' Apparently the wretched Behan made two children at the same time and one was born in Dublin, the other in New York, just about the same evening, thereby pleasing nobody, so to speak. I asked the taxi driver about the boom that was supposed to be in Ireland. 'The whore's bastards,' he said, 'are now spending our money on foreign journalists, telling these dirty lies about us and we dying of hunger. Is there no justice on this earth, or do we have to start shooting again?' Even so quite a number of tall buildings are sailing up to the high heaven around the centre of town. At the same time a lot of old women are on hunger strike in ruined unused jails where the inhabitants of fallen tenements have been put in 'cold storage', so to speak. Several more tenements have fallen during the winter.

I saw the ex Miss Rich with her daughter in a go car and I had forgotten to wear my dark glasses, so I had to look stolidly the other way. I hear they are selling 'holy pictures' of J.F.K. in the churches at Mass time, 'killed by the Communists' ....

It's quite warm in the flat and I have slept well so far .... Yesterday I listened to one of the races at Cheltenham, it sounded great, but I no longer have any desire to bet on these things ....

Dearest Kitty, I do hope you are well and happy. This missive has now gone far enough. I am already looking forward to seeing you when you get off the plane. It's not at all cold here, so I was right to bid farewell to the fair Astronomet overcoat.

Love from
Liam

---

434. KT TLS to Kitty Tailer
Panoramic, S. France   p.m. 8 April, 1964

Darling Kitty Pie,

Here I am in bathing trunks holding my stomach back and feeling rather good about everything. All that jazz thrust aside and my dance looking very like a winner at last, being on its last bloody legs, thanks be to whatever gods there are these days.

I went down to the post office early and got your letter, with enclosure, and to celebrate bought myself a dish of bacon and eggs with a grand café au lait at the Maison du Porto, all of which was excellent, especially your dear little letter. Thank you so much darling.

I hope everything goes wonderfully well in London and that they leave little Thomas with Kitty while they go cycling, or whatever the plans exactly are. In any case it will be wonderful for you to see the family. Now that your apartment is practically home and dry life will become much more full and resplendid for you, I feel. You might even [give] yourself without stint to the odd brioche. This last is, however, the French argot for a 'gut' or a corporation, the sort of thing I have. Even so my brioche, or *bedaine*, seems inclined to let itself be held in check.

I certainly will have the dance finished before you come, together with a few pages of the next chapter. Of course there will be a lot of rewriting and polishing of the dance before I'll bid it a final goodbye, but I'm rather pleased, especially as I had never complete faith in my capacity for doing it successfully. It was a tall order and there was a strong doubt about my stamina and intelligence.

What do you know about Santa Claus? I had one of those hunches about the horse, as soon as I heard the name muttered last winter before I left Dublin. However, I think it's about time to quit betting except on the smallest scale, the royal maximum being the doom of many men, as Davy Byrnes said in *Ulysses*.

I certainly agree about Goldwater. If he gets the nomination it will mean the Yids can collar the Republican organisation before the next election. In that way they would have both. It's like betting on pelota, when you move from blue to white and back again at the right moment.

Well Kitty, all my love darling. I must post this now and hurry back to get on with page six. I really am in a hurry to get rid of this burden. Thanks again for everything, *Siempre*

Liam

---

435. KT TLS to Kitty Tailer
[from Dublin]   p.m. 10 August, 1964

Darling Kitty Pie,

Thank you for the cablegram which came yesterday morning. I was so glad to hear you had got there safely. In spite of the plane's size on the ground it looked terribly small in the sky, and quite unfit to cross the Atlantic. I suppose by now you are ready to go on and that you have heard 'all about Laura'.

On this front all is quiet and well. Am into my chapter and have put the cigarette cartons down in the cellar, as I thought it would bring bad luck to throw them down the chute. The flat still looks beautifully clean, the way Kitty left it. I really will try to brush it now and again, especially the kitchen which depresses me terribly when filthy.

Yesterday I walked up to Croke Park and saw two wonderful Gaelic football games. One was very exciting because my county was trying to defeat Meath and did so to everybody's surprise. Like children the supporters of the losing team went away in dead silence, while the Galway supporters shouted, sang and cheered, swaggering back through the slums into O'Connell Street. They looked such strange young men and I saw a wonderful trio of terribly Nordic looking women from the Tuam direction, just about where you went to see your servant that day. They were very tall and gaunt and had light golden hair and wild blue eyes, just as if they had come off a Viking long boat. Then others, mainly young men, were so very dark and wild faced, purely Spanish. All from the one little place.

Everything seems to have died again, and quite a number of the writers in yesterday's English Sunday papers mentioned that Johnson probably started all the trouble to queer Goldwater's pitch. The *Observer* was quite snarky about it. I got a sort of whodunit that is quite fun, the life of Arnold Rothstein who was shot in 1924.[1] It is really better than a genuine whodunit, written by a Jew of course .... It was lucky I got that one on my way home after leaving you, because I bought two other books I had read before. What a day of money down the drain! I didn't go to the Horse Show after all ....

I got a letter from Pegeen. The lunatic has already begun to learn Greek and now knows how to say 'our car is green'. Of all the languages that could be of less use to her financially. It's not even classical Greek which would enable her to read Greek literature. It's her life. She said she had to stay in bed for five days after her return.

I shall be eager to hear whether you have turned over any tortoises or got some of their eggs, that would be rather wonderful. I mean turtles ... do they make the soup from the eggs or the flesh? I have never eaten any .... Dearest Kitty, you are so far away, and I love you so much. I wish you wouldn't go so far away. I also wish I had been less barbarous when you were here. Poor little Kitty pie, there is so little time left and I don't want to spend any of it waiting, waiting, and then waiting once more.

The dance has completely disappeared. This new world is so odd without the dance, quite another world. Maybe it will never come back ... Dear Isabel, I can hear the Paloma and the Ojos tienes again with nostalgia, now that the dance has gone. I played them yesterday for a long time.

I see that sweep ticket you bought lying on the desk. I forgot all about looking at the paper in question. '*Compra por cinco pesetas una centesima, la tirada esta noche en Francia!*' You remember the blind vendors in that appalling town selling lottery tickets?

You're going to have an awful job sorting out that stuff at Stamford. Certainly don't bother with any books of mine, except things written by myself, of course. And I do hope you get something for the flat. It's so beautiful, your flat. I often remember my trip of intimidation to Tourcoing [to buy tiles for Kitty's kitchen]. Naturally I refused to be there at the last moment. In any case I was not impressive, no cigar, no ten gallon hat. [i.e. the typical American.]

Goodbye now, darling beloved Kitty pie, and take great care of yourself so that I may see you soon again, ever so soon again and a tiny bit fatter. Maybe some turtle soup? Hope you find the grandchildren well down there. Goodbye again and all my deepest love,

Liam

[1] Leo Katcher, *The Big Bankroll: The Life and Times of Arnold Rothstein*, London: Gollancz, 1959 and 1963

436. KT TLS to Kitty Tailer
[from Dublin]   p.m. 31 August, 1964

Dearest Kitty Pie,

Just went downstairs and got your letter. I want to thank you for sending me the cable and talking to me across the ocean, very lovely, only I thought you sounded depressed and tired. Therefore I was delighted to learn just now from your letter that the doctor found you in excellent form and even better than last year. God Almighty! There's going to be no holding your energy from now on! ... This aged selling plater is by no means in that fortunate condition. Change of stable required. But then he might be like the famous German horse that wanted to be at stud when he was in training and wanted to be training when he got into stud, and loathed the chore of servicing more than one mare.

I have never in my life felt so unhappy in Dublin and bewildered by the horror of maybe having to die here. How odd to hate any place so much, yet I always did. Always. I'm getting nowhere with my book. Come to think of it I have written nothing here for years, not really. No doubt that bloody dance is still with me. I wrote it again and put it away carefully at the end of the rest of the MS, but does that really serve my purpose?

Joyce rang me on my birthday, but not Pegeen. Maybe she wisely felt that a birthday was not a thing I want to remember any more, if I ever did. Joyce says Pegeen passed her Russian exam and has been upgraded by the F.O. in the matter of pay, nothing to do with the exam of course. Joyce herself was having another concert, and is going off to France or Switzerland for her holiday.

Otherwise I live a recluse's life for the reason that I cannot afford to do otherwise .... In spite of everything I bought the London Jewish papers again yesterday and there was a funny piece about Shanghai shoppers ordering pants, I mean women of course, which were tapered down below. The sales ladies accused them of being modern revisionists! Wouldn't you think money would be saved in the present dangerous circumstances by such tapering – less cloth surely ....

I just can't stop reading this fellow Ian Fleming. It's a good thing he died, or I might go on reading the appalling bastard for the rest of my unfortunate life. I found out all the people he robbed for copy, mainly Dumas and Verne, although he didn't draw the line at taking chunks from respectable folk like John Galsworthy. Still, like Simenon, another great thief, he had a lot of talent and is quite delightful to read in parts.

I suppose you do not know when you are coming back? ... Dear Kitty, forgive this drivel, but I do feel terribly lonely and abandoned by everybody. Serves him right, says everybody, idle and without chores to do. However, the doing of this chore seems to require a more complicated organisation than I am able to afford, and certainly not able to organise without the sinews of war necessary for an old person to procure what he requires. A wounded cormorant does not attract support. It only attracts the dagger and the poisoned arrow of the hitherto too cowardly assassin.

I got another cold on Saturday while using the *'transports en commun'* to reach O'Connell Street and buy the *Herald Tribune*. A woman kept blowing myriads of germs, by means of coughing, into my face .... I finally took two more of those damned red pills last night and don't feel so bad this morning .... Still, there's no heat in this flat and it's already Winter. I might as well put on underwear and have done with it ....

Darling sweetie pie, *all* all my love, dear love, and love me kindly till we meet again. I kept remembering during the past few days sitting with you on the boat going across to the {?} islands and coming back again. How tender it was! How gentle! Also watching the crabs and little fisheen to which we threw bread. *Afuera,*

Liam

---

437. KT TLS to Kitty Tailer
[from Dublin]   p.m. 12 September, 1964

Darling Tired Sweetie Pie,

She who cooks and washes up and cares for children and then has to buy the liquor for Laura's party, to her I write two days beforehand, being now *très prudent* and *econome* by sending it ordinary airmail, it arrives at the same time for less money.

I have to smoke in order to write this chapter which intrigues me by its blasted and unexpected difficulty. After all it goes up and up and therefore has to be written the same way as the previous ones, only more powerful and fast.

I got your letter last night. The man got me out of bed at six o'clock to deliver. I felt you are rather sad. Because my last letter was sad? Yes it was, very sad. I am still sad but vainglorious. On his deathbed Plato rewrote the first page of his goddamn *Republic* which I could never read with pleasure or respect. Maybe my last words will have better luck with some future hapless creature cursed by my character and defects. In any case, despite bad headaches and solitude, I have again got carried away.

I happened to read the literary page of the *Daily Telegraph* the other night, having nothing else left by then (my Ian Fleming whodunits have run out, neither does Gibbon go with a pain in the forehead by day). This fellow was reviewing a book called *The English Short Story*, says he: 'The writer must be complimented on having the courage to mention Liam O'Flaherty, who has been most undeservedly and deliberately neglected and is now almost forgotten as a result and whose brilliance ... etc.' Well, I said to myself, this man knows a little about Liam O'Flaherty. After all, I deliberately saw to it, from away back as you say, that it was a good thing to get neglected, beginning with *I Went to Russia*, which thrust aside the Yids that were trying to use me as a battering ram for knocking the enemy Irish, continuing with *Shame the Devil*, which deliberately antagonised those that I suspected of corrupting me 'with enervating luxury and applause'. So here I am in solitude, trying to be a large fish that stays quietly at the bottom of the pool and ignores the silly bait which attracts small fry. That's all very well, said Kitty, *mais ... l'argent quand même.* If one could finish this the cursed money would come. If not, and I die in humiliating debt to my beloved, I die trying to reach the moon, or Mars, or Venus, or trying to uncover the unique and unfathomable gift that shines with divine splendour in the naked beauty of her omniscient eyes. *Afuera todo el mundo!* If that is true this chapter will be the best. But will it get finished?

My head hurts like hell. I feel certain that cigarettes are responsible. Yet I had to go out and buy another packet to relieve tension, or to act as bait, I don't know which. I wish another copy of that magazine *Revolution* could be bought here, but unfortunately the Russian employers have put their foot down. The local purveyor of left books and papers does not even sell *China Reconstructs. Le Monde*, however, is getting better and better on this great subject of the Communist heresy debate .... *Time* is sometimes good but generally bad these days. If they only readopted their old cynical attitude to everything, including politics and what are called Foreign Affairs. True enough this anachronism of the Presidential Election is beginning to wear thin. Malcolm X, in some article in the *Saturday Evening Post*, said that Johnson and Goldwasser are a wolf and a fox. To the negro it does not much matter whether it's a wolf or a fox that eats them, but he prefers Goldwasser since he is less clever and easier to use as a scarecrow to attract negroes into his Muslim camp. Bright fellow that Malcolm!

Come soon Kitty, though I feel that you are going to be delayed. I have tried to make this letter a little more cheerful. Did I, darling? If not forgive me and think of me kindly, think of me always, if not with love, then not with pity, but amusement. Then maybe I'll ride like a gentleman of the Warwickshire man's England, in blood and hand in hand to hell, amazing the welkin with my broken staves, of course staves of song. Please write as often as you can, Kitty. Your letters are all I get, the only words I hear that I love. God bless, love,

Liam

---

438. KT TLS to Kitty Tailer
[from Dublin 8 a.m.]   p.m. 21 September, 1964

Darling Kitty Pie,

   I got up foolishly a little after midnight and am now completely fagged out and hungry, without having any tea to make tea, but I have two eggs and some spuds, so maybe I should cook them and feel stronger. I had better wait until the shops open at nine.

Darling, darling, I don't know how to tell you how thrilled I was to talk to you yesterday morning. I felt so low, absolutely low and you raised me up, away up beyond all hope of going so far up at once. There I was down in the lowest and most horrifying cavern of despair and Kitty put down her little hand, on the tiniest wrist and lo! she was able to pull me up. Go stay there now, little man.

You must be a wreck yourself after all that rummaging in warehouses. Laura, of course, must be no bother compared to the pleasure of being in her company. Bicker as you may and indeed do, I suppose there is a deep and unbreakable bond between the two of you, so different from the tenuous and never quite tight cord that joins you both to your two brothers. *Moi, je suis tellement solitaire.*

Irene telephoned the other day and I was surprised at feeling glad to hear from her, but only on the telephone. I felt glad she was going to attend an oyster festival in Galway the following morning and therefore out of bounds. If people are not congenial mentally why see them? Yet one longs for companionship.

This Isabel and Gerald, [characters in *The Gambler*] the complicated son of a bitch! I am crawling ahead all the same. Maybe I'll get a few pages done before you arrive. I have been sleeping in my study for more than a week but shall move today into the bedroom. First of all I must put sheets on the damn bed, that will be a pleasant change. Today I must send out laundry. A huge bag of it has been standing in the hallway for several weeks. However, I did scrub the kitchen floor the other day. These are senseless words but really, darling, I can just barely keep my eyes open, I know you will forgive.

The Cockneys on this floor, Dreaper Clemence, are having another civil war. Clem has broken out again and his wife came into my flat yesterday week to telephone, because their own had been cut off. She rang the Moira hotel for news of him, without result. He had been gone for days. I saw during the week that the glass in their door was smashed and now a board has been put up as a temporary measure. I suppose he did it on purpose. There is another woman opposite me now, an old maid with a most charming voice and a mannish friendliness, at least she talks every time we pass. The O'Connors have also come back, I saw them yesterday. I had forgotten his face, so that I was puzzled for a few moment when the strange man with white hair and an idiotic grin waved his arm in a peculiar fashion .... To be quite frank, I should not regret leaving this place for ever and at once. Even so, I have no desire to die until my book is finished. What an extraordinary obsession! It is, of course, born of my love for you, both my desire to live in spite of everything, as well as the desire to write on and on to the bitter end.

I can hardly contain myself with excitement at the thought of seeing you soon. How kind you are to take an interest in this unfortunate person. How strange it must have been to talk to Katherine Hepburn again and to see Connie. I can't think of Hepburn vividly but I remember all about Connie. After all the poor woman followed a vision of beauty, which is a good thing to do, even though it turns into something sordid and terribly sad.

Well my beloved sweetie pie, I'll say goodbye now. I love you with my whole heart and soul. I read Hemingway's story about the bullfighter again. It was so good. Also his 'Fifty Grand' and 'The Killers'. *Afuera todo el mundo*, give my love to Laura too,

Liam

1965

---

20 March, 1965, O'Flaherty wrote a now rare letter to A.D. Peters from la Croisette, Cannes, France, held by B.O.M., accepting the terms demanded by Hilton Edwards and Mícheál MacLiammóir to release their interest in all dramatic and musical rights in *The Informer* in return for one half of the first two option payments received from Kermit Bloomgarten of New York. He also agreed to give Jonathan Cape ten percent of everything he received for dramatic and musical rights in *The Informer*, both on option payments and royalties. O'Flaherty said he would be in Cannes until the end of March, and on 23 March he signed a letter to Cape (drafted for him by A.D. Peters) in which the ten percent terms were set out. In March 1968, Bloomgarten's three year option expired, and though he had acquired the film rights from R.K.O. a Broadway production of *The Informer* never came off.

---

439. KT TLS to Kitty Tailer
[from Dublin]   p.m. 28 May, 1965

Darling Kitty Pie,

Here is the promised note which I am sending by avion express so that it may be there on your return. I got very worried on reading your first missive, in which you admitted having a nose bleed. I rang your place on Tuesday morning and found that you were not there ....

I finally have tackled my work, the go ahead part, with some sort of hope for the future. Indeed, I have turned on some unknown reserve of energy and I am vaguely confident .... I have received no news from Peters yet. No doubt the appalling New York Kike has found another way for being difficult, unless he has decided, as his kind often does, to do nothing further in the matter. It may be all for the best, as I would undoubtedly have a good go at Seabird Deux, on next Wednesday, if the dough had arrived.

The rates bill came and I paid a half gale, as they used to say, also a telephone bill that was only four pounds something. Otherwise nothing has happened ....

I rewrote that first 'lyrical passage', morning at Nîmes, which proved so difficult. The effort to put it on a par with the others, the soliloquy and the dance, was not altogether a success. However, it now possesses a neat and succinct superficies. Oh, what queer words! Perhaps, after all, we shall live to see the end of this 'intolerable affair', as '*le vieux* A.D. Peters' said about the musical ....

I am looking forward to your coming, darling. Even with the weekly visit of Mrs Fuller this business of looking after myself is a crashing power that devours energy. Even so, this recrudescence of hope is exciting. I smoke and drink but manage to keep on an even keel, which is unusual. One really does not know what to do with an unruly machine like mine.

I was terribly amused by your description of the Chinese show in Paris and read it to Barney Emmart, who laughed and laughed. He really is a very deep and intelligent fellow. 'She looked so young and gay, poised on a leopard skin rug before the blazing fire of pine logs.' After all, we have a few good moments from my long pregnancy. [i .e. with his book]

Hoping that everything is all right and that the nose bleed has not recurred, I'll finish this note and hasten to the G.P.O. and then get the laundry we left, which is still there. With Mrs Fuller coming that will probably be the end of my work today. In any case one can write anywhere, if the going is good and the pitching arm feels loose and intelligent up there on the mound.

Time had a delightful article about Manager Lopez of the Chisox. However, their efforts at praise generally put the voodoo sign on a guy, like they did last year with the Orioles.

Goodbye now, darling love, goodbye and good luck. Take it easy, play it very cool and close to the shift, since you don't wear a waistcoat.

Muireadach the Arrogant

---

440. KT TLS to Kitty Tailer
[from Dublin]   p.m. 23 July, 1965

Darling Far Away Kitty Pie,

This is really a bread and butter, rather than a re-establish contact letter, on account of the Pierrefitte book arriving unexpectedly last night. I thank you so much, for that disgusting man has apparently done a really good book on the Vermine Universelle.[1] I laugh, laugh and laugh. Just what I needed, a good laugh ....

I expect to get something done finally, now that my liver seems willing to do a little work downstairs. Can you imagine, I have still got four bottles of milk undrunk. Have I taken a dislike to that too? Jesus! Everything just can't die on me like horse racing.

I saw Francis Stuart in the street yesterday and we talked a while .... Really he had nothing to say. Did I?

It was wonderful while you were here, dear pie, although you never wore your beautiful overcoat. Even so, it was so nice doing nothing much, just loafing around, in spite of my liver it was really nice. Except that I cut up rough once, with the result I got shut up in the dog house for a little while. There you were, standing in the doorway of the Boeing plane, talking to the hostess. I was very worried until I got your cable to say you had arrived safely. Now I look forward to September. The main thing is to hold onto that regime.

... This time you never really got a chance to unload your jag, which appeared to be full-tanked and enthusiastic to spill. Thanks for doing all those things. There is little to be done now, except pay Mrs Fuller week by week and purchase some meat *de temps en temps* from Galloping Houlihan. I just adore those white scones, now that I toast them on both sides and spread a little honey on them hot. With tea that goes in a very refreshing manner ....

I'm inclined to agree, on due reflection, that the Kennedys are undoubtedly Full Blooded Sheenies of the very worst Scandinavian type, if not indeed Latvian Mockies. By now I daresay you and Laura have torn the cover off the ball, whacking it round Bayonet Farm night and day ....

How odd, I suddenly fell asleep right over the typewriter. It's only eight a.m., but of course I got up at two thirty. Even so, my liver does not seem exceedingly robust as yet .... By now, says Kitty to herself, he's dog tired of writing this letter and he's filling in with any rubbish that comes into his head. So darling pie, I send you my deepest and most true love from the inmost core of my heart, for ever and for ever, God bless Kitty and send her back to me. *Je n'ai que toi ... je n'ai surement que toi.*

Liam

[1] This might be a dig at Roger Peyrefitte's *La Nature du Prince* (1963) in which he attacks the Catholic establishment.

----

441. KT TLS to Kitty Tailer
[from Dublin] p.m. 20 August, 1965

Darling Kitty Pie,

I don't know whether this letter will reach you before leaving for the south on 25th. Let's hope so, although there seems a grave delay below there in New Jersey. By now I daresay you have returned from Rhode Island. You get around, you certainly do, whereas this fellow just stays in his stagnant pool.

I gave myself a real Marine Corps hair cut yesterday, and I feel as if I had caught another cold, but I daresay it's imagination .... Today I've got to take my laundry out in a taxi, which I hate .... The barber has a lot of news about dire happenings being in the offing. As there are no local papers barbers have a heyday. How the bastards hear these things is beyond my ken. Finally I said to him in a dramatic tone: 'Know what I heard?' 'What?' he said. 'Johnson is going to press the button on 31st of this month at noon sharp.' He stared at me and asked, 'What button?' 'Ha, ha!' I said with a maniacal grin, 'Funny thing is, none of us will know, because there ain't going to be anybody left.' It certainly kept the fellow quiet until I departed ....

Wait for the Arc de Triomphe and your packet on Sea Bird. Alas, the local boys are now talking darkly of the invincibility of Darkie's colt that had a cough earlier in the season and is now rarin' to put the kibosh on the Froggie. It's a good thing people will never learn a goddamn thing, otherwise where would the wide guys be? ...

I heard no more from London, Pegeen of course. Maybe she went to Greece. Or is she scouting for a Crematorium in which to bury her Vieux? Pity that Walsh did not bring the pony. They really are lovely animals. Remember we saw one in Connemara one day after lunch at an English hotel. There was a sick mare on the ground and they brought a rampant stallion hoping that his erect member would make her rise and take part in life once more. She paid no heed, poor thing, and they kept whacking at her with a stick. A horrid sight, yet he looked very gay, the stallion, with his grey hide and his proud member rampant. He was so small and compact, faintly reminiscent of the Mongol Tumans in which his ancestors ran, crossing the Himalayas and the great Russian steppes and then down into Europe: onto the high, broad plateau of Castille, with a squat blue-eyed and golden-haired rider on his back. How the hell did they get to that dreary mountainside? Certainly not with Subotai. Walsh must have a good eye and a horseman's heart.

I hope you will have a good visit in the south. Maybe you will turn a few turtles this time and sail up through the queer river with the moss grown trees overhanging the banks. Strange country! All the earth is so beautiful and so strange.

On Sunday I go to Croke Park again to see Galway play Louth. I met a strange creature from Rosmuc. He was a helper to a bricklayer from Belfast called Anstruther. The Rosmuc man told me he was 'a son of Lucas's little dove', to put it in translation. He told me he was deeply attached to Anstruther, having no children of his own and because Anstruther was 'fascinated by disaster' and consequently constantly got into scrapes. Thereupon he pulled the thinnest blade you ever saw from his thigh and said: 'With this knife I defend him against disaster.' It was a lovely phrase, *'Is ait leis an anacain.'*

Goodbye now, lovely Kitty, to whom I send my love, for ever and always, until the Mongols ride again.

                                                                        Liam

---

442. KT TLS to Kitty Tailer
from Dublin.   p.m. 25 September, 1965

Darling Kitty Pie,

I got your letter yesterday and now I know when you are likely to arrive, so that is most heartening news. I am already looking forward to seeing you get out of the plane and come down the ladder onto Irish soil, or cement. I am indeed happy that the time of your arrival is near and that presently I shall get out of here. Because of it I have had enough, by above the head, if you know what I mean .... Should not each cup, whether of superb wine or of deadly gall, drown the past with the future?

Today I am going up to Croke Park to the All Ireland Football Final, after posting this letter. Yesterday I went to Lansdowne Road and saw the local club playing Racing Club de France. It was indeed a rare and subtle pleasure and I enjoyed myself very much. The Parisians were excellent and outshone our fellows, both in the playing of the game and in their 'being'. It was like watching ... oh! what the hell interest could you possibly have in the damn thing? You are surely saying to yourself, 'Ducky's mind is blank and barren, so he has just let himself go, and being an old professional rubbish trots out without effort.' Quite true, I have nothing to say. Nothing happens and I am living in a vacuum, through which my unhinged mind wanders at a furious pace, driven by the unbearable agony of frustration. *Hèlas*! that Prix de l'Arc last year was really my last chance and I let it go, curse it! That is now twelve months ago and the agony is still just as poignant.

I saw Clifton outside the Shelbourne. I hardly recognised him, yet he was the same, except that his expression has become gentle and I realised for the first time his eyes are blue. He said he was waiting for a bus and must hurry away. Then he said, 'Do you have such a vulgar thing as a telephone number?' Due to some idiotic instinct of self-defence I gave him a wrong one. Then he raised his hand and rushed across the street to a large and very new looking Rolls Royce, the door of which was thrown open by a chauffeur as he approached. He disappeared hurriedly into the car and was driven away. The peculiar fellow invariably plays the same part ....

I got a postcard from that peculiar woman [Elizabeth Schnack] who translates some of my short stories into German. She said she was in Kerry on a holiday and intended to ring me on her way back. How the hell did she get my number? That will avail her nothing, however ....[1]

Please don't change your mind, because I can wait no longer. I just feel that it is *imperative* to go as soon as possible. All the greater hurry when one has nowhere to go. In any case, darling Kitty, I send you all my love in the meantime and I shall be counting the hours to see you appear from that plane and come down the ladder.

Le Barbare des Iles

[1] See Elizabeth Schnack's translated volumes of O'Flaherty's short stories *Der Stromer*, Stuttgart: Reclam, 1956 and *Ein Topf voll Gold*, Leipzig: Reclam, 1971.

For Kitty's birthday in December 1965 O'Flaherty wrote her 'The Nuptial Dance of Isabel de Casalva' inscribed 'To K.P. from Ducky Pie with eternal love'. Written by hand on the righthand pages of a ring-backed notebook this florid sketch is about two thousand words long, and reappears in *The Gamblers*. It begins 'As I lay naked on my back in complete darkness, stretched out flat and motionless above the luxurious ermine coverlet of her vast bed, the intense silence was ended by the faint tinkling of a guitarra.' Lights come on and

Isabel emerges from her dressing room totally enveloped in a red shawl. As the narrator watches and describes his emotions at the sight, Isabel's nuptial dance, within her shawl, reveals only her voluptuous face. The sketch is about 'passionate anticipation', accompanied throughout by the Spanish guitar music O'Flaherty loved, a vision in which Isabel becomes a butterfly. At the end Isabel returns through the curtained doorway of her dressing room, only to re-emerge: 'Then she ran forwards with a hoarse low cry and leaped headlong from the bedside straight into my widespread arms.'

1966

Darling Kitty Pie,

I am writing this today and will try to mail it on my way up to Croke Park, so that you may be sure of getting it down in Georgia, because I think means of transport, even by air, are bound to be lazy in that climate. I hope the G.P.O. is open, there are so many strikes now every week. Today the buses have decided to stay out permanently, or so they say, so I'll have a good walk [about two miles] to see Galway play Cork in the semi-final football.

Darling Pie, thank you ever so much for your adorable letter. I beg of you to slow up and let life go on at its own pace, otherwise you'll fold and they'll have to go out to the mound and order you back into the bull pen. I daresay you still have a lot left and there is no need to worry. I don't know what I've got left if anything at all, but I do know I'm in the ninth innings and one run behind and I'm just stepping up to the plate with two men gone. Ha, ha! (prolonged peals of sardonic laughter).

I did go to the horse show. Hardly anybody there and I felt I was looking at something dead. Yet the big hunter horses were so beautiful, and so out of place in 1966, after something, a thing called credit, has filled the roads with automobiles.

I have just finished eating an Irish stew that I cooked, not as good as yours. Everything else seems to be going all right in so far as the flat and Madame Full-air are concerned. The dullness and appalling boredom of Dublin life is also constant.

Le Monde is most melancholy about China, says war is inevitable, you know against whom. Today the *Sunday Times* piped in with the same theory I have been expounding for years, about Mao putting his country on a fighting basis away back in fifty-nine, with communes, etc. How he has now abolished his regular army as a final step, and left a chequer board covered with thousands of Chinas, each one of which has to be invaded and conquered, *ad infinitum* .... I feel unable to face the prospect of a third world war in my lifetime, and I'll just call it a day when it starts ....

I got a letter from Pegeen written, she said, on top of a Welsh mountain. Believe it or not, most of what she wrote was about the World Cup soccer football games. I daresay she hoped remarks of that sort might drawn an answer. Just for once I'll write her a controversial page about the modern 'defensive theory' in soccer playing!

I hope your visit south will be a success. I myself regard relatives with horror. They are inevitably poisonous attachments. They fill me with sadness, like visits to graveyards, since after all one's life is a perpetual progression, a perpetual dying and resurrection, like day following night and vice versa. What relation could there be between myself and what I have been yesterday, or the year before, or a decade ago? Are we not all the same, except people like you and I, I mean our relationship, which has remained unsevered, although on a different plane, until it is severed, at which point it will become rent like cloth back to its beginning, each rent a part becoming *no longer aware of the other*. As it is, darling, I am longingly aware of you the whole time. You keep going away so often. It's in your blood, like Laura, who keeps going away from you, even though she longs to see you again and indeed feels hurt at your staying so long away in Europe. Yet as soon as you come back she makes little trips away to show her spiritual independence. Just like myself! *Moi, je ne bouge pas, except toujours mes petites divagations, dans les bars* ... Good God! I have already begun to have indigestion from eating that stew. Never again! just what I always say after eating stew ....

Darling Kitty, hurry back and see me here. In the meantime all my deepest love and tenderness,

Le Barbare des Iles

---

444. KT TLS to Kitty Tailer
[from Dublin]   p.m. 26 August, 1966

Darling Kitty Pie,

I delayed this letter because there was no point in sending it sooner to the Colony Club. Thank you for your marvellous letter from Bayonet Farm, even though I got depressed by your description of your life as forlorn. After all, darling, the word is mine and I don't remember making you a present thereof. Tut, tut! Your life is not forlorn, you have advanced enormously in mind and the fact that you can now suffer far more than previously, is merely a proof of maturity. *'Beni soit le dieu qui nous a donné la souffrance.'* 'Out of the darkness I cried out to thee,' *et cetera*.

There you are, whirling on the treadmill of your endless journeys which will eventually bring you back to me, while I whirl on my own treadmill waiting, waiting for you and the lark that keeps escaping. Like the vision of beauty seen by an Irish poet, continually avoiding contact with its pursuer, who runs with bursts of madness in his running, through the glistening mist, the gambler's mirage of omniscient power ....

One would imagine from this rhapsody that all is well. If so, it is internal, because nothing has yet come forth. The ebullient and tumultuous ferment of fruition becomes ever greater and I do know that not only larks but a gentle horde of birds will sing in chorus their hymn to resurrected light.

Nightingales will sing at dawn and the mimosa will again be in bloom ....

All goes fairly well in the flat, except for the torment of waiting. I keep putting a pound under the circular rubber mat for Mrs Fuller, who cleans, scours and puts things astray. I see Junior now and then walking forth or back with supplies. He has now read *Famine* which he praised with the shrewdness of a military man. Quite a boy in his quiet American way, more Dutch than Anglo-Saxon.

I also met a Jesuit one day I went to have a snack at Jammet's bar counter. His name was Orr, he said, a descendant of the famous William Orr, one of the Belfast Presbyterian leaders of 1798. Funny his being a Jesuit. He told me he likes *A Tourist's Guide to Ireland* very much and wanted to buy me wine as a mark of his respect. An odd Orr and certainly an odd Jesuit, but then they are superlatively odd. He said they were getting fewer vocations in England and had to close one of their schools. 'Naturally,' I said, 'You can't expect to compete with Mao Tze Tung.' He looked at me closely and said, 'Sir, I quite agree' ....

I laughed and laughed over *Time*'s description of this un-American activities enquiry in Washington, especially the picture of its organiser, Mr. Pool, 'Cesspool Bill' somebody called him. The country is not dead yet, far from it. Furthermore, the Giants look like taking the Pennant after all. I now get the paper in Lower Leeson Street, near the Green. They carry a good line in foreign papers, there being a college near at hand, University College, Dublin, *librería de los estudiantes*!

Thanks for reminding me of the 'Barber of Trieste'. It was really good and would have been better if I had been in slightly better form. I now send you my deepest, deepest love, my beloved sharer of life.

Le Barbare des Iles

445. KT TLS to Kitty Tailer
[from Dublin]   p.m. 17 June, 1967

Darling Kitty Pie,

I got your letter just now, dated June 14th, which would be last Wednesday. I was surprised you had not got my letter, which I sent Sunday morning by air express. However, maybe Holmdel is just about as remote as Gortnagcapall in the matter of transport.

Your life sounds depressing on account of Barclay, poor man. It has to be borne or ended, and there is very little about death that is attractive, as you so correctly maintain again and again, so we may as well go on like that ridiculous character in Chekov's *Uncle Vanya*, after the guy makes a mess of a suicide attempt ....

Le Monde keeps coming fairly regularly, although it has now become quite different. All the outer *habiliments* of western European civilisation have fallen away and there stands *Le Monde*, all naked to the world as a Yiddish propaganda rag. However, they can't resist printing the news without comments here and there. The local Irish seem, as usual, utterly indifferent to what is happening in the world. They are now complaining loudly about the scorching heat. There has, in fact, been fine weather for six days in a row, which equals the record for the month of June set in 1884 ....

Darling Pie, I remember that blue dress well. You certainly looked very pretty in it, but then you always do! Sometimes it's unbearably lonely without you, very lonely indeed, especially when one realises how little time there is left and how uncertain things are in the world today.

Mrs Fuller keeps coming in. I saw her yesterday when I came back from seeing a ridiculous Texan film. It was a funny Western and people laughed at it, including myself. As I said, there was Mrs Fuller. As I came in without sound I found her sitting in the front room staring solemnly out of the window. She was most embarrassed, as I said in a remote tone: 'Glorious weather, Mrs Fuller.' I paid Quirke two pounds to clean the windows and now he talks to me again without an expression of hatred.

I got a note from Margaret Stephens [of A.D. Peters] about some people wanting to get out a short story collection, composed of the stories in the Cape volumes not yet included in paperbacks. In other words poorer short stories. They only pay one hundred and fifty pounds of which Cape takes half. I suppose seventy-five pounds is equal to the harm the publication will do to my by now non-existent literary reputation. In any case, I got one hundred and twenty pounds from Peters' office for this month. Sounds like the best I ever had so far, if one considers I have published nothing for nearly twenty years.

If one could only finish this book. If one could only get one's health back. Ifs were horses .... I was reading in some book I discovered about Caesar's affair with Cleopatra and the son that resulted. How odd it is that great men's children have almost invariably been worthless.

Yes, it must be tough on K. Hepburn if she really cared for Old Pot [Spencer Tracy died 10 June]. She must have to some extent, unless he was, so to speak her *Dada*, not just her big daddy but her Dada, like a foot fetish or similar.

Darling Kitty, I just thought how long it will be until I see you again and now I feel terribly miserable .... Maybe I'll send you a cable from the post office .... I hate sending one over the telephone because I hate spelling words, like 'u' for 'Ulick'. Well now, sweet Kitty, I send you all my love, peculiar as it is and sometimes *barbare*, until I hear from you again which will be soon I hope. Goodbye, darling love,

Le Barbare des Iles

Radio Telefís Éireann televised *Land* in eight half hour episodes during 1967.

---

446. KT TLS to Kitty Tailer
[from Dublin]   p.m. 8 July, 1967

Darling Kitty Pie,

Thank you for the cable, it cheered me considerably .... However, by now your grief must have wasted its venom to some extent. When one feels 'excessively' one is introduced to the reaction with excessive speed. Personally, as you know, I am a unitarian, entirely so. So that I spend my affection on one person almost entirely and the remainder on 'ideas', or to be exact, on abstract affections. It is probably better to be normal and to love all sorts of people a little and nobody to an extreme. Like on the market those who buy shares in hundreds of companies. In that way they save their bacon a while longer than the others. *Quand même, beni soit le dieu qui nous donnons l'extase*, if there is such a god.

Darling Pie, please get well and happy again ....

I got a letter from Pegeen. She said she is going to Greece for a holiday and calling on some German friend en route. I daresay she got tired waiting for me to invite her to come here. I really could not do so. I am unable to cope right now.

Dear one, please let me know your plans. Are you going south to Georgia again? My brain becomes more and more feeble. I can retain nothing apparently. Even simple paragraphs of a newspaper report I have to go over again and again, like an illiterate, to get the drift. All that is depressing. It might be a good idea to die slowly that way, by unnoticeable stages. Trouble is, one does notice and feel miserably affected. I must do something about this loneliness. Trouble is I avoid people when sober and can only enter into human association when I take a little drug of some sort, alcohol being the one in general use here which allows one to get in contact with people superficially.

Today, I am determined to go to the Phoenix Park races. Do you think I'll make it? very doubtful! ...

I am again reading that wonderful book about the Gobi Desert, written by those two elderly and distinguished lesbians, Mildred Cable and Francesca French, whichever of them really wrote it had great talent, not as a writer in the technical sense but in the matter of wisdom and sensitivity – quite remarkable.[1] Have also gone back to the Maupassant book you kindly procured for me. He was quite a man, *le petit Guy*. Apparently they do have proof that he inherited his syphilis from his mother, or from his reputed 'natural' father, Gustave Flaubert. Must be the mother because his brother Hervé died of G.P.I. also. In any case he was quite a man. Would he have been better under different circumstances? ...

Last night I was reading about the little islands, St. Honorat and Marguerite. Apparently the fiddler Paganini was buried on an islet for several years and then taken away to Genoa. He died of cholera at Nice. Perhaps a good scourge of plague would destroy the whole Riviera population!

Darling, I wish to kiss all yours away for ever more, all sad thought as well, to give you only laughter and the glorious exaltation of happy tenderness. How wonderful it will be to see you again, dearest sweetie pie! I hope it may be soon. After all this is July and something must happen soon. Soon I shall leave this marsh. Remember how the unfortunate Nietzsche was always yelling: 'Too long have I lain by this marsh.' After all I'm as crazy and feckless as he was. Pretty nearly, I'm afraid.

Goodbye now, darling and I send you all my love, all my most tender love.

Le Barbare

[1] *The Gobi Desert*, London: Hodder & Stoughton, 1942. These two missionaries, with Evangeline French, crossed the Gobi Desert five times, dressed as Chinese women. When this book came out Mildred was sixty-three and Francesca seventy. Their lesbianism is O'Flaherty's presumption.

---

447. KT TLS to Kitty Tailer
[from Dublin]   p.m. 5 August, 1967

Darling Kitty Pie,

I got a most beautiful [letter] from you yesterday and am writing this in response to your request for a final word before you leave. I got a charming letter from the Grand Hotel, saying there will be a room for me similar to the kind I usually have during my 'highly appreciated' visits. So there I am, looking forward to seeing you next Friday morning on the arrival promenade. I hope I shall be able to find it easily, you know how stupid I am about these things ....

I don't feel depressed at the moment, I suppose because I'm getting out of this filthy town next Thursday. You asked me if there was anything I wanted. I can only think of underpants, nothing else. I am now wearing the red ones ....

Yes, I read about the ructions in the United States. Not any more than usual, are they? In any case, disturbance of any kind is always a sign of life. his refers to urban riots. Here there is only apathy and futile mockery of the spineless. A jeer from twisted lips is a most depressing attitude towards the inadequacy of social life in this machine age. It's harder to dodge autos here than in Paris. People take a run at one and then blow their horns on purpose to annoy and terrorise ....

The Chicago Cubs are now falling back among the beaten, as they say about race horses, so I have lost interest in that too. My novel still stays with me mentally, but I can do nothing about it. I have a strong idea that I could do something and even finish it under the proper circumstances, whose identity I know, indeed clearly, without being able to procure. In the meantime dull-footed time goes marching on, towards an unseen frontier kindly kept concealed from our cowardly eyes.

I wonder should I take my black raincoat. Why black? I have none other .... Probably not, I like to ride light .... Remember that side road beyond Aix en Provence where we had lunch several times under the same tree? Where did it lead to? I tried hard but in vain to recollect the name .... Do you know Gibbon spelt Sète 'Cette'. The latter sounds more intelligible. Apparently there was a considerable battle there at a given moment, I was reading about it last night.

Well Kitty Pie, here goes now until Friday morning. I wish you the best of *bon voyages* and send you my deepest love from this tarnished and most decayed frame that once throbbed with the triumphant energy of youth.

Le Barbare

On 14 September, 1967, O'Flaherty wrote as from Dublin to Anthony Jones of A.D. Peters thanking him for putting through the sale of *The Assassin* to the B.B.C., and asking for his mail to be forwarded to Paris until further notice. The fee for television rights was three hundred and fifty pounds, and the fifty minute play, adapted by Hugh Leonard, was televised 1 October, 1968, as one of a series for B.B.C. 2 on 'The Jazz Age, tales of the twenties'. In November 1967, O'Flaherty agreed, in a note to Margaret Stephens, to the reprint of *The Assassin* by Cedric Chivers Ltd. (Lythway Press), against a ten percent royalty.

It was in the late sixties that the editor of this volume first met Liam O'Flaherty, with Kitty Tailer, at Hotel de la Paix in Geneva, Switzerland. They were staying there after a holiday in Tunis, where O'Flaherty said he admired the graceful carriage of the women and liked the people. The following personal impression of O'Flaherty, noted down at the time, may here be of interest. 'Still an active and energetic man of powerful physique, Liam looks less than his seventy-two years. He wore sunglasses until near the end of our meeting. He has piercing and slightly cold blue eyes. He is an excellent raconteur and a good actor. A mixture of a man of action and a sensitive introspective, he is self-centred, impatient and intolerant of views unless he admires or likes the person who holds them. I doubt whether he has any close friends and he probably needs periods of solitude interspersed with conviviality because he said he was interested in people more than in ideas. He needs people to define his own character, and likes an audience. He does his own cooking in Dublin, and is fastidious about diet, drinks wine or gin and dislikes whiskey. He still adores horse racing, follows rugby football and hurling. The Irish writer he most admires is Joyce. We did not discuss his attitude towards the Church but he said the beautiful sonorous Latin was "the only thing the Church has left", and now it only remains in *Ulysses*. He told a few anecdotes all based on opinion or characters. Beneath his verve and facial mobility he is a lonely and insecure man. He said in his youth he suffered from terrible bouts of melancholia inherited from his father. He still feels young at heart and prefers mixing with young people.'

In the late sixties, though most of O'Flaherty's work was out of print, interest continued in film rights. Those for *Famine* were, in July 1968, priced by A.D. Peters at thirty-five thousand dollars plus five percent of the film's profits, when a New York agent enquired.

448. KT TLS to Kitty Tailer
[from Dublin]   Friday p.m. 2 August, 1968
'My Pad'

Darling Little Pai Pai,

Here I am again, subject to the dreadful torture of writing a letter, but I'll do it and be damned to it. So you got there once again safe and sound. Stay that way, until your return, dear heart. Glad Laura did not fall down on the rendezvous and waved the plane onto the tarmac with her bullwhip. You must be in Bayonet Farm by now.

I'm keeping a level keel and feel surprisingly undespondent, in spite of the weather. It's sultry by day and cold by night and you know how I hate that .... Believe it or not they are rationing water in Sligo, Belfast and even in Mullingar. Novenas are pouring into heaven from the non- tourist areas, at a record breaking pace, according to the Celestial Correspondent of Radio Éireann .... Can't beat the Irish for insanity!

Well, I keep thinking how delightful you were, out at the awful Jesus place called Mount Carmel. You were really adorable and I remember your gentleness and charm, again and again, with deepest tenderness and joy. It is good to recall how you went to get a parasol for my head at the bullfight and then gave me your jacket to wear. I'm glad we went there. The bullfight was very good in my book. It was a great pleasure rewriting it and finding it still alive and full of energy ....

I hope things remain quiet on your sector of the front during Summer .... I get the paper nearly every day. In a way the election is just as dull as this year's baseball season. I do hope Humphrey does *not* get elected ....[1]

I got your schedule mixed up, but as far as I remember you are going to Peter's house[2] on the Island Martha's Vineyard first and then south? ... I adore the little Arab type espadrilles you got for me in Cannes, they are marvellous in this dry weather, as light as feathers and with a spring to them. I cut through the crowds like a catfish, in and out. The streets are crowded with tourists, hordes of students from all over Europe. Not that the hotel hawks get much out of them. It's nice to hear foreign languages spoken in Grafton Street, just as if Dublin were *really* a city.

Kitty Pie, I hope you are able to make your deadline this time. It would be so wonderful, that would mean your coming back next month, which is like next week, indeed like any moment now she'll be lifting the knocker.

I have got back into the habit of getting up at all hours, going to bed at all hours and eating at all hours. The most awful thing about this flat, run by my system, is opening and closing windows to avoid draughts. I've already had two since my return, however, I feel rather well and suffer from no other ailment. They have that new supermarket nearly finished. I'm so glad because I'm tired of the other shops ....

All those whodunits I brought back were frightful. The day has come to forswear those bloody things, they are worse than cigarettes. I've gone back to Gibbon.

Now, Kitty Pie, there seems no more room on this page, so I'd better go into my wind up and hurl my goodbye pitch in your beloved direction. Here it comes, Kitty Pie, a fast ball, just below the letters and right in there .... From that goddamn *Barbare des Iles* whom we left for dead, God knows where.

All my love, sweetheart
Poo, Poo

[1] Hubert Humphrey, currently U.S. Vice President, was elected as Democratic candidate for the November 1968 election, in which he was defeated by Richard Nixon (Republican).

[2] Peter is Kitty's son.

---

449. KT TLS to Kitty Tailer
[from Dublin]   p.m. 11 October, 1968

Beloved Kitty Poo,

This is just a hurried note to let you know that all is well *chez le barbare*. I have just finished the rewrite and finally made a good job of the change-over little chapter that follows the dance. It was over written in the first effort and showed signs of the lethargy that followed the monstrous and monumental dance, which felt overwhelming on copying it. Really beyond the beyond so far in its lifetime. Otherwise I feel a bit exhausted now, because I have been up and down most of the night and eating queer snacks now and again. I'm going right ahead now with the Epsom affair.

I got your telegram and was delighted that you found everything okay. I hope you won't lift anything, that's very important. Don't lift anything at all except a fork at table.

No other news, in any case it was only yesterday morning you went. I ran over to the top of the old building and saw the plane take off. I could see it in the sky for a long, long time. 'You be careful, Mr. Pilot,' I said, 'take Kitty home safely as she is the only Kitty I've got and she has to be fit to take me through the awful tunnel.[1]

I got *Le Monde* and they had an account of the bits of autoroute being done. One of them is the one from Orange to some other place and another, peculiarly enough, from Roquebrune to Mentone. Didn't know they had done anything beyond Nice, but I faintly remember you remarked on the Italians hard at work beyond the frontier. These autoroutes interest me for some reason. They are so beautiful to look at.

Do I or don't I hear from you before I leave on Friday? The *Barbare* is punctual. Let's hope all goes straight ahead now without a halt, as we can no longer afford halts.

I took the laundry and she said it would be ready. I'll leave a few weeks money for Mrs Gleeson. This trip is badly needed I think.

What do you know about Detroit? They squared the series at four all and the final was last night. I hope to get today's paper. Try to get *Le Drapeau Rouge*. I was also unable to get the result of last Sunday's rugby matches, but that is of lesser importance.

Goodbye now, Kitty Pie darling, because I am quite undone, and must walk down with this letter. That will loosen up the nervous system. *Olé los valientes!* ...

All the *Barbare's* love, all of it.

[unsigned]

On 7 December, 1968, Kitty Tailer, writing from Paris, sent Margaret Stephens a press cutting from the *International Herald Tribune* of 27 November, of Mary Blume's article ' '"Uptight" or the Ghetto's Generation Gap'. This described the filming of a play *Uptight* shot in Cleveland's black ghetto by Jules Dassin. The story opens on the day Martin Luther King was shot and is based, very loosely, on O'Flaherty's *The Informer*. Dassin wrote the script, and the star was Julian Mayfield. Paramount Pictures wrote to O'Flaherty about the screen credit, but he got no fee.

In 1968 Lythway Press, Bath (Cedric Chivers Ltd.) reprinted *Thy Neighbour's Wife*, *The Black Soul*, *The Assassin*, and took an option on *The Puritan*.

----

7 March, 1969, 'Going into Exile', adapted by Eoin Ó Súilleabháin, directed by Tony Barry, produced by Tom McGrath, was included in a Telefís Éireann series 'Stories of Ireland'.

---

450. KT TLS to Kitty Tailer
[from Dublin]   p.m. 22 April, 1969

Darling Kitty Pie,

Here is the promised note, being mainly information culled from the Almanach des P.T.T. 1969. Sunday eleventh May is the feast of Jeanne d'Arc. Thursday the fifteenth is the Ascension. Sunday the twenty-fifth is Pentecôte. Therefore, in my opinion, either Thursday the ninth or Tuesday the thirteenth would be best for the journey to Bretagne. Personally I vote for the ninth, the feast of St. Gregory, who had no great following that would clutter up the roads, but you'll make up your own mind as usual. Let's hope the weather on the bleak peninsula, so like this country here, is favourable.

Here it's typical April with rain and shine intermittent. The first flies have appeared in the flat, which is abominable. I hate the little creatures, but I daresay they have as good a right to live and fly about in search of food as I have.

The disturbances in the North are reaching a climax of some sort. Young squadrati are beginning to bomb police barracks with Molotoff cocktails and the local young men are anxious to go up there for the fun. However, I daresay the politicians of both camps are bound to come to terms and prevent the young people expressing their natural instincts for bagarrisme, if there is such a word for a bloody row. In any case, the poor Mr. Wilson seems doomed to play the valiant mouse on all fronts. Paisley is getting more and more followers down here and not among Protestants. 'You have to admire the whore,' is the usual expression used. I myself feel remote.

It is really extraordinary how much I hate any contact with society, whether good or bad. I ran into a few people, including Jim O'Byrne and my paratroop friend, who has returned from Anguilla and is now going out to Rhodesia to join Mr. Smith, odd creature with a child's innocent smile .... People are peculiar, most peculiar. I saw a lot of other men at Lansdowne Road on Saturday for the Leinster Cup Final (Rugby). You certainly get a collection of more or less interesting males (of the *barbare* type), but no interesting females. Wonder why? maybe they go away to wherever the money is.

I do keep worrying about your being alone in that flat and unable to get help if anything happened. Please be careful. Slow down to a crawl. I hope Pegeen is not conducive to too much effort. By the way, I can't open the closet where the soap and toilet paper are. I tried all the keys I found on a ring in the little bedside table and none of them fit. Are they the ones? ...

How long do you think the trip will be, so that I know how to deal with Mrs Gleeson when I'm leaving. I mean about money. When I'm talking to you on the telephone these things evade my scatterbrained memory .... Here is the end of this page, Kitty Pie darling, so once again I send you all the love in my deepest heart,

from *le Barbare* to Sweetie Pie

---

451. KT TLS to Kitty Tailer
[from Dublin]   p.m. 10 July, 1969

Darling Beloved,

I got your second letter yesterday and it was so beautiful that I almost wept with joy. Yes indeed little one, I was carried away onto the topmost height of rapture. Thank you Kitty Poo. By now you must be back from Rhode island and I hope you did not talk too much about Carthage, etc. to Farr, thus making him determined to hit the road at once in that direction. Also, please look after yourself down below in Georgia, Ma'am, nor try to do too much, because you have been doing too much, far too much, lately. Time enough when you get back to the dogs and what not, to let out a reef or two. The Martha's Vineyard adventure will still lie ahead.

I am at the moment on top of the world, as I am forging ahead with my work and feel the exaltation that comes from a feast after such a long famine, hovering on the brink of Avernus, that being the Roman Road to the nether world .... Even there they apparently charged for transport into the Devil's Den. Keep your fingers crossed for me, will you kid, so that the 'divine rose' may not fade too soon. For sure enough my rose has still too many thorns of unfulfilled desire.

I met Garech Browne and his personal secretary, or procureur, or whatnot, Des Mackie. They forced me to go out to Garech's house for dinner. He had a Horse Show troop of relatives and retainers, Lords and Ladies this and that .... I also met the painter Eoin Walsh, who told me a funny story about a literary row in a pub called Sheehan's, myself being the absent subject of the row. 'It was fierce,' Walsh said, 'About half swore that you are the world's greatest writer and the other half swore with equal passion that you are the worst.' 'Who won?' I asked. 'What,' he shouted, 'Those bastards wouldn't even try to pull a soldier off their sisters.'

I didn't go to the Horse Show. I'll maybe go to Croke Park instead, Kerry are playing Mayo, but then again I may not ....

I still think a lot of Tunisia and the *joute nautique* at Sète and the *sardañas* at Perpignan and the conversation with the former Rugby international at Cannet Plage. Is that the right name? Also the mountaintop where the air was good and the cowbells went on and on without respite. Thanks for that trip.

The weather is very sodden now and it's hard to breathe. Maybe it will let up shortly .... They still keep shouting and throwing stones at one another up in the North, while the northern government men are carousing with our government men here in Dublin. What scoundrels! They just keep up this tension in order to prevent union and their own dismissal. Everybody is turning against Israel here now. I have seen half a dozen letters in the *Irish Times*, one of their own papers, denouncing the Zionists. Goldie Meir seems to get their goat especially.

All my deepest love, beloved Kitty darling, right from my heart's deepest core. Take care of yourself and come back safe and sound to little ducky poo, who is such a fool, such a bloody fool. *Afuera todo el mundo*, we're going to win.

Le Barbare!

---

452. KT TLS to Kitty Tailer
[from Dublin]   p.m. 17 July, 1969

Beloved Kitty Pie,

The sun is still shining and I have been up since four as usual. It's nearly eight o'clock and I have had breakfast, a bath, and feel not so bad. However, the turmoil on this island is getting the better of me, as wars and rumours of wars always do. There are continual meetings here, with huge mobs marching on the various army barracks shouting 'Give us guns, you bastards, if you are afraid to fight.' Yesterday dockers tore the Union Jack from the British Embassy and the flaming remnants through the streets, the bourgeoisie are having kittens, not knowing what to do.

A commando of wild bearded creatures set off from The Bailey in three cars and a truck, shouting like Roman gladiators, 'We who are about to die ...' All very music hall and pathetic as popular tumults always are. Reminds me very much of Spain at the outbreak of the civil war, except that the fighting has not really started, if it ever does. If it doesn't the cause will be lack of material. Even Junior stopped me in the street and said: 'What the hell are you fighting Irish waiting for?' 'Hush,' I said, 'We're waiting for Lefty, he's the secret third person of the Mervin and Joe Trinity.' He looked at me in amazement – quite justified ....

I had to make a recording for Garech Browne, as I had given my word of honour to do so. Being Ireland[sic] the fellow who operated the machine in my flat was not quite sober so he made a proper balls of *The Ecstasy of Angus*, so I'll have to have another go next Thursday.[1]

Even Garech is acting on some committee or other. He says all his titled relatives, who have property in the North are doing things in their pants for fear of getting burned out. He seemed to take uproarious delight in their distress .... What a country!

I have absolutely nothing to read now except Gibbon and Flaubert's *Salammbô*. I get *Le Monde* the odd time, it's quiet again and even favours 'our cause', whatever that is. I was very amused to read about Giscard D'Estaing's *'parler'* over the television about devaluation. He used a blackboard and some chalk, like a schoolmaster, to set forth his Machiavellian ideas in triple talk that sounded really persuasive. Quite a gang, the present French government .... Certainly the English pound seems to have a dreary future, but I feel the dollar is sound. With all that industrial potential a fall seems impossible. On the whole things are not so bad. Anything is better than boredom.

I feel older every day and more uncertain on my legs, yet my brain functions. *A bas la vieillesse!* I get no mail, none whatsoever, except the odd letter from Kitty. I do hope you'll be safely back to Bayonet Farm by the time this note arrives. That will make it half way according to my reckoning. I miss you terribly, sweetheart. Yet time goes on, like a ferret in a rabbit burrow, inexorable. All this business of lying down and rising, cooking and washing myself and going out to buy things ... what horror! ...

Soon perhaps we'll go south again, somewhere, anywhere, together. And maybe pretty words will appear to take the place of those others that are getting tired of being repeated *ad nauseam*, beneath the lofty pale green dome of silent leaves. I love you dearest heart, with all the power of my own barbaric soul. Take it easy now pal, take it easy. Do as little as possible ... *Afuera todo el mundo* except us two,

Le Barbare

[1] The recording of *The Ecstasy of Angus* was issued by Claddagh Records, Dublin, in 1978 as part of a double album which also included '*Dúil*', 'Red Barbara' and 'The Stolen Ass' (CCT 15 & 16).

---

453. KT TLS to Kitty Tailer
[from Dublin]   p.m. 22 September, 1969

Darling Kitty Pie,

As you will have noticed this is a day late, owing to an untoward event. Yesterday the charwoman's son, a lad of nineteen, got drowned in the canal. Mrs Quirke told me as I was passing to get the papers and milk. For some reason I found the news a great nervous shock ... for a while I thought my nerves had folded, however, they are a bit better now. This is noon and I've just eaten. Naturally the charwoman is not coming. Poor woman, that horrible canal! And yet idiots go around campaigning against its removal.

I got your dear letter this morning, just an hour ago, when I went out for provisions. I worry about all these trials you have to undergo, especially the one due to that idiot dentist in Dublin. I felt sure he was no good.

I keep waiting for your arrival next Friday week. When you are here the worst things don't look so bad. After all, what else is there in life? Nothing of any great account. Let us be gay and make the hay of happiness while the sun of our propinquity shines. For long or for short, time ceases to exist and the divine rose of life, etc ....

They say Mao had a stroke and that he is in a state of coma. Of course we have heard that often. His death would be a catastrophe, because his successor would be the Little Tiger cat [Lin Piao], whom I suspect of wanting to conquer the world. These Caesars always do, whether they are Alexander of Caesar himself, or his second image Napoleon, or indeed the little Chinaman Lin of the perpetual mysterious smile ....

I met Junior the other day and he grabbed me powerfully and said he has read *I Went to Russia* and pretended to be outraged by my statement, which I had quite forgotten, that 'stockbrokers and preachers' were the scum of the earth, or similar. He said: 'I was a stockbroker once, sir.' 'So what, Mr. Van Dyke Cox,' I said. I don't know what he made of that. I wish he'd stop reading my book. He reads the queerest things like my *Life of Tim Healy*. I presume he gets them at the Royal Dublin Society place at Ballsbridge, the place where you heard Joyce play the piano. I got a postcard from her, written at Florence. She's there with her Dutch Jewish friend, the one who works at Geneva. Should she know Pat Kelly's daughter?[1] Doubtful! ...

Dearest darling pie, I still do keep thinking about Tunis and that whole journey. Rugby has begun again, but I have not yet been to see a game .... No French news arrives as I only get *Le Monde* or *Figaro* and they only deal with it on Tuesday, which hardly ever arrives for some reason. I send you all my love and will ring for a taxi because I still have twenty minutes left to make the deadline and get rid of this bundle [of laundry] that is standing in the hallway. I have stripped the damn bed, so I'll have to make it up myself when I return, or else sleep in blankets in my study. Kitty horrified. Take great care dearest. This little bereft person depends so much on your coming. The horrible *barbare*. Did you like *Le Barbare Enchaîné*? Better than *Le Canard* to a French satiric newspaper in any case. All my deepest love.

[unsigned]

[1] Refers to the editor, A.A. Kelly, then living in Geneva, who was told about Joyce Rathbone by Kitty shortly after this, see notes to 24 May, 1975, and first met Joyce in 1976.

454. KT TLS to Kitty Tailer headed 'Darkness at Noon'
[from Dublin]   p.m. 20 January, 1970

Dearest Kitty Pie,

The above is the correct address, but the date is not so correct because it is pouring rain and I have no intention of making my way to the former Nelson Pillar [blown up by a bomb in March 1966] in this downpour, so it has to be posted on Monday in South Anne Street.

My mind is confused and I feel I have already been here for several months, although it's only three days since my return .... The stove is carrying on with the job almost as efficiently as it has done for the past twenty years. Twenty years, how appalling! Some of the greatest events in history took far less. Napoleon did not last that long, neither did Alexander, nor Shakespeare, as far as I remember. Did the great Leonardo? So many people are just content to go on eating, sleeping and defecating. What horror! Roosevelt said what men fight for, indeed their *ultimate ambition*, is three square meals and a bed. What do they crave in the bed other than sleep? Eleanor? Ha! Ha! ...

It is always rather frightening to come back here after being in civilised France. Darling sweetie pie, thanks for the trip and the many views of white mountain tops seen from our free parking lot, where we just swung the car bonnet around to get complete coverage of landscape. Very charming in the evening and then downstairs to get a cup of tea or cold milk and watch the astonishing French babies trot around in their dainty Paradise suits .... Even so, that bloody room was a sort of death trap, especially the clouds of poisonous dust that rose from the queer material that covered the concrete. My throat at least feels infinite relief at being away from there and it has almost reverted to its former state of chronic, but mild, ill health. I regret not having seen our old woman again. Is she dead? She certainly was afraid of the devil and vaguely hoped I would come to her aid and plead in her favour to my relative. On further reflection I'm convinced that she took me for the devil's first cousin (on the mother's side) and not for *his divine darkness* as I at first thought. It was a beautiful *rencontre*, there on the mountain, Kitty Pie.

I certainly must, from here on in, do my very best to forge ahead, by hook or by crook, inch by inch, syllable by syllable. Anything smaller than a syllable?

I hope you are well? I do worry about you, because you are now almost as absent minded as myself and the least wrong move can be so fatal in the Paris streets ....

Well, darling beloved, I send you as *comme toujours* all my deepest love, such as it is, poor thing, having to live in a poor receptacle like myself .... Until next week, dearest Pie, keep looking after yourself carefully. At least it's a great relief not to have to read *Le Monde* every day .... You've to hand it to the French, Kitty, hand what? The wooden spoon for harsh wit.

Le Barbare damné des Iles

---

455. KT TLS to Kitty Tailer
[from Dublin]   p.m. 1 March, 1970

Beloved Kitty Pie,

Here I am again, darling, with one of my Sunday messages, the Gospel according to the *Barbare des Iles*. Thanks for the beautiful cable I got on Friday. I, too, am looking forward to Friday with a most eager heart. I hope you'll be there when I reach Le Bourget. And what are you going to wear? Fur coat I suppose, the weather still being like the Arctic.

I felt very lonely the whole time since you left, very lonely. Otherwise all is going well and the stove functioning to perfection. The only thing is one has to watch the grill which cooks at twice or four times the speed ....

Yesterday I went to Lansdowne Road to see the Scotland v Ireland game, instead of going to Jury's Hotel [to see the game on television] thinking a few hours standing in the bright sunshine would do me good. Good Lord! it was worse than the time I lost my hat and scarf. This time I saved the hat and lost the scarf. What a crowd, all of them urchins who took a delight in causing stampedes. Young males are appalling vicious. Still, I enjoyed the whole affair.

Wednesday night Garech Browne and his woman Tiger came and took me down to their place for dinner. I went because I thought he'd play the wonderful Romero record for me again. He did play a record of Romero's but it was the wrong one .... He's afraid that Tiger is going to leave him, which she quite flatly in my presence said she had every intention of doing. It was pathetic to see how heart-broken he is at the prospect. Of course, it may be a game on her part, trying to force him to marry her under threat of abandonment .... In any case, I said: 'My dear fellow, why worry? The pain of bereavement always gets silenced, either by death or by a resurgence of passion. Why worry so much about an evil that is transient?'[1]

Kitty Pie, what plans have you made? I don't care, I just want to be with you, but I do feel you shouldn't make too great an effort, so soon after your terrible [sic] in America. Just keep gently busy, that is best. I am not too downcast. My only worry is my advanced age and that there may not be enough time left to finish all I have to do ....

Le Monde is now coming regularly and the *Paper*. They both go on and on about Israel, *ad nauseam*.[2] There was some baseball news in the *Paper*, including a most vicious attack on Leo Durocher by Red Smith. There seems to be no law of libel in America. He'd get ten years for the sort of thing he wrote in England. Of course he's getting old now, poor man ....

I really don't know that it would be wise to stay in Paris for that match. What's the good of arriving early on Friday if we don't get out of town ... As I said, I'll row in with what ever plans you make.

Kitty Pie darling, I send you my deepest love, all of it. That sounds silly because there'd be none left if I sent all of it. Maybe the heart is a spider that spends its time spinning a new web of love. How charming! The little spider, hiding under a table in the corner, spinning away .... In any case this is from,

Le petit Barbare des Iles en attendant son arrivé vendredi

[1] On the face of it this is an insensitive remark, as the event referred to as 'terrible' in the subsequent paragraph was the death of Kitty's elder son, a diabetic from childhood, and the only doctor in a county of eight thousand people at Darien, Georgia. He died on 18 January, 1970, of insulin reaction while duck hunting from a canoe in the swamps near the Altamaha river.

[2] Constant terrorist attacks were taking place along the Israeli border, led by the Popular Front for the liberation of Palestine.

According to a letter from Anthony Jones (of A.D. Peters) to O'Flaherty of 19 March, 1970, 'The Bath' was to be a Granada T.V. play at a proposed fee of one hundred pounds, the adaptation to be done by Hugh Leonard. The fee was paid but this short story was never televised.

---

456. KT TLS to Kitty Tailer
[from Dublin]   p.m. 6 September, 1970

Darling Kitty Pie,

Here I am so depressed that I can barely understand what I am doing or why I'm doing it .... Will what I'm writing ever get to Holmdel? What happened to the letter I sent last Sunday? I answered your cable and I hope you at least got that ....

I caught a cold at Lansdowne Road yesterday, although it was a fine afternoon, and I was well buttoned up. I took one red pill last night and another this morning. Maybe that will pass. What does not pass, woman, is this bank strike. It is now certain that the miserable affair will not end before November ... so now I only have enough money to last me about ten or twelve days. A fine kettle of fish .... Do tell me quickly where the five are hidden, because the five might be the life saver ....

So you had a good trip. Thanks ever so much for the various communications. The postcard showing the fifteen mile long beach was suspiciously black near the sea's edge. Oh dear, I exclaimed, another sun-kissed beach with tar facings, considered very chic nowadays, even the Aga Khan's *colonie de vacances* for *les trop riches* has them.

It is now nine a.m. and I have already had lunch which consisted of a little grilled chicken and three potatoes ....

I did not get very far with this last effort to read *Salammbô* intelligently and not for the tale. Maybe I shall read *The Gamblers* again, although I no longer have any desire to do so. Like that queer American painter who had a curiosity shop in Dawson Street, downstairs: 'If I painted a picture now,' he said to me, 'it would be an antique at birth.'[1]

Darling Kitty, I wish you were here, or rather I wish that you and I were together some place and away from here. Soon! Otherwise I shall very probably consider that I've had enough, 'Like a foolish fellow that makes gay with superb wine in which a slow and tasteless poison has been dipped.' It was superb all right, at times.

I suppose you won't get this until your return from Georgia ... I hope you don't fly down there and back. Please talk to me on your return, or before you go, if you get this letter before then.

It was nice watching these young men playing rugby football again. There were only a few people on the stand and they were all gathered near where I sat, so we talked and discussed old and new times. Rugby may not be a gentlemanly game but gentlemanly people play it, and it also seems the only really international game, more like a religion than a game. There are still lovely things on this dark earth, even lovelier than a fleet of ships or a troop of horsemen, or a power of marching soldiers. I really do want to get as far at least as the point where he throws his gun in the water. I can hear the splash and see the widening circles of disturbed water in the night glare of the electric lamps. But surely also the scene at that delightful Château de la Chimère. What a lovely name!

Beloved Kitty Pie, would it be better not to love? Who knows? although that seems to be even worse. I daresay each one loves *à sa façon*. Remember my telling you about the old couple I watched going along the road to La Napoule by the sea's edge? Year after year I saw them walk hand in hand, then one year later I saw her alone with bowed head. So I bowed to her in silence.

Darling Kitty, thank you for everything. I'll make off now and go to the G.P.O. ... I hope you got the cable I sent, because the Irish telegram girl did not seem able to spell or read or understand what I said. Remember me to Laura and what happened to that German dog that nobody mentions any more? Did he prove to be a sinister Kraut after all? Goodbye darling love, I hope I may get news of you early next week. Four weeks from today will be the Arc de Triomphe but *pas pour nous, hèlas.*[1]

From the melancholy *Barbare des Iles*

[1] Kevin Monaghan

[2] The Arc de Triomphe Grand Prix race is run at Longchamp on the first Sunday in October.

457. KT TLS to Kitty Tailer
[from Dublin]   p.m. 20 September, 1970

Darling Kitty Pie,

By now you must be back in Holmdel for some time .... I don't know whether you have changed your mind about the date of your return to Paris? I have bought a ticket on Aer Lingus for Friday Oct. 2nd, which arrives at 10.30 p.m. No daylight trips there or thereabouts they said. Maybe the highjack raids, maybe just plain Irish cussedness ....

So what passes, woman, and this is not an idle question. Let us know, babe, what you got in mind. I had a postcard from Georgia. I envy you the few lungfuls of warm weather. Since September 1st we have had a permanent diet of rain here. Humidity one thousand percent. You can eat it like soup without teeth, it's so deliciously thick and soft. Real Dutch pea soup with a chunk of fat pig swimming around at random, with a grunt out of the creature, saving your presence, ma'am.

Yesterday afternoon I went again to Lansdowne Road and enjoyed myself looking at Racing Club de France play Lansdowne Club. Believe it or not there was a fellow playing wing three-quarter for Racing Club de France called Henri de la Rivière. He was really superb and I suddenly realised while watching him score his second brilliant try that he had written to me during last Summer from England, where he was spending some sort of work holidays for his degree in English literature, or some such thing. Point was he was writing a monograph or brochure, or whatever they call it, about my work and he wanted to know where he could get copies of *Skerrett* and *Famine*, etc. Of course I never answered the letter. I remember him mentioning he had to be back in Paris by end August as he was picked to play on the first fifteen of Racing Club this season. So there he was, Kitty Pie, the clever little devil, disgracing these big bullocking Lansdowne galoots, with his pernickety running .... Maybe if the little swift running tyke gets selected for the Quinze de France, as he surely will be, then maybe *le Barbare* will say, I'm going to say hello to that little guy. That's how *le Barbare* managed to get as rich as he is, doing the right thing every time, every time, Kitty Pie, every bloody time.

I got up early and had breakfast, worked and then went for the papers and milk at nine, had lunch at ten consisting of steak and fried onions, that may be a man's meal, you know what I mean, but it certainly left a taste in my mouth. It would be all right if I were not doing a no cigarette routine ....

For God's sake, Kitty, let me know as soon as possible what you have in mind and what to bring, because I am in ignorance of length of stay .... Poor bewildered *Barbare*, little he knew he would end up like this, a toe rag and a showboard to all and sundry, to all the low scum of vagabonds and base lackey peasants that keep the round of tippling at high noon, et bloody cetera. And just think he once drank the stale urine of horses and ate steak and onions that he should have scoffed like a wild beast.

Darling sweetie pie, write soon to Ducky.[ALS] All my love, *niña*! Give me some air I can breathe.

On 15 December, O'Flaherty wrote one of his rare letters to A.D.Peters 'please tell the New English Library [N.E.L.] to do whatever they want about the second volume of my short stories'. A.D. Peters had asked whether N.E.L. could exclude three stories from their second volume reprint of *The Short Stories of Liam O'Flaherty*, these were 'The Blackbird's Mate, 'The Sinner' and 'The Child of God'. The book had to be abridged to keep the price at five shillings for one hundred and twenty-eight pages. 'Benedicamus Domino' had been omitted in error from volume one, and thereafter O'Flaherty's permission had to be sought for changes. N.E.L. had bought the paperback rights from Jonathan Cape in 1966. Devin Adair controlled the hardback rights over six of *The Mountain Tavern* stories in the US, but the American hardback rights to the rest of this group of stories were free in 1971.

The short stories sold well in 1970. The Sphere paperback edition of *Irish Portraits: 14 Stories by Liam O'Flaherty* (selected from the three earliest collections) sold over eight thousand copies in six months.

---

458. KT TLS to Kitty Tailer
[from Dublin]   p.m. 20 June, 1971

Darling Kitty Pie,

Just got your letter and believe me that was a great relief as I was worrying terribly. My nerves, as you know, are not the best in Europe and it's no good saying to oneself, 'Well, it's only a couple of days since I saw her last.' However, now I know it takes a week for a letter to come from there to here, express or not, just as I said to you in Paris.

So the dinner is over by now and you may get a little rest. See that you take some, even if you have to poison a few dogs. Personally things are not too bad except that I have caught a slight cold and my finger nails are breaking, just as yours have been doing, although I think you told me some other damn thing cured that habit .... In any case my typewriting forefinger has to carry two bandaids to allow me to type in a mediocre fashion, as the Corkman said about Neenan's hurling. Yet we are not downhearted on this front by any means, we of the *Barbare des Iles* blood, seeing we are on our last chance, drinking at the Last Chance Saloon before hitting the Eternal Desert ....

I have withdrawn from human intercourse, so I don't know what gives on the Rialto. Except that I got two extraordinary postcards signed by Garech Browne, his father Dominic, Lady Tiger, Tauro, Mackie and a fellow called Maloney who is the court flute player and pipe in that peculiar mènage. They were in Aveyron. Tiger sent you her love.[1] They seem to be having a drunken spree to beat all sprees. Imagine Dominic getting involved with that lot, however poor chap, he has to take life as it comes ....

I keep thinking of all the trips we have made during the past two years, Tunis, Sardinia and Quiberon-Belle Ile. They are all so fresh and different from any other places we have visited together. Even so all the others too had something, good or bad. Of all the experiences during this last trip I like best the lane where we heard all the birds sing and saw the yearling bull suckle his mother. What a degenerate! I keep thinking once more of these two unwritten stories, 'The Blemish' and the one where a lizard is the centre piece, one that should be called 'Water' perhaps. I would like to get a book about fauna and flora of the American Western Desert, and especially anything that is written about the American desert lizard. Do you think you could scrounge around one day you are in New York? There are certain aspects of the background that I must find. Above all, what is the extent of a small lizard's awareness, the extent of sight and hearing, etc, ...
There are so many things in this world one does not know, or hope to know

... balls! Even so, these things that keep recurring and occupying space in the mind, without permission as a general rule, must be dealt with one way or another.

Darling Kitty Pie, you all just hurry on back to see me, heah? .... Unless some more of my fingernails fall off or break into fragments I might get going now and do something substantial, now that I have heard from you again and my maniacal forebodings have been proved false. All my love to my lovely and again to my dearly beloved ...

Le Barbare des Iles

[1] Tiger was Garech Browne's partner at this time.

----

459. KT TLS to Kitty Tailer
[from Dublin]   [envelope missing] July 1971

Darling Kitty Pie,

Thank you for sending the book on reptiles. Alas! they only give a list of different types without any information about their way of life and peculiarities. However, the pictures are useful. When this damn National Library opens, if it does, I'll consult the Encyclopedia Britannica. The place is now closed for repairs. In this country such a closure may last a long time. In any case I'm sorry to have put you to all that trouble, I wish the foolish *Barbare* had not thought of it.

I got a letter from Pegeen in which she said she is going to return from Russia on August 15th and that, for some reason, she would land in Scotland and enter Ireland at Larne, then go to Belfast and reach Dublin 16th or 17th August. Apparently she is then going on to see her mother, so I don't know what to say and have done nothing so far. Life has become a problem with which I am unable to cope. The least decision is beyond my means. Maybe tomorrow morning I'll feel able to ring her and say I won't be here. Of course it did not occur to her to say when she is leaving for Russia ....

By now you must be on that island [St. Simon's Island, Georgia]. You sound as if you and Laura are having a whale of a time with people coming and going. After all that is what you really like, with not a moment to spare and no time for the devil ....

This island goes on and on in the same insane way. The television becomes more and more a kind of Sunday School for Roman Catholic propaganda, with interviews with idiotic clergymen, pictures of De Valera with heads of monastic orders and what the Pope said about this and that. Even so I look at it every evening. It's better than being alone and going to bed at four or five in the afternoon and then waiting until three or four in the morning arrives so that I may get up without feeling I have been up all night.

I keep thinking of that French painter who lived alone in a frightful room in Montmartre, I mean the one that painted race horses. A fellow asked him did he feel hurt by spending his last years in abject penury. He just shrugged his shoulders and said, 'Well my dear fellow, a horse that has won the Grand Prix can't be sore at not having received the stake money together with the honour of victory.' He said he managed to live quite happily on one herring a day.[1] I don't believe a word of it, but painters are luckier than other artists being able to fiddle with their hands, making copies of life. I used to watch Asselin busy with his pencil, doing sweet bugger all.

I started reading an account of the Spanish civil war, the one by a fellow called Hugh Thomas,[2] until I almost screamed with horror at the vast and senseless tragedy of the whole thing. But then, in a very minor way, the same thing is happening in the North just now. *La vie est si triste et si con.*

I feel like the old man in my story called 'Galway Bay' when he was going along the docks with his old cow and he said to her: 'Poor old woman, what's going to become of the two of us.' At least the cow didn't care, or did she? Maybe the human brain is not such a great boon after all. Or do the brainless creatures we despise suffer as much as we do? Come on, *Barbare*, be as good as the old herring eating painter, at least as good as he said he was. After all, I still want to finish this book and vaguely believe myself capable of doing so. Under what circumstances? After all the insect I watched on a Donegal beach, the one that kept putting a tiny sliver of stone as a door covering the hole in which his wife had taken shelter to hatch, while I kept knocking it down with a little twig. He went on putting it back into place. Did the insect think he would really manage to keep it in place *finally.*

Oh Kitty Pie, what a sad little outpouring this is! But the law says one must always write the truth as one sees it. Always! I love you, Kitty Pie, that is the truth and must be said, *always* .... Goodbye dearest one, I hope the island will be happy making and that you won't long for the days when Thomas was little and asked for a whole bunch of toys. Goodbye now, darling, and be of good heart.

Le Barbare

[1] Probably Edgar Degas, whose race horse paintings O'Flaherty admired.

[2] Hugh Thomas, *The Spanish Civil War*, 2nd edition, London: Penguin 1965.

---

460. KT TLS to Kitty Tailer
[from Dublin]   p.m. 18 July, 1971

Darling Kitty Pie,

I am so grateful for the beautiful letter you sent me from Simon's Island which arrived on Friday. It was really delightful. Indeed, you now write better than I do, not that I fancy myself in that respect, but after all I am a 'pro'. I got a clear view of the whole setup, especially the young negro with the tie hanging down from an unbuttoned collar who said, 'Jeest'!

Well, in the meantime we had our conversation and I am pleased that you have finished that journey and only the other island, belonging to our friend Martha [St. Martha's Vineyard], remains to be crossed off your schedule. Then back again to eight Street the Peace [8 rue de la Paix] with bank and underground garage, and Rich Rock Stores in neighbouring Place Vendôme ....

I would just love a full dinner pail of achievement. Alas, I daresay such things will never again come to pass. The final deadline approaches, and old time is not dull-footed, or slow-footed, as gents like Euripides and Shakespeare pretend that he is. On the contrary he's a fast-baller, in fact a fireballer. I can't make out how long it is since I came back from Paris. It must be only a month or five weeks and yet I can barely remember what month it was that I returned. I got up last night at one o'clock, so now I don't know what day it is, even though it must be Sunday since I am writing this letter and nobody passes on the far Baggot Street that I can see through this window. It is now eleven o'clock and I've just finished supper, yes it must be supper, a boiled hen ... the broth was drinkable.

I heard a good one in the fish shop beyond the bridge yesterday, while buying some hake. The salesgirl shouted to a comrade: 'Is the hake gone up again?' 'No, not since the day before yesterday. Only the salmon and the sole.' 'The salmon again?' 'Yeah, it goes up every day almost.' It's like what they used to call, in the disease ridden old days, galloping consumption. But what disease is worse than inflation? The bastards leave bread and potatoes at a reasonable price still .... No doubt about it, Kitty Pie, we're hog tied ....

That television gets worse and worse. For how long was it hired? The only thing it is good for is sport .... People are not at one another's throats just yet. I hope that, now that July 12th has gone, things may quieten down. How bloody silly these islands are! It's no wonder considering the climate.

Sweetie, next Tuesday three weeks is 10th August, so you won't be so far away presently. It's really odd to have only one friend in the world, so far away. The old saying says, never put all your eggs .... Did you say you would telephone again before leaving? I can't remember things any more. I keep having to look in the dictionary for the spelling of the simplest words, it's frightening. Yet when I read the chapter that I'm doing, the eternal chapter as it is to be called henceforth, I feel at the height of my perceptions ....

I'm not even entitled to call myself *le Barbare des Iles*, owing to lack of primitive strength. Nevertheless, sweet Kitty, let us respect the one virtue that one still holds and brag about it in words, the power to love completely at least one being other than oneself. So here goes, darling pie, here goes, I'll make my way now to the G.P.O. and an airmail stamp will buy me ... boo ... hoo ... hoo. All my deepest love, darling

Barbare toujours

---

461. KT ALS to Kitty Tailer
For Kitty on her birthday 1971, [early December]
[marked] Cannes, A.M. France

La Mariposa,

Thereupon my eyes became spellbound by a painting of rare beauty. 'Oh!' I murmured.

It was the portrait of a butterfly hanging on the wall directly opposite the hearth, like the image of a tutelar household deity.

Resplendent in her majestic spread of four great black and yellow wings, all tailed, scalloped, ringed and hemmed in purple, scarlet and blue, the glorious queen of insects hovered above the moss-grown surface of a round forest pool, whose naked banks of sombre loam were decorated here and there by flowers of an exotic species, each one of them being merely composed of a single heart-shaped crimson leaf and a tall anthropomorphic stamen, proud with amber seed, that reached up craving to be touched by her divine magnificence.

The independent quarters of her royal canopy were tilted at random on their manifold and intricate hinges towards contrary directions, in order to point out with emphasis that her heart regretted the shameful necessity for making a decision of that gross nature. So too did the swollen bosses of her looped antennae, which twisted back and forth in the anarchic horror of despair, indicate loathing for the profession ordained by inexorable destiny.

That virtuous reticence was in striking contrast with the barbaric frenzy of her suitors, those left in hopeless anguish to the rear had already begun to droop their heads and shrivel, while the buoyant heirs still apparent, out in front, nearly broke loose from their pedestals trying to make contact.

As if to hide that outrageous exhibition of unbridled lust, a myriad tiny shafts of light poured from the tangled foliage overhead in a heavy rain of glittering silver dust.

Liam O'Flaherty

---

462. KT TLS to Kitty Tailer
[from Dublin]   p.m. 6 February, 1972

Darling Kitty Pie,

I keep worrying about your voice when we spoke to one another on Friday. You seemed agitated and worried. I hope that was a wrong impression, beloved one. Goodness knows, you have gone through a lot during the last months, what with Laura's operation and your damned tooth (which now gets another lease of life) and last but not least my unfortunate self, who always seems to sink back into the doldrums when least expected.

However, here in March and Spring and that famous line of Fitzpatrick's from *Omar Khayyam*: 'In the fire of Spring the Winter garment of repentance fling.' That does not sound appropriate, but you know what I mean. I always find it stimulating, the resurrection of life, everything stirring in the womb. Come to think of it, only human beings and some other disgusting forms of life don't find Spring necessary. They just procreate any time.

Unless you change your mind seriously you'll turn up here before Good Friday, and that will be wonderful, only three weeks or so distant. I think it's the most hateful day of the Christian year in a Roman Catholic country like this. It grinds one into the sordid earth. So we could read Gibbon together and recite my plagiarism: 'All religions are equally false to the philosopher.' ...

Didn't hear a word about Pegeen or if she got to London with all this dead weight of books, or did she get fired yet from her job .... I like the idea of you and Laura going back and forth together, between Holmdel and New York. For sisters you fit well, most of the time at least ....

Damned if I can understand why all the owners of property in the British Isles cannot stop quarrelling among themselves. They seem to be in such a bad way. I feel the revolutionary fever is rising again in France too, with Jean Paul and Madame Sa Petite Amie Serieuse de Beauvoir in charge of the Red Cohort. As de Gaulle said; 'They too are a part of France.' ...[1]

Everybody is very sore about the Welsh and Scottish refusing to play at Lansdowne Road, and rightly so.[2] Of course I think the bloody English are back of the whole dirty thing, or the Kike faces that now run the unfortunate country of Shakespeare, Gibbon and a myriad of other wonderful benefactors of humanity. Well, to hell with Rugby for this year. Perhaps there'll be a good race for the Cheltenham Gold Cup next week. I rather fancy Francis Flood's charge, Lady Something or Other. Maybe if you really come before

Easter we could go to Fairyhouse on Easter Monday in a hired car, as we did a long time ago ....

Beloved, I adore you
Le Barbare fantastique des îles

[1] Refers to Jean Paul Sartre and Simone de Beauvoir.

[2] Widespread I.R.A. bomb attacks caused this. The British Embassy, Dublin, was blown up 2 February, 1972.

---

463. KT TLS to Kitty Tailer
[from Dublin]   Tuesday, 29 August [1972]

Darling Kitty Pie,

Ever since we spoke across the Atlantic yesterday I feel overwhelmed with tenderness, because of your unfading and unmerited kindness towards this hapless *Barbare des Iles*. I wish I were with you when you sit in that chair to part company with a little of yourself, but I'll be with you in spirit, dear one. I never know whether it's best to make big or little of pain. Perhaps it's best to remind oneself that *'tout passe'*. How strange it is that the human animal, so coarse and unfeeling and even brutal, can be able to join so totally with another life that was originally alien, totally alien and unknown.

Soon now, in the Autumn fires of September, we'll fling the ragged garment of dying August, that villain that records my ever mounting {due?} with his Herculean hammer. I hope you don't change the date of sailing ....

It is very odd, Kitty Pie, that my brain is no longer able to get a clear conception of the passage of time. Is that the approach of senility? It's not yet a week since you flew away, in that huge Jumbo Jet, whose flight I watched across the southern sky, saying to myself: 'Jumbo, watch it fellow, because you'll be in trouble unless you carry my Kitty Pie safely to New York.' Even so, at times I get the idea that weeks and weeks have passed. That is rather frightening. Yet my memory with regard to my aged, but unfinished, manuscript is just as clear and sharp as ever, perhaps even more so.

I am reading Tacitus now. The translation is a bit annoying. I'll scout around Webbs on the sly for material about Greece, in case you still want to go there. Really I don't think driving there would be at all a prudent idea. The country is somewhat unsettled and to get around with a guide would be *de rigueur*. You might find out in New York whether these American Express 'short trips to places of interest' function there, like they do in Paris or Rome ....

I heard Jury's have really bought the Intercontinental but it's not certain to be retained as a hotel. The local boys sold the Italians fifteen thousand head of store cattle. That will keep their bookmakers in money for some time. They are going to sell this unfortunate island lock, stock and barrel, that includes the population too, the new slaves, added to the indigent Turks, Greeks, Wops, Yugos, Dagos and Pork and Beans ....

Darling Pie, I wish you good luck with your chair sessions and remember that amusing remark I made going through Hyde Park, laugh, pretty lady, laugh! I shall probably write another and equally unintellectual note next Sunday, because that is really the proper day to write. I mean the traditional one. Goodbye now, darling pie, and I send you my deepest and undying love. Long live Kitty Pie and Duckie Poo, *siempre*!

Le Barbare des Iles

---

464. KT TLS to Kitty Tailer
[from Dublin]   p.m. 12 November, 1972

Darling Sweetie Pie,

I got *L'Equipe* and the cheque for one hundred and sixty-five yesterday for air fare and telephone, which I think most unfair. I don't know what to say, like the little Yiddish song that you always found so like drawing one's fingernails along a smooth rock, 'Abie, Abie, my boy etc ....'

Do you know that Britain pays the crowd in the North four hundred million pounds subsidy per annum. Now Heath and Wilson have combined to threaten them with sweet bugger all unless they behave themselves ....

Darling, thanks ever so much again for the holiday, the glasses and the drops. I think they are doing a lot of good, although I'm not yet proficient at getting two bull's eyes. Mrs Gleeson left a note yesterday saying she cannot come until Thursday. What on earth would I do if she did not come at all?...This is one week and there are three more before I leave. I must go to Aer Lingus after I've lodged this cheque .... Damned if I know where you get the energy to keep going. I myself feel better than I have done for a long while. If the day is fine tomorrow I'm going to Howth, even though it's melancholy making to go there without you. Somehow I like it better than the animal park ....

I don't know what we decided about *Skerrett* and the other business, I mean Irene's daughter. You do just what you please without consulting me further, as I don't trust my judgement in the least ....

Well now, darling love, I'm going to put my name down for a ticket to Paris when I'm up town right now. Then you won't worry. Do you think I should buy a hat to go with my overcoat? My peculiar black cap will do. Maybe people will think I'm the common hangman, wow! Of course I could put a little plaque on the front saying '*Barbare des Iles*'.

All my deepest love, darling
[ALS] *de la part du Grand Barbare Deguelasse des Iles*

---

465. KT TLS to Kitty Tailer
[from Dublin]   p.m. 2 August, 1973

Darling Kitty Pie,

As I said during our recent telephone conversation, being of unsound mind undoubtedly, otherwise why subject myself to the torture of *two* letters per week, never mind here is the Thursday letter I promised. I'm sending the Thursday one to New Canaan and the Sunday one to the Park Avenue Club, in that way hoping to minimise the danger of one or both letters being thrust into a desk among forgotten knick knacks and thus never reaching their destination. A man might as well die for two letters as for one ....

I am writing a little every day but not much. While up at my bank this morning I brought the little black sack and made a tour of Moore Street, buying this and that. I certainly saved several return bus fares by so doing (*en passant* the ticket has now been raised to fivepence a head). Everything is much cheaper there and the sales ladies have become infatuated with my red jacketeen and white pants because they smiled at me and winked at me and one of them nudged me in the ribs and said: 'Whenever ye have anything good in yer mind come and say hello.' 'Indeed then I will, gorgeous,' I said. 'Do that, be God,' said she, 'and we'll have a hooley to beat all hoolies.' I even got some edible onions there, because this town has been out of onions for days. This Common Market is a proper .... Never mind! ...

I heard nothing about that visit to Thurles, Galway, Connemara and Gortnagcapall, but I judge Breandán [his nephew] is going through the motions with God knows who else, or how many, because there was an article today in the *Irish Times* about the Galway races, which appear to be on at the moment. Personally I have now become infatuated with cricket and look at nothing else.

I bought a book by Jean Paul Sartre just now, while I was out buying bread, pancakes and paying for the cleaners. I forget what the title is but the first two paragraphs, which I read in the bathroom after coming in, appeared to be quite good, except 'finicky' like all his work. However, '*il est quelqu'un', lui aussi.*

Darling sweetie pie, your two letters were adorable, and I am glad that an odd grand daughter has already turned up to wipe a plate or two. One even baked a cake! That's promising, only it does not go far enough. Somehow, I feel you'll be all right, because you were very fit basically before you left. Only thing is, sweetie pie, one has got to slow down coming through the home stretch, *slow down*. You must tell me what the medicos say .... I hope you are not worrying about Laura, it's bound to take a good while at her age to recover fully from an operation. As long as she chucks most of her committees and tribal festivities ....

Pegeen sent six more, I think six, of the bound Maupassants. They did not seem to be as well done as the others. When on earth is she going to stop sending them and how many of them are there? Reminds me of the story of a man who bought a pair of snails. In a couple of weeks they had bred thousands and millions of young snails, and so on, you know what I mean.

Goodbye now, darling beloved, and forgive the chattering folly of this extra letter, which will probably end up unread in a Bayonet Farm desk. it gives me a good moral feeling, having written it. Grab a pen and send me a little letter to this place, no matter how small, and scrub a couple of plates for me, willya, darling pie. Am I off my rocker? I certainly am stone cold sober, so it must be insanity. I love you, Kitty Pie, I love you with all my barbaric frenzy.

From *le Barbare des Iles lui-même*

---

466. KT TLS to Kitty Tailer
[from Dublin]   p.m. 13 August, 1973

Darling Kitty Pie,

I got your beautiful long letter from Holmdel yesterday. Thank you, dearest pie. I don't know how you find the time to write, considering the spate of cooking that keeps piling on and on, with relays of grandchildren that keep arriving, all with their beaks open. So today you are heading north towards somebody's hole, or whatever, I mean the island where the other part of your tribe is sojourning. I hope this letter will have arrived at the Colony [Club, New York] by the time you are returning ....

Believe it or not it is now only three weeks and a few days before I see you again. I hope this good weather lasts until then, because one gets a little work done in good weather .... As I go nowhere and see nobody there is hardly any news .... It is now a quarter to eight and I've been up since two. Stupid fellow! However, there is a football match at Croke Park today, so I will look at it on television and listen to it on Radio Éireann, because one talks and the other shows pics of what is happening.

Tomorrow and Tuesday the remainder of the Cricket Test Match, the second, between England and the West Indies will cheer me up. There was an appalling incident on Friday and for a good few moments it looked as if the English had a race riot on their hands, right in the heart of Birmingham, in the sacred precincts of the cricket club. The leading English player should have been called 'out' by the English umpire and he was not, so the West

Indian captain protested most violently and the whole West Indian team backed up their captain. The West Indian supporters on the stands went wild and poured onto the field. The police arrived and started swinging their truncheons. Then the West Indian supporters picked up the cricket stumps, *the sacred test cricket stumps were used for the first time in history during a riot.* There were a few heads broken and the B.B.C. announcer said there would be a 'tea interval' and went off the air. I don't know what happened while the B.B.C. was off the air. After tea had been taken, however, B.B.C. came on air again and apologised for the momentary interruption. Momentary hell! it lasted half an hour. Then the match continued as before. Everything happens, even in England, if one waits long enough .... Funny thing, the newspapers said nothing about the riot. Too busy talking about Watergate I guess ....

I cannot remember when I have had a bath last, or when I changed my pyjamas or bed linen. Maybe I'll let the whole thing go for another week .... I don't touch any red meat. In any case, even if I were tempted to touch where would I find some? All I see on sale is *fat* .... Poor Junior is hardly able to speak any more. Says 'Good morning' in a barely audible whisper. I don't know whether it's Dow Jones or the price of food. Interlocking I suppose.

The Horse Show came and went without me. I did see a few people while passing the Shelbourne who looked very horsey and met McCormick of Grange for a moment. He was blethering about John, Hans and Giovanni (I think it was). The international set only have 'first names' which you simply must know if you want to be known yourself and not treated as somebody who 'barges in the line out', or wears a made up tie! What a bore life is unless you are interested in the facts under discussion by fatheads. Ain't we all fatheads to somebody or other?

Kitty Pie, where have you been? I haven't had you around for so long, so long. Am I really going to the Cap 5000 motel this winter? I keep thinking how nice it would be to walk from there to the race track and maybe have lunch at that place. I got a wonderful lunch and there was a baby being christened. You know the place I mean. I do hope to have reached Monte Carlo by the time you get here [refers to his novel]. How wonderful to see a vague sign of daylight in the distance. And how sad, the divine rose of life cannot remain eternal for ever, only during the moment of writing.

All my love, darling pie, and all the love of
Le petit Barbare des Iles

---

467. KT TLS to Kitty Tailer
[from Dublin]   p.m. 26 August, 1973

Darling Kitty Pie,
This is Sunday once more, so I'm writing again to your Colony Club,

having missed writing Thursday's letter to Bayonet Farm owing to a not very serious indisposition, which has now passed, more or less .... I now feel better and having gone through my manuscript once more I feel quite well about things, apart from feeling 'The Dance' is not good. All this is very mysterious. It's now seven and I have been working for some time and feel rather muddled.

Darling, thank you for the letter I received yesterday, telling about your trip to the north, et cetera, together with the remark: 'And who did the driving? Who but Kitty.' Well, you'd be so mad if anyone else tried to do anything. Please let me know definitely when you are returning. I mean when you *really* are returning ....

Yesterday, while I was looking at the third test between England and the West Indies, an amusing thing happened. A solemn voice broke in upon the B.B.C. announcer's confabulation to say Scotland Yard wished him to say that a bomb had been planted at Lord's Cricket Ground and that the audience would have to evacuate the grounds until a search had been made. However, nobody wished to move and things went on for quite a while, with B.B.C.1 calling on eminent cricketers to give their opinion, most amusing looking types who agreed, with different accents of course, that the 'whole affair is utterly outrageous. I mean to say it's quite incredible that such an outrage could be perpetrated ... I mean, above all places *at Lord's* ... I mean, ah, as I said before, just incredible.' Well! It took them an hour to clear the people out and make a search. Then Scotland Yard announced that the whole thing was a hoax. A very dignified man with a white moustache, immaculately dressed, said to the B.B.C. man, 'What the devil are foreigners going to think of this sort of thing?' It was quite funny. Even so, I am glad Summer has more or less come to an end and Rugby is about to take over.

I got a postcard from Garech Browne, posted in Norway, with a picture of the most magnificent Viking ship I have ever seen. He said he was staying with a Guinness cousin, or cousine I imagine would be more true, and it was almost impossible to get anything to drink in Norway. Glad to learn that he appears to have forgotten my failure to turn up at the Shelbourne, where I had invited him to lunch weeks ago. Maybe he too failed to turn up.

Seems to me you are having the most successful American holiday for a number of years, all because you didn't have to go south. Much better to have those youngsters come to see you. No doubt about your failure to persuade Laura etc. What on earth would the poor girl want to see in Europe in any case. Like myself, she hates travel. She and Kate Hepburn had better hole up together. They seem to have a lot in common, apart from collecting bits of old glass and that sort of thing. Then there are the dogs ....

There were lots of little passages in my manuscript, or typescript, that gave me extraordinary pleasure. It was charming 'meeting' them again. Pegeen sent a whole lot of bound Maupassant books weeks ago and I have never written to acknowledge their arrival. Ain't that dreadful? I must be the most appalling father in Europe .... When virtue was handed out at the prenatal parade I certainly was ignored by the sergeant major, or whoever dishes out that sort of thing in the womb. Maybe some bloke whispered in his ear 'he don't need nothing from us, mate, the devil is going to look after him.' What a pretty picture, Kitty Pie. Well, to hell with them all, and you can take that as the last coherent word from your most loving friend,

Le Barbare des Iles

---

468. KT TLS to Kitty Tailer
[from Dublin]   Thursday p.m. [12 November, 1973]

Darling Kitty Pie,

Here is the 'rice and beans' letter I promised, I mean 'bread and butter' in our lingo, although life has been so appalling since my return to Dublin that 'prussic acid' would be better material for what is bound to be a lament.

The point is that the electricians have been on strike ever since, I mean the light and heat people. They go on and off at a brilliantly cunning and anarchic rate of torture. After talking to you on Tuesday morning I was unable to cook my early lunch because the stove ceased to function, and so on ever since. Fortunately I got out that big electric lamp you bought under similar circumstances, so I have been able to do a little reading in bed. Unless they get together and stop this torture, I really don't know how long I'm going to live on this side of sanity. Darling, you probably say to yourself that the dividing line, in my case, is very thin and almost indiscernible. I really am unable to write anything, darling pie.

I thought it very funny yesterday, when I was paying the electricity bill, their office was lit by a particularly miserable looking candle. 'Ha, ha!' I said aloud. Everybody looked at me in surprise as I pointed to the candle. The sodden wretches saw nothing odd in the electricity headquarters being candlelit ....

Saturday 5 a.m. I had to knock off, as the torturers put on their full offensive and I thought I was going *loco*. Yesterday noon I went to bed, having collected all the emergency food I could across the bridge, I mean food that does not need cooking, with a main basis of milk. Last night the light suddenly went on, for no apparent reason, at ten o'clock and it has been on ever since. It is now 6.45 a.m. and I'm afraid of 7 a.m. as it appears to be a favourite hour of opening a morning offensive .... I just took two red pills.

I'll try to post this in the Baggot Street post office beyond the bridge, as to walk up town seems an utterly impossible effort under the circumstances. This is Saturday, of course, and there is an international match at Lansdowne Road, Ireland against Argentina. I was hoping they would show it on television. The strikers might give us the weekend off and the game could be shown .... In spite of all that, Kitty, I don't believe that all is lost. But Epsom, it seems impossible to get out of Epsom. This morning I could do it, I feel certain of that, yet if I start after finishing this crazy letter the light will almost certainly go out. Presently I'll run out into Wilton Place, screaming at the top of my voice, 'I hate all my toys!'

Thank you ever so much for the trip, even for the gallerias and most certainly for the black unlabelled bottles that cost only two francs. Above all for the black-bottled wine that feared contact with the open air, in the house of *good cheese*. Maybe things will get better soon and I'll really hear from you tomorrow, but how would I know whether the telephone is working or not? ...

> Goodbye, darling pie, and all my forlorn love
> *Le Barbare Enchaîné*

At this time O'Flaherty wrote few letters except those to Kitty, more rarely to Pegeen, and very occasional short notes to his literary agents. A.D. Peters had died in 1972 and Michael Sissons had taken over. From 1974 Kitty Tailer kept only the two following letters.

1974

469. KT TLS to Kitty Tailer
Ducky Poo's Flop, Dublin   p.m. [? March, 1974]

Darling Sweetie Pie,

Your letter was the most beautiful thing I ever read, full of love and loyalty. Thank you, dear heart. I needed encouragement just then. Somehow the contest with life appeared to me totally lost. Now I am determined to go on, as long as you are by my side.

I am terribly sorry to hear Thomas is ill. I hope it's not serious? I too am counting the days that remain to be spent without your adored presence. It's already such a long time since I watched you walk down that long, long corridor at the airport. Since then you are always in the forefront of my thoughts. However, I am determined to make a great effort to get back into solid working trim. It seems years since I have written anything. I get a strange feeling, sometimes, that my world has disappeared and that it will remain *unregainable*. Away with these beastly and melancholy thoughts! As long as you love me, darling, life will always be a godly treasure of immeasurable beauty, and I do hope you will forgive all the torture and misery I have caused you.

You know my niece Maureen, who was going to marry a chap called Elliott? Well, I saw their picture in an obscure corner of the *Irish Times*. Apparently they got tied recently ....

Are you coming back here on your return to Europe, or do you land in France? Three weeks is not so long, is it? Then again, one feels it's far longer than eternity. If I could only get going again with my novel time would not drag so much, neither would this town seem so appalling.

I have to go out to eat today as Mrs Gleeson is coming. The Kelso laundry man came and gave me a receipt for two pounds sixteen shillings. That is, I have the receipt but do not remember giving him any money. I must have gone completely crackers .... Kitty Pie, this is getting to be intolerable. Don't worry, dear, everything is going to be all right.

I was relying on your visit State Side to give you a good rest from the constant peril of my company. In future, darling Pie, I'm going to try very hard to be a good boy. Damned if I have anything to read, I mean the filthy useless 'policiers' that I do read. What dishonour! ....

In a few days I'll write you a really respectable and civilised letter. In the meantime, adorable treasure pie, I love you beyond all bounds.

Le Barbare des Iles

---

470. KT TLS to Kitty Tailer
[from Dublin]   p.m. 9 September, 1974

My Darling Kitty Pie,

I got your letter last night and needless to say I was carried away, as always, by your beloved handwriting and words of tenderness, but when are you coming back? You forgot to say, although you have said so already and muddle-headed Bill (the one the German airmen used to call *'dumkopf'* or whatever during the war) has forgotten. Do say, Kitty Pie, when it is, so I can count the days like a child expecting a daidai, when mother comes home from the market, greedily counts the minutes. It seems so long, long, long since I saw you last, and I 'standing in the corridor *bei dem hohen* plane'. Well, sweetheart, things are not going at all bad with *dumkopf*. Looks like I might crack shortly round the corner and into the straight towards the winning post. *Olé!* I have *'une petite idée dans le tête'* that it might be nearly as good as we hoped ....

We'll go on lots more trips together .... There's a game at Lansdowne Road today, it's the Irish Rugby Football centenary and I suppose I should go to give a hand, but the weather looks as if it might pour.

When on earth are you coming back, Kitty Pie? There you are, barely out of sight at the end of that long bloody forlorn corridor, with me watching from the far end and I already shouting: 'For Jasus sake, girl, when are ye coming back?' Just like a man. I'll try and get a lot written before then. Cross your fingers.

The man on the radio, just now while I was eating breakfast, said the British Isles face a deadly and forlorn financial future. I nearly threw my teacup at the bloody radio .... I'm afraid I have become as ridiculous as a fictional absent minded professor. I see nobody, because really there is nobody to see. What a dreary town, unless one is a clergyman or a cattle jobber. When all is said and done France is the best of them, I mean countries.

You made a smart dip into the real estate wood pile when you signed on the dotted line for that apartment. With an underground pad for that reliable old trolley of yours. Unless Napoleon gets off his monument some night and drives it away to another bloody Waterloo. Let's hurry up and go somewhere, Kitty Pie. No matter where. I just want to be beside my girl, cuddling up against her all the while, like the old music hall song. Remember?

I think I'll go to the rugger match all the same. It looks like clearing up, but you just can't trust anything in this country, least of all the people and their weather. A proper lot of bastards. Goodbye for now, dearest and sweetest love of my heart.

Goodbye

Sa Majesté le Sacré Barbare des Iles

In 1974 O'Flaherty was awarded an Honorary Doctorate in Literature by the National University of Ireland, University College, Galway.

Famine was adapted for Radio Belge by Léon Darimont in January, 1975, sixty percent of the fee to O'Flaherty, the rest to Darimont.

Martin Sheen in New York wanted film rights of *Famine* for five thousand dollars but O'Flaherty would only accept three thousand dollars against a purchase price of thirty-five thousand dollars. Finally he agreed to two thousand dollars against a year's option against a purchase price of twenty-five thousand dollars. In the end, according to the A.D. Peters files, nothing came of this project.

1975 onwards

471. JR ALS to Joyce Rathbone
[from Dublin]   24 May, 1975

Dearest Joyce,

I want to thank you for having coming all that way to see me when I was badly laid up as the result of my accident.[1] I did really get a bad physical and spiritual shaking. Deserved no doubt, but that does not alter the fact that your gesture was tophole.

Thanks dear
Liam

[1] O'Flaherty had been knocked over in Dublin after alighting from a taxi, and broken a hip.

Joyce Rathbone has provided the editor with the following information about herself.

She was born in 1930 in New York, the daughter of Nellie Cohen, an American, and Liam O'Flaherty who became aware of his daughter's existence some two years later. Nellie Cohen married when Joyce was seven. Joyce was raised in London and legally adopted by her stepfather, so she assumed his name, Rathbone. When in her twenties Joyce decided to contact her real father and wrote to O'Flaherty in Dublin. There was no reply. She wrote again. Kitty happened to be in Dublin and saw the letter. In 1961 Joyce, who is a professional musician, went to Dublin to give a piano recital at the Royal Dublin Society and invited Liam and Kitty to the concert. Kitty came on her own and they met. Later Joyce met Liam for the first time in London. Joyce believes her mother met Liam through O.C., Liam's Communist friend, in London. Nellie was also interested in communism at the time.

The editor, A.A. Kelly, was in regular contact with Kitty Tailer during the period 1967-1990. As O'Flaherty aged and his health and energies deteriorated, especially after his broken hip in 1975, Kitty remained with him for longer periods, eventually moving into the Dublin flat where she remained in his last years.

Kitty was always helpful over research queries into the editor's book *Liam O'Flaherty the Storyteller* (London: Macmillan 1976). Up to 1976 meetings were in Geneva, where Kelly then lived, and Liam rarely travelled with Kitty, though both of them dined with the editor at home just before Christmas 1975, after Liam's accident. He looked healthy enough but had high blood pressure, and his memory had become patchy. He ate sparingly but enjoyed wine. Notes taken immediately after this dinner may be of interest.

'Liam had an old man's facility for living in the past. His first world war trench experiences seem to provide the most searing memories of his youth. His imagination, elusiveness, capriciousness, obstinacy and love of fabrication are still very evident. The pseudo-British accent (abandoned completely in his last years) seemed more marked than on our last meeting. The adoption of this seems part of his false front, his divided attitude to life and others, but he also has an admiration for the long-gone Great Britain of the twenties, especially London. He does not keep up with current trends. He reads a good deal but prefers old favourites except for Frank O'Connor, whom he admires. He was proud of having been in the Irish Guards, but would not talk about the Somme, as he was sickened by it. He said he used to think he was unfortunate, his ancestors owned a county, and he does not own a square yard, but he no longer minds. He complained about life in Dublin and said he had not been back to Aran for some time. He still loves horse racing.'

1976 was an important year for O'Flaherty. The publication of A.A. Kelly's critical study on O'Flaherty attracted more attention to his work, and Kelly introduced Liam to Seamus Cashman, of the newly formed Wolfhound Press, Dublin, with whom Kitty and Liam soon became friends. *The Pedlar's Revenge and Other Stories* (ed. A.A. Kelly) published 1976 by Wolfhound was well received, and the first of Liam's books to be published in Ireland. It was launched on Liam's eightieth birthday at the Arts Council in Dublin. Wolfhound have subsequently reprinted many of O'Flaherty's novels.

In 1977 Liam was persuaded to read on Radio Éireann 'All Things Come of Age' (28 June) and in December to record 'The Mermaid'. Subsequently Garech de Brún (Browne in the letters) of Claddagh Records, recorded 'Dúil', 'Red Barbara' and 'The Stolen Ass' which, with the previously recorded *The Ecstasy of Angus*, were issued as records C.C.T. 15 & 16 in 1978. Aged eighty, Liam was still lively, though very dependent upon Kitty.

In June 1978 the editor met Liam and Kitty in London, where they stayed for three days en route to Paris. That morning Liam had been to see the Irish Guards change outside Buckingham Palace. Because of heat and crowds they had only stayed for ten minutes, but it was surprising that he had wanted to go at all. Liam announced at this meeting that 'The Hawk' was his favourite story. He talked about his liking for Lorca's work, about how he came to write 'The Alien Skull' based on meeting a German in No Man's Land between the trenches. We all lunched in Joyce Rathbone's house. Pegeen O'Sullivan, O'Flaherty's other daughter, was also present.

In 1979 Liam was presented with the Allied Irish Banks Award for literature, adjudicated annually by the Irish Academy of Letters.

While in Dublin the editor met Liam and Kitty twice in September 1980. Their habit was then to go to the Baggot Street Mooney pub for lunch on Monday, Wednesday and Friday, and to another pub for sandwiches on alternate days. En route to the pub Liam looked for copies of *Famine* (Wolfhound, 1979) in the window of Parsons' bookshop, and went in to autograph a few copies. After lunch we returned to the flat, the rent of which had risen eight hundred percent since 1952! It was pleasantly but simply furnished with Velasquez prints (Liam's choice). His own first editions were in the study. Some fine leather bindings of Maupassant, done by Pegeen, were on the sitting room shelves. Liam reminisced about his childhood in Aran, how the house used to shake as waves pounded the nearby cliffs. He said he liked Shakespeare's sonnets and still read the daily paper. Kitty believed going back to Aran that Summer had upset him, for he had refused to spend the night there.

In 1980 Liam was able to give a reading at the 'Sense of Ireland' festival in London. Interest continued in film rights of his work, for example, John Boorman Productions took an option on filming *Famine* for five one-hour television episodes in 1979, the screen play to be written by Fred Haines. O'Flaherty signed this contract in Paris, December 1978. In March 1980 a six month stage option in *The Informer* was sold to Noel Pearson, Thomas Murphy to do the adaptation, and in the same year O'Flaherty refused an American request to adapt this book as an opera.

The Informer was staged at the Dublin Theatre Festival, October 1981, but not well received chiefly owing to poor staging. Box office receipts were good in the first week, then fell off and after the four week run the net losses were around twenty thousand pounds. The play went on to Louisville, U.S.

The last two traceable O'Flaherty letters are dated 24 March, 1980, and 26 March, 1981, both from Dublin, short notes addressed to Dr. Phillip Murray of Sligo, an admirer who collected O'Flaherty's work and sent him a case of wine both years. The thank you letters were probably written, certainly typed, by Kitty and Liam's signature is shaky.

In 1983 Liam was given honorary life membership of the Royal Dublin Society for his writing in Irish and English.

The last time the editor saw Liam was in April 1984. A member of the Aosdana, he was now blind in one eye and very deaf. A daily nurse was reading 'The Wave' aloud to him. An excellent bust of him had just been sculpted by Anthony Stones. Galway University was presented with one of these and the National Gallery of Ireland took another. Liam, his eyes as blue as ever, had become very thin.

Liam died 7 September, 1984, aged eighty-eight, in St. Vincent's Hospital, Dublin, after an illness lasting several months. His faithful companion, Kitty Tailer, was in another Dublin hospital at the time. The *Irish Times* devoted an entire page to O'Flaherty the day after his death, headed by an article entitled 'Liam O'Flaherty ends a long life of many diverse roles'. Only ten days before Francis Stuart had recalled their high old times together back in the thirties (the *Irish Times* 27 November, 1984, 'Recollections of a Great Spirit').

Liam's nephew Breandán Ó hEithir, wrote about his uncle in the *Sunday Tribune* on 9 September, 1984, known on Inis Mór at Willie Mhaidhc, and recalled their time together when Breandán first came to Dublin as a student.

Liam's last visit to Aran with Kitty in 1980 was described by Ulick O'Connor in the *Sunday Independent*, Dublin, 9 September, 1984. He quoted Neil Jordan's opinion of O'Flaherty as: 'A great, great writer, whose work must be unique in any language, any culture. His prose reminds me of those animal movements he describes so often, unconscious of itself, uncluttered by any intellectual veneer, with a springing grace permeating every element'. It was perhaps the loss of this spontaneity that hampered artistic endeavour in those latter years during which he struggled for so long over the unfinished *The Gamblers*.

Catherine Harding Tailer, that remarkably courageous lady, died in Dublin 31 August, 1990, aged ninety-one, and her ashes were flown home to the U.S. Her letters from Liam, which he never knew she kept, were amongst her papers. It is fitting that her loyalty and devotion should be thus immortalised, for such fidelity has become a rare virtue.

APPENDIX

Notes on unpublished fragments and O'Flaherty MSS which are referred to in, or provide additional background to, his correspondence.

HRHRC hold a five page undated MSS entitled 'The Adventures of General Michael Rathcroghan, chapter one'.

HLH (MS Eng 1056.2) hold a thirty-nine page Michael Rathcroghan MS, purchased with income from the bequest of Amy Lowell of Brookline. This Rathcroghan fragment is in two chapters, ironic and amusing.

Rathcroghan is O'Flaherty himself who (aged twenty-nine in the story) returns to Ireland after the war to find his parents very poor. He sets off to London to seek his fortune and after being fleeced of all his money drinking with an ex-Irish Guards friend, whom he has not seen for several years, he is introduced by this O'Hagan to the Neo-nihilist's Club and they get rid of the rest of his money. He then leaves the Soho lodging house and applies for a job as a night porter which he obtains in front of other waiting applicants by pretending to be a penniless gentleman. The story ends in mid-flow as Rath-croghan is shown his attic bedroom. He is to be paid £1 per week full board and work 9 p.m. to 9 a.m. at the hotel. This fragment reflects the actual welcome O'Flaherty would have got in Aran having fought in a war, of which they disapproved. In real life he got a job as a night porter (see *Two Years*.)

The Rathcroghan fragments must have been written over the period 1923-1926, as shown by references in the letter to Edward Garnett.

Also at HLH (same reference) is another story fragment 'A Day's Madness'. In this, after a false start (one page), O'Flaherty ran out of steam after eight pages, whereas in Rathcroghan he stopped at an interesting point after two well-constructed chapters, which could form a short story in themselves. 'A Day's Madness' seems to have started with some plan as it is marked, 'A Day's Madness – the Priest – the Seed'. In it the protagonist Dan Burke reflects O'Flaherty himself when he felt a neurasthenic attack coming on. Dan appears suddenly in the doorway of the Blake family kitchen. Matthew Blake is not there. Dan is large and powerfully built (like Gypo) with thick lips and a neck 'like the butt of a tree'. He startles Mrs Blake (aged sixty) dozing over her knitting. When he coughs for the second time and offers, with a yell, to baptise the cat, she passes out from fright. Her two children Con and Sheila are reading Euripedes *Alcestis* upstairs and hear their mother's fearful shriek. Sheila runs down to look and is terrified both by her mother's collapsed and ashen state, and by Burke. She rushes back upstairs saying her mother has had a fit and there is a madman in the kitchen. This fragment reflects O'Flaherty's state of mind when suffering from an attack, or an incipient one. Everything in this fragment goes to pieces, from his imagery (the man Dan's cough is compared to the first thud of a threshing machine), to his script which shows variable pressure. Irregular script is present throughout this fragment as if he is trying to write and describe a neurotic state of mind while actually experiencing it himself. But he fails to do so.

NLD hold interesting MSS (16,972) showing early attempts at what became *I went to Russia*. The first proposed title was *I See Red* and starts with a reflection on the suicide of Mayakovsky, who shot himself in 1930. O'Flaherty decides to go to Moscow to find out what caused this death. 'For, mark you, my own position was such as would afford the average Russian ample excuse for committing suicide. Yet I had no intention of doing so. My creditors had become exceedingly unpleasant. I had no money either to pay them or to meet my current expenses. I could not work. I was unhappily situated in many other ways. Further I had lost all hope in ultimately leading a happy life. I had ceased to believe that humanity was improving in any fundamental sense or that it was ever likely to improve. Indeed, I had reached such a state of morose cynicism that I believed in nothing except in a certain respect for the memory of the glorious past.' He goes on to say that he is only now inspired by racing and rugby football, and he sets out for Russia crying: 'God is Dead! Long live Lenin!'

He made six false starts before getting down to chapter one of *Lies about Russia* (his next title) and continued for fifteen chapters, parts of which do not match with the published text. O'Flaherty held a British passport at this time. Cancelled is a seven page critical passage about Norway, and a diatribe against Christianity. The few marginal notes and comments are probably by Edward Garnett.

Also at NLD (MS 16,973) is the text of a short story 'The Good God' which differs considerably from its final version as 'It was the Devil's Work', and contains some fine passages: and a violent Republican story, 'One Hundred Pounds' (4,000 words), no doubt then unacceptable to most editors but which should now take its place among O'Flaherty's work.

SELECTED CRITICAL WRITINGS ON
O'FLAHERTY

Bhaldraithe, Tomas de, 'O Flaithearta – Aistritheoir', *Comhar*, 25, Bealtaine, 1967, 35-7; 'Liam O'Flaherty – Translator(?)', *Eire-Ireland*, Summer 1968, 149-53.

Costello, Peter, *Liam O'Flaherty's Ireland*, Dublin: Wolfhound Press, 1996

Donnelly, Brian, 'A Nation gone wrong: Liam O'Flaherty's vision of modern Ireland', *Studies* 63, Spring 1974, 71-81.

Finlan, Michael, 'Journey from tumbled stones', *The Irish Times*, 11 Sept.,1984, 207-12.

Higgins, Michael D., 'Liam O'Flaherty and Peader O'Donnell, Images of Rural Community', *The Crane Bag* 9, 1, 1985, 41-48.

Kelly, A.A. *Liam O'Flaherty the Storyteller*, London: the Macmillan Press, 1976: 'Liam O'Flaherty's Balancing Act', *The Linen Hall Review* 5,1, Spring 1988, 5-7.

Kennelly, Brendan, 'Liam O'Flaherty, the unchained storm, a view of his short stories', *The Irish Short Story*, eds. P. Rafroidi & Terence Brown, Gerrards Cross: Colin Smythe, 1980, 175-88.

Kiely, Benedict, 'Liam O'Flaherty: A Story of Discontent', *The Month* II, Sept. 1949, 184-93.

Murray, Michael H., 'Liam O'Flaherty and the Speaking Voice', *Studies in Short Fiction*, V, 2, 1968, 154-62.

O Cuagáin, Proinsias, 'Dúil san Ainmhí Té ama I Scéalta Liam O Flaithearta', *Irisleabhar MháNuad*, 1968, 49-55, 57-9.

Ó hEithir, Breandán, 'O'Flaherty, last of a great breed', Dublin, *The Sunday Tribune*, 9 Sept., 1984.

Sheeran, Patrick, *The Novels of Liam O'Flaherty*, Dublin: Wolfhound Press, 1979.

Stuart, Francis, 'Recollections of a Great Spirit', *The Irish Times*, 27 Nov., 1984, 12.

Thompson, Richard J, 'The Sage who deep in central nature delves: Liam O'Flaherty's short stories', *Eire-Ireland* 18, Spring 1983, 80-97.

Zneimer, John N., *The Literary Vision of Liam O'Flaherty*, Syracuse: Syracuse University Press, 1970.

(Up-to-date details of O'Flaherty's work in print will be found in George Jefferson, *The Bibliography of Liam O'Flaherty*, Dublin: Wolfhound Press, 1993.

SUMMARY OF THE GAMBLERS

Liam O Flaherty's unfinished novel, over which he laboured for so many years, exists as a 40,000 word typescript, and although it contains some good passages, such as the description of a bullfight in Nîmes, it is in the main a disconnected, inconsequential story, full of superfluous adjectives.

The narrator is an American, Gerald McNiece, born 31 January 1912, a man shadowed by an unhappy childhood, who becomes an inveterate gambler, and indeed though he begins: 'It must be said at once that I have never, in cold blood, held father responsible for my sins,' his contradictory feelings for both his parents, and his jealousy of his weedy older brother Peter, who becomes a monk, haunt and distort his character throughout the story.

Gerald starts by admiring his father Jack for his physical beauty, athletic daring and poetic gifts. His father had married his mother, an American of French ancestry, in New York. She was a very rich orphan, thus the couple lived a life of 'carefree luxury' in California, then in France, where his mother became part of the Dadaist group. 'Those frail and exquisite creatures found her supremely feminine, like themselves, with the same flair for using refined cleverness as a substitute for instinctive power.' She wrote a long poem 'Paraclete', published at great expense, flattered by the social parasites by whom she was surrounded, but the poem was ridiculed by the American colony in Paris, so she and Jack sold their large house on Avenue Foche and became nomads, putting the two boys, like 'excess baggage', into an English public school. From now on Gerald becomes 'affected by the poison of exile and neglect'. He appeals to his father, game-hunting in Africa, who writes back: 'You must learn to play the game and to behave under all circumstances in a soldierly manner'.

Gerald's initial admiration for his father is destroyed when he is fifteen, at a bullfiight in Nîmes, to which both boys are taken, en route to their mother in Madrid. Jack McNiece, who likes showing off in public and had once taken part in rodeos, pays to be picador, is allocated a broken down horse, and the bullfight becomes a farce in which Jack becomes 'a ludicrous buffoon engaged in cruel play to entertain a bloodthirsty mob', for Jack is dislodged from the saddle and falls back into the corridor, furiously abused by the crowd, while the horse is disembowelled by the bull. What upsets Gerald is the way his father later distorts the episode and boasts about it. For the first time he sees his father as a poseur and a fraud. This realisation marks Gerald's passage into manhood. He quarrels with his brother en route to Madrid where they find their mother in a large rented house, now surrounded by a fresh group of parasites, while Jack has stayed behind on a debauch in Barcelona's Barrio Chino.

Gerald's mother is voluptuously beautiful 'her large brown eyes minutely spotted with gold, like a lark's eggs'. Her nickname for her husband, whom she loves in spite of his faults, is 'fidus Achates', after the faithful friend of Aeneas. She is now spending her money on a magazine called 'Fiesta' and she is still writing hopelessly bad poetry. She tells Gerald to help himself to her money. Both Gerald's parents are living lives out of touch with reality.

The two boys are next sent to various schools in different parts of Europe, lavishly supplied with mother's money 'the weapon by which she imposed her will', also 'the bribe through which she bought exemption from her duties as wife and parent'.

As a result Gerald starts betting, 'a much more potent anodyne than alcohol'. As a child he had often gone to Longchamps on Sundays with the family's French butler, and the fact that his mother is opposed to gambling of any kind adds to its attraction. By the time he is twenty-one Gerald has become as feckless as his father. He is pleased when his brother becomes a Franciscan monk, thus leaving him sole heir, though by this time his mother has squandered most of her fortune, and 'Fiesta' has expired after five years.

Meanwhile Jack McNiece, after physically assaulting his wife while drunk, has left for New York. Jack is now jealous of Gerald as a rival for his wife's funds. Gerald, to get more money out of his mother, and knowing how for her any form of art is a 'unique passion', pretends he is going to devote his life to sculpture, and goes to Paris. His mother tells him, 'just come to me at once whenever your wallet is empty', but Gerald believes that his father, now living in Cornwall, will prevent this, and installs himself in Montparnasse with the real intention of earning his living as a professional gambler. He pays to have a scandalous article with photographs written by someone else about his parents and their hatred of his father. He has become sycophantic to his mother, though try as he may he cannot crack his parents' relationship. With what he fears may be the last lump sum from his mother he continues to gamble recklessly.

Somehow Jack McNiece discovers that Gerald is responsible for the unpleasant magazine article and from Vienna he writes to tell Gerald that the article has brought his mother to 'death's door'. Fearful of having to learn his own living for a change, Jack threatens to take his son's life. Gerald then moves to an obscure hotel in Paris.

Knowing that he can no longer tap his mother for funds, Gerald tells his racing cronies that he will inherit more money on his twenty-second birthday and bribes his way into an illicit winnings scheme. He wins phenomenal sums. 'The marvellous intoxication of success made me totally indifferent to the means by which it was being gained. The fact that I had become a criminal rogue, who conspired with dishonest owners and trainers and jockeys to fix races, did not arouse the least feeling of shame or disgust in my corrupt mind', for there surely can be no depth of spiteful jealousy and unjust resentment to which the wounded vanity of outcast youth will not descend in search of vicious satisfaction.'. Gerald now realises he has drifted apart from his parents beyond recall.

At this point in his life Gerald encounters Isabel, Marquesa de Casalve, a rich and beautiful dark-haired widow, then living with the elderly Fuad Karami, a wealthy Egyptian, known as 'the Pasha'. Warned by Pierre Antoine and his other crooked confidants, that Isabel is known as 'the black spider', except that her embrace is far more deadly, Gerald nevertheless falls helplessly in love with her. Aged over thirty, she and her former husband wasted a fortune at the casinos, and since he died 'she has kept herself in clover by putting rich men through her hoop, one after the other. Yes sir! that Spanish vampire leaves all her victims cold, without a word of thanks or sigh of regret, as soon as the last drop of their blood has been sucked'.

Gerald, in the grip of another unique passion, ignores this warning. His mother now writes to say Jack (fidus Achates) has been helping in the Spanish civil war (the dates of which do not fit Geralds's given age), and is about to arrive in Paris to speak at a mass demonstration organised by the Popular Front. Jack knows Gerald has become a gambler and has threatened to attack him. Gerald, convinced that in any conflict he will end by killing his father, still loathing his father for the time he beat up his mother, decides he must leave Paris. He considers it a good omen that just now 'the Pasha' has returned to Egypt and Isabel sends for him. Reneging on his commitments in Paris, and 'carried up to the loftiest peak of unsullied worship' Gerald goes off with Isabel 'the black widow', driving her car right through the night six hundred miles across France to her home 'La Mariposa'. He has left one unique passion, his gambling, for another and the text ends with an ecstatic account of their union, only tempered by the insolent behaviour of the butler, Miguel, who appears to be Isabel's stepfather.

The description of Miguel gives a foretaste of what may happen when Gerald's money has run out! Meantime Isabel shows every sign of being as enamoured of Gerald as he is of her.

The description of Isabel's mariposa (butterfly) erotic dance, comes from a passage written to Kitty as a birthday present and later incorporated into this text.

The last Chapter (36) of *The Gamblers* suddenly jumps back to Derby Day 31 May, 1933. Gerald's mother is now living in Biarritz and writes to warn him to get out of Germany away from Adolf Hitler, the anti-Christ, so Gerald drives from Heidelberg, leaves his expensive car in Holland, and goes to Epsom to gamble at the Derby. It appears that this section may have come from a previous draft of the unfinished novel.

The text being unfinished the ultimate outcome of Gerald and Isabel's union is left in the air.

RECIPIENTS OF LETTERS

INTRODUCTORY NOTE
Recipients are indexed under the number of each letter.

MAIN INDEX

ACKNOWLEDGEMENTS

Thanks are due first of all to the British Academy, without whose Research Grant the expenses incurred during the compilation of this volume would have been prohibitive.

The editor is indebted to the following for their help during the lengthy task of preparing these letters: Pegeen O'Sullivan, who has given permission for the publication of her father's letters; Peter Tailer, who has allowed the publication of his mother's letters from Liam; Joyce Rathbone, the late Breandán Ó hEithir, Francis Stuart, Dr. Philip Murray, Sean J. White, Margaret Mary McQuillan of Harcourt Brace Jovanovich, Inc., Tom Maschler of Jonathan Cape Ltd., Livia Gollancz of Victor Gollancz Ltd., Seamus Cashman, Josh O'Donovan and Susan Houlden of Wolfhound Press who have been most cooperative throughout.

Gratitude is expressed to the staff of all the university libraries listed as holding letters of Liam O'Flaherty, especially to the librarians of Harry Ransom Humanities Center, Austin, Texas. The editor would also like to acknowledge some help in research from the following institutions: King's College Library, the University of Aberdeen; Miller Library, Colby College, Waterville, Maine; the location register of twentieth century literary MSS and letters at the University of Reading Library, Berkshire; John Rylands University Library, Manchester; George Arents Research Library, Syracuse University, New York; The British Library (newspapers) Colindale, London; Philip Wilkinson, librarian at the University of Southampton library; the University of Rochester Library, Rochester, New York; Stanford University Library, Stanford, California. Thanks are also due to A.D. Peters & Co. Ltd. (now Peters, Fraser & Dunlop Group Ltd), for allowing the inclusion of material from their files on Liam O'Flaherty now held by the Harry Ransom Humanities Research Center. Without the helpful cooperation and prompt attention of all these institutions and individuals this collection could never have been produced.

WORKS BY LIAM O'FLAHERTY
From WOLFHOUND PRESS

FAMINE

'The author's skill as a storyteller is at times breathtaking.
This is a most rewarding novel.'
Publishers Weekly

'I gladly accept one of the claims on the dustjacket of this novel:
"A major achievement – a masterpiece".... It is the kind of truth only a
major writer of fiction is capable of portraying.'
Anthony Burgess, *Irish Press*

Famine is the story of three generations of the Kilmartin family, set in the period of
the Great Famine of the 1840s. It is a masterly historical novel, rich in language,
character and plot; a panoramic story of passion, tragedy and resilience.

ISBN 0 86327 043 3

SHORT STORIES
The Pedlar's Revenge

'This valuable collection displays O'Flaherty's amazing range from a love
idyll between a wild drake and a domestic duck to the unspeakable
comedy of the appalling Patsa delivering the contents of his golden belly
under the influence of a cataclysmic purge, from the burning of young love
in that splendid story 'The Caress", to the rheumy old man sitting by the
roadside and failing to recognise, in the old woman who pauses in passing,
the warm love of his youth.'
Benedict Kiely

'... a gallery of human emotions, embracing a clutch of huge eccentrics,
sweet and sour remembrances of distant youth and vivid portraits of rural
Ireland ...'
The Sunday Times

ISBN 0 86327 536 2

THE BLACK SOUL

'The most elemental thing in modern Irish literature...'
AE

Intense, compelling, beautifully descriptive – as *Wuthering Heights* is to the Yorkshire moors, so *The Black Soul* is to the Aran Islands.

The sea roars dismally round the shores of Inverara. A Stranger takes a room on the island. Here lives a couple whose married years have been joyless – until the presence of the Stranger unleashes their passions . . .

For as spring softens the wild beauty of Inverara, the Stranger becomes conscious of the dark-haired Mary – how summer makes her shiver with life. He is the first man she has ever loved, and she thrills with sexual awakening.

But with autumn comes danger. Peasants mutter superstition against Mary; Red John laughs at nothing, there's murder in his eyes; and a madman's yell hurls the Stranger back to sanity . . .

ISBN 0 86327 478 1

THE WILDERNESS

'This allegorical story is the most ambitious novel O'Flaherty wrote.'
Dr A.A. Kelly

All efforts to attain happiness and beauty have failed because we have never known where God is. Outcast Henry Lawless has retreated into the wilderness – to find him. But the fairy glen he has chosen has its own laws, invisibly woven into the apparent calm. Does Patrick Macanasa's tribal claim, hovering in ever-increasing menace, hold a real threat? Is Eugene Raverty ready to wield the club of church power against the newcomer's startling beliefs? Or could the rebellious sensuality of Mrs Dillon, a symptom of the changing peasant class, devastate everything?

Stirring the conflicting desires of the glen, Lawless's search awakes ancient and unknown forces.

ISBN 0 86327 534 6

THE ECSTASY OF ANGUS

A Celtic retelling of the creation myth, seductive, exuberant and imaginative.

'Written with grace and feeling, it richly repays scrutiny.'
Irish Times

ISBN 0 86327 029 8

MR. GILHOOLEY

'A great, great writer, unique in any language, any culture.'
Neil Jordan

A powerful novel of love and intrigue.

Mr. Gilhooley, his lover Nelly – 'her sparkling yellow curls a golden treasure' – and their companions clash in an urbanised society for which they are quite unprepared. This is the underworld of 1920s Dublin.

Death, violence, sex, religion and love entwine and weave paths of good and evil in this powerful psychological thriller.

Mr. Gilhooley rivalled the fame of Joyce's *Ulysses* when it was first published, and was reviewed by W. B. Yeats as 'a great novel'.

ISBN 0 86327 289 4

THY NEIGHBOUR'S WIFE

'Raw, passionate stuff.'
Irish Press

Lily McSherry returns to her island home with her young husband. But her first love, Hugh, is now Fr McMahon, the local curate. O'Flaherty's famous first novel is a powerful story of conflict between religion and love, about choice and celibacy. The explosive and passionate story that unfolds is told in skilful, exacting prose.

ISBN 0 86327 328 9

THE ASSASSIN

'O'Flaherty's genius is at its best in registering mass emotion... There are some vivid sketches of Dublin's slums and night town.'
Irish Times

Based on an actual event, O'Flaherty's *The Assassin* captures a time and a facet of Dublin life in a way that no other fiction writer has succeeded in doing.

ISBN 0 86327 368 8

INSURRECTION

'Vivid, passionate writing takes the reader through the opening hours of disbelief, wild excitement and later horror as the Rising is established in the GPO.'
Electrical Mail

A novel of war, and of men's enchantment with it. On Easter Monday 1916, Bartly Madden joins Kinsella, the ascetic commander of a small band of insurgents, and Stapleton, a poet and anarchist. Only young Tommy Colgan is oppressed by the fear of violence ....

ISBN 0 86327 375 0

SKERRETT

'*Skerrett* is a classic.'
Irish Times

'Powerful in language, majestic in scope, utterly honest.'
Sunday Press

With a legend of trouble already behind him, David Skerrett comes to the island of Nara to teach the unbiddable children of an unruly people. From the very first moment there is struggle and conflict ...

ISBN 0 86327 369 6